D0152252

INFORMATION TECHNOLOGY

A LUDDITE ANALYSIS

COMMUNICATION AND INFORMATION SCIENCE

A series of monographs, treatises, and texts
Edited by
MELVIN J. VOIGT
University of California, San Diego

Recent Titles:

Alan Baughcum and Gerald Faulhaber • Telecommunications Access and Public Policy
Herbert Dordick, Helen Bradley, & Burt Nanus • The Emerging Network Marketplace
Sara Douglas • Labor's New Voice: Unions and the Mass Media
William Dutton & Kenneth Kraemer • Modeling as Negotiating
Fred Fejes • Imperialism, Media, and the Good Neighbor
Glen Fisher • American Communication in a Global Society
Howard Frederick • Cuban-American Radio Wars
Edmund Glenn • Man and Mankind: Conflict and Communication Between Cultures
Gerald Goldhaber, Harry Dennis III, Gary Richetto, & Osmo Wiio • Information Strategies
Bradley Greenberg, Michael Burgoon, Judee Burgoon, & Felipe Korzenny • Mexican Americans and the Mass Media
W. J. Howell, Jr. • World Broadcasting in the Age of the Satellite
Heather Hudson • When Telephones Reach the Village
Robert Landau, James Bair, & Jean Siegman • Emerging Office Systems
James Larson • Television's Window on the World
John Lawrence • The Electronic Scholar
Kenneth Mackenzie • Organizational Design
Armand Mattelart and Hector Schmucler • Communication and Information Technologies
Robert Meadow • Politics as Communication
Vincent Mosco • Policy Research in Telecommunications: Proceedings from the Eleventh Annual Telecommunications Policy Research Conference
Vincent Mosco • Pushbutton Fantasies
Kaarle Nordenstreng • The Mass Media Declaration of UNESCO
Kaarle Nordenstreng & Herbert Schiller • National Sovereignty and International Communication
Everett Rogers & Francis Balle • The Media Revolution in America and in Western Europe
Dan Schiller • Telematics and Government
Herbert Schiller • Information and the Crisis Economy
Herbert Schiller • Who Knows: Information in the Age of the Fortune 500
Jorge Schnitman • Film Industries in Latin America
Jennifer Daryl Slack • Communication Technologies and Society
Keith Stamm • Newspaper Use and Community Ties
Robert Taylor • Value-Added Processes in Information Systems
Sari Thomas • Studies in Mass Media and Technology, Volumes 1-3
Barry Truax • Acoustic Communication
Georgette Wang and Wimal Dissanayake • Continuity and Change in Communication Systems
Frank Webster & Kevin Robins • Information Technology: A Luddite Analysis

In Preparation:

Susanna Barber • News Cameras in the Courtrooms
Lee Becker, Jeffrey Fruit, & Susan Caudill • The Training and Hiring of Journalists
Thomas Lindlof • Natural Audiences
David Paletz • Political Communication Research
Jennifer Daryl Slack & Fred Fejes • The Ideology of the Information Age
Lea Stewart & Stella Ting-Toomey • Communication, Gender, and Sex Roles in Diverse Interaction Contexts
Tran Van Dinh • Communication and Diplomacy in a Changing World
Tran Van Dinh • Independence, Liberation, Revolution

INFORMATION TECHNOLOGY:
A *Luddite* Analysis

Frank Webster

Oxford Polytechnic, England

Kevin Robins

Sunderland Polytechnic, England

ABLEX PUBLISHING CORPORATION
NORWOOD, NEW JERSEY 07648

Library of Congress Cataloging in Publication Data

Webster, Frank.
  Information technology.

  (Communication and information science)
  Bibliography: p.
  Includes index.
  1. Electronic data processing. 2. Information
storage and retrieval systems. I. Robins, Kevin.
II. Title. III. Series.
QA76.W33 1986   004   85-46065
ISBN 0-89391-343-X

Ablex Publishing Corporation
355 Chestnut Street
Norwood, New Jersey 07648

Contents

For Liz, Frankie, and Isabelle
Rosemary, Dan, and Joe.

Therfore when I consider and way in my mind
all these commen wealthes, which now a dayes
any where do florish, so god helpe me,
I can perceave nothing but a certein conspiracy
of riche men procuringe theire owne commodities
under the name and title of the common
wealth.   They invent and devise all meanes
and craftes, first how to kepe safely,
without feare of lesing, that they have
unjustly gathered together, and next how
to hire and abuse the worke and laboure of the
poore for as little money as may be.

Thomas More. Utopia. 1516. Dent, 1937, p. 112.

Acknowledgements

This book has been a long time in the making. It began late in 1977 at Ealing College of Higher Education as a project examining the "political economy" of visual communication. Kevin Robins joined John Crowley and myself in that research which changed direction as the subject under study itself was changed by the conditions mapped in this book. John dropped out of the project early on, but he played an important part in getting it going. I thank him for that and his continued support.

A large part of the study was drafted for lectures when I was teaching at the University of California, San Diego, in 1981-82. There I had the privilege of discussing many of the issues with Herb and Anita Schiller, the stimulus of sitting in on Herb's classes, and the delight of their friendship and hospitality. Herb urged that I stop writing articles and instead produce a book on the topic. I hope he likes the result of his advice.

In California Sarah Carter and Richard Defriend (of the University of Kent) were extraordinarily kind and considerate. Also at UCSD Michael Schudson, Mel Voigt, Robert Meadow, and Dan Hallin were generous friends and colleagues whose interest in the issues was encouraging and supportive. Bill Loges and Kim Thompson were two of the many exceptional students at UCSD whose responses helped shape the book.

Librarians at Brunel University, especially the one to whom I am related by marriage, gave expert and enthusiastic assistance even when it interrupted Wednesday lunches. At Oxford Polytechnic Robert Murray was an intellectual prop, Steve Yearley (now of Queen's University, Belfast) a model of procedure, and David Pepper, Alan Jenkins, David Watson, Peter George, and Keith Lambe always ready to comment, query, and discuss. Peter Madgwick's unfussed assistance came at an opportune time, and his colleagues Cliff Wright, David Deacon, and Barry Axford provided the best kind of intellectual provocation and nurture one could hope for. Penny Smith took over my teaching for a term, and the smoothness of that transfer made the writing easier. In the polytechnic library Mrs. Cupples and Margaret Hutchings not only tolerated but welcomed my many requests. Sue Clay, a treasured student, wrote beautiful essays which lessened the isolation of writing.

I am, as ever, indebted to my parents, brother, and sisters for unwavering support. At home Liz Chapman constantly complained, especially as her pregnancy developed, but the dedication tells of her true role. Frankie interrupted—delightfully; Isabelle set the deadline for completion by her birth.—*Frank Webster, High Wycombe, November 1984.*

In and about Sunderland, special thanks are due to Rosemary O'Sullivan, Greta Mushet, and Sasha Brookes for their roles in promoting the cause of psychic and spiritual salvage. They have shed light where it was sorely needed. Through them I have a clearer understanding of what the "information society" will not provide, and an insight into what a different future might be. I am deeply grateful.

Particular thanks are also due to Mike Pickering who has always been good for a "canny bit crack," especially over a pint. I would like to acknowledge his continuing help—both intellectual and personal. At a distance, Les Levidow has been an invaluable support and facilitator. *Kevin Robins, Sunderland, November 1984.*

Since the views in this book are controversial, it may be especially necessary to state that we alone are responsible for them.

Chapter 1
Introduction: A Latter-Day Luddism

Are you not near the Luddites? By the Lord! If there's a row, but I'll be among ye! How go on the weavers—the breakers of frames—the Lutherans of politics—the reformers?

—Lord Byron to Mr. Moore, December 24, 1816

Early in 1813, Baron Thompson, called upon to sentence men found guilty of machine-breaking in the West Riding, took the opportunity to deliver a lesson in political economy. "Those mischievous Associations," he intoned, had as an objective

the destruction of machinery invented for the purpose of saving manual labour in manufactures: a notion, probably suggested by evil designing persons, to captivate the working manufacturer, and engage him in tumult and crimes, by persuading him that the use of machinery occasions a decrease of the demand for personal labour, and a consequent decrease of wages, or total want of work. A more fallacious and unfounded argument cannot be made use of. It is to the excellence of our Machinery that the existence probably, certainly the excellence and flourishing state, of our manufactures are owing. Whatever diminishes expense, increases consumption, and the demand for the article both in the home and foreign market; and were the use of machinery entirely to be abolished, the cessation of the manufacture itself would soon follow, inasmuch as other countries, to which the machinery would be banished, would be enabled to undersell us (Burke, 1966, p. 5).

Thus the learned judge addressed the Luddites before him in the dock. In so doing he not only offered a concise and orthodox account of an economic doctrine then making considerable headway in Britain, but he also cruelly parodied the views of those protesting workers who had joined into Luddite bands. Thompson's observations were widely reported in the contemporary press and in specially printed circulars. The economic doctrine became increasingly popular throughout the 19th century and is heard daily today. The parody stuck.

One can only speculate on the responses of the defendants who remained silent while several of their number were sentenced to be hanged for their part in organizations and activities which had resisted the introduction of new technologies. But if Thompson's words fell upon deaf ears that day in January 1813, the subsequent executions did not. They were to signal the end of significant Luddite opposition to mechanization in Yorkshire. The Industrial Revolution accelerated thereafter.

Nowadays, we no longer hang opponents of technological revolution. There is even small need to lecture recalcitrant workers; it seems that all that is required is to recall the specter of Luddism. Homilies of the kind offered by Baron Thompson are scarcely necessary (though they are delivered), because the very word "Luddite" so successfully abuses any opposition that his message gets through by default.

1

Luddism is portrayed as all that is negative, hopeless, and deluded. It is unintelligent, probably violent; indiscriminate and futile; the action of ignorant, backward-looking workers; anachronistic, brutal and destructive; lacking in imagination; opposed to progress. The accusation of "Luddism" has become a ritual incantation that forecloses debate on the social and political meanings, the causes and effects, of technological change. For all concerned, it is a charged and opprobious label: if you do not favor "progress," "improvement," the "new," the "future" itself, then you risk the dread charge being laid at your door.

Luddism in History

Between Justice Thompson and the contemporary image there is a direct line of continuity, but historians have shown Luddism in a different light. It was a part of the industrial unrest of the early 19th century which occurred in the context of profound changes in the structure of social relations right across society. These were most marked by innovations in the organization of work, but they spread far beyond the immediate process of production to the recasting of social space (towns, family, leisure, etc.). The chief instigators of such changes were a new breed of men, the modern businessmen, who preached and practiced the doctine of *laissez-faire*, then a rather novel ideology making great headway. Men like William Cartwright of Rawfolds, near Leeds, were fervent advocates of industrial capitalism; at the forefront of developments by virtue of their adoption of this forward-looking creed, it is not surprising to find an enthusiasm for new technologies integrated with their new political economy. These modern men placed great emphasis on the mechanization of plant, the centralized organization of production, the careful calculation of business, anything to improve output and the success of their enterprise. Such radicalism was seen as folly not only by many employees of the new men, but was also viewed with a jaundiced eye by numerous local employers who preferred to stick to the older, tried and true, methods. The latter were soon compelled to fall into line with the pioneers by the superior market performance of these whom Eric Hobsbawm (1964) has described as the "large modernized entrepreneur."

It would be a mistake to see Cartwright and his kind as mere technological innovators. Their stress on innovation and improvement is better seen as the material expression of an ideological zeal which contrasts with that of the small-scale 18th century masters (Berg, 1980). This is most evident in the shift from a paternal concern to the doctrine of contract which came to mediate more and more relations: in place of personal responsibility and responsiveness to those in one's employ, there came a commitment to wages, price, and profit. It was in this context of a shift in attitudes that technologies such as the hand loom made sense to people like Cartwright, since "sense" was measured in the precise terms of liberal political economy. For the *laissez-faire* capitalists, themselves usually the industrialists who owned or managed the larger factories, new machines and centralized production meant extra output, decreased labor costs, competitive edge, and more control over the labor process. Mr. Baron Thompson spoke their language.

It was against this backcloth that Luddism came into being. But this Luddism, the real Luddism, was not the cry of the empty gut against innovations which inexplicably (at least to the victims) threw people out of work. It was an answer from many ordinary people to changes imposed from above—to the accompaniment of much talk about "natural" economic laws and technological advance—which had repercussions on their whole way of life. Luddism was above all else an attempt by working people to exert some control over changes that were felt to be fundamentally against their interests. It was a protest, in the days before the existence of any organized trade union movement let alone meaningful political parties to represent the disenfranchised, against new modes of accountancy, employment patterns, work rhythms, authority relations, and industrial discipline. New technologies were a part of these changes, an integral part of them, and the Luddites steadfastly refused to regard them in any other way.

In recent years, a number of scholars, most prominently Edward Thompson, have examined these responses which were expressed in Luddism. These have shown that the Luddites were not frenzied bigots: on the contrary, they were usually well disciplined and organized. They did feel passionately about what was being done to them in the name of progress, but their actions were measured: their targets were by no means indiscriminate, but carefully selected with due regard to the actions, policies, and attitudes of the particular manufacturer. (Not surprisingly, Cartwright's factory—itself, significantly, well guarded—was the scene of the most vigorous Luddite assault in Yorkshire.) Most importantly, we now know that, despite the protestations of a long line of judges, politicians, and industrial managers, the Luddites did not protest against new machines *per se* but against the changed social relations which were being brought into being and of which mechanization was a part. Thus we find, for example, numerous instances of factories which used new machines being attacked, but only those worked by underpaid, untrained, and unskilled "colts" being destroyed.

Luddism, in short, was an answer—a political and moral response—from working class people to forces intent on destroying traditional social relations. It entailed an attempt to introduce alternative priorities to those being imposed by industrial capitalism. It was not a blind response, nor was it a matter of isolated protests, nor was it simply an industrial rebellion. It was a determined movement which shifted its scale of operations from villages across counties, which planned and practiced its sorties with some care, and which moved back and forth between armed raids on factories, industrial activity, and calls for political reform—in sum, what Edward Thompson calls a "quasi-insurrectionary movement" (Thompson, 1968, p. 604).

Luddism was a force which, if it looked back to better times in demanding "full fashioned work at the old fashion'd price established by Custom and Law," also looked towards the future times of labor organizations and aspirations. It does not deserve the sneering, indeed unthinking, dismissal it so frequently receives today. By most accounts this is not what it received from contemporaries; in spite of a large presence of troops, government spies, and rewards for informers, the detection rate for Luddite activists was remarkably small. The only satisfactory explanation is that Luddism enjoyed widespread popular, if tacit, support.

While it has been dismissed as a primitive form of resistance, appropriate to "societies where the patterns of industrialization were incomplete" (Thomis, 1972, p. 170), we would put forward a positive interpretation of Luddism as "an alternative political economy and morality to that of *laissez-faire* (Thompson, 1968, p. 603) because it carries an ethical response in opposition to the changes wrought upon society by the dispassionate logic of industrial capitalism. It offers another way of seeing to those blinded by the light of Baron Thompson's sentencing.

A Luddite Legacy

It is from this, the genuine history of early 19th century protest, that this book adopts, provocatively but seriously, a Luddite approach to information technology (I.T.) with two related maxims. The first celebrates the refusal of the machine-breakers to submit to "the imposition of the political economy of *laissez-faire* upon, and against the will and conscience of, the working people" (Thompson, 1968, p. 594). We acknowledge a debt to predecessors who would not readily succumb to changes in their way of life, unsatisfactory though it may have been previously, that were being introduced unilaterally by masters in pursuit of self-interest. At a time of most intense technological change against which there is little overt protest, we might instructively recall the Luddite resistance.

Second, reminding ourselves that the Luddites opposed not new technologies *per se,* but particular social arrangements that were embodied in processes of innovation, we take from the Luddites a theoretical and methodological principle. We feel able to identify with Luddism as a *critique* of developments which, because they are presented as mere matters of technical change, appear unstopable and unobjectionable. It seems to us that only a Luddite way of seeing can begin to query the conventional wisdom which presents technological innovation as asocial and neutral, yet inevitably to be accepted. A Luddite analysis is one which refuses to extract technology from social relations, one which insists that it must be regarded as inherently social and therefore a result of values and choices.

Invariably, the name of our eponymous hero, Ned Lud, is used to disparage those who criticize technological innovations. Mindless Luddites are lampooned as Canutes before the tide of progress. Behind this labelling of opponents there lurks an *implicit* theorization of technology. Technology here is conceptualized not as a social relation, but as a thing—a thing with a life of its own which subordinates people to its own logic.

Against this, a Luddite analysis, which does not imply a return to machine-breaking, proclaims that, to be understood and explained, technology should be regarded as expressive of particular structures of social relations. This is an important point. There will be some readers who, glancing at the title, will presume that this book is a tirade against the negative consequences of I.T. (unemployment, deskilling, etc.). However, we do not want merely to claim that there are unpleasant effects of the new technology. Our argument, the Luddite insistence, is that technology is an integral part of society, that technology incorporates social values. Our theme is that technologies—rather than the abstraction TECHNOLOGY—are part of the social process and that they are misconceived if removed from that context. We refuse to start analysis with technology and only then ask what will be the results of this thing. Rather, we commence with examination of the social relations within which technologies have been and are being developed, and thereby insist on the social constitution of technology.

This is the weight of David Noble's advocacy that Luddite intellectuals should "raise questions about technological development: about its design, its deployment, the reasons for its introduction, its technical and economic viability, and the causal connections between investment, innovation, productivity, competitiveness, and social welfare" (Noble, 1983c, p. 89). In this study, we try to reveal the social relations that I.T. embodies, the forces that account for its genesis, adoption, and use. In so doing we hope to fulfil a dual purpose, at once challenging the intellectual and the political credentials of those who would tell us that the "microelectronics revolution" has its own momentum which cannot be stopped.

The study is divided into three parts. In Part One, we look at conceptualizations of I.T. in order to reveal common assumptions and weaknesses across the range of interpretations. In Part Two, we examine the real social contexts within which I.T. has been nurtured and is being adopted. In Part Three, we return to our Luddite theme to present an alternative theorization and explanation of the "information revolution."

PART ONE

CONCEPTUALIZATIONS OF INFORMATION TECHNOLOGY

Chapter 2
The Selling of the New Technology

The promotion of the illusion of an "electronic revolution" borders upon complicity by intellectuals in the myth-making of the electrical complex itself. The celebration of the electronic revolution is a process whereby the world of scholarship contributes to the cults of engineering, mobility, and fashion at the expense of roots, tradition, and political organization.

—J. W. Carey and J. J. Quirk, 1970, p. 422

Bookstalls in airports, railway stations, chain stores, and news agents' are fascinating sociologically, since they give insight into the concerns of the mass market. Stocks are predictable: soft pornography, crime, science fiction, romance, international esponage, and romance predominate. Certain titles are found almost everywhere—*The Boys from Brazil, The Valley of the Dolls, The Day of the Jackal,* and *The Eagle has Landed* are obvious examples—as are authors such as Ken Follett, Len Deighton, Jackie Collins, and Harold Robbins. A little nonfiction sits beside the pulp novels, and this too has easily recognizable characteristics. It will surprise no one that a current best-seller is *How to Make Love to Your Man,* a thoroughly modern manual on how to be ladylike, attractive, and liberated.

The bookstalls have become particularly interesting since late 1978 because of the unanticipated appearance of a number of paperbacks that are concerned with a "nonsexy" topic—technology. As any publisher knows, technology does not appeal to a wide public: it is something for specialists, runs of a thousand or two, decidedly not the big time. Nonetheless, a number of titles have nudged aside stories about supermen, inter-galactic adventures, and erotic exploits. Titles such as *The Micro Millenium, The Third Wave, The Wired Society, The Micro Revolution, The Silicon Civilization,* and *The Communications Revolution* have achieved sales hitherto thought impossible for this subject.

Connoisseurs of the bookstalls will be puzzled by the presence of these books only at first glance, since a look at their covers explains their location. They are about a very special technology the discovery of which is set to change our lives more thoroughly than anything previously imagined. Their blurbs announce the content: "The Revolution that will change our lives" (Toffler, 1980); "A tiny fragment of Silicon that will change your life beyond recognition" (Hyman, 1980); "A revolution in technology that could bring the wholesale displacement of people from work by automation—by the robots of science fiction—or the chance of a glittering electronic future with infinite opportunities for everyone?" (Laurie, 1980).

These announce the arrival of something which will revolutionize our whole way of life—our work, leisure, education, politics, family . . . and even our sexuality, if we are to credit Professor Arthur Harkins, director of the graduate program in futures at the University of Minnesota. Harkins believes that by the year 2000

people will be "marrying" robots since, given that the "great bulk of human relationships are formulated on a ritualistic basis" (which is to say that "most humans,
in their relationships with wives or lovers, expect a kind of metronomic precision
of expected behavior and expected responses to occur over time"), even the most
intimate behavior is programmable. Because people "expect breakfast, lunch, and
dinner to be ready at a certain time, sexual acts to be performed at certain times
or in certain ways, the house to be a certain way, the vacation to be a certain way,
and the children to be treated a certain way," then these patterns can be duplicated
by a sophisticated machine which also incorporates personality traits, mechanical
sexual organs, and the warmth, texture, and smell of humans (*Computerworld*,
May 17, 1982). There will clearly be no way of escaping this new technology, and
thus it is not unexpected that Information Technology has entered the best-seller
listings. It is perhaps also a reasonable prediction that a future best-seller—after
How to Make Love to Your Woman—will be *How to Make Love to Your Android*.

The bulk of these popular books on Information Technology are as escapist and
unworldly as the rest of the pulp with which they displayed, despite their hard-
nosed tone and assurances to the contrary. Nevertheless, they do indicate the
arrival of a significant phenomenon. The development and future application of
Information Technology promises to have an influence on many aspects of everyday life. For this reason, there has been a justified fascination at the human ability
to create such a powerful new technology. An avalanche of futurist comment has
helped divert this nascent interest into apathy and awe.

Information Technology

Information Technology (I.T.) is a neologism (others are télématique, compunica-
tions, and informatics) coined to describe a tendency for computing and telecommunications technologies to integrate and converge. It is a generic term which en-
compasses word processors, office equipment, electronic mail, cable television,
videotex, robotics, television games, computer networks, and satellite communications. Its growth is being promoted by the rapid rise of microelectronics, which is
the source of dramatically cheapened computing capacity that is the enabling
technology behind recent developments.

Microelectonics is noteworthy because

- it is a heartland technology which has, in the manner of the steam engine,
petrol engine, and electric motor, application over an entire range of activities.
- it allows information to be handled almost everywhere it appears, since it:

  touches every function of sensing, of control, communications and information processing—indeed, just about every kind of work now performed by
  people or machines except generating power or propelling vehicles. It promises to extend the impact of all that has gone before and to impinge upon
  virtually every organised human activity, whether institutional or personal
  (Sarnoff, 1974, p. 31).

It is this availability of a cheap and reliable means of handling information that has led to the integration and convergence of computers and communications categorized by I.T. This is occurring because microelectronics can now be distributed in much wider ways than was previously possible, which brings about a need to tie together disparate operations. The Howlett Committee reviewed this trend thus:

> It has been obvious for some time that the running of a moderately industrialised economy requires the collection, storing, retrieving, processing and generally moving around of a great variety of information, numerical or otherwise, often in large volumes and often very quickly. The computer makes the first four of these activities possible on a scale which was unthinkable a generation ago and every modern state is now completely dependent on computers and allied devices. . . . The telecommunications system makes the transporting of information possible on the scale required and there is a corresponding dependence here too (Howlett, 1978, p. 1).

Because commentators have focused attention on microelectronics and the significance this has for computer applications, there has been a tendency to underestimate the symbiotic role of telecommunications. However, it is arguable that telecommunications is nowadays "the most important single business in Britain" (Conservative Party, 1979, p. 41), because it is not computers in themselves which are so crucial, but the ability to network computers, to extend computer communications on a widespread scale. Telecommunications, which itself integrates many aspects of computerization for information storage, exchange functions, and network control, provides this essential means of interconnexion (Baer, 1978).

The ability of telecommunications to transmit information presages a time when "information ring mains" will link departments in offices, headquarters to divisions, central offices to individuals; when automated factory production will be capable of control from a central unit; when the home will be able to access data banks in local, national, and international locations. . . . These prospects for an "electronic grid," enhanced by the increased carrying capacity of cable, optical fibre, microwave and satellites, have led writers to envisage an era of a "wired society" in which, in each home, office, shop, restaurant, school, bank, town hall, or wherever, there will be computer terminals linked to central processors which will create a situation in which the public have "information sockets like three-pin power sockets for electricity" (Barron and Curnow, 1979, p. 31).

Another important development made possible by the "tidal wave" (ibid.) of microelectronics is the emergence of industries supplying systems rather than separate products.

A number of reasons account for this:

- *integration:* one of the aspects of integration is the tendency for new products to subsume the functions of former ones.
- *convergence:* previously separate technologies are coming together with the imbrication of computers and communications.

• *product compatibility:* the trend today is towards the supply of data processing, communications equipment, and so forth as systems that are compatible in areas such as text editing, computing, filing, and reproduction.

It is for these reasons that AT&T projects that "More and more, the Bell System's services for business will take the form of comprehensive systems integrating virtually all aspects of information flow, encompassing voice, video, data storage, retrieval, processing and distribution, word processing and electronic mail" (*Annual Report,* 1980). Tying "together the products of... various sections" (Hitachi, *Annual Report,* 1980) is most readily seen in the office, but a similar process is discernable in goods being manufactured for the home which build upon television (for example, video cassette recorders, television games, viewdata). Thus AT&T observes that "the home communications market" is moving "in much . . . the same direction" as business "towards information-communications *systems.* We expect to equip the home of the future with facilities that meet a wide variety of needs: information, education, entertainment, and . . . the control of energy consumption (*Annual Report,* 1980).

Systems will increasingly replace products in three areas (which eventually will themselves integrate):

• *production systems:* automation of manufacture, instrumentation, robotics, computer-controlled engineering, etc.
• *office systems:* integrated systems for filing, typing, data/text processing and communication, copying, etc.
• *household systems:* home entertainment/information systems incorporating video, games, computing, television, teletext, etc.

It is clear that the shift towards systems of computer-communications will neither take place overnight nor be developed at an even pace. There are good social, economic, and political reasons why systems will be introduced into offices and large organizations before they fully enter the domestic sphere. And even in the office, systems will be built incrementally on a modular basis from present day products. Nevertheless, while conceding uneven development, and that the new builds upon the old, there remain unstopable pressures forcing the spread of I.T. systems.

From this it would seem that I.T. straightforwardly identifies a range of goods and services emerging out of the integration and convergence of computers and communications that are shifting away from disparate products towards systems. However, such a definition suggests too much neatness and fails to acknowledge both the generality and massive compass of the term. I.T. is in truth a vague concept, in principle encompassing any technology which handles information, though more often indicating the use of computers and communications together, that has been conjured to make sense of some deep-seated changes. In consequence, the category has a huge spread that makes it difficult to readily and comprehensively identify its constituents.

For this reason, some commentators have elided microelectronic applications in the field of product manufacture (e.g., robotics, control engineering) from the category, and have limited I.T. to those areas of use in more obvious information-processing spheres such as administration, education, government, and media. This does have the virtue of recognizing the major areas that are being and will be affected by the new technology. However, even this leaves I.T. with an enormous reach that includes "the actual equipment used to collect, store, process, transmit and display information. . . . (as well as the software that controls it) . . . and its interactions with human activities and the management systems necessary if the capabilities of new developments are to be fully exploited." In these terms, the title covers

> important sectors of the electronic components industry (with an emphasis on microelectronics), much electronic equipment (notably computers and their associated terminals, displays, etc.) and the whole communications industry, including the broadcasting authorities . . . (telecommunications) and the users and suppliers of information—industrial, financial, commercial, administrative, professional, and individual—because their activities will be affected by new forms of information handling   (ACARD, 1980).

Therefore, though I.T. is an amorphous term, we can identify the following sectors as central constituents:

- data/text processing equipment (computers, peripherals).
- data/text processing (software houses).
- data/text communications carriers (chiefly telecommunications authorities outside the USA).
- data/text communications equipment manufacturers (exchanges, satellites, etc.).
- significant parts of consumer electronics (e.g., video, television).
- electronic components (tv tubes, integrated circuits, etc.).
- office equipment (copiers, typewriters, word processors, etc.).
- information suppliers (online data bases, broadcasting organizations, etc.).

Futurism Wild and Sober

It is this arrival of I.T., unannounced and uninvited, which has been the occasion for the succession of "mighty micro" paperbacks. But the speculation has not stopped there. There has in fact been a much more sweeping response to I.T. Indeed, it is no exaggeration to say that the public has been deluged by materials such that it is hardly conceivable that anyone can be ignorant of at least some of its applications. The very scale of the response to I.T. compels us to take it seriously, though we cannot commend the flood of (mis)information that has burst upon society. To explain our antipathy, let us review some of the coverage of I.T. prior to analyzing its themes and assumptions.

I.T. has hardly been out of the media of late, whether as a regular source of accounts about economic restructuring caused by its take-up in the business press, features in the qualities, or breathless 200-word leaders in the tabloid newspapers. Television has put out programs—and series of programs—that commenced in Britain with a *Horizon* special and Christopher Evans's *The Mighty Micro* in 1978, and have appeared recurrently since on the likes of *Tomorrow's World, Nova,* and *The Burke Special.* Within the space of a few months, from nowhere, I.T. has permeated the media such that it has even entered the plots of soaps.

In these outlets futurism has been working as if there was no tomorrow to supply instant comment and projections. Wilson Dizard tells us that the

> vision of a plug-in future, of computers in the living room, of global tele-conferences, of robotics factories controlled by telepresence techniques, and of a new quality of life based on access to vast information resources is. . . too close to possible realization to be dismissed any longer as sci-fi fantasy (Dizard, 1982, p. 38).

With this we are away into speculation of a cashless society, an end to letters, telecommuting, shopping from our armchairs. . . . The *Futurist* magazine, surely the most excitable of all the prophets, repeats in each month's issue stories on the lines that we are "entering an era in which the science fiction of a decade ago is now technological reality," that an information rich future heralds nothing less than a New Renaissance for the West; that I.T. will rescue America from its present crises as the "new miracle brains" get into "everything from toys to kitchen equipment to machines that will play chess and backgammon," provide "automatic machines (that) will cut your lawn . . . then rake the leaves without human hands," let "capital . . . be generous with labour without significant cost to itself," hold down inflation . . . leaving a contented populace with time, inclination, and money so that "history's wheel, having rolled through despotism and oligarchy, may . . . because of the miracle chip, jam forever on democracy" (all quotations from the *Futurist,* August, 1981; cf., Cornish, 1982).

There are of course more sober prognostications than these. Comment becomes markedly less star-struck the shorter its span of prediction. The immediate prospects, delineated by politicians and businessmen in the main, wonder about the likely effects on balance of payments, European strategic relations with Japan and the USA, or organizational aspects of the "office of the future." Scenarios here outline painful effects on traditional operations, consider the need to invest in new technology, and the requirements of education to familiarize students with I.T. The talk is grim, realistic, and measured.

However, the sober and wild elements of futurism are usually wedded, in that comments imagine a dazzling future if only the difficult years of adjustment can be got through. For instance, James Callaghan, then Prime Minister, thought in late 1978 that "we may be on the threshold of the most rapid industrial change in history" which could bring "within reach of the budget of our people a range of goods and services they could never previously afford," but "we must prepare for it" because "we do not have time to lose" if we are "to reap the maximum benefit from the new technology" (Callaghan, 1978). This oscillation between tantalizing long-term prospect and formidable problems in the near future is characteristic of much of the presentation of I.T. It is, of course, the old theme of carrot and stick.

Government

The Conservative Government in Britain created a multi-million pound campaign—Information Technology Year 1982 (*IT'82*)—offering a program of travelling exhibitions, subsidized conferences, and demonstation projects. When it was announced "there were assurances that (it) will not dodge the issue of social change" (*Guardian*, 29 May, 1981), but what has issued forth amounts to nothing less than a massive propaganda exercise extolling I.T. By late 1982, its presenters had come to define it as a means of "informing and enthusing as many people as possible of the benefits of Information Technology" (*IT'82*, October 1982), and it was fitting that Margaret Thatcher, acknowledging the success of the campaign so far, promised that her government would "continue to encourage people to *accept* the new technology" (Thatcher, 1982, original emphasis).

To this end, *IT'82* produced an extensive advertising campaign featuring slogans such as "Has the revolution started without you?" "Is your seven-year-old better equipped to run an office than you are?" and "Is the technology in your local more advanced than the technology in your factory?!" Beneath such headings are messages, attractively illustrated, which tell us that I.T. is "transforming old industries, taking away boredom, removing danger, making factories cleaner, more pleasant places to work," that I.T. in the office will "take away an enormous amount of boredom from a secretary's life and provided a machine that is intrinsically interesting to use," that "caring for prematurely born babies, continuously monitoring them, and alerting hospital doctors and nurses whenever special treatment is needed, is just one area in which IT looks after people," that "from our earliest moments to old age, IT is involved in looking after us, and not just in terms of our health. IT is also helping to educate our children and to equip them to exploit fully the information revolution." *IT'82* produced an irregular newsheet in similar vein: the new technology is presented as a panacea for ills found in all spheres of life—and it reaches all spheres.

The campaign also encouraged the public to hurry and accept this "once-in-a-century chance to create new wealth, higher standards of living and a world in which routine and drudgery are alleviated and in which all of us have more time, freedom and ability to pursue our interests." And if these words of inducement ("The important thing to remember about the IT revolution . . . is that its effects are friendly") were insufficient, if one persisted in hanging back, then *IT'82* threatened: "one thing is certain about IT, if we don't learn its lessons now for ourselves; we'll end up having to pay someone else to teach us"; "The one thing that is absolutely certain is that if we don't adopt IT, our competitors will. They are already doing so"; "Without IT, Britain will decline—very fast"; "There's no future without IT."

Education

Education at all levels in the U.K. has been induced to act on I.T. (DES, 1978, 1979), harried by repeated calls for "an injection of technology into the curriculum" (Gosling, 1981, pp. 16-17) because the "task of education" is to help "our kind to make the transition to a new lifestyle" (Gosling, 1978, p. 39). In the upper ranges, extra resources have been made available for courses on microelectronics, computing, and electronic engineering, while research funds, cut almost everywhere else, have been forthcoming. "New blood" lectureships in British universities have overwhelmingly gone to I.T. and cognate subjects, while other disciplines have been heavily bled. Lower down the educational ladder there is a government commitment in the U.K. to get a microcomputer into every secondary school by the mid-1980s, special programs have been devised to familiarize the generation which will reach adulthood in the computer age; computer camps are encouraged as worthy holiday activities, and soon all Britain's 20,000 primary schools will have a computer. Needless to say, *IT'82* has singled out the schools for special attention. To this end posters, video material, films, and literature, all appealingly packaged, have been sent gratis to teachers. The campaign also subsidized 50 percent of a book—*Educating the Information Generation*—which was sent free to British schools early in 1983. The source of the rest of the costs, commercial sponsors, notably IBM, suggests the substance of this education. Such has been the success of these measures that the Microelectronics Education Program, a joint venture of the Departments of Industry and Education commenced in 1980, had its budget doubled and span of life extended to 1986 the better to continue its mission in schools (Fothergill, 1983).

Government can rely upon other agencies to complement this material. For example, the press is replete with messages for the younger generation, competitions to write essays on the microelectronics revolution, personal computers to be won, badges and leaflets to be sent for. The Disney organization supports the schools with its $800 million Experimental Prototype Community of Tomorrow (Epcot) which aims "to convince the general public that computers are as nonthreatening as Mickey Mouse—and infinitely more useful." Demonstrating the group's "underlying principle of using entertainment as a medium of public instruction," Disneyland (one of America's more visited amusements which is supplemented by major television and film coverage) will use Epcot's robots, moving replicas of living creatures, extensive terminals, and extravagant special effects "to portray processors as useful and approachable and to counteract the widespread perception of the machines as sinister and destructive entities" (*Computerworld*, March 8, 1982). AT&T features *Spaceship Earth* at the Epcot Center, sponsoring an exhibit which "depicts communications from the Stone Age to the Information Age" (*Annual Report*, 1982). The spectators will doubtless appreciate how wonderfully we have evolved, and shall continue to do so, if things are left in the safe hands of the Bell System (Bass, 1983). All this and Disneyland is but the most prominent aspect of a massive industry of toys, comics, and games which has hitched on to the I.T. juggernaut to sell its wares.

Advertising

Corporate advertisers have lately been spending fortunes, both extolling their produce and—with increased emphasis—urging public acceptance of I.T. and "the
future." A whole page is bought in the *Observer* newspaper (cost in 1983 £15,750)
to tell us that "Information technology has a long and benign history. The computer, the telephone, the telegraph, the printing press, the invention of writing itself—
all of them led to increased prosperity and universal improvement in the standard
of living." For all this and more to come, the paymaster adds that "Britain will be
grateful to Sinclair Research" (*Observer, 22 May, 1983*), and the advertisement is
repeated in other national press. In the USA, AT&T has been among the most
actively committed to "the great crusade for understanding" (Barnet and Müller,
1975, pp. 105-120), scheduling a regular series of prime-time television and newspaper advertisements which comment on an "Information Age" in the making.
The Bell organization incurs this expense because "We believe it is in the public
interest to see the benefits of that new age come to America as quickly as possible"
(Advertisement, *Wall Street Journal,* January 14, 1982).

United Technologies, buying space in *The Atlantic,* takes to heart the Mobil
organization's maxim that "business needs voices in the media" because "our
nation functions best when economic and other concerns of the people are subjected to rigorous debate" (Mobil advertisement, *Los Angeles Times,* April 6,
1982). To this end, United Technologies contributes to the "rigorous debate"
about technological innovation by vilifying "Misfortune Tellers" of the past through
choice quotation. Thus, "A sampling of the now-amusing statements of old shows
that naysaying is nothing new" precedes idiocies from a nineteenth century cleric
such as, "Rail travel at high speed is not possible because passengers, unable to
breathe, would die of asphyxia." Half a dozen of this sort of remark lead to the
sagacious conclusion of a "rigorous debate:" "Misfortune tellers with dark clouds
in their crystal balls have always been with us. Happily, so have innovators with
the vision and perseverance to reach successfully for the promise of technology"
(*The Atlantic,* April 1982).

Such appeals to favor change are commonplace in discussions of I.T. IBM is
especially in favor of progress and vehemently against those Luddites who hinder
innovation and the advantages it brings. The company presents history lessons in
the pages it buys:

> the action of the Luddites carries a very instructive lesson: it's not progress
> itself which is the threat, but the way we adapt to it. For without technology,
> a nation's progress would undoubtedly falter. Machines bring down the cost
> of production. Which in turn either creates greater profit for reinvestment,
> or holds down the costs of the product, so providing greater purchasing
> power for the pound. The result is greater wealth—the ideal climate for in-
> creased employment. And machines that relieve man of the tasks that limit
> his personal fulfilment. Smashing the clocks might destroy the mechanism
> of progress. But it will never delay tomorrow (Advertisement, *New States-
> man,* 25 May, 1979).

In such ways do corporate advertisers present innovation, seizing upon the idea of progress as an unqualified term of praise, tapping deeply-held beliefs of Western society (Pollard, 1968; Sklair, 1970; Bury, 1932).

Many of these advertisements are aimed at particular social groups rather than the public at large. Targeting messages in the business, political, and upmarket press that proclaim the electronic age is evidently directed at opinion leaders (the British government's "awareness campaign," launched by Labour in 1979, paralleled this in being aimed at "50,000 key decision makers" [*Electronics Times,* 11 January, 1979]). Given the socio-economic situation of such readers, one can safely assume that most will be predisposed to look favorably on I.T., so much of the propaganda will function to consolidate rather than change opinion. One may further speculate that, at such a time as we live, when I.T. is arriving amidst recession, uncertainty, and apprehension, there is a special psychological need for opinion leaders to be convinced that current developments which appear unstoppable are beneficial, and that the future will indeed turn out for the best. Only with this conviction can they operate effectively as mediators between government, corporations, and the wider public.

James Martin—and the entourage accompanying the James Martin Seminars—combines a boost in confidence in the future with the appealing promise of improved corporate productivity in the immediacy to those businesspeople able to attend his regular audiences in Amsterdam, London, Paris, Berlin, New York, Los Angeles, Chicago, Toronto, Atlanta, or Boston. All his activities evidence the breezy confidence and evangelical fervor of one sold on progress and the future and schooled in two decades with IBM. And of even more significance is that Martin represents only the best-known face of an unceasing round of conferences, seminars, and workshops designed to sell I.T. to educationalists, academics, business, community, and political representatives.

Visionaries and Realists

It has been a feature of commentary on I.T. that much has evidenced a coexistence of fantastic futurism with grave concern for the constraints of the here and now. We mentioned this paradox earlier, and would comment further on the popularity of the "visionary" and "realist" approaches. A great deal unites the two by switching back and forth from a scenario for the 1990s promising wonderful achievements to the disturbing and unsettled 1980s, and it has been choice of time scale rather than different conceptions of the significance of I.T. that has distinguished opinions. Thus, in spite of different emphases, it is hard to doubt that the presentation of I.T., both as a herald of better, even halcyon, days and as something which must be taken up immediately to avert a further plunge into recession, has been instrumental in effecting its unopposed introduction. The probability that foreign competitors will adopt I.T. before us, and thereby gain markets at our expense which will worsen recession, is constantly held out as the reality which demands rapid take-up of new technology. It is such a prospect that induces the Trades Union

Congress to pressure "Britain to be in the vanguard of technological change" (TUC, 1979), and, as this present difficulty imposes itself, the long-term futurist nirvana is drawn upon as a source of morale.

When one looks at statements from politicians about I.T., one sees serious concern for immediate problems, though the electronic idylls are always on the horizon. But what is still more striking than this is the astonishing unanimity about I.T. in the political sphere which in fact serves to denude the issue of politics in any meaningful sense. In Britain, Labour and Tory spokespeople are in accord that I.T. presents the possibility of renewed glory—provided it is quickly taken up. For example it was James Callaghan who noted that 1978 "has proved to be the year when Britain woke up to microelectronics," urged the nation to meet head on the challenge of I.T. and strive for its rewards. If we do not adopt it, he went on, "and other major industrial countries adapt . . . then the prospect for us will be of stagnation and of decline" (Callaghan, 1978). In exactly the same way, Kenneth Baker, by 1981 the Minister of Information Technology in a Conservative administration, stressed the "enormous opportunities" I.T. held for the country, so long as we were not "left behind in this technological race. We shall have to run fast to keep abreast of our European partners, and we shall have to run very fast to keep ahead of the newly emerging countries (since) we cannot resist the trend of progress" (*Hansard*, 11 July, 1980, col. 933-934). A full-scale debate on I.T. in the British Parliament held in 1980 underscored this remarkable consensus, members agreeing that "it is difficult to decide who is a Conservative and who is a Socialist in this debate" (ibid, col. 955), that in speeches "there has been a lack of political partisanship and a genuine desire to explore the problems and possibilities of modern technology" (col. 993), that a "feature that has characterized this debate already is the lack of party controversy" (col. 993). All this is uniformedly technocratic, denying a politics of technology on the center-stage of the polity.

We are not the first to note this consensus. Revealingly, a commercial organization, Acorn Computers, underscored it in a full page advertisement in the *Guardian* newspaper (8 June, 1983) on the eve of what was one of the most polarized and bitter political campaigns in post-War history. The text ran:

Whatever the differences between the three major parties . . . we're happy to report a certain amount of accord on, at least, one important issue. All three parties have recently affirmed their commitment to the continuing growth of information technology and to the vital role of the microcomputer in education and industry. Whoever wins tomorrow, therefore, it is certain that the microcomputer has an increasing role to play.

Acorn unabashedly staked its claim as "one of the handful of companies that has helped Britain achieve this position" as it insisted that I.T. "is basic to the future growth of this country," prior to concluding: "Isn't it reassuring to know that, whoever is drinking the champagne on Friday, there is a shared determination to keep that industry ahead in the world?" It is fitting that a commercial outfit should in its puffery voice approval of this consensus, since it recalls an earlier example of assurances that certain things are beyond debate: as Acorn's interests in I.T. coalesce with those of the nation, so too did General Motors' with those of America. We may ponder the likely effects on public attitudes towards I.T. when political representatives—not to mention a surfeit of media, education, and business opinion—present such an undifferentiated response.

So have gone—and continue to go—the instant analyses of I.T. We have been swamped with projections and recommendations which acknowledge I.T. will have an enormous social effect, that its adoption is unavoidable, and that in the long run it will be a fine thing for us all. These deserve closer inspection.

Technology is Benign

Technology is presented as, on the whole, benign. Typically "most of the changes are changes for the better: better education, better news media, better forms of human communication, better entertainment, better medical resources, less pollution, less human drudgery, less use of petroleum, more efficient industry, and a better informed society with a rich texture of information sources" (Martin, 1978a, p. 15). To be sure, there are references to potential ill effects, generally of a transitional nature, but the overwhelming image is one of a "benevolent technology" (ibid.) which may create an "electronic renaissance" (Williams, 1982, p. 280).

In spite of the fact that reports, especially in the media, present a picture of there being a choice to be made between interpretations that are either optimistic or pessimistic, there is no balance between alternative views. The roseate picture of a post-industrial wonderland far outweighs references to the possibility of mass unemployment and authoritarian states.

Technology as Spectacle

Technology is presented as a spectacle, as something which can evoke only a gee-whiz, awed response, since it entails regarding technology as a phenomenon that has arrived in society from out of the blue, although it will have a devastating social effect. This conception of a desocialized technology which is set to have the most far-reaching social effects inevitably leads to Callaghan-like calls to wake up to the unexpected arrival. We are so accustomed to preceiving social change in these terms of a history of technological development ("the Railway Age," "the world the steam engine made") somehow removed from human intent and decision that the most recent developments are readily framed in this way (Williams, 1974, pp. 9–31). History comes to be seen as a history of technological innovation, contemporary Britain the product of a "remarkable series of inventions" (Landes, 1969), microelectronics but the latest stage of this progression. History—technological advance—comes to have its own logic and drive which shapes the society though it is devoid of social value. In this framework technology is assumed, crucially, to be separate from society at its outset (apparently having arisen from some internal process in some wierd and wonderful place such as Silicon Valley) only to be introduced at a later stage as an independent variable which is the primary cause of social change.

Because futurists, in adopting this perspective, accept as their starting-point a completed technology, they are impelled to offer the public no role other than that of consumer of the latest gadgetry. Ignoring the processes by which technology itself comes to be constituted means that one is restricted to consideration only of the likely impact the latest product will have. Such a procedure, as Young observes, necessarily excludes the public from any meaningful say in technological change, since its presentation leaves one with nothing other than the sense that "This is beautiful, fascinating; I have been enlightened. It is serious but very palatable fare—to be consumed" (Young, 1979).

So long as consideration of technology starts from the technology as it is, then discussion can only be limited, restricted to the social implications of a constituted technology, and ignorant of the whole series of social choices that have been exercised in the production of the technology:

> What the media treat is the "impact" of such development. Where were those media when they were being conceived and prepared for market? Today is yesterday's *Tomorrow's World*, but what debate occurred before Raymond Baxter and Co. were allowed to televise what's in store for us? (Ibid.; cf. Gardner and Young, 1981).

W.A. Fallow, chairman of Eastman Kodak, in a recent speech to shareholders unassumingly revealed the misguidedness of regarding technological innovation in the manner of futurists when he informed his audience of Kodak's criteria for development of new products as follows:

> Last year, Kodak spent more than $615 million on R&D (research and development), ranking it among the top ten U.S. companies in total research expenditures. Right now, while we are meeting here, there may be a Kodak scientist . . . making an exciting new discovery in photographic imaging, electronic imaging, or their related fields. Such discoveries can lead to whole new technologies.
>
> About ten years ago, for example, the continuous wave dye laser was invented during research at Kodak. . . . Over the last decade, it has revolutionized the field of spectroscopy. But Kodak has never produced such a laser for market, and so far we have no plans to do so. That market has never had the earnings potential to justify the cost of developing it.
>
> I think the point is clear. Just because Kodak knows *how* to make a product doesn't mean we *should* make it. . . . From now on, Kodak's success will depend on our ability to apply the right mix of many technologies, in those markets characterized by solid growth potential (Fallow, 1982).

To take Mr. Fallow seriously—and, as head of one of the world's leading corporations, he merits taking seriously—is to refuse the starting point and therefore subsequent analysis of almost all commentary on I.T., and to start re-examination of the relations between technology and society from a perspective which rejects all talk of their separation.

Technology is Neutral

Because technology is believed to be asocial, it is also seen as neutral, a tool to be used either appropriately or not, depending on the motives of a society. From this assumption of neutrality, most comment on I.T. asserts that the new technology offers choices. We shall have more to say about this rhetoric of choice, but here we offer Dizard's alternative of a "life-enriching culture in the 21st century" or "collapse into political latitude, economic stalemate, and social fragmentation" (Dizard, 1982, p. 1) as representative of a recurrent theme.

Across the spectrum of politics, one finds assurances that the "technology itself is neutral: it is the way it is applied and used that determines the effects on people" (GMWU, 1980), and from a such a proposition the idea of choice is irresistible. Moreover, if I.T. is socially neutral and leaves policy choices to the public, then on what reasonable grounds can it be suspected?

Inevitability

It is paradoxical that these presentations of I.T., so often professing "choices" that the new technology allows, invariably carry an underlying inevitability. There is total agreement that I.T. must be adopted—and as quickly as possible. Thus Large's "in a competitive world there is no alternative to using the chip as quickly and widely as possible" (Large, 1980, p. 12), and Hyman's "the new technologies need to be introduced rapidly and creatively" (Hyman, 1980, p. 123), are unexceptional statements among the futurists.

As we have noted, commentators across the political divide insist that I.T. cannot be rejected. Tory Kenneth Baker, for example, asserts that "The inevitable logic is that we must accept the technologies" (*Hansard*, 11 July, 1980, col. 938), and he finds an echo in Labourite John Evans' words that "The British people in all walks of life, whether they are employers, trade union members, politicians, or academics, must recognise that we have to accept the advent of the new technology" (Ibid., col. 1000). Moreover, though we are told in the U.K. that the Social Democratic Party has "broken the mould" of orthodox allegiances, the fracture has not affected reaction towards I.T., leading member Shirley Williams concurring that "there is no alternative to adopting the new technologies" (*Guardian*, 18 November, 1980).

This inevitability has been reinforced by a historical legacy of what has been called the "ideology of industrialization," by which is meant a tradition of thought which perceives technology as a hidden hand in development apart from the social issues of power and control. David Dickson summarizes:

The message of this ideology is that industrialization through technological development is a practical—rather than a political—necessity for achieving social development. It implies an objectivity to the process, and seeks to remove it from debate on political issues. It thus gives a legitimacy to prophecies that appear to promote the process of industrialization, often regardless of their political, or even social consequences . . . To stand in the way of technology is, almost by definition, to be labelled reactionary. Industrialization is equated with modernization, with progress, with a better and healthier life for all (Dickson, 1974, p. 42).

The Past in the Future

If one queries the advantages—or the need—of accepting today's technological innovation, one is frequently protrayed as an unworldly romantic in sharp contrast to the this-worldiness and foresight of its advocates. This charge castigates a deep-rooted tradition in England of a rejection of "industry" in favor of a retrospective ruralism (Newby, 1980). It is a remarkable feature of industrial capitalism that, throughout the transforming experiences of the past three centuries, the ideas of rural life have "persisted with extraordinary power" (Williams, 1975, p. 10): "*Real* England has never been represented by the town, but by the village, and the English countryside has been converted into a vast arcadian rural idyll in the mind of the average Englishman" (Newby, 1979, pp. 11-12). This idealization of the countryside, especially the agricultural past, in the most thoroughly urbanized country in the world is evidenced in much literary and cultural output which extends from the beginnings of industrialization through writers as diverse as William Blake, Charles Dickens, and D. H. Lawrence, to current vogues for Laura Ashley dresses, earthenware pots, and nostalgia for anything rural and it can easily be shown to be misleading, ignorant of the misery, oppression, and deprivations of pre-industrialism (see, for example, George, 1962). Subscribers to a rural idyll are too often ignorant of history—the real history of the countryside in which life "was as hard and brutal as anything later experienced" (Williams, 1975, p. 31)— to be taken seriously. Because of this, opposition to new technology is readily smeared and thereby discounted by association with a tradition which can appear to desire a return to the impoverishments of an earlier time. Drawing on this imagery, Wilson P. Dizard can sneer at and condemn the "disturbing tendency to retreat from the implications of the new machines, to deny the possibility of a viable technology-powered democratic society. These anti-technology forces, the new Luddites, seek solace in astrology, artificial Waldens, and bad poetry" (Dizard, 1982, p. 15).

Paradoxically, however, and possibly because ruralism is so deeply entrenched, perpetrators of the new technology have often tried to steal the clothes of these opponents even while ridiculing their proposals. This is achieved by projecting a return to the past in the future, the recovery of a golden age with 21st century comforts, by suggesting that adoption of I.T. will effect a return to a lost way of life. We see this posture in the language of those who envisage the re-establishment of domestic production in the era of the electronic cottage, a period when community will be regained in a wired society, a time when pollution disappears due to "technologies that are environmentally sound . . . and nondestructive of the ecology" (Martin, 1978a, p. 4).

This capacity to combine rejection of I.T.'s critics with the argument that I.T. satisfies the requirements of their criticism is remarkably common. Dizard, for example, jettisons "antitechnology forces" for their naivety and immediately proceeds to hymn the "search for a new Eden through the melding of nature and the machine" that is a "powerful force propelling us toward new forms of post-industrialism" which, in the "information age," brings "electronic salvation within our grasp" (Dizard, 1982, pp. 22-23). Alvin Toffler dismisses "critics of industrialism" who picture the "rural past as warm, communal, stable, organic, and with spiritual rather than purely materialistic values" because "historical research reveals that these supposedly lovely rural communities were . . . cesspools of malnutrition, disease, poverty, homelessness, and tyranny, with people helpless against hunger, cold, and the whips of their landlords and masters" (Toffler, 1980, p. 135). Toffler categorizes those who praise "pre-technological primitivism" (Toffler, 1970, p. 284) as a "small, vocal fringe of romantic extremists" that is "mostly middle-class, speaking from the vantage point of a full belly, blindly indiscriminate" and guilty of desiring "a return to a world that most of us—and most of them—would find abhorrent" (Toffler, 1980, p. 167), going so far as to label these "future-haters" sufferers of the pathology "technophobia" (Toffler, 1970, p. 233). Nonetheless, our best-selling futurist is no apologist for industrialism. On the contrary, "Second Wave systems are in crisis" (Toffler, 1980, p. 139), and their institutions "crash about our heads" (p. 367) due to crises of ecology, work satisfaction, and even intimate relations. But from the ashes of this collapse, salvation rises in the form of "third wave civilization" which is set to supercede "second wave" (i.e., industrial) society. Here the electronic cottage will facilitate the development (and re-establishment) of the "prosumer" who combines the role of consumer and producer while working from home. Such a trend offers a return to lifestyles that were "common in the early days of the industrial revolution among farm populations," though now one can "Imagine this life pattern—but with twenty-first century technology for goods and food production" (p. 294).

Add this together, and what is offered is a "practopian future" (p. 375) which looks much like—but is also much more than—the romantic visions of the past. In like manner, James Martin contends that:

> Local communities in the future may grow more of their own foods and provide their own daily needs. They will have offices for white-collar workers plugged into nationwide telecommunications networks. They will have satellite stations or other links that provide the same television facilities as in the big cities. The local bread and vegetables will be better than those that are mass-packaged for nationwide distribution. Much of the drudgery of commuting will be ended. . . . For many the lifestyle of rural communities with

excellent telecommunications will be preferable to that in the cities (Martin, 1978a, p. 191).

The moral of all such propaganda—as if one could have missed it—is simply that

> Rather than lashing out, Luddite-fashion, against the machine, those who genuinely wish to break the prison-hold of the past and present would do well to hasten the . . . arrival of tomorrow's technologies . . . [because] it is precisely the super-industrial society, the most advanced technological society ever, that extends the range of freedom (Toffler, 1970, pp. 282–283).

Neo-McLuhanism

Though this futurism which imagines "people living in what one can recognise as the old pastoral ways . . . but possessing great power because they have internalized the communication and productive capacities of the urban-scientific-industrial phase" (Williams, 1975, p. 331) has recently experienced a resurgence, it has a lengthy tradition. This was developed, especially in the United States, during the nineteenth century as a distinctive "industrial version of the pastoral design" (Marx, 1964, p. 32), found its exemplar in Walt Whitman's celebration of the "body electric" (Bentall, 1976), and drew together a "powerful metaphor of contradiction," "a strong urge to believe in the rural myth along with an awareness of industrialization as counterforce to the myth" (Marx, 1964, p. 4, 229).

The most prominent recent member of this tradition was Marshall McLuhan. He himself had, significantly, a biographical connection with both the English school of literary criticism which held to the notion of a disappearing rural "organic community" and the "industrial pastoral" of his native North America (Fekete, 1978). Moreover, most of the contemporary writers on I.T. ought to be seen as being squarely within this tradition and its McLuhanite emphasis on the "electronic sublime" (Carey and Quirk, 1970). Indeed, the presence of elements of McLuhan's work can be sensed in all the books, articles, and television presentations to which we have referred. For example, Anthony Smith's *Goodbye Gutenberg* (1980), both a substantial book and a BBC documentary broadcast in 1980, constantly reminds us of McLuhan's *Gutenberg Galaxy* (1962), and, though he never in fact mentions his mentor, Smith's exercise should be seen as a sequel to McLuhan's. Elsewhere McLuhan is unabashedly rehashed: James Martin believing that I.T.'s promise of satellite-age democracy will fulfil McLuhan's ideal of a global village (Martin, 1978a, pp. 75-76); Sam Fedida and Rex Malik (1979) announcing their debt to McLuhan on the opening page of their report on viewdata; and Joseph Pelton, whose fantasia of the "telecity" in an age of "Global talk" is simply vulgar McLuhanism (Pelton, 1981b).

Technological Determinism

It is apposite that we recall McLuhan here, first to indicate the tradition in social thought of "the machine in the garden" (Marx, 1964), and second—and more important–to point out the technological determinism which underpins the futurism now in vogue. Starting out from the technology, this comment is invariably determinist, since, acceding to the technology as it is, it then asks and only asks–what are the social implications of this technology? The technology is assumed to be a major–and insolatable–variable which causes social change, and, whether or not writers take a strong or soft line as regards the degree of causation, they all remain within a determinist frame.

In the light of recent concern with I.T., we believe that it is now appropriate to revive the criticism of McLuhan's faith in the electronic millenium, since his work represents an extreme formulation of technological determinism and today retains a certain veracity as a version of the belief that technology is the motor of history. As McLuhanism resurfaces, it is salutary to indicate its two central traits. One, technology is considered a determining factor within society, for McLuhan *the* determinant factor: "All media work us over completely. They are so pervasive in their personal, political, economic, aesthetic, psychological, moral, ethical, and social consequences that they leave no part of us untouched, unaffected, unaltered. The medium is the message" (McLuhan, 1967, p. 26). The difference between McLuhan's advocacy of "utter human docility" in the face of technological change, and the now common statement that we must "adapt to the world of the silicon chip" (Burkitt and Williams, 1980, p. 154), is only one of emphasis (and not much of that). Two, as detailed earlier, technology is detached from its social context and treated as an isolated phenomenon.

The conception of a determining technology is found in all popular (and not so popular) presentations of the new technology. A characteristic metaphor is that of an alien, extra-social invasion which cannot be prevented from effecting massive changes in social arrangements. The imagery of revolution created by such invaders has become the stock-in-trade of futurist offerings, and examples are legion: Burkitt and Williams commence with "A mysterious force has come into our lives, working silently, screened from the human eye, and understood by only a tiny few. It is smaller than a fingernail, thinner than a leaf, and is covered with microscopic markings. It is powered by minute amounts of electricity . . . yet it is probably one of the most significant machines ever made by man: the silicon chip" (Burkitt and Williams, 1980, p. 9). Alvin Toffler, writing of the "great, growling engine of change–technology" (Toffler, 1970, p. 25), envisages a "dramatically new techno-structure for a Third Wave civilization" (Toffler, 1980, p. 164) which is a "powerful tide . . . surging across much of the world today, creating a new, often bizarre, environment in which to work, play, marry, raise children or retire" (pp. 17–18). Frederick Williams contends that "our lives will never be the same again" because of the "miracles of electronic communications" (Williams, 1982, p. 9, 18). Joseph Pelton believes the "process(es) of technical modernization, automation . . . are seemingly irresistible forces" (Pelton, 1981b, p. 203). Christopher Evans opens with "This book is about the future. . . . It is a future which will involve a transformation of world society at all kinds of levels . . . It's a future which is largely moulded by a single, startling development in technology whose impact is just beginning to be felt. The piece of technology I'm talking about is, of course, the computer" (Evans, 1979, p. 9). Occasionally, some of these writers, aware that it is looked on with disfavor by most serious students, disclaim "naive technological determinism" (Gosling, 1981, p. 8). At the same time, they hail a "microelectronics revolution which is changing and shaking our whole contemporary world," bringing about an "explosive reconstruction of human society and life" (p. 81, 83).

Recalling these features so much in evidence, it is important to emphasise that this neo-McLuhanite perspective involves a focus on technology to the exclusion of social phenomena—the social is always adaptive and secondary to technology—and in doing so it "abolishes history," thereby removing "questions of human need, interest, value or goal" (Fekete, 1973, p. 80, 78). From this perception of desocialized technologies, McLuhanites then identify an astonishing causal capability in the technology: the technology is transformed into a *deus ex machina,* influencing society yet beyond the influence of society. It is in this way that McLuhanism is a type of "technological fetish" that is idealist in spite of its ostensible materialism. Though materialist in focusing on the things of this world (and how can one be more materialist than when concerned with technology?), the approach is idealist in so far as it excludes the world from these things to which it ascribes such social significance.

Technological Socialism

There is one other feature of futurism which deserves elaboration—the aspiration towards a similar society to that offered by socialists *without* need for socialist commitment or action. This projection rests on the adage that socialism is a fine dream but is practically unattainable. Now, thanks to I.T., runs the argument, the dream can be realized without the unpleasantness of political struggle. The idea that we may, following technological trends, be on a path which will produce a better society (one which will make manifest the ideals of many socialists) in a smooth, evolutionary manner is a favored theme of futurism. It often merely suffuses prediction, making its presence felt in assurances that the information society will be a caring, communal, service-oriented one, but the appropriation of socialist language and vision can be quite explicit. Thus, for Anthony Hyman, "the magnificent generosity of the new technology is at last beginning to make it possible for society to move in the direction of its old dream, never realisable but a splendid goal, the dream that was appropriated by Marxism and then lost in the monolithic politics of the twentieth century: from each and all according to their inclination; to each according to need" (Hyman, 1980, pp. 126–127).

On occasion, this type of comment presents I.T. as the means to achieve a recognizably socialistic society while also claiming it is a challenge to all orthodoxies. James Martin, for instance, impatient with the uptake of I.T., appeals to "young people especially" as he lambasts all who oppose the good life promised by the new technology, and his attack includes "corporate Luddites" who "attempt to prevent the spread of new technologies which they fear will harm their profits" (Martin,

1978a, pp. 14-15). He announces himself a veritable firebrand, the champion of technologies that "are in conflict with the established order" which are bound to "encounter fierce opposition from vested interests" (p. 15). Alvin Toffler is still more of an extremist, insisting that all ideologies are conservative when contrasted with his allegiance to the "super-struggle for tomorrow" between "those who try to prop up and preserve industrial society and those who are ready to advance beyond it" (Toffler, 1980, p. 453). He rings the death knell on Marxism—"The farther we move beyond industrial mass society the less tenable the Marxist assumptions" (p. 436)—and (less vigorously) on capitalism, which is "tearing apart under the impact of an accelerating wave of change" (p. 247). Toffler, eager for battle, denounces "Marxists and anti-Marxists alike, capitalists and anti-capitalists, Americans and Russians [who have been] bearing the same set of fundamental premises" . . . Both were apostles of indust-reality" (p. 115), both "basically committed to preserving the dying industrial order" (p. 453). Our hero berates the cowardice of those who find "frightenening . . . the prospect of deep political change," and contemptuously throws aside those "pseudorevolutionaires"—"Archaeo-Marxists, anarcho-romantics," etc.—who are "steeped in obsolete Second Wave assumptions" (p. 456). The real revolution is coming, states Alvin Toffler, and this "third wave" will bring down all "second wave elites." It is fortunate that all we need to do is catch the third wave as it rises and let it carry us safely to a shore offering material abundance, personal satisfaction, and communal bonds while it swamps all obsolete political interests.

There are other futurists who put a different inflection on the issue, though they share the domain assumptions. The promise of I.T. is seized upon by Christopher Evans to at once propagandize for Western capitalism and preach the immanence of "paradise" here, where "the emancipation of Man from the need to work for his living will have been achieved" (Evans, 1979, p. 150-151). With Toffler and Martin, Evans believes that "the production of fantastically cheap devices will, at long last, make the humanistic dream of universal affluence and freedom from drudgery a reality" (p. 207), which means that the world will change "and for the better, and without the long-awaited revolution of the proletariat" (p. 205). However, this practical attainment of socialism via the microprocessor, since it is a "creature of capitalism" (p. 209), will highlight the "inherent advantages of the capitalist system," because I.T. could only have developed "through go-for-broke capitalist exploitation" (p. 207).

Therefore, pace Toffler, Evans announces the "decline of communism" because the "most striking feature of Russia . . . has been its failure to get anywhere near, let alone catch up and overtake, the living standards of its capitalist rivals" (p. 206) and, with the "surge of affluence" the "Computer Revolution" is bringing in the West, "even the most ardent Marxist" will be forced "to bow to the overwhelming testimony of the microprocessor" (p. 208), since "the Communist world . . . in the absence of capitalist incentive, is bound to lag further and further behind" (p. 207). Casting an eye over Chinese and American rapprochement, Evans considers that "the message of the microprocessor and the fact that it is a creature of capitalism may already be getting through" (p. 209), before concluding that the "absolute dependence of mass microprocessor technology on capitalist production and distribution methods could well be the first nail in the coffin of doctrinaire Marxist thinking" (p. 207). Professor W. Gosling has already buried Marxism. Having shifted from a university chair to the post of technical director of Plessey Electronic Systems, he brings all his scholarship to voice what Hyman, Toffler, Martin, and Evans assume. The senior Plessey managers who heard his lecture must have been relieved to learn that "Karl Marx's lack of understanding that technology is not static was one of the things, along with his psychological naivety, which made his theoretical ideas such a poor guide to policy" (Gosling, 1981, p. 67).

We scarcely need say that this promise for the future indicates no real socialist commitment on the part of these writers. It is but a consequence of I.T. that we will arrive at the humanization of capitalism (Hyman, Martin), perhaps with communism's collapse (Evans) or the convergence of all systems into a new civilization (Toffler). However, the hold of these commentators on a vision of the future which is socialistic is significant in one particular respect: they monopolize discussion of the future when those whose aspirations and ideals they steal appear unimaginative, reactive, and defensive. When faced with the arrival of I.T. socialist responses, concerned chiefly with negative effects, have appeared pessimistic and even reactionary. It is in this way that propagandists for I.T. have stolen a march on the Left. It is they who have confidence, they who welcome the future, and it is they who, ironically, foresee the possibility of socialism within I.T. itself.

Conclusion

The speculation about I.T.'s social import seems to us to have two effects worth special emphasis. The first is that it manages to dominate discussion in a straightforwardly quantitative manner which makes it difficult for alternative perspectives to be heard. Analyses of I.T. are almost totally one-sided, so that public debate and discussion is markedly impoverished. Second, the major consequence of this presentation of I.T., while it may not persuade the populace to wholeheartedly welcome the new technology, is to create a general sense of acquiescence to innovation. We believe this happens because I.T., without discernable origins, is something ordinary people cannot understand. The technology is a mystery and remains a mystery even when its technical functions are explained in simplified terms, because its genesis—its social history—is ignored. In this way, technology is placed in a tradition of science fiction as an arrival—fortunately benign—from another galaxy: as Margaret Thatcher appositely observes, "Information Technology is friendly; it offers a helping hand; it should be embraced. We should think of it more like *ET* than IT" (Thatcher, 1982, p. 29). Without history, I.T. becomes an unstoppable force which, though incomprehensible to natives, is understood sufficiently for them to realize that it must change their whole way of life.

For good or ill, we are obliged to adjust to the things that have arrived unannounced and unexpected. Understandably in these circumstances, a common response is one of apathy. The technology has been imposed upon us irrespective of our wishes or even imaginings, and it seems that there is little we can do other than accede to its dictates. Hence we often witness a resigned acceptance of the inevitable, a sense of helplessness, and a feeling of stale familiarity and apathy after constant but uninformative media exposure.

Starting with the palpable hereness of I.T., and only then moving to consider its social influence, is to accept from the outset that technology is in crucial ways out of our control. And it is because almost all comment on I.T. unquestioningly adopts this framework that its function is in effect to sell it to the wider public. That, in general, I.T. is said to be beneficient makes it that much more palatable, and that much futurism promises it will bring about a socialistic idyll makes it that much more appealing at the same time as radical critics must appear dog-in-the-manger, but these are essentially embellishments, since the starting-point—the technology in and of itself—means that alternatives are blocked from the beginning.

Finally, because futurism, wild and sober, takes on a aura of realism by commencing analysis with the technology itself, it contains a deep irony. Starting "realistically" with I.T., it can quickly and impatiently extrapolate to the wildest imaginings (or, if it so chooses, fix on the shorter-term prospects), all the while insisting that such dreams are but potentialities of technology which is here today. The irony is that such prospects are but castles in the air, since to start with the technology which is here in the world without looking at the world which developed and is developing the technology is to ignore realities that thwart futurist dreams ever being realized. Futurism fails to face up to the social realities that are embodied in technologies that have been created and are now being expressed in the application of I.T. The procedure is something akin to starting with sight of a tiger in the bush and then imagining all manner of things it might do (attack that deer? have a sleep? run in that direction?), ignoring the whole time that the animal has been previously incapacitated by drugs, training,and perhaps extraction of teeth by someone who has carefully bred his pet and who remains constantly in control.

In spite of all the assertions of commentators on I.T. that they are coming to grips with existing realities and extrapolating only upon these—"the aim of this book . . . is . . . to illustrate that tomorrow began yesterday and that the options sharpen and tighten every day" (Large, 1980, p. 13); "I am under no Pollyannaish illusions" (Toffler, 1980, p. 19)—we charge that these writers are profoundly unrealistic from start to finish.

We would also note that this writing on I.T., in spite of—or rather because of—its "real-world" starting-point, exemplifies what Roland Barthes termed "the creation of myth." Effective mythology is not sustained by outright lies, but through what Saul Bellow has called "concealment through candour": "Myth does not deny things, on the contrary, its function is to talk about them; simply, it purifies them, it makes them innocent, it gives them a natural and eternal justification, it gives them a clarity which is not that of an explanation but that of a statement of fact"

(Barthes, 1973, p. 143). This seems to us precisely what comment on I.T. achieves: it talks endlessly about the new technology, realistically, candidly, tangibly; but because it never comes to terms with the social relations of the technology and remains stuck in an account which accepts its "naturalness," the talk amounts to a snow job. Myth "has turned reality inside out, it has emptied it of history and has filled it with nature, it has removed from things their human meaning so as to make them signify a human insignificance" (Ibid., pp. 142-143).

All this is functional to those interests aiming to exploit I.T. for their own purposes, because it deflects attention away from the powers behind the technologies, disarms critics both with abuse and the prospect of an easily attainable electronic fairyland (provided we do not resist its application in the here and now), and above all credits I.T. with an independence from society, with a naturalness which renders it incomprehensible as a social, value-laden, phenomenon. It is in ways such as these that comments on I.T. "proclaim the future in word and . . . desert the future in fact (Carey and Quirk, 1970, p. 396).

Chapter 3
Daniel Bell: The Myth
of Post-Industrial Society

The term which gives this book its title ... is ... but a catchphrase, a simplification which, like all such phrases, cheers the semiskilled intellectuals who
want a ready formula (this is the function of ideology) to explain complex
events. For any analytical purposes, the phrase confuses more than it enlight-
ens, because it erases the crucial differences between contending groups—differences arising out of interests, ideas, policies, and purposes, differences
which are the stuff of politics.

—Daniel Bell. *Sociological Journeys.* 1980a, p. 142.

It if was merely a matter of I.T.'s arrival being accompanied by McLuhanite
futurism, then our response would be straightforward, because such ideas are too
simplistic to be entertained as serious appreciations of new technology. However,
those seeking acceptance of I.T. can find credentials and credibility in the publications of a leading American sociologist, Daniel Bell. His evocation of a post-industrial society (hereafter PIS) and, more recently, its synonyms knowledge and
information society, with their close association with technological development,
give authority to pronouncements on prospects to be brought about by I.T.

It is Daniel Bell, the indefatigable exponent of PIS and "advanced capitalism's
most persuasive advertising man" (Giddens, 1981a, p. 21), on whom purveyors of
I.T. most rely for intellectual support. We see this debt, most often unacknowledged,
in hosts of statements ranging from AT&T's announcement of an immanent Information Age of which they declare themselves a part, through the countless, assump-
tively uncontentious, references in newspaper articles, lectures, and books to the
post-industrialism now in the making, to the new journal titled *The Information
Society.* All such indicate what is now a conventional wisdom for which Daniel
Bell undertook the groundwork, and they are tribute to the success of his endeavor,
begun in the late 1950s, to delineate PIS.

Ideas surely have their time. Just as few Thatcherites or Reaganites will have
read the works of Friedman, while most draw upon his authority, so few ideologues
for I.T. will be intimate with Bell's oeuvre though all pay homage to PIS. This
worldly popularity is a remarkable achievement for a writer who presents "the
concept of a post-industrial society [as] an *analytical construct,* not a picture of
a specific or concrete society" (Bell, 1976, p. 483), rather as "an as if, a fiction,
a logical construction of what *could* be" (p. 14). While Bell refuses to descend
from the heights of ideal-type analysis, down in the broadrooms, television stations,
classrooms, and political hustings his forecasts are seized on with alacrity. As early
as 1969, Andrew Schonfield observed that the notion of PIS had "already passed
into the folklore of forward-looking business executives with a large research-and-

development budget to justify" (Schonfield, 1969, p. 24). Since the arrival of I.T., this folklore has spread as only rumor can.

Why is Bell's concept nowadays so resonant? That PIS serves as a smoke-screen for I.T.'s strategists is part of the reason, but Bell is something more than this. He is an intellectual of a high order who, ensconced at Harvard, has no direct interest in I.T. Indeed, it is because he is a free-floating intellectual of formidable talent that he can so readily be adopted as an ideological lodestar. This is a role he is not new to, having acted a lead in the "end of ideology" saga in the 1960s, but it is also wrong to see him as a neo-conservative thinker. He is not in accord with Reaganite policies, is a critic of Friedman and Hayek, and has a longstanding affinity with Keynes (Bell, 1962, ch. 4).

In fact, Bell's major characteristic is a liberal and academic outlook that is most evidenced in his commitment to a doubting and questioning ethos, in this endorsement of a "God that Failed" mood of many one-time leftists which is manifested in accession to "irony, paradox, ambiguity, and complexity" (Bell, 1962, p. 300). It is suggested in his considerable knowledge of literature, languages, sociology, and economics that finds expression in sources ranging from Aeschylus to Walter Benjamin, Dante to Gide, Genesis to the Rand Corporation, which cannot sit easily with straightforward business and political programs. The diversity and exoticism of Bell's learning, his "restless vanity" (Bell, 1980a, p. xxiii) that produces a compulsion to cite, footnote, and qualify, finds accord with perception of "the complex, richly striated social relations of the real world" (Bell, 1962, p. 25) and cannot readily embrace party politics.

In addition, his knowledge of the Left, achieved by personal involvement and study of socialist politics and philosophy from childhood and youth in the Lower East Side of New York, provides Bell with sensitivity towards ideas and movements which he retains though he now finds them distasteful. As such, his writing is characterized by an informed anti-Marxism, a suspicion of overt and combative political commitment of whatever kind, and a pronounced skepticism: in his own words, "anti-ideological, but not conservative" (Bell, 1962, p. 16).

It is these qualities, learned, literate, and wary of commitment, that both strengthen Bell's liberalism and, paradoxically, fortify his contribution to conservatism. It is Bell's engrossment with complexity and his presentation of complexity in erudite form, so long as it takes as its major opponent radical positions, which makes his work attractive to conservative forces, though it professes to be liberal itself.

It has long been so with Bell. A generation ago, conservatives found in *The End of Ideology* (1962) confirmation of their anti-communism and affirmation of their Americanism, though the book expressly professed the moderation of a disillusioned red. Contending that "old passions are spent," since "the American intellectuals (have) found new virtues in the United States," the tract mapped "a rough consensus among intellectuals on political issues: the acceptance of a Welfare State; the desirability of centralized power; a system of mixed economy and of political pluralism" (Bell, 1962, p. 404, 311, 402–403). Yet this book, embedded as it was in a liberal outlook that stressed the virtues of middle-of-the-road policies, was also readily adaptable to conservatism in that it gave an intellectually impressive defence of the status quo that was susceptible to conservative distillation by way of the formula: "the world today is complex and dense, so we can't talk seriously of radical change, so let's affirm the virtues of our institutions, be cautious and, above all, anti-Marxist."

This is why we designate Daniel Bell a "cold war liberal" *par excellence:* his work, at once lauded as liberal in the USA, demurred at McCarthyism and presented it with legitimations for its actions. Bell could not interpret McCarthyism as part of a "traditional conservative heritage" (Rogin, 1967, p. 5), since to him America was a pragmatic and pluralist society, so it was to be explained as merely the "disquiet of the dispossed" encountering "deep changes in the social structure" (Bell, 1963, pp. 16–17), the excesses of which were temporary, a consequence of "a panic by Senator McCarthy and other right-wing Republicans" conducted "not always with scrupulous regard for civil liberties" (Bell, 1967, pp. 185–186). At the same time as Bell presented McCarthyism as an aberration created by the spread of liberalism itself that was following occupational and educational change, he time and again conceded the case of witchhunters. First, in arguing that communism itself was to blame for McCarthyism ("most of all, communism has spawned a reaction, an hysteria and bitterness that democratic America may find difficult to erase in the bitter years ahead" [Bell, 1967, p. 16]); second, accepting "the fact that Soviet Russia was the principal threat to freedom in the world today" (Bell, 1962, pp. 310–311) and that there was a consequent "need for containment" (ibid., p. 14; cf. Kolko and Kolko, 1972, pp. 329–358); third, that liberals had underestimated the communist threat at home, since "numbers alone were no criteria of Communist strength" because "the Communists by operating among intellectual groups and opinion leaders have had an influence far out of proportion to their actual numbers" (Bell, 1963, pp. 46–47); fourth, that Communism "As a conspiracy, rather than a legitimate dissenting group, [was] a threat to any democratic society" which "May have to act against that conspiracy" (Bell, 1963, pp. 58–59; cf., Caute, 1978, pp. 51–53).

It is this sort of argument, produced by an avowed liberal in the name of liberalism, which is manna to conservative America. While he could ring his hands at the excesses of McCarthy, he could account for it as but a "status panic" responding to changes brought about by the extension of liberalism itself, at the same time as conservatives, thanks to those like Bell, could present America as a pluralistic, tolerant, and democratic society which must, for continuity, excise Marxists.

It may appear removed from the concept of PIS and I.T. that we resurrect Bell's earlier writing and identify his outlook as liberal *faute de mieux* and sucor to conservatism. However, Bell's early work is closer to his more recent concerns than might be imagined, in that themes have been remarkably consistent over the years (Kleinberg, 1973). We review some of these below, but here affirm our perception of Bell's world-view as one which, itself liberal, finds concordance with conservatism. *The Coming of Post-Industrial Society* (1976) performs a similar function to that of *The End of Ideology:* in the service of conservatism, it professes its own liberalism and provides conservative forces with liberal credentials. Let us look at that work more closely.

Post-Industrial Society

Bell argues that America is leading an advance into a new society from pre-industrial, though industrial, to post-industrial society which is marked by changes in social structure (Bell, 1976, p. 116). He is emphatic that PIS will come into being through changes in social structure rather than in politics or culture, which he regards as separate realms of society (we return to this anti-holistic maxim). He describes PIS thus:

> in the economic sector, it is a shift from manufacturing to services; in technology, it is the centrality of new science-based industries; in sociological terms, it is the rise of new technical elites and the advent of a new principle of stratification. From this terrain, one can step back and say more generally that the post-industrial society means the rise of new axial structures and axial principles: a changeover from a goods-producing society to an information or knowledge society; and, in the modes of knowledge, a change in the axis of abstraction from empiricism or trail-and-error tinkering to theory and the codification of theoretical knowledge for directing innovation and the formulation of policy (Bell, 1976, p. 487).

Bell integrates these constituents of PIS. The shift to a service society heralds the pre-eminence of the professional and technical class whose major characteristic is working with information and knowledge. And the category of services which is decisive for PIS, since it "represents the expansion of a new intelligensia" (p. 15), is that found in health, education, research, and government.

Alongside these occupational changes, information increases quantitatively, but also qualitatively because in PIS "Theoretical knowledge . . . become(s) the matrix of innovation" (p. 344) as a "knowledge theory of value" replaces a "labour theory of value" (Bell, 1979b, pp. 167-168). This means that actions in PIS start from known theoretical principles, the practical applications of which call for the marshalling of quantities of data. An important facet of PIS is evidenced in activities that range from technological innovation (theoretical possibilities are known at the outset; the detail of experimentation, design, and production are contingencies) to social and economic planning (for example, government policies follow from accredited models which are implemented in view of empirical data). This "centrality of theoretical knowledge" contrasts with the empiricism of industrial society where changes were from "inspired and talented thinkers who were indifferent to science and the fundamental laws underlying their investigations" (Bell, 1976, p. 20).

Information and knowledge are therefore central to PIS. In addition, because their "codification" is necessary, I.T. is essential because only "computers have provided the bridge between the body of formal theory and the large data bases of recent years" (Bell, 1976, p. 24). This key role for I.T. as the means of codifying theoretical knowledge is made still more significant by the need of PIS for the "management of organized complexity" (Bell, 1979b, p. 166). That is, such is the complexity of life in PIS that "intellectual technologies" are required that are capable of ordering and processing "the transactions whose huge numbers have been mounting almost exponentially because of the increase in social transactions" (ibid., p. 172). Such features mean that I.T. will come to be in the information society that road and rail transport were to industrialism, "the central infrastructure tying together a society" (Bell, 1979d, p. 22).

With the rise of the professional and the prominence of information/knowledge, there is increased planning evident in government strategies and corporate goals. This is at once a consequence of the "centrality of theoretical knowledge" which allows "the conscious, planned advance of technological change" (Bell, 1976, p. 26) and a guarantee that PIS will not be controlled by a technological elite. Because planning is at the heart of PIS, its members will be able to control their destinies in an unprecedented way. Thereby, politics will become the lever of society; the "post-industrial society will involve *more* politics than ever before, for the very reason that choice becomes conscious and the decision-centres more visible" (Bell, 1976, p. 263).

Moreover, with the increased significance of planning along with the spread of professions and services, PIS develops less concern with "economizing" (maximizing economic return for individual interests) and more with a "sociologizing" mode of life ("the effort to judge a society's needs in more conscious fashion . . . on the basis of some explicit conception of the 'public interest' " [Bell, 1976, p. 283]). That is, political decisions, the collective will, come to be paramount, expressed in such things as where to allocate research and development funds, environmental protection, and social policy. In parallel, companies fall into line with the "sociologizing" ethos and adopt socially responsible policies. All such manifest the "new consciousness" of PIS which, as a "communal society" (p. 220), promotes the "community rather than the individual" (p. 128) as the central unit. And while planning is crucial for this change in value—once one plans, one controls, and one's vista extends beyond the narrowly economic—the expansion of the service sector hastens it along since this incorporates a nonprofit and community outlook. The end result is that PIS is a society concerned with the quality of life rather than the quantity of goods, a game between persons which is both caring and expert.

Finally, PIS's new capabilities and needs mean that the "manual and unskilled working class is shrinking in the society, while at the other end of the continuum the class of knowledge workers is becoming predominant" (Bell, 1976, p. 343). Already the "United States has become a white-collar society" (p. 134), and "the heart of the post-industrial society is a class that is primarily a professional class" (p. 374). Since this is so, Marxist thought is redundant: "If there is an erosion of the working class in post-industrial society, how can Marx's vision of social change be maintained?" (p. 40). In PIS the "labour issue" is "no longer central" (p. 164); class and class consciousness will decline in a society stratified on a hierarchical but graduated and meritocratic scale, and tensions will shift from classes to "situses" such as between universities and corporations.

PIS certainly flatters the I.T. pioneers. How could such people object to a scenario that places themselves—the "scientists, the mathematicians, the economists, and the engineers of the new intellectual technology" (p. 344)—as the "new men," assures them that they deserve their esteem since "a meritocracy principle . . . is central to the allocation of position in the knowledge society" (p. 44), and proclaims I.T. an element without which PIS would collapse? Moreover, PIS at once boosts the self-importance of the I.T. personnel—"in the society of the future . . . the scientist, the professional, the technicien, and the technocrat will play a predominant role in the political life of the society" (p. 79)—while simultaneously insisting there is no danger of them gaining disproportionate power, since "the initiative in organizing a society these days comes largely from the political system" (p. 119) and "the technocratic mind-view necessarily falls before politics" (p. 365). And neither will PIS be a stodgy system. Though class antagonisms will diminish conflict there will be aplenty in the "situses" of society.

Above all, PIS will be a liberal society, the community being to the forefront, with "more conscious decision-making" (p. 43); more politics as "Participation become(s) a condition of community" (p. 128); more professional, service oriented and interpersonal. It will be one where argument will be the norm, but this will be a healthy tension unlike the destructiveness of class conflict. To cap it all, PIS promises the demise of Marxism. For the I.T. devotees, the picture is wonderfully appealing—IBM and AT&T executives can push out their jaws, assure themselves that they are not fogeys, acknowledge that operating in PIS will be tough, but they can do it.

PIS and Sociological Theory

While it is easy to see from this why those involved in deploying I.T. find the "fiction" (Bell, 1976, p. 14) of PIS attractive, Bell does create something which should be treated seriously, not least because he draws on, in an informed way, a long tradition of sociological theory. *The Coming of Post-Industrial Society* is pervaded by a concern to establish links with the great tradition. Acknowledging that "we are all *epigones* of the great masters," (p. 54) many pages are stalked by Weber, Durkheim, Marx, and lesser classics, as Bell, seeking to "restore some of the informing power of the older modes of social analysis" (p. 10), announces himself part of this lineage. It is in his discussion of and connection with antecedents that Bell's work is lifted above that of most users of the concept, and it is a reason his writing appears authoritative. We believe that, in tracing Bell's indebtedness, we can reveal shortcomings in the entire enterprise.

Max Weber

Unquestionably, the major influence on Bell is Max Weber, from whom he derives his ideal-type mode of analysis, key concepts, and philosophical outlook. There are other thinkers on whom Bell draws, notably Emile Durkheim,whose concern with social integration has become an obsession with Bell in recent years, and Saint-Simon, whose emphasis on the rise of science and engineers is a recurrent theme. However, these are overshadowed by, and to a large extent incorporated into, the main theme of PIS which Bell takes from Weber, that of rationalization.

Krishan Kumar has observed that "Almost every feature of Bell's post-industrial society can be seen as an extension and a distillation of Weber's account of the relentless process of "rationalization" in western industrial societies" (Kumar, 1978, p. 235). We agree and will elaborate this, but it is worth noting that Bell thinks rationalization is something more than Weber's key concept, it being "the major underpinning of sociological theory" (Bell, 1976, p. 341) itself. For Bell, while it is with Weber that "the concept of the rational moves to the very centre of sociology" (ibid.), the "tendency of civilization . . . to become more rational" (ibid.) is also the chief concern of Durkheim's *Division of Labour in Society,* and it was Saint-Simon's "insightful, if neglected" (p. 55) contribution to be "the father of technocracy" (p. 343) by predicting the growth of the engineers and the associated shift to the "administration of things–the substitution of rational judgment for politics" (p. 77). Durkheim and Saint-Simon thus are perceived as being complementary to Weber, for whom "the master key of Western society was rationalization, the spread through law, economy, accounting, technology, and the entire conduct of life of a spirit of functional efficiency and measurement, of an "economizing" attitude . . . towards not only material resources but all life" (Bell, 1976, p. 67).

Bell identifies rationalization as a pervasive feature of industrial society which is "organized around a principle of functional efficiency whose desideratum is to get 'more for less' and to choose the more 'rational' course of action" (Bell, 1976, p. 76). But it is something more than this. For Bell, rationalization is also the means of accounting for industrial society's evolution into post-industrialism. This is an odd explanatory principle in view of the absence in Bell's writing of causal analysis, but it is the case that in *The Coming of Post-Industrial Society* many changes are described, tendencies reviewed, characteristics identified–and then ascribed, post hoc, consequences of rationalization.

Bell "foregoes causality but emphasises significance" (Bell, 1976, p. 12), preferring to think in terms of an "axial principle" which is "an effort to specify not causation . . . but centrality" (p. 10). But throughout *The Coming of Post-Industrial Society*–a work quintessentially concerned with social *change*–there is a tacit reason given for the documented trends. Though nowhere in the long book is there an examination of, say, how and why there has come to be "intellectual technology," we are presented with a description of what it is and what it does, for which Bell, in spite of explicitly foresaking causal analysis, offers as explanation a logical construct–rationalization. Never empirically demonstrated, rationalization operates as a causal mechanism by imputation, so we have the paradox of Bell's refusal to examine causality at the same time as he proffers rationalization as the primum mobile of change.

This simultaneous refusal of causal analysis alongside imputed causality lets us identify in Bell's work a contrast between its substantive appearance and its lack of historical specificity. *The Coming of Post-Industrial Society* is in this way "a catalogue of effects without causes" (Abrams, 1982, p. 116), an instance of that peculiarly "ahistorical historicism" (Abrams, 1972, p. 25) devoted to forecasting on the basis of established trends, yet empty of practical analysis. What Bell presents is a picture of PIS in the making, a mass of sign-posts that indicate the direction of change, and the idea that rationalization is the power of change, but this power is nowhere shown in actual operation. PIS emerges out of industrial society, we recognize its coming in the form of services, extended education, a "new consciousness" and so on, but the only causal mechanism we are offered is the hidden hand of a "principle of functional efficiency" (Bell, 1976, p. 75) which is instrumental in changing the world though never seen to be involved in the world.

There are other features of Bell's adoption of rationalization as the master key to account for the creation of PIS. An important one is the assumption that the developments which give rise to PIS are socially neutral, though they are socially significant. If services are to extend, if professions are to enjoy an unprecedented expansion, if I.T. is to form the infrastructure of PIS, then they are neutral in so far as they are results of rationalization. This does not mean that these aspects of the social structure do not pose questions for the polity and culture; it is just that these changes in themselves cannot be reduced to matters of human interest, value, or ethics, since rationalization endows them with a quality which is sui generis.

The assumption of change being neutral holds in spite of some of Bell's own observations. For example, he states that "intellectual technology" is a social requirement of the age we are entering, as are inventions "responses to social need and economic demand" (Bell, 1976, p. 205). Elsewhere he writes that "the conscious, planned advance of technological change" (p. 26) has arrived. On the surface, such statements, suggesting that technological change is socially induced, imply that Bell rejects the currently fashionable view that social change results from new technologies which are themselves asocial.

However, while he does say that technology is created by society, Bell does not differ in any significant way from the technological determinists we encountered in the previous chapter, because he contends that there is a deeper cause of change of which technology is a manifestation–rationalization. Thus, while I.T. may result from social pressures, for Bell the social is itself motivated by a technical force–the requirement of greater efficiency. I.T. is therefore developed for what Bell forwards as a social reason–the rational solution to the needs of society–which is paradoxically independent of the social. He claims that technology is created by social needs, yet these needs are strangely lifeless. They are not matters of debate, interest, conflict, and value–what most people think the social is about–but rather matters of rationalization, a force which pervades society and poses needs left, right, and center that is itself bloodless, inhuman, desocialized.

This raises the question of determination, and technological determination in particular, in Bell's work. Since he so rarely presents concrete analyses of change, this issue is especially difficult to examine. He is too wily to fall for the charge of being determinist, and explicitly abjures it (Bell, 1976, p. 12, 38-39), but because of his presentation of rationalization as the reason for change, Bell is determinist only at a deeper, more abstract, level than his more vulgar followers. The difference between those who tell us that technology shapes the world and Bell's claim that it is rationalization which is the key to change, is that he read Max Weber and has managed to thematize the idea of rationalization onto a 20th century stage. As a conception of development, rationalization as a neutral yet determining force is little different from those of the cruder propagandists when brought to bear on I.T. The new technology is to both camps simply more efficient than previous ways of managing, and therefore must be adopted. It is, once manufactured, inevitably to be introduced and must shape social relations.

It is worth pinpointing the determinism underlying Bell's theory to highlight its commonality with salespitches for I.T. which resort to PIS for credibility. It is persistently in evidence in his recourse to rationalization as an account of change, though by virtue of this concept Bell can veer from an extreme social to technological determinism without abandoning an underlying determinism—the dull compulsion of "more for less." Nevertheless, because technology is a major expression of rationalization, Bell leans towards technological determinism and thereby accords with most futurists. Take, for example, his thoughts on "productivity" which "allows the social pie to expand" (Bell, 1976, p. 155). He continues: "Technology . . . is the basis of increased productivity, and productivity has been the transforming fact of economic life in a way no classical economist could imagine" (p. 191). It is this productivity that "has been the chief engine of raising the living standards of the world" (p. 188), which are the basis for PIS. A result of more productivity is the spread of services, since, as national income rises, so expenditure on services grows. In turn, this brings about a service society and the new consciousness that characterizes PIS. Elsewhere, the requirements of productivity impel educational expansion, changes in the occupational structure, and more long-term planning. At almost every point of his analysis, Bell's premise is technology's capacity to increase productivity, the constraints this imposes on social structure, and the way it lays the basis for PIS. When the miasma of qualification is penetrated, it is hard to image a more technologically determinist position.

If Bell's exposition of *The Coming of Post-Industrial Society* depends on rationalization being the motor of change with the presumption that it is neutral yet socially determining, how is it that, encountering a lengthy tradition of thought which ridicules such postulates (see Goldthorpe, 1971; Peel, 1971), PIS has had so much success? Giving people what they want is surely one part of the answer, but another is that Bell practices what can only be called an intellectual cheat which apparantly endows PIS with characteristics the opposite of those which we have delineated.

Bell argues that, with the advent of PIS, important changes appear which mark a break with industrial society. The crucial factor in this transformation is a challenge to the motive that made industrial society such a success and paved the way for PIS. As Bell puts it, the "development of every advanced industrial society, and the emergence of post-industrial society, depends on the extension of a particular dimension of rationality. But it is precisely that definition of rationality that is being called into question today" (Bell, 1976, p. 342). He believes that PIS challenges the economizing mode of industrial society in developing a "sociologizing" outlook which queries what were once given ends. These assumed a goal of maximum productivity for self-interest, but the "sociologizing" mode of PIS forwards different ends based on a communal ethic that can challenge rational means. Bell suggests that PIS, being planned in terms of community wishes, is in a position to freely choose its destiny: "Perhaps the most important social change of our time is a process of direct and deliberate contrivance. Men now seek to anticipate change, measure the course of its direction and its impact, control it, and even shape it for predetermined ends" (Bell, 1976, p. 345). We have seen that the rise of scientists and engineers, theoretical knowledge, and so forth places a novel emphasis on planning, and we have been assured that this will not be the fiat of technocrats, since it "gives rise to new social relationships and new structures which have to be managed politically" (p. 20). This is in part because the new "sociologizing" mode arrives to query and supercede the rationality that was once dominant, but, in addition, the capacity to plan which was endowed by industrial society itself means that in PIS people can decide for themselves how they want to shape their society, though this might mean planning for ends and means that undermine rationalization itself.

Since PIS "seeks to control its own fortunes, the political order necessarily becomes paramount" (p. 13), and since politics "is always prior to the rational, and often upsetting of the rational" (p. 365), Bell is able to assert that PIS will be epitomized by the very reverse of the determinism we have argued is a central feature of his work. How can one charge that he is determinist when he tells us, again and again, that "control of society is no longer economic but political" (p. 373)? How can Bell be so accused when he states that PIS will be a veritable political hothouse, decisions being made in the polity which ramify into all corners of society such that even technological innovation will come a matter of political debate and decision?

The only answer is that, by an astonishing sleight of hand, Bell at once insists that PIS will witness the predominance of politics and at the same time refuses to examine the relation of the polity to the social structure, changes in which, it will be recalled, have laid the foundations for the political take-over in PIS. We are told that these "separate realms" have reversed roles, but Bell presents neither an explanation for this reversal nor an analysis of how they crossed over. This is an evasion which takes us to central weaknesses of Bell, and it echoes a dilemma faced by an influential tradition of Marxism. By examining Bell's relation to Marx, we can explore these weaknesses further.

Daniel Bell and Marxism

Bell situates his work in relation to Marxism in two connected ways, empirically and methodologically. He asserts that, because he "rooted social change in social structure or institutions" rather than in "mentalities," "the source of our interest in social change is necessarily Marx" (Bell, 1976, p. 55). What follows this is an assurance that "we have all become post-Marxists," since Marx's predictions have been empirically falsified. We want to review this line of descent from Marx in the writing of Daniel Bell, but to get to it we prefer to take what might at first appear a detour by tracing a more conceptual, yet simultaneously more personal and political, lineage that further reveals Bell's debt to Marx's "great antagonist" (p. 67) Max Weber.

The link here is made by the late Hungarian Marxist Georg Lukacs, an "extraordinary man" (Bell, 1962, p. 441) who haunts many pages of Bell's output and is regularly exorcised because, we believe, his ideas undermine the PIS enterprise and bring into question much of Weber's work itself (Lukacs, 1972). In a fascinating essay, Bell discusses the connections between Lukacs and Weber and, after some impressive detective work, discovers that Weber formulated his well-known distinction between the "ethic of responsibility" and "ethic of ultimate ends" (Weber, 1967) as an expression of his "own anguish" (Bell, 1981, p. 540) at seeing his most brilliant student, Lukacs, opt for allegiance with the Communist Party as a solution to the philosophically-formulated problem of alienation.

There is nothing novel about depicting Lukacs' unexpected political commitment to the "proletariat" as a "missing term in a geometrical proof" (Stedman Jones, 1971). But in the case of Bell his observations on this issue are revealing, both because they emphasize his own affinity to Weber, and because they demonstrate his aversion, not just to Marxism in general, but specifically to the Marxism professed by Lukacs. We refer here to Lukacs' maxims that Marxism is to be regarded as an activist theory of change and as one which rejects the proposition that capitalism is susceptible to division into separate parts. These interpretations are distasteful to Bell, who distrusts Lukacs' militant political message and who is antipathetic to holistic analysis, to the claim that society should be viewed as a totality. Both these objections are principles around which the theory of PIS revolves.

Recurrently and from his earliest pieces, Bell is drawn to embrace Weber's dichotomy of an "ethic of responsibility" and an "ethic of ultimate ends," to endorse the former and reject Lukacs' acceptance of the latter. This of course fortifies Bell's refusal of Lukacsian Marxism, but one can go further to point out that here it is possible to discern ways in which Bell's personal make-up, political predilection, and intellectual pursuits are interlinked.

Bell concluded his early study *Marxian Socialism in the United States* (1952) by recalling Weber's advice that "He who seeks the salvation of souls, his own as well as others, should not seek it along the avenue of politics" (Bell, 1967, p. 193), which indicates his sense of disillusion with his own, 1930s generation. But Weber marked Bell more profoundly than this. Weber's principles had in fact provided this anti-Marxist tract with its thesis, since Bell—the repentant and reformed socialist— had made the argument that the reason for the Left's failure in the USA was its lack of pragmatism. Because it had clung doggedly to socialist goals, it had been incapable of making serious political inroads in America; because it had not opted for an "ethic of responsibility," it had fallen on barren soil, left to rave about "ultimate ends" in a political wasteland: "The socialist movement, by its very statement of goal and in its rejection of the capitalist society as a whole, could not relate itself to the specific problems of social action in the here-and-now, give-and-take political world" (Bell, 1967, p. 5).

It is not unusual for early writing to be derivative, but what is remarkable is that Bell's indebtedness to Weber has remained. The insistence that moderation is all that is acceptable in the body politic, its promotion to the status of an explanation for the particulars of American history, and the view that political effectiveness requires the renunciation of socialist goals does more than underscore Bell's own dislike of extremist politics, serving also to emphasize his world-weariness, his readiness to insist that complexity is reason enough to abjure radical solutions, his distrust of totalistic political programs. Daniel Bell, "a lifelong Menshevik," sums it up thus: "The ethic of responsibility, the politics of civility, the fear of the zealot and the fanatic—and of the moral man willing to sacrifice his morality in the egoistic delusion of total despair—are the maxims that have ruled my intellectual life" (Bell, 1981, pp. 550–551). Herein lies a key to understanding *The End of Ideology:* the book is a hymnal "for those who take on responsibility, who forgo the sin of pride, of assuming they know how life should be ordered or how the blueprint of the new society should read, [whose] role can only be to reject all absolutes and accept pragmatic compromise" (Bell, 1962, p. 302). It is this same ethic of responsibility which characterizes PIS, which is a dense society; liberal and pluralistic, with "more participation . . . than ever before in political life" (Bell, 1976, p. 469); replete with interest groups located not in classes but in "situses" which have jettisoned class struggle but continue and perhaps encourage group conflict (p. 482) within bounds that call only for piecemeal social changes; an order in which there is stratification but of a reasonable type, multifaceted and meritocratic. Bell's PIS ought not to be seen as that which is developing, but rather as that which ought to be coming into being according to the tenets of "responsible" thinkers.

It is appropriate that Bell reveals his personal, political, and intellectual affinity with Weber in the context of rejecting Lukacs, but there is another reason for this dismissal. This lies in the particular type of Marxism favored by Lukacs. Again and again, Bell objects to the "Hegelian-Marxist mode which sees society as a structurally interrelated whole, a totality organized through the economic system" (Bell, 1974a, p. 23), asserting that he does "not believe that societies are organic or so integrated as to be analysable as a single system" (Bell, 1976, p. 114), and this reaches back over 20 years (Bell, 1962, p. 99). Lukacs is most frequently cited as an instance of the holistic fallacy (Bell, 1980a, pp. xiii–xiv, 329; 1974b).

It is axiomatic to Bell that against "holistic views of society, I would counter-pose the argument that, at most times, societies are radically disjunctive" (Bell, 1980a, p. 329). He himself divides, quite arbitrarily, society into three parts:

> the social structure, the polity, and the culture. The social structure com-prises the economy, technology, and the occupational system. The polity regulates the distribution of power and adjudicates the conflicting claims and demands of individuals and groups. The culture is the realm of expressive symbolism and meanings (Bell, 1976, p. 12).

It will be remembered that *The Coming of Post-Industrial Society* is concerned only with one of these elements, the social structure (Bell, 1980b).

What is noticeable about this strategy is that:

• Bell is incapable of offering any justification for it and does not attempt to do so (cf. Ross, 1974).

• The most cursory review of social realities attests to the interpenetration of these realms (vide the economic significance of culture, the connections between politics and economic affairs).

• While Bell is confident that PIS will be politically directed and thus different from industrial society, nowhere does he reveal how or why this switch of levels will be effected.

• Bell's concerns are insistently with the interrelationships between realms (ques-tions are posed from realm to realm throughout his work), yet nowhere does he examine the character of these relations (Steinfels, 1979, p. 169)

We return to this last point, since it reraises the vexed question of determina-tion, but here we state bluntly that Bell's anti-holism is unsupportable, indefen-sible empirically, and conceptually gauche. It is, however, crucial for PIS to be sustained because, were it not for the "disjunction of realms," Bell would be com-pelled to examine uncomfortable questions such as the relation of politics and economics, or culture and politics, which only by virtue of his self-imposed anti-holism can he evade.

If we have shown that Bell is primarily concerned to exorcise Lukacsian Marx-ism's politics and holistic methodology, we are still left with his belief that "we have to begin with the predictions of Marx" (Bell, 1976, p. 56). And, though he re-jects Marx on the grounds that his predictions have been falsified by history, he insists on paying tribute to him as one of his "own masters" (Bell, 1962, p. 48). Bell does this by contending that the roots of PIS are actually traceable from Marx's later, unfinished, writings that were eventually published as *Capital*, Volume III. Here, in what Bell calls "schema two" of Marx, are trends that Marx observed "with extraordinary acuity" (Bell, 1976, p. 59) and which undermine the "theoretical simplification" (ibid.) of "schema one" that had envisaged class polarization, the concentration of capital, and revolution. Marx's "empirical description," inchoately sketched in *Capital III,* revealed characteristics both at variance with Marxism and fundamental to Bell's description of the evolution of PIS. These were:

● "With the rise of a new banking system," capitalism became dependent on "the savings of society as a whole" rather than on those of a small property-owning class.
● The ownership and control of the corporation became separated, and a "new category of occupation," professional managers, developed.
● The growth of "white-collar work" was at the expense of manual (proletarian) jobs (Bell, 1976, pp. 59–60).

Bell, seizing on trends Marx himself suggested, recuperates the master to discredit Marxism the more effectively. He tells us that the old Marx repented of his middle-aged idealism, realizing "in the later years . . . accurately the shape of things to come" (Bell, 1976, p. 56). The classic statement of Marxism's disproof on these lines is Ralf Dahrendorf's outline of a "decomposition of ownership," "decomposition of control," and "decomposition of labour" (Dahrendorf, 1959), a study which "undoubtedly influenced" (Bell, 1976, p. 37) Bell's formulation of PIS. Such arguments used against Marxism highlight Bell's commitment to what is the solid plank of most contemporary anti-Marxism, the managerial revolution hypothesis, which holds to the view that capitalism has been superceded because of an increase in white-collar professional workers. We do not debate this contentious thesis here, but it is revealing to note that PIS revolves on its acceptance, offering the paradox of an apparently novel theorization being in fact highly unoriginal (Janowitz, 1974, p. 232).

We respond to Bell's fatal embrace of Marx by noting that he knowingly oversimplifies a man to whom he has "devoted half [his] life" in study (Bell, 1976, p. 196). The duality Bell constructs between a dreamy propagandist and a sober and perceptive intellectual is unfair to Marx—and Bell knows it. Elsewhere, for instance, he has written that "Marx was 'inconsistent,' and it is this inconsistency which allows so many individuals to construct their 'own' Marx;" that "on no single theme associated with Marx's name . . . is there a single unambiguous definition of a concept" (ibid.; cf., Gouldner, 1980). It is Bell's willingness in developing PIS to preclude other interpretations of Marx which returns us to his unrelenting rejection of Lukacs.

Lukacs is particularly pertinent as a riposte to Bell's falsification of Marxism because he represents a Marxist tradition which denies the validity of disproofs couched in Bell's terms. When Bell pronounces Marxism out of date because of empirical developments, he must ignore Lukacs, since the latter, anticipating Bell in replying to similar criticsms of Marxism offered at the turn of the century, declared that Marxism "does not imply the uncritical acceptance of the results of Marx's investigations" (Lukacs, 1971, p. 1), but rather should be seen as a method of analysis that lays emphasis on examination of historical processes within a holistic framework. It is revealing that what Lukacs seeks to establish as the major heritage of Marx is what is most antipathetic to Bell's endeavor. Moreover, because

Lukacs' focus of attack in *History and Class Consciousness* was not anti-Marxists, but interpretations of Marx by other Marxists, his contribution is a reminder of an ironic feature of Bell's anti-Marxist outlook. This is that, at a fundamental conceptual level, Bell remains ensnared within a Marxist paradigm against which Lukacs contended 70 years ago.

Residues of Marxism have often been discovered in Bell's writing. Victor Ferkiss considers him a "quasi-Marxist" (Ferkiss, 1979, p. 74); Ian Miles judges his work a form of "vulgarized Marxism" (Miles, 1978, p. 70); Seymour Martin Lipset labels it "an apolitical Marxism" (Lipset, 1981, p. 22); and Andrew Schonfield thought PIS "fairly familiar Marxist stuff" (Schonfield, 1969, p. 20). In addition, others have noticed the receptivity of Soviet and East European thinkers to PIS, the communist idea of a "Scientific-Technological Revolution" being "closely akin to that of Post-Industrial Society" (Lipset, 1981, p. 23). Sol Encel regards them as "strikingly similar" (Encel, 1979, p. 38), while Kumar discovered in Eastern Europe "an extraordinary willingness to accept the idea . . . of a post-industrial transition" (Kumar, 1978, p. 193). The question is: how can Bell deserve such designations from his reviewers and such accord with his enemies when his "entire mode of thinking . . . is distinctly . . . anti-Marxist" (Bell, 1973, p. 745)?

Discrediting Marxism by empirical falsification and rejecting Marxisms that endorse totality as a concept, Bell fails to see the congruence his own procedures have with much Scientific Marxism (Gouldner, 1980). One principle common to Bell and this version of Marxism is that there are separate levels of any society (the economy, polity, culture, etc.). Thus, where Bell contemplates "disjunctured realms," Scientific Marxists insist on "relative autonomy" for the parts. And though these Marxists denote the primacy of the economic level "in the last instance," while Bell projects a complete separation of levels, there is no real difference, since "relative autonomy" can readily means absolute autonomy (the "last instance" never comes, and how relative is "relative"?).

Another commonality, contingent on the former, is Bell's recourse, time after time, to a base and superstructure model of society. His concept of PIS, proposed as a theory of social structure only, is presented as the foundation of future society, irrespective of its politics or culture. Bell's contention is that social structural trends are leading to PIS where, at some indisclosed point, politics will become supreme. We have here the assertion that it is the social structure, that it is changes in economy, occupational structure, and, especially, in technique, which lay the basis for PIS. And this stands in spite of his manifestly contradictory claim that the levels of society are separate from one another: without social structural change, there can be no PIS.

In consequence, Bell, rejecting Marxism for its economic determinism (Bell, 1976, p. 85), rests his account of PIS on the same metaphor and the same sort of determinism as Scientific Marxists who posit that the economic base shapes the superstructure, certain features being prerequisites of PIS regardless of activity in other realms. We are not alone in recognizing this congruence. S. M. Lipset, for example, has written that

Much of the analysis of Post-Industrial society may be seen as congruent with (or derivative from) the Marxist orientation of historical materialism, which is based on the methodological premise that the principal determining factor in social development is change in the technological structure, that the cultural and political "superstructure" vary with the base level of technology (Lipset, 1981, p. 23).

In presenting the social structure as the basis of PIS, Bell accedes to a deterministic form of analysis. Moreover, his presumption of a social structural base necessarily leads him to view certain social trends as asocial though they have profound social implications. Here, Bell repeats another maxim of Scientific Marxism, that certain phenomena, technology and economy especially, are essential to society while in crucial ways beyond social influence (see Chapter 4).

Commenting on Marx's categories of analysis, Bell at once reveals his one-sided interpretation of Marx and indicates his agreement with a particular Marxist exegesis. He says that, for Marx, "the economic substructure of society, the mode of production was divided into two parts—the social relations of production (property) and the forces or techniques of production (machinery)" (Bell, 1976, pp. 40–41). Bell then states that "along the axis of property, we can post a scheme of feudalism, capitalism, and socialism. Along the axis of technology, we can stipulate a scheme of pre-industrial, industrial, and post-industrial" (Bell, 1974a, p. 23). Here, Bell, like Scientific Marxism, presents forces and relations of production as separate, related, if at all, only externally. In this way, he desocializes productive forces, positing at one level the sphere of social relations (where property is divided out) and at quite another the productive relations which are rendered purely technical. He then goes on to contend that "the forces of production (technology) replace social relations (property) as the major axis of society" (Bell, 1976, p. 80), because "what has become most important is the emphasis on technique and industrialisation" (p. 41). At a stroke, Marxism is disproven by the fact that the sphere of production has displaced in significance that of social relations (though it decidedly affects the latter). In short, the asocial foundation of society has proved so effective a motor of change that Marx's thought on class conflict has been nullified by the triumph of Weberian rationalization.

This interpretation flies in the face of Lukacs, who emphasized that productive relations were integrally social, that no part of society could be prized apart from the rest, while arguing against other Marxists who, like Bell, were suggesting that occupational change and economic growth were outdating Marx's propositions. This tradition of Marxism continues in Eastern Europe and the Soviet Union, and is exemplified in the technicist concept of the Scientific-Technological Revolution which so echoes Bell's PIS that he cannot resist drawing on it (Bell, 1976, pp. 105-112).

It is by attesting that Marxism is reducible to a base/superstructure metaphor which entails conceiving of one level of society that is asocial yet, more or less, determining of all else, that Bell can at once reject the Marxist stress on conflict as outdated and retain a "vestigial Marxism" (Floud, 1971, p. 25) by himself proposing a base/superstructure model. In doing this, Bell in effect Weberianizes Marx by defining "productive forces" as the sphere of technical rationality. And it is by virtue of this separation out from society of a level concerned solely with, and shaped by, rationalization that Bell endorses a convergence theory of development in terms of social structures. Thus Bell, reviewing the work of Czechoslovak Radovan Richta (Richta et al., 1969), can endorse a version of Marxism in declaring that:

> With the Richta study, we come full circle. The vision here, out of Marxist theory, is what might be called a post-socialist society. That society is also post-industrial. But such a society merges . . . with the post-capitalist societies in that the new determining feature of social structure . . . is the scientific and technological revolution, or what I have called in my writings the centrality of theoretical knowledge as the axial principle of social organisation, while the character of the new stratification system will be the division between the scientific and technological classes and those who will stand outside (Bell, 1976, p. 112).

In response to this one can only say that Bell's Marxism—and the Scientific Marxism with which he is in such accord—is a simplification of Marx, because the "notion of an 'authentic Marx' is inherently absurd [since] no protean thinker can ever be given a single, unambiguous reading" (Bell, 1980a, p. 114). At the least it excludes the entire tradition of Critical Marxism (Gouldner, 1980) from Lukacs, through the likes of Horkheimer and Marcuse, to Habermas and Williams writing today, for all of whom the idea that "social structure" or the "productive forces" are "separate realms" motivated by an asocial force (whether rationalization or scientific progress) is alien. Bell's anti-Marxism is characterized by a definition of Marxism as a predictive theory that has been empirically falsified (and thus its political appeal is removed), but he himself adopts a similar conceptualization of society as Scientific Marxism that encounters the same problems of determinism while it desocializes spheres of human activity.

Conclusion

Daniel Bell is to be taken seriously chiefly because those committed to I.T. woo the populace with appeal to his vocabulary and authority. But, looking behind the concept of PIS at Bell's interpretations of Marx and borrowings of Weber, we can see a familiar and stale perspective on the new technology, the same one we encountered in the previous chapter. It is one which presents technology as asocial (and thus neutral), the fruit of an abstraction called rationalization which, because it is more "efficient," must be adopted, though it will decisively shape social relations.

Chapter 4
Scientific-Technological Revolution

The kind of person who most readily accepts Socialism is also the kind of person who views mechanical progress, *as such,* with enthusiasm. And this is so much the case that Socialists are often unable to grasp that the opposite opinion exists. As a rule the most persuasive argument they can think of is to tell you that the present mechanization of the world is as nothing to what we shall see when Socialism is established. Where there is one aeroplane now, in those days there will be fifty! All the work that is now done by hand will then be done by machinery: everything that is now made of leather, wood, or stone will be made of rubber, glass, or steel; there will be no disorder, no loose ends, no wildernesses, no wild animals, no weeds, no disease, no poverty, no pain—and so on and so forth. The Socialist world is to be above all things an *ordered* world, an *efficient* world. But it is precisely from that vision of the future as a sort of glittering Wells-world that sensitive minds recoil. Please notice that this essentially fat-bellied version of "progress" is not an integral part of Socialist doctrine; but it has come to be thought of as one.

—George Orwell. *The Road to Wigan Pier.* 1937, p. 166.

A public opinion poll published in Britain late in 1982 revealed that the plethora of material about I.T. has been effective: most people are now convinced that I.T. will cause wide-ranging changes in society, and the majority of these believe the changes will be for the better (*Guardian,* 8 December, 1982). The two-dimensional salespitch—I.T.'s introduction is inevitable and good for us—appears to have been a success, notably for the government publicity campaign which fittingly received tribute from the Prime Minister herself for "generating enormous enthusiasm throughout the country" (Thatcher, 1982).

However, the apologists for I.T. have not been entirely triumphant, since disturbingly large minorities remain unconvinced of the new technology's benignity. Indeed, as much as 34% predict increased unemployment in its wake, and only 35% hold a "favourable impression in general" of I.T. (*Guardian,* 8 December, 1982). Skepticism, ambivalence, and even hostility are not restricted to the U.K. A recent high-level working group of representatives from Japan, Italy, West Germany, Britain, Canada, France, and the United States, established at an economic summit held at Versailles in 1982 to report on "technology, growth and employment," thought this lack of enthusiasm an international problem. Accordingly, it advised governments that "More attention to the problem of public acceptance of new technologies is needed" (Command 8818, 1983). We may expect the propaganda to continue.

Exorcising the Ghosts

In view of this widespread suspicion, it is not surprising that even the enthusiasts respond to doubts about I.T.—the better to smooth its introduction. Margaret

Thatcher, for instance, recognizes "the very understandable fears that people have about the impact of new technology on their lives and jobs," and she appreciates "there will be difficult changes and some problems of adaptation." Nonetheless, she is encouraging, having "no doubt whatsoever" that "Information Technology will mean new wealth and new jobs" in the future. For those disposed to think otherwise, the Prime Minister voices a threat which is regularly on the lips of I.T.'s advocates: "Unless we successfully develop and harness the new technology in our factories and in our offices, we shall simply not be able to compete with other countries which do. And if we lose this race, we shall be priced out of not just particular products or processes, but out of whole industries. Then, jobs really would be lost" (Thatcher, 1982).

Christopher Evans concedes that the unemployment threat "has a thread of realism in it" (Evans, 1979, p. 94), then schoolboyishly announces that, since I.T. will bring wealth to us all, we should not worry about worklessness but rather look forward to "affluent redundancy." Likewise, Peter Large envisages that "During the 1980s work might become available only to eighty per cent of the population" (Large, 1980, p. 160). His counsel, however, is "don't blame the computer, blame the people" (p. 151), though the "issue is not essentially a party political one," being rather a matter of querying the "work ethic" which will involve "struggle between radicals of many persuasions and the deeper conservative power structures of Western European societies" (p. 160). Large's solution to the problems created by I.T. thus accords with most I.T. fans in recommending that "policy should not be to prevent labour displacement, but to make it acceptable, by ensuring that it does not convey social hardship or stigma" (Barron and Curnow, 1979, pp. 232-233).

Burkitt and Williams, commenting on reports of massive job losses resulting from I.T., agree that "there is no doubt" that the effects "will be traumatic" and admit that people "are understandably alarmed at the thought of unemployment (Burkitt and Williams, 1980, p. 42). They are honest enough to find this vexatious, but try to mollify readers by presenting a mostly favorable prospectus laced with reminders of the uncertainties of prediction—particularly when predictions are unpleasant. Thus "people have long been making forecasts . . . . which have turned out to be wholly false" (p. 43); "A study of the unemployment effects of the introduction of computers into the British civil service has shown how unjustified early predictions were" (p. 45); "computers can sometimes create jobs rather than destroy them" (p. 46). But these authors cannot in the end avoid the stubborn fact that I.T. is job-reducing, whatever precision is lacking in prediction. They exasperatedly conclude that "if jobs can be done efficiently with technology it is a waste of time and money to work in the old ways. Automation can help us save, by using our time more economically. There is no virtue in doing needless work" (p. 52). Such realism insists that I.T. is a *good thing*, whatever it might do to one's livelihood, and one had better accede to it: "instead of fearing the consequences of the technology —and therefore resisting its introduction—we would be aware of its likely effects.

This will help make the transition as smooth and painless as possible and we can use microelectronics to benefit all people" (ibid.).

Some consideration of the blemishes of I.T. is therefore found in the writing of most futurists, though the troubled words of Burkitt and Williams are rare. Much more common is to mention a few negative consequences and then to belittle them by suggesting they are resolvable by either more technology, changed attitudes which involve no practical actions, or minor social engineering. It is hard to take seriously identification of the problems surrounding I.T. which bring forth such ready answers. Since the overwhelming message of most futurism is that I.T. is an undisguised blessing, while technological redundancy and the like are local difficulties—if difficulties at all—that will be easily overcome so long as we embrace the new technology, it is appropriate to regard such frivolous commentary as an attempt at spiking the guns of "future-haters."

The Left's Analyses of I.T.

However, consideration of some of I.T.'s negative aspects by its propagandists does allow us to move to discussion of a significant minority response to I.T. It has been characteristic of trade unions and most of the Left to adopt a pessimistic attitude towards I.T. Comment from such quarters has been predominantly gloomy in outlook in contradistinction to the optimistic scenarios sketched by the likes of Evans, Martin, and Large. In the following pages, we delineate the main features of the labor movement's response to I.T. in order to compare them with those of the I.T. acolytes. Extending from this, we then examine the wider issue of the Left's conceptualization of the relations between technology and society. Finally, we analyse ambiguities and ambivalences towards technology in the writings of Marx and Engels, because these thinkers serve both as an intellectual source to many contemporary Leftist commentators, and, through their paradoxes, as a means of clarifying difficulties with the Left's response to I.T.

Predictions "that by early in the next century it will require no more than ten per cent of the labour force to provide us with all our material needs" (Stonier, 1980a, p. 305) have induced many on the Left to paint a bleak, dystopian picture of the future. The employment impact of I.T. has for obvious reasons been the major cause of anxiety for the labor movement, and most analysts from that quarter envision significant job loss. Chris Harman's assertion that "the microprocessor is being transformed into the means of destroying millions of people's jobs" (Harman, 1979, p. 4) is characteristic of socialist and union representations that foresee "enforced unemployment" (CIS, 1978) growing alarmingly. When placed in the context of recession, international competition, and the current political climate (factors stressed by these commentators), the introduction of I.T. is seen as likely to exacerbate problems: "the situation is made very much worse by the rapidly increasing use of electronic hardware such as computers and their tiny offspring the microprocessor. It is the use of this equipment which will enable rationalization to occur with a vengeance" (Hines, 1978, p. 2). Clive Jenkins and Barrie Sherman image a "jobs holocaust" (Jenkins and Sherman, 1979, p. 182), a "collapse of work," resulting from I.T.'s application that will create massive "structural unemployment" in the U.K. by 1990. The Labour Party agrees, believing that "If microelectronics is let loose in a free market economy, the consequences will be disastrous (Labour Party, 1980, p. 24). To these writers the future is grim, likely to be "one in which there is little or no economic growth and the people of the U.K. are divided into those who number in their households at least one paid worker and those who, because they do not, are largely reliant on whatever unemployment compensation it is decided they should receive" (Hines and Searle, 1979, p. 64).

It is the consensus of trade union opinion in Britain that most of I.T.'s effects will be unpleasant, and the threat of unemployment and deskilling of work, the vulnerability of women, and health and safety risks are especially common concerns (Robins and Webster, 1982). However, despite widespread apprehension in the trade unions about the likely effects of I.T., there is little sign of resistance to its introduction. On the contrary, they are virtually unanimous in favoring its acceptance and regard its adoption as unavoidable. Typical statements come from ASTMS (Association of Scientific, Technical and Managerial Staffs), which "accepts the introduction and need for the new technology" (ASTMS, 1979); the GMWU (General and Municipal Workers' Union), which believes that "Britain probably does not have a choice about whether it accepts technological change in the future" (GMWU, 1980, p. 11); and APEX, which concedes the "argument that a negative approach to new technology would not be in the long term interest of the living standards or employment prospects of trade union members" (APEX, 1979a, p 60).

This acceptance of innovation coexists with a belief that technology is a neutral force, summarized in a TUC (Trades Union Congress) document as follows: "Whether technology will prove to be a friend or foe will not depend on the technology itself, but on its application and the policies adopted by governments, trade unions and employers" (TUC, September, 1979, p. 7). Such a point of view, usually supported by a line of reasoning which argues that technology will bring real benefits to society that later on can be divided in an equitable way, is frequently reiterated. A TGWU booklet, for example, states that "the real problem is not whether technological development by itself is good or bad. That is a misleading way of looking at it. The important issue is the control of technological development" (TGWU, 1979, p. 3), and an APEX conference motion, successfully adopted, recognizes "that these technologies can mean either a better working life and increasing prosperity for British workers, or a massive increase in long-term unemployment and falling living standards" (APEX, 1979b).

On the political stage proper, the British Labour Party endorses the same notions of neutrality and inevitabilism in stating that "microelectronics is a dramatic and fundamental stage in the evolution of technology. . . . We cannot, and should not hold back the tide of its applications" (Labour Party, 1980, p. 22), while regarding it "as an instrument to change the quality of social relationships within the community" (p. 37).

The Left's Conceptualization of the Relation of
Technology and Society

These responses to I.T., in face of bleak prognoses of its effects, carry with them a formulation of the relation between technology and society which has a long history on the Left. This is one which, adopting a perspective that envisages technology as "one of the engines of economic growth" (ibid., p. 5), also perceives I.T. as a phenomenon that can, in the right circumstances, be a tool for public well being. Technology is therefore regarded as a neutral instrument, open to use or abuse depending on whom wields power in society.

It is only by separating out technology from society in this way—only by removing technology to a level which is independent of social relations—that the Leftist pessimists can resolve the contradiction of bleak predictions of I.T.'s likely effects with acceptance of its introduction. Since technology is seen as autonomous from society, it can be regarded as potentially progressive, however much it might be misused by capitalism. The corollary of this conception of I.T. is that a constituted technology is socially and politically acceptable, since in itself it is unobjectionable.

Trotskyists

This image of I.T. being a technology which is potentially liberating but in likely danger of manipulation by reaction is very common on the Left. We find it in one of the hardest-hitting examinations of new technology from the Socialist Workers' Party. Chris Harman voices a classic use/abuse perspective when he writes:

> Just as the great advances in the physical sciences in the first half of this century were transformed into the murderous weapons that gave the world Hiroshima and Nagasaki, so the microprocessor is being transformed into the means for destroying millions of people's jobs and making the rest even more tedious and dehumanised than before.

This is the present position, but I.T. could be a means of effecting socialism, of

> making possible the translation into reality of the age-old desire for a society from which toil has been banished and in which human beings control their own destinies.

Used appropriately the new technologies

> could do away with the toil and tedium of much work forever. They could produce a society in whch mining accidents only "maimed" robot miners; in which clerical workers turned into the office for only a couple of hours a day and engaged in leisure pursuits while machines did the rest; in which shift-work was unknown except for a very narrow range of occupations like nursing and firefighting; in which the tedium of the assembly line was a nightmare from the past; in which even the handicaps associated with natural afflictions like deafness and blindness were overcome (Harman, 1979, p. 4).

There is this promise, argues Harman, but under capitalism "all these possibilities are developing in a society which cannot take advantage of them. Instead of creating new hope, the microprocessor is creating new fears of mass unemployment."

Base/Superstructure Metaphors

As one moves through the political spectrum to the Right, this image of the use/ abuse of a neutral technology holds constant. In addition, there is a recurrent adoption of the metaphor which divides society into a base and superstructure, the former regarded as a level separate from the latter yet simultaneously an essential support for it. We refer here particularly to the presentation in socialist analyses of I.T. of the idea that technology, while neutral and therefore dependent on political programs for significance, is also an essential prerequisite for fulfilment of social needs. Thus, one often encounters references to the "new social structure which the chip could . . . create" (Labour Party, 1980, p. 35) on the Left that suggest technology is a determinant—more or less—of social relations. Harman, for instance, is not unusual in writing that "the new technology is going to revolutionize the working lives" (Harman, 1979, p. 28) of people, for good or ill.

We shall need to return to this issue of how technology might be at once both neutral and determining, subject to social control while socially controlling, but at this stage we would emphasize the congruence of Left wing perspectives on I.T. with conservative proponents: all regard the new technology as neutral, its adoption as inevitable, and as—more or less—determining of social relations.

Socialists

Characteristics found in the Socialist Workers' Party pamphlet are well in evidence in the Labour Party's document on microelectronics. This insists that socialists must "ensure that microelectronics is a boon rather than a bane for our people" (Labour Party, 1980, p. 22). Labour is convinced that I.T. will be abused if left to a Thatcherite administration, because the "current recession exacerbated by the Tory Government's deflationary policies is the worst possible background for the adoption of new technology" (p. 24). Under the right circumstances, however, Labour believes that "new technology could create a historic stage in the development of a socialist caring society, in which the quality of life for every individual is enriched" (p. 38). That is, "Provided that our party policies for reflation and full employment can replace Tory monetarist deflation and recession, new technology offers the opportunity of increasing living standards" (p. 23) which presage an era generous in provision of "own time," with short working hours allowing people extensive leisure to be spent in "enriching community and person-to-person services" (p. 37).

Jenkins and Sherman

The evocation here of I.T. being used to provide "own time" echoes the advocacy of Clive Jenkins and Barrie Sherman, who offer one of the most pessimistic projections of I.T.'s influence in foreseeing in the U.K. something like five million out of work in the next decade, whatever is done by politicians. They present a grim prospect: "Remain as we are, reject the new technologies and we face unemployment of up to 5.5 million. . . . Embrace the new technologies, accept the challenge and we end up with unemployment of about 5 million" (Jenkins and Sherman, 1979, p. 113).

Caught in this double bind, one might anticipate despair at the certainty of 20% unemployment, but not from Jenkins and Sherman. Their conception of technology enables them to swing from extreme pessimism to the wildest optimism, because I.T., being neutral, can under appropriate political direction be used in acceptable ways: "The new technologies are not something to be feared. If the right planning, the right political attitudes and the right political decisions prevail, then the world could be a far better place to live in" (p. 157). Their recommendation is for a "leisure society," which simply means that we should abandon the work ethic and pay people generously to be idle. A straight-forward political decision could mean, contend Jenkins and Sherman, that "the 'collapse of work' may be referred to in historical terms as the 'ascent of leisure' " (p. 13).

This rejection of the ideology of work and its replacement with a leisure society is not a simply a matter of choosing a more humane policy towards the new technology (though it requires that), since it depends on acceptance of I.T. to provide the wealth which will allow the luxury of leisure for all. Therefore, for all the easy talk of choice as regards I.T., its introduction is both inevitable and determining. It is inevitably to be adopted, since "if the rest of the world . . . adopts the new systems, our products and services will be more expensive, old fashioned, less competitive, and would lose export markets as well as domestic sales . . . . In the cold wind of world competition and our exposed position . . . the new techniques must be adopted" (p. 150). It is determining since only the "new technologically based society" (p. 124) can "enable society to pursue the goals that it chooses" (p. 160) by generating the means to found a "leisure age."

In this projection we have once again the trilogy: technological innovation is neutral, inevitable, and determining. Assumed to originate at a level somehow autonomous from social relations, it is also assumed to be at once determining of society and susceptible to manipulation by political strategies.

Harold Wilson

Shifting further to the Right, though remaining in what might still be regarded as a left wing spectrum, we come to Harold Wilson. In 1963 he delivered what was to be a strategic speech at the Labour Party Conference. In his address—*Labour and the Scientific Revolution* (Wilson, 1963)—the future Prime Minister proclaimed that "we must harness Socialism to science, and science to Socialism" as he insisted that the "white heat of this revolution" was integral to socialism. Wilson's speech anticipated much of today's comment and concern about I.T., but more significant are the assumptions he shares with others on the Left.

First, there is the notion of a neutral technology the use or abuse of which depends entirely on the choices of political parties. Wilson charged that "technological progress left to the mechanism of private industry and private property can lead only to high profits for a few, a high rate of employment for a few, and to mass redundancies for the many." This could be rectified by voting Labor since the free-floating technology allowed the electorate "the choice between the blind imposition of technological advance, with all that means in terms of unemployment, and the conscious, planned, purposive use of scientific progress."

Second, despite this ethos of a neutral technology enabling the exercise of choices, it must be accepted:

> Let us be frank about one thing. It is no good trying to comfort ourselves with the thought that automation need not happen here; that it is going to create so many problems that we should perhaps put our heads in the sand and let it pass us by. Because there is no room for Luddites in the Socialist Party. If we try to abstract from the automative age, the only result will be that Britain will become a stagnant backwater, pitied and condemned by the rest of the world.

Third, there is technological determinism, an insistence that technology is the precondition, the basis, for socialist construction, promising "to provide undreamed of living standards and the possibility of leisure ultimately on an unbelievable scale."

Wilson's keynote address allows us to appreciate the extent of agreement towards technological innovation held far across the political spectrum. We want especially to indicate in the following pages the assumptions—assumptions which serve to depoliticize, to arrive at a tacit consensus about, crucial aspects of change—Wilson shares with not only the labor movement thinkers referred to above but also with liberals and Soviet Marxists. The link with liberals may have been suggested to readers familiar with Sir Harold Wilson's politics, but more revealing still is that his theme—the "Scientific Revolution"—calls to mind the Soviet concern to associate communism with a "Scientific Technological Revolution." Indeed Wilson explicitly formulated an intention of "restating . . . Socialism in terms of the scientific revolution" and called attention to "the formidable Soviet challenge in the education of scientists and technologists, and above all, in the ruthless application of scientific techniques in Soviet industry." The Soviets have long made the connection sought by Wilson. Demonstrating the commonality of approach towards technology of Western liberals and Soviet theoreticians, we can underline an extraordinary degree of convergence of thought and social arrangement.

Westerners and Soviets

J. K. Galbraith's writings offer a useful means of illuminating this commonality. Galbraith, a lifelong Democrat who regards himself as "being a general mainstream reformist" (*Times Higher Education Supplement* 25 February, 1977, p. 7) in the Keynesian tradition, published *The New Industrial State* in the late 1960s, a work centrally concerned with the import of technology in the post-war period. The book is critical of both conservatism and radicalism, attacking the latter because it refuses to recognize that "decisive power in modern industrial society is exercised not by capital but by organization, not by the capitalist but by the industrial bureaucrat" (Galbraith, 1975, p. 17), and the former because it subscribes to a "myth of the system" (p. 349) which, "whatever its formal ideological billing, is in substantial part a planned economy" (p. 26). In examining who nowadays exercises power—the "technocracy"—and why industrialism is "extensively replacing the market with planning" (p. 349)—the "imperatives of advanced technology"— Galbraith reveals an approach remarkably similar in conception to that of Harold Wilson.

Galbraith's contention is that nowadays "the imperatives of technology" determine social arrangements: it is the requirements of advanced technological production which organize social systems. In particular, advanced technology gives rise to the "necessity of planning" (p. 35), which renders obsolete market mechanisms for determining economic performance while also calling for "specialized knowledge, talent or experience" (p. 86)—the "technocracy"—to run industry. Galbraith is obviously more of a technological determinist than the politicians to whom we have referred, but he is not fundamentally different. He shares with those previously mentioned the perception of technology, though it is socially determining, as also neutral, "as an essentially technical arrangement for providing convenient goods and services in adequate volume" (p. 391).

What is significant about Galbraith is that he is an influential and persuasive thinker in the center of the political spectrum and to the right of those previously discussed, who yet accords with their view of technology as neutral, yet socially determining. What is still more interesting about Galbraith's book is its conclusion, from his premise of a neutral yet determining technology, that *all* industrial societies are converging: "there is a broad convergence between industrial systems. The imperatives of technology and organization, not the images of ideology, are what determine the shape of economic society" (p. 26).

It is this claim that East and West are becoming alike which turns our attention to Russia and Marxist conceptions of the relations between society and technology. In the Soviet Union, writers have been quick to reject the convergence thesis as enunciated by Galbraith. The ideological implications of agreeing to the proposition that communism is in fundamental ways akin to capitalism are unacceptable (Gouré et al., 1973). At the same time, the idea of a Scientific Technological Revolution has enjoyed a great deal of currency in that country over the past generation (Hoffman, 1978). In truth, since the early years of the Russian Revolution there has been a commitment to rapid technological development. Lenin made important concessions to technologists in the years following 1917 by championing a policy of concessions with control towards scientists and engineers who were often opponents of the Bolsheviks, arguing that "It is necessary to grasp all the culture which capitalism has left and build socialism from it. It is necessary to grasp all the science, technology, and art. Without this, we will not be able to build life in a communist society. And this science, technology, art is in the hands and the heads of the specialists" (quoted in Bailes, 1978, p. 52). Later, Stalin and his associates vaulted technology to the very center of the Bolshevik program: as they "moved from their underground past into the rapid modernization of the 1930s, they increasingly emphasized the scientific basis of their hegemony, and particularly their accomplishments in technology as evidence of their right to rule" (ibid., pp. 383-384).

This has provided the legacy for contemporary theorists of "the spreading scientific and technological revolution, unparalled in scale and in its results and consequences" (Fedoseyev, in Dahrendorf et al., 1977, p. 84). Though Galbraith's "imperatives of technology" is rejected, what remains is essentially the same conception of science and technology. The Scientific Technological Revolution (STR), contend the Russians, is a neutral phenomenon which can be used or abused depending on the appropriateness of political programs: "it is precisely upon . . . the social organization of their (people's) activity that the manner in which scientific and technological achievements are used depends" (ibid., p. 91). Chastising "bourgeois conceptions of the scientific and technological revolution" for regarding it as "an absolutely independent and decisive factor of contemporary history, standing above society" (ibid., p. 90), Pyotr Fedoseyev is blind to the irony that his own conception of the STR is one in which the social enters only post hoc as a distributor of technology's bounty. In his theory, the STR has its own dynamic which will "radically change the entire structure and components of the productive forces, the conditions, nature and content of labor" (ibid., p. 88), *after which* society can allocate its produce.

The difference between the Galbraithian and the Russian theorization of technology is only in the Soviet insistence that capitalism will misuse modern technology. The conception of technology as autonomous holds constant, though it is claimed that in the West this potentially liberating instrument is misapplied because here the system is antagonistic to its positive use (cf. Marcuse, 1958). Soviet thinkers go so far as to assert that the STR will increase instability in the capitalist societies, since their social relations will necessarily conflict with fast-advancing technology. Conversely, the Soviet Union's development towards communism is assisted by and in harmony with technological innovation. It is in this sense that we are to comprehend Pokrovsky:

> The STR does more than aggravate all the former contradictions of capitalism, it engenders new ones. . . . The most acute of the present-day social problems is the threat of rising unemployment through the growth of production automation. . . . A working people's state possesses the necessary economic and administrative levels for applying the results of the scientific and technological revolution in the interests of all society—so as to satisfy people's material and spiritual needs. With the development of science and technology, physical labor becomes enriched and more creative . . . in the economic competition between the two systems, scientific and technological progress in the socialist countries not only strengthens socialism, it also has an international

political and social resonance; on the one hand, it shows capitalism's incompatibility with the humane tasks of ever creative human thought and, on the other, it points to the broad prospects for countries and people during this process and demonstrates the possibilities for an ever fuller satisfaction of the material and spirtual needs of all members of the socialist society (Gouré et al., 1973, pp. 101–102).

In this formulation we are presented not only with the assumption that technology is neutral, but also the belief that it is a crucial—to an unspecified degree determining—ingredient of socialism. Appropriately applied, the STR "creates for this new society (communism) an adequate material technological basis" (Richta, in Dahrendorf et al., 1977, p. 59; cf. Richta et al., 1969). Witnessing the re-emergence of this favorite Marxist metaphor of base and superstructure, pertinent questions can be posed: What is the precise degree of technological determinism in the evolution of socialism? At what point does the (technological) basis of socialism give way to the superstructure? To what extent do Soviet theorists of the STR "reduce an analysis of revolutionary forces to the progress of science and technique?" (Touraine, in Dahrendorf et al., 1977, p. 110). Here we do not try to answer these questions, but in raising them we can emphasize the conceptual affinity of Soviet Marxism, liberal Western theorists, and socialist and trade union accounts of technological change.

Bernalism

We might pause at this point to remind ourselves that this perspective on technology—neutral, inevitable, determining—is not confined to the thinkers already mentioned. It has a lengthy history in Britain among the Left discussion of which will serve both to sketch intellectual origins and to illuminate some of the Left's vacillation towards technology. Bernal's writings have been especially influential, to such an extent that the group's biographer can argue that "Bernalism," developed in the 1930s, was able to "enter into mainstream politics" in the early 1960s speech of Harold Wilson referred to above. Wilson's enthusiasm for "the white heat of this revolution" was "subscribing to Bernalism pure and simple" (Werskey, 1978, p. 15, 320). Since Bernal was a self-confessed Marxist, a committed Communist, an admirer of the Soviet Union and much influenced by Russian views on the relations of technology and society, it is clarifying to elaborate on the means by which a consensus could be achieved that ranged from this political pole to that of "a future Prime Minister" who attempted "to put British capitalism onto a more scientific and managerial basis" (ibid.).

Bernal's best-known book is *The Social Function of Science* (1939), and it is one which "rests upon . . . paradox" (Werskey, 1978, p. 190). Divided into two parts—"what science does" and "what it could do"—the first part of the book is an exposition of ways in which the capital market restricts, distorts, and diverts technological innovation, thereby "tending to become more and more a factor blocking technical progress" (Bernal, 1939, p. 132) as it searches after "immediate profitability" rather than the "most valuable" applications (p. 133). Here the paradox of Bernalism intrudes, since, while regarding capitalism as something intrusive into the process of technological change which must render this a social creation, throughout his work also runs the view that capitalism is merely misusing a science and technology which under a "planned system" would be unleashed to provide for the whole of society. Bernal is here both "asserting and denying the "class character" of science," on the one hand regarding it as a product of capitalist values and relations that is irredeemably marked by class differences, while on the other hand seeing it as a "quasi-human entity endowed with extraordinary capacities" (Werskey, 1978, pp. 186–187) so much so that it is the "chief agent of change in society" (Bernal, 1939, p. 382).

It is because Bernal adopts this contradictory view—science and technology are at once capitalist science and technology and independent, potentially progressive, determinants of social change—that he could find agreement with such diverse thinkers as Soviet apologists and Harold Wilson. Moreover, it is surely because Bernal developed a conception of science and technology which was at once socially situated *and* socially independent that his doctrine of a use/abuse approach to technology became so attractive to the Left. This could allow condemnation of capitalism's misuse at the same time as it foresaw this science and technology being inherited and encouraged to provide material sufficiency for a viable socialist society. This amounts to the Left having its cake and eating it: technology under capitalism is not only abused but it is also retarded and misshapened in design; nonetheless, under socialism this same technology can be put to good use at the same time as it becomes more plentiful. "Bernalism" retains the traits of neutrality, inevitabilism, and determinism, but only after it performs a volte-face on its accusation that capitalism produces capitalist technology. It has to do this about turn because, if it was consistent, it must either challenge the technologies produced by capitalism or else consider the possibility that politics are irrelevant in a world in which technology is the motor of change.

The Left, Technology, and the Division of Labor

J. K. Galbraith's writings are illuminating when compared to Marxist thought for another reason. This is found in his definition of technology as "the systematic application of scientific or other organized knowledge to practical tasks" the most important consequence of which is "in forcing the division and subdivision of any such task into its component parts (Galbraith, 1975, p. 31). Galbraith's conception of technology is that of an instrument which will "divide and subdivide tasks" (p. 32) the better to enable efficient production. From this perception of technology being a neutral if determining matter of task specialization and fragmentation that allows greater productivity follows the characteristic Galbraithian emphasis on expertise, authority, hierarchy, and management.

This stress on the intimate role of technology in the division of labor poses serious problems for Marxists. By raising the issue of the connections between the demands of efficient production and the division of labor, Galbraith reveals that Marxists must consider questions of the relations between efficiency, division of labor, authority, and the meaning of work under socialism and the socialist critique of capitalism. If technology must bring about the division and subdivision of work in order to assure material plenty, then socialism itself becomes problematical, since its ideals may be undermined by the corollaries of technology, authority relations, fragmented labor, and so forth. Thereby a tension is manifested between the requirements of socialism for material sufficiency and for egalitarian goals and end of alienation. By the same token, the Left's critique of capitalism loses much of its force if socialism continues with technologies and modes of work which sustain inequalities and dissatisfying labor.

Galbraith is not of course the original formulator of this problem. It is to Max Weber, the classic theorist of rationalization as the key factor in the making of the modern world, to whom we must refer for the most sustained challenge to socialism. It was Weber who, speaking in 1918, referred to the technical limitations that would be imposed on the Bolshevik revolution as "the first fact which socialism has to reckon with: the necessity for years of specialist training, for increasingly extensive specialisation and for administration by a specialist civil service. . . . The modern economy cannot be run in any other way" (Weber, 1918, p. 197). The requirements of efficient production Weber contended, would subvert the "great experiment" (p. 215) then commencing in Russia. While he thought this would be evidenced predominantly in bureaucratization, the implication is that technology—and the organizational impositions it carried with it—are complementary and inescapable (cf., Giddens, 1971, Ch. 15).

Moreover, if socialism is to be defined in terms of the production of sufficiency —a long tradition on the Left—then the corollary is that the technology which makes possible this production and the specialization and hierarchical relations that go with it are also to be regarded as neutral, inevitable, and, more or less, determining of society. To this extent, however, they then run counter to much Marxist thought which rebels against the alienation created by fragmented labor and the inequalities which its organization requires. If socialism is seen as the satisfaction of material wants, and if this calls for technology of the kind Galbraith describes, then we are also forced to conclude that the convergence he envisages is inescapable. However, this in turn subverts the socialist enterprise in so far as "the differences between capitalism and socialism become blurred, particularly from the standpoint of ordinary workers in advanced industry" (Gouldner, 1980, p. 273).

This is an issue of fundamental importance to the Left's analysis of and response to I.T., since it can result in perceiving new technologies as a means of securing untold material plenty which will lay the basis for socialism and, as such, is exceptionally hard to resist, whatever short term consequences its application might have. Conversely, if I.T. is viewed as a product and purveyor of capitalist relations, as not simply a means to increase production but more a way of retaining and extending the dominance of capital, then the Left can vigorously and unhesitatingly oppose it.

However, if one looks to the East, one kind of answer is found, though we interpret Soviet commentators to be advising socialists in the West to regard I.T. as that which lays the material basis for socialism, encouraging them to see I.T. as a future inheritance which happily may hasten the death of its capitalist parents. Back in their own country, there is a commitment to technological development so fervent that it is presented as synonymous with communism, a constant refrain which asserts that more technology indicates a further progression of Marxist ideals. We might understand this better if we remember that, from the earliest days, the Bolsheviks defined socialism as, above all else, provision of sufficiency to the populace. By the 1930s the industrial achievements of the Soviet Union had become a means of legitimating communist domination, the Bolsheviks claiming the right to rule "not only as the avant-garde of the industrial proletariat, but on the basis of their ability to transform nature and society" (Bailes, 1978, p. 383). Though it was under Stalin that egalitarianism was abandoned in favor of rapid industrialization, it was Lenin who mapped this course from the early days when he defined socialism as "electrification plus soviets" (cf. Medvedev, 1971).

It is well known that Lenin was an enthusiast, not only for technology, but also for the organizational arrangements that Galbraith insists are its inevitable accompaniment. He was advocating "Soviet Taylorism" as early as 1918 on the grounds that socialism demanded efficient production of goods and that this was to be effected by neutral yet socially determining technologies and techniques. For example, moving a resolution to "provide for the introduction of the Taylor system" into Russia while making industrial indiscipline a *criminal* offense (in the West it met only with dismissal), Lenin said:

> Big capitalism has created systems of work organization, which, under the prevailing conditions of exploitation of the masses, represent the harshest form of enslavement by which the minority . . . wring out of the working people surplus amounts of labor, strength, blood, and nerves. At the same time they are the last word in the scientific organization of production, and as such, have to be adopted by the Socialist Soviet Republic and readjusted to serve the interests of our accounting and control over production on the one hand, and raising the productivity of labor, on the other hand. For instance, the famous Taylor system, which is so widespread in America, is famous precisely because it is the last word in reckless capitalist exploitation. One can understand why this system met with such an intense hatred and protest on the part of the workers. At the same time, we must not for a moment forget that the Taylor system represents the tremendous progress of science, which systematically analyses the process of production and points the way towards an immense increase in the efficiency of human labor. The scientific researches which the introduction of the Taylor system started in America . . . yielded important data for allowing the working population to be trained in incomparably higher methods of labor in general and work organization in particular.
>
> The negative aspect of Taylorism was that it was applied in conditions of capitalist slavery. . . . The Socialist Soviet Republic is faced with a task which can be briefly formulated thus: we must introduce the Taylor system and

scientific American efficiency of labor throughout Russia by combining this system with a reduction in working time (Lenin, 1969, pp. 79–80).

With Lenin, we have a straight-forward rendition of the use/abuse doctrine: Taylorism is good for socialism but bad under capitalism. He not only regards technological innovation as inescapable because it is efficient, but also insists that capitalism's technical organization of work is to be adopted by the Soviets. Aided by the popularizer of Russian Scientific Management, Alexei Gastev, whose ideas "owed as much to American industrial engineers and capitalists . . . as . . . to Marx and Engels" (Bailes, 1977, p. 374), Lenin's recommendations made headway in Bolshevism's home (Sochor, 1981). We might add that it is significant that, in spite of the anti-capitalist rhetoric, the only difference Lenin foresees with Taylorism's use in Russia is that the workers will be treated to a reduction in working time. Nowhere is there questioning of the division of labor and authority relations which is the price of more leisure. It was in response to this that Weber could triumphantly announce the vindication of his thesis that socialism conflicted with technical efficiency, that egalitarianism was incompatible with rationalization: "the Bolshevik government . . . has now gone over to the reintroduction in those factories which are working at all . . . of a piece-wage system, for the reason that output would suffer otherwise. They leave the industrialists at the head of the concerns, because they alone have the expert knowledge" (Weber, 1918, p. 215).

Adopting the proverbial metaphor of base and superstructure, Lenin constantly reiterated that material sufficiency was the axis of Bolshevik policy, and this is still the case. However, it begs the vexing questions: to what extent, precisely, is this base the determinant of all else? to what extent does this reduce socialism/communism to a matter of technology? When contemporary Soviet thinkers write that "scientific and technical progress is the principal lever for the creation of the material and technical basis of communism" (Fedoseyev, in Dahrendorf et al., 1977, p. 100) they are certainly true to Lenin, but one must ask to what degree does this exclude other factors such as work satisfaction, inequality, and even politics?

One answer, irresistable to such points of view, is that technology is *totally* determining of socialism. This is implicit in Lenin's advocacy of Taylorism plus "reduction in working time," and later Soviet writers have extended this to project a working day of only four to six hours in the period of advanced technology. Assumed here is that socialism is to be discovered in nonwork: the supply of leisure due to technology's generosity becomes the measure of socialism, while work, it is tacitly conceded, will remain undesirable and alienating. Not only is this to abandon an important element of the socialist critique of labor under capitalism; it is also precisely that which appeals to conservative enthusiasts for I.T. who herald a future leisure society.

Moreover, in the Soviet Union, technology can be seen as even more of a means of achieving socialism since it can also be presented as a means, ultimately, of removing the alienation brought about by the division of labor. It is projected that some time in the future not only will there be generous provision of leisure, but also that in the workplace automation will do away with specialization, fragmentation, and the need for authority. As G. Shakhnazarove states: "Often in seminars and lectures the question is asked: 'Who will do the 'dirty' physical work under communism?' .... All such particularly laborious and "unpleasant" work will be done by *machines* " (quoted *in* Gilison, 1975, p. 145). Again, what is striking about this formulation is that it concurs with conservative Western analysts of I.T. who regard innovation as likely to proceed through stages of mechanization (when, as Galbraith suggests, it will increase the division of labor) to automation, which will unify the whole process under the control of autonomous professionals (see below pp. 128-129).

The convergence theorists in the West, intellectually out of favor at home, hereby enjoy a convergence with Soviet analysts of science and technology (cf. Daglish, 1972). Daniel Boorstin's belief that "great technological change . . . seems somehow a law unto itself, to have its own peculiar vagrancy" (Boorstin, 1978, p. 24) is echoed in the postulation of a relatively—how relative?—autonomous "spreading scientific and technological revolution, unparalleled in scale and in its results and consequences" (Fedoseyev, in Dahrendorf et al., 1977, p. 84). It is not surprising to read the complaint of Michel Bosquet that

> The elites of both sides now have the same ideology, broadly that of the Harvard Business School, whose disciples are currently organizing courses in Moscow: the same hierarchical division of labor and the same military discipline in the factories of Detroit and Togliattigrad, Chicago and Minsk" (Bosquet, 1977, p. 75).

Marx and Engels

This interpretation of the role of technology—what might be called the technological route to socialism—has not only provided a springboard for recent theorists of the STR, but also draws upon distinct elements of the thought of Marx and Engels. Within the corpus of these two are found conflicts that provide for differing traditions of Marxist analysis of technology which are themselves an instance of "primary Marxism's" "nuclear contradiction" that has generated and recurrently reproduces the opposing perspectives of scientific and critical Marxism (Gouldner, 1980, p. 14). Alvin Gouldner performed a magnificent task in clarifying ways in which Marx's thought "shuffles back and forth" (p. 79) between science and critique, to supply a wider context from which we will extract aspects most relevant to theorizations of technology. These revolve around the differing conceptions of Marxian method (whether historicist and holistic, or structuralist and intent on dividing society into separate levels) and differing interpretations of the causes and resolutions of alienation.

Critical Marxism

It is not hard to find in the writing of Marx reference to the "mystification of the capitalist mode of production, the conversion of social relations into things" (Marx, in McLellan, 1977, p. 504). Much of his energy was expended in demonstrating that things which appear to be beyond the influence of society are socially constituted. His major target was what he termed the capitalist reification of economic categories, such as profit, money, the market, and labor, whereby the social character of these terms is obscured when they are presented as eternal verities. Technology is also often described in this way: "Nature builds no machines, no locomotives, railways, electric telegraphs, self-acting mules, etc. These are products of human industry; natural material transformed into organs of the human will over nature, or of human participation in nature" (Marx, 1973, p. 706).

While Marx here emphasizes the social construction of technology, elsewhere he goes further to claim that this is intrusive into the actual technology, it being "the material embodiment of capital" (Marx, 1970, p. 427), the "development of the means of labor into machinery (being) not an accidental moment of capital, but rather the historical reshaping of the traditional, inherited means of labor into a form adequate to capital" (Marx, 1973, p. 694). In this way, technology ought to be perceived as a product of capitalist development, as constitutive of capitalist social relations, and as a means of perpetuating those relations. Because it incorporates capitalist relations, technology per se contributes to the alienation of workers. It is an embodiment of a relation of domination which relegates the worker to an appendage of the machine that appears "alien, external to him." (Marx, 1973, p. 695). Because "the appropriation of living labor by capital is directly expressed in machinery," the worker's "own labor power [is] devalued. . . . Hence we have the struggle of the worker against machinery. What used to be the activity of the living worker has become that of the machine" (Marx in McLellan, 1977, p. 379).

The division of labor is also conceived as an element of this social process. Just as capital builds into machinery the values of subordination (technologies are devised to control the worker by usurping skills, reducing initiative, and so on) and profit maximization (technologies are designed not for human need but for profitability), so too is the division of labor shaped. Relations of work organization are not to be seen as neutral requisites of some hidden hand of efficiency but rather as historically and socially specific: "division of labor in the workshop, as practiced by manufacture, is a special creation of the capitalist mode of production alone" (Marx, 1970, p. 359), being the "recognized methodical and systematic form of capitalist production" (p. 363).

In these ways, technological changes and the organization of work, far from being autonomous, are constantly at "the service of capital" (p. 361), which has brought them into being. Marx therefore argues that machinery is an expression of capital's power and priorities:

> The special skill of each individual insignificant factory operative vanishes as an infinitesimal quantity before the science, the gigantic physical foces, and the mass of labor that are embodied in the factory mechanism and, together with that mechanism, constitute the power of the "master" . . . in whose brain the machinery and his monopoly of it are inseparably united (p. 423).

Technology is not something which happens to be abused by the "master" from the outset, the intention has been to consolidate and perpetuate the relations of capital and labor and these are duly incorporated into machinery and organizational arrangements. Because this is so, these not only express capital's interest by deskilling labor wherever possible by designing skills into machinery or breaking down activities into more elementary parts, but also relegate the worker's role to that of machine-minder, to performer of functions so fragmented that they cannot be identified with. Technology and the division of labor under capitalism thereby condemn the worker to an alienated existence: "The work of directing, superintending, and adjusting, becomes one of the functions of capital" (p. 331). A consequence for the worker is "life-long annexation . . . to a partial operation, and his complete subjection to capital" (p. 356).

It is these formulations which give credence to a critical Marxist tradition that sees in technical change the incorporation of value. From such a perspective, I.T. can be perceived as a capitalist technology, as something comprehensible only when situated within a specific historical and social context, as something which assumes and perpetuates the subordination and alienation of working people. The methodology of this Marxism is insistently holistic and historicist, refusing to extract technology from the complex of social relations that constitute a society. Its political corollary is an expression of hostility towards innovations which are regarded as tainted by capital.

Scientific Marxism

However, the writings of Marx, and still more clearly of Engels, do not unequivocally support this line of thought. In spite of such remarks, Marx also made observations, indeed many observations, the implications of which are in sharp contrast. Thus, at the moment of his writing that technology entailed capital's values, he could contend that this same technology could also be neutral and thereby amenable to use by socialists after their seizure of power. Examples are numerous, but this is an especially direct statement:

> while capital gives itself its adequate form of use value within the production process only in the form of machinery and other material manifestations of fixed capital, such as railways, etc. . . . this in no way means that this use value—machinery as such—is capital, or that its existence as machinery is identical with its existence as capital; any more than gold would cease to have use value as gold if it were no longer *money*. Machinery does not lose its use value as soon as it ceases to be capital. While machinery is the most appropriate form of the use value of fixed capital, it does not at all follow that therefore subsumption under the social relation of capital is the most appropriate and ultimate social relation of production for the application of machinery (Marx, 1973, pp. 699–700).

Marx's writing is peppered with these sort of remarks which are palable sources of a use/abuse approach to I.T. In *Capital,* for example, he extends this idea of alternative uses of technology when chastising those of his contemporaries who fail to distinguish opposition to "the capitalist employment of machinery" from opposition to "machinery itself" (Marx, 1970, p. 441). Marx thundered at the apologist for technological innovation who attacked critics of the current application of new technology:

> Any employment of machinery, except by capital, is to him an impossibility. Exploitation of the workman by the machine is therefore, with him, identical with exploitation of the machine by the workman. Whoever, therefore, exposes the real state of things in the capitalistic employment of machinery, is against its employment in any way, and is an enemy of social progress! Exactly the reasoning of Bill Sykes. "Gentlemen of the jury, no doubt the throat of this commercial traveller has been cut. But that is not my fault, it is the fault of the knife" (ibid., pp. 441–442).

Marx and Engels are as one on this conception of technology which "in the hands of the producers working together [can] be transformed from master demons into willing servants. The difference is as that between the destructive force of electricity in the lightening of the storm and electricity under command in the telegraph and voltaic arc" (Engels, 1971, p. 145). Marx thought it obvious that "the way in which machinery is exploited is quite distinct from the machinery itself. Powder is still powder, whether you use it to wound a man or to dress his wounds" (Marx, in Marx and Engels, 1982, pp. 99).

Statements on these lines render Marx's approach to technology much more ambiguous than might first appear. Further, it is necessary to remember that, throughout his work, Marx regularly revealed an admiration for the productive capabilities of capitalism, not least because of his frequent evocation of a stages view of development in which capitalism's growth is presented as purposeful both to gestate the proletariat and to supply it with the material basis for founding socialism (see Avineri, 1969; Marx, 1950). This radical evolutionism is the unmistakable message of a number of his studies—particularly *The Communist Manifesto*—and its weight is that capitalism is functional to the socialist future—as is its technology.

More than this, Marx on occasion admits that alienation is to be ended not simply by overcoming the market system wherein the worker's "life-activity is for him only a means to enable him to exist" (Marx, 1967, pp. 20–21). Though Marx's depiction of alienation is most often associated with his diagnosis of labor as a commodity, as something the worker "sells to another person in order to secure the necessary means of subsistence" (ibid.), it does have other dimensions (Mészáros, 1970). We have noted the alienation which Marx claimed was entailed in the capitalist division of labor and its associated technologies, and we shall return to this, but for the moment emphasize another aspect which is better understood in consideration of his conception of "freedom," since it reveals interesting attitudes towards technology.

To appreciate Marx's notion of freedom, we have to realize that he believed "conscious life activity directly distinguishes man from animal life activity" (Marx, 1975, p. 328). He though that human beings, in their labor, produce objects that are expressions of themselves: "man reproduces himself not only intellectually, in his consciousness, but actively and actually, and he can therefore contemplate himself in a world he himself has created" (p. 329). This postulate is of course the axis of Marx's argument that under capitalism, where the worker's labor is "a commodity which he has made over to another" (Marx, 1967, pp. 20-21), alienation is endemic since the fruits of one's labor are but so much in wages. However, if this process of self-realization through one's work is for Marx what separates humans from animals, people nevertheless remain animal to the extent that they must eat, drink, and procreate. Contemplating these essentials, Marx introduces an important idea, the notion that a certain level of material sufficiency is a prerequisite for non-alienated activity. That is, humans cannot be free from alienation until their basic needs are satisfied. Animals "build nests and dwellings, like the bee, the beaver, the ant, etc. But they produce only for their own immediate needs or those of their young . . . they produce only when immediate physical need compels them to do so" (Marx, 1975, p. 329). A person, on the other hand, "produces even when he is free from physical need and *truly produces only in freedom from such need*" (ibid., our emphasis).

It is this precondition for freedom, this essential ingredient for self-realization, that introduces into Marxism the idea of technologies and techniques which are required to fulfil this need. From his early writings there is an insistence that without freedom from basic needs political change is futile. Thus, in *The German Ideology* he could assert that "the development of productive forces . . . is an absolutely necessary practial premise, because without it privation, *want,* is *merely* made general, and with *want* the struggle for necessities would begin again" (Marx and Engels, 1976, p. 49). When Marx returns to this notion in later writing, he even extends it in ways that are surprisingly reminiscent of some recent commentators on I.T. In a famous distinction, he states that "the realm of freedom begins only where labor which is determined by necessity and mundane considerations ceases; thus in the nature of things it lies beyond the sphere of actual material production" (Marx, in McLellan, 1977, p. 496), following this separation of the "realm of freedom" from the "realm of necessity" (p. 497), with the insistence that "the true realm of freedom . . . can blossom forth only with this realm of necessity as its basis. The shortening of the working day is its basic prerequisite" (ibid.).

What we have here is not only the separation of society into levels—a base and the rest—but also the suggestion, which recurs in Marx, that it is in nonwork that freedom is to be found. Implicit is acknowledgement that labor of necessity is an unavoidable evil, that some alienating work is the price of freedom gained outside of that work, and that some work may contribute to the very malady that it is presumed to prepare the basis for overcoming. Here we must recall an affinity with many enthusiasts for I.T. who promise what Marx appears to require—time to do one's own thing free from want, while work is performed by automated machinery which leaves the populace free to enjoy the "affluent redundancy" of a "leisure society." For a Marxist analysis of technology it poses major problems, not least the query that, if capitalism could supply a reduction in working time sufficient

to create generous leisure without privation, then is it necessary to struggle politically against capitalism? Why not follow the tide of capitalist technology? When
Marx writes of socialism that it will reduce "the necessary labor of society to a
minimum, which then corresponds to the artistic, scientific, etc. development of
the individuals in the time set free, and with the means created, for all of them"
(Marx, 1973, p. 706) there is apparent an awkward convergence with contemporary
conservatism (cf., McLellan, 1976, pp. 299-303).

This pointing to a shortening of the working day as a basis of socialism (without
jeopardizing productivity) is also, as we have seen, at the core of Soviet theorists
of an STR. A consequence of this target is the acceptance of a neutral level of production which in turn accepts that the organizational arrangements involved in
attaining that production are similarly neutral, inevitable, and—up to an undisclosed
point—determining of the social relations which are to be built upon it. Engels,
writing in 1872 when Marx was still very much alive, candidly stated this requisite,
since "a certain authority, no matter how delegated, and . . . a certain subordination, are things which, *independently of all social organization,* are imposed upon
us together with the material conditions under which we produce and make products circulate" (Engels, in Marx and Engels, 1958, p. 638, our emphasis). Weber
could not have put it better. If we accept that there is a prerequisite of a basic
level of production prior to politics (or freedom), then a certain amount of technological take-up, division of labor, authority, and unpleasant labor must be regarded as unstopable.

Further problems this entails are made clearer in examination of Marx's views on
the division of labor (cf. Rattansi, 1982a,b). We have already revealed that Marx
contended that the capitalist division of labor was alienating. However, on other
occasions he indicated that the division of labor of itself was alienating. For example, in *the German Ideology* it is argued that "as soon as the division of labour
begins, each man has a particular, exclusive sphere of activity, which is forced
upon him and from which he cannot escape" (Marx and Engels, 1976, p. 47). In
this case, only abolition of the division of labor (and the technology that is integral to this division?) can end the fragmentation this creates: "the division of labor
implies the possibility, nay the fact, that intellectual and material activity, production and consumption, devolve on different individuals, and that the only possibility of their not coming into contradiction lies in negating in its turn the division
of labor" (p. 45). However, we have also seen that the "realm of necessity" denies
the possibility of ending the division of labor—and in turn denies the possibility
of entirely eliminating alienation. Marx's early ideal of "communist society, where
nobody has one exclusive sphere of activity but each can become accomplished in
any branch he wishes" (p. 47) had, by the time of *Capital,* given way to the admission that

> All combined labor on a large scale requires, more or less, a directing author-
> ity in order to secure the harmonious working of the individual activities, and
> to perform the general functions that have their origin in the action of the
> combined organism, as distinguished from the action of its separate organs.

A single violin player is his own conductor; an orchestra requires a separate one" (Marx, 1970, pp. 330–331).

It is ironic that Marx's onetime dream that with a "communist organization of society there disappears the subordination of the artist to local and national narrowness, which arises entirely from the division of labor," because there will be "no painters but at most people who engage in painting among other activities" (Marx, in McLellan, 1977), resurfaces in more modern Marxist thought when technology is seen as the means of achieving this goal by completely automating production. Marx himself said nothing on this possibility, but it is embryonic in his thought and we ought not to be surprised that so many Marxists, East and West, have stressed the technological resolution to alienation.

The Marxist Legacy

We have emphasized these dimensions of Marx's thought because they have such profound implications for contemporary responses to I.T. from people on the Left who trace a genealogy from Marx. Gouldner poses the dilemma forcefully:

> If socialism premises a release from scarcity based on increased productivity, it therefore premises the requisites of that increase. These include continued use and development of advanced technology in industry, the continued existence of the very division of labor and the entire system of authority and subordination on which the application of technology to industry depends and, with this, the very human stultification that machinery and that division of labor imply (Gouldner, 1980, p. 272).

This appears to us to be the major inheritance of current left-wing analyses of technological innovation. Technology might well be regarded as abused by capitalism, but it will not be seen as constitutive of capitalism. Followers of Engels, perhaps approaching by way of Bernal, will contend that capitalism even stifles technological change, having become a "hinderance to the development of production" (Engels, in Marx and Engels, 1958, p. 376), while simultaneously "clashing with the obsolete system of social relations . . . [and] further aggravat[ing] the contradictions of capitalism" (Fedoseyev, in Dahrendorf et al., 1977, p. 95). With Engels, much Marxism today will assert that socialism will bring technology "deliverance from these bonds [which] is the one pre-condition for an unbroken, constantly accelerated development of the productive forces, and therewith for a practically unlimited increase of production itself" (Engels, 1971, p. 148). This view, what Orwell complained of as the "fat-bellied version," of socialism as a system that can best assist the growth of technology and satisfy the material aspirations of the people while giving them adequate time in which to enjoy them, is but a logical extrapolation of traits in the corpus of Marx and Engels. From this point of view, technology, whether used or abused, is in a real sense supra-social at the same time that it is the foundation of the coming socialism.

I.T. and the Challenge to the Left

The difficulties with these conceptions are numerous, but, to repeat, not least is specifying the precise degree of determination: how much technology is sufficient for socialism? How much technology, division of labor and authority relations are necessary—and acceptable to socialists, given their effects on workers—to serve as prerequisites? Engels was not precise, but he had no doubt that a developed degree was inevitable, scorning socialists who attacked "the principle of authority" thus: "Wanting to abolish authority in large-scale industry is tantamount to wanting to abolish industry itself, to destroy the power loom in order to return to the spinning wheel" (Engels, in Marx and Engels, 1958, pp. 636-637).

Moreover, these questions call forth the further, still more important, assault on Marxism: to what extent can technology per se—this technology which both Marx and Engels agree is essential for socialism though developed by capitalism—lead us to socialism? This is not a frivolous issue, given the cornucopia of futurism projecting precisely this—material plenty without the need to work—"without the long-awaited revolution of the proletariat" (Evans, 1979, p. 208). A hint of this is in Marx's rhapsody on the "realm of freedom," and Engels arguably came still closer to endorsing it in suggesting that communism would only be fully attainable when automation managed to abolish the division of labor (Levine, 1975).

André Gorz

But we need not look to Engels or peer into Marx to discover suggestions of a technological route to socialism, since, in a recent book, André Gorz, a prominent New Left thinker, articulates this very theme. Gorz endorses an idea frequently evoked by socialists repelled by work under capitalism (and actually existing socialism) who perceive in leisure a potentially genuine socialist lifestyle. This is the premise of STR theorists as much as it is that of Michael Harrington who, like his Soviet counterparts, sees technology as its means of attainment: "Freedom will not be discovered within technology, but by means of it, i.e., through the diminution of the working day and a vast, qualitative increase in leisure time . . . socialism seeks the abolition of compulsory labour. Its decisive means of production is leisure" (Harrington, 1974, p. 161).

Though he cannot pretend that automation will develop to such a degree as to entirely abolish the unpleasantries of the division of labor—and therefore urges socialists to resign themselves to the inevitable alienation this entails—Gorz occupies the same platform as Harrington. Writing of the "post-industrial neo-proletariat" (Gorz, 1982, p. 69) Gorz advises the Left to jettison the orthodox call, a "philosophy of the proletariat (which) is a religion" (p. 21), for struggle to control work: "workers' control" is an anachronism because work is unavoidably unsatisfactory. What the Left ought to recognize, attests Gorz, is that "The logic of capital has brought us to the threshold of liberation" (p. 74). This "liberation" induced by capitalism itself is from work by means of advanced technology.

Gorz's recommendation—that of Jenkins and Sherman, Peter Large, and Alvin Toffler in Marxian garb—is for a leisure society: political struggle nowadays is for Gorz a matter "no longer of winning power as a worker, but of winning power no longer to function as a worker" (p. 67). It is his belief that we are moving towards a "dual society" which can subsidize from one part the leisure activities that take place in the other. Arguing that in face of a rapid technological change the demand for leisure is "the only realistic and practicable solution" he contends that high technology vigorously applied in one sector of society will assure the efficient production of goods while the other—the "sphere of autonomous activity" (p. 93) —will be where, using "convivial tools," socialism (leisure) will be achieved. Socialism thereby is to be created by a flight from work, although the latter must supply the materials for this leisure-oriented socialism. Here it is essential that Gorz draws on the base/superstructure metaphor of Scientific Marxism to support his thesis: "The extension of the sphere of autonomy is thus predicated upon a sphere of heteronomous production which, though industrialized, is restricted to socially necessary goods and services that cannot be supplied in an autonomous manner with the same efficiency" (p. 101). There is a price to be paid for the rewards of this dual society which is that, to satisfy "primary needs" (p. 97), some work must be performed in stultifying conditions. The sop is the abundance of leisure in an age of material plenty.

Gorz is illuminating chiefly because he writes as a Marxist and directly about new technologies. He argues that I.T., "According to whether it is a politics . . . of the Right or the Left, . . . may lead either to a society based on unemployment or to one based on free time. Of all the levers available to change the social order and the quality of life, this is one of the most powerful" (pp. 136-137). Of course, as with many conservative ideologues for I.T., there is no doubting which choice a Leftist should make, nor that Gorz is offering no choice at all when it comes to acceptance or rejection of such a progressive technology as I.T. Indeed, he is disarmingly realistic about this, recalling Galbraith in stating that "The rules, regulations, and laws of a complex society dominated by large-scale structures are the result of technical imperatives" (p. 92). Pervading the entire book is this inevitabilism, an assumption that technology is socially neutral, yet also determining the very possibility of socialism. For this reason, political style aside, it is a conservative tract, technocratic in all except its hopes for the content of leisure. Gorz's message is one of retreat from politics and political struggle, since—though he fails to pose the obvious question himself—his theory removes the need for politics. There is no reason, given his views on the capacity of technology to provide the leisure and sufficiency that will enable socialism to be viable, why we should not see capitalism adopting the same technology (which after all it has created) nor seeing it as able to produce the same leisure facilities. As we have observed, apologists for I.T. promise precisely this.

Revealingly, Gorz's concerns were presaged over 20 years ago by no less a thinker than Daniel Bell who recognized the import of data-processing systems

(Bell, 1962, p. 265) which promised a "new character to work, living, and leisure" (p. 268) and noted the enduring theme of leisure as compensation for alienating labor that is rehashed by Gorz. Bell commented on the fact that "what workers have been denied in work, they now seek to recapture in manifold ways. Over the past decade there has been a fantastic mushrooming of arts-and-crafts hobbies, of photography, home woodwork shops with power-driven tools" (p. 259). This is recognizably the convivial style of life that Gorz would appear to desire and even think of as socialist. Not so Bell. He added that, "while this is intrinsically commendable, it has been achieved at a high cost indeed—the loss of satisfaction in work" (ibid.). The guru of I.T.'s conservative enthusiasts appears here more discontented with the negative effects of advanced technology on the labor process than Marxist André Gorz.

Gorz's work is not to be dismissed as an idiosyncracy. We are struck by the assumptions he shares with nonradical theorists who discern convergence between industrial societies due to technological imperatives; we are skeptical of his theorization of technology as asocial yet socially determining; we do query the evolutionism in the book; and we do question Gorz's separation of society into distinct realms. But we do not regard him as exceptional. He writes as a Marxist in the tradition of Scientific Marxism which has presaged all of his insights, including the theme of socialism as affluent leisure.

Conclusion

The conclusion we draw from this journey through the Left's analysis and response to technology is that it reveals a remarkable consensus as to how it should be approached: neutral, inevitably to be accepted, and, more or less, determining. From this we must note that, rhetoric apart, the differences this position has from those selling I.T. are minimal: "Marxism is infatuated with the bougeois society it despises. If Marxists wanted to expropriate the expropriators, they also fell in love with their instruments: science and technology" (Jacoby, 1981, p. 5). Analyses of science and technology which conceive of them constituting a "genuine revolution" (Benson and Lloyd, 1983, p. 16), whether they are of the Left or Right, inescapably concentrate on how best society can adjust to what is "the technical base of the economy" (p. 190). From such a perspective, science and technology—the productive forces which form the STR—rather than people are the motor of change. The latter are merely required to adapt to the new circumstances created by the STR, preferably to enjoy its bounty with the guidance of a well-intentioned and kindly state (p. 203 passim). We think this affinity of opposite political poles testifies to the survival of that "identical reification of process" Edward Thompson (Thompson, 1978, p 270) described as shared by conservatives and communists in the 1950s. The rest of this book is dedicated to detailing how I.T. should be understood, in contradistinction to the above, as a social relation (Young, 1977).

PART TWO

THE SOCIAL CONTEXTS
OF INFORMATION
TECHNOLOGY

Introduction: The Rhetoric of Choice

> "there's small choice in rotten apples."
> —Shakespeare

The first part of this book has argued that, across the spectrum of comment on I.T., from James Martin's enthusiastic bubbling, through Daniel Bell's sociological conjectures, to André Gorz's socialist futurology, a number of interconnected assumptions hold constant: that technology is a neutral, asocial phenomenon which is yet more or less determining of society and must be acceded to. We contend that this is a misconception of I.T.—and of technological innovation tout court—and we shall undertake the detailing of an alternative. However, before commencing this critique we want to draw attention to a further characteristic which complements these others and is found in most considerations of new technology. This is to refer to the recurrent assertion that I.T. offers unprecedented opportunities for us to control the future direction of society: a wave of scientific and technological innovation, so runs the argument, presents us with *choices* in the making of which we can shape our destinies.

The Two Industrial Revolutions

It is nowadays readily conceded that the first industrial revolution was a frightful experience for many of those who lived through it. There is much agreement that bad housing, inadequate nutrition, oppressive conditions of work, poor health care, and widespread child abuse were instance of the ravages that industrialization wrought on the common people. There is nothing necessarily radical or even condemnatory about this concession: indeed such an admission, like that which concurs with Marx's diagnosis of 19th century laissez-faire capitalism, frequently bespeaks the conservatism of those who urge us to "look what we have come through" as post-capitalism has emerged and brought with it unimaginable wealth, meritocratic education, the welfare state, citizenship rights, and the like.

Daniel Bell adds to this the perception that the "Industrial Revolution" was a term applied retrospectively to events and processes that had taken place during the late 18th and 19th centuries, noting that the concept was the creation of the historian Arnold Toynbee in 1884 as a title for a series of lectures which aimed to review the previous century. The first "Industrial Revolution" was only recognized with hindsight: "those who were living through the industrial revolution never knew they were living through such a revolution" (Bell, 1979a, p. 13). For those living "in the eye of the hurricane" (ibid.), experiencing what are now seen as monumental historical developments, there was little if any appreciation of the range and scale of change which the word "revolution" connotes.

These observations are connected since, it is suggested, because the industrial revolution was so much an uncoordinated and undirected affair, the creature of "inspired and talented tinkerers" (Bell, 1976, p. 20) stumbling in the dark to improve this or that machine, capture a market here and there, refine a process or product wherever the need arose, then mistakes were made and many people suffered from the consequences of development. Not knowing quite what they were doing, lacking any over-all plan or strategy for change, as well as not having the means, technical or social, for consciously guiding change, the pioneers of the industrial revolution were not in control of that which they were forging. Because of this environmental pollution, maltreatment of the young, appalling sanitary facilities—all those features which are conjured in the phrase "Dickensian England"—are both explicable and in some way forgiveable because contemporaries did not know what they were doing. Acts committed in ignorance (but what about Podsnap?) are less reprehensible than those knowingly executed.

Today we face the prospect of a second "Industrial Revolution" to be ushered in by I.T. This time, however, we are aware of the potential reach and enormity of the forthcoming revolution: we are able to "self-consciously witness" (Bell, 1980c, p. x) this major series of changes on the eve of their occurrence. Moreover, knowing the costs of the first industrial revolution as we stand on the threshold of the second, by carefully *choosing* (the key word) the appropriate policies I.T. can be used as a means of leading us to "the good society" (call it "post-industrialism," the "information society," what you will) in a more or less painless way. Sensitive to the social costs of the preceding industrial revolution, we can today avoid repetition of previous mistakes and move consciously towards an enlightened "silicon civilization." In the contemporary world, we have the ability, technically and socially, to design societies as we think fit. Thus Daniel Bell:

Today, with our greater sensitivity to social consequences and to the future . . . we are more alert to the possible imports of technological and organizational change; and this is all to the good, for to the extent that we are sensitive, we can try and estimate the consequences and *decide which policies we should choose*, consonant with the values we have, in order to shape, accept, or even reject the alternative futures that are available to us (Bell, 1980c, pp. x–xi; our emphasis).

The Ethos of Choice

Let us strike the keynote, choice, before pursuing our tune. We stand today at a crossroad, attest commentators on I.T., and we are free to choose our route: we have the technological means, the necessary vision and the historical understanding to select which direction is deemed best. "One of the most intriguing features (of the future)," claims Christopher Evans, "will be the way in which the new, freely communicating societies will control their own destinies" (Evans, 1979, p. 216). Because we know history and thereby what to avoid, and because we are aware of what the new technology can do before it does it, judicious assessment can lead us to better things: "It [the future] could be stultifying or enlightening. The choice is ours" (Williams, 1982, p. 14).

This ethos of choice manifests itself on all points of the futurist compass, where there is agreement that "we have arrived at a point at which public decisions are becoming imperative" (Dizard, 1982, p. 118). Australian Labor Minister Barry Jones posits a popular alternative that "Technology can be used to promote greater economic equity, more freedom of choice, and participatory democracy. Conversely, it can be used to intensify the worst aspects of a competitive society, to widen the gap between rich and poor, to make democratic goals irrelevant, and institute a technocracy" (Jones, Barry, 1982, p. 254); and Anthony Smith is convinced that "a vast area of choice is open to societies: to use the opportunities to reduce centralization, say, or to increase it; to continue to press for economic growth or to stabilize; to increase disparities between developed and nondeveloped societies or to close them" (Smith, 1980, p. 20).

Centralization or Decentralization?

So it goes. It would be possible to list many more instances of the choices that I.T. supposedly allows (in television programming, in work organization, in educational methods. . .), but here we focus on the most frequent evocation, which offers as alternatives centralization or decentralization. I.T., it is claimed, can give either greater concentration of power or more devolution depending on how society decides to arrange its politics, business, administration, education, leisure, and so on. Bell puts it thus:

The new revolution in communications makes possible both an intense degree of centralization of power, if the society decides to use it that way, and large decentralization because of the multiplicity, diversity, and cheapness of the modes of communication (Bell, 1979d, p. 36).

Where Bell leads, the lesser futurists follow. Thus Anthony Smith states that "Whether we have 'big' or 'little' government, whether we become a gregarious or a lonely society, individualistic or regimented, is largely a result of the way we choose to use the technology" (Smith, 1980, p. 324). Peter Large suggests that "If every home had a viewdata tv set, then democracy could—if we wanted it—become literally government by the people, and instant government at that, with daily push-button voting even on secondary issues" (Large, 1980, p. 65). And Murray Laver contends that while "computer-based information systems could be used to concentrate power [they] could equally well be used to implement a policy of radical decentralization. The choice is ours" (Laver, 1980, p. 10). Britain's ebullient Minister of Information Technology, Kenneth Baker, urges that we

> "recognize that there is a dilemma at the very centre of the use of the new technologies. They can be used to bring all these advantages which I believe will develop more quickly and more beneficially in a free and open system with the minimum of central controls. But they can also be used to control and manipulate people. They could be used to indoctrinate people. They could be the most effective weapons of control that any dictator has ever had in his hands, the nightmare of 1984. So there is a choice as to how we use these technologies and how we allow them to be used" (Baker, 1983a, p. 8).

The Rhetoric of Choice

This posing of choices by I.T. is of course not surprising in view of the insistence of commentators that the new technology is neutral. Being "just like any other technology, I.T. is intrinsically neither good nor bad. Everything depends on how the country adapts itself to using information technology" (Marsh, 1982, p. 638), which "really is neutral" (Laver, 1980, p. 10). From this presupposition, the language of choice is irresistible.

However, in spite of I.T. being aloof from the stresses and strains of human value, thereby allowing for the exercise of choice as to its uses, there are three ways in which presentations of I.T. contradict the proposition that choices are waiting to be made that will determine its applications. The first is that the scenario most often presented—either centralization or decentralization—is not a credible alternative, since the advantages of the latter so overwhelm those of the former. Who but an authoritarian would argue for centralization? Who but a crazed person could propose, in an age in which it is commonplace to deplore large bureaucracy, a build-up of central controls? The whole either/or debate is a fraud which characteristically poses as a choice a "path to greater freedom or to 1984" (Baker, 1983a). Where a choice is offered between what "Schumacher elaborated [as] his appealing ideas on small is beutiful just at the moment when technology was creating the possibility of realizing some of his dreams" and "the Big Brother Society" managed by "faceless bureaucrats" (ibid.), there is in effect no choice on offer. Similarly, when

Anthony Smith counterposes "individuation" and "regimentation" and elaborates the former as analagous to the ancient Alexandrian library, there is no genuine alternative being offered. Who could opt for centralization when available are "opportunities for individuals to step out of the mass homogenised audiences of newspapers, radio, and television and take a more active role in the process by which knowledge and entertainment are transmitted through society?" (Smith, 1980, p. 22).

There is a second way in which the language of choice can be seen as rhetoric. This is found in an underlying inevitabilism that characterizes writing on I.T. We observed earlier that much of this is presented in terms of an economic imperative of having to respond to foreign competitors who are adopting I.T., cheapening production, and thence threatening and capturing our markets. A complementary way of presenting I.T. as a fait accompli is to argue that it is such a marvellous gift that only an idiot would want to turn it down. This message is simmering beneath the surface in the words of Baker and Smith, but it comes to the boil when King rejoices "that the potential benefits which will flow from this new technology are so enormous that there will be no question of avoiding or slowing down their actualization" (King, 1982, p. 25). Peter Marsh, writing in the *New Scientist,* is not far removed from such reasoning when he laconically observes that "Britain is quite at liberty to ignore the technology and pursue its own unique way of doing things. But then it would have to face up to the fact that, by comparison with much of the rest of the world, it would grow steadily poorer with no chance of arresting that trend until well into the next century" (Marsh, 1982). Who, being compos mentis, could see here a realistic choice?

The third contradictory feature is evident in something related to this inevitabilism, but which merges into technological determinism. This is seen in Dizard's statement, following his assurance of the existence of choice, that, like it or not, a "strategy will emerge by design or default" (Dizard, 1982, p. 19) by which society will adapt to I.T. Similarly, Kenneth Baker's contention that "a choice exists and we will have to decide what we want" precedes by a few words an uncheering, "the stark choice for British industry is to Automate or liquidate" (Baker, 1982). What this all amounts to is that, whether or not we exercise choice, the new technology is here to stay, will impact on us enormously, is an offer we cannot refuse.

This capitulation to technology—whatever we may choose, it will shape our destinies—is also present in the restriction of choices to I.T. itself. In accepting as a starting point the technology which has arrived ready constituted, this ethos of choice in fact limits real choice to that which has been pre-selected. Pertinent and practical questions surely are: Why has a technology, which we are informed can do function a, b, and c from which we may choose, been developed in the first instance, and what choices have been excluded in the process of innovation? Whose interests lie behind research and development programs, and what is their significance? Asking these questions, it will be clear that choices may have been excluded before we are ever told to choose.

Finally it is worth stating that, in spite of all the words that have been written on the choices offered by I.T. in spite of the constant references to how *we* may decide upon our futures because of this wonderful innovation, there have been few instances of people being allowed any real choice to date. Which factories have allowed choice to the employees as to adoption of robots or computer numerical control? Where are the offices in which the typists have been allowed choice as to whether or not they adopt word processors, new forms of copiers, and the like? Where are the banks in which the employees were offered the choice of automation or continuation of traditional services? Of course, this too is rhetoric, since I.T. has been and is being designed, developed, and installed with minimal public account-ability (and that which does take place is premised upon management being able to initiate new technologies).

Beyond Choice

It is our view that this talk of alternatives from which we may choose should be seen, as Vincent Mosco argues, as a "non-scenario" which functions as yet another means of imposing I.T. on the public by presenting it "in the spirit of the marriage vow. . . . [as] something we must accept, through thick and thin, for better or worse" (Mosco , 1982, p. 4, 6). Who can seriously object when we are insistently informed that I.T. is open to manipulation in whatever ways we so desire? For good or evil, reaction or progress, large or small. . . .What can one complain about when the new technology is entirely malleable? We would find less of a cause for concern if this rhetoric of choice were restricted to advocates of I.T. who have an identifiable interest in its introduction that would warn us to be suspicious of such language. However, such a scenario is adopted across the political spectrum, and we find even on the Left and among trade unions a similar endorsement of the tech-nology being neutral, potentially to be used purposely or abused.

Since our position is easily misunderstood, it merits stating that we are not con-tending that the decisions people make in the course of their lives are insignificant. Nor are we saying that responses to I.T. are irrelevancies. Rather, our claim is that current discussions of I.T. which emphasize a freedom to choose in fact positively delimit genuine choices being exercised, since they so obscure realities. Continuously asserting that I.T. provides choices here, there, and everywhere paradoxically restricts real choice because it diverts attention from analyses which could reveal the realities of the introduction and development of I.T., wherein which meaning-ful decisions are to be made, at the same time as it disarms what can be healthy suspicion about technological change by presenting innovation as a neutral process.

It is our belief that purposeful control over destinies can only come about when real social processes are revealed. Our claim is that genuine choices can be made only when circumstances—*here* I.T. is shaped in *these* ways for *those* interests; *there* are factions implementing I.T. in *these* forms for *these* reasons with *those* consequences—are accurately appreciated. Some years ago, Herbert Schiller ob-served that the "road to the social use of technology runs through the rugged ter-rain of interest groups, privileged classes, national power, and self-satisfied decision-makers" (Schiller, 1970, p. 150). The rugged terrain within which I.T. is located, so long as the facile language of choice is dominant, will not be mapped. That would be to the advantage of identifiable groups in society whose interests are advanced by the conception that technical change is inherently neutral. We see it as the major task of this book to commence examination of the social contexts and meaning of I.T. so that a better starting point can be arrived at, from which decisions of substance can be made, than that which is currently ascendant.

Chapter 5
I.T. and Work

Poetry? It's a hobby.
I run model trains.
Mr. Shaw there breeds pigeons.

It's not work. You don't sweat.
Nobody pays for it.
You *could* advertise soap.

. . . . . .

How could I look a bus conductor
in the face
if I paid you twelve pounds?

Basil Bunting, "What the Chairman told Tom." From
Collected Poems, Oxford University Press, 1978, p. 118.

Introduction

It is a commonplace of sociology that work is not to be defined by what is actually being done at any particular time. The meaning of work is not inherent in performance but is contingent upon the interpretations of actions—reading a book, chopping a tree, excavating an archaelogical site, digging a hole can be either leisure or work depending on the context within which it takes place.

Recognition of the social construction of work is a significant intellectual and political insight because it turns attention away from assumptions and assertions of its naturalness and inevitability towards the contexts which have given rise to contemporary definitions. We so readily take for granted that work is our destiny, something that most of us must endure, that to recognize it as artifically created presents us with a new, disturbing, and revelatory way of seeing.

Lately it has become instructive to be reminded of this sociological truism because so many commentators, dismayed by unprecendented levels of unemployment, have begun to tell the populace not to worry about the decline of work and are recommending as a solution to worklessness the abolition of work, which is perceived as having been an onerous and unavoidable imposition upon the human race until the advent of the electronic age. To argue that work is not natural, that it is a social construct, is to refuse facile considerations of the removal of a hitherto unpleasant affliction which is externally imposed and to insist that to understand "work" we must understand the social relations that formed it and within which it functions.

Pre-eminent amongst the contexts which have created work as we know it has been the development of industrial capitalism which, bringing about the system wherein an employee contracted to sell his or her labor for a specified period at a particular price, introduced as the prodominant meaning of "work" that activity, employment, which one undertakes to make money. Conversely, activities that are often mentally and physically demanding that are undertaken nonremuneratively (child-rearing, community projects, political and trade union organization. . .) are regarded as nonwork or, nearer the mark and revealing of the conception of paid employment in our society, "voluntary work."

A consequence of this was that work came to be regarded as time rather than task-oriented (work starts at 8 a.m. sharp and stops at 5 p.m., rather than when the cows need milking, the fields ploughing, a job lot completing), thereby placing an unprecedented emphasis on the "proper use of time" (Smiles, 1891, p. 12), the clock as an "oracle" which Gulliver assured the Lilliputians "pointed out the time for every action of life," and the spread of industrial conflict as in large part struggles over the length and cost of time. With capitalism, "Time is now currency; it is not passed but spent" (Thompson, 1967, p. 61). A cognate feature was the development of leisure, defined in opposition to work, as time free from paid employment. Relatedly, there came about the widespread notion that work is largely a means to an end, a burdensome necessity which provides money to spend in those "little islands of freedom called 'leisure' " (Coates, 1967, p. 75). This is, of course, to identify, albeit loosely, the phenomenon of alienation which is so characteristic of work nowadays. It is to recognize that a predominant meaning of work as so much wages contains the paradox that, for many people, it lacks intrinsic meaning, is reducible to so many pounds, shillings, and pence and apparently little more. It is to perceive work as a sacrifice of one's life, an unwelcome diversion and diminishing intrusion into one's *real* life which is *lived* outside of work.

This idea of work and time spent at work as "the stuff between pay packets" is a major feature of the experiences of people over the last two and more centuries. It is a remarkable indictment of our social arrangements that they produce and perpetuate work that condemns much of people's lives to such manifest dissatisfaction, that inflicts upon "the walking wounded . . . violence—to the spirit as well as to the body" (Terkel, 1977, p. I; cf., *Work in America,* 1973). And, in arguing that this is consequent upon a conception of work as time bought and reluctantly sold, we remain acutely aware of the compounding effects of much work being, historically, and still today, physically arduous and even dangerous, machine-paced and repetitious, fragmented and stultifying (Samuel, 1977).

In spite of these aspects, which must be emphasized in any serious study, work has not entirely negative connotations. For a start, the term insistently seeks to escape its dominant meaning of paid employment to reach a wider, more dignified notion, such as in "working in the garden" and "working on a problem." This intonation, submerged much of the time, suggests that people search to find in their interpretation and experience of work a sense of purpose and worth lacking in its more common themes.

What we can glimpse in shifting definitions of work, in this secondary yet widespread use of the term, is an attempt to appropriate work from a restrictive and dulling monetary contract towards a means of self and social expression. Studs Terkel, in his remarkable interviews that allowed Americans to talk uninhibitedly about their working lives, "was constantly astonished by the extraordinary dreams of ordinary people" (Terkel, 1977, p. 14). An extended definition of work beyond the denigrating process experienced by the many is a key aspect of those dreams.

No doubt this alternative definition could be called something else, perhaps "occupation" or "labor," and indeed it is often referred to as a "hobby" or "pastime," but we think it is revealing that most often other words are not recoursed to, and an attempt is made to confer on the common term another meaning. This suggests a great deal about our society and the relations it contains, when people so contest vocabularies: the refusal to entirely concede work to wage labor is an acknowledgement that something is worth fighting for, is an indication of a desire for work to mean much more than a waste of energy and demeaning of self.

We have said that work is recognized as important to people, as important enough to apply the term in spheres of life that are valued for much more than their economic return. In stating this, we intended to signify a qualitative meaning and would emphasis that this is a widely held perception, but we would add to it the fact that work—work in the dominant sense of "remunerative employment"—is also quantitatively of great significance to people. Since it is an activity that occupies a large proportion of most people's daily lives, it is not surprising that, investing so much of their waking hours, they strive to make it of significance (Garson, 1977). Indeed, what is astonishing about the conditions of work in our society is that so many people, for so much of their time, are compelled to endure work which can evoke from them only a minimal commitment and often impels them to recourse to survival strategies such as "fantasizing," "skiving," and the proverbial "clock-watching."

Nevertheless, giving so much of their time and energy, people will respond even to stultifying work by trying to and often succeeding in creating something of worth. And it is here that we can see positive features of work—in the comradeship of the factory, the sociality of the office, in the "if it wasn't for the people, I couldn't stand it here" syndrome.

In addition, and connected to this, work is central to one's conception of self and social worth, it is crucial to identity and self-esteem (Fox, 1980). All of us are aware—and if our attention lapses our procket books remind us—of the evaluation of work in our society which, at first glance, renders in both economic and prestige ways greater rewards to white-collar occupations (revealingly not defined as "workers" but as "professionals") than to manual workers. This is not surprising; since society has defined what work will constitute and how it will be interpreted (as so much time for so much money), it also produces valuations of the worth of those performing the work which in turn it will try to have accepted by its members. Hereby, work is implicated in the overall web of social relations in society; it tells us a great deal about people, their economic prospects, their political outlook, their self-opinion, their position in the hierarchies of esteem.

With this in mind, we would make another observation. We take as a maxim that "dignity is as compelling a human need as food or sex" (Sennett and Cobb, 1973, p. 191), that there is a hunger for it in all but the most defeated and destitute of people (and perhaps even here too), and that wherever affronts to that search are made manifest—in interpersonal relations, in media representations, in political hustings, in the family—they will be resisted. Throughout the society, we can see this process of resistance, rejection, distancing, nuancing, negotiation, and re-interpretation (Cohen and Taylor, 1978), impelled by the search for positive identity. It is in evidence in the most abject of conditions, such as high security prisons (Cohen and Taylor, 1972) and concentration camps (Ginzburg, 1968), and can be expressed in denials of the most compelling forces, for example, where those living in poverty reject the label of being poor. Since poverty remains a turpitude in our society, we ougnt neither to be appalled nor gladdened that "about half the chief wage-earners or heads of households with incomes below the state's poverty standard, or on the margins of that standard, said they never felt poor" (Townsend, 1979, p. 425). Their denial is an assertion of the human need for dignity in face of assaults upon it. A similar process is in evidence in struggles over work.

This is an extraordinarily complex and variable phenomenon fraught with conflict and doubt. A person's work, mediated by his or her occupational title, is the major indicator of class, education, cultural patterns, and economic standing, all of which carry evaluations which may be accepted, rejected, or negotiated by those so identified. Those occupying what are seen as the lowest positions in our society— those whose work is manual, dirty, and disagreeable—often, if not always, will contest, here aggressively, there covertly, there ambivalently, the given hierarchies of work.

What is recognizable in these processes is that work is a terrain of struggle for much more than wages and costs, important though these are. It is also a locus of conflict over values, perceptions, images of worth, and worthlessness. Since this is so, it is not then surprising that work is often interpreted in contradictory ways. For instance, certain work may be diminishing and widely regarded by its performers in an instrumental manner, but for those involved there is much more at stake than surviving the monotony of the line for a sum of money—there is the real danger of *themselves,* especially those lower on the social scale, being reduced to the value of their economic returns and demeaning work, becoming that which the pay slip and routine of the work tells them that they are.

An understandable response, an understandably human response, is to re-interpret the situation, to distance oneself from the ascribed role that is relegating of the self, to forge alternative definitions which may lead to work, while remaining alienating, being cut through with other sorts of meaning. Examples are legion: the car worker who hates the work but lauds his contribution to the economy; the farm worker who receives a pittance yet proclaims his role in feeding the nation; the factory operative oppressed by the line but enjoying the camaraderie of the plant. . . . This contrariness of work experiences, this response to the impoverishment of so much work practice and wider social valuation, paradoxically can create a commitment to work, can produce a perspective which at once can despise work and yet gain real value from it which in turn betokens a commitment.

No doubt some part of people's attitudes to work can be explained in terms of indoctrination. It would, for instance, be possible to construct a history of the work ethic ("He who shall not work shall not eat," and so forth), the socializing role of education, religion, and managerial ideologies as means of inculcating work discipline, punctuality, and the like. And it would then be possible to contrast such analyses with the overwhelming tedium and strain of so much work in an illuminating manner. Recognizing that work is for many people distasteful and ruinous of human potential yet often accompanied by a strong desire to continue in work, it is attractive to argue that this desire is but the deception of an outworn morality that in the post-industrial society may be abandoned.

Such an enterprise, while it has its uses as an exercise in demystification, is flawed in the way in which it separates out, neatly and decisively, the practices of work (monotony, repetition, routine, etc., which are assumed to have been inevitable until the arrival of our high technology era) from its cultural valuations (the work ethic, ranking of occupations, distribution of incomes, and the like), with the two aspects being exogenously related.

Just lately, this separation has become something of a fad as commentators encourage us to forego the "purely cultural" (Stonier, 1983) ethic which impels us to want to work and to instead embrace a "Leisure Society" premised on the affluence produced by the microelectronics revolution. This is an especially appealing formula in the current period of high and rising unemployment. The problem of unemployment—that the unemployed want work and suffer badly for want of work—could, runs this thesis, be solved by a mere cultural adaptation, simply a change of attitude, thanks to the generosity of I.T. Simultaneously, the need to undergo what is freely acknowledged as debilitating and soul-destroying work, to earn money in order to *live* elsewhere, is removed by enlightened beliefs.

These theorizations are discussed at some length in Chapter 6; here we restrict ourselves to indicating the false dualism—the practice of work here, the attitudes to work there—that it embraces. Doing so, it is worthwhile emphasizing that the unemployed want work not least, but not only, because of their material shortages, because life on social security is grim. It is then important to ask why this should be so *now*, given the stupendous wealth our society currently enjoys. Asking that question is to answer it with the retort that paltry handouts to the workless are *not* indications of a mere lack of generosity on the part of the wider society. They are much more of a sign to the majority of deviance, of wrongdoing to be avoided, of the undeservedness of the poor. Conversely, and crucially, they are a justification of the rewards to the worthy, the better off who remain in work. They are, in short, an indication that work is connected to a web of relations which extend throughout the society.

It is worth emphasizing that work, while it is in general an activity restricted to a particular locale for a given number of hours, cannot be accurately perceived in narrow focus. Relations of work spill out into the wider sphere and the wider sphere spills in—in attempts to justify what goes on in the workplace ("this is the rate for the job for that sort of skill") and in efforts to legitimate the status quo ("my skills and my diligence gain me this sort of income and this sort of life style which project this sort of image"). None of this is surprising given that work itself, work defined as paid employment, is a social construct. Having been produced by social arrangement, it is only to be expected that society puts particular valuations upon it. It is for this reason that it is mistaken to perceive the work ethic and the possibility, by ending it, as a resolution to the problem of unemployment, as though it is purely exogenously connected to work itself, as somehow an extra inducement to win the hearts and minds of the participants. This is false. The work ethic is both a cultural *and* a material conception without which it is hard to conceive of our social system continuing. *Not* because its demise could stop people wanting to work (the usual retort of the already privileged who are assured they made it by their commitment), but because it could seriously challenge the distribution of income and wealth across the society. If it was not for the work ethic and the sobering but reassuring lesson of the workless, how could the present hierarchy be sustained? In reply, here those high in our society justify their positions always, but always, in terms of this work ethic, and, often sotto voce, of those undeserving minions who "live off the state."

What we are saying here, against those who would have technology abolish work, and society then change its valuation of that work, is that it is salutary to be reminded that work is a social creation and has long been so. The problem of work as perceived by many futurists is one that has been to date an unavoidable necessity which only today can be technologically abolished. Work (there) can be extinguished smoothly so long as society (here) amends its conceptions of work and worklessness. However, the social character of work compels us to recognize that there is nothing natural about work which is to be made technologically redundant. It forces us to look seriously at, not work, but the society which has brought work into being. If we do this, we can avoid a misleading focus on work in itself, as a problem hitherto unsolvable, and acknowledge the wider social relations of which work is an integral part.

We are scathing of solutions to the appalling levels of unemployment (and to alienating work in general) in terms of the recently resurrected idea of an escape from work thanks to the largesse of high technology because the proposition rests upon a dualist perception—work as a practice which is inherently onerous separate from the cultural value that inculcates a desire to work. The division ignores the complexities of work, its ambiguities and ambivalences, is blind to the conditions which have produced and perpetuate both the practices and the values. Further, to divide work into two independent dimensions is to overlook the fact that the perceptions and conditions of work are not only deeply interwoven but also that they are in large part the products of struggle.

Society has never been at one as regards work, because it has always been cut through with conflicts—conflicts over the distribution of resources, evaluation of worth, allocation of time,—and over work. It is axiomatic to our analysis that explanations of the meanings of work and the circumstances of work are to be sought in the struggles for work—a struggle which extends far beyond the work place into wide social relations, but which finds an important locus in this major activity of a people. Recognizing this, we believe that much of the reason for work being alienating is to be found in examination of the monetary contract between employer and employee, which is always more than an economic relation since it insists upon the subordination of those in employ, their exclusion from decision-making, the persistent attempt to increase the intensity of their labor. However, it is also in relations of work that we find reason for positive characteristics—a sense of purpose, even of fulfillment. This is a paradoxical situation: stultifying conditions are resisted, the resistance blunts the pain of work and even can bring rewards from work, the resistance—the lived experience of the work process—ironically generates consent to the condition against which the resistance is aimed. This may be paradoxical, but it is commonly found even in arduous and unpleasant labor. Thus Bill Williamson, recalling his grandfather's work in the coalfields of North-West Durham, observes that

> It is difficult for non-miners to appreciate that such work, despite its difficulties, can bring satisfactions. My grandfather, like many others, was proud of his skills as a hewer. He enjoyed the company of other men. He liked the conversation—the crack, as he called it. He took great care in his work and enjoyed seeing jobs done properly, with precision (Williamson, 1982, p. 85).

It is paradoxical, but to be expected in a society which does so much to thwart the dignity of so many people ("This is the sort of work, this the sort of wage, for your sort of people. . ."). It is the visceral refusal to accept indignity. For those without work, the threat to dignity is worst of all—though they struggle still to counter the insults and deprivations, often denying the palpable facts of their condition—because, being out of work, they are removed from an important theatre of struggle. The unemployed, the idle, are beyond the pale of a society that has created the category work, with all of its impositions nevertheless part of society.

Our thesis is that work is a central sphere of conflict in our society over human values and valuation. What the dichotomy of those who wish to abandon the work ethic entails is abandonment of the gains—as well as the losses, to be sure—in that relation of those who have little or no say in the organization of work, the introduction of new technology, the division of income, the patterns of recruitment, etc., i.e., those occupying the subordinate positions in our society. The prescription is superficially attractive (who can support unhesitatingly the life-restricting labor of mass production?) but has to be recognized as capitulation to one side, the powerful minority one, of the struggle over work. It means that the "Leisure

Society" will be heralded as the product of capital; the "collapse of work" will mean banishment from employment on the terms set by those who presently decide upon most features of our society.

Employment/Unemployment

I am convinced that the substitution of machinery for human labour is often very injurious to the interests of the class of labourers.

—David Ricardo. *The Principles of Political Economy and Taxation.*
1821, p. 264.

Since the public became aware of I.T., the major concern in Western Europe has been its potential to reduce employment. The question "will I.T. create or destroy jobs?" has been understandably pressing and ought to be addressed. A good many articles, reports, and polemics have been delivered on this topic which has divided authors broadly into two camps, the optimists, who contend that new technology holds out the prospect of more jobs in the long term although there may be a temporary period of adjustment to be endured, and the pessimists, who provide a bleak picture of structural employment being exacerbated by I.T. This analytical division does reflect a real distinction, but it is much less clear-cut than it appears and, as we shall show, the opponents hold important principles in common. Further, it is also widely, though not universally, recognized that the debate is not a matter of two equally convincing interpretations. The evidence has been growing that I.T. is, on the whole, job-reducing; as Guy de Jonquieres of the *Financial Times,* an I.T. enthusiast, observes:

Most authors are honest enough to acknowledge that it is hard to make precise predictions but have concluded gloomily that more chips will probably mean fewer jobs (*Financial Times,* 15 July, 1981).

The Optimists

This group is found almost entirely in the world of government, media, and business, and has responded to I.T. by interpreting it as yet one more step in the march of progress, as the commencement of an era which is looked forward to with optimism for the "countless opportunities to enrich and improve our national life," for the "new possibilities Information Technology has to offer" (Thatcher, 1982). It was in these terms that Kenneth Baker spoke in the House of Commons debate on I.T. in 1980, and his derogatory remarks on the "pessimists" are common features of the presentations:

Today we are discussing an industry that will provide enormous opportunities for employment and British industry. I am not one of those who believe that the development and use of information technology will produce widespread unemployment. I believe that it will create a large number of job opportunities. I disagree with the views expressed by Mr. Clive Jenkins [a trade union leader] who, in the past, has voiced the unemployment argument. From the rather smooth and sophisticated exterior of Mr. Clive Jenkins there is a nasty little Luddite trying to break through. The job opportunities in the British hardware and software industires are enormous (*Hansard*, 11 July, 1980, col. 933).

The Lessons of History

A favored theme of the optimists is to recall history as a means of discrediting critics of I.T. and of removing the apprehensions of those likely to be affected by the new technology. The "we've heard the prophets of doom before and look how well things have turned out" argument is succinctly expressed by Patrick Jenkin, the Minister for Industry under Mrs. Thatcher until 1983:

> Fears that automation will inevitably lead to higher unemployment are not new. In 1811 the Luddites rioted and destroyed the textile machinery which they saw as a direct threat to their jobs. Yet employment in the textile industry proceeded to grow during most of the 19th century. Nor was this an isolated example. In the same century, the fastest growing industries, in terms of employment, were those based on new technology. Railway employment rose from 29,000 in 1851 to 320,000 in 1901; in chemicals, employment over the same period trebled; and in metal manufacture employment nearly trebled.
>
> The last century demonstrates clearly that, despite the fears to which new technology gave rise, technology promoted employment. More recent history repeats the lesson. Considerable concern was expressed in the 1950s and early 1960s about the impact of automation on jobs. Nonetheless, employment in the U.K reached record levels towards the latter part of the 1960s. Despite the evident lack of competitiveness of much of the British economy, and the impact of the first oil crisis, total employment showed no overall fall during the 1970s, a decade which witnessed the widespread diffusion of computers (Jenkin, 1983, p. 526).

Swings and Roundabouts

In spite of this confidence that I.T. brings "good news for jobs throughout the U.K." (Thatcher, 1982), most optimists are not so convinced that it will have such an unblemished effect. Indeed, the major trait of the optimists is the assertion that the employment impact of I.T. will be one of "swings and roundabouts," with job loss here and job gain there, but in the end some sort of equilibrium achieved. Though this prospect will unavoidably entail dislocation for some workers, it is not an unhappy one, since alternatives will be presented by new technology that on balance will extend opportunities. Thus, innovation will "inevitably involve both job displacing and compensatory job creating mechanisms" which in the long run should be "beneficial to both output and employment (Sleigh et al., 1979, p. 106).

This scenario has been present from the early days of the debate, being clearly enunciated by James Callaghan, the then Prime Minister, in a speech that brought the issue to a wide British public late in 1978. Here Mr. Callaghan spoke at length of the "rewards and penalties" of I.T. as he asked that "we work together to ensure that the challenge we face is turned into an opportunity grasped." He addressed the nation thus:

microelectronics evoke a mixture of fear and excitement. Fear, yes. We can all understand the worry about the impact of this new technology on jobs. There can be doubt about it, the new technology will involve some crucial job losses in a number of industries. Where those jobs consist of dull and repetitive work on the assembly line or in the office, this is not an unmixed curse provided there are *new* ones. But interesting and rewarding jobs will be lost too. We have had some experience of this in our industrial history. In this century, both over automation and the coming of the computer, the predictions were of ever increasing unemployment. But, in fact, until the oil price crisis of 1973, the industrialised world enjoyed a longer period of sustained full employment than at any time in history.

Now we may be on the threshold of the most rapid industrial change in history.

And we must prepare for it.

It will put within reach of the budget of our people a range of goods and services they could never previously afford. Pocket calculators have already become almost as common as transistor radios.

Secondly, there is great potential for more exports, output and investment. So there should be job gains as well as job losses.

. . . . let me list some of the potential job gains.

There are the jobs actually *making* the microelectronic devices. . . . .

There are the jobs applying the technology—the opportunities in software and systems design.

Even more important, there are new products and new services which will become economic for the first time. One change that is foreseen is that the new technology will make possible improved communications systems which will eventually allow many people to work more at home . . . such a development will mean a massive purchasing of electronic equipment, and thousands of workers would be needed to make it (Callaghan, 1978).

Mr. Callaghan's assurances can be given a gung-ho rendition on crossing the Atlantic, where the Ganleys cavalierly observe that

Fears for jobs have been omnipresent whenever changes in technology take place, and they have been justified. Those employed in one sort of communications concern have often found themselves jobless. Conversely, new types of jobs have sprung up in the new concerns, which offered more opportunity in the long run. What did the first telephone operators do for a living before the advent of the telephone? They were telegraph boys—subsequently put out of work! And what will telephone operators do for a living as the computer takes over? They will move on to the next rung of the next ladder (Ganley and Ganley, 1982, p. 12).

Innovation is an Evolutionary Process

The presentation of I.T. as having "a mix of job creation and job displacement effects" (NEDC, 1978a, p. 3) is not restricted to political speeches or sloganizing historical reviews, and a number of reports have offered more sustained analyses within such a framework. They have also elaborated upon it to argue that innovation will be evolutionary. Mr. Callaghan himself drew upon one of the first of these reports, which was produced by the Central Policy Review Staff (CPRS) in support of his conclusions.

The *Social and Employment Implications of Microprocessors* (CPRS, 1978) commenced with what has become a feature of optimistic analyses by attacking "Those who have predicted large scale increases in unemployment" because of I.T. on the grounds that they "implied certainty where none exists" (p. 1). This retort to what are regarded as overexaggerated predictions of large-scale redundancies is characteristic of the optimists, who are persistently replying to the fears, which have been widely publicized in Western Europe, that I.T. is a job-killer. Examining nine case studies, the CPRS contends that job losses and gains will broadly balance, that "the technological changes in most industries are likely to be evolutionary rather than revolutionary, and the consequent employment effects are likely to be slow to show themselves and in most areas to offer reasonable opportunities for planned adjustment" (p. 13).

The CPRS performs an important service in reminding commentators that I.T.'s employment influences will be shaped considerably by the particular conditions appertaining at the time and location of technology's introduction. There is a real "need for caution in any simple predictions about the effects of microelectronics on employment" (p. 12), and the CPRS's case study approach reveals the variability of effect. However, the problem with their analysis is, on their own admission (p. 12), its superficiality. This criticism was answered in a later government publication.

The themes of the CPRS were echoed and amplified in a major report from the Department of Employment which appeared 12 months later (Sleigh et al., 1979) and quickly became the mainstay of the optimistic position. As with the CPRS paper, Sleigh et al. counselled care and qualification in analysis, which they contrast with the wild assertions of "pessimists." Indeed, their study team was established "in part to respond to this alarmist thinking . . . [that] jobs will be lost" (Sleigh, quoted in Forester, 1978). The report is critical of the "far-reaching economic assumptions" (Sleigh et al., 1979, p. 1) of forecasts which suggested large-scale redundancies, rejecting

> many of the "models" produced in relation to micro-electronic technology [as] unlikely to offer much help in forecasting the outcome in the short, medium or long term with any accuracy. They tend to ignore both the indirect macro-economic effects of new technology and the complex inter-relationships between sectors. Furthermore the speed of diffusion of new technology is often assumed to be much faster than either past or present experience would indicate (p. 106).

Emphasis upon the overriding importance of the practical contexts into which I.T. will arrive leads Sleigh's team to place the new technology as part of an ongoing trend of innovation. Having visited more than 60 organizations in the U.K., U.S.A., and Japan, they conclude that "In general the impact upon employment of microelectronic technology will be gradual rather than revolutionary" (p. 109); for instance, in the office area "movement towards the full electronic office system will probably be slow and patchy" (p. 58), while "In many areas of industry which are already automated (especially in the process industries) the main effect of new technology will be the introduction of more sophisticated control systems, with negligible effects on overall manpower levels" (p. 107).

Institutional versus Occupational Analysis

Since the perspective of these two reports is of a national, macroeconomic kind, it is worth complementing them with the most thorough examination to date of I.T.'s impact at a local level. Kenneth Green, Rod Coombs, and Keith Holroyd (1980) undertook, in late 1978 through 1979, an investigation of the employment effects of microelectronic technologies in the Tameside (Greater Manchester) area. It should be said that Green et al. do not subscribe to an optimistic position. On the contrary, their theme is that "the effects of the micro revolution will continue to affect Tameside industry till at least the end of the century putting an increasing number of jobs at risk" (p. 114), and they do project a decisive job loss in the region because of I.T., estimating that "between 3½ and 9½% of jobs in Tameside and 3–10½% of jobs outside Tameside held by Tameside residents will be at risk in the 1980s as a result of the diffusion of micro-electronic equipment and products" (pp. 115–23). Nevertheless, while it is misleading to place the findings of this study in the optimistic camp, it does offer support for one or two of the optimists major principles.

Scrutiny of 50 Tameside companies, and interviews with in excess of one thousand, led to the discovery that I.T. was variable in impact. Green et al.'s explanation for this provides a tacit criticism of some predictors of large scale job loss who decontextualize their projections in looking at a particular occupation, find a new technology which could fulfil that role, and then, assuming that the innovation will displace the worker and those like him, extrapolate to a national level a figure for likely job loss. The mistake is that this ignores the "detailed specific knowledge" (p. 80), the concrete local circumstances (size of workplace, distribution of staff, modes of organization, peculiarities of market structures, etc.), which influence the adoption of new technologies. In response to this the Tameside survey opted for "an institution-based analysis of potential labour displacement rather than the occupation-based method" (Green and Coombs, 1981, p. 45) favored by most other writers.

Green et al. do not take this recognition of the significance of context in technological uptake as a means of entirely rejecting pessimistic scenarios (Green et al., 1980, pp. 13–52). However, their emphasis on the importance of local circumstances does accord with that of the CPRS and Sleigh et al. In addition, they agree that "the 1980s [will be] an evolutionary rather than a revolutionary phase in the introduction of microelectronics" (Green and Coombs, 1981, p. 49) and that "it is fair to say that it [their projection of job loss] is probably lower than the job loss that many have assumed will result from the microelectronic revolution" (Green et al., 1980, p. 117).

New Jobs

The optimistic projections are not restricted to an insistence that I.T.'s effects will be incremental and/or more or less balancing. There are other emphases that can be discerned among the hopeful, one of which is to focus upon the prospect for job creation because of I.T. Perhaps the most quoted report on these lines— that I.T. would bring with it a net growth in employment—is the least read. We refer here to the report of a study group headed by Jerry Wasserman titled *The Strategic Impact of Intelligent Electronics in the U.S. and Western Europe, 1977- 1987,* which was produced by the international business consultants Arthur D. Little in 1979. This examined I.T. markets and applications in America, France, West Germany, and the U.K., concentrating on four sectors—automobiles, business communications, industrial controls, and consumer products. It contended that, although some industries would decline, the fast growth of new sectors would provide a net growth of about one million of which 40% would be in Europe (*Engineering Today,* 27 March, 1979, p. 10; Kendall et al., 1979, p. 399).

The Arthur D. Little study, reputedly costing one million pounds to prepare (*Financial Times,* 20 March, 1979), is undoubtedly of significance to any debate on the effects of I.T.—hence its widespread citation. Unfortunately, it is unavailable to the public (even the specialized academic public), having been sponsored by 60 clients from government and industry and sold at $35,000 per copy. It is revealing that the difficulty of access to this report, presumably because its sponsorship puts it out of copyright, has not prevented it being used as evidence for an optimistic future, though most of the details appear to have been gleaned from a press conference held by Wasserman in 1979 to announce its conclusions. While this is illustrative of a theme of this book—that information supplied as a commodity means that access will be restricted by market criteria—it renders the findings of dubious authority.

There are, however, other areas to which the optimists can point for evidence of job creation. One such is computing, where a report for the Electronic Computers Sector Working Party of the National Economic Development Council found a shortage of "at least 25,000 people" with computer-related skills in 1980 (of whom about 16,000 are programmers and analysts) in the U.K. (NEDC, 1980). Another occupation experiencing a shortage of personnel which was "widely reported" to Sleigh et al. (1979, pp. 84-90) is electronic engineering. Yet, another expanding area is cable television, where a government White Paper believes that "New jobs will be created both short term during the construction phase, and long term"

(*Home Office and Department of Industry*, 1983, paragraphs 34-38, 217), Conservative M.P. Raymond Whitney thinking "it is probable that tens of thousands will accrue from this development" (*Hansard*, 2 December, 1982, col. 474). The herald of this good news was a paper published by the Information Technology Advisory Panel (ITAP, 1982) which was enthusiastic about the potential of "thousands" of new jobs being generated. In a parliamentary debate which followed the ITAP report, numerous members endorsed John Spence's view that this area of "Communications is an enormously important job generator" (*Hansard*, 20 April, 1982, col. 206).

It is noticeable that, as regards cable, there is a reluctance to quantify the promised expansion. Since the penetration of cable in the U.K. is minimal at the moment, it would seem clear that it will lead to extra jobs. However, this does assume straightforward addition, something which has been challenged by pessimists. For example, a report prepared by the Greater London Council envisages cable possibly causing the destruction of 25,000 jobs, such as in entertainment, as a result of cheap imported materials undermining the domestic industry (Greater London Council, 1982, pp. 64-66; cf. Jefferson, April 1984).

More Service Sector Jobs

Connected to the belief that I.T. can lead to additional jobs is an emphasis among optimists on a realignment of employment such that, while the primary and secondary sectors may be hit, sometimes hard, by technological innovation, those displaced will be able to find work in an expanding service sector. As Peter Marsh has it, "The creation of jobs in the service sector acts as a sink for those people who cannot . . . get the employment they expect in manufacturing industry" (Marsh, 1981, p. 161). This view is at the heart of Daniel Bell's theory of a "post-industrial service society" which will be paid for by wealth accruing from automation of agriculture, mining, and manufacture, this income being spent on the consumption of extra services. It is closely allied to the notion of a coming Leisure Society.

Since we consider both propositions in the following chapter, we may simply state that the expansion of services is frequently recoursed to by the optimists. Thus, Mr. Callaghan in 1978 found some comfort for those threatened by technological redundancy in the rise of "new services" (Callaghan, 1978), while asking "Where will the new jobs be?", Chancellor Nigel Lawson answers for the Conservative Government that they lie in "a rapid growth in service employment" (Chancellor of the Exchequer, 1983). Sleigh et al. went even further, to argue that the "growth of employment in services in not necessarily associated in the long run with a loss of jobs in the secondary sector" (Sleigh et al., 1979, p. 106), with "growing employment in the services . . . consistent with a growth in the secondary sector" (p. 7). This is a valid point, though especially sanguine when contrasted with the 30% decline of the manufacturing workforce in the U.K. from 1974 to the close of 1982 (*Economic Trends*, (353), March, 1983, Table 36). More characteristic reasoning is evidenced in the words of Bruce Gilchrist of Columbia University:

That's where the growth is . . . from writers to people servicing electronic equipment. The impact of computers on employment will be somewhat less as more people enter the service industry. You can't get one waiter to serve twice the number of people, whereas in a factory, automation can cut the labor force in half (*Datamation*, May, 1980, p. 50).

Another version of this optimistic theory—somewhat more attractive than Gilchrist's vision of more waiters counterbalancing jobs lost in manufacture—is Bell's view of more professionals in employ (Bell, 1976, Ch. 2), a vista given a gloss in Tom Stonier's advocacy of "a massive expansion of both education, and research and development" (Stonier, 1983, p. 13) "to provide new, mainly information skills which will be useful in a post-industrial economy" (p. 138), such that "education will grow to become the largest industry in the post-industrial society and its number one employer" (p. 18), followed by the likes of "tourism" (pp. 164–68).

Competition

The preceding discussion has omitted what is the most striking feature of the optimists—and of most of the pessimists—analyses of the employment effect of I.T., which is one that allows for varying interpretations within a shared framework. This is manifest in a stress on the threat and promise I.T. poses to our economy's competitiveness vis-à-vis other nations. The argument is that I.T. will be adopted in a dynamic and competitive economic milieu. Because of this, optimists contend that new technology, rapidly accepted, will increase productivity and thereby competitive edge which will be translated into market growth and in turn more employment: "We can then become more competitive, sell more goods and employ more people" (Jenkin, 1983).

In this light, the employment effects of I.T. should be seen as the employment effects of cheapened production, and market share as a matter of economics rather than technology. Technological unemployment is now no longer the key issue, the "all-important variable" being "the adaptability of the U.K. economy" (CPRS, 1978, p. 5) to the new situation. Straight-forward prediction must therefore be abandoned since "it cannot be stressed too strongly that the overall impact on jobs will depend crucially on an unforeseeable economic climate" (Sleigh et al., 1979, p. 1).

This framework, which rests upon the undoubted fact that I.T. is not introduced into a steady state economy, can remain optimistic, although ready to concede that I.T.'s more immediate effects are to displace labor. Thus, few commentators would deny that "higher productivity implies less employment for the same level of output" (CPRS, 1978, p. 4), and Margaret Thatcher herself accepts that "This is always the problem with new technology—at first it reduces the number of jobs" (*Observer*, 8 May, 1983). However, this is temporary because this "direct effect" of innovation is merely "the net change in the number of jobs before account is taken of output changes." With improved productivity (and hopefully the bonus of better quality) from I.T. comes "increased demand for our goods and services, which in turn gen-

erates higher output and employment. Profits also increase, inducing higher investment and R&D expenditure thus creating jobs. Finally, investment in robots and
other microelectronic-based equipment provides opportunities for domestic producers of such capital goods to increase output and employment" (Jenkin, 1983).
In short, things may start badly for the employed, but "Later, [new technology]
makes possible all kinds of production that wasn't possible before, which *increases*
jobs" (M. Thatcher, *Observer,* 8 May, 1983).

Something else follows from this perspective. An emphasis on I.T. as an integral
element of economic competition poses more than an opportunity to seize new
markets—it also raises the unavoidability of its adoption given that our competitors
are also taking it up. The optimists have been quick to point this out. While usually
cheerful in announcing the glittering prizes I.T. offers, they have not been slow to
proclaim the impossibility of pessimists' positions. It is usual for them to deny the
bleak outlook projected by those who regard I.T. as labor displacing, but it is even
more common for the optimists to argue that nonacceptance of I.T., because it will
reduce our international competitiveness while increasing that of other countries,
will of itself decimate jobs in the U.K. because other nations will underprice us.
Acceptance of I.T. may be risky, but rejection is a recipe for certain high unemployment. From this perspecitve, I.T. must be accepted because failure to introduce
it will bring about a worst case scenario. With speed and good fortune, new technology can stimulate growth in the economy and thereby more jobs; to hesitate,
doubt, and vacillate is to guarantee a slide into the abyss. In sum, I.T. must be
accepted; it is a fait accompli; there is no choice about it, because, "while it cannot
be said with certainty that successful adaptation is bound to result in full employment it may be said with absolute certainty that failure to keep abreast of our
competitors in technological change will lead to higher unemployment" (Sleigh
et al., 1979, p. 9). Here is an echo of the inevitabilism we heard in Part One.

The Limits of Optimism

Most of the criticisms of the optimistic outlook will be made below when considering
the views of pessimists. Nevertheless, a few remarkes can usefully be made at this
juncture. First, it is undoubtedly correct of the optimists to query abstract projections of the impact of I.T. on employment. New technology may have enormous
potential for job reduction, but the particulars of organization, region, economic
climate, and so forth are important variables. While these vex the task of projection,
they are the substance of the real world. However, it should also be apparant that
these optimistic outlooks, while often strong on voicing complexity, are weak on
projection, often resorting to hope and assertion to keep up their spirits. This
weighs especially heavily against the most authoritative report which, having examined numerous cases to illustrative the variability of technological innovation's
effects, "makes no specific predictions about the employment impact of the application of micro-electronic technology since it sees this as depending crucially upon
the complex interplay of macro-economic and technological factors" (Sleigh et al.,

1979, p 2). Recognition of the limits of sweeping projections premised on naive assumptions is no substitute for detailed and meaningful estimation. Too often the optimistic view relies on its criticism of pessimists to support its own undemonstrated assertion that things will turn out well in the end.

Second, there is the difficulty of resolving the conflict between the argument that I.T. is part of an ongoing, gradualist process of change with the insistence that "we do not have time to lose" since "our success will depend on whether we can adopt this new technology fast enough" (Callaghan, 1978). If, to hasten I.T.'s introduction, the "people of this country must get a bit of push [because] We are instinctively an indolent nation" (Ferranti, *Electronics Times,* 11 January, 1979), then how can this square with the reassurance that "the speed of diffusion of new technology is often assumed [by pessimists] to be much faster than either past or present experience would indicate" (Sleigh et al., 1979, p. 106)?

Third, while the optimists validly make play with elements of the economic context into which I.T. is introduced in order to assure people that it will not dramatically destroy jobs, they do so at the expense of underestimating—and often entirely neglecting—both the fact that the major feature of the current economic climate is recession (of which more below) and that other nations are pioneering stategies on exactly the same assumptions as their own. Across Europe, leading nations, entrapped inthe slump, "are all looking to new technology as the panacea. The developments in electronics are recognized as providing new markets of enormous potential. Cable TV, satellites, telecommunications equipment, and computers are the major growth areas" (Locksley, 1983, p. 129). Thus, in France, there has been developed, both under Giscard d'Estaing and Francois Mitterand, a national policy for rapid adoption of *télématique* that is premised on the recommendations of the Nora and Minc report presented to the president in 1977. The strategy outlined by these authors places I.T. at the center of a policy which aims to make the French economy more competitive than its rivals (Dodsworth, 1982). The consequences of *télématique* for employment, attest Nora and Minc, are dependent on the speed of adoption of I.T. since this will crucially influence the opportunities of capturing overseas markets and attaining growth to supply compensating employment:

"What effects massive computerization will have on employment depend on a balancing act, the outcome of a race between the reduction in manpower linked to increased productivity and the increase in markets resulting from a higher degree of competitiveness" (Nora and Minc, 1980, p. 33).

It is the same story in Japan, West Germany, Italy, the United States, and even New Zealand (Gidlow, 1982). In short, every advanced capitalist society is rushing to adopt I.T. as a means of improving its current competitive position and thereby mollifying technology's employment consequences. America's current "stunning leap into total automation" is being effected on the grounds of a need to "maintain the U.S. lead in industrial productivity" in face of concerted challenges from abroad. The assumption is that the "new wave of factory and office automation in the U.S. will raise the productivity of American workers . . . and increase the ability of domestic industries to compete with the imports that have eaten away at America's industrial strength" (*Business Week,* 3 August 1981, p. 58, 67).

With all nations adopting I.T. in haste as a means of encroaching upon one another's territory and defending their own, the possibility of new technology achieving savings in production costs with no country making market gains must be entertained. The myopia of the optimists in regard to this, the threat of international competitiveness being maintained at the current level with less people in work, is an astonishing oversight.

The Pessimists: A Shared Framework

Though it is fair to categorize as pessimists those, usually academics and trade unionists, who foresee I.T. producing high levels of unemployment, the difficulty of separating predictors into two clearly opposing camps becomes evident when one recognizes that what both usually share is the conviction that the economic context into which I.T. is entering is a crucial variable. They agree that I.T. must be accepted, because our competitors will otherwise undercut our prices. While the optimists greet this challenge with relish, and believe that we can steal a march on other nations (thereby increasing our employment at their expense), the pessimists think that, even if we do achieve competitive edge, our workforce will be severely depleted by I.T. Vide Chris Freeman:

> If we do not keep up with the international race in the use of microprocessor technology, then we risk becoming more uncompetitive in terms of world trade, so that even before North Sea oil expires, the problem of growth and levels of employment in the British economy would be even more severe than it is today. If we adopt this revolution enthusiastically in every branch of our economy and make it the cornerstone of our industrial strategy, then we also risk accelerating the scale of labour displacement through the very success of this technical revolution (Freeman, in Forester, 1980, p. 316).

Colin Hines is typical of the pessimists when he follows a depressing review of the structural unemployment he believes I.T. will bring about with resignation to the inevitable:

> All this is not to say that a Luddite-smash-the-computer-response to these developments would be appropriate; the need to remain internationally competitive leaves us with little alternative but to increase their application, since most other leading industrial nations already make more use of computers and microprocessors than we do in Britain (Hines, 1978, p. 5).

Similarly, the trade unions, though generally pessimistic as regards job prospects, overwhelmingly recognize that I.T. must be accepted, because "if British industry is to compete successfully in world markets it must keep pace with technological innovations occuring in other countries" (APEX, 1980, pp. 51-52). The Trades

Union Congress enunciates this theme, which its members resignedly accept (Robins and Webster, 1982), with some enthusiasm in producing a report remarkably similar to those of the optimists. Arguing that the challenge of I.T. must rapidly be responded to by Britain being "in the vanguard of technological change," the TUC urges that we grasp "the unique and unparalled opportunity . . . for Britain to improve its economic performance and also its competitiveness in world markets" (TUC, 1979). Presenting its views, the TUC joins Sleigh et al. in declaring that it "rejects the determinist view that the advent of microelectronics must inevitably be associated with a particular level" of unemployment since "a higher rate of economic growth . . . [can] guarantee effective demand for the increased output that new technology can make available." Ipso facto Britain must accept I.T. because "those countries whose industrial enterprises adopt this new technology into their products, their manufacturing processes and their services will enjoy trading success and economic growth" (TUC, September 1979, p. 16, 29).

The TUC's enthusiastic response is not that of most trade unions in the U.K., but it does articulate the shared framework of the pessimists and the optimists which regards adaptation to I.T. as unavoidable. Here again surfaces the inevitabilism we have previously observed: I.T. is arriving whether we like it or not; there are no choices other than how best to adapt to the unstopable. I.T. scares the pessimists, and they hope to ameliorate its effects by enlightened state action; the optimists are bullish, relishing the prospect of beating the French, Germans, Japanese, and Americans.

We might enhance understanding of this fundamental agreement by reminding ourselves of David Ricardo's well-known views on technological innovation. Writing 170 years ago, he agreed with the diagnosis of the pessimists as regards the loss of jobs through innovation, but insisted upon new technology's adoption for reasons which at once underscore those of the optimists and the pessimists and undermine their principles:

> if a capital is not allowed to get the greatest net revenue that the use of machinery will afford here, it will be carried abroad, and this must be a much more serious discouragement to the demand for labour than the most extensive employment of machinery; for while a capital is employed in this country it must create a demand for some labour; machinery cannot be worked without the assistence of men, it cannot be made but with the contribution of their labour. By investing part of a capital in improved machinery there will be a diminution in the progressive demand for labour; by exporting it to another country the demand will be wholly annihilated (Ricardo, 1821, p. 271).

Ricardo finds some accord here with the analysis of both pessimists and optimists to the extent that he argues that economic constraints make inevitable the adoption of new technology whatever its consequences for employment. However, he poses the economic, not in terms of the nation state in competition with other nations—the unit of analysis of pessimists and optimists—but of capital, arguing that if resisted this will take itself abroad. In addressing himself thus, he raises a question which neither pessimists nor optimists, fixed on the national consequences of international competition, seriously consider: that is, to what extent are their assumptions of national boundaries falsified by the presence nowadays of transnational corporations and the international movement of capital? We return to this below (see also Chapter 7).

What is a Pessimist?

Having indicated the deep-seated agreement of all sides of the debate, we return to examination of the arguments of the pessimists. At the outset, it bears stating that to be a pessimist is not what it was a few years ago. In 1979, when the first predictions of I.T.'s effects were being produced projections of between 2½ million and 3½ million (10-15% of the workforce) being put out of work by the end of this decade were regarded as "very pessimistic" (*Financial Times*, 29 March, 1979). Nowadays the analysis of the *Cambridge Economic Policy Review* (1979), which estimated, at the upper level, 2.7 million unemployed by 1985 appears positively optimistic in view of the climb from 1.3 million in 1979 to 2.9 million by the close of 1982 and 3.2 million by February 1983, according to official statistics which understate the problem (*Economic Trends*, 353, March 1983).

Pessimistic Projections

There are, broadly, four types of pessimistic analysis of I.T.'s effects, namely:

• a *technological* approach (e.g., Barron and Curnow, 1979), which projects from technological potential the likely effects on occupations.
• a *sectoral* approach (e.g., Jenkins and Sherman, 1979), which assesses the likely impact by estimating I.T.'s applications in industrial sectors.
• a *historical/technological* approach (e.g., Stonier, 1983), which marries extrapolation from past trends in employment with estimates of the impact of I.T. on existing labor.
• a *case study* approach (e.g., APEX, 1980, and other trade union surveys).

Cases studies are used in all of the other three approaches, and indeed the categorical divisions are frequently crossed. All such methods are open to criticism, though few are quite so naive as Sleigh et al. purport, since often they recognize such problems as the representativeness of their cases, the import of prevailing economic conditions, and the complexity of circumstances on the ground. It is useful to review some instances of these studies.

Iann Barron and Ray Curnow's report to the Department of Industry, submitted in January 1978 but kept under wraps because of its gloomy prognosis (*Financial Times*, 13 November, 1978), argued that "Should the displacement consequences put forward . . . take place in a society experiencing low growth and balance-of-payments problems, we may be contemplating levels of unemployment c. 10-15% of the workforce and more" (Barron and Curnow, 1979, p. 201) by the close of the

1980s. They list the following occupations as 'at risk': proof-readers, library assistants, mail carriers, telegraph operators, draftsmen, programmers, accountants, financial advisory, administrators, secretaries, billing clerks, keypunchers, cashiers, filing clerks, meter readers, shipping clerks, tv repairmen, plateprinters, telephone repairmen, light electricians, machinists, mechanics, inspectors, assemblers, operatives, material handlers, warehousemen, sales clerks, stock clerks, compositors. (p. 191). Their forecasts "are totally surprise free, and represent the working through of known technological concepts and capabilities" (p. 43).

The best-known pessimistic prediction comes from Clive Jenkins and Barrie Sherman (1979), with estimates that the U.K. will experience a 20% rate of unemployment by 1990 since "whichever road we take work will collapse" (Jenkins and Sherman, 1979, p. 113). Their argument hinges on an estimate of new technology's potential to increase productivity in the context of international competition. If the U.K. adopts I.T., it will remain competitive, but with the loss of five million jobs. If it does not, the country's competitive edge will decline, with the loss of five and a half million jobs.

A third study which projects widespread unemployment from I.T. is the historical review of Tom Stonier which suggests that, by early in the next century, "it will take no more than 10 per cent of the labour force to provide us with all our material needs" (Stonier, 1983, p. 122). Stonier contends that there is a long-term process which results in a declining demand for labor that he terms the "ratchet effect." While there are cyclical periods which affect employment patterns, there is an underlying structural pressure which "invariably represents advances in technology affecting labour requirements directly or indirectly" (p. 99) that assures that, during a period of boom, employment never reaches the level of an earlier cyclical peak. This ratchet effect is a key feature of the current period and results in high unemployment. Though caused by technology, it is not a matter of direct labor displacement by innovations; it is rather that "In bad times labour-intensive, low-productivity operations are most likely to be closed, while in good times technologically advanced, high-productivity systems are introduced. Thus there appears a wave of unemployed workers during a recesson of which only a relatively small proportion may be reabsorbed as times improve" (pp. 108-109).

These predictions of the effect of I.T. on employment represent the more general attempts to forecast the future. There are many others which foresee "automatic unemployment" (Jordan, 1981) that are less wide-ranging, aspects which we consider below, but two comments may be made at this juncture. The first is that none of these three studies oppose the introduction of I.T., although it will exacerbate unemployment. On the contrary, they urge its rapid adoption and even are sanguine about its long-term potential. Barron and Curnow's statement that "the improvement in productivity that information technology will allow is inherently "good," because it can be converted into greater leisure or a higher standard of living" (Barron and Curnow, 1979, p. 232) is shared by Jenkins and Sherman and by Stonier, and these postulates make it questionable quite how pessimistic such studies really are.

Second, it seems clear that it is an impossible task to precisely gauge the accuracy of these estimates. They are premised on I.T.'s potential, but underplay the complexity of the contexts within which it will appear. However, this is not reason enough to reject them, still less to conclude that prediction is impossible. They are useful reminders of I.T.'s potential, all things being equal. Things are not cateris paribus, of course, but if we can assess more of the particulars of contexts these pessimistic projections can still help towards sound forecasts of the effects on employment of I.T.

Economic Growth, Labor Decline?

To do this, we must first turn to the major context, the current economic climate, into which I.T. is being introduced. It is clearly impossible to quantify exactly new technology's role in causing today's high levels of unemployment in the U.K. Indeed, it is possible to argue that failure to adopt I.T. quickly has contributed to the demise, because "we have been overtaken by competitors in fields such as cash registers, food processing equipment, process instruments, machine tools, printing machinery, and even in ships' chronometers . . . we have failed to recognise new opportunities until others have produced the products" (ACARD, 1978, p. 24). Such a point recalls the urgent theme that I.T. must be adopted because the international economy is ever-moving and that failure to adapt entails "greater threats to employment than the displacement of labour by machines" (ACARD, 1979).

However, if I.T.'s role in bringing about the present crisis, directly or indirectly, is uncertain, a key issue that can be addressed is whether growth in the economy will allow for an increase in employment. I.T. will be implicated in economic expansion, and the hope of many is that this will be sufficient to enable a spread of job opportunities. However, there is evidence to indicate that, even where there is growth, I.T. can thwart this being translated into more jobs.

The assumption of many commentators is that economic growth will demand more labor—and among some optimists there is an assumption that increased productivity achieved by new technology will automatically translate into more employment—but this is questionable, since growth could take the form of investment in capital goods (more I.T.) rather than in labor. There is some evidence for this in the series of reports from the NEDC sector working parties in recent years. These enable us to examine employment patterns in a major growth area of the economy, I.T. itself. The NEDC, reviewing all its sectors in the spring of 1983, concluded that "there have . . . been significant manpower reductions in the growth industries such as electronics, due to changing technologies and to the improvement of productivity" (NEDC, 1983a). It appended various tables to its report from which may be distilled the following illustrative figures:

• the electronic components sector increased output between 1975 and 1981 by almost 100%. At the same time it reduced its workforce by about 18%.

- the electronic capital equipment sector increased output by 45%, yet shed 8% of its employees.
- the electronic consumer goods sector held output stable, while reducing its employees by 28%.

Even the rapidly expanding area of electronic computers has not increased employees dramatically, and employment in the computer hardware and services industry grew only 1-2% between 1971 and 1978 (NEDC, 1979), though it is true that there is a labor shortage in this arena.

Telecommunications tells a similar story. Though it is destined for rapid economic growth, it appears likely that, even with this, it will shed labor because of I.T. While Sleigh et al. believe that new technology's impact is "not likely to be major" (Sleigh et al. 1979, p. 75), the NEDC telecommunications sector working party could only hope in 1978 that "the level of employment (will) fall . . . less dramatically than in recent times" (NEDC, 1978c), later observing that in the telecommunications equipment industry "Manufacture of electro-mechanical equipment, which is relatively labour intensive, is being phased out and replaced by electronic equipment. Employment in the industry has therefore fallen from 88,000 in 1973 to 65,000 in 1981 over a period in which output has more than doubled" (NEDC, 1983a, p. D4). In 1982, British Telecom complemented this in announcing plans to increase productivity per man by 50% by 1987, thereby gaining an expansion of output with 7% less labor (*Observer*, 29 August, 1982, p. 11). The privatized British Telecom, in its first report, posted £1.5 billion profit (50% up on the previous year) in March 1985, due mostly to an 8% volume rise in business, though between 1982 and 1984 it reduced its staff by 16,500 (7.5%) with plans for further lay-offs in the immediate future as it continues to implement automation.

Clearly, these sorts of savings may be made not merely by technological innovation, but what is undoubted is that I.T. is implicated in getting greater productivity out of employees, and growth is no guarantee of retaining an existing workforce. Indeed, the *Financial Times* recently reported "a broad academic consensus that the British economy can absorb growth of three per cent a year for several years without adding to employment" (Hargreaves, May 20, 1983). This point is complemented by many observers of "sunrise industries," those rapidly expanding high technology companies on which many hopes for future employment are placed, which are described as capital- rather than labor-intensive and thus likely to offer few vacancies. The following is typical: "the new industries based on electronics have little effect in reducing unemployment. In the past year, five electronics firms have either expanded or set up new factories in Glenrothes, creating work for a couple of hundred people" (Marsh, 1982, p. 634). On the same lines, but turning to Europe's biggest private sector employer, Jenkins and Sherman report that Philips "has estimated that even allowing for a three per cent annual growth rate in turnover over ten years, by the end of that period it will be 56 per cent overmanned" (Jenkins and Sherman, 1979, p. 87).

The same pattern is observed among the large I.T. corporations. At Plessey, in 1978, there were 58,700 employees which were reduced to 42,900 over the next 4 years while sales with price stability grew from £611 million to £963 million (*Plessey World*, July, 1982). Throughout this period, regular reports emerged from Plessey that gave new technology as reason for diminution of staff. For example, the *Financial Times* reported on 1 February 1979 that 4,000 workers had been made redundant since 1974 at the Edge Hill, Liverpool factory due to the replacement of electro-mechanical telephone equipment by electronic exchanges—and added that a further 1,000 were to go that year. In May 1983, a further 389 losses were announced at the same factory because, as a company spokesman said, "The labour demand is falling with the introduction of new machines" (quoted in *Guardian*, 21 May, 1983).

The Plessey chairman informed shareholders that, because his company had "anticipated . . . the new growth field of Information Technology . . . our long-term business strategy has proved right. I am happy to add that our shareholders have benefited accordingly" (*Plessey Report and Accounts*, 1982, p. 5) . Meanwhile, the number of employees continued to tumble, falling to 38,657 by October 1, 1982.

General Electric Company's recent history is much the same: in 1980, it had 153,000 employees in the U.K.; by 1982, 145,000, though during the same period sales from U.K. operations had increased from £2.5 billion to £3.1 billion—a 24% increase in revenue alongside a 6% decline in staff (profits in the same period grew 40%) (GEC, 1982). ICL, Britain's major computer manufacturer, after plunging into debt in 1981, returned to profit in 1982, but with one difference—it had lost 10,000 personnel, one third of its complement, in the intervening period (*ICL Annual Report and Accounts*, 1982). The company managed to generate about the same amount of revenue in 1982 as in the previous 2 years, with 30% less employees.

The editor of *Electronics Weekly* summarized the position in an eve-of-election leader thus: "There can be no doubt the electronics industry and the major companies have flourished under the last government (1979-83). . . . The other side of the coin is shown by the estimated 100,000 jobs lost in electronics since Mrs. Thatcher came to power" (June 8, 1983, p. 6). The Plessey directors quoted approvingly Kenneth Baker's assertion that "Britain's economic prosperity depends upon the success with which we manufacture its (I.T.'s) products and provide and exploit its services." This may be so, and the leading corporations in the business are experiencing sustained growth. However, in the same speech Baker observed that I.T.'s "potential for increasing efficiency [was] immense." The question whether these increases are of a magnitude to fuel growth at the same time as they reduce labor demand—giving what is now called "jobless growth"—has to be considered in view of the recent record of major contenders in the "fastest-developing area of industrial and business activity" (all quotes from Kenneth Baker, cited in *Plessey Report and Accounts*, 1982, p. 5).

The Pessimists and History

The optimists do not have a monopoly on history. Their look into the past to contend that, since earlier technology and unemployment fears came to nought, we should cast aside worries about I.T. has been challenged on a number of grounds. First, there is the point that I.T. is arriving and finding applications at an unprecedented speed. Compared with the development of other "heartland" technologies, such as steam power and electricity, which took decades to permeate society, I.T. gives little time to adjust. It is arriving today on a "tidal wave of microelectronics" (Barron and Curnow, 1979, p. 14), "rushed along by a torrent" (p. 47) of innovation. While optimists regularly contend that I.T. will have a gradual impact, their time-scale remains, in historical terms, remarkably short. No one denies that the new technology will be pervasive by the end of the century. Compared with our forebears, we have little time to adjust and the pessimists feel we lack the necessary time.

Second, pessimists lay stress on the current recession as an unpropitious context in which to automate (from the point of view of the worker) since "unlike previous periods of rapid technological innovation . . . there is no expanding economy to cushion the blow and reabsorb workers in new growth areas" (CIS, 1978, p. 1). With I.T. being introduced during a period of declining employment in manufacture and with little prospect of service sectors expanding significantly, there is no prospect of jobs saved by I.T. being compensated for elsewhere.

Third, Christopher Freeman and colleagues at the University of Sussex Science Policy Research Unit have been at pains to recast the automation debate of the 1950s and 1960s, arguing that today's I.T. is an integral part of that same history. Their case is that

> radical innovations may tend to be "job-generating" in their early stages but "job-displacing" as they mature. In the early stages there is no standardisation and often competing designs. Many new entrants come into the new industries and services attracted by the growth and profit prospects. Because of the absence of standardisation and of major economies of scale, many processes are highly labour-intensive, so that the job-generating effects may be considerable (millions rather than thousands).
>
> However, as the new technology matures some standardisation takes place on the basis of the most successful designs and techniques; production and distribution economies of scale become increasingly important; firm size and capital intensity tend to increase. Employment grows more slowly or stabilises. In some cases secondary "job displacement" effects in other industries or services may become very important (e.g., the effect of railways on canals, of electrification on steam, or of microelectronics on some sectors of mechanical engineering and services) (Freeman, January, 1978a, p. 9).

This thesis, which draws on Schumpeterian concepts and on Kondratieff's notion of long cyclical waves of development, contends that, at the outset of major inventions and innovations, growth of labor is characteristically encouraged as the "swarming of imitators," enters the market and jostles for position. Additionally, it was "not until the late sixties [that] the computerisation process [was] beginning to release labour, the rate of diffusion up to this date being so fast that more labour was required in computer construction than released by computer usage" (Stoneman, 1976, p. 189). Nonetheless, as time passed, the electronics industry itself "has become more capital intensive, the rate of growth of employment has diminished and the absolute level of employment has actually declined or stagnated in some sectors even where sales and investment continue to expand" (Freeman et al., 1982, p. 101). There remain some growth points for employment even today, but the trend after a generation and more of the genesis of I.T. is generally negative for jobs as "one of the main thrusts of new investment in the immediate future seems likely to be designed to exploit the labour-saving potential of the technology in other industries and services" (ibid., p. 126).

Why Technological Innovation?

Consideration of motives is not often admitted by economists whose proper focus is costs and revenues. Whether I.T. will increase or decrease jobs seems devoid of value and belief: if the market expands, more employment will or will not be generated regardless of what people think. However, in trying to assess what is likely to happen, it appears to us worthwhile to state and cite what is the overriding motive for the introduction of I.T. I.B.M. says it straight:

> At a time when world economies are straining for answers to high inflation and lagging output, the demand for information products continues to outrun supply.
> Why? The answer lies in the world's need for more productivity. Manufacturers seek lower costs on the plant floor. . . Governments at all levels search for ways to serve many needs while staying within limited budgets (*IBM, Annual Report*, 1981, p. 6).

This imperative is the driving force behind both production and use of I.T. (cf. CSE, 1980, ch. 1), and the economic pressure seems to us especially likely to encourage labor displacement in a period of depression. No doubt there are those who would argue that such an orientation could of itself create jobs, since venality leads to greater competition and thereby market expansion which translates into more jobs: economic self interest and the "hidden hand" of the market are said to work wonders. We have already cast doubt on the necessary connections between growth and more employment, but we would emphasize also that, in the foreseeable future, the context of severe recession combined with a motive of maximization of economic return from technological innovation is likely to increase unemployment. Albury and Schwartz appositely comment:

> "Capital is in crisis and it is responding to the sales pitches of the microelectronics industry to try to cut what costs it can by installing cheaply produced

microelectronics-based office machinery in banks, the state bureaucracies, corporate headquarters and even education" (Albury and Schwartz, 1982, p. 140).

Changes in the Labor Force

The introduction of I.T. will clearly be influenced by the size and characteristics of the labor force. In Britain, the most striking feature is the growth of the population of working age, which expanded by 700,000 between 1977 and 1981 and will continue to grow by over 750,000 between 1981 and 1986 (*Employment Gazette,* April, 1981, p. 167) consequent upon the working through of the baby boom of the 1960s. This is especially serious because, while the numbers leaving school, where activity rates are highest, are at near record levels, those reaching retirement age are rather low.

Earlier predictions of labor force size had been even more serious, since they had projected from rising activity rates of women that the labor force would rise to 28 million in 1991 from 25.4 million in 1975 (*Employment Gazette,* September 1978, pp. 1040–43). However, the problem of how to absorb these extra numbers into the workforce has been mitigated by declining activity rates caused by early retirements and a fall in married women seeking work. A previous estimate had even thought that this would be sufficient to allow the labor force actually to decline marginally between 1977 to 1981, despite the growth of the population of working age. However, as things turned out, activity rates held up more than expected between 1979 and 1981 and the work force grew slightly, and now it is anticipated that the effect of declining activity rates will only reduce to 500,000 the number of new jobs required in Britain by 1986 to cater for school-leavers. (*Employment Gazette,* February 1983, pp. 50–54).

It was possible to absorb an increased labor force between 1961 (23.8 million) and 1979 (26 million) when unemployment rose at a slower rate than the availability of jobs, from 1.5% to 5.7% (*Social Trends, 13,* 1983, pp. 51-64), chiefly because this growth was caused almost entirely by married women seeking work and in large part entering, often in a part-time capacity, an expanding service sectore (notably health and education). At a time when this sector is retrenching, it is hard to see ways in which the growth of school-leavers can be managed. Unemployment in Britain rose from 1.2 million in 1979 to well over 3 million by the end of 1984, a dismaying statistic which only worsens the problem of creating employment opportunities for an expanding labor force. The same demographic trend is evident all over the industrialized world.

Mulinational Corporations and Investments

I.T. is an industry with an international market dominated by transnational corporations competing for these sales (see Chapter 7). While it is understandable, given their immediacy, that the employment implications of I.T. are considered solely at a national level, some consideration of the interests and characteristics of multinational corporations is essential to assess its true significance. Indeed, the pivotal role of multinational corporations in I.T. and advanced economies generally raises serious questions as to whether discussion of employment patterns and policies restricted to a particular country are altogether relevant, since the internationalization of capital undermines the possiblity of "any national economic coordination which might be achieved" (Scott, 1979, p. 171).

In all advanced societies, economic units have undergone rapid and accelerating concentration during the twentieth century. In the U.K., a small number of corporations holds the keys to the economy, with the hundred largest manufacturing firms accounting for over 40% of net output by 1970 (Aaronovitch and Sawyer, 1975) and likely to be responsible for two-thirds by the end of the 1980s (Prais, 1976, p. 7). The top hundred manufacturing companies also account for over one-third of the entire labor force in private sector employment (Marsh and Locksley, 1983, p. 39), and over 70% of employees in manufacture work for organizations with at least 500 on their payroll (Westergaard and Resler, 1975, pp. 151–52). Concentration has been accompanied by a growing internationalization of affairs and, while not all large corporations trade abroad, as a rule there is a correlation between size and foreign marketing. The pattern is repeated in all the advanced capitalist societies, though the U.S.A. and Britain are at the forefront of these processes (Holland, 1976). In this situation, it is self-evident that the policies of multinational corporations are important for employment prospects.

There are three connected aspects of I.T. of particular interest as regards multinationals. First, because I.T. manufacture and service are dominated by transnationals, a number of characteristics of its supply, production, and use are evident, most revealing of which are the global strategies that are entered into by the corporate leaders (Sciberras, 1977). We elaborate elements of these in a moment. Second, I.T. is a technology which is especially amenable for the co-ordination of dispersed enterprises. Because "with satellite, Jamaica, Barbados, and Taiwan are, for most intents and purposes, no farther away than the data entry room down the hall, the typing pool upstairs or the data processing shop in the next building" (McCartney, 1983), it allows both I.T. suppliers themselves and other multinational corporations to better operate on an international scale. Indeed, the requirements of globally dispersed corporations have been seen as a major factor encouraging the rise of the new technology (D. Schiller, 1982a,b). This can have consequences for employment, since control of production and the movement of information are facilitated by I.T. and result in the corporation being less restricted to national frontiers. Third, developments in I.T. find a ready response in multinational corporations because a major characteristic of high capital is a commitment to high technology. Large firms are usually capital rather than labor intensive; for instance, the hundred largest firms in the U.K. "spend about half as much again on capital per person employed as do the remaining smaller firms" (Prais, 1976, p. 9). I.T. presents itself as a further stage in this growing trend of capital intensification.

With these aspects in mind, we can make another point: private corporations invest wherever they can best further their own interests (Baran and Sweezy, 1973).

Multinational operations are not exempt from this principle and in some ways are particularly well placed to invest freely. Calculation of these interests is clearly a complex matter of labor costs, workforce skills, transportation, communications, political climate, strategic location, and so on. I.T. reduces some of these difficulties (for example by enhancing the flow and handling of data and reducing costs of transport), and may encourage organizations to disperse, especially those which already have international outlets.

We may illuminate something of capital's modus operandi by looking at recent events in Britain. While investment here has declined in recent years, notably in manufacture, which has experienced a 40% decline in investment in plant and machinery since 1979 (Vines and Taylor, 1983), private investment overseas has increased since 1978 by 116% to £35.4 billion, with £20.7 billion of that being achieved in 1981-82 alone (*Economic Trends,* (353), March 1983, p. 89). At the same time, overseas investment in the U.K. public and private sectors totalled £16.7 billion (p. 90).

These figures underline the fact that advanced capitalism, seeking to best maximize its interest, has an international constituency and that, at least in the case of the U.K., domestic investment is currently less attractive than that offered abroad. Multinational corporations are, by definition, well situated to operate on an international scale so it is no surprise to see them closely integrated with these trends. Indeed, an analysis in *Labour Research* (1983) reveals that overseas production accounts for 44% of the output of Britain's top 50 private manufacturing companies in 1981-82, a figure which compares with 39% for 1980. I.T. companies are well to the fore of this process, with overseas production now accounting for 35% of the total turnover of the eight largest corporations in the electrical/ electronic sector, up from 29% in 1980-81.

These production patterns and the investment trends they entail translate into jobs. For example, GEC, Britain's biggest private sector employer and a company with subsidiaries in every continent, raised its employees overseas from 36,092 in 1981 to 43,456 in 1982, while in the U.K. its workforce fell from 156,392 to 131,752 between 1981 and 1984. Though the impact on employment of these patterns is not traceable to a direct displacement effect of I.T., what is undoubted is that I.T. corporations, along with other capital, operating globally, readily invest—and thereby transfer labor—where it best suits their interests.

Britain is obviously not alone in having private capital invest where it can best benefit itself. Philips, one of the world's biggest I.T. operations, is part of the same trend, having commenced a strategy of rationalization of its European facilities, which resulted between 1980 and 1981 in a 30% increase of investment in the U.S.A. and Canada (to 15% of corporate assets) with a parallel rise in sales in North America (Philips, *Annual Report,* 1981, p. 16) and a reduction of its European workforce from 200,000 to 165,000 since 1980 that has left 20 plants closed and production units transferred to larger units (Jonquieres, 1982).

For high technology, transnational corporations investment in the United States is readily explained in terms of the scale and strategic import of this market, but other considerations lead to the channeling of funds and production to alternative areas to the domestic country. A favored sphere has been the Third World, especially the Far East, where low wages, disciplined workers, and I.T.'s cheapness of transport have been incentives. *Semiconductor International* (February 1982) reported on 1980 average hourly pay as shown in Table 1.

Table 1

Country	Wage ($)	Wage and Fringes ($)
U.S.A.	5.92	8.06
Hong Kong	1.15	1.20
Singapore	0.79	1.25
South Korea	0.63	2.00
Taiwan	0.53	0.80
Malaysia	0.48	0.60
Philippines	0.48	0.50
Indonesia	0.19	0.35

Philips is candid about this inducement, noting that

for a country with high labour costs such as the Netherlands, there is the fact that rationalisation of a production process makes it possible to look for an appropriate place in the world in which to locate that process. . . . Another aspect of this picture is that the highly rationalised production of electronic components results, among other things, in labour-intensive, but nevertheless simple operations which can be "farmed out" to countries with an adequate supply of the necessary type of labour. Deliberations in this respect, both now and in the future, can lead to the conclusion that a more favourable location than the Netherlands can be found for certain industrial activities elsewhere in the world—a conclusion which the entrepreneur cannot ignore (Philips, 1979, p. 6).

Putting these deliberations into practice, in a strategy spanning a decade of placing "a considerable portion of its labour-intensive activities in developing countries . . . [where] a large supply of unskilled labour exists to be tapped" (Catz and Heller, 1973, p. 73), Philips increased investment projects between 1980 and 1981 106% and 18% in Latin America and Asia, respectively, while simultaneously reducing by 17% that in the Netherlands. Meanwhile, the corporation managed, between 1979 and 1981 to rid itself of 13% of its European labor force and 8% world-wide, though that in Asia expanded and in Latin America remained stable (calculated from *Annual Reports* 1979-81).

Atari, then a subsidiary of Warner Communications, provided a vivid instance of this process when, late in 1982, it axed 1,700 of its workforce in Northern California (24% of its total) and moved its manufacture of home video games to Hong Kong and Taiwan (*Guardian,* 24 February, 1983). And *Datamation* reports a trend for

American I.T. companies to "buy foreign" when it comes to the labor market and describes instances such as the Philippines which

> With one of the lowest wage scales outside India, Indonesia, and South America . . . [has] managed to attract significant offshore development. Most of the activity is based in the Philippines' own version of the Silicon Valley near the Manila International Airport. American companies operating here include Data General, Intel, American Microsystems, Zilog, and Advanced Micro Devices (McCartney, 1983).

Similarly, the *Financial Times* writes that, in Singapore, "no sector has grown more rapidly than electronics, which now concentrates on micro-assembly and component manufacture. . . . Major plants are operated by Texas Instruments, National Semiconductor, and Fairchild—all American concerns" (22 November 1978). A survey of the American electronics industry in 1983 found that 48% of corporations with over 1,000 employees would be expanding overseas investments in the near future, and listed countries in order of preference. The U.K. and West Germany, being politically stable and strategic markets, top the poll, but high in the ratings are Mexico, Taiwan, Singapore, the Philippines. The report observed that

> Still popular targets for U.S. electronics investment are South East Asia and the Far East, although former havens for investment such as Taiwan, Singapore, and Malaysia have seen some of their support dwindle, as countries like the Philippines, India, Hong Kong and South Korea have all experienced improvement in their positions (Electronics Location File, 1983, pp. 4–6).

Meanwhile, a targeted area for American investment is the Caribbean, where "Barbados rose by 12 points in the table (to 16th) and Jamaica by 14 (to 21st). Also, Costa Rica became the highest new entry in 1983's Survey, moving into 25th position, while another newcomer, St. Vincent, has come in at 37th place."

We are not attempting to describe and chauvinistically deplore a transfer a jobs from the first world to the third, though it ought to be seen as part of a new international division of labor whereby "under transnational corporate direction, production in conventional industrial goods and services is being transferred world wide to sites with impoverished workers, tax exemptions, and complaisant governments" (Schiller, 1981, p. 15). In spite of this, most high technology production and application will remain in the metropolitan centers. Our concern here is to underline the fact that capital in general, and noticeably corporations involved with I.T., move their production where it best suits them. It would appear that this often results in the closure of plants which are expensive to maintain, chiefly due to labor costs, in the advanced capitalist societies, and transferring them, or more commonly part of them, abroad. This process is one which need not directly involve the substitution of workers for I.T., but it is one which is aided by the new technologies and undoubtedly results in the transfer of employment.

It is important to consider the significance of international transfers of investment capital and labor requirements, but it would be a mistake to assume that this entailed a straight-forward exchange of jobs to locations with the advantage of cheaper wage rates. I.T. does encourage this movement of functions, but it also assists the trend amongst large corporations to invest in capital rather than labor-intensive production. This is to return to the point made earlier that economic growth is no assurance of increased employment, since technology may account for expansion. With multinational corporations, this is clearly the case.

While the cost of labor may not be crucial within the third world, it is important in the advanced societies. This is, of course, a reason to move plant to countries such as Taiwan. However, at the same time, the metropolis is the main market and as such an incentive to corporations to locate facilities there (which is not to mention that the third world is politically volatile). I.T. can offer a solution here because it can allow production to be situated "back home," but in a capital intensive manner. It was because of this that *Business Week* could report in 1982 a return to the U.S.A. of some electronics corporations as follows: "Both Motorola Inc. and Fairchild . . . have recently moved some lines back to the U.S. where modern computer-controlled assembly of chips costs the same as using Asian labor" (March 15, 1982). So long as wages are not onerous on the corporation, the metropolis is preferred. Moreover, multinational corporations can combine domestic and off-shore production, as Robert H. Conrads, a Los Angeles management consultant explained, by, for example, retaining volume production abroad where labor requirements might be high while constructing domestic sites "for less labor intensive [tasks], employing a limited number of higher level workers, including engineers and administrators. The assembly production that is kept at these complexes will be highly automated" (quoted in McCartney, 1983, p. 117).

Multinational corporations get not only this from their global reach and I.T. They can also effect a switch, to whatever degree they decide, back to the metropolis on terms which benefit them most by situating production on the fringes of the core markets, thereby assuring lowest-possible labor costs with ready access to the most lucrative markets. Such appears to be the strategy of a wave of notably American, West German and Japanese investment in high technology in recent years in Scotland (where "Silicon Glen" is located between Glasgow and Edinburgh) and Ireland, where "it seems increasingly evident that gaining access to the whole E.E.C. market is an important consideration" (Jonquieres, 1983a). Ireland in particular has been attractive to American electronics companies, being the third most popular place in the world for their overseas investment (Electronics Location File, 1983). Low labor costs compared to neighboring European countries, generous subsidies from the Irish Industrial Development Authority, and high productivity resulted in over three-quarters of U.S. companies in the Republic describing their profits as good in May 1983 (Annual Investment File, 1983, pp. 6–7). Though they are located on the fringes of the market where labor is cheapest, these moves do not bring many jobs (the average electronics company in "Silicon Glen" employs 200; Crisp, 1983), are often created to finish and package part-assembled goods from Japan and America, and are usually highly automated as "the direct result of many more companies using micro technology to cut labor costs" (Connor, 1981).

The role of transnational corporations in employment patterns and their connections with I.T. are as yet poorly understood, and we cannot begin to quantify their implications, but what we can say is that their resources, their marketing strategies, their interests, and I.T. itself give these companies a facility to locate jobs where it best suits them. (Ernst, 1983, ch. 6). In turn, the likelihood is that this leads either/or to transfer of production to parts of the globe where labor costs are low and to domestic investment on the metropolitan fringes in capital rather than labor intensive methods. Either or all ways, the suggestion is that transnational corporations are unlikely to generate employment and very probably will reduce manning levels in the advanced societies.

Though he did not say it in so many words, E. Bradley Jones, president of the American corporation Republic Steel, emphasized this outcome in an interview with the *New York Times*, October 11, 1981, when he described the emergence of "geo-economics" as "a way of saying that the trading nations of the world are stepping up their intermingling of resources, manpower, technology, and capital." He continued to observe that, with the blurring of national boundaries, two elements in particular, capital and information, have been crisscrossing international boundaries "with growing ease and speed." As an example of this, which without I.T. would be unthinkable, he cited Ford's Escort, which is assembled in three countries from parts made in nine. As a result of this interaction—which is especially evident in the I.T. manufacture industry itself—Jones believes that companies will have broader supply options. Such a trend, he said, could "provide alternatives to increased costs, inadequate quality, and sluggish productivity" (*New York Times*, National Recruitment Survey, October 11, 1981, p. 5). We have spelled out some of the meanings of these alternatives above, and return to them in our final chapter.

Slow but Steady Diminution

We referred earlier to Green et al.'s estimate that in Tameside there would be steady loss of jobs throughout the 1980s of around 3 to 10%. This has been supported by a large-scale survey conducted by the Policy Studies Institute (PSI) early in 1981. Reviewing twelve hundred manufacturing firms selected for representativeness across industrial sectors, PSI found that among those using I.T. the majority had experienced and anticipated no significant changes in employment (Northcott and Rogers, 1982, p. 56). However, this study, which was restricted to examination of I.T.'s direct effects on production and processes in manufacturing industry and excluded other kinds of application (such as office work), did find that

with the establishments with process applications, for every one which has experienced an increase in jobs as a result of using microelectronics, three others have experienced a decrease, and a similar or greater disparity is expected in the next 18 months. With the establishments with product applications, however, the position is reversed—for every one which has experienced a decrease in jobs about three others have experienced an increase, and a similar or greater disparity is expected in the future   (ibid., p. 57).

Because product and process uses of microelectronics do not balance out, process applications being more widespread than the production of goods containing microelectronics, the overall prediction is for a net decline of employment (p. 60; Northcott and Rogers, 1984).

Areas of Job Loss

Pessimistic analyses of I.T.'s effects on employment are studded with instances of dramatic and not so dramatic job loss. We cannot hope to cover all of these, but review a few for illustrative purposes, prefacing our remarks with the point that, while the representativeness of these cases is debatable, the pessimists are able to present many more examples of I.T.'s applications that are likely to lead to job loss than optimists have of job creation through new technology.

There is common agreement that employment in certain areas has been and will be hit especially hard by I.T. Watch-making is a case in point where electronics has had a sweeping impact, reducing the Swiss industry's labor by about 40% between 1970 and 1978 (Rothwell and Zegveld, 1979, pp. 136–38). Printing is another area which I.T. has and will markedly effect. Since the late 1960s, the mechanical process of typesetting based upon hot lead has been replaced by computerized typesetting with photo-composition as the predominant technological method. In this way, traditional skills of printers such as composing and reading are eliminated, and the means eventually will be available for direct entry for journalists and writers that bypass printers (Hills, 1980). The introduction of I.T. has been a particularly hard-fought issue in the British printing industry since the mid-1970s (Martin, 1981), where attempts to innovate have met well-organized unionization. Nonetheless, printers have been on the defensive (Gennard and Dunn, 1983) as employment in the U.K. dwindled between 1977 and 1981 by 4%. Revealingly, within this overall decline of printers nationally, those employed in the publishing of newspapers, where there has been the most determined resistance from the workforce (and the most vitriolic attacks on it) numbers have held steady, the general decline being accounted for by printers of periodicals, bookbinding, and other publishing. Indeed, in the whole category of paper, printing, and publishing, *all* groups have lost members since 1977 *except* for newspaper printers (Central Statistical Office. 1983, p. 115). Rupert Murdoch's introduction of new technology at his News International plant in London that led to dismissal of 5,000 printers early in 1986 may well mark the reversal of this resistance.

Office Automation

While pessimists examine other industries and occupations at risk from automation in keeping with their view that "information technology will directly influence the efficiency of 95% of the economy" (Barron and Curnow, 1979, p. 227), the office is picked out for special attention. It is office automation, the various uses of I.T. in the office relating to the handling of textual and numerical information, which "is expected to grow rapidly and to be the single most important use of information technology in the long term" (p. 142). Word processors, desktop computers, facsimile equipment, and the like are already extending into the office, and, in the future, the development of information networks within and between organizations promises the "electronic office." Because the office is a lucrative market, the efforts of most I.T. corporations are directed towards the "office of the future," attracted by yearly growth rates of anything up to 40% (*Financial Times*, April 13, 1982).

Offices are prime targets for I.T. applications because their major raw material is information, whether in the form of sales, orders, customer services, personnel records, marketing, merchandising, advertising, or enquiries. This information is received, processed, stored, and transmitted within the office network, and it is here that I.T. equipment is being introduced on a modular basis. Further, the office—sometimes referred to as an "information factory"—has lacked automation in the past:

> Twentieth century offices are being run by 19th century office methods. ...While the office is the organization's information and communications' nerve center it has not seen much of the technological advances that have brought computer technology to other line functions such as accounting and production (Press Release from First Office Automation Conference, Atlanta, cited in McCuster, 1980).

While rationalization of office work has been taking place over generations (e.g., typing pools, shared secretaries, copying), this process has not to date evidenced any large scale commitment to technological investment, most being brought about by reorganization rather than technological innovation. This is now changing as companies, in the words of a computer research manager at Amoco Production Co., begin "looking at things that are being done in the office and trying to better mechanize them" (cited in McLellan, 1980).

There are many reasons why the office is a target for automation. Not least are changes in occupational structure and modes of employment that have resulted in a rapid rise of white-collar employees who may be regarded as "information workers." The growth of the service sector, in which a majority of workers are white-collar, is related to this (Bain et al., 1972). It is estimated that over 40% of workers in the U.K. were white-collar by 1971 (Brown, 1978, p. 68) and the *Labour Force Survey* calculates that over 49% were such by 1981 (*Labour Force Survey*, 1982, table 4.8). Though most of these are located in the service sector "something like a third of all employees in manufacturing are white-collar workers" (Kumar, 1978, p. 207), the Department of Employment recording an increase in administrative, technical, and clerical workers in manufacturing industries from 23% of total employees in 1964 to 30% by 1981 (Central Statistical Office, 1971, table 144; 1983, table 6.4).

These developments mean that

Work for an increasing proportion of the population, indeed, no longer means manual labour—or even manual labour with the assistance of mechanical power—but the manipulation of symbolic materials in an office, or the processing, in some way or other, of people (Brown, 1978, p. 71).

I.T. can automate aspects of these sorts of work. While new technologies will surely impact on most white-collar work, where it can deal most effectively and even substitute for it is in the areas of least skill and maximum routine—that is, the lower levels of nonmanual labor, chiefly clerical employment (office machine operators, typists, clerks, secretaries, and the like), which by 1981 accounted for 17.4% of employees in Britain (*Labour Force Survey*, 1982, table 4.8), having risen from 14% in 1971 (Routh, 1981, pp. 5, 45). This accords with international patterns. Since the bulk of such work is performed by females, their vulnerability to I.T. is discussed separately below.

While this spread of white-collar work is undoubtedly an important factor, along with the contingent information explosion, explaining the genesis of I.T. in general and for the office in particular, it is not the only reason for a spate of innovation directed at this area. Offices are also expensive: A.D. Little consultants (1979) estimate that the salaries of office workers rose in real terms 7% per annum between 1974 and 1978, during which period I.T. costs plummeted. Other sources claim that as much as 50% of a company's costs go to office functions, with upwards of 80% of these being absorbed by wages (Rothwell and Zegveld, 1979, p. 139), and that on current trends these overheads will reach half the cost of sales by 1988, against having been less than one-third in 1976 (*Financial Times*, April 18, 1983). Sir Robert Telford, managing director of G.E.C.-Marconi Electronics, sums up:

the office remains the most labour-intensive sector of industry and commerce with capital investment in automation systems being less than one-tenth of that on the factory floor. While the labour costs are rising at a rate of between 6% and 8% per annum the cost of electronic automation has been falling at a rate of between 10% and 20% (*Financial Times*, 30 December, 1978).

Labor-intensity of office staff is complemented by low productivity such that "over the past ten years, while the working population has increased by 6%, the growth of office staff in Western Europe and the U.S. has been around 45%. Yet when general productivity has gone up by 80% in that decade, office productivity has gone up only 4%" (Lloyd, 1979). These factors combine to make capital investment in the office an attractive proposition to reduce labor costs and increase productivity.

This is the prospect which disturbs the pessimists, who believe that I.T. will create major redundancies in office work. Items in the *Financial Times* (April 18, 1983) which declaim that "the white-collar sector—there are five million people

involved in administrative and clerical roles in the U.K. alone—is ripe for a major
shakeout of the kind seen in recent years in manufacturing," that "administrative
overheads are still out of control in most West European companies and particularly
those in Britain," and which favorably report that in other countries "cost-cutting
has been achieved mainly through office automation and computerisation," por-
tend unemployment for many.

There is something of a gap between perceived need, corporate motive, and the
practice of substituting machines for office workers. For instance as recently as
1980 only one of four offices in the U.K. had a photocopier, one in ten a data
processor, and one in forty a word processor (Jonquieres, 1980a). While this undoubtedly understates the intrusion of technology into larger officers where economies of scale make it a more attractive proposition, it is a reminder of the distance yet to go before automation is achieved. In addition, though there have been
claims, especially from manufacturers, of large increases in productivity from office
machines, the measures can be problematical (for example is productivity calculated by jobs completed, speed of processing, or quantities of information processed?). Moreover, there have been cases where I.T. has been introduced into the
office and appeared cost-effective in terms of cost per item of produce, but savings
consumed by production of extra copies of documents, more drafts and the like
(*Economist,* January 30, 1982, pp. 93-94). It is also the case that I.T. consultants
agree that new technology will be used efficiently in the office only if organizational changes are introduced with machinery, few savings being made by direct replacement of employees by technology (cf. Naffah, 1979; Price, 1980; Sachs, 1981), a
factor which can complicate measures of technology's displacement of personnel.

These caveats aside—all of which repeat the truism that technology enters
specific contexts which affect its capability—numerous commentators foresee
many office jobs disappearing through I.T. There is no disagreement that those
most immediately vulnerable are the 25% of employees which falls into the less
skilled white-collar category "clerical and other non-manual" below the managerial
and professional groupings (*Labour Force Survey,* 1982, p. 17). Barron and Curnow
contend that, in the U.K., there are one million secretaries and typists, 750,000
administrative workers, and 400,000 managers, the lives of whom will be changed
significantly by the automated office (Barron and Curnow, 1979, p. 151). Given
the potential of I.T., these authors believe it "may lead to serious labour displacement in secretarial, typing, administrative and management staff" (pp. 152-53).
Similarly, Nora and Minc are sure that in the office I.T.'s effects "on employment
will certainly be massive, even if the characteristics of this form of economic activity do not currently make a statistical evaluation possible" (Nora and Minc, 1980,
p. 37). McDonald and Mandeville, considering only word processors, believe that
"between 17% and 23% of employment in the typist/secretary" grade could be
saved by their adoption" (McDonald and Mandeville, 1980, p. 146), and Emma
Bird also estimates that up to 17% of typing and secretarial jobs will disappear by
1990 (Bird, 1980, p. 39). The most cited projection is that produced by Siemens
of West Germany in 1978. Classifying office work into three types by length and

degree of verbal communication with others, Siemens concluded that 43% could be "formalized" and approximately 25% automated (Morgenbrod and Schwartzel, 1978).

These estimates, some abstractions while others are extrapolations from case studies, suggest that I.T. does generally reduce employment in the office and almost invariably increases output. APEX (Association of Professional, Executive, Clerical and Computer Staff), while unwilling to offer an overall prediction of job loss, provides numerous cases where I.T. has reduced office jobs (APEX, 1980, ch. 2), observing that especially vulnerable were mail room clerks, filing clerks, routine clerical and administrative jobs, cashiers, printing and reprographic staff, typists and secretaries, supervisors, and first line managers. Frances McMahon's investigation of word processors in major installations in the U.K. found that "Productivity was increased in all cases and by as much as 300%. In all but two cases, typing and secretarial jobs were reduced by between 3 and 73% (McMahon, 1980, p. 36). This research revealed the unsurprising fact that most office machinery was introduced to save money by increasing production. The Prudential Assurance Company, Britain's largest insurer, evidenced the same outlook in announcing late in 1982 a reduction of 18% of staff from its general household and motor insurance division in tandem with starting "to introduce new office technology" (*Guardian*, 7 October, 1982). The financial editor of the *Guardian* observed that, while "general insurance business is very largely a clerical function: moving bits of paper around and taking a series of fairly routine decisions on what should be done about them ... office technology is leaping forward," its application encouraged by the fact that the insurance "industry [is] under immense pressure [and] the big composites have started to look at their costs." Nora and Minc said much the same thing in the late 1970s when they estimated "job savings of approximately 30% are now possible within 10 years" in insurance (Nora and Minc, 1980, p. 35). Such calculations are especially grim when one considers that insurance has long been an expanding employer, the workforce having increased in Britain by over 11% between 1978 and 1981 (*Employment Gazette*, February 1981, p. 66; December 1982, p. 510). The Prudential's decisions announce the turning of this expansionary tide.

It would be possible to continue listing cases of job loss and/or productivity gains consequent upon automation of office functions. Individually, all would be questionable as to their representativeness. Nonetheless, what is striking is this: to our knowledge the introduction of I.T. in offices has nowhere led to increases in staffing. Aimed at saving costs, I.T. in the office could, of course, in conditions of considerable expansion, increase labor. But, in the current climate, this is unlikely. On the contrary, what has been the result is at the least greater productivity from the same number of employees and, more regularly, more output with less staff.

The Demise of the Service Sector?

Pessimists have decisively rejected the idea that any job displacement I.T. might bring about will be compensated for by an expansion of the service sector. On the contrary, while they acknowledge that services have grown considerably throughout the twentieth century, they contend that I.T. will actually have its major impact in this area for the very reason that it is a technology designed and developed to handle more efficiently information which is the stuff of much service sector work.

It is this emphasis of the pessimists on I.T.'s potential to halt what appeared till recently an unstopable historical trend which takes the issue of "the impact of microelectronic technology upon service-sector employment. . . [to] the heart of the argument about the effect of new technology upon overall employment levels" (Sleigh et al., 1979, p. 52).

Thus, Nora and Minc argue that while the service sector has to date absorbed workers either displaced from the primary and secondary sectors or entering the labor market for the first time, we have now reached the "breakdown of this adjustment mechanism" because "with telematics, the service sector will in the coming years undergo a jump in productivity comparable to the gains in productivity enjoyed by agriculture and industry in the past twenty years" (Nora and Minc, 1980, p. 34). Raymond Curnow adds that

> Historically, displacement of labour from the manufacturing sector has occurred over a very long period and has previously been absorbed into the socalled service sector, e.g., office or government functions. Unfortunately the advance in the technologies is associated with such service functions. Labour displacement is taking place in retail distribution networks, banking, insurance, and with the coming of the word processor, in large or specialised offices also. Since more people are engaged in office work than manufacture, the impact here may be very large (quoted in *New Scientist*, 8 June, 1978, p. 666).

Since we consider the relation between I.T. and the "service society" in Chapter 6, we shall truncate our comments here. What we seek to demonstrate in the following pages is, first, that expansion of the service sector is unlikely in the foreseeable future, and second, that I.T. will be able to reduce a number of key service sector jobs. Either way, optimistic vistas of more service work are mistaken. Clearly, the effects of I.T. on office work discussed above are pertinent to this issue, since much of such work is accounted for by the rise of the service sector.

That public expenditure, a major element of services' revenue, has been and is being cut has meant that the service sector will be unlikely to absorb extra workers (Harris and Taylor, 1978). Policies towards public expenditure in recent years have reversed a trend of expansion in a sphere which employs about 30% of the workforce. Though by no means all of public expenditure goes on services, it is the case that apart from some of the public corporations (7.5% of the laborforce in mid-1982 and itself in decline) such as gas and coal, the bulk of the public sector is composed of services. In fact, some two-thirds of public sector employment is in the "other services" category, with about one-eighth in transport and communications (which is often included under service sector occupations) and only one-seventh in production industries such as mining and quarrying, manufacturing and construction (*Economic Trends*, (352) February, 1983, pp. 82–89). Key service occupations, funded from the public purse, have been reduced lately. Thus central government and local authorities (accounting for 10% and 12.5% of the employed labor force in 1982) both shed labor between 1981 and 1984, and these reductions were effected in services which, until 1979, had experienced sustained growth. That there is a close tie between public expenditure and service sector work, and that the former is being reduced, necessarily limits expansion of the latter.

Moreover, though the service sector in the U.K. grew without interruption since the Second War, expanding from 10.4 million in 1961 to 13.4 million in 1979, that year marked its apogee, and by 1981 it had fallen back to just on 13 million (*Social Trends, 13*,1983, p. 54). It is true that services have been less hard hit by recession than manufacturing (which shed over 1 million workers between 1979 and 1981), something which has resulted in their percentage of total employees continuing to grow (from 46.7% in 1961 to 61.3% in 1981), but there is nothing in the statistics which suggest that they are a refuge for those displaced from other sectors.

Though the category "services" is a miscellany which defies easy generalization, it is possible to deduce some significant conclusions from available data. Two services in particular are often seen to be especially important absorbers of those displaced by I.T., namely education and health. It is certainly the case that both have expanded considerably: employment in education by local authorities rose from .8 million in 1961 to 1.5 million in 1981, to represent 11.5% of the total service sector labor force, and the National Health Service expanded over the same period from .6 million to 1.3 million, some 10% of service employment. Nonetheless, even assuming that these occupations are relatively aloof from automation, there are signs that they will not significantly expand in the future. Employment in local authority education actually peaked in 1975 at 1.6 million and remained at that level until 1980, since when it has lost numbers. Health employment followed a similar pattern, though it has continued to rise to an all-time peak of 1.3 million in 1981. However, since 1 million of this is female it is questionable whether it could absorb the predominantly male workers made redundant in other sectors. Moreover, since health's growth has levelled off recently, this casts serious doubts on hopes that it is set to markedly expand.

Banking

Closer analysis of the service sector shows that some occupations which are significant sources of work are particularly vulnerable to I.T. Banking, insurance, and finance are cases in point. We have already commented on insurance as open to large-scale automation. Before turning to banking's susceptibility, we would observe that this whole sector, which in the U.K. experienced an almost 100% expansion between 1960 and 1980 when it grew to 1.3 million employees (about 9% of total service sector work) had its forward march halted that year. Whatever was the cause of this, it is further grounds for doubting a continuation of service sector growth.

It is because banking is an activity especially open to automation that many feel jobs will be lost in this sub-sector, which accounts for about 28% of all insurance, banking, and finance employment. The spread of electronic banking (automated teller machines, point-of-sale terminals, on-line account handling, the range of electronic funds transfer facilities (see Marti and Zeilinger, 1982)), en route to a "cashless society," have all raised fears amongst banking employees for their security. (BIFU, 1979). Nora and Minc believe that "the installation of new computer systems would permit employment reductions affecting up to 30% of the personnel over ten years" (Nora and Minc, 1980, p. 34), though redundancies would not be of quite that order. Two recent studies predict losses in banks of between 10 and 12% by 1990, one arguing that, in Britain, the five major clearing banks, an oligopoly accounting for most banking employees, would decline by 12% (Coulbeck and Shaw, 1983); the other, conducted by Emile Kirschner of Essex University for the Commission of the European Communities, concluded in May 1983 that up to 10% of banking jobs are at risk in Europe (*Guardian*, 1 June, 1983).

The optimistic retort to this is that banks have long been computerized, and, while the recent wave of innovation is acknowledged, the belief is that this "will make it easier for banks to contain staff growth" (Sleigh et al., 1979, p. 66) rather than cause displacement. The fact that banking as an employer is now stagnating is itself significant, as it follows years of growth of around 3% per annum (*Financial Times*, 9 July 1982), but there are other reasons why it is likely to ebb appreciably. One is that, in the U.K., banking staff account for two-thirds of operating costs, and are thereby the most likely source of savings. In truth, labor costs have long been a key consideration influencing automation in banks. Though past technological innovation did not create unemployment, it is scarcely a comfort, since computerization of accounts and money transfers over the past generation has accompanied sustained growth of the industry. The consequence of rapid expansion accompanying automation was that the banks took on extra staff, but not nearly so many as they would have had to had not machinery been introduced. Lloyds Bank, for example, estimates that without mainframe computers they would require almost 50% more staff (*Economist,* October 2, 1982, p. 88). Of course, one could contend that this simply highlights the fact that technology rarely directly displaces workers, that the context of introduction is crucial. This is so—but today's contexts are not propitious.

Labor in banks is particularly vulnerable at the moment because a new climate of competition combines with the recession to target staff costs for reduction. The recent entry into the banking market of outside interests which see banking services as attractive and logical extensions of their operations calls for a response from traditional operators. While the recession is squeezing profitability, building societies, securities houses, and retailers are new competitors for checking accounts and the like. Both of these developments put pressure on the banks to cut overheads.

I.T. can appear an outlet for this pressure. Bird's report that "In the U.K. almost two thirds of all staff in the major clearing banks are involved in payment services and at least half of these are performing straight-forward clerical duties" (Bird,

September, 1980, p. 43), is an invitation to automate. For instance, automatic tellers, which have grown rapidly in the last four years, have been estimated each to save 1.32 full-time staff (*Financial Times*, 9 July, 1982). In addition, over 80% of European bank jobs are in branches which are both expensive to run and amenable to replacement by electronic self-service systems. Pactel consultants observed in 1980 that, because of this, 5% of present manned branches will be closed and there will be 10% fewer staff in Western European banks by 1990 (*Computer Communications, 3* (4) 1980: 190).

Recent developments in British banking are foreboding. In June, 1983, Barclays Bank announced a program of branch closures as part of the reshaping of its network, and this news was quickly followed by the news that the Midland Bank was streamlining its business. This involved continuation of staff reductions begun in 1981 which led to a loss of 4900 jobs (9%) by 1983, and the projection of a further 3000 to go by 1986—a total reduction in excess of 14% over 5 years and a dramatic reversal of employment trends in banking. These cuts are motivated by a drive to greater efficiency, and the majority of the Midland's closures will affect small, labor intensive branches. The Midland's retrenchment does not involve the greatest proportion of losses in British banking, the laurel going to the Royal Bank of Scotland, which plans to shed 18% of its personnel by 1987. Job reductions are one facet of the new emphasis on efficency; "the clearing banks are also using new technology as the second prong of their attack on costs, with rapid increases in their networks of automatic cash dispensers" (*Guardian*, July 12, 1983).

Retailing

The "distributive trades," an amalgam of retailers and wholesalers, is undoubtedly an important employer of labor in Britain, accounting for over 20% of the total service sector and about 12% of all employment (*Employment Gazette*, December 1982, pp. 507, 510). However, there can be little hope of this sector expanding in the future, since it has failed to do so over the past 20 years (*Social Trends, 13,* 1983, p. 54) in spite of profound changes in size, organization, and turn-over of the concerned groups.

Though I.T.'s impact on this sector will be highly varied, since there are an estimated 250,000 businesses and 350,000 shops in the distributive trades (D. Harris, 1983, p. 6), it is assured that it will be widely adopted for reasons of more effective stock control, reduction of theft, and staff savings (Musannif, 1983). Few commentators, either pessimistic or optimistic, find great concern for possible large-scale job through I.T., though Sleigh et al. report that in this sector staff savings of up to 15% will be made "in clerical functions backing up retailing operations" (Sleigh et al., 1979, p. 72) which will be absorbed by internal redeployment. However, this may not be feasible if planned market growth fails to materialize. Moreover, growth in all likelihood will be at the expense of smaller retail outlets (continuing a long-term trend) which could result in serious indirect unemployment effects as smaller, more labor-intensive distributors lose their markets to the larger companies that are at the forefront of technological innovation (Arnold et al., 1982, pp. 90-96). The effects of I.T. on the distributive trades are imprecise, but one finding is widely accepted: no commentator can be found who believes that I.T. will enable this sector to appreciably expand employment in the future (cf. Powell, 1983).

Civil Service

To date I.T. has not led to net redundancies in the civil service. New technology has been introduced and has proved economical when applied. For instance, word processors were found to be "well worth while provided the workload is carefully analyzed and selected and the aptitude of individuals is taken into account" (Smith, 1979, p. 88), and word processors were able to increase productivity between 40 and 200% for materials which go through a number of drafting stages (*Word Processing by Computer,* 1978, p. 3, passim), with "overall gains in productivity fluctuating between 20% and 70%" (Unit of Manpower Studies, 1978, p. 8). The development of an "information grid" for the civil service (B.T. Campbell, 1982, pp. 188-95) is being encouraged and government is now the largest single computer user in the U.K. (*Financial Times,* January 8, 1979; Goodman et al., 1980), but, where necessary, staff have been able to be absorbed.

However, prior to discussing whether the age of redeployment of automated civil service workers is coming to an end, there is an important preliminary point to be made. This is that the civil service is currently contracting as an employer. It did grow considerably as an employer throughout the 1960s and 1970s but has fallen since 1979 to about half a million staff. The civil service, which occupies about 4 to 5% of service sector employment, has stopped expanding. This indicates that, as with distributive trades and insurance, banking, and finance, one cannot look to these services for job opportunities for workers displaced elsewhere.

Moreover, there are reports now appearing which suggest that sections, at least, of the civil service are endangered by I.T. Not surprisingly these are the labor intensive, hence expensive, spheres, notably social services which accounts for almost 20% of the nonindustrial civil service workforce and the inland revenue which takes up about 14% (Central Statistical Office, 1983, p. 120). In the current economic and political climate, any shakeout of labor seems unlikely to be redeployed.

Two examples may illustrate this development. The first is an agreement reached between unions and management on new technology which cleared the way for far-reaching changes in tax offices. This followed the adoption of a plan to computerize the income tax system in Britain using a string of regional computer centers communicating with video terminals spread around Pay-As-You-Earn (PAYE) offices. According to the *Financial Times* "The agreement guarantees that . . . the Government will not demand compulsory redundancies as a consequence of the introduction of new technology. . . . But it does specify that a number of jobs will be lost as a result of the introduction of new technology—though these will be dealt with by a mixture of natural wastage and redeployment" (April 13, 1982). *Computing* (16 July, 1981) elaborates by quoting a civil service paper (*Efficiency in the*

Civil Service, 1981) which argues that "An intensive search for cost saving applications of new information technology is an integral part of the drive for efficiency" and follows this with a report that PAYE computerization will cut 7,000 jobs from the Inland Revenue. In a situation of overall decline in employment in the civil service the emphasis on reductions must be "natural wastage"—i.e., net job loss.

The second case is the planned "Social Security Operational Strategy," a £700 million twenty-year project, which will link micros in benefit offices to seven area computers feeding in turn into a huge data base in Newcastle. While this would "dramatically reduce paperwork and duplication in handling 25 million benefit claims a year" presently done by 117,000 civil servants who deal with 30 different types of benefit and refer to 100 instruction manuals and could save £1.9 billion, "the string in the tail is that most of this would come from staff cuts—possibly as many as 20,000 to 25,000 by 1995" (Ring, 1983).

Leisure

Though we have summarily reviewed well over 50% of the service sector in terms of employment, there is another very significant grouping which deserves mention. This is the rag-bag of occupations named "miscellaneous services" that holds a number of jobs ranging from "betting and gambling" and "motor repairs" to "laundries." This category has risen slightly since 1978, to 2.5 million employees in 1981 (*Employment Gazette,* February 1981, p. 67). It represents 19% of service employment.

Of particular relevance to the I.T. and employment debate is that this category includes "leisure" work, a type seized upon by a number of enthusiasts as a means of absorbing displaced labor in a rich "post-industrial" society of the future that can afford such luxuries. Since we elaborate this topic in the following chapter we

Table 2

	1978	1981 (in thousands)
Hotels and other residential establishments	280	270
Restaurants, cafes, snack bars	171	195
Public houses	251	246
Clubs	109	134
Catering contractors	72	77
Cinemas, theatres, radio, etc.	102	98
Betting and gambling	94	97
Sports and other recreations	106	137
Total	1185	1253

merely consider leisure employment here to observe the following patterns. Taking our categories from *Social Trends,* we may tabulate leisure industries in Britain from census data for 1978 and 1981 as shown in Table 2.

These occupations constitute about 10% of service sector employment, so there is not doubting that they are significant areas of work. Nonetheless, what is striking is that their growth is modest wherever it is evident, averaging only some 6%. The category sport and other recreations stands out as the only sharp expander, at 31%. However, since this accounted for only 1% of service sector employment in 1981, it has to experience unimaginable growth to significantly influence the total labor force. Those who hope for a "vast extension of the leisure industries" (Large, 1980, p. 30) as in some way compensating for technologically-induced unemployment are unrealistic.

Conclusion

It was not the purpose of this review to arrive at a precise figure which generalized the impact of I.T. on employment. As we have seen, this will be much influenced by the contexts within which it is introduced, and we are ready to concede that variations of these make exact prediction impossible. However, recognition that technological innovation takes place in the ruck of socio-economic conditions is not reason enough to throw up one's hands in dismay in pronouncing prediction impossible or, in cheerfully confessing that things are so complicated, arguing that with luck change will not be particularly tumultuous. It is reason to look determinedly in an attempt to identify the key contexts into which I.T. is arriving in order to achieve some valid estimations.

In our view some things which can be ascertained are

• I.T. has a range of applications which result almost invariably in increases in productivity.
• it is being introduced at a time of recession, though, even in areas of growth, employment does not necessarily expand.
• demographic trends exacerbate the problem of I.T.'s introduction.
• in all advanced capitalist societies the new technology is being introduced to meet the threat of other nations which could result in cheaper production, less employment, and no overall economic change.
• it is being introduced overwhelmingly to save on expenditure in order to increase profitability and/or efficiency rather than to increase employment.
• key developers and users are multinational corporations which have world-wide strategies and a commitment to high technology which militate against investment in the relatively expensive employment sectors of metropolitan centers.
• service sector employment is not increasing at the moment and is likely in future to decline in significant areas because of the application of I.T.

For these reasons we feel confident in stating that I.T. will bring about further unemployment.

I.T. and the Work That Remains

> The Chairman. "Is it not the purpose of the advocates of scientific manage-
> ment to apply it to all classes of work whether it is machine work or any
> other kind of work?"
> Mr. Taylor. "It certainly is, sir."
>
> —F. W. Taylor, *Testimony before the Special House Committee.*
> 1912. (1947c, p. 126)

Prospects for employment appear bleak and the uptake of I.T. will not help
matters. Nevertheless, we have to remind ourselves that, even if unemployment in
Britain were to rise over the next 5 years to the 20% levels predicted by the most
gloomy, the bulk of the population will remain in work. This of itself has profound
implications for any estimation of response to new technology, though to hint here
that the majority may be beyond the reach of I.T. in not our point, since it is likely
that even those in employ will be impacted by technological change. *Business Week*
(August 3, 1981, pp. 58–67) suggests that almost half of all jobs will be affected by
factory and office automation in the near future while the Arthur D. Little consultancy expects between 40 and 50% of all American workers to be making daily use
of electronic terminal equipment by 1990 (Giuliano, 1982, p. 128). The future is
one in which a minority is likely to be made technologically redundant, although
most of the remainder will be influenced by new technologies at their place of
employment. Because of this, it behooves us to consider the effect that I.T. will
have on the work that remains, to ask what it will do to levels of skill, job statis-
faction, occupational roles, and the like.

To adequately examine this at the moment is an impossible task, because there
is both a shortage of empirical evidence available and conditions are changing rapidly.
Moreover, this uncertainty is compounded by the fact that it is difficult to do
justice to the range and diversity of I.T.'s effects, to detail its impact on *this* occupation, in *that* work environment, under *those* conditions of employment. Nonetheless, conceding that I.T. will have differential effects on work dependent upon a
number of factors (employers' practices, union strength, market location, investment patterns, etc.) which make tackling the topic in a few thousand words awesome, we do feel that it is feasible to review the likely direction of change and
known features with some confidence by drawing upon past trends, empirical
evidence which is available, and theoretical traditions that try to make sense of the
relation between technology and work.

Proletarianization or Professionalization?

Opinion about the effects of I.T. on work usually falls into one of two schools
of thought, and assumptions of Marxian and Weberian sociology have underpinned
most comment. The optimists are Weberian and regard technological innovation as
an expression of the rationalization of society which stimulates a process of profes-

sionalization. From this perspective, the increased influence of the expert is both manifest in and encouraged by the application of advanced technology, the aim of which is to increase efficency and produce yet more sophisticated and efficient technologies. As we have seen, the evolutionary principle which underpins this approach (high technology = high skill = higher technology = higher skill) is in evidence in Bell's theory of post-industrial society. It gets a vulgar rendition in the everyday claims that I.T. will do away with "the repetitious, machine-dictated tasks" (Hyman, 1980, p. 44) of work and leave people free to move on and up to more interesting and stimulating tasks. The opinion is frequently voiced that new technology best does boring jobs that no one actually enjoys, so it is all to the good if these are automated and workers then left free to do more exciting things. On these terms, a technology which, say, can effectively take over the counting of notes in a bank, or the calculation of interest in a building society, or replace the mundane activity of copy-typing is to be welcomed as liberating the worker from alienating circumstances, as the provider of opportunities to channel his or her energies in more invigorating directions—from bank teller to financial advisor, clerk to mortgage broker, typist to personal assistant.

Against this is the pessimistic writing, stimulated by the writing of the Marxist Harry Braverman, which places at the center of analysis the motives and interests of those introducing and developing new technologies. Because capital seeks to achieve the best return from its investment, from this perspective I.T. is viewed as a means of more effectively extracting productivity from the work force. Braverman thus sees I.T. as an integral part of the struggle between labor and capital, a means to better exploit the working class, one which weakens its capacity for resistance and reduces its circumstances such that it downgrades its skills even to the extent of proletarianizing nonmanual labor. This Marxist account assumes that technology mediates the relation between capital and labor and that it is shaped to the former's advantage: that, far from being rational, it is politically skewed since it expresses "the transformation of science itself into capital" (Braverman, 1974, p. 167).

Mechanization and Automation

This review suggests that the two interpretations are diametrically opposed. At many levels, practical and philosophic, they are irreconcilable, and we expand upon these differences below. However, there does appear to be some degree of congruence when it comes to empirical description of what may actually happen where new technology is introduced. This can be clarified by examining a distinction drawn by optimists between mechanization and automation. Jon Shepard (1971) developed this distinction in a study of office automation in the late 1960s that was influenced by the pioneering work of Robert Blauner (1964). On this account, mechanization involves the fragmentation and specialization of particular jobs, which brings about a greater division of labor with consequences for workers of more repetition, more mundane tasks to fulfil, more monotony, a reduction in skill, and less satisfaction with work. Shepard illustrates this with the example of "the punched-card system of data processing," the result of which was that "increasing numbers of office employees became operators of special-purpose machines as their sole function" (ibid.) and experienced the sort of "monotony and repetitiveness long attached to much factory work" (Shepard, 1971, p. 52, 53; cf. Hoos, 1961).

As we shall see, this is very much the prospect delineated by Braverman. However, the gulf between the interpretations reopens when the optimists insist that mechanization is but a *temporary* feature of technological progress which will be superceded by the automation of activities. Automation is an integrating process which draws together a number of previously mechanized tasks under one technology and leaves the worker with a more skilled, responsible, and enriched job. It thus assumes "the absorption of repetitive tasks by computers" (Shepard, 1971, p. 52), and is to be seen as the culmination of a journey, the unpleasant aspect of which is mechanization that must be endured in order that the satisfying destination might be reached: "automated technology returns to the . . . worker the freedom and control, purpose and function, and self-involvement in work that mechanization has taken away" (p. 5).

Bravermanseque reports reject this view that mechanization is an interruption en route to further professionalization, on the grounds that such faith in "an evolutionary perspective" (Shepard, 1971, p. 119) is misplaced, and introduce two general objections. The first is the question of time-scale. What Shepard regards as a temporary feature, Braverman sees as a continuing process of deskilling. We shall have more to say about this image of a unidirectional decline of skill later, but postpone our qualifications to note Braverman's second—and we believe more pertinent—objection to the evolutionists, which is found in his stress on the conflict of interests and motives which shape the development of technologies. It is the absence of analysis of interest and motive, questions of who gains, why, and to what end that most markedly distinguishes Marxian from Weberian accounts, and it is this difference which leads Marxists to put at the center of study the problem of control in the workplace. Because these principles have profound implications for understanding the effects of technological change, it is necessary to examine some tenets of this perspective before we ponder the practical issue of the impact of I.T. on work.

Taylorism

Harry Braverman's book *Labor and Monopoly Capital: The Degradation of Work in the Twentieth Century* (1974) draws much of its strength from an interpretation of the writings of F. W. Taylor (1856–1915), the father of "scientific management." The specific features of scientific management do not require review here, and it will suffice to say that they are usually manifested in specialized organization of labor, piece work, time and motion practices, and an individualist appeal to homo economicus. What does require discussion is, however, the significance of Taylorism for modern management.

Braverman's insight into Taylorism is his recognition that control of the labor process requires a new strategy in the modern plant, because it is no longer adequate for capital to hire labor with requisite skills and leave production up to it and/or to personally oversee those in one's employ. Braverman understands that Taylorism was a necessary adjunct to large-scale production which demands not just the "engineering of things" but also the "engineering of people" (Noble, 1977, pp. 263-264), a "technology of social production" (ibid., p. 258) to meet changed conditions.

Taylor argued that this was to be achieved by management acting upon three interconnected principles, namely:

• clarification and identification of the constituents of a job independently of the worker (i.e., defining precisely the job to be done rather than leaving the detailed arrangement to the hireling).
• separation of the conception of a job from its execution (i.e., distinguishing the thinking from the doing of work).
• use of knowledge of the labor process to control its execution.

Braverman put it thus:

if the first principle is the gathering together and development of knowledge of labor processes, and the second is the concentration of this knowledge as the exclusive province of management—together with its essential converse, the absence of such knowledge among the workers—then the third is the use of this monopoly over knowledge to control each step of the labor process and its mode of execution (Braverman, 1974, p. 119).

Taylor's principles boil down to emphasising that management must effectively manage by thoroughly *planning*, by preconceptualizing, the labor process, and they underline his legacy to succeeding generations of management as "the aggressive attempt to gain management control over the special knowledge of production" (Edwards, 1979, p. 104). Braverman exaggerates the degree to which management does achieve monopoly over knowledge of the labor process, but does encompass the key elements of Taylorism and identifies its importance.

This is why it is an injustice to criticize Braverman on the grounds that many of Taylor's arrangements were not put into practice. As Taylor himself observed, "piecework was really one of the comparatively unimportant elements of our system of management" (Taylor, 1947c, p. 6), the particulars of scientific management were secondary to the "complete mental revolution" (ibid., p. 27) which was entailed in the detailed planning of the work activity by management. Taylorism's contribution to management was to recognize that control of work in the modern organization called for least possible dependency on employees and this could be achieved only when work was "fully planned out by the management" (Taylor, 1947b, p. 34) to the extent that "there is hardly a single act or piece of work done by any workman in the shop which is not preceeded and followed by some act on the part of one of the men in the management" (Taylor, 1947c, pp. 44–45). There was nothing especially novel in what Taylor did in terms of incentive schemes or supervisory practices, as he himself acknowledged (1947b, pp. 139-140); but what was innovative was the message that management's role was

> the deliberate gathering in . . . of all of the great mass of traditional knowledge, which in the past has been in the heads of the workmen, and in the physical skill and knack of the workman, which he has acquired through years of experience. The duty of gathering in all of this great mass of traditional knowledge and then recording it, tabulating it, and, in many cases, finally reducing it to laws, rules, and even to mathematical formulae, is voluntarily assumed by the scientific managers (ibid., p. 40).

Industrial sociologists have claimed that the "chief innovation of Taylor consisted in measuring the time taken for each part of an operation instead of proceeding as others . . . had before him, to the measurement of the total time of an operation" (Friedman, 1955, p. 52). Our comments above make it clear that this, though a feature of Taylorism and the popular image of scientific management, is not our view. Nor is it what Harry Braverman regarded as Taylor's special contribution. What Braverman recognized was that Taylor drew attention to a need for management to control work in a new way, the prerequisite of which was detailed knowledge of its functions in order that "Any possible brain work should be removed from the shop and centered in the planning or laying-out department" (Taylor, 1947a, pp. 98-99). From this, "the key to scientific management" (Braverman, 1974, p. 113), could, and very likely would, follow precise measures of output, job fragmentation, specialisation, and the like. But the really distinguishing feature of Taylorism is the emphasis on planning as the sine qua non of management so that it could attain "control over work through the control over the *decisions that are made in the course of work*" (ibid., p. 107, original emphasis).

To be sure, some of Taylor's recommendations have not been carried out and some were no doubt misguided (Kakar, 1970), but this ought not to lead us to underestimate the significance of his thought, which is as much a matter of its being a sign of the changed conditions and requirements of American industry in the early years of the twentieth century (cf. Nelson, 1975) as its educative impact on managers. This qualification aside, and though few organizations adopted his principles hook, line, and sinker, thousands of plants did introduce elements of scientific management, and within the space of a decade or so it "had achieved a degree of popularity and acceptability that earlier proponents would not have foreseen in their most euphoric moments" (Nelson, 1980, p. 201; cf. Montgomery, 1979a, ch. 5).

But Taylorism is not reducible to a set of practices; its legacy is what Braverman discerns, a methodology for management which has so permeated the fabric of the modern corporation that it is taken for granted, a "basic philosophy of work organisation which has dominated the administration of work through to the present day" (Hill, 1981, p. 27). Its "fundamental teachings have become the bedrock of all work design" (Braverman, 1974, p. 87), and even the much vaunted (and marginal) instances of "job enrichment," "worker participation," and "human relations" industrial practices show little divergence from Taylor's principle that management's prerogative and purpose is control over the overall design of jobs, allocation of roles, and co-ordination of the enterprise.

A Dynamic of Deskilling

If we concede Braverman's interpretation of Taylor, then there does appear to be here what Craig Littler has called a "dynamic of deskilling" (Littler, 1982, p. 52). There is for instance an intent to deskill the worker when Taylor writes of his concern with "gathering in of knowledge which . . . has existed, but which was in an unclassified condition in the minds of workmen, and then the *reducing* of this knowledge to laws and rules and formulae" (Taylor, 1947c, p. 41, emphasis added). Given the impetus of management to extract the maximum return from the labor of its employees, it is likely that Taylor's claim "that the cost of production is lowered by separating the work of planning and the brain work as much as possible from the manual labor" (Taylor, 1947a, p. 121), in being met, will result in manual labor being allocated roles which have been designed to involve a modicum of intelligence, that assume and emphasize specialization of function, minimization of skill requirements, and reduction of training time (cf. Davis et al., 1972, pp. 65-82); all of which encourage the replacement of skilled by unskilled labor as well as facilitate the speed-up of work at the behest of management. Though we have stressed that Taylorism is primarily about control of work processes by managerial development of knowledge, diligent planning, and preconceptualization, and we can readily agree that this control can be exercised by a number of strategies (the carrot, the stick, the conscience, the persuasion. . .), it is empirically the case that managements have in the main operationalized their plans in terms which Taylor would have much approved—carefully designed routines, standardized procedures, specialized tasks, and similar "low trust" roles for employees, (cf. Fox, 1974). And here it is salutary to note that a recent survey of work design in forward-looking "experimental" manufacturing companies in Europe, where each design had been given "attention as an innovation in the improvement of work life," discovered that the overriding concern of the planners was with "efficiency and technical merit" (Lupton and Tanner, 1980, p. 231), while workers' conditions, experiences, and desires were well down the list of priorities. This, be it noted, in the organizations that are "forward-looking."

Organization and Technology as Values

Braverman's identification of Taylorism as a managerial attempt to wrest control of the labor process from workers by planning, designing, and conceptualizing it, by seeking a monopoly of knowledge of work, leads on to the claim that the technicalities of work organization are not simply matters of efficiency but rather expressions of domination. When a planning department introduces standardized modes of operation, when tasks are divided and subdivided, when each element is carefully costed and timed, then all of these organizational arrangements, specifications, rules, and procedures presented in the name of efficiency are in fact modes of continuing the subordination of workers and an attempt to better the return on investment of capital. Organizational techniques are value-laden: they are political.

Something else follows from this perspective. If management's search for control is discernable in organizational arrangements, it then follows that technological innovations, as products of management, are also expressions of the struggle for control, developments of planning departments which look for better ways of exploiting employees. In this light, machinery is to be regarded as part of the gathering in of knowledge of the labor process by management. It is to be perceived as the fruition of a planning operation whch has observed and even anticipated the labor process, discerned the skills necessary to effect production, and then moved to incorporate these as far as is practical into technologies. Machinery is therefore a logical concommitant of Taylorist organization, since it "offers to management the opportunity to do by wholly mechanical means that which it had previously attempted to do by organizational and disciplinary means" (Braverman, 1974, p. 195). Technologies thus are not to be regarded as separate from the rules of a work organization: both are expressions of Taylorist principles to be seen in unison—as the French put it, as la technique.

Fordism

Braverman argues that the organizational and technological arrangements of production lead characteristically to the deskilling of workers because the planners regard this as the best means of perpetuating their control. Henry Ford's automobile plant at Highland Park, Detriot may be taken as a classic instance of this process, whereby the operation of an intricate machine is rendered an unskilled occupation by organizing work of a highly specialized kind on assembly lines where machines themselves often undertake the skilled functions. Ford's development of the assembly line may be viewed at one level as the direct application of the Taylorist principle of division of labor into minute parts by a management, cognizant of the detail of the manufacturing process, which decides that the work can best be controlled by having many simple operations that can be performed by unskilled labor and paced by the speed of the line. However, at another level, the assembly line advanced upon Taylor by from the outset incorporating into machinery skills which otherwise would have to be done by labor. The following illustrates this duality:

> Go into Highland Park on a June day in 1914; pick out one of the simpler operations, the assembly of the front axle. . . . What would you see? A chain-driven assembly line, looking like a broad chute, encased in smooth sheet metal, moving slowly but inexorably forward; a series of axles, perhaps six feet apart, fastened securely to the chute; a continuous metal trough running

down its center, containing small components; on each side of the chute, intent workmen . . . doing just one job each to the axle which slowly moves towards them and slowly recedes.

You ask the boss, "How many operations?" If you have thought of the axle as a simple part, you are astonished by his reply, "Fifteen." Sure enough, you see men whose function is to join parts together and insert a bolt; others who put nuts on the bolts; others who tighten the bolt and insert cotter pins; one who uses a hand-lever arbor press to impose the inside ballbearing cone upon the stub-axle; and another who applies a more complicated machine to bring steering-arms and stub-axles into combination. The boss will tell you that each different component of the axle represents an elaborate amount of machine work. For example, the stub-axle connecting-rod yoke has undergone eleven different drillings, filings, reamings, millings, countersinkings, and the like in eight different machine tools before it reaches the assembly line. The boss will also inform you that everybody is constantly studying a further simplification of assembly line procedure. Thus the job of joining the steering-arm with the stub-axle was performed in three operations; the new machine does it in one! (Nevins, 1954, p. 505; cf. Beynon, 1973; Garson, 1977).

It was this phenomenon, Fordism, which heralded the arrival of what Edwards (1979, ch. 7) has appositely called "technical control" of work, an application of scientific management which controlled by way of machine-pacing of easily-replaceable unskilled labor that undertook the 7,882 different jobs in the factory (Ford, 1923, p. 108) where each operative was limited to one or two elementary tasks such that "The man who places a part does not fasten it. . . . The man who puts in a bolt does not put on the nut; the man who puts on the nut does not tighten it" (p. 83). We are not suggesting that the high technology and acute degree of division of labor characteristic of Ford's factories and motor-car manufacture in general were the only means of control of his work force (see Meyer, 1981, Ch. 5), but we are arguing that, in the years following the development of Taylorism, the adoption of flow-line assembly and advanced technology in the leading manufacturing enterprises can be viewed as an important extension of the basic principles of scientific management.

It is hard to disagree with Braverman that such developments have led to low-level work. The goal of capital accumulation is a continuous stimulant to deskill existent work, and though Braverman does not adequately deal with new occupations that may themselves be products of the needs of capital, it is clear that, in manufacture at least, where technology of a Fordist variant has made most inroads, low skilled work is the norm, because high technology has been planned for and accompanied by minimal requirements of worker initiative, know-how and sensitivity. A factory worker put the enigma thus in the mid-1960s:

Complicated new machinery doesn't make the worker's job any more rewarding: the effect is the opposite. Less, rather than more, skill is required. As machines grow more complex so they become more self-reliant. They need less looking after; and they get it (Fraser, 1968, p. 13).

The consequences ever since the diagnosis of "Forditis" (Meyer, 1981, p. 41) in terms of worker dissatisfaction, boredom, anguish, and alienation are commonplace. A result of this has been high levels of absenteeism, sabotage, apathy, and similar forms of resistance (see Ditton, 1972, 1979). In turn, management has tried the palliative, notably in times of full employment and worker insubordination, of a variety of Herzbergian "job-enrichment," "quality of working life" schemes (see Herzberg, 1968; Weir, 1976). Our view is that these attempts to remove alienation and engender commitment by bundling a number of soulless tasks should be seen not only as managerial strategies, carefully wrought plans, to better control in their interests when other factors make crude versions of Taylorism untenable, but also as isolated instances, as "exotic gardens in a desert" (Assen and Wester, 1980, p. 237) which, if tempting mirages to liberal academics and executives are arid from the perspective of the workers for whom they are devised (cf. Guest et al., 1980).

Information Technology and Scientific Management

I.T. can be regarded as a continuation of the application of Taylorist and Fordist principles in contemporary manufacture (Cooley, 1981a,b). The technological innovations currently being made in the automation of lines, robotics, computer numerical control, and the like can be seen as part of management's strategy to fulfil the twin goal of controlling work and upping production. The new technology can be viewed as an expression, a material embodiment, of management acting upon its thorough understanding of the labor requirements of modern production. This understanding displays both a suspicion of the labor force (that workers are unwilling to give their best) and a low priority in the design of jobs for the quality of work. It is only in this way that one can appreciate the language of Russell A. Heddon, president of Cross and Trecker Corporation, when he observes that computer-controlled machine tools are simply "taking more of the skill off the shop floor and putting it into the computer" (quoted in *Business Week*, August 3, 1981, p. 63). This is an attempt by management to increase its options for control—their computer will contain the skills once the domain of employees—and it illuminates a distrust of workers, though the changes in relations are almost always couched in terms of a more rational way of doing things.

Barry Wilkinson's writings (1983a,b) on microelectronics in engineering factories located in the West Midlands of England usefully emphasize that technological innovation is not the consequence of happen-chance discovery. He rejects studies that restrict analysis to the impacts of innovation, because these presuppose that technology has simply arrived on the scene to make its effects known as a more rational method. Against this "behavioural science," Wilkinson contends that technological innovations are matters of values, decisions, motives, and interests; that, prior to their arrival, social relations have influenced them. In this way, Wilkinson reveals that I.T. concerns human choices, but these choices are restricted to managements—those privileged people "with the power to choose, choices which reflect their intentions, ideology, social position, and relations with other people in society" (Noble, 1979, p. 19)—because the planning of innovations is their prerogative and is guided by their interests. Grasping this, one can recognize the extent of the permeation of Taylorism in our society: technology is nowadays the major characteristic of industry, and it is the outcome of management's study of the labor process, its knowledge of work, its plans for production.

Wilkinson's study of I.T. in modern factories is critical of Braverman's somewhat deterministic argument that organizational and technical changes automatically do down the worker. He stresses that technological innovation is a "negotiable phenomenon" (1983a, p. 94) not only between workers and managers, but also between varying managerial styles. To this extent he appropriately reminds us that technologies which potentially deskill may not necessarily be applied or applied in the most ruthless manner if managers do not consider that conditions merit such a course of action (cf., Jones, Bryn, 1982). Such decisions may be made on the basis of management having a sympathetic attitude towards employees; they may prefer the responsible autonomy of employees to the direct control of more strictly Fordist strategies (cf. Friedman, 1977); their actions may even be shaped by workplace traditions and attitudes (cf. Burawoy, 1979).

However, this qualification having been made—recognition that conditions on the grounds are complex and variable, and that a feature of Taylorism is that it allows for management options—Wilkinson's studies reinforce the fact that it is management which has the opportunity to "incorporate their perceived interests into the technical organisation of the factory at the expense of the workers' interests" (Wilkinson, 1983a, p. 92); that, when it comes to technological innovations, workers are always responding to management initiatives; that humane management is exceptional; and that, in conditions of recession when competitive edge is crucial, the urge to maximize output is likely to impel companies to take aboard technologies that will dictate the pace of work and, in deskilling the job, allow for faster production and cheapened wage rates, moving towards the position where the "ideal worker is essentially mediocre, working steadily at an average pace, accepting meekly the dictates of the technology" (Blackburn and Mann, 1979, p. 107).

Of his cases, Wilkinson is able to produce one optical company which is purposefully trying to avoid I.T. deskilling its labor force. This is in itself rare, but too much can be made of it. Perhaps most important is to realize that this small plant is out of step with the leading manufacturers for whom have been devised machines which make redundant the skills of lens makers, that this enclave of the industry is trying to alleviate the worst excesses of "a Tayloristic technology designed to deskill what is traditionally a craftsman's domain" (Wilkinson, 1983a, p. 47). The optical company's attempt to retain the dignity of its workers is not only out of step with its own industry; Wilkinson's work also shows that it is apart from the trends at other plants taking up I.T. Here there is an overwhelming desire to implement technologies which do deskill in order to seize or tighten control on the shop floor. The plating company which took on new technology primarily to weaken its employees may have been extreme in locating the controls of its new technology behind a wall "for no other reason than to prevent workers tampering with them, and management have made no secret of the fact that the intention is to wrest control of the plating process out of the hands of a problematic workforce" (ibid., p. 36), but its reasoning was much more in accord with the generality than the squeamish optical company.

Printing

The history of the printing industry provides another, notably sharp, instance of a decline in craft skills as a result of sustained technological innovation. A number of factors have combined in recent years to intensify competition in the British printing industry: the export market having been hard hit by the value of sterling, declining newspaper circulations, the spread of instant print shops, and in-house printing are just some of the reasons for the present situation. With wages taking up some 25% of costs in printing (Pike, 1980) and the unions having long ago established relatively favorable conditions (termed by some "restrictive practices"), it is not surprising that labor relations have become a focus of conflict in recent years. Much of the conflict has concerned technology which is seen by management as a means of ameliorating their positions at a time of stress. The potential of new printing technology is well in evidence in the United States, and it is a potential which many print workers in the U.K. fear.

The effect of the new technology has been to break down the skills of print workers, such as traditional setting of presses by replacement with computerized techniques, en route to finally by-passing printers altogether with direct entry by originators of text into automated systems (front end systems) of production. As we have observed, fewer print workers will be required in the future, but as this diminution is achieved the existant labor is seriously impacted. Already, I.T. is breaking down discreet skills that provided the basis for printers in Britain to have 10 separate craft unions in 1948—today only one remains (Gennard and Dunn, 1983, p. 17). The unions are now on the defensive as the foundations of their past control of productions processes—specialized knowledge—are undermined by technologies that incorporate their expertise (cf. Duhm and Mueckenberger, 1983).

In the early 1960s, Robert Blauner conducted an analysis of printers which argued that they "have a non-alienated relation to their work, which . . . recalls the craftmen of pre-industrial times" (Blauner, 1964, p. 35). "Work for craft printers," he went on, is "not a means to life, but an expression of their selfhood and identity" (p. 56). He documented their job security, their high degree of independence of supervision on the job, and the range of skill acquired over long apprenticeships which gave to printers a sense of "professional standards of the craft" such as a commitment to "quality workmanship" (p. 47), all of which traits identified the printer as an elite with "the highest level of freedom and control in the work process among all industrial workers today" (p. 56).

Blauner's description, arguably out of date even then, concluded with a prescient comment: "it is not certain how long printers can maintain this position, for technological innovations and economic developments threaten to eliminate not only the typesetter's control but the job itself" (Blauner, 1964, p. 57). Looking back, we can see that printers in Britain did hold to their position until recently, but conditions of recession, competition, and more determined management are rapidly taking printing from "a technologically conservative industry, whose production methods had remained relatively stable since the late 19th century . . . to one of the most technologically sophisticated industries, with a high reliance upon computers" (Martin, 1981, p. 335).

The consequences of "automated printing facilities that vastly undermine the traditional craft skills of hand compositors and linotype operators" (Wallace and Kalleberg, 1982, p. 321) are well documented (cf. Winsbury, 1975; Zimbalist, 1979). The major skill of the modern printer is typing, a far cry from the craft expertise of the compositing, plate-making, and presswork of the past, and a change particularly threatening because, being a feminine skill entering an overwhelmingly male trade, portends "girl-like status for the printers (see Cockburn, 1983): as a printer put it to Cockburn: "It took me six years, perhaps eight, to learn how to be a good comp and operator. You could take any competent typist from out on the street and I would maintain that within two months she could be doing my job" (ibid., p. 114).

In Britain, where the printing industry is highly organized, the resistance to innovation at management's behest from unions whose strength is their total control of what they do (Stansell, 1981) has been vigorous and has created an immense amount of opprobrium from advocates of "progress." To date, print workers, able to restrict entry to their occupations, have been able to retain the label skilled for work that is little more than typing, but this is only a holding operation, signifying a condition where the skill has been denuded from the worker yet the workers' combined strength has remained formidable. It is widely believed that "the print unions are fighting their last battle" (ibid.) against the apparently unstopable "tidal wave of changing techniques sweeping over this industry" (National Graphic Association, Assistant General Secretary, 1978, quoted in Gennard and Dunn, 1983, p. 20).

These developments are presented as merely a matter of technological progress, self-evident improvements that must be adopted. But such a presentation ignores the fact that they are evidence of an often fierce struggle between employers and employees to control the work process. Managements are introducing new print technologies because it restructures existent relations and weakens their dependency on what have at times been recalcitrant, and have always been expensive workers. New technologies are not simply brought in on grounds of efficiency, but more importantly to "further the interests of employers" who are "consciously motivated by profitability criteria" (Wallace and Kalleberg, 1982, p. 321). Today, the employers, strengthened by the growth of oligopoly and squeezed by competitors and recession, are able and willing to try to resolve their difficulties by the adoption of Fordist modes of production, by putting into place technologies that have been designed and developed to take over the functions of workers and reduce employers' reliance on skilled labor.

The Rise of White-Collar Work

We have seen that scientific management has found extensive application in industry, and that most of this has adopted Taylorist organizational techniques and Fordist technologies. However, there has been a development which has run parallel with this and which has been caused, in some degree, by it. We refer here to the growth of white-collar workers, perhaps the most observed sociological trend of the twentieth century. It was inherent in Taylor's advocacy of meticulous planning in order to take the conceptualization of work out of the control of the workforce that management would grow:

> This new division of work, this new share of the work assumed by those on the management's side, is so great that you will, I think, be able to understand it better in a numerical way when I tell you that in a machine shop, which, for instance, is doing an intricate business . . . [there] will[be] one man on the management's side to every three workmen; that is, this immense share of the work—one-third—has been deliberately taken out of the workman's hands and handed over to those on the management's side (Taylor, 1947c, p. 44).

Taylorism presupposes a battalion of overseers, measurers, plotters, and planners to investigate, design and supervise scientific ways of work and David Montgomery notes that "everywhere scientific management was introduced, it required a vast proliferation of supervisors" (Montgomery, 1979b, p. 10). Some idea of the scale of this expansion can be gained by recording the growth of supervisors at the Ford Motor Company: between 1914 and 1917, the number of men directed by a single foreman fell from an average of 53 to 15, a growth in supervisors of some 350% (Meyer, 1981, p. 56; cf. Arnold and Faurote, 1915).

Nowadays, about one-third of all employees in manufacture are white-collar workers. Of course this expansion is only in part the result of Taylorism. Within manufacturing companies, the growth of marketing staff has complemented the burgeoning number concerned with organizing and overseeing the labor process. In addition, the spread of local and national state employees—educationalists, social services employees, etc.—has contributed to a general rise in services sector employment which has resulted in almost half of the labor force now being nonmanual workers.

Fordism of the Office

This has presented a major problem for capital of escalating costs. We have already adduced reasons why the white-collar occupations are now being targeted as a prime area for automation, and in the following section we analyze its major victims—women. Here, however, we are at pains to thematize the problem of white-collar work for management as predominantly an issue which calls for changes in modes of control so as to allow nonmanual labor to be performed more cheaply. In anticipation of this, we are already being swamped by conferences and consultants' brochures promising to "solve the problem of office productivity" by carefully conceptualizing the information routines of nonmanual workers and supplying the requisite machinery to speed or reduce the information flow at a cost-effective rate. "The primary reason to plan at the corporate level is to increase profits by maximizing return on investments in office systems," states consultant R. W. Ketron as he urges' scientific management to enter the office (Ketron, 1980, p. 138). White-collar staff, those who once took over the conceptual skills of manual workers, are finding themselves being managed: "The men who applied Taylor to the workers are now themselves Taylorised" (Kumar, 1978, p. 293).

White-collar work is of course highly stratified, especially on lines of gender, which allows for different forms of control to be undertaken by management, but until recently the chief mode has been what Edwards (1979) has called "bureaucratic." That is, loyalty, application, and diligence have been attained by offering the white-collar worker a career pattern, annual increments, a high degree of informality in terms of dress, time-keeping, and generally superior conditions of employment.

There are signs that this is changing as what might be termed the Fordism of white-collar work is undertaken by means of I.T. This builds upon and consolidates a good deal of the Taylorist managerial arrangements that already have been applied in the larger offices over past decades, as "management experts of the second and third generation after Taylor erased the distinction between work in factories and work in offices, and analyzed work into simple motion components" (Braverman, 1974, p. 319). Given the variation of size and circumstances of white-collar work, any complementing of Taylorist administration by technical control will inevitably be variable, and this itself assumes that efforts have previously been made to seriously detail the labor processes of offices. But what is for sure is that, as the price of I.T. continues to fall and costs of office staff rise, there will be sustained attempts made at rationalizing office work. As this is undertaken, it will be the least-skilled lower-level forms of work which will suffer Fordism. Those furthest down the road, those in which "the conversion of the office routine into a factory-like process in accordance with the precepts of modern management" (Braverman, 1974, p. 347) is most established, those which already have a high degree of specialization of function, numbers enough to attract economies of scale, and a significant penetration of technology, will advance most rapidly. It is for this reason that major innovations are being made in government agencies, finance houses, banks, insurance companies, large corporations, and the like, where work can be surveyed and then readily structured into repetitive and quantifiable tasks which facilitate the use of machinery (Duncan, 1981, pp. 191-198).

Elmer Staats, Comptroller General of the U.S.A., evoked the scientific management assumptions behind recent developments in an address to the 1980 Federal Office Automation Conference in Washington. Here he called upon management "to carefully *plan and monitor* the organizational and behavioral changes that will occur as offices move further toward automation." When Staats offered "six elements for effective use of office automation as a productivity tool," we witness as paramount the Taylorian precepts of management as the conceptualizer and workers the executioners of whatever is planned for them by those thirsting after more productivity. Thus:

1. *productivity improvement* must become a goal of every agency.
2. proper evaluation of office systems must be completed and procedures streamlined *before* proceeding with the development of office automation systems.
3. *cost* benefit and *cost* effective studies of the most appropriate technologies should be conducted.
4. the human and user interface with the technologies must be *well planned* in the development of new systems.
5. an evaluation of the system's impact on *productivity* and delivery of services should be conducted.
6. top management must be committed to the development and effective use of these systems (*Datamation*, January, 1981, pp. 67–68, emphases added).

Fordism of office work is the "outcome of deliberate planning by work-design specialists" (Salaman, 1981, p. 119) whose concern is not with improving the lot of the workers but with getting maximum return from their labor. To this end, they will carefully monitor labor processes, then plan to make those function to best effect. Today the work designers have technology, where before their main resource was organizational arrangement. In the past, their resolutions were in accord with those recommended by Taylor: specialization, routinization, fragmentation. Building upon these innovations have appeared the I.T. consultants who announce that skills of workers can now be built into machinery (spelling, calculation, filing, etc.). As this occurs, the office worker is set to repeat the pattern of the factory worker: machines will perform the skilled tasks and the worker, following its dictates on some specialized function, will be reduced to the role of a "feeder": "At this stage clerical work becomes manual work" (Salaman, 1981, p. 119).

Consequences of office work which is highly structured and automated are easily predicted. As with manufacture, when scientific management intrudes, the most likely applications are roles that are repetitive and tedious and technologies which take away the initiative of workers. The work is low in skill, mundane, and dissatisfying. Already there are signs that the estrangement this engenders in office workers can constitute a "people problem" (*Datamation*, Jan., 1981, p. 71) which can negatively affect production. As on the factory line, the white-collar workers can become sullen and uncooperative when faced with machinery which "requires people to do things in new ways, to be more orderly and disciplined, to follow more structural procedures, to give up a lot of comfortable habitual ways of doing things in order to gain advantages in efficiency and control" (Bambrough, 1980, p. 19).

Worker dissatisfaction is of course not a worry of management—until it intrudes upon performance. Consultant Clive Malpas-Sands, however, whispers disquiet that office automation may be proceeding too much on the Fordist lines in trying to achieve technological solutions to the problem of productivity while still requiring worker input to be effective. "Most dangerous of all," he notes, "this automated process inevitably attacks the traditional method of carrying out tasks without considering the possibility of worker alienation" (*Computing,* 9 July, 1981). And another consultant responds with advice which is currently in vogue: "for sustained productivity . . . you need a mix of discretionary and repetitive jobs (because) you must get people involved" (*Datamation,* January, 1981, p. 71). Part of this involvement—which never extends to the design of technologies and allocation of any but the most lowly of roles—is the massive propaganda campaign we are undergoing celebrating the progressive wonders of I.T. No doubt another element will be the employment of labor relations experts, ergonomists, and the like to stimulate participation, inculcate a sense of belonging, and encourage adjustment to machinery which has been developed to perform labor processes more effectively than people.

Scientific Management and Computing

Using I.T. as a means of Fordism of office work can present problems for management. Roger W. Ketron, a senior consultant with Citibank's Systems Consulting Services, outlines some when, describing the "centralized data processing system" of the Continential Bank of Illinois (a centrally managed and controlled facility which provides remote access to terminals distributed throughout the company's international offices) as "the least expensive method in the long run for providing automation to a large organization" for both data and text handling, he observes that the "Implementation of this approach requires strong central control of all information processing." There is nothing in this with which most managers would disagree: the centralized system would give them immediate access to their whole network; it would place employees at the behest of whatever software was applied at the core; it could isolate the terminal operators and reduce them to the role of feeders of a distant system over which they have no control. It "may alienate various sectors of the organization" as they find themselves by-passed and ignorant of the workings of the organization, and, as we have seen, this can cause difficulties for companies if their staff are dissatisfied, but this is not the major problem of such a system, the attraction of which is enormous for an organization which wants to thoroughly plan and implement strategy through its information system. The real snag is that the system "fosters a tremendous dependence upon one part of the organization—the information processing division—since the technicians in the central computing facility are the only ones who can maintain the required complicated systems." Our consultant wryly adds that "Such dependence may not ultimately be healthy for the overall organization" (Ketron, 1980, p. 140). The problem with I.T. as a tool to attack the problem of office productivity is that it requires construction and operation by another group of workers that is given power over an entire organization. I.T. might well be the deskiller of a great deal of white-collar work, but to implement the technology which does the deskilling requires computer workers.

In Britain, the potential of computer programmers in particular was illustrated during the 1979 Civil Service dispute. The unions involved in this affair, groups representing chiefly clerical and administrative workers, withdrew only a few key members working in computer centers which serviced the whole civil service network. The "action soon paralysed the whole operation" of the civil service, though the unions were able to continue to pay the wages of these key colleagues out of contributions from the vast majority who were still employed, though unable to do much because the computer system went down (*Computing*, October 14, 1982, p. 24).

Managements are well aware of this power grouping and have "made it clear that they [are] not willing to leave the on the job behavior of their programmers to either luck or goodwill or even to constant barrages of company propaganda" (Kraft, 1977, p. 7). They therefore respond in a variety of ways. Perhaps the most common reaction is that adopted by the Civil Service itself, which makes pay awards to computer workers above that of their colleagues in an effort to separate them from fellow employees. Another tack is to form a back-up system which can be brought into operation should the primary system to threatened. According to *Computing* "Many organisations such as banks and airlines already have fully manned back-up installations which duplicate the workload of the main system" (October 14, 1982, p. 25).

However, these are really only short-term and superficial responses to the problem of computer workers being indispensible because of their specialized knowledge. More fundamental resolutions are being developed to reduce the difficulty which involve applying Taylorist principles to occupations that themselves are major agencies of Taylorism. That is, over the last generation or so, though more urgently in recent years, managers, aware of the power (and related cost) of computer staff, have looked concertedly at their work in an effort to detail its constituents and from the strategic position of this knowledge to commence wresting control from computer personnel by the practices of routinization, specialization, and standardization—familiar Taylorist procedures—and even by applying computer technology itself where feasible. The story of this endeavor has been one of a sustained and often successful attempt to deskill computer work in a battle for control which, as Joan Greenbaum claims, has seen the occupation "transformed from worker-regulated processes to management-controlled tasks" (Greenbaum, 1979, p. 13). It is worthwhile looking more closely at this history, since it illustrates the "dynamic of deskilling" on a white-collar, professional group that is surrounded with an aura of high tech which much comment suggests will be a source for skilled and satisfying jobs in the future.

Philip Kraft argues that the history of computing has been one of a determined "effort by computer makers and buyers to find social and technical ways of routinizing the work and deskilling the worker" (Kraft, 1979b, p. 140). He observes that, in the early days (shortly after the Second World War), to be in computers was to be working at the highest reaches of professional skill, perhaps even to be a "programmer artist," with "a machine-language programmer . . . [being] someone comfortable with abstract logic, with mathematics, with electrical circuits and machines, and often with some substantive field as well, e.g., aerodynamics or cost-accounting" (ibid., p. 142). Because of its novelty and embryonic state, there was also an "absence of a clear-cut division of labor in the programming workplace: every programmer did more or less the same thing as every other programmer" (Kraft, 1979a, p. 5). Not surprisingly, in this situation computer experts were in short supply, could indulge in considerable job changing, and enjoyed premium salaries (Greenbaum, 1979, Ch. 2).

From a manager's point of view, this was chaos; there was a growing need for computer workers, management was not at all sure of what they did, they were expensive and liable to leave whenever it suited them, and there were few standards, so that, if a key worker did leave, a whole operation could be jeopardized. Some discipline, some control, had to be introduced. The first major step to bring computer work within management's domain was to initiate the separation of roles of systems analyst from that of programmer, an instance of the commencement of the division between conceptualizer—the person whose job was to liase with customers to define needs, requirements, and feasibility—from that of performer of the more mechanical task of putting detailed instructions into the machine. Later, this separation, an early effort to divide head and hand, was refined by the further division of operator from programmer, whose job was to undertake the most routine and repetitive actions of coding. It need scarcely be said that, in the pioneering days, these distinctions were fluid, but the point is that they were the start of a managerial attempt to rationalize on its terms. Part of this strategy for control was also the very real differences of salary scales, status, and authority accreditations which over the years were increasingly formalized.

There was also developed a number of high-level languages, notably Cobol and Fortran, that enabled the separation of programming operations from knowledge of the engineering of the computer itself. With the establishment of distinct programming languages packaged/canned programs could be provided for common applications, such as payroll calculations, that, though requiring considerable expertise in their design and creation, were to be used by operators with minimal computer knowledge, which in turn increased the division of labor within the computer field by expanding the employment of low skilled computer workers such as applications programmers. Packages were soon available for many routine programs which would be put into use by operators with but a few months' training in computing.

There was still lacking a means of standardizing the production of programs themselves. This was becoming an increasingly acute problem as the costs of software rocketed and of hardware fell, while the demand for applications rapidly rose. As an answer to this difficulty—how to increase the productivity and reliability of programmers—"structured programming" was begun and continues to be refined. In essence, this is a means of producing computer programs by following rules that are both detailed and specified. It entails breaking down complex problems into successively larger number of less complex ones, until a stage is reached where a solution to each problem can be shown to be mathematically correct. Structured programming is "not so much a language as a method of using a language. The programmer is told what instructions to use, what logic to follow, and what routines to insert in the program" (Greenbaum, 1979, p. 181). At a further stage, the instructions can be separated into sub-elements (modules) which are also standardized but amenable to preparation by more specialized, more easily trained and less skilled personnel.

> Structured programming, in short, is the software manager's answer to the assembly line, minus the conveyor belt but with all the other essential features of a mass production workplace: a standardized product made in a standardized way by people who do the same limited tasks over and over without knowing (or needing to know) how they fit into the larger undertaking (Kraft, 1979b, p. 149).

The assertion of managerial control over computer work by the division of labor, standardization of task, creation of precise rules of procedure, etc.—processes which have entailed an overall deskilling of the profession—is ongoing, and we do not want to suggest that programming is as yet a rudimentary skill. Computer work has undergone such an explosive growth in applications and personnel that attempts at scientific management of the industry have inevitably only been partially successful (cf., Cornford and Friedman, 1984, p. 23). But the point is that the harnessing of the labor under management's control started long ago, and that already there are signs of the results. Many computer workers possess but an aura of skill: their daily work is little more than specialized clerical labor.

Attempts to control computer work continue. In a twin strategy of making computers user friendly—useable by the general public with a minimal amount of instruction—and simplifying the production of programs themselves to make the work possible for nonexpert, easily-replaceable, and cheaper labor, efforts are being made to manufacture software which allows almost anyone to program. To this end, the British government in 1983 pledged £350 million to the creation of the fifth generation computers. These will, among other things, incorporate artificial intelligence in the machines, thereby by-passing much programmers' work by embodying it in the design stage. And this is not a future possibility. James Martin, upon hearing of Alvey's plans, castigated its spending of public monies to produce software already available. "Use-it," Martin claimed, was a facility already available which designs mathematically correct systems and generates bug-free codes to run them. Martin added that this would unavoidably reduce present requirements for programmers, observing that "programmers are happy to automate other people's jobs but unhappy when it comes to automating their own" (*Computing*, May 26, 1983, p. 4).

In another instance, the *New Scientist* (29 July, 1982) quotes the then head of I.C.L., Rod Wilmot, as having "an objective of increasing the productivity of the data processing department and allowing the individual to get direct access to data," a two-pronged strategy which means that, on the one hand, the "sort of productivity yardsticks once applied only to factory workers are now being thrust on white-collar software experts [as] their employers are measuring programmers' industry in terms of the number of lines of code they produce or the hours they spend each day on their terminals." and, on the other, that by supplying software of a particular kind to "senior managers [they] can by-pass programmers altogether." The question of how skilled programmers can be compelled to "make applications programmes in one tenth the time that it takes using existing I.C.L. systems tools" while managers lacking computing skills can by-pass their own programmers is answered by the "data dictionary" I.C.L. has produced, which contains two packages—one a "systems software" package, the other a "standard software" package. The data dictionary is a creation drawn from previous models of business computer requirements, and can be used to "simplify the production of new programs by both experts and the people who are actually going to use them." It is, in sum, an elaborate package which makes the application of computers a matter of effective use of a dictionary rather than thorough mastery of a language.

I.C.L. is not alone in attacking the hold of computer professionals. A recent report in the *Financial Times* (21 September 1983) tells us that I.B.M. is well on the way to "moving its computing emphasis out of the data centre and towards the individual manager." Noting the frustrations currently experienced by managers dealing with the traditional data processing professional (jargon, little sense of urgency...) and realizing that many executives would undertake their own computing if the procedures to do so were readily available and comprehensible, I.B.M. has "made available through its computer services operation simple ways in which executives could carry out their own computing." Results of this endeavor are a new software named "Intellect" which make possible computer use by a manager "in exactly the same language as the thought in his mind," i.e., allowing "natural English communication between men and machine" within a training period of just one week. "Intellect," complemented by cheaper and more versatile hardware and other advanced software means, of course, that the data processing center—and the experts operating in that center—are relegated in importance.

Of course, these examples are of trends which are still in process, and we do not want to suggest that programmers are about to be made extinct. Clearly, packages can only be created to allow the by-passing of computer workers and/or the reduction of programming itself to a mundane task where tasks are predictable and more or less standard. And, though the user friendly systems are becoming increasingly sophisticated, the expertise of programmers will be necessary in many specialist functions. Yet the signs are clear, despite the need for these qualifications. Work fragmentation and general deskilling of programming will continue, not because of technological imperatives, but because of management's need to achieve the best possible return on investment, a goal that requires wresting control from a group of employees which, left alone, will prove expensive and possibly obstructive. This is all the more acute nowadays, when the costs of software outstrip those of computer hardware by anything from five to ten times. In this situation, the managerial response of "how can we get more for less out of our programmers?"—

and the consequences of trying to by-pass, simplify, or specialize their functions—were predictable. To the extent that Taylorian principles of management—"gathering in of knowledge which . . . has existed . . . in the minds of workmen, and then the reducing of this knowledge to laws and rules and formulae"—find application in computer work, it is only the most recent "of white collar occupations to be forced into conventional industrial moulds" (Kraft, 1977, p. 98). By the same token, it is no surprise that many computer workers "complain of boredom, lack of interest, and the loss of self-esteem" (Greenbaum, 1979, p. 163).

The Fordism of Professions?

Though it is undoubted that the major applications of I.T. will be found in the least skilled and therefore most readily mechanized jobs (those with little to lose are most likely to lose it), the application of Taylorist and Fordist techniques in computer work does suggest that some work currently considered professional could be endangered. Mike Cooley offers a number of examples, ranging from university teaching and architectural design to medical practice, where computers which incorporate the skills of professionals find application (Cooley, 1981a). There are many others where one could envisage I.T. leading to the downgrading of a profession, the most prominent of which perhaps is school-teaching, where computer-assisted learning could substitute for teachers, and some sort of "assistant" could fulfil the role of overseer of the children. We offer another case to exemplify the capability of I.T. to take over the skills of a profession, both to illuminate its dangers and because its practitioners appear complacent about the situation.

The profession of librarianship has been much excited by the advent of I.T. in general and the development of online information services in particular. The idea of an information society has an obvious attraction to those at the center of information collection and dissemination, and the thought of vast data banks which can be remotely accessed is appealing to anyone interested in such work. The librarianship profession finds itself in a maelstrom of change in traditional practices, with anything and everything from cataloguing methods through to book issue affected by new technology. A widespread feeling among librarians is that they will emerge from this with an advanced, high tech image that will mark an end to the unworldly and undervalued stereotypes of old (Williams, 1978).

Brian Nielson (1980) finds this especially the case among online librarians. Currently, anyone wanting to make use of such a facility must approach a librarian skilled in the operation of automated retrieval systems, aware of the names and locations of data base sources, access protocols, command languages, system features, and indexing and coding practices of the requisite data bases. In addition, the librarian will need to be au fait with the user's discipline, capable of helping him or her formalize and narrow their inquiry for the exercise. Because of this, the online librarian currently receives much status from users who are dependent upon his or her expertise as the gatekeeper of the system. Moreover, the librarian finds the situation flattering because he or she is also required to spend lengthy periods interviewing clients in order to prepare search requests–a classical professional characteristic.

All of this is appealing to the librarianship profession, since it promises more skills and a enhancement of image in the eyes of clients. However, what mars the picture is that it ignores the motive behind the development of online facilities, one which is determindly seeking to make the systems user-friendly, seeking to mechanize functions currently performed by librarians. Though at the moment online information retrieval is a specialized task, there are already available "options capable of guiding a child through the mechanics of a search" (Magrill, 1978, p. 78), and programs are under way to make these systems even more transparent. Online is fitting into a familiar pattern; high technology leads to simplification of use. And the reasons are obvious: the vendors of online systems and the data banks which they access want to sell to more than just libraries and have their eyes set on markets such as corporations that could need to purchase their information. Similarly, libraries incur major expenses on their professional staff; a reduction in dependency, the replacement of professional staff by assistants with minimal training, would clearly cut these costs.

These innovations presage a time when online users will avoid having to enter libraries altogether. In the meantime, they are a sign that technologies, if temporarily requiring skilled intermediaries, are set to have built into them levels of sophistication which will make professional skill unnecessary. A result will surely be that the professional online librarian role will be reduced to that of a typist keying in details for the user, en route to ultimate redundancy. In this way, it will follow the path of other librarianship skills, notably cataloguing, which are increasingly produced at a central source and bought ready prepared by others who wish to adopt them.

Technological Innovation, Social Change and Skill

It has been our thesis that technological developments are to be seen as part of the growth of scientific management, the crucial characteristic of which is an impulse to control work by monopolizing its conception and that this does not necessitate the details of Taylorism–specialization of task, time and motion schedules, etc.– since these are options that may or may not be put into practice. However, the instances we have cited, and it appears almost wherever else one looks, reveal that the implementation of management strategies have had negative effects for skill of workers, and that they have been brought in on Taylorist lines of routinization, standardization, and fragmentation, often to the accompaniment of use of machines which subsume workers' skills. Wherever feasible, scientific management has brought about organizational and technological arrangements which have resulted in working people being machine-paced, having to endure repetitive work in highly structured roles, and experiencing deeply-felt alienation.

We ought not to be surprised by this. Changes in manufacture, in office work, in computing itself, and even in the employment of professionals are not intended to benefit those on the payroll. They are conceived and developed outside of their control to increase the return, to better the efficiency, of the organization. That such rationalization might mean a diminution of skill and satisfaction among the workforce is beside the point so long as they do not adversely affect output.

It is worth emphasizing here that the majority of people in our society have minimal levels of skill, because it flies in the face of a received wisdom which tells us that all new technology is progress that somehow upgrades its operators, and which labels almost anyone going to work wearing a jacket and tie "professional" and those working with complex machinery as "skilled." Krishan Kumar reminds us of "one of the commoner ideological features of industrial society, whereby social processes are disguised by formal acts of reclassification and re-labelling" (Kumar, 1978, p. 262), such that all workers associated with technology, in whatever capacity and with whatever skill, are considered at least semi-skilled. Just because of this—and nothing more than changes of classification—there has been this century a massive decrease in "unskilled" workers and increase in "semi-skilled." Against this twaddle, it is salutary to note the research of Blackburn and Mann which, looking at some 75 to 80% of the male manual workforce in Peterborough, found that 87% of these men used less technical skill in their jobs than they would have required in driving to work, and that "most of them expend more mental effort and resourcefulness in getting to work than in doing their jobs" (Blackburn and Mann, 1979, pp. 121, 280). And it is hardly possible to blame these men for not trying to extend themselves. On the contrary, challengingly skilled jobs for the bulk were simply unavailable: since 85% of these workers had the capability to do 95% of all the jobs, any individual choice was restricted to different kinds of "Mickey Mouse" work.

Braverman is most effective in puncturing the inflated sense of "skill" so much heard from the proponents of the knowledge society. Amidst all the talk of a need to equip the forthcoming generation with skills, the like of which the older generation can scarcely conceive, it is sobering to be reminded that "It is only in the world of census statistics . . . that an assembly line worker is presumed to have greater skill than a fisherman or oysterman, the forklift operator greater skill than the longshoreman, the parking lot attendant greater skill than the lumberman or raftsman" (Braverman, 1974, p. 430); that the categorization of much nonmanual work as "professional" disguises the fact that the mass of these are low-level clerical employees. Detailed evidence of a fall in skill may be hard to gather, but the decline in apprenticeship periods from between 7 and 5 years to 2 or 3 years, and British Goverment Training Centres where a trade such as electrician or plumber can be learned in 6 months, are suggestive of it and ought to be set against the persistent complaint of managers that they cannot get skilled laborers. To be sure, 6 months can give someone a skill (or, as Braverman would have it, "dexterity") compared to the uninitiated, but Braverman is right to rage against the demeaning of the word when nowadays

> the worker is considered to possess a "skill" if his or her job requires a few days' or weeks' training, several months of training is regarded as unusually

demanding, and the job that calls for a learning period of six months or a year—such as computer programming—inspires a paroxysm of awe (Braverman, 1974, p. 444).

On similar lines, it may surprise, but it is nevertheless the case, that in spite of heady calls for a massive expansion of education for forthcoming information work, in spite of the image of future generations emerging from our schools with an abundance of skills, we already have a problem of *over-education* for the jobs that are available. As early as the late 1960s, Ivar Berg (1970) argued that this was the case, and more recently Randall Collins (1979) has reiterated that, apart from a few key professions, the skills required of jobs are learned after entry to those jobs and not at the schools (cf. Rumberger, 1981). Credentials, certification, call it what you will, the connection between educational diplomas and the requirements of available jobs is at best tenuous. There may be little doubt that paper qualifications are required to gain entry to a job, but as a rule the work itself has little if any need of them (Burris, 1983). That one requires some formal qualification for almost any occupation nowadays is bitterly ironic in view of the minimal levels of skills most of them require.

But this image of a fall from grace, a collapse of the skilled artisan, cannot altogether be sustained. The very fact that scientific management assisted the rise of white-collar workers challenges the generalization of declining skill in an uninterrupted way. There is a "dynamic of deskilling" which is powered by the impulse of employers to reduce costs, but this does not mean that new, even skilled, roles are not created, though these may themselves be rationalized later on. If this was not the case, we would be hard put to explain the genesis, under capitalism, of occupations such as computer science. Moreover, we can also recognize that, notably within the service sector but also in manufacture, there has been a significant increase in professionals among the rapid rise of white-collar occupations. A glance around at occupations such as accountancy, law, science and technology, social work, and education readily reveals that there has not been a decline of skill across the board. In an age when the title "professional" is ascribed to almost anyone from army recruits to car salesmen to brain surgeons, the word has been demeaned, but some social changes have brought into being what are unarguably highly skilled occupations, and have expanded considerably some already established at the turn of the century. In the U.S., for instance, "professional and technical" occupations grew as a proportion of the total workforce from 4% in 1900 to 15% by 1970 (Dunlop and Galenson, 1978, p. 25, Table 1.11; Ginzberg, 1979), while in Britain, Guy Routh has calculated that "professionals" grew from 4% in 1911 to 11% by 1971 (Routh, 1980, p. 5), and the 1981 census recorded that 27% of the British labor force was "managerial and professional." Though we would quibble with definitions, there is no denying that there has been both a proportional and absolute expansion in professional work, which must lead one to conclude that, while many jobs have been deskilled, notably in manufacture, there has also been some increase in skilled work.

We think this has neither compensated for the loss of skills in the bulk of occupations nor that much of this is safe from deskilling by "scientific management." Yet is it possible that rapid growth of a particular occupational sphere can mean that, in the midst of scientific management being applied, there can still be an absolute growth of skilled personnel. This appears to be the case with computing, where there has been such a demand for the work that absolute numbers of skilled people, notably systems analysts, have increased at the same time as the work as a whole has been deskilled by division of labor, routine, and the like. Indeed, while programming packages have been developed to simplify computer operations and to increase the productivity of programmers in particular, demand has been such that the numbers of systems analysts needed to examine situations and prepare procedures for computer applications have grown dramatically. Because of the pace of take-up of computers even programmers have expanded while being Taylorized, but analysts have increased even faster.

Mechanization and Automation

With these observations we can return to our discussion of mechanization and automation and the debate between Marxian and Weberian interpretation of change. It is important because proponents of the distinction between mechanization and automation would sweep aside the gloomy picture we have drawn with the optimistic assertion that technological change heralds a better quality of working life in the long term. The crux of this position is that change is a matter of rationalization which, if having unpleasant consequences for some people in the short term, will not permanently disadvantage them. On the contrary, it sees in the evolution of the professions the prospect of an upgrading of low-skilled work which will be subsumed by machinery at the same time as compensated for by more professional labor. Frederick Taylor was an enthusiast of this position, voicing the belief that scientific management, if negatively affecting some jobs, would open up opportunities for workers to better themselves. Thus the

> demand for men of originality and brains was never so great as it is now, and the modern subdivision of labor, instead of dwarfing men, enables them all along the line to rise to a higher plane of efficiency, involving at the same time more brain work and less monotony. The type of man who was formerly a day laborer and digging dirt is now for instance making shoes in a shoe factory. The dirt handling is done by Italians or Hungarians (Taylor, 1947a, pp. 146–147).

A more attractive version of this is that of the "utopia of automation" (Salaman, 1981, p. 117) which leads to an upgrading of the skill of the worker because high technology integrates a number of mechanical tasks, thereby giving control over a system to the worker who can then exercise discretion, initiative, and a range of intellectual abilities where appropriate:

> automation increases the worker's control over his work process and checks the further division of labor and growth of large factories. The result is

meaningful work in a more cohesive, integrated industrial climate (Blauner, 1964, p. 182).

If mechanization, even of skilled tasks, can be taken to such an extent as to automate a process which will leave workers in control of an entire system demanding greater skill in generally more pleasant conditions, then is this not a positive development, a reskilling trend which should be encouraged even if having unfortunate side-effects in the short term? In addition, since automation will integrate what are tedious and isolated jobs—for example assembly line work—is it not arrogant and callous to resist it since it will free workers from tedium? Moreover, even if automation leads to there being less people employed in particular occupations, then there is no need to worry because the increased productivity it allows will pay for other professional vacancies, notably in services, which have been growing throughout the century.

There are three retorts to this prospect. The first is the obvious point that automation at the expense of large numbers of jobs is scarcely a viable choice for many people, especially at a time of depression. It is asking a great deal of employees that they take on trust that professional jobs will be produced to compensate those displaced by automation. And it ignores the potential of these jobs to be negatively impacted by technologies. The second objection is to challenge the distinction that is drawn between mechanization and automation. The presentation of the two as alternatives is only supportable at an abstract level, and, in practice a line is hard to draw. There will be some circumstances in which innovation will allow a few workers to retain enhanced control, perhaps with extra skills, in charge of a system, but more common has been the introduction of technologies which do automate a great deal of work, but which require a worker to perform rudimentary tasks as an adjunct of the machine (Bright, 1958). Indeed, this has been our case where we have argued that Fordism is a variant of scientific management which involves the embodiment of workers' skills in machines. This is usually accompanied by a high level of division of labor (mechanization), but, as the technologies have been developed on Fordist lines, these divisions have been reduced *without* making the worker's job more satisfying. Those left still perform rudimentary tasks on a machine which incorporates more and more of a production process.

The third cirticism is to challenge the view that automation, when achieved, does appreciably increase the skill and satisfaction of work. Blauner's example was process work in a chemical plant, highly automated systems handled by central controls where workers monitor automatic systems, adjusting dials, gauges, and valves as required. The image is one of expertise, education and work satisfaction. Theo Nichols and Huw Beynon castigate this "sociological stereotype" and offer a very different finding in their study of a large chemical producer. For a start, they discovered that "control room operatives" were a minority of the work force: "For every man who watched dials another maintained the plants, another was a lorry driver and another two humped bags or shovelled muck" (Nichols and Beynon, 1977, p. 12). Blauner's heroes, those who monitored production technologies, were certainly better off than the majority who did "donkey work"—"everybody knows that" (p. 21)—but their work induced tension, was tedious, boring, lonely, done on a shift basis, and trained for on the job with skills limited to the particular process for which they had been instructed (pp. 18-29). The "scientific workers" performing this automated work scarcely found contentment in their labor, and the findings of Nichols and Beynon suggest that the future—the automated future—will be familiar: bored workers guided by written instructions watching the dials of a system which is alien to them.

Conclusion

Seeing I.T. as an integral element of the spread of scientific management deeper into both manual and nonmanual labor, we cannot be sanguine as to its effects. Its introduction has nothing to do with improving the quality of working life, just about everything to do with assisting the greater efficiency of the organizations within which it is applied. To this end, managements, true to Taylor and Ford, have initiated and developed I.T. as a key component of control of the labor process. Undoubtedly, there will be some cases of an increase in skill resulting from adoption of I.T., possibly where a work force is decimated and those remaining learn new ways of operation, but the bulk will be a well-known kind: machine-pacing, diminution of worker initiative, a pervasive sense of alienation.

We are aware that the emphasis of our analysis towards managerial strategies of control has underplayed both the significance of resistance at the workplace to these changes and the part played by people's orientation to work in responding to new technologies. We are conscious that experiences at school, political conditions, family expectations, personal ambitions, and the like influence and shape responses to events in the office and factory. We return to these issues, but would make a preliminary observation at this stage of our account. Generally experienced as alienating and threatening to those targeted in manual and nonmanual work, across the board the response to innovation seems to be one of resignation when faced with what appears to be unstopable, but this is especially so in white-collar sectors where "helplessness and hopelessness" (Prandy et al., 1982, p. 180) is prevalent. This is particularly the case as regards women, who are both most vulnerable to technological assaults on their work and more likely to attach low importance to their labor, seeing it "very much secondary to being a wife and mother" (Beynon and Blackburn, 1972, p. 148). Because women have been allocated the least rewarding, most menial and mundane work in office and factory, it is important to recognize that scientific management has been directed chiefly at them. At the same time, men, notably in office employment which has expanded rapidly and taken aboard a disproportionate number of women at the lower levels, have been able to enjoy relatively privileged conditions—especially so in promotion which they have gained over the heads of women as white-collar work has grown— even while Taylorist methods have been impacting on that sector (Stewart et al., 1980, Chs. 6-7). These gender divisions call for further examination.

I.T. and Women

At both ends of the job scale women are struggling: many are finding themselves thrown onto a hostile labour market, displaced from the older dying industries and with no new skills to offer or prospect of retraining.

Others are becoming increasingly aware that their once secure office jobs are now in jeopardy—threatened by the "savings" of new technology, and new "traps" in the shape of homeworking are opening up.

Still others, working within the data processing industry, are reporting that the recession is bringing with it reactionary attitudes to women at work—especially those in senior positions with young children.

—*Computing*, 7 October, 1982.

Fifty-one percent of the British population is female. About one-fifth of this is under the age of 16 and a further eighth is retired. Almost all of the remainder of women fall into one of two categories, either "economically active" (working or seeking work) or "housewife." Since men hardly ever are homemakers, while 26% of women are housewives, it is not surprising to find that only 37% of all females were economically active in 1981, compared to 59% of males (*Labor Force Survey, 1982*, Table 4.3, p. 14). However, for women aged over 16 the proportion economically active rises to 47%, and for those between the ages of 16 and 65 it is in excess of 60% (*Social Trends, 1983*, Table 4.3, p. 52). Notwithstanding the questionable assumption that housework is economically insignificant (Oakley, 1974, 1981), that women in 1981 accounted for 40% of the total British work force is undoubtedly an important proportion (cf. Mackie and Pattullo, 1977).

Increase in Women's Economic Activity

One of the most commonly observed social trends in recent years is an increasing propensity for women to work (Manley and Sawbridge, 1980). All manner of statistics highlight this development, though in truth the growth of women's participation in the labor force can be exaggerated. Their proportion of the labor force was 30% in 1911 (Wainwright, 1978, Table 3.2), and 70 years later it had extended only another 10%. In spite of this qualification, there has been an especially marked increase in female employment since the Second World War, notably between the 1960s and mid-1970s when the female proportion of the total leaped from 32.5% in 1961 to hover around 40%. This trend is shared by other advanced societies (I L O, 1976)—and indeed globally, women represent about 35% of the work force (Seguret, 1983, p. 295). For example, in 1960, 33% of the American labor force was composed of women, and this had risen to 42% by 1980 (Hacker, 1983a, p. 130; cf. *OECD Observer*, March 1983).

In Britain, the total labor force grew from 18.4 million in 1911 to 26.1 million in 1981. This was in part due to a steady growth in population, but is not the main explanation. The key factor has been changes in economic activity rates of the sexes. In 1931, 91% of men over the age of 15 were economically active. By 1981, although total numbers of economically active men had risen from 14.8 million to 15.5 million, this had not kept pace with the growth in the adult male population (which had risen from 16.3 million to 19.9 million), and only 78% of adult males were economically active. Conversely, while, in 1931, 34% of adult women were economically active, by 1981 47% were in such a position, and the total figures for economically active females had risen from 6.3 million to 10.5 million (out of a total of adult females which had expanded from 18.3 million to 21.7 million). What this means is that, over a period of 50 years, while the labor force grew 24% (21 million to 26 million) women accounted for 84% of this rise and their contribution had far outpaced anything that could be accounted for by demographic rates.

Married Women's Increased Economic Activity

Women's increased activity in the labor force has been due to the growth of married women's participation. Thus, between 1931 and 1981, while 4 million extra females became economically active, the number of economically active married women increased during the same period by 5.7 million (Brown, 1978, Table 2.2), the imbalance being the result of the greater popularity of marriage nowadays (Thompson and Hunter, 1978, p. 86). Such has been the significance of married women's entry to the labor force that an increase of over 2 million in between 1961 and 1981 was entirely due to their increased participation (*Social Trends,* **13**, 1983, p. 51).

By 1981, some 65% of economically active females were married (*Labour Force Survey,* 1982, Table 4.2), compared to 15% in 1931 (Brown, 1978, Table 2.2). These figures are complemented by the proportions of married women who work, there having been a steady and sustained increase over the last half century from 10% in 1931, 22% in 1951, 42% in 1971, to 49% in 1981. There has been some stabilization of this increase in recent years, consequent upon increased fertility rates and lower employment opportunities due to the recession (*Employment Gazette,* February, 1983, p. 51).

Economically active married women cross all age groups, and the rising proportions are not restricted to any stage in the life cycle. Hence, between 1961 and 1979, when the activity rate overall rose from 30 to 50% for married women, for those aged 20 to 24 the increase was from 41 to 59%, for those 25 to 44 it was 33 to 59%, and for those over sixty from 7 to 10% (*Social Trends,* **13**, 1983, Table 4.3). These figures encompass the child-bearing years, so it is not surprising to learn that a clear majority (54%) of women—married or nonmarried—with dependent children work (*General Household Survey 1980,* 1982, Table 5.7, p. 97). In turn, these statistics underline the fact that "the increase in female participation is not due entirely to greater numbers of young women entering the labor market, but far more to women re-entering after having children and those staying in the labor market without interruption" (*OECD Observer,* March 1983, p. 29). This is an international trend (Scott, 1982, p. 146).

Women's Jobs

If women, and married women in particular, account for a large segment of the labor force nowadays, what sort of work do they do and where is their work located? Looking at employment on an industry basis, we find that, in 1981, while the service sector in Britain accounted for 62% of all employees, some 78% of female workers were in this sector where they constituted 54% of total employment (*Employment Gazette,* December 1982, Table 1, p. 505). Women have been closely connected with the expansion of the service sector, which grew some 30% between 1960 and the late 1970s. For example, between 1951 and 1981 an additional 3.2 million (46%) women became economically active in Britain, while 2.5 million (56%) extra women found employment in the service sector, 78% of the increased economic activity of women being absorbed by the growth of service industries. This is again an international trend, where women in advanced societies are disproportionately in service employment (Werneke, 1983, pp. 28-29; OECD, 1979, Ch. 1).

Women are not only concentrated in the service sector, they are also disproportionately found in certain occupations (see Hakim, 1978, 1979, 1981). Though not substitutional, there is a close connection between the expansion of the service sector and white-collar occupations (Kumar, 1978, pp. 206-208). By 1981, the service industries accounted for in excess of 60% of employment. Since we know that about half of all workers in that year were white-collar and that 30% of employees in manufacturing were of this kind, we can estimate that more than three-quarters of all white-collar work is now located in the service sector (calculated from *Employment Gazette,* December 1982, p. 505; Central Statistical Office, 1983, Table 6.4). Because the "expansion of the service economy, with its emphasis on office work, education, and government, has naturally brought about a shift to white-collar occupations" (Bell, 1976, p. 17), and because this has been accompanied by the growth of female employment, it is to be expected that women largely have taken on white-collar jobs. By 1981, 61% of women's employment was of a nonmanual kind, and women accounted for 53% of all nonmanual workers (*Labour Force Survey,* 1982, Table 4.8, p. 17).

Women may be a majority of white-collar workers, but they are not randomly distributed among white-collar occupations. Indeed, the largest category of female white-collar work is "clerical and related," which accounts for about one-third of all women's work, 40% of the work of women in full-time employment (*Employment Gazette,* November 1982, p. 481), and three-quarters of which is performed by women. Figures such as these indicate that women occupy the lowest ranks of white-collar work: for example, while 32% of women employees were "clerical and related" in 1981, only 7% of men were so, and, while 42% of women were in the lower ranks of white-collar labor, only 13% of men were so. Put otherwise, 70% of clerical and related and other nonmanual occupations were held by women, compared to their occupancy of 35% of "managerial and professional" posts (*Labour Force Survey*, 1982, Table 4.8).

For these reasons, the shift towards white-collar work, which has readily been acclaimed by post-industrial theorists as indicative of a new professional information age, should be seen as the spread predominantly of low-level nonmanual labor of a "white-blouse" kind (Westergaard and Resler, 1975, p. 291). Clerical work has risen from 30% of all white-collar work (and 5% of all occupations) in 1911 to 37% (14% of all labor) by 1971, during which period the proportion of women in clerical work rose from 20% to 70% (calculated from Routh, 1980, Table 1.1, pp. 6-7, 24-26). The 1981 *Labour Force Survey* found that 46% of all white-collar jobs were classifiable as "clerical and related and other nonmanual occupations," of which the vast majority was performed by women.

Female overrepresentation on the lower rungs of white-collar work is highlighted by analysis of occupations in terms of male and female constitution. Typists, shorthand writers, and secretaries are almost totally (99%) female; office machine operators are 86% female; clerks and cashiers 62%, and so on (cf. Dex and Perry, 1984). A similar pattern is evident in the nonindustrial civil service, where, in 1982, women accounted for 81% (97,038) of "clerical assistants" and 61% (113,399) of "clerical officers," which are the two lowest grades; conversely, women accounted for tiny proportions of the top grades, such as 3% at deputy secretary, 5% under secretary, 7% principal, and zero at permanent secretary (Management and Personnel Office, 1983, Table 2, p. 12). The story is much the same in the U.S., where, in 1980, 35% of all women's work was clerical (and 80% of all clerical work was undertaken by women), while just 17% was professional and technical, and 7% managerial and administrative, with 99% of secretaries, 97% of typists, 96% of keypunch operators, 93% of bank tellers, and 90% of billing clerks and bookkeepers being women (Hacker, 1983a, pp. 127-131). And the pattern is similar in all advanced societies (cf., Werneke, 1983, pp. 29-31; I L O, 1976).

Women and Part-Time Work

Women are not merely concentrated in low-level, white-collar work, they also constitute a high proportion of part-time employment. Indeed, in excess of 90% of part-time work is female and over 40% of all women workers are part-timers. While part-time work accounts for 20% of total work only 2% is performed by men, the remainder being undertaken by women (*Employment Gazette*, November 1982, Table 5, p. 481). This ought not to be surprising in view of the very large numbers of married women who work while they take major responsibility for family arrangements, but it is significant that, while married women accounted for 27% of all people in employment in 1981 and two-thirds of all women employees, 53% of them worked 30 hours or less per week, which is the official measure of part-time work. As such, married women undertook over 80% of part-time employment

(*Labour Force Survey,* 1982, Tables 4.6, 4.9). This compared with 4% of men who worked less then 30 hours per week, one-third of whom were over retirement age (*Employment Gazette,* November 1982, p. 477). For women, part-time work is on the increase having expanded 26% between 1971 and 1981 (ibid.).

Part-time work is concentrated in particular occupations, with catering, cleaning, hairdressing, and related jobs accounting for 39% of all female part-time work, and the next largest category is "clerical and related," where 20% of women's part-time work is located (ibid.). Britain appears to have an especially high proportion of part-time female workers, though in E.E.C. countries, on the average, almost a quarter of women are part-time (Robertson and Briggs, 1979, p. 677), in the United States the figure is about one-third (Hacker, 1983a, p. 118), and everywhere female part-time work is extensive (Seguret, 1983, p. 297).

Remuneration

Women earn less than men. The following figures, taken from the 1982 *New Earnings Survey,* illustrate a well documented phenomenon. In April, 1982 men who worked full-time in nonmanual occupations averaged £178 for 38.2 hours per week, while women in full-time nonmanual employment earned £104 for 36.5 hours per week. Women, therefore, received 58% of the male weekly wage and 61% of the hourly rate. Though total figures are less in manual occupations, the differentials between the sexes are similar, with women receiving 60% of the male weekly wage and 68% of the hourly rate (*New Earnings Survey,* 1983, Part D, Tables 86–87). For all full-time work, women receive about two-thirds the weekly reward of men, slightly more (72%) on an hourly basis. While women who work full-time lag behind men, those in part-time employ—two in five of all employed women—do even less well. In nonmanual occupations, part-time women receive just over half the hourly rate for men and 83% that of their full-time female colleagues (Webb, 1982, Table 6.5, p. 121). In the U.S., Hacker reports that full-time female job-holders in 1981 earned 59% of their male equivalents (Hacker, 1983b, p. 27). In Britain, the proportion of income going to the female sex seems not to have markedly altered since the mid-1970s (Webb, 1982, pp. 123–124), while in the United States it has held steady since 1960 (Hacker, 1983b, p. 28).

Women and Trade Unionism

Women are underrepresented in trade unions (Aldred, 1981). It is true that unionism amongst women increased until the late 1970s as part of the general expansion of organized labor and greater female economic activity (cf. Bain and Price, 1972; Price and Bain, 1976). Nonetheless, while 63% of men in Britain were unionized by 1979, only 40% of women were in the same position (Price and Bain, 1983, Table 3). Since white-collar occupations are less unionized than manual jobs (by 1979, about 40% of trade unionists were nonmanual, with a density rate of 44% in white-collar employment), and women are mainly found working in these posts, their lower level of organization is to be expected (cf. Coote and Kellner, 1980). Britain is of course somewhat unusual in having over half of its work force unionized. Even so, the sexual disparity is evident in the United States, where 23% of employed workers are unionized, though only 16% of women are organized (Hacker, 1983a, p. 137).

Even where women are unionized, they are underrepresented in union structures, such that, even where they constitute a majority of members, they usually command only a tiny minority of full-time positions (Wainwright, 1978, Table 3.14) and never more than 20% (Webb, 1982, pp. 154–160). Low rates of female participation in trade unions, expressed in terms of membership, attendance at meetings, service in official positions, or whatever, are readily explained in Britain by the large amount of part-time work which is undertaken by women that necessarily excludes them from many aspects of the work environment and, more generally, by the imposition on women of major responsibility for domestic arrangements (cf. Myrdal and Klein, 1956). That the 25-34 age group are least unionized is easily understood in the light of the constraints of domesticity at a time when women are most likely to have young children on their hands. Whatever may be the explanation that women are not well organized makes them especially vulnerable on the labor market.

Women and Unemployment

According to *Social Trends* (13, 1983, Table 4.13), women comprised 29% of the unemployed in 1981. Since they then accounted for 40% of the work force, it would appear that they are more resilient to the recession than men (cf. Niemi in Amsden, 1980, pp. 325–349). However, this prima facie case requires qualification, first by the fact that women's unemployment is often underestimated because of the disproportionate number of women who do not register as unemployed. In Britain, if one does not register as unemployed, then one is not so categorized, though for many women there is little point in registering their worklessness because they are due no benefits from the state. The *Employment Gazette* (June, 1983, pp. 265–267) estimates that 400,000 (16% of the total unemployed) fail to register their unemployment, of which 68% is female.

The *Labour Force Survey* of 1981, when assessing unemployment rates, accounted for nonregistration. On this basis, it found that 37% of the unemployed were women and that 9% of women were unemployed, compared with 9.9% of men. While this would appear to more or less equalize male and female experiences of worklessness, there are disturbing signs that women's positions are especially vulnerable. To date, service sector employment has been less hard hit by recession than manufacturing, with the latter accounting for three-quarters of all confirmed redundancies in Britain between 1977-1982, when rates of labor reductions in manufacture vastly outstripped those in services (*Employment Gazette,* June, 1983, pp. 245–56). Though textiles and clothing, manufacturing industries in which women are 59% of all employees (*Employment Gazette,* December, 1982, Table 5, p. 508), have been badly hit, and women situated there disproportionately so (Huws, 1982a, pp. 55–61), that the service sector has been relatively spared the ravages of the recession has proved to have been a bulwark for female employment. The effects of recession being sectorally unequal has meant that, because the distribution of male and female employment is also sectorally unequal, it is men who have predominantly been at the sharp end of closures and labor reductions. In this case, however, what requires explanation is why women's unemployment represents such a high proportion as 37%, when services, where three-quarters of all women work, have been relatively unscathed. The answer must be that, though sectoral divisions are protecting women's jobs at one level, at another women are being displaced before men. The perception here of discrimination against women is made more disturbing in view of the service sector having stopped expanding in recent years, and concerted attempts being made to cut down on labor there.

Women on the Labor Market

There are some who see women's role in the expansion of service industries and white-collar work as the commencement of a "female-centered economy" (Bell, 1976, p. 146) which is identified as an ingredient of "post-industrial society." Moreover, new technology, assisting the coming of the information age in which nonmanual, professional work predominates and services abound, also promises a time when women will have the same opportunities as men, because the "post-industrial society, in its initial logic, is a meritocracy" (ibid., p. 409). Still others, echoing Professor Bell, foresee new technology offering to upgrade female work, to lift it from the ruck of semi-skilled labor, by for example changing the role of the personal secretary to that of "administrative secretary," which anticipates a time when "secretarial jobs will soon require a master's degree in business administration and will be regarded as an entry level into management" (Bird, 1980, pp. 48–49).

Against the ways in which post-industrial writers take up certain superficial features of social trends to project a meritocratic and professional future, we emphasize the characteristics of female labor reviewed above. It is true that women account for most of the expansion of the work force and now constitute 40% of the total, that they chiefly perform nonmanual work in the service sector. But to construct a social theory and future scenario on the basis of these trends, without looking more closely at their characteristics, is a calumny. Peering beneath the surface, one sees that women's work is performed in the lower rungs of the hierarchy of jobs, is concentrated in a limited range of occupations, is 40% part-time, undertaken mostly by married women, is poorly paid relative to men, and is underrepresented in trade unions. In addition, women "tend to monopolize occupations which not only have a low economic return, but which are lacking in subsidiary economic benefits, have limited security of tenure, and offer little in the way of chances of promotion" (Giddens, 1981a, p. 288). Moreover, the bulk of women's work—54% falls into just two occupational categories, "clerical and related" (31%)

and "personal services" (23%) (*Employment Gazette,* November, 1982, Table 5, p. 481)–is "typically feminine," an extension of woman's domestic role such that, whether office wife, waitress, or cleaner they are performing services that are characteristically subordinate to men, roles which presuppose men occupy the leading posts that require being cared for (cf. Beechey, 1977). Such work is amongst the least skilled across the range of occupations, and serves to illustrate that women work on the periphery, their jobs located in a "secondary labor market" (Edwards, 1979, p. 167), where they are systematically disadvantaged (Beck et al., 1980). In all of this, there are few if any signs of an impending meritocracy.

There is another reason why we have gone to some length in this section to stress the ascertainable features of female employment. It is an oppositional point, aimed at the surfeit of talk which goes on and on about the potentialities of I.T., the choices that it offers our society. It is one which emphasizes that I.T. will be introduced into a preconstructed social context. This focus switches attention from what I.T. can do towards the issue of which ways the existent society shapes I.T. In this way, it counters futurism's glib rendition of choices by insisting on the limits received conditions place on the implementation–and even imagination–of alternatives. In the key sphere of work, the fact of women's subordination is the overwhelming social reality into which I.T. is being introduced. Assessment of I.T.'s likely impact has to come to terms with this practicality, the hic et nunc of women's inferiority (cf. Kahn-Hut et al., 1982).

There is something else to note about women's work. Though the popular image of the machine worker is one of the male, in fact a somewhat greater proportion of women work with machines (Form and McMillen, 1983, p. 154). The data in support of this statement come from the United States, but there is no reason to suppose that it differs markedly in other advanced societies, and at the least we can be sure that a large majority of women use machinery in their work. In short, women are already familiar in their employment with machinery, its adoption is no new thing to them, and further mechanization will build upon an established foundation. We would add to this two further observations. First, technological innovations have never been introduced with random effects on the work force. This has been the case historically and remains so today. Technology has most impact– enough of an impact to dictate the pace of work, remove initiative from the operative, or even to do away with a need for an operative–upon workers whose labor is most routine, fragmented, and unskilled, or, at the least, whose work is amenable to division in such ways that it can be made unskilled and thereby open to mechanization. Second, and connected, women are concentrated into occupations which are in general of low skill. It follows from this and the other weaknesses of women that they are a ready target for technological rationalization (Turner, 1980). Moreover, while it is possible that the very cheapness of female labor may be a barrier to technical displacement–and however derisory this sort of reasoning, a factor delimiting the introduction of machinery can be an abundance of cheap labor–it hardly needs stating that, in a period of economic stringency, even the cheap, especially if they are unresisting or unable to resist, are expendable. It is with these points in mind that we turn directly to examination of I.T.'s implications for women, agreeing and indeed insisting that "the vulnerability of many women's jobs to microelectronics is a function of the types of work women do" (Arnold et al., 1982, p. 120), that women's weak position in the labor market makes it likely that they will be adversely affected by I.T.

I.T. and Women's Jobs

Numerous writers have noted that women's work is endangered by I.T. (cf. Downing, 1980, 1983; Barker and Downing, 1980; West, 1982; Werneke, 1982; Bird, 1980; Huws, 1982a, b; Arnold et al., 1982). No one suggests that all women's occupations are equally at risk or even that all are at risk, but it is because women disproportionately work in low-skilled, most often white-collar occupations where they deal routinely with information that their labor has every likelihood of being automated. In addition, commentators, discerning the preponderance of white-collar work in the service sector, believe that it is especially this—particularly the lower-level, least skilled white-collar work in this sphere—which will be mechanized now and in the immediate future; thus the European Trade Union Institute states: "Because of the high proportion of women in tertiary sector jobs the disproportionate impact of technological change upon tertiary sector employment will have a disproportionate impact on women's employment" (European Trade Union Institute, 1979, p. 102).

Undoubtedly their weaknesses vis-à-vis employers (the accepted norms of feminine behavior, the high rate of part-time employment, the low level of unionization, the common view that married women are a "soft option" for cutting jobs because their right to earn their own living is not fully accepted) are important contributory factors, but that so much women's work is especially susceptible to take-over by I.T. is the major cause of concern. As low-skilled information workers, women are most readily replaced by technologies the purposes of which are to better handle information. It is primarily for this reason that trade unions, especially those with a high female membership, have been quick to sound the alarm bell, deducing from the available evidence that "aggregate employment in occupations traditionally filled by women, at present levels of workload, could fall substantially as a result of technological innovation" (T U C, September 1979, para. 62, p. 26).

In the following pages, we give most attention to the effect of I.T. on women's work of a white-collar kind, and, as such, our focus sectorally is the service industries where most nonmanual labor is located. However, though it receives much less attention than the service sector, there is evidence that in manufacturing, where 19% of women in Britain find employment, 60% of whom work at the semi- and unskilled levels like assembly line operation, I.T. is not only reducing jobs but also that where "new technology is introduced into mixed workplaces, women's jobs are much more likely to be affected than men's jobs" (Huws, 1982a, p. 105). This is in line with the point made previously that women, sectorally protected from the recession, appear to do particularly badly in terms of overall unemployment because of sexual discrimination.

Routine White-Collar Work, I.T., and Women

I.T. promises to usurp many office functions currently performed by women: transcribing, storing, retrieving, calculating, and the like will be reduced as new technology enters office work in a big way. We have already drawn attention to the vulnerability of office work to I.T. (see pages 140-143) and may note that to date "the preponderance of evidence is pessimistic" (Werneke, 1983, p. 60) as to the effects of I.T. on females in low-level, white-collar work. A widespread feeling is that the "majority of women office workers will not find their jobs more interesting; many will find they have no job at all, and the majority who remain in office work will find they are subject to new, more intense and depersonalized forms of control" (Downing, 1983, p. 40). These effects are by now fairly well documented, and, insofar as they are common to other low-skilled work, have been examined in the previous section of this chapter.

For the purposes of focusing on the new technology's implications for women, it is appropriate that we amplify them here.

Job Loss in Office Work

Earlier, we offered reasons why offices are on the brink of major automation (see pages 140-143), which boil down to a search for maximum efficiency, for increased productivity, and for greater control of the information factory. Characteristic reasoning of the office automation advisors is that new technology is at last cost effective when set against wage rates. For example, Mackintosh consultants reported in 1980 that, while secretarial labor had been increasing at a compound interest rate of over 15% since 1975 and postage costs by over 20%, the price of electronic mail devices had been moving in the opposite direction. The attractions of new technology for cost-conscious employers soon becomes irresistible in these circumstances. Of course technology is not absent from contemporary offices, but recent innovations mark a big leap forward in office automation, while the sphere has long been, relative to manufacture, short of mechanization. Judith Wainwright reviews:

> To date, the average "modern" commercial organization has computerized approximately 20% of its information, using conventional data processing. The remainder contains large amounts of textual information which is expected to be tackled by the next generation of computer systems—office systems. Word processing, currently a rapidly growing area, is the base through which many of these systems will evolve (Wainwright, 1982, p. 22).

Numerous estimates of the amount of job loss have shown a range from single figure percentages upwards to 30 and 40%. No one has come forward with evidence (or even with strenuous assertion) that suggests that office employment is set to expand appreciably. Behind all these projections lies the reality that it is primarily female jobs that are at risk, that the spread of I.T. will "have a particular critical importance for working women" (McLean and Rush, 1978, p. 44). Given the distribution of office work by sex, this could scarcely be otherwise. An I.T. consultancy underscores this point in producing the diagram shown in Figure 1, which represents the distribution of office personnel by number. Recalling that the overwhelming majority of secretaries, typists, clerks, and cashiers are women, and that these occupations, being the least skilled and most predictable in terms of function, are more readily automated, it is abundantly clear that the most likely candidates for displacement by I.T. in the office are women.

As we have previously observed, the impact of I.T. will be variable, subject to differences of office size, particulars of operation, market position, and even regional labor distribution (Bird, 1980, Figures 9-10, pp. 28-29), but the overall direction of change and the areas of job losses appear fixed.

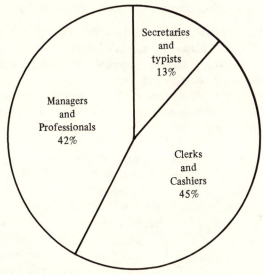

Figure 1. Distribution of office workers by number (Infotech, 1980, p. 52)

A reduction in office jobs for women is especially worrisome because, as Hazel Downing notes, "office work stands out as perhaps the cream of the choice, offering clean, comfortable, respectable work with the possibility of promotion up through the secretarial hierarchy" (Downing, 1980, p. 275). To make this statement is not to glamorize the female office worker as "a modernized Horatio Alger heroine" (Mills, 1953, p. xi), and in truth much of such labor is dull, repetitious, and stupifying, but it is to acknowledge that where work options for women are decidedly few, then the choice between an operative on the assembly line at an electronics factory, charring for the better off, or secretarial work is easily made in favor of the latter. To intrude upon opportunities for women in the area which is most attractive to that sex is therefore especially serious.

Natural Wastage

A recurrent theme of commentators is that, though office jobs performed by women will be reduced by I.T., there is some consolation to be found in the fact that in "the great majority of cases, these job losses are taking place by natural wastage, rather than actual redundancies" (Huws, 1982a, p. 105). Frances McMahon is not unusual in reporting from her survey that

> In all the cases I studied not a single person was made redundant. The jobs were reduced by natural wastage. When a person left the company they were simply not replaced. Thus the net number of secretarial and typing jobs is continually reduced even though no one can actually say "I was made redundant by word processing". . . . It works the other way as well. Fewer new typing jobs are being created. Instead, when companies need more productivity they simply purchase another word processor (McMahon, 1980, p. 38).

This does have a mollifying effect on those directly involved, since no one is declared redundant against his or her expressed wishes (which is not to say that subtle and not so subtle pressures are not applied, for example by older employees being urged to voluntarily retire in order to save the posts of younger colleagues with family responsibilities). It is because it blunts the pain of those personnel who must encounter a reduction in complement that trade unions in Britain invariably attempt to negotiate "natural wastage" as the means of achieving targets set by management.

However, as regards women especially, the euphemism is pernicious, since it can operate only because of the peculiar features of their employment. This is to refer to the high turnover of women in work, frequently observed, and having obvious causes such as the demands of child-birth, women's responsibility for children and aged parents, or the priority of a husband's work which may require women to give up their own jobs to move with their spouse's career. It is because of the fluidity of female employment that policies of natural wastage can be more or less readily implemented, but while superficially satisfactory because it averts much unpleasantness and confrontation, it has attendant dangers. It is not a more humane managerial strategy for tackling a diminution of staff, some carefully devised plan of enlightened firms, but simply a product of the peculiarities of women's employment. Ostensibly a means of treating women considerately, it represents a draining of the pool of female jobs which to date has been necessary to allow women to find work in circumstances that result in their entering and leaving employment at more regular intervals than men. As the total pool is reduced, those women leaving posts by natural wastage will find it correspondingly more difficult to achieve entry elsewhere.

Organizational Change

It is a commonplace of advisors on office automation that direct substitution of workers by machinery is usually untenable. To maximize efficiency considerable reorganization of office functions and personnel ought to accompany the introduction of new technology (cf. Sachs, 1981; Mertes, 1981). To date, office reorganization has of itself been a major means of increasing efficiency, with staff being elaborately divided according to tasks in order to allow for standardization of procedures which are a prerequisite for increased productivity. In turn, such organization has encouraged the development of machinery to perform what are elementary tasks (Mills, 1953, pp. 192-193). To this extent, technology and organizational change have developed symbiotically, though machinery has historically lagged behind organizational rearrangements.

The need to harmonize organizational change and technological innovation is well illustrated by Texaco's restructuring of its London offices. The replacement of conventional electric typewriters by word processors did not of itself bring about the increases in productivity of an order such that, from 750 staff being serviced by 100 secretaries in 1977, by 1982 1000 staff could be adequately serviced by 70 employees located in administrative support centers. To reach a level of 30% reduction of secretaries, 150 managers at Texaco had to give up their personal secretaries—or, rather, 150 secretaries had to be taken away from their one-to-one relationships with their superiors in separate offices and reallocated where they could be more productively using modern technology. Texaco looked at the traditional office functions in their London offices and observed that the "army of secretaries" was being used inefficiently, because up to 80% of their time was being taken up with nontyping duties such as dictation, figure work, making coffee, and travelling back and forth to the photocopying center. A change to administrative support centers was the determined upon source: the consequence of these capital intensive sectors was greater efficiency at Texaco—and a lot more typing from the relocated specialized secretaries who more than managed to cover for the one-third of their colleagues who had left (Kransdorff, 1982).

Deskilling

The organizational changes that accompany technological innovation in the office have major consequences for the workers. The Texaco case makes this evident, and it does not take much imagination to envisage the typical daily work of women in administrative support centers. Not only can employment itself be jeopardized by these developments, but also I.T. can lead to greater specialization (more typing, less of the variety of traditional office work), machine-pacing, and less skill required by the operative (Downing, 1980, 1983). The new technology, introduced into an appropriately designed "factory office" (Braverman, 1974, p. 299), removes a great deal of the diversity from office work as maximum efficiency is aimed for, and the operative is kept busy in the word processing center. In addition skills of office workers—knowledge of filing systems, well-produced typing, shorthand, ability to spell, numeracy—become less necessary as technology is able to incorporate these abilities (for example, by audio dictation, electronic typewriters, central processing, or pre-programmed word processors):

Typists, mail sorters, telephone operators, stock clerks, receptionists, payroll and timekeeping clerks, shipping and receiving clerks are subjected to routines, more or less mechanized according to current possibilities, that strip them of their former grasp of even a limited amount of office automation, divest them of the need or ability to understand and decide, and make of them so many mechanical eyes, fingers, and voices whose functioning is, insofar as possible, predetermined by both rules and machinery (Braverman, 1974, p. 340).

It is most common to illustrate deskilling of office work by pointing to secretarial functions, but it extends much further across the range of office jobs, for example the development of online systems in banking, insurance, and building societies undermine requirements of numeracy and calculation as transactions are fully automated, with the customer being dealt with by an employee whose job is only to key into the terminal a name, account number, and particulars of the deal. All the detail is done by the central processing unit (calculation of interest, balance, and the like).

It may seem paradoxical, but it is the case that the splendid new technologies aimed at the office require less skill from their operators. Undoubtedly, the new machines are awesome at the outset and a period of training is required before they can be effectively used. Yet this is generally short, of a few days duration, and once procedures are mastered it is possible to see that losses in the range of function have taken place as the expensive technology demands intensive use to justify investment, and that it has had built into it skills that were once the province of the operative. The manufacturers of I.T. make no secret of this, Fujitsu, for example, stating in its 1982 report that

> In modern society the trend is towards even more sophisticated and highly integrated computer and communications networks. At the same time, the trend is toward more sophisticated interfaces for more simplified operation of the equipment that accesses and connects these systems (Fujitsu Ltd., *Annual Report*, 1982, p. 4).

And I.B.M. makes much the same point when defining word processing—the centerpiece of the office of the future—as "the simplification and improvement of traditional typing, secretarial, and clerical functions through a managed system of people, procedures, and modern office equipment" (quoted in NALGO, 1980, p. 14).

We may save ourselves repeating much of our earlier comment on the work implications of I.T. consequent upon this most recent development of Fordism by reviewing tenets of a paper—*The Impact of Office Automation upon Job Content and Function*—by Leela Damodaran, an ergonomist employed at the Human Sciences and Advanced Technology Research Group of Loughborough University. Damodaran (1980) presents a diagrammatic representation of the job requirement changes in secretarial work which follow the adoption of word processors (Figure 2). The specialization, and narrowing, of function is obvious here, though

Figure 2.

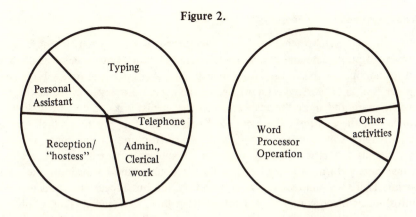

Damodaran goes further in clarifying the meaning of I.T. when she tabulates a number of "characteristics of a successful word processor operator." For those who consider that the specialization contingent upon the use of word processors is not necessarily restrictive—after all, a range of tedious activities can be happily replaced by a single stimulating and challenging one—these are revealing. They include:

- preference for working with machines rather that with people.
- willingness to remain at a work station for prolonged periods of time.
- low vulnerability to distraction by noise and activity around them.
- ability to work under pressure of time deadlines.
- accustomed to close monitoring of output.
- ability to translate accurately from dictation.

These are assurances that office work in the age of I.T. will be stultifying for many of the operatives. We would add that we find unacceptable any suggestion that these are traits natural to women—though already dormant myths are being revived that women are suited by nimble fingers and an ideal temperament which is passive, patient, and painstaking (Scott, 1982, p. 140). While we reject the idea that the makeup of women fits them to the demands of I.T., we do accept that the qualities required of many future office workers will be those of an ability to accept machine-pacing, to accede to close supervision, the persevere with rarely-interrupted keying. As Glenn and Feldberg presciently put it:

> old skills have been made trivial and opportunities to develop new skills have been reduced. Such traditional specialities as stenography and book-keeping, which require extensive training, have been displaced or simplified beyond recognition. The skills now required are more *mechanical*, as in operating a xerox machine, *lower level*, as in typing addresses on automatically typed correspondence, and/or *more technical and narrow*, as in the administrative support center (Glenn and Feldberg, 1979, p. 61, original emphasis).

Mental versus Manual Labor

This recalls an earlier theme of this chapter, that it has long been an aim of management to perpetuate and extend the division between mental and manual labor, and to monopolize the former. That management seeks to retain for itself the conceptual aspects of work, the knowledge of the overall processes, while making the workers more and more "hands" who perform menial tasks, is not for reasons of caprice. On the contrary, there are solid reasons for this situation which revolve around capital's attempt to best effect its return from investment. Since a factor, often the major factor, of outlay is the cost of labor, it is evident that the ambition to maximize return will require that the optimum value be made of the labor process. There are numerous ways of achieving this, but a recurrent one is to wrest control—or as much control as is feasible—from those performing labor. Control is a matter of seizing the initiative, of making oneself less dependent upon one's employees, and a key way is to break down the skills, especially those reposited in brains, of those in one's hire. Major ways of achieving this are to fragment a job by specialization and to routinize its functions. As this is effected, as work processes are planned by management on the basis of repetition of elementary tasks, management is less dependent on its employees and concomitantly strengthened. As management draws the design of work into its domain and reduces its employees to executors of mundane tasks, workers are denuded of mental skills and increasingly transformed into manual workers. We have seen this happen, under the guise of rationalization, in many production processes where nowadays the most refined goods (cars, televisions, electronic components, etc.) are manufactured by semi- and unskilled workers performing banal tasks on assembly lines where it is high technology conceived and implemented by management which contains the real skills, but we now witness this extending into white-collar labor.

There have, of course, long been attempts made to more effectively manage office work, and a number of people have examined earlier attempts to increase productivity there. In general, a prerequisite of greater productivity is for management to increase its control over the labor process such that speed-up can be best effected. To this end, mechanization often follows organizational changes that have simplified tasks. C. W. Mills wrote a generation ago of the reorganization of information work which he believed was a pre-condition of office automation. In the then "new office," Mills foresaw the future, one of "factory-like operatives in the white-collar worlds," which followed when

> the new office is rationalized: machines are used, employees are machine attendants; the work, as in the factory, is collective, not individualized; it is standardized for interchangeable, quickly replaceable clerks; it is specialized to the point of automatization (Mills, 1953, pp. 206, 209).

Social reorganization of the office (shared secretaries, typing pools, specialization of function in clerical activities especially) has been accompanied in the past by technical innovations, though this was on a modest scale and Mills overestimated the speed of its development; but I.T. promises to change this trend, to allow technical solutions to the problem of low office productivity, to extend to white-collar employees methods well known to manual workers.

The further control of the work process that I.T. allows can take a number of forms. One method is for terminals to be linked to a central processor which responds, for example, to an entry from the terminal operator of a customer's inquiry at a travel agency. At the depression of a few keys (dates, proposed destinations, etc.) the central computer, appropriately programmed beforehand at the behest of management, performs all the requisite costing exercises, literature searches, timetabling accounts, flight schedules, etc. formerly done by clerical workers. As this takes place, the operator is reduced to the level of a keypuncher; the skill of the job is in the machine which incorporates functions previously undertaken by people. Where once the travel agent's staff needed to be numerate and well versed in a range of forms and literature, the work can now be done with a minimal amount of training. Indeed, the best indication of this is that it is now possible to do it oneself from home with a viewdata set.

Another way of increasing control is by fragmenting a job, by increasing the division of labor to such a degree that the isolated specialist is unable to comprehend the whole. Thereby, the individual task is not only mindless, but the worker is ignorant of the overall processes. This in itself enhances the control of management, which does grasp the whole, and it also makes the work of individual operatives more readily amenable to speed-up since it is simple and routine. However, though this reorganization is often a prelude to mechanization and invariably accompanies it, it does present problems of monitoring diverse functions. In the past, elaborate systems of personal supervision have been the favored solution, but these of themselves are expensive. I.T. comes to the rescue of management, as its capabilities allow for the recording of the output of employees with accuracy and ease. Chris Harman (1979, p. 11) cites from the *Financial Times* of 1 November 1978 one word processing system, called Mastermind, which has a display terminal which

> provides complete information on the status of up to two hundred active dictation and transcription jobs in the center. A disc memory offers a permanent, unlimited archive of the completed work. A companion report printer provides detailed daily, weekly or monthly summaries of input and output activities.

The company that developed Mastermind, Dictaphone, is the U.K. market leader in centralized dictation systems which, according to the *Financial Times* are "designed to connect with the dictation input system and log every item of work and check its progress. Depending on the configuration in use, the supervisor can locate any single item of work by author, subject matter, typist or other categories and discover its exact status." This trend towards automatic work control certainly increases the surveillance capability of management, and it has an added advantage: such production-control systems by "assessing the typist's known speed and amount of outstanding work . . . result [in] the fastest turn-round of work for everyone" (Wilkinson, 1982). Harman appositely adds that "the electronic time-and-motion man has entered the office with the microprocessor" (Harman, 1979, p. 11).

It was again Harry Braverman who most clearly perceived the relations between fragmented work, deskilling, and mechanization, that behind these developments was the search to increase the productivity of employees. As we enter an era of extensive automation of office work, "the drive for speed has come to the fore" (Braverman, 1974, p. 335). In consequence, we should not be surprised that, amid all the changes of organization in the new office, the "visual display unit operator can spend her entire day at the keyboard, with no opportunity for a walk, a chat or an extended lunch break. The intensity of the work is greatly increased. Word processors make you work harder" (Craig, quoted in *Computing*, 21 May, 1981). With the establishment of these patterns come "bonus systems, à la factory production . . . introduced in many offices by which vdu operators are paid according to the number of key depressions an hour" (*Computing*, 21 May, 1981).

In addition, it is not unexpected that companies which introduce I.T. into their offices attempt to extend the length of the working day. Having invested large amounts of capital in office technologies, it is only sensible to keep them constantly in use in order to recoup expenditure. To this end, following the example of factory work and of many computer installations, it is predictable that shift working will be introduced into some areas of office work. This is most likely to occur where large organizations have pioneered centralized word processing, as, for example, at Security Pacific National Bank where machines are kept busy at three shifts per day in a center where 50 employees serve approximately 800 persons (Ketron, 1980, p. 140). Moves to shift working have long been recognized to be detrimental to social life; their extension to areas traditionally occupied by women can scarcely be interpreted as an advancement of their position, though no doubt the eulogies praising the possibilities of combining work and home by typing through the night are being scripted.

Limits on Career

Women have long been restricted in their access to the upper echelons of whatever work they are engaged in (and some work they are restricted even from entry into). Yet another barrier to promotion for women appears to be I.T. This happens because, as the technology is adopted in situations which call for a restructuring of work roles, it further isolates operatives from more desirable career possibilities by being more highly structured than in the past. Operatives of machines are given specified roles and remunerations, and the chances of moving beyond say word processing are limited. That these people are women—and chiefly married women, who are often working part-time—makes it that much easier to keep them in lowly places. Moreover, the new jobs that are created by I.T. which are attractive, rewarding, and skilled, notably design, installation, and maintenance of the equipment, go overwhelmingly to men rather than to women.

Hence women became increasingly vulnerable to further automation of traditional clerical work because they were unable to move up to the new jobs at the technical level. With increasing automation, the male/female stratification in the office became even more pronounced (Werneke, 1983, p. 61; cf. Huws, 1982a; Arnold et al., 1982, p. 68).

Differential Effects of I.T.

Numerous commentators have drawn a picture similar to the one sketched above of the office being mechanized primarily at the expense of women. However, while this is the trend, it is in need of qualification. It is, for instance, clear that the pace is being set in the larger organizations, where economies of scale are most beckoning, management most sophisticated, and technology already well advanced. For this reason it is in banks, insurance companies, headquarters of national and international corporations, and the like where I.T. is most visible. As a result, "choices among different work structures now available to workers will be considerably narrowed for those working in large organizations" (Glenn and Feldberg, 1982, p. 208) before the squeeze is put on smaller enterprises. Added to this is the fact that not all female office workers will be impacted the same. Within this category are numerous gradations of skill, strategic location, corporate ethos, and the like. In particular we ought to beware equating female office workers with personal secretaries. In Britain, there are over three million clerical and related female workers, but only one-third are classified as secretaries and typists (Bird, 1980, p. 26). Within this latter group, only a minority are personal secretaries, so we may be reminded that most female office workers are performing work as filing clerks, mail sorters, invoicers, photocopy operators, switchboard operators, and the like. Discriminating in these ways, it is self-evident that I.T.'s effects will be differential. Because this is so, there will undoubtedly be offices and jobs where new technology actually enhances the work of, for example, some secretaries. For instance, if a word processor is introduced for use by a single secretary without changing the demands upon her, then, as it merely substitutes for her typewriter, she may enjoy its extra capabilities, and, if she is the sole secretary in a small office, since her other functions will continue, the effects of the word processor will be limited to a small proportion of her day. By the same token, such an office would be ill-advised to purchase a word processor, because it could hardly be justified in terms of cost.

Again, the effect on the operator of I.T. will be experienced differently depending on where she has previously been employed. If, for example, the word processor operator previously worked in a typing pool, then the new technology may enhance her work, since with the original she was tied to a machine anyway, the work was just as routine and repetitive, and the novelty is simply a more versatile keyboard.

For this reason it was predictable that in the civil service—a huge organization already elaborately structured on the lines of scientific management—there "is general but not universal enthusiasm among typists for the equipment, an appreciation of the quality of the output and a widely held belief that operation of the equipment provides enrichment of their task" (*Word Processing by Computer,* 1978, p. 23). Conversely, a personal secretary shifted to an administrative support center is liable to feel the move negatively, missing the contact with colleagues, the variety and control over her work (cf. Arndt et al., 1983). Finally, there is the halo effect of working with I.T. (computers!) to be considered, which may, at least in the short term, lead some women to welcome the new technology, something complemented by the prestige associated with being a minority for the period until I.T. becomes pervasive.

To date various statements have been made public that describe the vagaries of response to and effect of I.T. as somehow in balance; that, while there will undoubtedly be some negative aspects of I.T., the positive features will cancel out the unpleasant. It is a travesty to contend that the effects are counterbalancing. The reality is that they are predominately in a negative direction (cf. West, 1982; Crompton and Reid, 1982), that "the first piece of information that hits you like a cattle prod is that there are at least two types of word processor operators," one which "loves the things" and constitutes "at most a quarter" of office workers who will be reskilled as it is introduced, the other, the outright majority, which "would otherwise be found in a typing pool" (Warr, 1980). Karen Nussbaum summed up the situation in the *New York Times* thus:

> The use of word processors has meant a slight improvement in the working lives of some clerical workers because it has removed the drudgery of repetitive typing. . . . But for millions of others, it has meant that they are assigned to centers where they do nothing but babysit machines for eight hours (*New York Times,* 11 October, 1981).

It is churlish not to acknowledge that there will be some circumstances in which I.T. will be of benefit for some people. Nonetheless, it is naive to fail to see that for the bulk of office workers I.T. portends a decline from their current position.

The Decline of the "Social Office"

Hazel Downing reviews the qualities of a good secretarial worker. Beyond shorthand and typing speeds are a range of other requirements which are characteristically feminine—good dress sense, neat appearance, pleasant manner, nice elocution and grammar. . . . These "skills," "the training for which she will have received simply by growing up," are expressions of patriarchy in the wider society and are manifest in the office, where women are expected to gossip, to make coffee, run shopping errands for their male superiors, and generally soothe their employers (Downing, 1983, p. 42). While patriarchy is most obvious with regard to secretarial jobs, it extends to the lowest-level typing jobs and is a means of controlling women workers and an excuse for paying poor wages. Typically,

> women are 'treated' to candy on holidays, jewelry on their anniversaries with the company. . . . 'Niceness' is stressed throughout the company, to create a pleasant atmosphere. The 'niceness,' which extends to sharing work loads, helps the women cope with the strains of constant supervision and rigid formats; it also enables the company to continue imposing 'unreasonable' demands (Glenn and Feldberg, 1979, pp. 66–67).

This profoundly disadvantages women, but it does enable them to have considerable control over the tempo of their work and it gives to the office a relaxed, personalized feel, a social quality in which a chat is normal during working hours, where there is no clocking on or off at 8 in the morning and 4 in the afternoon, where the unrelenting monotony of the assembly line is absent. In addition, just as the housewife has her expertise even where it is limited to the kitchen, so does the secretary have her expertise as "office wife" in her knowledge of her domain, the filing systems, diary arrangements, and personal contacts.

It is certainly the case that this depiction of the social office has long been out of date as regards the large bureaucratic organizations, but the point is that I.T.'s introduction into the office nowadays, impelled by the desire to increase control of the labor process and extract greater productivity, threatens to end the social office in hitherto spared areas (Barker and Downing, 1980; Forester, 1980), to bring about the "conversion of the office routine into a factory-like process in accordance with the precepts of modern management and available technology" (Braverman, 1974, p. 347). Just one consequence of this, but an important one for many women office workers, is the removal of a significant element of the secretarial career structure. Because I.T. brings about changes in the office, and in particular because it reduces the number of personal secretaries in an organization, the opportunity to achieve reflected status by becoming the secretary of someone high in the organization is reduced. While this may be an illusory form of mobility, it has long been the major expression of secretarial success, which the spread of centralized typing systems, shared secretarial services, and the like undermine.

Feminization and Proletarianization?

The foregoing has argued that the future of office work

> will resemble the automated factory in most important respects: a few highly trained systems analysts and programmers at the top, segregated in almost every conceivable way from the mass of "proletarianized" office workers at the bottom. These are likely to be mostly keypunch operators, a job that "can be learned in a matter of a week of two," and carries almost no prospects of promotion or the opportunities to learn new skills (Kumar, 1978, p. 210).

This interpretation of a downgrading of much nonmanual work has a lengthy history in social analysis, ranging from Lewis Corey's identification of "The 'new' proletariat . . . of lower salaried employees" (Corey, 1935, p. 260) in the America of the 1930s, which was echoed in Klingender's (1935) thesis of the proletarianization of clerical labor in Britain, through C. W. Mill's insistence that "the white-collar people . . . are in exactly the same property-class position as the wage-workers" (Mills, 1953, pp. 71-72), to Harry Braverman's powerful claim to witness the degradation of work in the twentieth century such that "traditional distinctions between 'manual' and 'white-collar' labor, which are so thoughtlessly and widely used in the literature on this subject, represent echoes of a past situation which has virtually ceased to have meaning in the world of work" (Braverman, 1974, pp. 325-326).

These arguments do have a great deal of validity, though there is an over-eagerness to downplay palpable differences between occupational groups which still exist (Parkin, 1972, 1979). However, perhaps even more serious than this qualification, the thesis of proletarianization must be conceived in recognition of the fact that it has taken place and is continuing to occur in occupations which are predominantly female and/or which have undergone feminization often simultaneous with restructuring (cf. Beechey, 1982). Because of the location of women in our society, because of attitudinal and structural limitations placed upon women (Feldberg and Glenn, 1982, p. 75), while much white-collar work is being demeaned, since it is "carried out by women with reduced aspirations . . . [and little power] . . . proletarianization is much weaker than it appears at first glance" (Crozier, 1971, p. 19). The consequence of this is that where feminization occurs, though the work may have undergone a reduction in skill, it is unlikely that the participants will take on a proletarian outlook. Though women suffer lower wages, poorer career prospects, and less skilled work than men, they complain less about this and are in no position to complain more. Therefore, though I.T. is more of a threat to women than to men, gender differences are an important variable in assessing the results. This is of such import that already research has revealed the

> irony . . . that even though women are assigned to technologically more restrictive work than men, and though women suffer relatively more from technological change, women's job satisfaction and machine liking differ little from men's (Form and McMillen, 1983, p. 175).

Women taking over what were once male occupations at the same time as the work is changed by organizational and technological innovations is no new thing. Feminization has long been evident in clerical work (cf. Anderson, 1976), tailoring, (cf. B. Taylor, 1983, pp. 101-117), education (cf. Banks, 1971, pp. 144-145), and has been threatened in printing (cf. Cockburn, 1983, Ch. 6), and this has often accompanied changes in the labor process.

We can offer an example of a parallel process of deskilling and feminization of an occupation by looking at computing itself, where the proportion of computer operators in the United States who were female rose from 29% in 1960 to 63% by

1982 (Hacker, 1983b, p. 29). We pointed out in the previous section (pp. 143–148) how computing, the deskiller of others' work, is itself subject to deskilling (Kraft, 1977), but gender factors are integrally connected to this process. Joan Greenbaum has argued that "within only twenty years, job fragmentation and deskilling have degraded the jobs of computer workers, as much as computer work has affected legions of clerical and production workers" (Greenbaum, 1979, p. 159). What has accompanied this has been that women have been allocated the lowest grades involved in computing and, relatedly, under-represented at senior levels where the "most skilled suboccupations [are] thoroughly male-dominated" (Kraft, 1979a, p. 17). Kraft noted that as early as 1970 women were under-represented among systems analysts and over-represented among the more mundane programmers, though still a minority of the total of what was then an especially attractive occupation (Kraft, 1979b, p. 152). By 1980 in the U.S., women accounted for 23% of the elite systems analysts, 31% of the second division programmers, 59% of the third category computer operators, and 92% of the bottom level key entry operators. Their representation had increased across the board, but notably in the lower rungs of the occupational category (Gilchrist et al., 1983, p. 102). Women have entered computing as the work tasks have been segmented and reduced to less skilled operations and have been restricted in opportunities of entering the upper echelons of the profession, but the fact of their entry has assisted the containment of dissatisfaction over changes in the work.

It is difficult to determine exactly the degree to which feminization of itself lowers the prestige and reward of a job. In some cases, there is evidence that feminization per se leads to a lowering of status and even to changes in definitions of skill. For example, Michèle Barrett observes that

> Compositors have traditionally been successful in establishing their work as highly skilled, and there is considerable sympathy for them in a situation where automation is threatening to strip these workers of a bargaining position that rests on these skills. Yet the same technological developments also threaten to radically "deskill" many secretaries, since work processors render obsolete the editorial and layout functions formerly required in typing. Typists, however, have not achieved the same success in gaining commensurate recognition of these skills. If the compositors stand to suffer from these developments, the secretarial workforce faces the threat from a far weaker position (Barrett, 1980, pp. 168–169).

This instance reveals that even conceptions of skill are problematical and much dependent on a group's power over definition, and that gender relations play a significant role in this process.

It seems to us inescapable that, nowadays, low-level clerical work especially is set to undergo further deskilling, and that because this is performed by women there are major consequences for both the respondents and the wider society. We are not suggesting that women performing clerical functions find them unalienating, but we do feel that the reality of their, socially induced, lower likelihood of protest should be acknowledged. In addition to this, because we are discussing the effect of technology on a group of people who, on the whole, share homes and incomes with working men, it is essential to cognize the consequences of these relations for class structure and consciousness in a period of rapid adjustment.

Cutting into Management?

There are some commentators who concede that the office is the locus of I.T.'s applications and that this may displace and deskill employees, but who do not believe that the clerical levels are its major target. On the contrary, a number of I.T. consultants consider that "managerial productivity has surpassed clerical and secretarial productivity as the priority aim of office automation" (Kleinschrod, 1981, p. 27).

There is a prima facie case to be made for this thesis on grounds of efficiency and economics. Though estimates vary, there is no disagreement that, though numerically outnumbered, managers and professionals take the lion's share of all office wages. Infotech (1980) offers a pie graph to illustrate this position (Figure 3). The *Economist* reports a different estimate from the American management consultants, Booz, Allen, and Hamilton, which reveals a similar situation where "a colossal 75% of total office costs goes on managers, only 12% on secretaries," and adds that "little investment goes into productivity-enhancing equipment for managers: only 29% of total office investment at present is spent on equipping the

Figure 3. Distribution of Office Workers by Cost

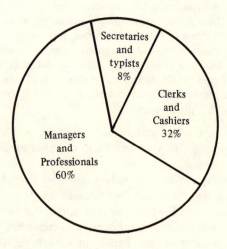

[expensive] manager" (January 30, 1982, pp. 93-94). The logical deduction from these figures is clear, and the editor of *Computing* articulates it as follows:

> Just over 65% of the white-collar wage bill goes on managers and professional staff in the office, so a small amount in cost displacement in this area would contribute significantly to the overall productivity of the office (June 4, 1981, p. 18).

On this evidence, there would appear to be little reason to fear for women. Because "a major proportion of the paybill is spent on the executive" (*Economist*, January 30, 1982, pp. 93-94), then managers and professionals are the endangered species. Moreover, numerous writers have also observed that one significant group of women in the office—secretaries—are actually not only scarcely worth automating because they are cheap, but also rather difficult to automate, since so little of their time is actually spent at the keyboard. Again estimates vary, but it is common to calculate that only 10-15% of a secretary's time is spent typing, while the bulk is given over to running around the organization with messages, answering the telephone, acting as receptionist, and the like. On the other hand, the "typical manager, whose salary is three times that of a humble secretary, spends over 50% of his time producing, reading, or discussing documents" (ibid.). Clearly we have identified the major information worker where I.T. can have most applications.

It is our view that the fact that greater potential savings by automation are found among management is no comfort for women in the office. It is undoubtedly the case that personal secretaries do not sit at the typewriter a great deal, but there is evidence that this is changing. Rosalie Silverstone and Rosemary Towers interestingly report on this in their 1982 survey of London secretaries thus:

> In 1970 when a similar survey was completed, 70% of secretaries worked for one person only. By 1981 the proportion had dropped to 50%. This trend is likely to continue, leading to a reduction in "personal" secretaries and an increase in "team" secretaries (*Guardian*, 9 February, 1983).

This development merely generalizes what we have seen in the case of Texaco: the effort to cut costs, with which I.T. is intimately involved, calls for reorganization of office workers. To this end, secretaries are being rearranged so as to be working more effectively at machines. The shared secretary, the typing pool, and the administrative support center are signs that the under-used female office workers are being put to more intensive labor. Currently secretaries may not be devoting a large proportion of their time to typing, but automation can occur here on a satisfactory basis if accompanied by reorganization.

While in some quarters there will be opposition to the loss of the status symbol of a personal secretary—another factor often discerned as limiting the impact of I.T. on women in the office—in the long run such paternalistic practices will not spare more than a few. The search is on to save money in the office, and those at the front line, those most expendable, are the least resistant and least skilled—i.e., women. That some of them are currently not heavy users of machinery is no great stumbling block, provided the office is appropriately designed for an influx of I.T. In addition, when one talks of secretaries it is important to note that the term is a catch-all which includes anything from 16-year-old telephone answerers to personal assistants of directors, so that I.T. will quite readily find applications in some secretarial work with minimal rearrangement. On top of this, that secretarial work constitutes only one-third of all female clerical work indicates that I.T. has much scope outside of that category.

We agree that some managers are threatened by I.T., but this will not be a random group. It will be the lower levels of management on the whole that are attacked by new technology, those whose jobs are most routine and least skilled. Braverman saw this as likely a decade ago, when he observed that "management is now nerving itself for major surgery upon its own labor limbs," that "the object of this attack is no longer just the clerk but the comfortable arrangements made by their own managers" (Braverman, 1974, pp. 343–344). That junior management is not safe from I.T. is no sign of a rescue of women office workers. On the contrary, it underlines the point that, in the search to save money and control work processes by using I.T., the lower one is in the hierarchy, the more vulnerable is one's position. That some levels of management are within the sights of the technological innovators cannot make any more secure the sitting ducks.

Working from Home

The foregoing will have made clear that I.T. holds little promise for women at work. Suffering, relative to men, prior to its introduction, the new technology will build upon and consolidate their subjugation. As a final comment, however, we are obliged to make mention of I.T. for extending home-working for women. There has recently been a gush of comment to the effect that, because of the communications capabilities of the new technology, much work can now and in the future be performed from home. An end to commuting and business travel, the end of the centralized office where people gather to work, is envisaged as teleconferencing, computer networks, and the like link up dispersed locations and do away with traditional methods of work. It has been suggested that this networking potential of I.T. will be a godsend to women, since it will enable them to combine the roles of mother, housewife, and worker in an era of the "electronic cottage."

We do not believe that this will happen, for a number of reasons. Of course there are the much publicized instances of professionals, such as systems analysts and journalists, who may find remote site working advantageous, but, in the main, the prospects for women are poor (cf. Huws, 1984). There is little doubt that, in the long term at least, home-working will extend, but our reasons for suspicion revolve around the fact that, historically, home-workers have been the most disadvantaged of all. Home-workers are in general an especially vulnerable group of people, keen to work, but unable to enter the labor market on equal terms with others because of commitments (young children, aged parents, invalidity, etc.) which keep them at home. Employers have in the past been quick to exploit the weaknesses of these people, to pay low wages in return for long hours. As I.T. develops, the likelihood is that the preponderance of work done at home will be that which is most readily monitored—typing of reports and similar routine clerical work. In turn, the women allocated such jobs will be paid chiefly by output rather than at a weekly rate, since hours of work will be flexible and typing easily recorded. The home-workers will also be responsible for auxiliary costs such as lighting and heating. Above all, they will be isolated from other workers, which will make them especially weak in negotiation with employers. All of this is to say that home-working will be introduced on the basis of existent social relations, that, far from resolving the problems of women whose work opportunities are restricted because of their gender, it will exacerbate them. Moreover, women working from home by way of I.T. will also find that their traditional roles as homemakers will be reinforced. This will be in a situation replete with further technology for the kitchen and lounge which will contribute yet further to female subordination. Since this aspect of I.T. merges the work and leisure effects, we will return to it in later chapters.

Chapter 6
I.T. and a Service/Leisure Society

The "realm of necessity". . . . has highly elastic, perhaps ineffable boundaries; in fact, it is as "necessary" socially as the vision one has of freedom.
To separate one from the other inexorably is sheer ideology, for it may well
be that freedom does not "base" itself on the "realm of necessity" but
really determines it.

> — M. Bookchin. *Toward an ecological society.* Montreal: Black Rose
> Books, 1980, p. 129.

Introduction

The prospect of the development of either or both a service or a leisure society
is especially appealing to enthusiasts of I.T. who connect their coming with technological change. There are various interpretations of what precisely a service or
leisure society will look like, but each hinges on I.T. as a prerequisite, because
advanced technology will provide the necessary wealth to pay for more services
and leisure. Increased affluence is the necessary foundation upon which the new
society will be built, and without I.T. an increase is unthinkable.

Three scenarios have been offered which overlap in particular presentations,
namely;

• while employment in manufacture will fall because of I.T. compensatory opportunities will be made available with the *expansion of service occupations* which will
be funded by the riches realized from automated production.

• jobs will be lost to manufacture because of new technology, but these will be
mopped up by an *increase in leisure services* which will be required in the affluent
electronic age. As Margaret Thatcher put it, "Leisure is a big *industry.* . . . There is
great industry in other people's pleasures" (September, 1983).

• the collapse of manufacturing work will be of such a scale, and service jobs
themselves will also be negatively impacted by technological innovation, that the
end of full employment must be acknowledged. However, because the society
which adopts I.T. will be extraordinarily wealthy, it will have the opportunity to
behave generously towards those displaced by removing the stigma of unemployment, paying them a handsome social wage, and allowing them to become pioneers
of a *leisure society* in which more and more of the people enjoy "affluent redundancy" (Evans, 1979, p. 94).

There is a fourth position which can be distanced from the foresaid that contends that I.T. will cut a swathe through employment in the formal economy but
that the resultant worklessness will be cushioned by the spread of activity in the
informal economy, centered around the household and locality, which will be aided
by I.T., because this makes technologies that people can afford in order to do
things for themselves available at cheap rates.

On the surface, each of these prospects is plausible, even attractive, both as on-going trends and as solutions to the problem of technological redundancy. Since we regard all of them as misconceived, it is useful to examine each in turn to delineate underlying weaknesses.

Expansion of Service Occupations

The most sanguine view of the future is that in which I.T. rapidly arrives, profoundly affects existent conditions, but helps bring about a superior alternative. Kenneth Baker describes this accelerated evolutionism thus:

> In the early 1950s in Britain around 40% of the workforce was in manu-facturing, by 1970 it had fallen to 37% and by 1981 to 28%. This trend will continue as American experience has shown, but I do not believe this will lead to massive unemployment since more and more people will be needed to provide the service activities which the new technologies are already stimulat-ing (Baker, 1983a, p. 3).

On these terms, I.T. "will reduce the number of people involved in the actual manufacturing process" (ibid.), but there is no cause for alarm, since services will correspondingly expand to take up the slack. Moreover, services will not merely substitute for jobs lost in manufacture: they are also of a more satisfactory kind for the workers (providing a service for people rather than fabricating a thing) and for the society at large (a service society is more "caring" than a goods—producing one).

Because of this, it is not surprising that the idea is attractive to those on the Left as well as to Conservatives of Mr. Baker's hue. For example, Clive Jenkins and Barrie Sherman believe that I.T. could enable the expansion of education and health services which could to some extent compensate for job losses elsewhere as well as mark social advance. They write that an "explosion in employment is possible in all of these people-oriented service industries" (Jenkins and Sherman, 1979, p. 169), and the message is that such a development would be politically progressive. The British Labour Party goes further in proposing that the unemploy-ment caused by I.T. could be channeled into some kind of services to represent a form of socialism. Viz:

> It is possible that many of those whose work may be wholly or partly dis-placed by microelectronics in the decades ahead might choose—if the choice were offered to them—to spend more of their own time in enriching commun-ity and person-to-person services. . . .Socialism is not merely a concept of creating a constitutional framework for economic and social advance and transformation. . . .It involves the idea of a caring society. Could we regard the chip. . .as an instrument to change the quality of social relationships within the community? (Labour Party, 1980, p. 37).

The congruence between Margaret Thatcher's claim that "many, many new jobs will be in the service industries" (September, 1983), and the socialist conviction that there is a need for more services, is striking. Both present as some sort of ideal a service society—the free marketers believing that this will come about because wealth created by investment in production will lead to increased consumer demand for services, the socialists convinced that the new technology will generate sufficient wealth to subsidize an increase in services.

Post-Industrial Society as a Service Society

We shall come back to these propositions, but, because the prospect of more service employment arising as work in manufacture declines is not the preserve of politicians, we can focus discussion on a more academic presentation. This returns us to Daniel Bell, because the concept of post-industrial society (PIS) is intimately connected with the growth of services, I.T., and the spread of information work.

Bell's presentation of his thesis opens with a description of changes in employment patterns by sector. Adopting Colin Clark's (1940) three-sector model of society (primary ⟨extractive⟩, secondary ⟨manufacturing⟩, and tertiary ⟨services⟩), and drawing on Fuch's delineation of the "transition from an industrial to a service economy" (Fuchs, 1968, p. 1), Bell outlines the well-rehearsed theme of a decline in primary and secondary sector employment and its transference to the tertiary or service sector.

The Service Society is an Information Society

For Bell, services in general indicate the coming of post-industrial society, but it is the especially rapid growth within them of the "professional and technical class" (Bell, 1976, p. 17) which is most important because its expansion supports his claim that post-industrialism is not only a "white-collar society", but also that it is one where the "professional" is predominant. Because of this PIS is a "knowledge society" (p. 242), for the professional's work chiefly involves using and generating this resource. Thereby, a post-industrial society is not merely a service society, it is also an information society in which "the weight of society. . .is increasingly in the knowledge field" (p. 212).

What Daniel Bell is pointing to here—that the fastest-growing service sector occupations are those which handle information—has received much publicity from devotees of the information society who often have recourse to his concepts. Indeed, the terms "post-industrialism" and "information society" are treated as synonymous in popular depictions of the future. Tom Stonier, for example, writes that a "post-industrial economy is one in which both the number of people employed in manufacturing and the proportion of the gross national product going to manufacturing industries has taken second place to the service sector made up of information, not domestic, operatives" (Stonier, 1983, pp. 23-24). And those who perceive this growth of information work as a key element of increased services do not see it solely as a switch in available jobs. It is also, as with Bell, regarded as an improvement, because information operatives are thought of as part of the professionalization—indeed embourgeoisement—of the whole society.

Bell himself has taken to distinguishing three types of work, namely "extractive," "fabrication," and "information activities" (Bell 1979b, p. 178), the balance of which has changed over the years such that in PIS the "predominant group consists of information workers" (ibid., p. 183). The promotion of information work to this central position in his analyses of post-industrialism draws upon the well-known studies of Marc Porat (1976, 1978) which delineated the growth of informational activities until they accounted for almost half of the American labor force by the late 1960s, a claim complemented by Barron and Curnow's estimate that "information occupations . . . amount to 65% of the working population" (Barron and Curnow, 1979, p. 19).

Bell is aware that information work extends across sectoral categories, but nowhere does he pursue this point. This is not surprising, since it is central to his thesis that service sector growth is the major stimulus behind the development of a post-industrial information society. His acolytes adopt a similar perspective, contending that a shift from agriculture and manufacture to services marks the coming of the information age. G.T.T. Molitor puts it thus:

> The high point of American work force employment in manufacturing . . . came in 1920, when 53% of the work force was so employed. In that year, 28% of the workers were engaged in agriculture and extractive industries, and 19% were employed in information, knowledge, education, and other service enterprises. . . . Economically, politically, and socially, the importance of manufacturing is fading fast. By the year 2000, a mere 2% of the American work force will work in agriculture, 22% will be in manufacturing, and 66% . . . will be allied with information (Molitor, 1981, p. 23).

The Service Society and I.T.

There are three ways in which I.T. is crucial to PIS. First, because post-industrialism's major resource is information, there has to be a technology able to handle it,and advanced computer/communications are this management tool. Second, technological innovations hasten the arrival of the information society by automating much agriculture and manufacture, thus freeing workers to fill vacancies made available by the expansion of services. Third, and most important, advanced technology is the means by which the service society is funded. This is necessary because services consume wealth rather than create it. When a patient sees a doctor, a student consults a teacher, or a client meets with a social worker the exchange may result in better health, more wisdom,or an improvement in family relations, but none of these outcomes is an object with marketable value. On the contrary, these are services which are a drain on society's resources, which it must subsidize from its wealth-creating sector. Services must be paid for, personnel must have incomes to live, and it is this which the manufacturing and agricultural sectors provide. They supply the means that we might enjoy the luxuries of a service society. It is fortunate for us that technology has and is so revolutionizing the primary and secondary sectors that we can afford lots of services. Without technology to enable an excess of production PIS would be but a pipe-dream. Ipso facto, if we are to sustain services and even have more of them, we must encourage I.T., because it will boost the productivity of industry and agriculture.

Moreover, adoption of I.T. is made more pressing because services, since they are matters of qualitative relations rather than quantities of output, are performed by people rather than by machines. In turn, there are unavoidable limits on the productivity of service workers, since one cannot readily mechanize a "relation between persons" (Bell, 1976, p. 155). On the one hand, this is a fine thing for employment, since services opportunities are constantly made. On the other hand, they are very expensive, since service costs cannot be much reduced by machinery. The upshot is that further pressure is placed on the wealth-creating sector of society—the goods-producing element—to increase its output by constant automation, in order that more services (and proportionately more service jobs) may be funded.

We have argued already that, in spite of absence of analysis of change in Daniel Bell's model of the transition from industrial to post-industrial society, he does impute causal explanations which are deterministic. We are reminded of this determinism when he presents the "theorem of Christian Engel" (Bell, 1976, p. 128) as sufficient explanation for the expansion of services. Engel's law has it that, as a society gets wealthier, so is it likely to spend proportionately less of its income on the necessities of life and more on new needs which can now be afforded. For Bell, this accounts for the growth of service employment: we have got richer because technology has increased production; as we have prospered, so we have looked around for ways of satisfying other needs which cannot be met solely by material objects but require services; therefore, service occupations have grown. It must be the case, reasons Bell, that, because there is a lot more service sector employment nowadays, the citizens of the emergent post-industrial society, affluent beyond the imaginings of their predecessors, are consuming a lot more services performed by people.

We shall return to the ex post facto logic in evidence here—services have manifestly grown, and their rise is accounted for by a German statistician's theorem rather than by empirical causal examination—but, with the point made that the service society depends on high productivity in the wealth-creating sector, we can go back to our opening remarks concerning politicians' responses to I.T. What is striking is how much Conservative and Socialist analyses share with Bell. The service society is regarded by all as a novel and desirable order, a humane and caring one that is achievable, the basis for which is advanced technology, since how else can services be afforded? There is no questioning of the goal of services and none of the technological prerequisites. All that is a matter of contention is whether market mechanisms or state direction should be the interim strategy. Professor Bell feels a "convincing case for the primacy of the market and for a market system" (Bell, 1979b, p. 196) has been made, but really this is of little consequence given the deep-seated consensus amongst the parties.

Increase in Leisure Services

Margaret Thatcher is a figure of some influence, so her views are worth listening to. It is commonly agreed that employment in the primary and secondary sectors will decline, but the Prime Minister refuses to be downcast. She is confident that new opportunities will present themselves in service sector expansion, but not in all services (she has a well-known distaste for services that are funded from the public purse). Mrs. Thatcher's rhetorical question, "Where do new jobs come from?" is answered in her identification of leisure as an employer set to grow. She tells *The Director* that

> we must also expect a lot more of our jobs will come from the service indus-
> tries—from the McDonalds and Wimpeys, which employ a lot of people, from
> the kind of Disneyland they are starting in Corby. . . . Who in pre-war days
> would have said there would be such a big nursery garden industry? But you
> go and buy a rose in a pot and put it in your garden. So more leisure can also
> create jobs (September, 1983).

Two months later, her Chancellor, in a more weighty publication, announces that, while jobs in manufacture are likely to decline, a solution to mass unemployment lies "in private services, including information and entertainment services and leisure activities" (Chancellor of the Exchequer, November 28, 1983, 4.3).

The assertion that leisure occupations will grow considerably in the future is part of the same argument that we are set to enter a service society. Mrs. Thatcher's disavowal of services funded from general taxation should not divert attention from the fundamental agreement her proposals have with those previously reviewed, though her predictions of an expansion of the "happiness industry" may have an especial appeal. Peter Large is not so discriminating in foreseeing "the expansion of education and community work and a vast extension of the leisure industries, so that the former factory hand retains self-esteem through wider knowledge, service to others—and becoming the local golf champion" (Large, 1980, p. 30). Similarly, Tom Stonier considers that "the leisure industry belongs to the happiness industry, but so does a good part of education, health and social care. It is these areas which will become the most important areas of economic activity of the future as robotized systems secure materials production" (Stonier, 1983, p. 212).

The basis for these scenarios is that I.T. will bring such riches to people that they will have excess money to spend. Leisure is an obvious place to spend this (and people will have more time to dispose of in leisure pursuits—see below) which in turn stimulates employment. It is perhaps not surprising that intellectual commentators see education as the most desirable sort of leisure work to increase. In this regard, Barry Jones is typical in identifying a "post-service society" where "education is the area with greatest potential . . . followed by home-based industries, leisure and tourism, skilled craftwork, and welfare services" (Jones, Barry, 1982, p. 40). A recurrent image is of a vast growth of education in the information society where short working hours and wealth in abundance allow for the pursuit of education for its own sake, for self-development, for convivial lifestyles. All this is to be paid for by "machine-created wealth" (Large, 1980, p. 153). It may not be quite such an attractive vista for some as Daniel Bell's professionalized knowledge society, but it undoubtedly shares the same premises.

Leisure Society

Consideration of the possibility of increasing work in leisure services takes us into discussion of a theory which at once distances itself from talk of there being full employment in the future at the same time as it endorses the same underlying principles as those who envisage further tertiarization. Many commentators believe mass unemployment is here to stay and even worsen as I.T. spreads. However, they also feel that this enforced leisure can, with appropriate policies, be turned into a socially desirable condition.

As we have seen (pp. 120–127), the evidence suggests that it is doubtful whether service employment will continue to expand in the context of recession, and, even if it did, its growth will be subject to considerable automation by I.T. Already the service sector is stagnating, and with public expenditure, which accounted for the majority of service sector expansion during the 1970s (Robertson et al., 1982, pp. 50–51), being reduced, the likelihood is that things will worsen (cf. Briscoe, 1981). Many have predicted, and evidence supports the view, that the "industrial-ization of service" (Levitt, 1976) will denude service employment, and, though there is likely in the foreseeable future to be a continuation of the trend towards a greater proportion of the labor force being employed in services because the slump is more severely hitting manufacture, and work there is most easily automated, the service sector cannot be looked at as a means of absorbing large numbers of displaced workers.

This being so, the idea of extending leisure rather than work opportunities has become especially attractive to many commentators on I.T. It ought to be said that this is not always a matter of conversion when faced with the intractable problem of high unemployment. There are those whose belief in "progress" is such that they can conceive increased leisure as simply an extension of long-term historical trends. On these lines, Peter Large cites a Delphic Poll conducted in 1978 which predicts the decline of the average working week to just 20 hours by 1999 (Large 1980, pp. 26–27). However, much more common are those advocates of increased leisure who are haunted by the spectre of mass unemployment. Even the ebullient James Martin imagines that new technology will produce such massive rises in output for most occupations that measures to avert large-scale redundancies will be required. To this end he recommends "a reshuffling of work so that everyone works shorter hours" (Martin, 1978a p. 212). In this way, the familiar themes of job-sharing and shorter working hours are put forward as both the reward for accepting I.T. and the means of ameliorating its employment effects.

To the trade unions, job-sharing and increased leisure are ways of retaining the status quo, but to James Martin they are signs of a revolution in Western thought. With the arrival of a 3½-day week in a high tech society, he envisages that the moral imperative that drives people to labor will collapse: "The Protestant ethic will have given way, perhaps to attitudes closer to those of Athens in its prime, perhaps to new attitudes unclassifiable in terms of past history" (Martin, 1977, p. 7).

Martin's depiction is not quite the same as that of other futurists. It is widely believed that, while job-sharing is on the right lines and that it might be a useful holding operation, I.T.'s massive impact must be more resolutely encountered. The likelihood of enormous numbers of unemployed turns other futurists squarely towards the "Protestant work ethic." Unlike Martin, they do not believe this will give way. It is their contention that sustained efforts must be made to change the work ethic in order to make acceptable upwards of 20% of the labor force out of work. If only, they claim, we could change attitudes towards unemployment, I.T. could be welcomed without qualification. Such is the popularity of this attitudinal solution to the problem of mass unemployment that we may usefully review some of its proponents.

Patrician Conservatives

In Britain, prescriptions for a leisure society from a number of leading Conservative politicians have attracted considerable attention since the discovery of I.T. James Prior, Peter Walker, and Francis Pym, all experienced government ministers and prominent Tory "wets," have at one time or another expressed disquiet about the rapid rise of unemployment and the probability that technological innovation would exacerbate the problem. Francis Pym, for example, thinks that "over recent years new technology has come out of the science-fiction books into our lives . . . [and] this whole process will have the most profound influence on the working lives of everyone in this country" (Pym, 1983). The Right Honorable gentleman fears that because of this "What we are facing is a reduction in the demand for labor in manufacturing industry. If we go on allowing the effect of this reduced demand to express itself through unemployment, we will only create permanent mass unemployment." This bleak prognosis of a new age is so compelling, and Thatcherite monetarism so inadequate a response, that the tradition of Conservatism which Pym represents cannot remain silent: "Some things are of too overwhelming and pervasive importance to be left to the natural ebb and flow of life. This is one of them." If laissez-faire policies are slavishly adhered to while I.T. sweeps across the economy, they "will divide the country between those who work and those who don't. It will be unacceptable economically, socially, politically, and, I would add, morally too" (Pym, 1983).

Pym's solution to this twentieth century problem of the "two nations" depends "on throwing out traditional notions of employment," massively increasing leisure while removing "the stigma and futility of mass unemployment" and thereby hastening a time when instead of as now reading, "unemployment up a million," we might read "leisure time doubled for two million" (Pym, 1983).

His answer is not novel. It echoes James Prior's recommendation, made shortly before taking up a post as Minister of State for Employment, that "If we do have to face higher unemployment, let's not despair. It may well be that in the next ten, fifteen, or twenty years we will have a new philosophy towards unemployment. We may have to move away from the Protestant Work Ethic" (March 21, 1979). Peter Walker put it more prosaically: "Our attitudes to automation verges on the lunatic. We should rejoice and create a society in which the machine works twenty-four hours a day. . . . Uniquely in history we have the circumstances in which we can create Athens without the slaves" (*Guardian*, November 19, 1980).

Trade Unions, the Left, and Leisure

We have discussed the attraction more leisure has for the Left (see Chapter 4), so we may be brief in reminding readers that the concept of a leisure age as a solution to unemployment is popular amongst radicals. Clive Jenkins and Barrie Sherman are the best known writers in this vein, where to combat unemployment they urge a "revolution in attitudes" (Jenkins and Sherman, 1981, p. 185) which will end "two centuries of propaganda" (Jenkins and Sherman, 1979, p. 141) of the work ethic, and advocate, in place of usual union calls for job security, a "whole life security" (p. 163) in the form of an assured social wage for all, and abandonment of the ideology of work such that "whether in or out of work people should be wanted and secure, their families not discouraged, and the unemployed themselves not made to feel inadequate" (ibid.).

These two unionists are prepared to support the widespread plea for more educational provision which might provide some additional employment, but this they insist is to be regarded primarily as a means by which newly leisured groups can divert and enhance themselves—i.e., "People should be enabled, if they wish, to use education and knowledge as an end in itself, to treat it as a leisure activity" (Jenkins and Sherman, 1979, p. 167). In this sense, education becomes pleasurable rather than instrumental, an occupation rather than work (Schaff, 1982, pp. 346-349), a sign that the information age has attained a stage of development where labor is unnecessary for survival, and people have real choices in how they spend their time (cf. Anthony, 1977).

Len Murray, then head of Britain's trade unions, forwarded views akin to those of Jenkins and Sherman in an interview with the *Guardian*. Realizing that a return to full employment in the immediate future is unlikely, he felt it behoved the labor movement to question its assumption of the value of jobs for all. In 1983, he did not "think full employment is necessary or desirable," that "things have changed and we should not assume that our working patterns today should be the pattern for the future." Continuing, he observed that "it's a good thing that people should have more time to engage in creative non-employment" and that "inevitably, we are moving into a situation where leisure is forming an important part of our everyday life. So that the issue is that in order to preserve living standards there will have to be an agreement about who gets what, and how work is divided. . . . We must try to get a proper distribution of work and that can only be done by tackling the question of leisure as well" (*Guardian,* August 26, 1983; cf. Clemitson and Rodgers, 1981).

All this and more is reiterated in the writing of Andre'Gorz, a prominent French neo-Marxist thinker. Gorz enunciates much the same message as Pym, Prior, Walker, Murray, and Jenkins and Sherman, in a Marxian idiom. Thus, he looks at new technology and pronounces its effect to be a reduction in employment. Traditionally, the Left would have sought to protect workers' livelihoods and therefore to resist technological redundancy, but Gorz thinks such a strategy wrong-headed. Since "people aren't particularly keen to be employed full time all year round" (Gorz, 1983b), the aim of socialists should be to gain free time, to negotiate shorter working hours "so that everyone may work *and* work less and less, while enjoying a guaranteed income" (ibid.). Gorz's view is that "liberated time" (Gorz, 1983a, p. 213) is a more worthy cause than pursuit of "an obsolete religion of work" (ibid., p. 216). His vision of the "post-industrial neo-proletariat" (Gorz, 1982, p. 69) is of a class which abjures the fight for full employment in favor of one aimed at "winning the power no longer to function as a worker" (p. 67). The future need is to "extend self-motivated, self-rewarding activity" (p. 87)–i.e., to extend leisure: "the right to enjoy rather than sacrifice our lives, to cooperate rather than compete, to be ourselves rather than cogs of a big machine, needs to be a central political concern" (Gorz, 1983b).

I. T. and Leisure

There are a number of features of these depictions of a leisure society. Not least is the quite extraordinary amount of agreement on the desirability of more leisure (the precise amount required is unclear, but all seem to want more of it), and this consensus extends to broad acceptance that a society which had more leisure would be "humane, caring, creative and harmonious" (Jenkins and Sherman, 1981, p. 165). But there is a more fundamental congruence than this which centers on the role to be played by advanced technology. All of these thinkers forward the view that a *change of attitude* will be required to break the work ethic and establish a leisure orientation which will then be feasible because I.T. will create the requisite *increase in wealth* to pay for the extra leisure. The premise of all these commentators is that I.T. will provide the material foundation to fund more free time, and that this will come about without guilt or recrimination by altering *attitudes* about the *distribution* of resources, the *supply* of which is taken to be a result of a separate sphere of *production* which is technologically secured.

As such, the way of seeing is the same as the apparently oppositional views that service sector work and/or more leisure jobs will absorb employees displaced from manufacture or agriculture. There, the theme was that wealth generated from increased productivity could pay for more service occupations: here, the central idea is that such wealth can support a life of idleness.

For example, Francis Pym observes that if we are to change "the entire way in which we think about our working lives," then this "will only be affordable through sustained economic growth." Therefore the prerequisite for the new age is rapid uptake of I.T. such that a reduction in hours of work will be achieved "without harming productivity or competitiveness" (Pym, 1983). Jenkins and Sherman are entirely orthodox: "Our propositions for embracing the new leisure, indeed the leisure shock itself, are premised upon a growth economy and this growth is premised largely upon the use of microelectronic and other technologies,, (Jenkins and Sherman, 1981, p. 70). Ditto Mr. Murray, when he asks "How do people define full employment in 1983?" and answers his own question with "by reducing the working life and the working week, largely through development of new technology" (*Guardian*, 26 August, 1983).

André Gorz falls into line with these writers, though in an especially illuminating way because of the baldness of his assertion that I.T. provides an essential part of a "dual society" which supplies the materials to satisfy "primary needs" (Gorz, 1982, p. 97), upon which basis the "sphere of autonomous activity" (p. 93) can be erected. Gorz, explicitly evoking the Marxist tradition which distinguishes an economic base (of which technology is an integral element) from a superstructure where "disposable time" can be located, lets us see that this perspective is shared by Marxist and Conservative politicians alike. *At the heart of all the analyses of a leisure society—and of service society predictions—is a metaphor which poses a wealth-creating level of society distinct from that of wealth-consuming.*

Gorz is candid about this and insists that "in complex, industrialized societies... socially necessary activities are necessary not to self-based responsible individuals but to a material system that still has the character of a huge machine" (Gorz, 1982, p. 91). Here he tells us that "socially necessary activities" require large organizations for production, high technology, and a complex division of labor. This is, he concedes, inevitably alienating for the worker, but I.T. does provide the opportunity to reduce time spent in producing the necessities of life which in turn offers a plentitude of free time. Thus "the sphere of autonomy is still based on a sphere in which the production is heteronomously socialized. It is because of this efficiency and its productivity that we have instruments and time that permit a growth of autonomy, as well as a rich and diverse choice of activities" (Gorz, 1983a, p. 220). Writing thus, Gorz recalls the distinction drawn by Marx, which is a bedrock of "Scientific Marxists," between the "sphere of necessity" and the "sphere of freedom." He acknowledges this and adds that the former "could be reduced but never entirely eliminated [but] by recognizing its inevitability, not by denying its existence, will it be possible to reduce its importance as much as possible and, as a result, ensure that its logic does not dominate every type of individual activity" (Gorz, 1982, p. 95).

Gorz's position, accepting a "realm of necessity" within which undesirable work will never be completely done away with, is not, of course, quite so sanguine as that of some other futurists who believe that production can either be automated altogether or sufficiently to make the work there interesting. Gorz believes that the "technical imperatives" (Gorz, 1982, p. 92) of the productive forces will always impinge upon workers to make life for them unpleasant even if of short duration, though there are some, for instance Daniel Bell, who suggest that technology, by ending mechanical tasks that are alienating, is allowing automation to such a degree that the "rhythms are no longer that pervasive. The beat has been broken" (Bell, 1976, p. 162). But these differences are epiphenomenal, for the framework remains a shared one; there is some part of the system which meets material necessities on which basis may be constructed leisure or services. When Gorz writes that "material production is subject to natural necessities" (Gorz, 1982, p. 96) which have distasteful consequences for workers, but that this can, because of technology, be reduced to "as brief a time as possible" (p. 96) while we can "use the goods it supplies. . .to enlarge the sphere of autonomy" (p. 101), he is agreeing fundmentally with Bell's claim that "basic needs are satiable, and the possibility of abundance is real" (1976, p. 465), so that services aplenty can be provided in post-industrial society. Both accept that "reality is made up of distinct levels" (Gorz, 1982, p. 118), that a crucial level is the one which supplies necessities, that if productivity here can be raised, one can either or both reduce working time spent in that level and purchase more services or leisure.

Consensus

We have criticized these perceptions at length in Part One of this book, so we may merely restate that they offer a technological route to either more services or leisure. This is because the metaphor of base/superstructure (or wealth creating/consuming) assumes a separation of society into two realms, one of which, the base, is in some way removed from the rest of society yet crucial to the remainder because it is from this base which wealth emanates. The assumption is that this sphere is neutral, merely producing the goods, the bounty of which will be used in the superstructure. Though the base is devoid of social relations, it is yet determining—more or less—of social relations elsewhere, because they are dependent on the technologies/wealth produced by it. In short, in the whole way of seeing, whether expressed by André Gorz, Francis Pym, or Daniel Bell, "one finds the most dismal cobwebs of othodox Marxism" (Bookchin, 1980, p. 294) coexisting with the grime of Conservative orthodoxy wherein economics, technology, production, science, and the like are placed at one fundamental level of society, and ethics, morality, consumption, ideas, etc. at quite another (although somehow the latter is determined by the former). We do not wish to straightforwardly repeat our earlier criticisms, but we can recast them by examining further inadequacies of service/leisure society scenarios.

The Role of Services

Economists have often observed that the division of employment into three sectors, primary, secondary, and tertiary, by Colin Clark, Daniel Bell, and others is more than classificatory, since it carries both explanatory and evolutionary assumptions of change: it suggests that increased productivity in the primary and secondary sectors is "the motor that drives the transformative process" (Browning and Singelmann, 1978, p. 485) onwards and upwards on a progressive trajectory.

There are numerous criticisms of this, but here we would emphasize two. The first is that the stages view of development—from pre-industrial to industrial to post-industrial society—is historically cavalier. Just as the "over-tertiarization" of Third World countries, nowadays regarded as a sign of maladjustment, indicates that there is no historical insistence that an industrial base be founded for services, so too is there little evidence to suggest that any of the advanced societies have progressed from a situation of majority employment in industrial production to one in services. The most spectacular change has not been a change from factory to service employment, but from agriculture to services. Moreover, even in Britain, historically the most industrialized of societies, the proportion of the labor force occupied in manufacture has been remarkably stable at 45–50% between 1840 and 1980 (Brown, 1978, Table 2.4, p. 66), and it is the collapse of manufacturing industry due to recession rather than underlying trends of employee transfer which has quite dramatically reduced this proportion to about one-third. All this is to say that talk of evolutionary shifts from one sector to the next is at the least dubious. Other than in England, nowhere has a majority of the population at any time worked in industry, and even in this country it is hard to sustain the argument that employees have shifted in any sequential way. The additional fact that service employment expansion has been in large part the result of women's entry to the labor force, often in part-time roles, casts still further doubt on the contention that there has been a transference of employment from one sector to another. It is clear that employment patterns cannot be explained, still less predicted, by models of evolution which contend that shifts take place because one sector's productivity is such that workers can be moved elsewhere; occupational distribution cannot be accounted for by the creation of wealth in one realm which pays for employee expansion in another.

The second criticism of this evolutionism helps us to make sense of employment patterns while revealing further difficulties with the developmental model. A starting-point for this attack is the observation that "services" is a residual category which accounts for anything not classifiable in the primary or secondary sectors. It is "a rag-bag of industries as different as real-estate and massage parlors, transport and computer bureaux, public administration and public entertainment" (Jones, 1980, p. 147). Our point in stressing the generality and left-over constitution of the service industries is that the classificatory convenience which separates the tertiary sector from others is misleading. It is the social construction of the category services as industries apart from—yet dependent upon—the fruits of manufacture and agriculture which misleads commentators and enables some to suggest, with superficial force, that services will expand on the basis of increased productivity in the primary and secondary sectors. However, it is only at a conceptual level that the service sector can be regarded as distinct from yet dependent on other areas of society.

This comes clear when, following Jonathan Gershuny, we further explore the meaning of services. Paradoxically Bell's theory of a post-industrial society replete with services, nowhere explicitly defines what a "service" is. Throughout his writing, the service sector is contrasted with the industrial sector, and we are told that post-industrialism comes with a change "from goods to services," but despite this he never tells us directly what a "service" is. However,

> it becomes obvious by contrast with the nature of goods; goods are material, permanent, made by people using machines, which are sold or otherwise distributed to people who thereafter may use them at will. Services, we infer by contrast, are immaterial, impermanent, made by people for people (Gershuny, 1978b, p. 56).

Bell's entire theory of PIS as a distinctly different stage of development requires that service work is perceived as the opposite of goods production, because it is the supply of services—those "games between people"—which distinguishes PIS from industrial society, where most workers are employed in the fabrication of things. It is Bell's claim that, at a certain point, when industrialism generates sufficient wealth, service employment grows in response to the new affluence. A society moves out of industrialism when it has excess wealth to spend which it will lay out on immaterial services (education, advice, health care, entertainment. . .) that do not produce tangible things but rather consume resources. This is, of course, to recall Engel's theorem which is axial to Bell. Perhaps more significantly, it is also to recall the insistence of so much Marxism that the material base of society is the prerequisite for all else.

The premise of this model of change is challenged when one examines the substance of service work (services in terms of occupation rather than sectoral categorization) and the relations between the tertiary and other industrial sectors.

It is apparent upon closer examination that service occupations, defined as those the outputs of which are nonmaterial or ephemeral (Gershuny and Miles, 1983, p. 47) are not restricted to the service sector. An accountant working in a bank or in an electronics factory can be categorized as belonging either to the service or industrial sector, though the work changes scarcely at all. Similarly, a carpenter working in a college of education or on a building site can be in either category; there are managers in hospitals as well as in automobile plants. What this suggests is that industrial classifications do not illuminate the type of work performed, and many producers of goods can be found in the service sector, while many nonproducers are in the primary and secondary sectors. Gershuny and Miles calculate that as much as half the growth in service occupations is a result of intrasector tertiarization rather than inter-sector shifts (Gershuny and Miles, 1983, p. 125). When a manufacturer expands the white collar staff, perhaps in marketing, training or personnel, the firm is certainly taking on service workers, but who would seriously suggest that this is dependent on some autonomous productive sector? Much more convincing is the argument that such changes are to better allow the company to stay in business, to facilitate its productive activities by capturing markets, teaching workers to be more efficient, and more carefully selecting staff. They are expressions of an increased division of labor within and between industrial sectors. It must be that we reject the presentation of the service sector as some sort of parasite on the industrial base, if one can recognize similar occupations across the sectors: people doing the same work across industrial sectors cannot in one context be using up resources while in another creating them.

This observation brings into question the use of envisaging society in terms of separate levels, but the definite rejection of such a way of seeing comes when one looks more closely at the service sector itself. What one discerns is that a good deal of service sector work is engaged, not in consuming the wealth supplied by industry, but in assisting its generation. Gershuny, arguing that "the growth of the service sector of employment. . .is largely a manifestation of the process of the division of labor" (Gershuny, 1978b, p. 92), leads one to realize the "systematic link between the secondary and tertiary sectors" (Kumar, 1978, p. 204) and the consequent absurdity of sharply distinguishing realms. Browning and Singelmann, for instance, distinguish "producer services," such as banking and insurance that are largely "a reflection of the increasing division of labor" (Browning and Singelmann, 1978, p. 489) and are chiefly engaged in providing "services to producers of goods" (Singelmann, 1978b, p. 30). It is only by donning a pair of theoretical blinkers that one can perceive services as distinctly apart from production activities, and the following observation from Gershuny is subversive of all theorizations which foresee services springing from the take-up of I.T. by industry.

> the important thing to note about tertiary industry is that though it does not directly produce material goods, a large proportion of it is closely connected with the process of production in the slightly wider sense. The distribution industry, for instance, does not itself make any material object, and yet is an integral part of the process of making things—if products cannot be sold they will not be produced. Similarly, the major part of finance and insurance is taken up with facilitating the production or purchase of goods . . . though, in 1971, nearly half of the working population were employed in tertiary industry, less than a quarter of it—23.1%—was involved in providing for the final consumption of services (Gershuny, 1977, pp. 109–110).

Even education, which appears on the surface to be an archetypical Bellian service as a nonproducer which consumes resources, owes much of its growth to the wider society's need to systematize the training of its work force, to engage in research activities to improve industrial productivity, and the like.

Remarkably, Daniel Bell himself gives the lie to his own methodology in commenting upon the naivety of gross national product measures which calculate public services as debits. As Bell observes, this ignores the very real contribution such services can provide, because "the value of health services is measured by the costs of doctors' fees and drugs, not by the reduction of time lost on account of illness;

the value of education is measured by the cost of teachers' salaries, equipment, etc., not by the value imputable to the gain in pupil knowledge" (Bell, 1976, p. 281). To all of this, one can only assent. It is an error to categorize without qualification an effective health service which may return injured workers quickly and in full health to the labor force, where once their ailments may have resulted in permanent disability; it is folly to assume that production owes nothing to a well-schooled populace which is literate and numerate; it is an absurdity to imagine that producer services such as advertising are other than "intermediate inputs to the final product" (Gershuny and Miles, 1983, p. 13). This being the case, one must then ask why Professor Bell persists in retaining his model of society as one which projects a goods-producing sector apart from (yet funder of) its services.

Services and Manufacture

The notion that services are readily separable from other work activities, let alone industrial sectors, is false, and this of itself indicates our preference for a more integrative perspective. We may elaborate on the need for a more complex under-standing of services and a more holistic framework by drawing further on the work of Gershuny and Miles. In their study *The New Service Economy* (1983), they re-view difficulties associated with defining services and suggest the connections be-tween services and manufacture.

They distinguish four meanings of service, namely:

• *service industry*, which is all those firms and employers whose product is not a tangible good.
• *service occupations*, which are jobs that are not directly involved in production.
• *service products*, which are goods that perform service functions such as house-hold goods.
• *service functions*, which involve service work but which do not necessarily figure in the money economy.

We have argued that analysis of the service industry and service occupations undermines the base/superstructure metaphor upon which theories of a service society depend, because, although not directly involved in production, much of service industry and many service occupations are extensions of the division of labor rather than a sign of entry into a new era of consumption. We examine service functions towards the close of this chapter, but in the following focus on service products to further emphasize the wrong-headedness of separating goods-production from services-consumption.

In a number of propositions, Gershuny and Miles turn on its head Engel's theorem as they remind us of Bell's ex post facto logic which explains the growth of service sector employment in terms of society accruing wealth which it decides to expend on services. Bell, starting from the palpable fact that there is more service employment, deduces its expansion from Engel's rule that, as one gets wealthier, so one's additional income is spent on services. People must be spending more on services, argues Bell, since there are so many additional service workers around. A problem with this is that Bell fails to look at what service workers actually do, and, as we have seen, a great deal of service work is to be accounted for by the division of labor to make more effective the production of goods.

Another problem with Bell's account is that he fails to consider that people might satisfy service requirements by investing in goods rather than service workers. Gershuny and Miles come to this by reversing Engel's theorem, by wondering whether the case has not been that, rather than increased riches leading to extra expenditure on personal services to satisfy needs, a relative increase in the cost of service workers along with cheapened service products becoming available might have led to the satisfaction of service requirements through the purchase of goods rather than the employment of people. Gershuny and Miles argue that, over the years, services have not managed to achieve the productivity increases of manufacture, the result of which is that charges for services have risen relative to the price of manufactured goods. Figures from the Department of Employment support this with estimates that, between 1963-1983 in Britain, the cost of services grew 12.4% in real terms while durable household goods fell 36.7%. (*Economic Progress Report* (161) October, 1983, Chart 2). In this case, Gershuny and Miles argue that Engel's theorem still holds, people still want services, but the cost of having that service performed by another person becomes unattractive when set against the price of buying a machine to do it. In turn, this consumer demand for services in the form of goods "can. . .produce pressure for innovation in service provision" (Gershuny and Miles, 1983, p. 42), which means that service requirements impact on manufacture itself. Instances such as the automobile industry and consumer electronics are pointers to the trend of fulfilment of services by goods rather than through employment of service workers. Gershuny himself claims, with impressive empirical documentation, that the spread of service products signifies the growth of a "self-service economy"—almost the antithesis of Bell's service economy (Gershuny, 1978b, p. 81)—which is likely to continue to intrude into both service sector and service occupation employment.

The Myth of the Service Society

We return to the self-service economy below, but what we stress here is that these service products "form a fundamentally importance source of change in the overall industrial structure" (Gershuny and Miles, 1983, p. 121). The "industrialization of service production" (p. 84) is pointer to what others have called "consumer capitalism," where the production and consumption of goods and services are to be regarded as intimately connected. And they underscore a theme running through this book, that to conceive of society as divisible into distinctly separate levels is mistaken. The historical record shows that "the economies of the Western world during the 1950s and the 1960s were dominated by the consequences of social and technological innovations in the nature of provision for a particular range of service functions, namely transport, domestic services, entertainment" (p. 121); that, far from the economic and technological "basis" of post-war societies determining the amount of wealth available to pay for more service workers, the major activity of the "base" was the manufacture of service products that could substitute for service workers. Bell's theorization—and the other lesser offerings—cannot begin to account for this, since an adequate explanation must jettison insistence on separate realms of society.

Jobs in Leisure?

The hope of some that we are set to significantly increase jobs in leisure comes to grief on closer analysis. Though there is some difficulty in defining precisely what leisure jobs are, available data suggest that, over the past decade, they have grown but little (for men only 3%, and for women 14% between 1974 and 1981 (*Social Trends*, 13, 1983, p. 145), from a small base and even using the generous definitions of government statisticians—ranging from hotels, public houses to betting and gambling—they constitute no more than 4-5% of total employment). Only in the wildest projections can one foresee a transfer of work to this area sufficient to absorb even a small proportion of the present unemployed.

The theory also rests on the assumption that leisure activities will be labor-intensive, in the future, calling for much interpersonal contact between leisure worker and leisure taker. But one has only to think of that major leisure activity—television viewing—to consider that goods may well be a major means of satisfying leisure interests. Indeed, as we show in Chapter 9, a striking feature of leisure nowadays is that so much of it is in the form of technologies which enhance television—video, television games, home movies, viewdata, cable, and the like. To be sure, these require personnel to supply programming (though few if any additional workers in the manufacturing sector), but, looked at in the round, the numbers are small, there being in the whole of Britain less than half of one percent of the work force occupied in radio and television services, plus the film industry, in 1981 (*Employment Gazette*, May 1983, p. 5).

In spite of such sobering figures, the appeal of leisure jobs continues to surface. Tom Stonier, for instance, offers tourism as a major employer in post-industrial Britain, since "it is a large employer of the unskilled and semi-skilled. . .and it is an ideal buffer against the vagaries of the international economic climate" (Stonier, 1983, p. 165). It is his claim that the "historical heritage" of this nation—anything and everything from Buckingham Palace to "satanic mills and back-to-back houses" (ibid.)—meant that, even by the late 1970s, "tourism had become a bigger industry in Britain than automobiles" (p. 166), that there is much employment in showing "people who enjoy the warmth and the light, the good food and good health of post-industrial society the debt we owe our forebears" (p. 167).

Leaving aside the question of the desirability of a large-scale switch to tourist occupations (do we want to follow Grenada?), we may state that, even in the 1970s, the tourist industry employed considerably fewer than Stonier suggests, and is not likely to sustain significant growth in the future. In 1981 in Britain, there were 340,000 employees in motor vehicle and parts manufacture, 211,000 in repair and servicing, with a further 240,000 involved in their retail distribution and filling stations, making 791,000 in the trade, not counting those indirectly involved, such as those producing sheet metal for the manufacturing process. Tourism was composed of 33,000 in "tourist offices and other community services." If we are generous and add to this those employed in hotels (many of whom depend not on tourism but on business travellers), we get another 226,000, and no doubt there are several thousand people in restaurants who gain some sustenance from tourism (*Employment Gazette*, May 1983). But, however much we stretch the categories, however much we hope the future holds more Wimpeys and McDonalds, tourism cannot even match employment in automobiles let alone offer an answer to the problem of mass unemployment (see Tourism statistics, *Employment Gazette*, January 1986, pp. 19–20, Tables 8.2–8.9).

Dreaming of a Leisure Society

If we cannot look to the leisure industry to significantly create jobs, and if it is demonstrably the case that service sector employment is neither expanding nor conceivable as a luxury built upon industry's productivity, we come, like so many others who search for an answer to mass unemployment, to leisure itself. Characteristic of a plethora of "realistic" thinkers is Thatcherite Hector Laing (Chairman of United Biscuits) who concludes that "as the old industries shed people they are unlikely to re-employ them even as the economy recovers. The new industries won't absorb these people either, never mind the extra people that are coming on to the market" (*Financial Times*, January 7, 1983, p. 13). From this assessment, solutions couched in terms of reducing the amount of work done in order that the little that remains might be more evenly redistributed—by early retirement, job-sharing, shorter hours, and longer holidays—and changing the work ethic that the unemployed and the wider society might be accommodated to worklessness and less work have an irresistible attraction. We believe these are empirically misinformed and conceptually flawed. Let us show why.

Enforced Leisure

The first point is that several million people are well advanced towards a leisure existence already. These are the unprecedentedly large numbers of unemployed who are suffering enforced leisure. Their condition is not enviable. All the available evidence, accessible to anyone who cares to look, attests to the material deprivation of the unemployed (in Britain, the disposable income of an average worker with a nonworking wife and two dependent children falls by 47% on becoming unemployed, and it drops 74% for unemployed single workers ⟨*Observer*, 14 August, 1983⟩), their earnest desire to find work at rates even well below their previous incomes, their susceptibility to illness both mental and physical, the strain on family life, and the struggle to retain dignity. (see, inter alia, Miles, 1983;

Brenner, 1979; Jahoda, 1982; Coffield et al., 1983; Marsden, 1982; Sinfield, 1981; Seabrook, 1982a; Economist Intelligence Unit, 1982).

We might fruitfully explore why those presently in enforced leisure are left to suffer so by a society that, by almost any historical or comparative measure, is extraordinarily wealthy. Why have leisure attitudes not already made inroads into the national psyche? As a prelude to this investigation, we must note that the work ethic is alive and well in contemporary Britain. Its advocacy as a means of self and social development, the positive side of the work ethic, is a regular theme of Thatcherite politics which "believe in the puritan work ethic" that "honesty and thrift and reliability and hard work and a sense of responsibility. . .are not simply Victorian values. They do not get out of date. . . . They are part of the enduring principles of the Western world" (Thatcher, 28 January, 1983; cf. the premier's sermon on the moral impetus to work reported in *Guardian*, 5 March, 1981). The Conservative government of 1979, re-elected for another term in 1983, fought consistently, openly, and unashamedly on a platform of "rewarding entrepreneurs" who "work hard" with "drive and inventiveness" (Thatcher, October 14, 1983), to which end they promptly redistributed wealth away from the poorer to the more affluent class, the reduction of tax rates to the rich being a practical expression of this doctrine which contributed to the top 5% of the population increasing their share of the nation's wealth from 43 to 45% in 1981 (*Inland Revenue Statistics, 1983,* HMSO, pp. 39, 50, tables 4.8, 4.9).

Margaret Thatcher's beliefs find an echo in the wider society, evidenced not only in her electoral success, but also in the negative side of the work ethic which labels as work-shy and culpable those out of employment. Though economists talk of "structural unemployment" and Mrs. Thatcher of a "world recession [which] has brought high unemployment to almost every country" (October 14, 1983), the image of the "scrounger" is widely adhered to in modern Britain and hardly seems to have shifted over the past decade (Brown et al., 1983). An EEC report published in 1977, which found that an astonishingly high 43% of British respondents agreed that unemployment was caused "because of laziness and lack of will-power" (EEC, 1977), indicates that periodic media campaigns against "the Welfare Scroungers" (*Daily Mail,* 22 September, 1976; cf. Golding and Middleton, 1979), however much they might contribute to opinion, also strike a chord in the wider populace. For supporting evidence, we may look to the recent research on attitudes towards the unemployed by psychologist Adrian Furnham, who found that "people not on social security tend to have more negative attitudes towards those that are" (Furnham, 1983, p. 147), that commonly-held beliefs are that the workless are "fiddling," abusing social security by overclaiming, moonlighting, and such like. Similarly opinion polls regularly report that substantial numbers of people believe many of the unemployed do not want work (Boer, 1983).

It is this attitude which Nigel Lawson, the Chancellor of the Exchequer, articulated when, proposing a cut in the real value of unemployment benefit, he was asked whether he thought the present levels acted as a disincentive to work. He replied without hesitation: "I think there can be no doubt whatsoever" (*Guardian*, 4 July, 1983). And when Norman Tebbitt, a senior minister of the Crown, spoke on May 13, 1983 of unemployment being "socially acceptable at a higher level when benefits are generous than when they are non-existent," he was voicing at once the widely-held prejudice that the workless are somewhat featherbedded, in receipt of something for nothing, and giving the lie to the one-time truism that a return to pre-war levels of unemployment would not be tolerated. The cliché of the 1960s, that anything more than 5% unemployment would lead to social unrest that would be hard to contain, has been revealed as a nonsense by the reality of the recession being a disciplinary influence rather than a radicalizing force. The brutal truth is that high levels of unemployment have led to quiescence and the reassertion of orthodox values (cf. Moore, 1978; Runciman, 1966). This is at least in part a reason for the appeal of the ethics of Thatcherism, and is suggestive that unemployment rates of 20% or even more can be contained while the work ethic thrives; that we can expect the unemployed to continue to feel "*ashamed* of being unemployed," while many others continue "talking about lazy idle loafers on the dole and saying that these men could all find work if they wanted to" (Orwell, 1937, p. 76).

We do not want to argue that attitudes towards the workless are altogether negative: like much else in our society they are shifting and ambiguous. But, as a counter to heady talk of ending the work ethic, we must at the outset emphasize the *lack* of any significant change to date, though there are many unfortunates already compelled to live in a leisured condition. That these attitudes remain is reason to suspect that they are far more deeply entrenched, considerably more interwoven into the social fabric, than those who urge a change of mind suppose.

Job-sharing and Reduced Working Hours

A cognate issue is that of working hours. It is a commonplace that the shorter working week, earlier retirement, and longer holidays are signs of a long-term evolutionary progress towards a leisure society and indicative of the waning of the work ethic. Those who see here a resolution to unemployment—with hours of work few enough to enable jobs to be shared around with extra leisure for all—can positively bubble. Thus the labor editor of the *Financial Times* opens a story titled "How industry could adjust to soak up unemployment" with a premonition that "Those of us who work for forty hours or longer will soon be in a minority, and may even have to face charges of being anti-social for being so. . . the workaholic may soon be seen as being as much an outcast as the alcoholic" (*Financial Times*, 27 January, 1982). These projections must come to terms with a number of stubborn facts (cf., House of Lords, 1982, pp. 93–101):

• though it is undeniably the case that hours of work have fallen considerably over the last hundred years, since 1945 "the average (working week) has hovered around forty" (Meyersohn, 1975, p. 45). It is quite astonishing that the announcement of an agreement between management and unions for a 39-hour working week, as has occasionally happened in the past 5 years, is greeted as a breakthrough, when advances over the past 40 years have been minimal and official statistics show that

> the median number of hours worked by full-time male workers in 1981, at around 40 hours a week, was very similar to the distribution in 1971. This stability is not surprising; over the same period the normal weekly hours. . . of full-time manual workers declined by only one per cent (*Employment Gazette*, November 1982, p. 481).

● trades unions' negotiation of shorter working hours have largely been a covert form of wage bargaining which has established a reduced basic working week in order to boost earnings at overtime rates. Formal hours may have declined here and there, but in practice little has changed. In Britain in 1981, while over 40% of men in full-time work undertook a 40-hour week, nearly 25% worked 45 hours or more, and 5% reported a normal working week of over 60 hours (*Employment Gazette*, November 1982, Chart 4, p. 482).

● available evidence on circumstances in which shorter working hours have been arranged indicates that reductions in working time do not lead to extra employment opportunities, because hourly productivity tends to increase to compensate for the drop in working hours (White, 1980; *Employment Gazette*, October 1983, pp. 432–436).

● managements have persistently opposed attempts to lower working hours on grounds that this would mean higher costs, less competitiveness, and ultimately fewer jobs. In the context of crisis, this is an impulse to increase working hours rather than reduce them (cf. Anglo-German Foundation, 1981). It is for this reason that Ford resisted worker calls for a 39-hour week until 1982, and British Leyland motors was prepared to withstand strikes and worker discontent during 1981–1983 in order to cut back on breaks, speed up the track, and lengthen the night shift. And the attitudes evidenced in these particular cases were made general at the Confederation of British Industry's 1983 annual conference, where delegates "overwhelmingly endorsed a resolution attacking the move for shorter hours" (*Guardian*, November 9, 1983). Philip Stephenson captured the mood of conference when he rejected the "manifest absurdity" of calls for shorter hours. "The only way," he continued, "to create more jobs. . .was to increase working time" to match the challenge of "Japan and the Far East where most operatives worked for between 50 and 60 hours a week" (ibid.).

● attempts to introduce job-splitting schemes in Britain have been largely unsuccessful, despite financial incentives from government. The problems of organization, career structures, and the unwillingness of employers and employees to share jobs has led to only just over 300 cases being reported over the first 5 months of a scheme which allowed employers to claim £750 for each existing full-time post that was split in such a way as to give part-time work to people who would otherwise be unemployed and in receipt of benefit (*Guardian*, 19 July, 1983).

● though there has been some early retirement in Britain over the past few years, as late as 1979 some three-quarters of men aged 60–64 were in the work force. This figure is exceptionally high (in the U.S. it was 63%, in Germany 40%), but thoughts of making a reduction encounter the difficulty of funding early retirement. A *Financial Times* journalist, reporting these figures, noted that proposals to reduce the age of retirement had been warned that its cost would be prohibitive at a time when pensions and associated benefits already consume 17% of Britain's public expenditure (Hargreaves, January 24, 1983).

• hopes that part-time work might be extended to share full-time jobs run up against the fact that it is almost all (over 90%) performed by women, has been a manifestation of their entry to the labor force, is low-skilled, limited in range, usually temporary, and poorly paid (*Employment Gazette,* November 1982, pp. 477–486). These patterns are a historical legacy and cannot easily transfer across the gender divide.

The Conceptualization of a Leisure Society

The above shows that there is no easy way by which a leisure society might be brought about. Little progress towards such an order has been made, the work ethic is still strongly felt, and the "notion that ordinary workers have much more leisure time at their everyday disposal than before the war is a gross misconception" (Westergaard and Resler, 1975, p. 84). Nonetheless, optimists could persist with their argument, contending that these are but obstacles in the way of changing attitudes to adjust to the new age, that the proselytizers of a leisure society must persist in the face of sharp opposition in voicing the view that the "work ethic is a proposition bred by mercantilism out of the Reformation. It is only by recognizing its irrelevance to modern conditions that governments can begin to think straight about employment" (Wedell, 1983). So long as it is the case that "80 per cent of the potential labor force is needed to earn enough to pay everybody, there is room for more flexible measures for the other 20 per cent" (ibid.), and there is a strong argument for persisting with the mission to convert people to a new ethos however awkward the arrangements might be. So long as there is a material plentitude and the promise of yet more to come, then there is a case to be made that the main task is to change attitudes to work so that all might enjoy the future wealth without stigma.

The problem with this is not simply that it must encounter profound practical difficulties, but that it is also theoretically miscast. And it is so in the same way as with those who project a service society, in that the framework of analysis is one which assumes the separation of society into different levels. Thus it repeats the service society mistake in presuming there is an economic/technological base which throws up resources to be consumed at a separate level by services or leisure. The two do not come into contact with one another (yet the former is in some way the determinant of the latter): one is asocial, neutral, a "natural" arena of production, the other the sphere of choice and valuation.

The leisure society perspective not only repeats this error but also continues to produce other dichotomies which are untenable. The most prominent of these antinomies are technology and society, work and the work ethic/leisure ethos, necessity and freedom, economy and beliefs. All share a presentation in which the former is conceived as a desocialized realm where arrangements impose themselves—through natural needs or due to the search for efficiency—upon human beings, rather than being human creations. And the latter realm is presumed to be where the action is, where values, desires, and subjectivities thrive. We have argued earlier against this fallacious vision of technology and society which carries with it the paradox of being deterministic at the same time as it talks endlessly of choices to be made. Here we extend the argument to comment on the opposition of work and the work ethic and necessity and freedom.

Work and the Work Ethic

The concept of a leisure society for which we now have the wealth to pay, provided we change our opinions about work, rests upon the assumption that work is a given phenomenon, an imposition which is unpleasant but unavoidable. It has an inherent logic which imposes upon workers generally debilitating conditions. Because of this, attitudes towards work are regarded as exogenous, as embellishments which persuade people to undertake necessitous but laborious tasks. This dichotomy—work has to be done, the work ethic is propaganda to get people to do it—is the axis of those who, seeing now that so much work can be done by machinery, announce the death of the work ethic and the birth of a leisure age. No longer required to brainwash people to get work done, we can now abandon outmoded ideas.

The trouble with this conception is that work cannot be desocialized, because any historical analysis reveals it to be a social construct. And because we are so familiar with this social phenomenon which is work that we assume its naturalness does not make it any the less social. The creation of factories, time-sheets, wage rates, supervisory roles, specialized tasks, assembly lines, finished products, and so forth—the very stuff of work as we know it—are all artificial processes, human fabrications. With this insight, dualist perspectives break down. The notion that work (there) can be extinguished smoothly so long as society (here) amends its opinions is no longer tenable. Acknowledgement of the social character of work compels us to see that there is nothing naturally imposed which is about to be made technologically obsolete, and leads us to look seriously, not at work as a thing in and of itself, as an inhuman activity apart from society, but at the society which has brought work into being and now proposes its abolition.

If we realize this, that work does not have to be abolished to allow us to be human, but that being humanly created it can be humanly reshaped, we can raise a most serious question mark over the desirability of a leisure age. The question of import becomes: what has made work, the work we must endure, so onerous that thought of escape is so ·alluring? Göran Palm, in his sensitive account of work at the giant Ericsson plant in Sweden, vividly evokes this issue. He chronicles the brutality of the work that must be done, the human waste when people think "that the most important thing in work is that the working day should end as quickly as possible" (Palm, 1977, p. 113). He reports that

> It seems so self-evident to most of these employees that the working day is there to be passed as quickly as possible that they seldom even think of the fact that *it could* be different. There are constant complaints at LM workshops but seldom about this particular aspect, seldom about the fact that there is something wrong with the work itself. . . .It is almost as though a law of nature prevailed (p. 123).

But witnessing the stultification that is the lot of so many workers—as leisure futurists do—Palm refuses to blame work itself for this—as leisure futurists do—by resisting the tautology that "work is work." On the contrary, he points out that alienating work ought not to be reason for welcoming its abolition, but for condemning its architects:

> the very fact that this way of experiencing working hours is common entails a pretty crushing judgement of those who have organized and distributed the jobs at LM. And not only at LM. They have organized these tasks in such a way that those who have to carry them out do not feel satisfied until the tasks have come to an end, i.e. when the Bell rings. They have organized these tasks in such a way that those who have to carry them out concentrate on getting through them as quickly as possible so that they can go home (p. 123).

Advocates of a leisure society assume as irrelevant the social factors that have led to work being what it is today. But the past weighs heavily on the present and future, and even the recent history of work provides an instructive lesson. This is a history which in the last century is intimately connected to technological changes. These are regarded, like work itself, as somehow natural, in that they are presented as neutral developments which come upon us and represent progress. However, like work, technology is a social construct, and is revealingly examined from such a point of view. Refusing to see technology as a thing apart from society, we can recognize that in this century, notably in manufacture, technologies have been purposively designed and developed as a means of getting more out of employees. Nowhere have engineers or investors seriously considered creating machinery which might ennoble work (cf. Noble, 1977). Throughout, the aim has been to maximize output while minimizing the role of worker who threatens—as a human being who is unpredictable, and as an economic cost—to interrupt that pursuit. The consequences of machinery and organizational changes, technological and technical refinement, have been that workers have had imposed upon them tasks which are routine and fragmented.

This is not happenchance. It has taken place because the overriding concern of those who make decisions about research and development programs, purchase of machinery, and deployment of workers approach with the principle in mind of how best to effect a return on their investment, and Information Technology is part of this process. Presented as an unearthly discovery, its history reveals that it has been guided by the powerful's search for greater return from the lower orders. To this end, corporations are investing heavily in computer-communications equipment to improve the productivity of even their nonmanufacturing personnel. The workers whom it impacts will in the main experience job loss, more machine pacing, restrictions on the variety of tasks, a loss of control.

The hapless employer will reply that he exists in a competitive world—the "real" world (but this is a value too!)—and he must take up new technology to keep his business going. The more optimistic will insist that cheapened production, even if it reduces jobs in the short run, will in the end generate more jobs as extra markets are captured. The less sanguine tell us that maybe more jobs will not follow in the wake of economic expansion, but at least with growth we will be able to be kind to the displaced. One can scarcely credit such logic; the worker is told to accede to a technology which has been designed either to do him out of a job or to make his work more constrained in order that the employer might get more for his investment and, if things turn out alright, perhaps the work ethic will be changed.

Not only is this unreasonable, in that it asks the worker to trust to the judgement of those who have major responsibility for making work what it is with little consideration for the well-being of the worker, but it also ignores other dimensions of the work ethic which make it much more than a means of getting people to work by telling them that they ought to go, in that it connects with and helps justify the wider distribution of income and wealth. That is, the very people who are most actively taking up new technology are the same ones who are insisting that we cut back on public expenditure, reduce the burden of the welfare state, and revamp the tax system to stimulate the initiative and inventiveness of the entrepreneurs who will lead us out of the abyss. It is for these people that Mrs. Thatcher speaks in almost every speech which recites privatization, reduced public expenditure, and technological innovation as the way forward. The people who gush forth about "Britain having lived beyond its means for too long," at a time when official figures reveal that those living on the margins of poverty leapt 30% between 1979 and 1981, to almost one in four of the population (*Guardian*, 1 November, 1983), are those most avidly urging upon us new technology in the name of a work ethic which will reward the "lean and fit" and squeeze out the "indolent and fat." It is because the work ethic is much more than an additional input to work, because it is connected to the wider web of social relations in society, that we cannot expect it to give way if and when we emerge from recession. Does anyone believe that today's entrepreneurs, suffused with the work ethic, will then with aplomb agree to greater taxation to fund the "new consciousness" (D. Bell) of a leisure society? It is no wager that these same people will be those who insist on retaining their "hard-earned rewards" gained "by working all hours" in the name of the work ethic and, in the name of the same work ethic, refuse to give more to the workless.

Dignity at work

Insisting that work is a social product, asking what sort of society is it that has brought us to the position of considering a leisure age, the foregoing is deeply suspicious of those who would have us throw off the work ethic. We add a further gloomy note. There are those with compassion who look to I.T. to ease the burdens of the poor even while it takes away what work remains for them. There is much that is admirable in this tradition, and it has a lengthy history of struggle for reform of wages and welfare, but it does seem to us to have capitulated at a quite crucial point in accepting a definition of work as something which must be endured, a sacrifice of one's life performed for so much money. Krishan Kumar reminds us of this when he recalls that the waves of radicalism that swept England during the early decades of the nineteenth century were chiefly artisanal protest against novel forms of work which could be compared adversely to alternatives still alive in the collective memory. The rise of trade unionism signified acceptance of the ways of work that capitalism decreed with struggles limited to wages, safety, and social benefits (Kumar, 1983, p. 16). Palm puts this onto a contemporary stage:

> The annual wage increases, the increasingly laboriously raised real wages, holiday compensation, overtime compensation, supplements for inconvenient working hours, weekend supplements, transfer grants, severance pay, etc.—all of these are undoubtedly and unreservedly appreciated by those who have benefited from them. . . . The successful wage struggle has helped lift the working people out of the poverty, slums and undernourishment which still prevailed well into the twentieth century. Tuberculosis has been eradicated, as have the cockroaches. Modern dwellings, comfortable clothes and fast cars have come instead. And yet: are not all these improvements remote from man as a worker, man as a human being who sits at his or her machine or works on his or her components? (Palm, 1977, p. 126).

There are many who recognize the scars that work as it is inflicts upon people, and it is understandable that they see in I.T. an opportunity to heal these by destroying that work. After all, obliteration of this odious thing is but the logical extension of unionism and much socialism which has fought for leisure time demands, for sufficient money from work to spend in leisure, and for longer hours for leisure. We cannot agree with these diagnoses. Because work has been devised as burdensome is not reason to capitulate to the notion that work is so awful that we should be glad when a technology arrives which promises its abolition. It is reason to fight for dignity at work, for technologies which enhance human labor, rather than diminish it. The fight ought not to be for the continuation of demeaning work, still less annihilation of that labor which is available, but for labor which is not demeaned. Anything else is to concede the "unilateral right enjoyed by management to organize, arrange, mechanize, automate, distribute, take apart, check and transfer both work and workers as they please" (Palm, 1977, p. 141).

Freedom and Necessity

The preceding remarks are as applicable to Marxist André Gorz as they are to Tory Francis Pym, since both postulate an asocial sphere of work which may subsidize leisure. As we have seen (Chapter 4), a good deal of Marxism defines its political goals in terms of more leisure which may ultimately be completed by total automation. Here we draw attention to the Marxist framework, not to reiterate the convergence with conservative thought, but because it allows us to comment upon another dimension of this agreement which is especially alluring at a time of rapid technological innovation.

We refer to the common notion that there are in society a specifiable number of needs which must be met before one can indulge in leisure. It is a common-sense proposition which runs along the lines that one must eat before one can play, provide housing before one can relax, warmth before rest. . . . In Marxist terminology, the "realm of necessity" is prior to the "realm of freedom": until a material basis is secured, people cannot even begin to consider breaking the chains of an oppressive political system. Central to this is an evolutionary view of development, the proposition that, until such time as the productive forces secure an adequate supply for needs, socialism is unattainable; the idea that capitalism is a progressive force in so far as it unleashes material abundance. As far as technology is concerned, this Marxist approach adopts, with some qualification, an *inheritor* policy: let capitalism develop the productive forces until the stage is reached when the proletariat can take them over. From this point of view, technology and work are in an important sense asocial, impositions of necessity which must be endured until such time as technology can undertake all onerous labor. The advent of I.T. is regarded from this point of view as a means of more readily satiating needs in a manner that will make work—an activity forced upon us by necessity—less necessary. The Marxist stress on the limitations imposed by needs fatally embraces the conservative view that advanced technology has such productive capabilities that work in future will hardly be necessary. What is the purpose of arguing for socialism, if I.T. will bring it in its wake?

The presentation of needs which must be satisfied by technology and/or work as a prerequisite for political debate assumes a realm of the natural which ought to be challenged. To ask the questions "what are needs?" and "what is the relationship between this necessity and freedom?" is not only an assault on familiar Marxist tenets, but it is also to query the necessity for much of what I.T. promises to do for us.

Bookchin has spent a good deal of time pointing to the absurdities of the Marxist separation of the "realm of necessity" from the "realm of freedom" (Bookchin, 1982, p. 10, passim). He ridicules the contradictions inherent in this divorce of realms—one oppressive the other liberatory—at the same time as Marxists claim that necessity conditions freedom. In remarks that are particularly apposite to Gorz's depiction of a dual society where short working hours in objectionable circumstances are compensated by affluent free time, Bookchin derisorily observes that insofar as self-management, self-activity, and selfhood are the very essence of the "realm of freedom," they must be denied at the "material base" of society while they are presumably affirmed in its "superstructure". . . . On the other hand. . .we must further conceive that this dehumanized realm of necessity—riddled by "imperious authority" [Engels] —can somehow enlarge the class consciousness of a dehumanized working being into a universal social consciousness. . . .we must conceive that this free society can remove hierarchy in one realm while "imperiously" fostering it in another, perhaps more basic one. Carried to its fullest logic, the paradox assumes absurd proportions. Hierarchy, like overalls, becomes a garment that one discards in the "realm of freedom" only to don it again in the "realm of necessity." Like a see-saw, freedom rises and falls at the point where we place our social fulcrum— possibly at the center of the plank in one "stage" of history, closer to one end or another at other "stages," but in any event strictly measurable by the length of the "working day" (Bookchin, 1980, p. 127).

Marxism is trapped into proposing that the human being is "born like the trolls of old when the sun goes down and which dies when the sun comes up," ensnared in relegating work and leisure (or necessity and freedom) to different worlds, which results in people being "invited to split themselves in two" (Palm, 1977, p. 151). Because of an unexamined conception of need, Marxism is both determinist (technology and/or the productive forces come the motor of history) and hopelessly ambivalent (it must offer separate poles of freedom and necessity). To the extent that Marxist thought is ensnared in this way of seeing, Bookchin's dismissal of Marxism is deserved:

the "realm of necessity" can never be viewed as a *passive* "basis"; it must always infiltrate and malform the "realm of freedom". . . Marx's tragic fate can be resolved into the fact that, integral to his entire theoretical edifice, he colonizes the "realm of freedom" by the "realm of necessity as its basis." The full weight of this theoretical approach, with its consequent reduction of social relations to economic relations, of creative to "unalienated labor". . .of individuality to embodied "needs," and of freedom to the "shortening of the working day" has yet to be grasped in all its regressive content (Bookchin, 1974, p. 26).

Given the fatal attraction of Marxism to the metaphor of base and superstructure (or necessity and freedom), the time may have arrived when Marxists must renounce their Marxism if they are to comprehend the significance of I.T.

Need is a Social Construction

There will be readers who agree that the precise relation between the realms and the degree of determination between the levels of necessity and freedom are problematical, but who are not prepared to jettison the framework. Common sense tells us too insistently that food, clothing, and shelter are necessities, are prior to politics and perhaps even consciousness. Many can accept that Palm identifies a real difficulty for Marxists when he asks:

Clearly those who are hungry must first have enough to eat. . . . But how far above the starvation level does this rule apply? Is for example pudding more important than the dignity of work? Is owning a pedigree dog more important than the dignity of work? Is freedom in a house of one's own more important than freedom at work? (Palm, 1977, p. 130).

But many fewer will accept this as reason enough to reject the idea of needs being a natural requirement that is an axis of all approaches to I.T. which envisage the new technology as the herald of an era in which needs are satisfied and in which, on the basis of a technological resolution to the problem of need, leisure (or socialism or services) may be constructed. Against this, with Bookchin, we insist that the realm of necessity, the needs which we are assured shape work as we know it, are *not* natural facts which at last can be done away with by a wonderful technology. On the contrary, "Need itself is a socially conditioned phenomenon" (Bookchin, 1980, p. 129).

A starting point for establishing this claim might well be anthropology. Marshall Sahlins makes the point that needs may be satisfied in two ways, either "by producing much or desiring little" (Sahlins, 1974, p. 2), and in his studies of tribal economies reveals that the leisure society can be attained by having modest needs. Thus, "hunters and gatherers work less than we do; and, rather than a continuous travail, the food quest is intermittent, leisure abundant" (p. 14). What we have here is a truism—the "original affluent society" is one where needs are defined unambiguously and are therefore satiable in conditions where "people do not work hard" (p. 17)—that economic organization (and work, production, need, etc.) is "a category of culture" (p. xii) rather than of nature. But though this is a truism, it is nonetheless subversive of most projections, Marxist or otherwise, of services or leisure that assume the pre-existence of needs independent of social values.

Drawing attention to the relativity of needs, we can return to our own society with the query: what are the social conditions that define needs here? We do not get far with Engel's theorem (accepting for the moment the separation of wealth and need which the maxim entails), since the claim that, as wealth increases, so additional needs are generated, is thrown into doubt by the prior question: why do we need to increase wealth in the first place? We certainly do not advance much in trying to compile a list of physical needs, since even categories such as housing and food raise questions of size, architectural design, variety, taboos, modes of cooking, quantities, and so forth.

A better answer is found in Sahlins' remarkable assertion that "modern capitalist societies, however richly endowed, dedicate themselves to the proposition of scarcity. Inadequacy of economic means is the first principle of the world's wealthiest peoples" (Sahlins, 1974, p. 3). On these terms need cannot be a basis of our society which, upon being met, can give way to more leisure because the dynamic of the system is premised on an inability to satisfy "infinite needs" (p. 39). The raison d'être is not to fulfil need and then relax, but to continue the process of capital accumulation which requires the continual creation of need in order that the market might avoid stagnation. It is for this reason that capitalist societies can never satisfy needs. Because the market is not merely a way of allocating resources, but also a means of keeping the show on the road—without being able to sell, without being able to attain growth, the system atrophies—needs cannot be allowed to be satiated. It "can never be possible to define what would constitute *enough;* the ancient dream of sufficiency, as soon as it comes close to realization, has to be jettisoned, because it is not compatible with the economies of the west" (Seabrook, 1980, p. 439). All talk of I.T. being able to "supply all our material needs within 20 to 30 years" (Large, *Guardian,* 6 April, 1983), and futurism Left and Right is riddled with such talk, is subverted by the fact that in capitalism needs are infinite (Leiss, 1978). Once this is accepted, we must abandon ideas of work sharing, increased leisure, etc., because these solutions are dependent on the assumption that "there is a fixed amount of work to be done" to satiate limited wants. But there "cannot be 'too many workers' so long as there are unsatisfied human needs" (Brittan, 1983), needs in capitalism are insatiable, and therefore the root idea of leisure society theorists, that unemployment is caused by there being excess production to fulfil needs, is untenable.

If needs cannot be regarded as finite, they also cannot be seen as inchoate expressions of consumers' desires. A popular opinion has it that consumer demand for satisfaction of needs determines productivity activity, but if this were so a great deal of corporate activity would be endangered. It is our view that much marketing, design, and salesmanship indicates the attempt of the industrial system to "adapt belief to its needs" (Galbraith, 1975, p. 272). This is to suggest that consumption and production in capitalism are integrally connected, a principle opposed to the linear thinking of those who assume that, first, there are pre-given needs, that these are then met by production, and that, later on, leisure can be expanded.

Essential to comprehend this unity is the notion of capital accumulation, which is a constant pressure towards discovering needs, giving rise to the situation where "wants are increasingly created by the process by which they are satisfied" (Galbraith, 1979, p. 238). There is now a sizeable literature documenting "the management of consumer demand" (Galbraith, 1975, p. 273), the stimulation of needs by advertising, marketing campaigns, regular redesigns of products, media parades, the display of goods in brightly-lit arcades (cf. Ewen, 1976). It is now recognized that the rise of advertising was much more than a mission to inform customers of what was available; it was a means of exercising some control over markets for goods in order that corporations could be better regularized, growth better planned, manufacturing made more efficient (Pope, 1983). In our society, need is defined by a market system which promises to satisfy it at the same time as it can never allow satiation to be achieved. This paradox, that modern production promises to satisfy all needs, yet constantly requires the generation of further needs, means that we must abandon conceptualizations of society which entail different levels. If the creation of needs is essential to the continuation of capitalist production, then what sense does it make to distinguish separate realms of necessity and freedom?

Finally, demonstrating that needs are insatiable in a market economy, and that this undermines projects of needs being assuaged and a leisure age introduced, the Left, which so often equates the realm of freedom with leisure, faces a disturbing irony. This is that a major locus of capital accumulation, both of goods and services, is the realm of freedom itself. In so far as leisure, free time, has been achieved, it has also in large part been colonized by some of the most dynamic elements of capital. The entertainment business, the happiness industry, portents of a leisure age we are told will transcend capitalism itself, are areas in which some of the most energetic examples of capitalist enterprise are found. This being so, when the leisure industry is so central a feature of contemporary capitalism, how can one begin to divide this society into levels wherein necessities and freedom are divorced?

The Informal Economy

Earlier in this chapter, we drew upon the work of Gershuny to demonstrate that the growth of services could not be seen as representing a new society, but that service occupations, service products, and the service sector should be regarded as integrated phenomena. We recoursed to Gershuny's depiction of the connections between manufacture and service products as a means of underlining the fallacy of conceiving society in terms of separate realms. Not only is Gershuny's work a direct assault of Bell's post-industrial society theory; it also contains materials for a critique of all anti-holistic methodologies. This being so, it is ironic that Gershuny himself sketches a future scenario which is open to similar criticisms to those levelled above, in that he draws upon a "dual economy" (Gershuny, 1978b, pp. 150–151) model of development. Because we believe that he accurately delineates ongoing empirical trends which he theoretically misconceives, we elaborate upon the "self-service economy."

Gershuny counters Bell by showing that, while service occupations and the service sector have grown, consumption of services has, if anything, fallen over the last 20 years or more. While people are more affluent, they have not spent additional amounts on personal services, but more on service products, because, while they want more service functions, the costs of personal services have grown while those of service goods have declined in price. To the extent that Engel's theorem holds, Gershuny argues that it is met by products rather than by people, a possibility not considered by Bell but borne out by spending patterns.

He projects a bleak future, envisaging sustained decline of employment in manufacture and the service sector with the spread of I.T., and concluding that the prospect is one "of declining wages and rising unemployment. Our socio-technical system is stagnating" (Gershuny and Miles, 1983, p. 125). However, set against this decline of the formal economy is growing self-service activity which uses goods from manufacture for people to do for themselves in the informal economy (where goods and services are produced without declaration to state authorities). This is by no means unproductive (Rose, 1983), whether undertaken in household, community, or the black economy, and is "often more satisfying than routine deskilled employment" (Gershuny and Pahl, 1980, p. 7). If self-service is on the increase, while unemployment in the formal economy is in decline, then it can be regarded as something of a substitute, at least a palliative, for unemployment. In this way new technologies, while denuding opportunities in the formal economy, can have beneficial consequences in stimulating alternatives in the informal arena; "it is at least possible to consider technological change as not merely piling on the misery to our stagnating socio-technical systems, but as forming a key element in the transformation to the new types of socio-technical systems" (Gershuny and Miles, 1983, p. 128).

In this way it is possible to welcome I.T. in spite of its job-reducing consequences in the formal economy, because "with appropriate public policies the informal economy may be adapted to socially progressive ends" (Gershuny and Pahl, 1981, p. 83). Gershuny and Pahl accept that "the efficient industrial production which is necessary to compete in international markets, means reducing employment" (Gershuny and Pahl, 1980, p. 9), advocating in reply "a much more flexible approach to how all work gets done" (Gershuny and Pahl, 1981, p. 85) which involves "sharing jobs among those who want them and exploiting the promise of the informal economy" (p. 88). Their suggestion is for men to emulate traditional female patterns, "which might involve a period in the formal economy, then a period in the domestic economy with young children, followed by a period of part-time or "voluntary" work before returning full-time to the formal economy" (p. 87).

Since they accept that "we cannot escape the development of some form of dual economy. . .[So] we must set about designing an acceptable form of it" (p. 85), most attention is to be focused on the informal economy to make acceptable new circumstances. This is revealed as a sphere which has "some highly desirable characteristics—autonomy, variety, greater use of personal skills and initiative and so on" (p. 81) that can be presented as an alternative to formal employment, provided enlightened social policies are adopted by government. Their depiction of work in the informal economy converges with many leisure society theorists: it may be unpaid, but provided it has a supply of goods from manufacture and is not impoverished it can be defined as "constructive, social functional unemployment" (p. 81). It can, in short, be regarded as the sort of worthwhile leisure activity foreseen by futurists who envisage a dual economy that, because it is productive in one sector, can free people from work and give them free time to do their own thing elsewhere.*

---

*Pahl's recent book (1984) appeared too late to be considered here. The study provides important evidence about activities in the household, and revealingly insists on a wider conception of work than employment. However, while it is "largely a refutation" (p. 11) of his earlier views, Pahl underestimates the significance of employed work, because of his focus on the home appears to regard it as a palliative to macro-economic problems, and, most serious, fails to examine how the "one economy. . . is becoming increasingly pervasive, dominant and destructive of alternative ways of getting by" (p. 134).

The informal economy has been seized upon by I.T. zealots who recognize that it will create high unemployment but wish to gain acceptance for it. Bob Tyrrell of the Henley Centre tells us that the informal economy is not only "genuinely productive" but that its existence and vibrancy questions the "conventional wisdom that has it that only work can meet our need for social status, psychological fulfilment, structure to our day and economic return" (*Guardian*, 16 February, 1983). Des Appleton trumpets the same message when he claims that the "rediscovery of the household as a significant unit is another example of change in work organization; already anecdotal evidence exists of traditional work being transferred to the home through the facility of micro-techology" (*Guardian*, 19 October, 1983). And just in case we have not yet appreciated that unemployment caused by I.T. is no bad thing, since the informal economy, helped by I.T., provides even more satisfying work than before (call it leisure-as-work), Professor E. G. Wedell spells it out in recommending that we make "the market sector of the economy. . . fully competitive" (which entails much labor reduction) while providing "adequate subsistence" to "those not needed in the market economy," so that they can keep busy "working for themselves and their neighbors." Already, opines the learned professor, "the growth of the voluntary sector and the informal economy demonstrates" that "people have begun to develop in these directions," so this policy would merely be following the wishes of the populace (Wedell, 1983). The informal economy shows that unemployment is not so bad; encourage I.T., and we will have enough wealth left from the market sector to make it even better when there are many more redundancies. Why, the *Economist* informs us, such is the scale of the "do-it-yourself economy" that it "probably absorbs over half of the hours during which Britons work." With all this action, there is no reason to fear unemployment, since the "domestic economy" is a safety net. It even, continues the esteemed journal, could mean that with all this productive activity in the home that the workless are contented Tories—certainly it "helps to explain why a lot of Britain's 3 million unemployed are still voting for Margaret Thatcher" (*Economist*, March 5, 1983, p. 36).

With all such prognoses, we are back on an already very familiar terrain. What is recommended "as the post-industrial transition gathers pace" is a "dual economic strategy" where the home and neighborhood are allocated extra resources to compensate for redundancy consequent upon "the creation of a slimmed-down formal economy which is competitive and efficient" (Robertson, 1983). Instead of leisure or services as result of or panacea for I.T., we are offered the joys of the informal economy, a more personal, rewarding, perhaps more efficient society that (a sop for the radicals) may even lead "to the decline of money and its tyranny and then to the making of a non-economic society" (Burns, 1975, p. 245).

There are numerous difficulties with this resolution to the problems of "post-industrialism" (see Henry, 1982, pp. 466-473), but we focus on two. The first is that it is only at an abstract level that the informal economy is likely to compensate for unemployment. Given the fact that those who are displaced from the formal economy are the most vulnerable, the poorest and least skilled, it is the case that these will be least able—and the least likely to be given help—to take advantage of the informal economy's potential (where they will share the condition of the most systematically disadvantaged group in our society and by far the most numerous in the informal economy—women). Lacking the skills to be creative and the capital to invest in goods to allow them to be productive, these are the people most likely to be found "doing nothing" in their unemployment (cf. Marsden, 1982, pp. 229-231).

A more serious weakness of the informal economy as resolution to unemployment is that it reproduces the same problem, evident in theories of leisure and services, of arbitrarily separating social realms. We can investigate this further by noting the willingness of the informal economy's advocates to accept that consumer needs from the household at once provide a link with the manufacturing sector (a demand push), while also assuming that these needs are autonomous of the market economy. The perspective assumes that informal economy wants are a stimulant to the goods-producing sector at the same time as these needs (what Gershuny calls "post-industrial values") are self-generating. It is striking that, throughout his writing, Gershuny accepts as natural the part of Engel's theorem which assumes a "hierarchy of needs" that are met in stages moving from "basic necessities towards luxuries" (Gershuny, 1982, p. 496). As we have seen, this is by no means obviously so, and need is a social category. But Gershuny will have none of this, arguing that, as we get richer, so we self-originate needs for more luxuries, which in turn stimulate industry. It is our view that this linear thinking—we get richer, new needs are generated, these impact back on manufacture, manufacture supplies the goods to satisfy need—is a misconception. While manufacture clearly does provide goods that substitute for some services (washing machines for laundries, vacuum cleaners for domestics) it is by no means certain that consumer needs so dictate. The production of goods to substitute for personal services might well be planning on the part of corporations in the formal economy. Perhaps more telling, there are many other goods for which the consumer never asked that are provided by manufacture, and a need then discovered or created. Whoever wanted or even imagined a need for cable television, tv games, video discs, personal computers?

It is our contention that the growth of the informal economy has much to do with capital's identification of a major market, that, rather than having been lured into the area by consumer demand, capital has stimulated needs, the better to effect its sales. To some extent, goods from manufacture to the home can be seen as a response to pre-existent monetary exchanges, in that industry saw a way of supplying a technology which could substitute for a service worker. But to a larger degree, it is a sign that capital, recognizing the long-term trend of privatization, has targeted the home as a major growth area. That so much I.T. for the home is an extension of the television is both recognition of a likely market and a determination to create more consumer need for activities which already account for 35% of leisure time (Martin and Mason, 1982, p. 203).

This intrusion of capital into the informal economy not only challenges the idea that consumer demand/needs are determining of what is manufactured, but also it questions the assumption of the independence of the informal from the formal economy (cf. Kumar, 1979, p. 23). Against the view, which suggests that the informal economy is a self-initiated development which imposes demands on the formal economy, this position claims that the connections are more integral. It does not deny that people strive to build for themselves meanings and things of worth, but it does state that business has entered the private sphere to better its interests, which often entails creating consumer needs. On these terms, there is a close connection between the growth of the self-service economy in which the "household becomes more self-sufficient. . .inward-turning and less sociable" (Gershuny, 1978b, p. 148), and the formal economy, which is more than a reaction to the wishes of the former and has much to do with corporate strategies that nurture the process of privatization. From this point of view, the growth of the informal economy offers little hope to the unemployed because it is regarded as a part of the spread of capital into expanding markets (and because this is so, when the household lacks spending power, capital is less interested in it, and thus we have the situation that informal economic activity is most pronounced in employed homes).

Our emphasis here is on the intentionality of the formal economy, which Gershuny regards as some lifeless respondent to "final demand" (Gershuny, 1982, p. 497). To delineate the intrusion of capital into the household in recent years is to raise serious questions about the assumption that this is simply answering the call of the consumer and to postulate that capital has its own interests to serve in developing in this direction (see Chapter 9). And to conceive of the informal economy as some haven from the ravages of capital, to picture it as the straightforward expression of consumer needs to which an inert manufacturing base passively responds, is to close one's mind to some of the most audacious corporate strategies currently being effected.

Conclusion

C. Wright Mills wrote 20 years ago that "the effective way to plan the world's future is to criticize the decisions of the present. Unless it is at every point so anchored, "planning" disguises the world that is actually in the works" (Mills, 1963, p. 303). When we read in our newspapers and see on our televisions promises of a coming leisure society, perhaps even more services, or the phoenix of a do-it-yourself lifestyle, it is as well to be reminded of Mills' words. The future we are told, from Left and Right, is to be built upon a technology which will enable us to afford all these extras. It will give us more time off, better services, the tools to do our own thing at home. The point of this chapter has been that leisure or services or the informal economy are not by-products of new technologies, that heady talk of such largesse is ignorant of "the world that is actually in the works" of present-day developments.

Services, leisure, and the informal economy and the range of technologies that are supposedly going to pay for them are instances of change, but they are changes in which capital's search to accumulate plays a leading part. To be sure, many services, a good deal of leisure, and much activity in the home and neighborhood have been wrested from capital or have been preserved, and these still require defending, but to project as expansion of services, leisure or the informal economy as a transcendence of capitalism is absurd: "the talk of change turns out to be changing people so that they fit the modified needs of cold economic processes; and the only revolution turns out to be the revolution of the fixed wheel" (Seabrook, 1982b, p. 47). Ironically the search to accumulate has, since the war, been directed in large part into leisure, services and the household. Capitalism's expansion has not only been international, but also new domestic "territories have. . . continued to be opened up all the time, conquered, colonized, annexed" (Seabrook, 1983). The magic of the marketplace has extended aggressively into services, leisure, and the home, and this penetration has even accessed what were once private domains. This is new, but it is a novelty exploited and engineered by capital itself.

Chapter 7
I.T. and Corporate Capital

I once asked a press agent for a computer company what was the reason for all this enthusiasm. He held a hand before my face and rubbed his thumb across his fingers. "Money," he whispered solemnly. "There's so goddamn much money to be made."

—Tracy Kidder. *The Soul of a New Machine.*
Harmondsworth: Penguin, 1982, p. 20.

Introduction

Xerox Corporation is a world leader in reprographics, and its range of copiers, duplicators, and electronic printing systems means that it is destined to play a pivotal role in any information society. Its dazzling array of word processsors, data networks, and work stations are the stuff of futurists' dreams. But Xerox itself has a proper sense of priority. Refusing to be awed by the wonders of new technology, it lists its five operational principles on the cover of its 1982 annual report. Top of that list are the words: "We exist to earn profits."

Coming from one of the world's major suppliers of I.T., it is a useful reminder of something which receives far too little attention from the post-industrial prophets, though the import of this ethos can scarcely be exaggerated. In the current climate of frenetic endorsement of change, of breathless celebration of a new era, one can usefully emphasize the role of established concerns. Along with Herbert Schiller, we would insist that "contrary to the notion that capitalism has been transcended, long prevailing imperatives of a market economy remain as determining as ever in the transformations occurring in the technological and informational spheres" (Schiller, 1981, p. xii). Encountering talk of a "new age" being brought about by I.T., it is important to realize that corporate capital is integrally connected with and initiatory of the new technologies. To ignore the presence of capitalist interests, to turn a blind eye to their goal of expansion, to overlook the significance of market criteria in the genesis and uptake of I.T., is something akin to studying the workings of the body while foregoing examination of the heart and head.

Corporate Requirements and Corporate Principles for I.T.

Virtually no corporation is aloof from I.T. and the bigger the organization the more it is needed to process information, coordinate disparate sites, and network within particular locales. For this reason, the history of I.T. ought to be seen as closely connected with the expansion of corporate capitalism as a whole. Dan Schiller has demonstrated that, as corporations grew inside the leading capitalist nation, so did America lead in the development of I.T., since "only telematics could control and unify the complex industrial and commercial operations thereby engendered under centralized corporate demand" (D. Schiller, 1982a, p. 4), and that it was pressure from big business users especially which has brought about the deregulation of communications as the means of providing I.T. facilities best suited to their purposes. By the same token, I.T. has been developed in line with the requirements of expanding transnational corporations, it being the

> same group of heavy corporate users of telematics which . . . has become a guiding force in an evolving domestic policy for U.S. telematics, [that] *today likewise demands expanded and integrated telematics services in the international arena*. These major corporate users require global rebuilding of telecommunications network facilities just as they earlier pushed for domestic upgrading of the network (ibid., p 101).

If it is the requirements of particularly American corporate capital which provide the setting for I.T.'s development there are some actors on stage playing especially prominent parts. These are a privileged group of corporations involved in the supply of I.T. goods and services. They are themselves at the forefront of users—it is characteristic that Xerox has "moved aggressively towards automation" (*Annual Report*, 1982, p. 5) of its production operations, and that I.B.M. uses its Satellite Business System network to handle more than 160,000 calls per day for the company's internal telecommunications requirements (*Annual Report*, 1982, p. 10)—but it is their location at the center of the I.T. industry itself which makes them most important. They find I.T. essential, not only as a tool for their own use, but also as a source of enormous market opportunity. These pressures have as a rule combined to make them especially eager to ally with business users to urge on government policies towards I.T. which favor "liberalization" of one-time state monopolies (notably telecommunications), the better that they might take advantage of opportunities to supply I.T. chiefly to corporate concerns and always on market principles. The machinations of these corporations are of such significance that they merit close inspection.

The Information Business

There are two major reasons why these suppliers have great interest in I.T. The first, already mentioned, is that there is an enormous market. Estimates vary as to its worth and likely expansion, but all are stupendous. For example, Mackintosh Consultants (1980) in 1979 thought that the world market for electronics, then worth $246 billion, would rise to $765 billion by 1990 (at 1979 prices). More recently, I.B.M. has estimated global demand for I.T. products and services will be $1,400 billion by 1992. Daily, such figures are reproduced in the business and technical press, and, with such potential rewards, it requires little imagination to account for the interest of capitalist enterprise.

Second, and related, because I.T. represents a move towards convergence and integration of once disparate industries, there is often not only a desire but a necessity for affected corporations to move with technological trends. The spread of I.T. is creating a new industrial situation where, as the chairman of Plessey has observed, "telephone, communication, data processing and electronics are increasingly converging into a huge fast-advancing industry" (*Sunday Times*, 22 October, 1978). This in turn brings into conflict previously unrelated corporations which once had established interests in products and processes (typing, computing, communications, copying, etc.) that are now usurped by the reach of I.T. Because "integrated information systems will require·co-ordination between the fields of computer technology, telecommunications and office equipment," corporations are busily restructuring having recognized that now it "will not suffice to be a specialist in only one" (Ericsson, *Annual Report*, 1982). This reorganization to meet the challenge and opportunities of I.T. is expressed in processes of vertical and horizontal integration (placing under one holding facilities for end-to-end production and regrouping around a coherent range of products).

The Strategic Role of Transnational Corporations

While it is as yet unclear precisely which corporations will maneuver themselves into a position of market supremacy, we do know who the contestants in this struggle will be. The I.T. industry is already dominated by a select and powerful group of transnational corporations. Tory M. P. Ian Lloyd suggested this in 1980 when he observed that "Almost by definition, I.T. is an international technology, with an international research and developing support base, and an international market at virtually all levels" (*Hansard*, 11 July, 1980, col. 982). Mr. Lloyd's notion of international is limited, in that the players are all from North America, Europe, and Japan, but insofar as he draws attention to the only organizations able to operate on this scale—transnational corporations such as I.B.M., A.T.&T., N.C.R., Olivetti, Siemens, Philips, Ericsson, I.T.T., Hitachi, Burroughs, Honeywell, Matsushita, N.E.C., Xerox, R.C.A., G.T.E., Sony, and Northern Telecom—he is accurate. It goes without saying that the participants are well aware of this situation, I.B.M. for instance advertising that "Information Technology is of course an international business" (*Times*, Dec. 1, 1983).

Within this elite, some corporations are better placed than others to take advantage of the changed I.T. industry. Those with established strongholds in *telecommunications equipment production and/or services* (A.T.&T is the most prominent) and *computer manufacture and services* (especially I.B.M. and the "Seven Dwarfs") are well situated, followed by companies positioned in the lucrative *office equipment* segment (e.g., Xerox, Olivetti). Other participants may be less centrally involved at the outset (though overall scale, wealth, and strengths can make up for disadvantages) and more or less dispersed. There are three overlapping categories here:

- *electronic and electrical conglomerates*, e.g., I.T.T., Philips, G.E.C., Siemens, Hitachi, AEG-Telefunken, Ericsson.
- *communications conglomerates*, e.g., R.C.A., Thorn-E.M.I., C.B.S.
- *outside corporations* seeking an entry to I.T., e.g., Shell, G.M., Coca-Cola.

All of these corporations are multi-million (and most often multi-billion) dollar organizations and are advantaged on the I.T. market in a number of ways. In particular they have

● the necessary resources to offer *systems* of compatible equipment and services which smaller competitors cannot afford. The major participants in I.T.'s leading sphere—the office sector aimed primarily at business users—are required to offer integrated information networks, and all have in recent months produced a system. Philips is typical when it reports that

> In the field of office automation we can now offer a complete range of systems. Our developments in this field are aimed at creating compatible and flexible systems for data and text processing, which are linked by a local network that can form part of a larger switching configuration. . . . In this way, our product policy ties in with the demand, which is shifting from separate units to integrated systems (*Annual Report*, 1982, p. 31).

● an *international reach and global strategy*. We have seen (pp. 109–115) how this confers advantages as regards labor supply and deployment, but it is also vitally important in the I.T. industry, which provides the data processing and communications infrastructure that underpins the increasing internationalization of political, economic and social affairs. The I.T. suppliers are not limited by national boundaries, and—at one with major customers—distinguish their operations and markets in the broad categories of Western Europe, North America, and the Far East. It is as a "global planner" (Barnet and Müller, 1975) that we are to appreciate I.B.M.'s self-assessment of its being "in a good position to take advantage of the growing worldwide demand for information processing products" (*Annual Report*, 1982, p. 2), and the Nippon Electric Co. (NEC) revealingly brags that "worldwide . . . information networks are becoming a reality," that "C&C" (integrated computers and communications) are "the very foundation of NEC's Universe," that wherever "the world environment grows in complexity"—in the home, business, and society at large—"NEC is certain to be there . . . one of the largest electronics manufacturers in the world today" (*NEC's Universe*, 1982).

● the resources necessary to *enter and sustain* a significant presence in the I.T. field. These prerequisites are always prodigious, the huge financial outlays being especially important in:

> (1) undertaking the inevitably costly *research and development* (R&D) programs necessary to develop advanced technology and to achieve and retain competitive edge. Sophisticated technology has long been a defining characteristic of transnational corporations, but circumstances have led to competition being expressed largely in terms of technological advantage in I.T. At the moment, innovation is at a premium because it is the locus of struggle for market leadership. The same reason accounts for the current extraordinary rate of technological change, with the product cycle lasting perhaps 3 or 4 years, while a few years ago it was a decade or more. It is this thirst for market edge in the I.T. business which leads transnationals to invest heavily to secure innovation. In turn, high

levels of investment in R&D at least in part account for the mind-boggling speed of recent technological change. Spending on R&D is proportionately high, as a rule being about double the expenditure of other sectors. However, it is the absolute costs of R&D which underline the advantages of the transnationals: examples of spending in 1981 were:

I.B.M., $1.6 billion
I.T.T., $1.1 billion
Philips, $1.1 billion
Siemens, $1.2 billion
General Electric, $1.6 billion

These occupy the upper levels of expenditure, but even at the lower ranges expenditures are in the hundreds of millions of dollars (e.g., in 1981 Texas Instruments spent $373 million, Digital Equipment $251 million, Plessey $203 million, R.C.A. $461 million). At the forefront stands AT&T's Bell Laboratories (which, under the 1984 divestiture, remains intact), which during 1982 employed more than 25,000 people, including 3,300 with doctoral degrees and another 6,000 with master's degrees, and handled a budget of $2 billion (*Annual Report, 1982*, p. 19). The only rival to this was I.B.M., which between 1977 and 1982 spent $8 billion on R&D, $2.1 billion in the final year alone (*Annual Report, 1982*, p. 8).

(2) paying the high premiums for *entry or relocation* in the I.T. environment. Huge sums are required to gain control of strategic plant and expertise in I.T., and it is the transnationals which have the resources to practice the favored method of acquisition as a means of restructuring. Since entry into I.T. requires "massive amounts of capital" (*Business Week*, October 11, 1982, p. 63), all but the super-rich are debarred. What super-rich means, we show below.

I.T. is Restricted to the Mighty Few

Characteristics such as these cast doubt on extravagant claims that I.T. is an entrepreneur's paradise. This is a favored theme of futurists and in Britain finds expression in media eulogies of the business acumen of computer supremo, Sir Clive Sinclair. Knighted for his entrepreneurial success, it is true that Sinclair has achieved considerable sales in personal computers. But is is quite wrong to take this market and the achievement of Sinclair's rapid entry as characteristic of I.T. Indeed, it is because the personal computer market is relatively tiny that it has, to date, been left free for small entrepreneurs, while the leading I.T. corporations go for the large markets in communications and computing. Figures are inexact, but the order of magnitude can be appreciated by the *Financial Times'* estimate that the world market for personal computers was $11 billion in 1982 (21 June, 1982; since this included machines costing up to £10,000 it also covered small business computers) which is about 7% of the business of managing, processing, and transmitting information (*Financial Times*, 11 April, 1983). Sinclair Electronics' turnover in 1983 was $80 million, which is miniscule when set against I.B.M.'s $34.4 *billion* the previous year. Moreover, the world computer leader did launch a personal computer aimed at small businesses rather than the home in 1981 (because of this, it cost considerably more than the hobbyist machines offered by Sinclair), and by 1983 had seized 30% of the market (*Financial Times,* October 25, 1983), indicating that the leading IT companies, when and if they judge it to be opportune, can enter these fields and rapidly establish dominance.

The inescapable reality is that the I.T. business overall is restricted to a few giant (if currently competing) oligopolies at home, and even more so abroad, of a size without precedent. When Jaques Maisonrouge, chairman of I.B.M. Europe, insists that "we are great partisans of the free enterprise system" (quoted in *Financial Times,* 2 March, 1981), this has to be interpreted as the freedom to compete in a match from which all those who lack hundred-million-dollar and more resources are excluded. (As if to confirm our point, Sinclair's company was swallowed then spat out by Robert Maxwell's printing and media conglomerate early in 1985.) Much more representative than Sir Clive Sinclair's $80 million sales are shown in Table 3.

Of course, these are gross totals which disguise important differences between corporations, and they exclude state holdings which can be substantial (e.g., in France the leading I.T. groups are nationalized, yet have revenues of some billions of dollars), as well as finance houses' investment (Hamelink, 1983) and the interests of oil companies (see below). Nonetheless, they do make clear the colossal scale of the I.T. industry where, for example, Wang Laboratories, with sales in 1982 of $1.2 billion, can be described as a "small company" when set against the major "corporate goliaths" (*Financial Times,* 18 March, 1981).

The I.T. transnationals know it is the case that "a relatively small number of very large companies account for a major proportion of worldwide sales" (I.T.T., December 31, 1981, p. 7). Siemens too is aware that its scale confers considerable advantages, boasting that it is "among the few suppliers on the world market who combine the three 'C' technologies (communications, computers, components) under one roof: technologies which shape the course of future developments in communications [because] Only a company which offers a full range of communications products and services can also provide comprehensive customer-oriented solutions to the future" (Siemens, n.d., circa 1980). Acting on this recognition, Olivetti has entered a number of strategic alliances and acquisitions to strengthen its position vis-à-vis other transnationals. A remarkable instance of its perception that the "challenge offered to us by the new industries cannot be countered by purely national policies" (*Annual and Extraordinary General Meeting,* 7 April, 1982, p. 12) was the agreement reached with AT&T in December 1983 by which Bell took a 25% holding in the Italian company as a means of distributing its goods and services in Europe, while AT&T will do the same for Olivetti in America. The *Guardian's* report of the reasoning behind the deal sounds the refrain of giant corporations operating in a world market wherein the nation state is insufficient for their needs: the hundred-million-dollar-plus deal had been made, said Olivetti's chairman, in order that the "partnership would be able to face the competition

Table 3

Corporation	Base	1982 Revenue in Billions of Dollars
AT&T	North America	65.8
IBM	North America	34.4
General Electric	North America	26.5
Siemens	Europe	17
Hitachi	Japan	16.3
Philips	Europe	16.1
ITT	North America	16
Matsushita Electric	Japan	14.9
GTE	North America	12.1
Eastman Kodak	North America	10.8
Toshiba	Japan	10.2
Westinghouse	North America	9.7
Xerox	North America	8.5
RCA	North America	8.2
GEC	Europe	8
3M	North America	6.6
Mitsubishi Electric	Japan	6.2
Schlumberger	North America/Europe	6
Sperry	North America	5.6
Honeywell	North America	5.5
N.E.C.	Japan	5.5
AEG-Telefunken	Europe	5.5
Thorn-E.M.I.	Europe	4.7
Sony	Japan	4.5
Texas Instruments	North America	4.3
Control Data	North America	4.3
Hewlett-Packard	North Amrerica	4.3
C.B.S.	North America	4.1
Burroughs	North America	4.1
Digital Equipment	North America	3.9
Motorola	North America	3.8
Time Inc.	North America	3.6
N.C.R.	North America	3.5
Fujitsu	Japan	3.5
L.M. Ericsson	Europe	3.2
Olivetti	Europe	2.5
Northern Telecom	North America	2.5

with I.B.M. and Japan in office automation. Olivetti had not chosen a European partner because it was already Europe's biggest company in the field" (*Guardian*, December 22, 1983). Europe, one of the three richest areas in the world, cannot support a partner of sufficient means to effectively compete against Japanese and American corporations, so Olivetti must ally with AT&T in order, in the words of chairman Carlo de Benedetti, that it may "compete with I.B.M. on a world level" (quoted in *Computing*, January 12, 1984, p. 16).

In face of this situation, a few mega-corporations are developing systems to sell on a global market; others will survive only by adopting the role of clients and subcontractors to these concerns, or by establishing a particular niche in the industry which is of no great significance to the leaders. Either way, as ticks on the back of rhinos or mice under the table, there can be no doubting where real power lies.

Oligopolistic Competition

If the preponderence of transnational corporations makes a nonsense of I.T. presenting a free market, it is not the case that there is no competition. Because of the technological trends and market requirements that have given rise to I.T., corporations are susceptible to the lure of huge potential profits and simultaneously threatened by the intrusion of competitors into their own domains. The ultimate winners cannot yet be identified, but what is preordained is that transnational capital, dominant at the outset, will be ascendant at the close.

The struggles currently taking place are especially fierce, because there is both high demand for I.T. and the technology subsumes functions once the undisputed reserve of specialist corporations. This mix results in what Olivetti describes thus: "The growth rates of the sector in which we operate are probably unique in the current phase of world industrial development. The basic features of the sector are extremely rapid technological evolution accompanied by the entry of an increasing number of new competitors, attracted by these growth rates, and facilitated by the technological developments which have lowered barriers to entry" (*Annual General Meeting,* 8 May, 1981, p. 10). A consequence is that, where formerly AT&T could dominate telecommunications inside the United States (with about 80% of the market), I.T.T. could sit at the forefront of international communications, and I.B.M. could monopolize world computing (with 60–70% of the market), nowadays the situation is more fluid. To prosper in the rapidly expanding field of I.T., corporations are required to offer systems which incorporate previously separate products and services. Where once Olivetti could concentrate on typewriters, it now needs to offer systems which contain the functions of typing, computing, printing, and communications; where once I.B.M. could concentrate on computing, it is now required to offer systems which include typing, computing, printing, and communications; where once I.T.T. could be satisfied with international communications, it is now having to produce systems which offer data networking and text processing; where once G.T.E. could concentrate on telephony and consumer electronics, it has been pressured to offer systems that include data transmission and computing; where once Xerox. . . .

It is in this context that huge corporations are now competing aggressively for future expansion and market share. The situation is uncertain, shifting, even competitive, but it is one restricted to titans. What can compete with A.T.&T.'s revenue in 1982 of $65.8 billion and net profit of $7.3 billion (the largest corporate profit in the world that year), or I.B.M.'s sales of $34.4 billion and $4.4 billion profit (the second largest corporate profit of 1982)? The answer is the cluster of I.T. corporations which also have billion-dollar incomes, the couple of dozen nation states with a gross national product to match, and perhaps a few new entrants.

New Entrants

Prominent among the latter are oil companies, amongst which Exxon was the leader until 1984 (the largest income receiver of all corporations, with $97.2 billion in 1982). A review of Exxon's excursions into I.T. is revelatory. Back in 1979, Exxon's chairman, Clifton Garvin, indicated three future directions for his company: oil, gas, and petrochemicals which would continue to be the major segments of the business; alternative energy sources, such as oil shale and coal; and "opportunities outside the energy field ... which utilize our experience and skills, or which are the outcome of advanced technological development" (quoted in *Financial Times*, December 18, 1979, p. 17). I.T. had been identified as a source of investment.

That same year, Exxon purchased Reliance Electric, a maker of electric motors, for $1.2 billion. This controversial take-over, justified by Exxon as necessary to allow the manufacture of an energy-saving electronic device, falls into Garvin's second category of corporate development. However, from the point of view of Exxon's structure and strategy, it can be regarded as bridging the gap between its energy operations and its attempted shift into the electronics industry.

For over a decade, Exxon had been acquiring companies in the information processing business, taking on 15 or so such ventures in the early 1970s. By expending large sums of money—by 1978 it had already spent $80 million (*Datamation*, July, 1978, p. 169)—Exxon quickly established a foothold in the office and communications systems fields, notably with Zilog (microcomputers), Vydec (word processors), Qwip (facsimile equipment), Qyx (electronic typewriters), and a Communications Systems Group which specializes in voice response systems. In the early 1980s, most of these were consolidated into Exxon Office Systems, which in 1981 introduced the "Exxon 500 Series Information Processor," the "initial work station in an evolving line of systems products for the office" (Exxon Corp.: *Annual Report*, 1981).

Exxon Office Systems created the third largest marketing force in the office equipment industry (*Business Week*, August 24, 1981, p. 87) and, according to the Yankee Group, was expected to account for up to 10% of the information processing market by the end of the 1980s (*Computing*, August 6, 1981, p. 9). Despite this, Exxon's I.T. ventures were a consistent drain on the corporation's resources, with losses running into hundreds of millions of dollars (*Financial Times*, 8 February, 1982). In 1980, for instance, Exxon's Information Systems Group (Exxon Office Systems, Zilog, and a collection of smaller companies) lost $150 million on sales of $270 million (*Business Week*, August 24, 1981, p. 87), and by 1981 some $500 million had gone into Exxon Office Systems without realization of any profit. The upshot of continued losses was Exxon's dramatic decision to withdraw from the office systems business late in 1984.

What is most significant about Exxon's sally into I.T. is that it could afford the hundreds of millions of dollars entrance fee and sustain losses for years which for most other companies would be disasterous. Because of its enormous resources,

Exxon's losses in I.T. were in fact relatively insignificant, since these interests accounted for less than half a percent of total sales, and debits of hundreds of millions of dollars "seem like loose change" (*Business Week*, 24 August, 1981, p. 87). Though Exxon made a mark in the I.T. industry, it expected that office equipment and communications would have accounted for less than 5% of total revenues by 2000. That, as an absolute sum, would be about 5 billion dollars at current prices, but to Exxon it is a minor investment.

Telecomputerenergetics

Exxon's adventures indicate not only the immense wealth necessary for participation in the I.T. industry, but also an attempted move by numerous oil companies into (and for some pretty quickly out of) what Joseph Pelton calls "telecomputerenergetics" (Pelton, 1981b, pp. 46–51). Many of the entrants to I.T. are prodigiously rich oil corporations which foresee a time when oil begins to run out. A small instance of their "scramble to diversify" (Dafter and Betts, 1981) in the growing area of I.T. (of which they are heavy users, computer-communications being essential to manage their dispersed enterprises) in the U.K. is that half of the seven investors in Machine Intelligence Research Affiliates (a company based in Edinburgh University working on artificial intelligence) are from the oil business (*Computing*, 11 August, 1983). A bigger case is the involvement of British Petroleum (1981 revenue $52.2 billion, profit $2.1 billion), which already owns Britain's biggest computer software company, Scicon, in Mercury Communications, a telecommunications network established in England to rival British Telecom (B.T.). The original backers of Mercury were Cable and Wireless, British Petroleum (B.P.), and Barclays Merchant Bank. In 1983, when the latter, after spending £35 million, withdrew its 20% holding, £60 million had been invested, another £200 million was required for the next phase of development, and estimates were that £1 billion could be required over the next 15 years (*Economist*, March 12, 1983, pp. 41–42). B.P. and Cable and Wireless took over the complete Barclays' interest because they "have the cash to follow through with the investment," which is "so enormous that few companies would be able to afford it" (*Guardian*, 17 November, 1983). B.P.'s withdrawal in 1984, after reconsidering Mercury's prospects, negates neither its search to diversify nor the scale of investment in I.T.

In the United States, there is a similar trend. Getty Oil (1982 revenues $12 billion), in 1979, took an 85% stake in the cable service Entertainment and Sports Programming Network, an investment consolidated the following year by purchase of interests in film companies that would access movies for Getty's cable television operation (and Getty Oil was in turn swallowed by Texaco—1982 earnings $47 billion—early in 1984). And Atlantic Richfield (1982 revenues $26.5 billion) recently entered a joint venture in America with L.M. Ericsson involved in cable making, software, and telecommunications equipment manufacture. Relatedly, Schlumberger Limited is a company closely involved with the oil industry which has recently made significant moves into I.T. This transnational—registered in the

Dutch Antilles with headquarters in both Paris and New York—had revenues of $6 billion in 1982 (net income $1.3 billion), largely from its oil drilling services. This requires considerable use of I.T. and was no doubt a factor in Schlumberger's purchase of Fairchild Camera and Instrument, the fifth largest semi-conductor manufacturer in the United States, for $425 million in 1979 (*Financial Times*, 22 May, 1979), its take-over of Manufacturing Data Systems (MDSI), a computer services concern, for $190 million in 1980 (*Financial Times*, September 19, 1980), and acquisition of Applicon, a computer-aided design/manufacture supplier, in 1981, in exchange for 4 million Schlumberger shares valued at $224 million (*Annual Report*, 1981, pp. 38-39). MDSI and Applicon became part of a new subsidiary, Computer Aided Systems, in which role they will support their parent, but also enter other markets in the burgeoning I.T. industry. In this way, Jean Riboud, Schlumberger's chairman, reckons "diversification into electronics will help [the company] ride out swings in the oil business" (quoted in *Economist*, January 8, 1983, p. 54). General Motors (1984 revenues $84 billion) is involved in a cognate industry which it believes faces inexorable decline. As a safeguard GM took over Hughes, the giant U.S. electronics, aerospace and defense group, for a staggering $5 billion early in 1985 (Dodsworth and Taylor, 1985).

In Britain, in common with most other advanced capitalist countries, the state monopoly over communications has been removed, and this has been accompanied by a great deal of rhetoric that "competition should be allowed" (Baker, *Hansard*, 14 June, 1982, cols. 596-597). The sums involved in the I.T. sphere, and the characteristics of the new entrants, throw a revealing light on the limits of this competition.

An Overarching Computing/Communications Information Industry

It is important to emphasize that much of the current rivalry between giants in I.T. stems from a trend towards an overarching information industry which threatens to break down barriers separating what were once distinct areas. Whether one starts from particular technologies, corporate structures, or market features, the conclusion is unavoidable that we are en route towards a much larger and more integrated industry. As the Information Technology Advisory Panel points out, "the communications' needs of homes and businesses appear to be converging" (ITAP, March, 1982, p. 17); the home of the future, offering integrated tv-based systems for entertainment, education, purchasing, and accounting facilities is not radically different technologically from the office of the future which provides a number of functions via data processing and communications networks linked to visual display units. Because of the potential rewards, most corporate activity is directed at business information systems and digital networks, but a similar technology is used for the domestic I.T. systems, and often the same corporations are involved in both fields. As competition between the giant corporations works itself out, as both domestic and business sectors become imbricated, we shall see the emergence of mega-companies with interests in office equipment, communications, data processing, cable television, broadcasting, and so on, as they compete for supremacy over what has been called the "information grid" (cf. Dordick et al., 1981).

Though, at present, the process of forming an integrated information industry is at an early stage, and the business sector is moving fastest towards the electronic office, it is already more than embryonic. The Nippon Electric Company (NEC), for instance, describes itself in a way which deserves lengthy quotation:

> NEC is constantly involved in constructing and laying down the building blocks for tomorrow's "C&C" Universe.
> Telecommunications? There are NEC digital switching systems of every range and capacity. And to help transmit massive volumes of information, NEC continues to pioneer in the development of fiber optic communications. There are NEC submarine cable communications sytems, facsimile equipment, not to mention the simple telephone handset. NEC satellite and microwave communications systems, aviation and space electronic equipment, laser communications sytems. Each is part of our total commitment to better communications.
> At the same time, NEC spearheads the development of another vital ingredient in the "C&C" mix—computers. From small systems to mainframes, from voice-actuated devices to sophisticated controllers, NEC computers are all around you. At home, in the office, in business and government.
> And then there are electron devices. NEC is easily among the world's top manufacturers of semiconductor devices. Smaller and smarter ICs, LSIs, VLSIs (very large scale integration), bubble memories and other components have earned NEC a reputation as a leader in this field.
> To help usher "C&C" into the home, NEC is working toward a computer control center which would enable programmed operation of everything from the latest appliances and environment control equipment to home entertainment electronics and communications tools. Heading this list of wide-ranging "C&C"-based development in consumer electronics is the NEC personal computer, already making its mark in both business and at home.
> And, of course, there are NEC's "C&C" systems.
> So there we have it. NEC's Universe in a galactic nutshell. A full spectrum of *communications* equipment merged with *computers* for every conceivable application. And at the core, *electron devices*, the indispensable source from which "C&C" draws its power (*NEC's Universe*, 1982, p. 13).

Illustrative of this trend from the direction of technology, we may take the case of satellites, which play a major role in long distance national and international communications. There are traditional distinctions between satellite manufacturers, operators, and programmers, and there has to date been a concentration on business and military markets. However, since satellites require enormous investment (for example, the Satellite Business System (SBS) consortium had sunk almost $1 billion into its business communications satellite by 1982 without making any return—*Economist*, 14 August, 1982, p. 22) it is not unexpected that interested parties often extend beyond manufacture to operation at the same time as they widen their markets to maximize return on their outlay. For example, it is a short step from supplying military and business users to offering domestic customers satellite communications (SBS commenced this in 1982); little more towards offering satellites not only to network broadcast television but also to transmit direct to the home (Hughes recently invested $500 million in a satellite which will be given over largely to cable television—*Economist*, December 11, 1982, p. 46); and it is not so far to project satellite manufacturers moving beyond carrier functions to offering either or both data processing and television programming (as does RCA).

Similar trends are evident in the U.K. where, for example, the newly-privatized British Telecom (B.T.), already in a commanding position in the telecommunications network, has extensive interests in building cable television systems and from 1983 to 1985 partnered in a consortium (United Satellites) with British Aerospace (1982 revenue $3.6 billion) and GEC (1982 revenue $8 billion) to build and operate a satellite intended to supply both business communications and pay-tv services. B.T.'s extension beyond telephony is obvious (and, in the long term, the integrated digital networks towards which telecommunications companies are moving could usurp the functions of cable), but so too is the spread of GEC, a company with major interests in satellites, telecommunications equipment, cable TV, office systems, and television manufacture. Similarly, organizations developing cable television services find no technical reason to stop at TV provision, since cable can be a means of entering telephony. Because of this, Mercury Communications, set up to provide a national telecommunications network for business users, has negotiated with cable TV suppliers to use their networks to extend into domestic telephone services, as well as to enhance their business network by linking with local cable to offer additional functions such as electronic mail and teleconferencing.

In the Far East, the Matsushita Electric Industrial Co. (1982 revenue $14.9 billion), the world leader in consumer electronics (under brand names such as National, Panasonic, Quasar, and Technics) with a complete range of video, TV, and audio equipment, has decided to concentrate in the future on business customers. Already it has a substantial robotics production facility, but "sees greatest opportunity in office automation" (Smith, 1983, p. 101) to which end it has entered the market for copiers, word processors, and computers (in association with both IBM and Fujitsu). And an even bigger Japanese Company, Hitachi (1982 revenue $16.3 billion), has a still more extensive reach across the I.T. spectrum.

Turning to North America, we can cite RCA as indicative of this development. Thornton Bradshaw, its chairman, recently laid down his company's future as being "in the interrelated areas of communications technologies, consumer and government electronics, and entertainment and information services" (*Annual Report*, 1981). This reveals an astonishing range of connected goods and services, which include TV manufacture, the television network NBC, video equipment, cable TV equipment and programming, a global telecommunications network, private telephone systems, data communications, and satellite manufacture and operation. While RCA is especially well placed to provide the "home-information system" (*Business Week,* August 17, 1981, p. 86) with "television sets that, with a minimum of extra wires and attachments, could have plugs for games, computers, videodisk players, and cassette recorders" it has strengths in communications and is "planning to go after more industrial and commercial business" (*Wall Street Journal,* 4 March, 1982) for which it will require investment in computers and data processing.

Though it is clearly an example of the move towards an overarching information industry, vertically integrated yet straddling domestic and business markets, RCA's progress is by no means assured, precisely because this trend is being affected by the challenge of others, not least IBM and AT&T, which, coming from different directions, promise to meet head on with RCA some day. In fact, RCA (1982 sales $8 billion) has in recent years encountered difficulties such as a $400 million plus loss in computers in the early 1970s (*Business Week,* September 25, 1971, pp. 34–36) and misdirected diversification into businesses such as Hertz car and truck rental and frozen foods (Thackray, 1976), so much so that "some Wall Street observers say that all the company's problems make it ripe for a takeover" (*Wall Street Journal,* 4 March, 1982). Bendix (1982 revenue $4.1 billion) threatened even this in 1982, thereby revealing the enormous stakes involved in the shift towards a unified information business. And in December 1985 General Electric acquired RCA for $6.28 billion, dramatic evidence indeed of the trend which RCA itself exemplified.

Corporate Restructuring

Because of present conditions and future potential in the I.T. industry, there is considerable restructuring and regrouping among the corporate interests. RCA's reasoning is representative of all the leading contenders:

> our vision is directed at developing products for the growth markets of the 1980s. Toward that end, we continued to restructure our operations on the premise that electronics is the foundation of our corporate strategies and the key to the company's successful performance in the years ahead. Our restructuring involves divesting those operations that do not fit the pattern of RCA's basic businesses (RCA. *Annual Report,* 1980).

Statement after statement from company boards attests to concerted and speedy action to seize advantage, slough off redundant elements, consolidate around key products and services, reorganize domestically and internationally to best meet the opportunities of I.T. From Minnesota Mining and Manufacturing (3M) comes recognition of a changing marketplace, notably "in such fields as electronics, information processing, and communications," which calls for a "restructuring into four business sectors based on related technologies [which] would better prepare 3M to meet the challenges of continued growth and profitability during the rest of the decade and perhaps beyond" (*Annual Report,* 1981, pp. 4–6). A truly global transnational, with 52 principal locations outside the US, 3M is certain that this "new organizational structure"–one part of which includes the Electronic and Information

Technologies division, which accounts for one-third of 3M's $6.6 billion 1982 revenue and includes copiers, office communications, data terminals, and related technologies—will enhance "the global perspective we bring to our products and businesses" (p. 29) by "even closer integration of 3M's U.S. and International businesses" (p. 7).

From Eastman Kodak (1982 sales $10.8 billion) comes news that dominance in camera and film is no longer adequate for its worldwide operations; that a new structure is required "to emphasize the company's interests and capabilities in electronics" (*Annual Report*, 1981). This will help keep Kodak ahead in its traditional domain, but acquisition of Atex Inc. in 1981, a designer of computer-based systems for text preparation and processing, its Ektaprint range of copying machines, and its microfilm products which can combine "sophisticated micrographics hardware, a powerful microcomputer, and specially designed software, to provide electronic access to both on-line data and documents" (*Annual Report*, 1982, pp. 17–18) are also signs that "the company plans to use electronics to enter new markets" (Moore, 1983, p. 121).

From Olivetti comes the announcement that "profound changes are taking place in our sector in methods of production, sales strategies, and the structure of the competition" in which the company "is fully involved . . . because its business lies in the most dynamic sector of the computer industry (*Annual and Extraordinary General Meeting*, 7 April, 1982, p. 9). This has resulted in many millions of dollars invested outside of Italy, notably in the U.S., where seven new companies were bought in 1982 alone and 19 investments have been made since 1980 compared to four in Europe (*Economist*, September 3, 1983, pp. 66–67). At the same time Olivetti has leapt to number two position in Europe's data processing industry (behind I.B.M.) as it continues to extend its range way beyond its traditional typewriter products to include all "the most advanced areas of information processing, that is office automation systems, distributed systems for specialised applications, telematics and personal processing systems" (*Annual and Extraordinary General Meeting*, 8 May, 1981, p. 76).

From Fujitsu comes the message that, in 1981, the Communications and Computer Systems Groups, after 20 years' existence, were "superseded by a new corporate structure" which "reflects Fujitsu's belief in the interdependence of computers and telecommunications, and is aimed at greater flexibility to meet the future need for integrated information processing and communications systems" (*Annual Report*, 1982, p. 2). From Philips, between 1978 and 1982, came a steady stream of pronouncements springing from recognition of a need for "more far-reaching rationalisation, production concentration and regrouping of existing activities . . . in our enterprise" (*Annual Report*, 1979). By 1981, this was "going according to plan" in search of "sufficient profitability" (*Annual Report*, 1981), and it involved a vigorous program of acquisitions and deals with noncompeting companies which have included the purchase in America of Magnavox (consumer electronics), Signetics (semiconductors), and GTE-Sylvania (televisions), and in Europe a controlling interest in Grundig (consumer electronics) late in 1983, and agreements with Sony to market audio disc systems and AT&T (see below) for telecommunications equipment. In tandem, the Dutch corporation formed a new service company, Philips International, which would lay down "world product policy," thereby having responsibility for the "preparation and support of total company policy" (ibid.).

One could continue with such cases of corporations gearing up for the changed I.T. circumstances. These reviews cannot capture the complexity and scale of the restructuring of organizations which are huge entities, employ thousands of people in disparate and manifold locations, and involve millions upon millions of dollar transactions. But the point is clear: corporations with interests in I.T. have all commenced profound and rapid changes to meet the new conditions.

The I.T. Industry in the U.K.

Though the major players are found in the United States, where over half the world's leading transnationals are based and the largest domestic market is located, there are substantial concerns in Western Europe and Japan. These are eager to extend beyond their national—and continental—markets into the lucrative North American scene to gain outlets and strategic advantage to compete with U.S. corporations on a global scale. Siemen's increase in 1982 from 17 to 41% of its foreign capital investment going to the U.S. is illustrative of a priority shared with Olivetti, Philips, GEC, and all other leading I.T. businesses. We review some important features of the U.S. scene below, but in the following pages we describe the fast-moving I.T. situation in Britain, since it reveals both general features of the industry (oligopolistic competition, international enterprise, rapid restructuring, concentration on business systems) and the extraordinary size of the I.T. industry worldwide, by showing that the British corporations, enormous by most standards, are small fry in a global setting. The fact that the U.K. is one of the most wealthy societies in the world (in 1979, only six other nations—the US, Japan, USSR, West Germany, France, and China—had a larger gross national product), with substantial I.T. corporations, yet is dwarfed when set against the chiefly American companies in the information business, is testament to the realities of industrial domination.

Three corporations (GEC, Thorn-EMI, and Racal) head the British effort in I.T., with three others (Plessey, Ferranti, and ICL) playing a strong supporting role. In addition, British Telecom (B.T.), with revenue of £7.7 billion in 1984, the biggest and most strategic British I.T. venture, has a key role to play within both the domestic and international communications networks. Though it recently joined with private corporations and is enthusiastically developing a strategy in accord with market principles, because it has an important legacy of public service, and government will retain a major shareholding for some years to come, we comment on its role in the following chapter.

All the British I.T. corporations have made significant acquisitions and internal changes in recent years to bolster their position. The biggest by far, GEC, with some 300 subsidiaries around the globe (1983 turnover £5.5 billion) is a general electronics and electrical concern, making products ranging from consumer goods to telecommunications equipment. It has many interests in I.T. and in the late 1970s and 1980s has been busy acquiring companies which have particular attractions. With huge capital available (£1.3 billion as of March 1983) for investment, the purchase of office equipment firm A.B. Dick (for £52 million), Scriptomatic (£12 million), an addressing machine producer, plus a 30% share in Cortex Corp., a software firm, indicate both GEC's commitment to developing strengths in the U.S. market and its rather cautious moves, a number of which have involved licensing deals with foreign corporations (e.g., Hitachi for television manufacture, Northern Telecom for telecommunications exchanges).

When GEC bought out A.B. Dick, this was a sign of its identification of office equipment as a crucial market (Wilkinson, 1978). Working from its established strengths in communications, GEC reorganized its divisions in 1981 to form GEC Information Systems (GECIS) in order to

> co-ordinate the GEC effort in the field of information technology, including the "electronic office." The company brings together the Private Systems and Telephone Divisions of GEC Telecommunications Ltd, GEC Computers Ltd, Reliance Systems Ltd and GEC Viewdata Systems. The wide product range of these companies, together with A.B. Dick Ltd, enables GEC Information Systems to provide integrated information networks based on voice and data switching systems, computers, word processors and local area networks (*Report and Accounts*, 1982, p. 30).

This subsidiary offered "a comprehensive range of products and systems" (GEC. *Review of Operations*, 1983, p. 10) and commenced a major marketing operation in the US, but was reorganized in 1984 following poor performance, an indication that GEC's wide spread at the expense of depth puts it at a disadvantage in the crucial office systems business.

GEC has substantial interests in other I.T. spheres, notably in defense and space products (through its Marconi subsidiaries especially), military communications systems, and cable television (GEC was one of the 11 successful applicants for a license to build a cable network in Britain, gaining the Windsor area late in 1983).

GEC made a bid for Decca late in 1979 but was beaten to the merger by Racal Electronics, which paid £106 million for the company early in 1980. Racal, for long the most profitable European electronics firm, took over Decca partly for its established position in "electronic warfare" (where Racal started out in business and what fuelled its dramatic growth over 14 years from sales in 1969 of £8.8 million to £763.6 million in 1983), but it also had a lot to do with Racal's extension into data communications (which by 1983 accounted for about one-third of revenue). Racal quickly reorganized Decca, selling off parts which did not fit into its corporate strategy.

During 1979, Racal announced a move into computer-based office systems by setting up Racal Information Systems and buying, along with other companies, Telesystems Network of Chicago, a firm specializing in data and text protocol converters, devices crucial for computer information networks. In 1981, it brought out a new multi-function office computer, the Series 6000, and with PLANET, its local area network which enables word processors, computers, printers, and terminals to communicate, Racal aims to "meet the growing demand for fully integrated information systems in offices and industrial complexes" (*Annual Report and Accounts*, 1983, p. 3). This will compete with Xerox's Ethernet local network in North America, where Racal, via its Milgo and Vadic outlets, achieves 30% of its sales.

While Racal is going with the trend of all the major I.T. corporations in seeking to win orders in computer/communications for the office, it has not left other areas unattended. In 1983, it was awarded a license to operate a nationwide telecommunications service based on cellular radio technology which will "provide portable access to the public telephone network on a vast scale" that in turn will mean Racal "will be ideally placed to supply and maintain complete systems anywhere in the world" (ibid.). In addition, Racal, in partnership with Oak Industries of California, entered the cable television business in 1983 when it won the contract for Croyden Cable.

Thorn, which acquired EMI late in 1979 for £114 million, lacks strength in the office systems market, being an oddly heterogenous company with chiefly consumer electronics, defense, and engineering interests. Its major money-maker is consumer electronics, which accounted for 69% of profit on sales of £2.7 billion in 1983, and it is here that Thorn-EMI is founding its strategy for domestic I.T. systems. It was this which stimulated its interest in EMI, a deal that "could not have been supported for its immediate benefits in terms of present profits but its importance in our strategies for the 1980s is of great significance" (*Report and Accounts*, 1980). Thorn's plans to move towards the manufacture of integrated entertainment/information systems explains the appeal of EMI, since the latter has substantial interests in music and film and thus complements Thorn's manufacturing operations with programming: EMI's "extensive operations in the production and distribution of films for the cinema and programmes for television and home video complement the Company's comprehensive and dovetailing Home Entertainment activities" (*Report and Accounts*, 1982). To this end, Thorn divested EMI holdings extraneous to corporate strategy.

This vertical integration has been effected along with a policy of horizontal integration, Thorn-EMI extending its range of consumer electronic goods to include almost every conceivable I.T. gadget for the home—video disc and cassette, audio equipment, television, viewdata, teletext, etc. With EMI under its wing and a chain of rental outlets to bridge the gap between manufacture and customers. Thorn-EMI can offer "new products for those new markets just when the customer requires it" (*Thorn-EMI 1980*, n.d.). More recent products and services have been fitted into Thorn-EMI's grand design. It has won three of the eleven cable franchises (Coventry Cable, Ulster Cablevision, and Swindon Cable Services) and is enthused "by the prospects which we see arising for the Company from the forthcoming expansion of broadcasting by satellite and cable tv" (*Report and Accounts*, 1982).

The dark spot for the company is the Japanese giants which dwarf the British company and are especially strong internationally, where Thorn-EMI gains 40% of its revenue.

The fate of the other corporations in the British I.T. industry is more precarious. None of them is in an especially favorable position, economically or strategically, and there have been signs that they (or parts of them) might be absorbed into one or other of the leading groups, though recently they have substantially reorganized and have managed to achieve much increased profits which have kept most predators at bay. Plessey, a defense and telecommunications group with sales in 1983 of £1.1 billion, underwent a shaky period in the late 1970s, but with a very large stake in telecommunications equipment (in 1983, this accounted for 47.2% of revenue and 57% of profit) and important defense contracts, has emerged as a powerful force. In 1980, it announced that it had "developments in progress covering a comprehensive range of data, voice and digital systems products" (*Report and Accounts*, 1980), and, seeking to offer "more and more the total technology approach" (Chairman, *Report and Accounts*, 1983, p. 6), it entered the office equipment market with Plessey Telecommunications and Office Systems, which will use the company's private digital exchange as the hub of its sales effort in offering an Ethernet-type network.

Between 1978 and 1983 Plessey's regrouping led to the disposal of over 20 subsidiaries and 26% of employees, but sales grew 66% and profits 167% (*Report and Accounts*, 1983, p. 5). With continuing workforce reductions accompanied by vigorous economic growth, a determined and coherent managerial plan for future development, its local network products, and international reach (42% of sales in 1983 were overseas) Plessey is a significant contender in the I.T. business. Nevertheless, it recognizes that this technology "requires a new order of strategic thought and consideration" because "the huge scale of effort and enterprise required will only be met by stronger association with other companies" (Chairman, *Report and Accounts*, 1983, p. 7). This is especially the case as regards the U.S. market, into which Plessey has been trying to expand (in 1983, North America accounted for 13% of turnover). To meet this challenge, Plessey bought the Stromberg-Carlson Corporation from United Technologies in 1982 for some £30 million as a vehicle to sell its exchange equipment in the U.S., and the same year it established a joint venture with Scientific-Atlanta Inc. to strengthen its communications interests. While Plessey is strong in switching equipment, it has been weak in cable tv and satellite communications, which the Scientific-Atlanta link will bolster in the British company's "plot to win 5% of the world's telecommunications markets by the end of the 1980s" (*Economist*, January 8, 1983, pp. 59–60). Connectedly, Plessey won franchises to participate in two of the eleven cable tv ventures in the U.K. in 1983.

Ferranti, a company specializing in defense electronics which was bailed out of bankruptcy in the mid-1970s, looked a likely candidate for merger with GEC or Racal in the early 1980s. Since then, it has enjoyed rapid growth (sales rose between 1980 and 1983 from £214.6 million to £372.2 million, while profits trebled), but its relatively small size and lucrative defense contracts still make it vulnerable. Its size limits its ability to provide systems and, recognizing this, Ferranti has consciously sought to find openings for particular products in lush markets, most recently in the office equipment sector. In addition, in 1981 it formed Ferranti GTE to manufacture telecommunications equipment, a deal which gave Ferranti the backing of a leading U.S. corporation (which has sales more than 50% in excess of even GEC), in return for giving GTE access to the British (and European) markets.

International Computers Ltd. (ICL) was until 1984 the U.K.'s major computer manufacturer. Formed in 1968 by a Labour government initiative, ICL held 35% of the British computer market (about the same as IBM), but its concentration on mainframes led it into severe difficulties in the late 1970s, when technological changes and more intense competition undermined its position. After privatization in 1979, ICL suffered intense crises between 1980 and 1982, with a £50 million loss in 1981, managerial upheavals, threats of take-over from Sperry and Control Data after oil giants B.P. and Shell had refused to take an interest and selling to Philips, Siemens, GEC, Hitachi, Fujitsu, and Toshiba had been considered, and the urgent need for a £200 million loan from government. A new managing director, Robert Wilmot, was hired from Texas Instruments in 1981, followed in 1983 by the arrival as chairman from British Leyland of Sir Michael Edwardes, a militant industrialist. At the close of 1983, ICL had a profit of £45.6 million (92% up on 1982) on sales of £846 million. The price was profound reorganization which cost one-third of ICL's employees their livelihoods in the space of 2 years (*Financial Times*, May 25, 1983).

From the outset, Wilmot pushed the company into data communications, especially in the office sector, since he acknowledged the imperative of reacting "to the changes in the computer world with the increasing importance of telecommunications" (*Guardian*, May 12, 1981) to provide a "womb-to-tomb networked product line." ICL also tried to strengthen international operations, though with little success, since in 1982 it lost 9% of its European sales. Nonetheless, about 40% of ICL's revenue is from exports, and, to reinforce its position, the company negotiated deals with Fujitsu to gain access to microchip technology, and with Mitel of Canada to sell telecommunications equipment. In spite of these efforts to move with the I.T. trends, ICL's future was uncertain; it is small in relation to the world's major computer manufacturers, all of which except Sperry have plant in Britain, and, as the *Economist* observed, "Most of the recovery so far has come from the sacking of 10,000 workers and cutting stocks and working capital" (December 11, 1982) rather than expansion of market share. Its absorption by STC (see below) in 1984 was not unexpected.

There are two additional companies worthy of note. Cable and Wireless (C&W) is a recently privatized telecommunications concern with the bulk of its interests overseas, a legacy of the British Empire (Barty-King, 1979). In 1982, it made a profit of £157 million on sales of £403 million, and has moved into the domestic telecommunications market with a large, since 1984 total, stake in the Mercury project. It has a similar, though more modest, investment in the U.S. British Aerospace (BA) is a world-ranking supplier (1982 revenue £2.4 billion) of communications satellites, which in 1981 began to develop with IBM and British Telecom plans to produce an advanced communications service to link business users in Western Europe. It was the subject of take-over bids from GEC and Thorn-EMI in 1984. Its production of satellites inevitably means that BA's constituency is far wider than the tiny British Isles.

The reach of these latter in particular—BA's world marketing and C&W's overseas locations—and of the I.T. corporations in general reminds us of a crucial issue easily overlooked in describing a particular nation's representation in the industry: how does one ascribe corporations as belonging to individual countries? Reviewing these businesses, we should remember that, while they have large indigenous markets and production facilities, as transnationals they have substantial plant and sales abroad. That their headquarters and majority stock are in the U.K. is of course of great significance, but we ought to realize that national labels are rather loose when describing corporations which traverse the globe to find avenues for their goods and services, and areas in which to produce them; that perhaps the major feature of transnational corporations is their international reach rather than national location; and that their strategies and characteristics increasingly distance them from the domain of any one country as they exacerbate "the long-run trend . . . toward the dwindling of the power of the nation state relative to the corporation" (Johnson, 1975, p. 83).

With this in mind, it is most important to note that among the biggest I.T. enterprises in the U.K. are subsidiaries of foreign transnationals, examples of which are IBM United Kingdom Holdings (1982 revenue £1.5 billion); Standard Telephones and Cables (STC, ITT's U.K. division, which since late 1982 has been 35% ITT owned, after the parent divested stock to appease British sentiment), which grossed £628.5 million in 1982; and Rank-Xerox (51% Xerox), which had sales of £1.3 billion that year. Giants in their own right, these can call upon the massive resources of the larger groups to which they belong to provide technologies, R&D, and preferential intra-company pricing. The absorption of ICL by STC/ITT late in 1984 is at once testament to the power, reach, and resource of that organization, and a sharp reminder of the difficulty of designating national labels.

Developments in Britain illuminate general features of the I.T. industry: companies are busily restructuring; all have resources running into the hundreds of millions of pounds and an international strategy. On a world scale these are relatively minor participants;* nevertheless, the process of jostling and maneuvoring for

---

*Because of this British companies are vulnerable to competition from the dominant U.S. and Japanese suppliers and, to protect themselves, constantly under pressure to enlarge. Thus the *Financial Times* recently noted that developments "seem to argue for further rationalization of the British electronics industry to produce fewer, stronger groups of international scale" (Jonquieres and Stone, 1985) and an industry minister complained that "GEC and Plessey are way down the international ranking list in size" (quoted in *Computing*, 20 June 1985). Not surprisingly, then, there is much talk of mergers and takeovers. In the opening months of 1985 these included Thorn-EMI being absorbed by Hanson Trust, British Aerospace by GEC, STC by British Telecom, and Plessey and GEC to unite with world-ranking communications manufacturers. Undoubtedly the next few years will see the realization of at least some of these proposals.

market supremacy is representative of what is happening in all advanced capitalist countries at national and international levels, and the conclusion is unavoidable; the "post-industrial society" is being shaped by transnational corporations now engaged in an unprecedented struggle that is bringing into conflict previously discrete sectors in a world market.

Strategic Alliances

In the midst of this competition is the paradoxical appearance of what the *Financial Times* describes as "a new zest for strategic alliances" (October 25, 1983). Wherever market advantage might be snatched without jeopardizing corporate position, collaborative projects are entered into. These, often involving dozens of cross-licensing deals and numerous joint ventures between individual companies, form a "boundlessly dense and virtually unprobed network" (D. Schiller, 1982a, p. 111) which we may illustrate with the following:

- Xerox ($8.5 billion in 1982 revenues) and Siemens ($17 billion) have agreed to integrate their product lines of office systems, Xerox's local area network being linked to Siemens' automated exchange products.
- IBM ($34.4 billion) and Matsushita Electric ($14.9 billion) are collaborating on small business systems.
- Olivetti ($2.5 billion) has arranged with Hitachi ($16.3 billion) to sell the Japanese company's mainframe computers in Europe and has agreed with Toshiba to collaborate on office automation equipment in Japan and Europe (*Financial Times*, 14 May, 1985).
- Fujitsu ($3.9 billion) and ICL ($1.2 billion) agreed in 1981 that Fujitsu's largest computers will be sold under ICL's name in Europe, its existing technology will be licensed to ICL for computers, and it will supply ICL with microelectronic devices for the latter's small computers.
- AT&T ($65.8 billion) and Philips ($16.1 billion) agreed in 1982 jointly to market telecommunications equipment in Europe, the Middle East, and parts of Latin America.
- Xerox ($8.5 billion), Intel ($899.8 million), and Digital Equipment ($3.9 billion) have combined to produce the Ethernet local area network.
- Ferranti ($558 million) and GTE ($12.1 billion) have joined to sell telecommunications equipment in Britain.

Computer-Communications in the United States

In the I.T. industry, the most certain development is that towards computer-communications systems for business use. It is here—in office automation and local, national, and international data/text networks—where the stakes are particularly high and the rewards potentially enormous. It is for this reason that, as we have seen, most corporations in Britain develop, as a priority, data processing/communications networks for business users.

Contestants approach this market from particular backgrounds, but all must extend beyond their traditional domains. Copiers must be made intelligent, office machinery must be made compatible, communications must carry data and text as well as voice. . . . An important division remains between corporations able to offer systems for use within the office (if from a computer origin, they horizontally integrate to network the machinery; if from communications equipment, they try to produce an office system built around an automated exchange) and those experienced in communications services which present enhanced data and text facilities. But this division cannot long hold and has already been broached because of technological advance, market inducement, and corporate design. In the U.S., where the telecommunications service company has long been a major equipment manufacturer, the breakdown is most evident. Because it is here that the really crucial developments are occurring—crucial because they will have repercussions throughout the world, since, while the American domestic market is of major importance, it is never sufficient for the leading transnational corporations in I.T. or for their major, transnational, customers—we review the situation.

The history of computers and communications in the United States over the past decade and more has been an immensely complex one, full of expensive litigation, detailed legislation, and tortuous planning, but it comes down to this: the long-held "natural monopoly" of AT&T over domestic telecommunications has become untenable as the demands for data/text processing have extended to require the movement of such information both within and between sites. Corporate users in particular have voiced a need for a communications infrastructure which the "universal service" of AT&T can provide, but not at attractive cost to business. Relatedly, corporations in the information business, perceiving and acting upon the potential market for those able to move as well as process information, have joined forces with the likes of IBM and Xerox to insist on the deregulation of AT&T, that they might win some of the communications traffic which they regard as the extension of their present operations. AT&T, seeing its monopoly endangered, initially counter-attacked, but only half-heartedly, it too acting in the knowledge of vast rewards to be gained from its own entry into computer-communications, as time went on becoming more willing to trade off for market freedom less central elements of its network, particularly those of least profitability which service the domestic customer. The outcome, still in process but now clear enough, is that the information business in the United States—notably the supply of computer communications but extending into computer bureaus, data base management, and the like—is that a few mega-corporations are fighting among themselves for prominence in an industry dedicated to meeting the requirements of predominantly business users.

The leading protaganists in this war are AT&T and IBM, with the phalanxes of Xerox, ITT, GTE, RCA, and Wang among a few others playing important supporting roles. Beyond these—though they often extend far beyond the epicentral struggle over computer-communications—are major corporate initiatives in cable television, satellite production and operation, and other information/entertainment spheres. Dan Schiller (1982a) has performed an important service in documenting and explaining the events which have led to the present condition of the American industry. Since it is not necessary to repeat his argument, we limit ourselves to comment on some recent maneuvors to emphasize the powers and priorities of the designers of the "information society."

AT&T

Over 50 years ago, AT&T (the Bell organization) was granted a "natural monopoly" over telecommunications within the U.S. In recent years, this has been eroded, culminating in the break-up of the company in 1984 amidst much talk of deregulation, of ending monopoly to cultivate the fruits of competition. AT&T is a peculiarly American institution in that, in most societies, the natural monopoly of telecommunications has been placed in the hands of state-run companies rather than private capital. Nonetheless, in practice whether state-run or a private corporation telecommunications monopolies have not acted noticeably differently in the past, all having been imbued with authority to provide a national service. Similarly, all are changing in the same ways: AT&T's deregulation is paralled outside the United States by liberalization (and often privatization) of the network by states acting upon the same principles in response to recent changes.

It is important to understand that events at AT&T and in the drawn-out government investigations represent changes guided firmly by market considerations (Brock, 1981). On one side, for over a decade there have been insurgent corporations attempting to breech AT&T's monopoly, and in recent years their calls to offer, for example, data processing *and* communications, have become insistent. In response, the Federal Communications Commission (FCC), which oversees communications, has steadily opened up the network to AT&T's competitors. On another side, corporate users have become an increasingly important market both to AT&T and to other corporations intent on offering information services, and, as such, have been both an inducement to change existent regulation and a pressure group urging that any change is beneficial to themselves. On yet another side has been AT&T itself, which has seen technology and customer requirements make anachronistic the 1956 legislation which limited it to common carrier activities while confirming the right to monopoly.

Responding to these pressures, the FCC, in a series of decisions which culminated in a December 1980 judgment (Computer Inquiry 11), has attempted to placate the new arrivals and business users at the same time as assuaging Bell's ambitions. The end result was that the FCC exempted from regulation "enhanced" communications services and equipment (i.e., computer-communications) from which Bell had previously been excluded, while ruling that AT&T could only enter through a separate subsidiary (to protect competitors being swamped by the might of the Bell system). This gave the green light to unfettered competition; in the words of FCC Commissioner C.D. Ferris, "Now communications business entrepreneurs can be sure that the marketplace and not the government will decide their fate" (Ferris, 1980).

This FCC decision was confirmed and amended by the 1982 Justice Department's anti-trust settlement with AT&T, which broke up the monopoly by ruling that Bell should divest itself of its 22 local companies. What was left was a structure worth over $40 billion which achieved revenues of $33 billion in its first year of operation, that retained long distance telecommunications lines, Bell Laboratories (for R&D), and Western Electric (for equipment production); that is, a vertically integrated corporation offering equipment manufacture through to services unencumbered by previous needs to subsidize local operations, and free to enter any market it chose. In a market society, that choice is obvious—that which provides most reward, namely business computer-communications. AT&T, having lost two-thirds of its assets by value while retaining stocks that provide half of its former revenue and over 60% of its profit, has emerged as a leading contender for supremacy in the I.T. business that takes as its major priority the requirements of corporate users. The company is now able to enter office automation—to which end it will horizontally integrate—as well as other fields like cable at the same time as, with regulation abandoned, it will be allowed to challenge for world-wide markets. The prospect is, in the words of the *Wall Street Journal*, of a "glamorous high-technology concern that could dominate the emerging age of information . . . in computers, broadcasting, cable television, publishing, and electronic parts and equipment manufacture" (21 January, 1982).

At a glance, it is easy to see deregulation and divestment as some sort of defeat for AT&T. However, loss of regulated monopoly and subsidiaries, far from stripping AT&T of its powers, is thought by many commentators to have enhanced them. The *Financial Times* wrote that "AT&T has done very well" (January 11, 1982) and Richard Wiley, former chairman of the FCC, saw the anti-trust agreement as a "brilliant masterstroke" which let Bell rid itself of costly local phone company operations in exchange for entry to lucrative markets: AT&T, he continued, "kept the moneymakers they already had, and won the right to go after everything else on the high-revenue side" (quoted in *Wall Street Journal*, January 11, 1982). In short, it is best regarded as an instance of the widespread corporate restructuring which is taking place in all I.T. concerns, this time with the complication of state intervention (though intervention strongly in favor of corporate goals).

AT&T has for some years been gearing itself for computer-communications. In 1978, it announced its projected Advanced Communications Service, which was intended to provide for a shared data communications network, the interfacing of incompatible terminals and computers, various data communications facilities, and overall maintenance and management of the network. Though delayed, this, renamed Advanced Information Systems (AIS), commenced operation in 1983, offering "a systems approach" (*Annual Report*, 1982, p. 23) to the information needs of business and government agencies. Building on its prodigious resources and telecommunications strengths, AT&T seeks to take network protocols and architecture out of the hands of computer vendors and put them into its network. To this end, it is horizontally integrating in the computer-communications area, using its switchboards as the hub of its strategy. It has in-house facilities for satellite communications, videotex, teleconferencing, and computer equipment manufacture, and in 1983 arranged licensing deals for computer software with Intel, Motorola, and National Semiconductor (*Financial Times*, 16 May, 1983) because, in the words of a former Bell manager, AT&T "definitely have ambitions of providing full systems solutions for meeting the office-of-the-future needs" (quoted in *Datamation*, June, 1982, p. 28).

While AT&T is maneuvering in the U.S. I.T. market, this colossus is also moving fast on the international scene. The new legislative climate has permitted AT&T to reach beyond America, and it has responded with alacrity. Commenting that the "marketplace AT&T International seeks to serve is a global one" (*Annual Report*, 1982, p. 23), Bell got a listing on the London Stock Exchange in 1982, bought a 45% holding in an Irish telecommunications manufacturer Telectron to access the European market, and took a 25% stake in Olivetti of Italy to strengthen its entry into office automation markets. More dramatic still, AT&T negotiated in 1982 an agreement with Philips for joint production and sales of digital switching equipment outside the U.S., at a stroke gaining access to Philips' sales network in 63 countries for its advanced technologies. Greeted with awe around the world, this agreement brought together two companies the sales of whose telecommunications divisions surpass those of the rest of the world industry combined. Recurrent rumours on Wall Street in the spring of 1985 that AT&T was planning to bid for Digital Equipment Corporation, America's second largest computer company, underline the prodigious resources it brings to its challenge on the I.T. market.

ITT

With AT&T seeking increasingly to integrate computers and telephones into new communications systems and determinedly moving internationally, other concerned corporations have responded with alacrity. For example, ITT, a company formed a half a century ago when it took over overseas telecommunications upon restriction of AT&T to the U.S. mainland, is using its resources as the largest telecommunications company in the world (after AT&T) to consolidate internationally and to attack the liberalized home market. Already possessing data processing and communications business in Europe, with integrated manufacture and service facilities, ITT now "believes that the United States markets for telecommunications equipment may become more competitive and present greater opportunities to attain a significant position" (ITT, December 31, 1981, p. 3). Though the company requires more computer products to fully enter the electronic office field, it has acquired word processor manufacture capability and software expertise, and can offer digital switching, telephone hardware and maintenance, and data bases, as well as access to its own international communications network to corporations with appropriate requirements (Hargreaves, 1982). Its Dialcom service already provides computer functions for an information network used in American hotels which offers electronic mail, current news, stock market information, airline schedules, etc., and ITT's Communications Operations and Information Services (COINS) group provides integrated facilities which include long-distance telecommunications within and outside the U.S., record and facsimile transmission, and various value-added services. Though the company is only beginning to compete with AT&T and others over communications-computer business, it has a long-term strategy which must lead to confrontation (Sharpe, 1981).

IBM

On the same day that the Justice department settled its case with AT&T, it dropped a 13-year-old suit against IBM, the world's dominant computer manufacture and service power, that had charged it monopolized the field. This was a signal that IBM would be left unhindered in its challenge for similar markets to AT&T. IBM makes no secret that "it is our goal to compete in, and grow with, the information industry in *all* its aspects" (*Annual Report*, 1981, p. 3; cf. Malik, 1975). To this end, it has extended its already integrated computer lines to incorporate advanced communications facilities and redoubled its efforts to retain supremacy on international markets.

In 1981, IBM commenced a profound restructuring of its internal organization to meet the new opportunities of I.T. It currently offers a comprehensive range of office equipment from personal computers through to large mainframes, sets computer standards, offers customized information services and videotex. Significantly, in 1983 it took a 15%, and in 1984 a total share in Rohm Corporation of California, a telecommunications equipment manufacturer, which followed a venture with Mitel to supply switching technologies. Still more illustrative of corporate trends is IBM's involvement in Satellite Business Systems (SBS), which offers to major business users computer data communications, telecommunications, electronic mail, teleconferencing, and facsimile transmission. By early 1982, SBS had been extended to carry international communications, and the following year made available channels for pay-television services. Though SBS originated as a joint venture, by 1984 IBM had increased its share to a dominant 60%. But IBM's most decisive move in computer communications came in June 1985 when it announced the acquisition of up to 30% of MCI Communications, AT&T's chief rival in the U.S. long-distance telecommunications market (though it has only a small percentage of the total market), with MCI taking responsibility for the SBS facilities. The *Financial Times* reported on its front page that this "agreement brings IBM, the dominant force in the world computer industry, directly into telecommunications in the most dramatic example yet of the growing convergence of the two rapidly converging technologies" (26 June, 1985). With MCI having expanded across the Atlantic in recent years, the deal also provides a 'possible basis for IBM's long-held dream of a global communications network linking computers around the world' (*Financial Times*, June 27, 1985). More than anything else, it indicates IBM's transformation into a communications company that will fight for every aspect of the computer and telecommunications market. While most of IBM's recent commitment has been inside the U.S., it has followed this path of consolidation of its computer dominance and extension into communications around the world (Jonquieres, 1983a,c).

Xerox

Xerox planned to offer an inter-city data communications network in 1978, but this scheme—Xten—was shelved (after purchase and resale between 1979 and 1982 of Western Union International, a telecommunications business, and major internal changes following declines in profit) in favor of concentration on a local network for offices, named Ethernet, which Xerox offers in association with Intel and Digital Equipment. This provides for the interconnection of office technologies at a local level in a way analogous with a ring main. With products ranging from standalone electronic typewriters to work stations which incorporate computing, text editing, graphics creation, and communications functions, Xerox may not offer the distance network of competitors, but it is strategically placed in the office of the future. Arrangements with Siemens of West Germany to market Ethernet in Europe have helped it establish an international standard for local networks.

Other Corporate Interests

There are a number of other important participants in the U.S.—and international—computer-communications industry. These include GTE, America's second largest telecommunications corporation, which took over the value-added common carrier Telenet in 1979 and restructured it as part of GTE Communications Network Systems, able to market national and global voice and data communications. Pursuing the computer-communications market, it divested itself of its considerable television production segment, combined with Telenet financial data bank services, and bought the Sprint long-distance network in 1982 while entering the European market in association with Ferranti. At the local level, Wang Laboratories has produced an intra-office network called Wangnet, the fruit of a policy of integrating office automation technologies, which will rival Xerox's Ethernet. Sperry Univac has enhanced its computer range by integrating products with its Sperrylink office system network, and in 1981 Hewlett-Packard introduced its "Interactive Office" concept, which allowed it to enter "the substantial and growing market for office computer systems" (*Annual Report*, 1981).

In addition, the U.S. scene is more crowded by the presence of transnationals from Japan and Europe. We have already noted the British interest in North America, but there are more substantial forces. Though the heights of the domestic market for communications and computers are well nigh impregnable (the network is firmly in the hands of AT&T, and IBM is way ahead of its rivals in computers), the particular mix which is entailed in the electronic office is attractive to major

Japanese conglomerates. So too could Philips, with its Sopho-Net private networking system which can connect any make of data, text, or imaging device to any other with complete transparency, make inroads into established U.S. markets, provided it is able to negotiate appropriate deals with well-paced U.S. companies, thereby complicating still further an already fastmoving and shifting situation.

Mastery of the Information Business

Even this sketch of the North American situation makes some things remarkably clear: the I.T. industry is currently in a state of turmoil, the locus of which is data processing and communications for business users, a consequence of which is rapid restructuring by corporations which, if predominantly concerned with their domestic markets, always look beyond the Pacific and Atlantic for growth. It is also evident that, in the U.S., the predominant forces come from one of two directions, computer manufacture and services or telecommunications, and the meeting points are integrated office systems and/or national and international networking of such systems.

Of course, the conflict is not as yet so sharp as to endanger major corporations; the situation is fluid, and there is enough demand to allow for general growth while the main participants are keeping themselves away from out-and-out confrontation. Nevertheless, conflict between these mega-corporations, especially IBM and AT&T, is inescapable, given market and technological trends, for what is at stake "is mastery of the business of managing, processing and transmitting information" (*Financial Times*, April 11, 1983). Moreover, though all the significant players in the North American business are giants on a world scale, the two behemoths, AT&T and IBM, stand out from the rest by virtue of economic resource and strategic position. Nowhere else is there a communications corporation which enjoys AT&T's advantage of a huge network as well as facilities for producing equipment, and IBM's revenues exceed the sum of its six closest competitors in computers. Therefore, the likes of Control Data Corp., GTE, and Sperry will "compete for the crumbs, but it will be very hard to pick up the bigger chunks or large accounts that both IBM and AT&T will think of as rightfully theirs" (Wohl, 1982).

Other Areas of I.T.

Our discussion has concentrated on the most lucrative areas of I.T. because this is where the major corporations are most involved, and it is from where, once infrastructures are laid, these companies may expand into other spheres from positions of prodigious strength. However, I.T. is so extensive that there are other sectors, such as defense systems, factory automation, and microchip production, which at first look unconnected to business computer-communications and which we have not mentioned. It is important to see these as related to developments in computer-communications as a whole since, though the most frenetic activity is taking place in business information systems, these are all being drawn into the maelstrom.

Microchip suppliers are entering traditional computing, factory automation is increasingly merging with the electronic office, military communications companies are involved with civil systems. Whichever direction one comes from, the borders of corporate activity are becoming blurred.

In this light, particularly noteworthy are cable services, phenomena receiving much publicity as innovations for the domestic consumer. As a different market with its own history of corporate participation, it is to be expected that cable would not involve the same groups as those supplying businesses, and this is to some extent so, partly also because the home is a much less economically attractive venue. However, because it is still a significant market and, because cable can provide the channels for information movement for both business and domestic users and thereby presages the convergence of entertainment and business communications over the same networks, it is of interest to I.T. corporations, either as an alternative to or as an enhancement of established communications channels. At the moment, this is evident from the activities of Plessey, GEC, STC, and British Telecom in the U.K., which are all heavily involved in plans for cable television.

Even where I.T. corporations involved in computer-communications for business users do not participate, it is important to recognize that cable is dominated by large corporate capital (cf. Compaine, 1979, Ch. 7), which is often moving beyond cable into business areas. Whether as equipment suppliers, operators or program providers, a combination of these, or all three together, the presence of large corporations is unmistakable. In North America, the major cable TV providers are media conglomerates which include Time Inc. (1982 revenue $3.6 billion) with its American Television and Communications operations, its joint venture, with MCA ($1.6 billion) and Paramount Pictures (a subsidiary of Gulf and Western Industries which had sales in 1982 of $5.5 billion), called USA Cable Network, and Home Box Office, the biggest pay-TV service, with around 50% of the market; and Times Mirror (1982 revenue $2.2 billion), with its Times Mirror Cable Television operation and part-ownership of the Spotlight pay-TV program services.

Beyond media conglomerates are large diversified corporations. A major participant of this type is Westinghouse (1982 sales $9.7 billion), which in 1981 bought the cable TV operation Teleprompter for $646 million and placed it within Westinghouse Broadcasting and Cable Inc. Westinghouse, best known for its massive involvement in nuclear energy, has extensive television and radio interests, participated for a time in a joint venture with ABC (1982 sales $2.6 billion) called Satellite News Channel, and has budgeted $1.2 billion for investment in cable between 1982 and 1987 (*Business Week*, October 11, 1982, pp. 77–78). In addition, the company has a large stake in factory automation, which includes the robotics manufacturer Unimation. General Electric (1982 revenue $26.5 billion), also with large interests in factory automation and computer services, has developed broadcasting and sufficient cable interests to rank in the cluster of elite U.S. concerns, and with its takeover of RCA in 1985 moves close to the very top. Yet another participant is Coca-Cola (1982 sales $6.2 billion), which bought Columbia Pictures in 1982 for $692 million and quickly moved into cable as an outlet for its purchase.

Paul Betts sums up the American situation thus:

Some of the biggest names of corporate America are now investing hundreds of millions of dollars in cable. The Rockefellers, Getty Oil, the major communications conglomerates like Warner, CBS and ABC, the Hollywood studios and the publishing empires are all seeking a major piece of the business. Westinghouse has already invested in excess of $1 billion in cable. And with the deregulation of telecommunications, the giant American Telephone and Telegraph company is now entering the fray (Betts, 1982).

With such participants, this *Financial Times* correspondent does not anticipate that the present turmoil will do anything other than bolster the hold of the "few dozen major companies with the financial muscle, marketing and programming resources to capture the lion's share of the business" (ibid.).

In Britain, the situation is much the same as in the U.S. (Economist Intelligence Unit, 1983). Though the market and contestants are correspondingly smaller, the estimated costs of entry into cable are £30–35 million (*Investors Chronicle*, 2 December, 1983, pp. 16–17). Here there are no restrictions to ownership of equipment, operation, or programming (Home Office and Department of Industry, 1983), so it is no surprise to see consortia of large interests that include American capital.

Cable TV is the fiat of multi-million-dollar enterprises in all advanced capitalist societies, and whether these come to it from a background in telecommunications, broadcasting, movies, newspapers or finance, all the participants have enormous resources. Moreover, because cable services are but one wing of an increasingly indistinguishable electronic information/entertainment business, they cannot be understood unless seen as elements of one massive industry that is dominated by corporate capital. On all sides, "the centrality and importance of the emerging *relations between* sectors" (Golding and Murdock, 1977, p. 25) is the accompaniment of this integrating movement. We have seen that numerous corporations involved in the computer-communications arena have entered the cable industry, but, even if from other directions, they move into and beyond cable: Warner-Amex offers security and financial services on its Qube cable network; Time Inc.'s subsidiary Manhatten Cable TV devotes much of its network to communications requirements of business users; Home Box Office has moved into movie production in a venture (Tri-Star Pictures) with Columbia Pictures and CBS: Clyde Cablevision will offer both entertainment and business services to the companies with premises in central Glasgow. The process is of course uneven and complex, but there remains an inexorable trend towards integration—always accompanied and guided by large corporate capital.

This then is the situation that confronts us: amidst interminable discussion of changes in the I.T. industry, one thing remains constant—led by computer-communications for business, and increasingly moving towards integration, it is a business monopolized by transnational, especially American, corporations. This is a far cry from the idea of a rational, managed "information society": the chaotic, confrontational strategies shaped by market forces and aggressive competition between powerful capitals. Whatever the outcome of the present wave of struggles between large-scale capital, one thing is certain—the dominance of still bigger capital over the emerging information grid. An elite of transnational corporations will supply I.T. goods and services on an international stage.

Corporate Control Shapes What I.T. is Developed

There will be readers, many intensely interested in new technologies, who will question the relevance of the foregoing. To these people, the technology itself is the key factor, and the manufacturer merely the provider. Anthony Hyman's belief that "it is an open question whether Europe would not be better off simply following the main IBM line" (Hyman, 1980, p. 13), suggests this line of thought, that, if transnationals can most effectively and efficiently supply the I.T. hardware, then there is much to be said for their predominance. And Edwin Parker says it bluntly: the "issue is *not* who owns or operates the hardware facilities. The issue *is* whether the facilities, however owned, are accessible for use by all members of the society" (Parker, 1976, p. 20).

With this, we are back to familiar debates: whether technology is neutral, used or abused depending on the motives of operators. It is premised on a distinction between hardware and software, the former regarded as inert, while the latter is seen as value-laden, possibly biased (a television program, etc.). Our review of corporate involvement in the information business does reveal that much software (computer programs, data bases, media) is in the hands of large capital, and we shall comment further on implications of this, but more important, our descriptions must shake confidence in the ready distinctions drawn between medium and message that pave the way for commentators to welcome I.T. from whatever direction it arrives.

The difficulty is not only that transnational corporations frequently supply both hardware and software as a combined package (in cable as owners and operators, in computing as equipment suppliers and operational designers) and increasingly are "selling solutions to problems, not just raw computer power" (General Electric, *Annual Report*, 1981, p. 9), but also that we can see in describing company strategies that the very technologies that are produced, the very hardware which appears asocial, are manifestations of corporate priorities, are results of select businesses identifying certain developments as more important than others. To believe that computer communications for business users, far and away the most sought after market, are simply neutral developments is surely untenable, given our identification of the prioritization of this area—and the reason for that prioritization—by the leading manufacturers and users. The stark reality is that these are systems developed to serve the intracorporate needs for which they were designed" (Tobin Foundation, 1982, p. 25). Pioneered and produced for identifiable social needs, it is surely reasonable to suggest that a different constituency and different manufacturers might produce different technologies. It is only by closing our minds to the possibility of alternative technologies—though a constituted technology is so palpable that the positing of imagined alternatives is sorely difficult—that we can assume as natural the results of the focus of leading transnational corporations on the "electronic grid" within and between offices.

Any review of company statements reveals time and time again that Xerox's guiding principle—"We exist to earn profits"—is shared by all corporate contenders, and is why they have identified computer communications for business, since it is here that the largest sales might be found. It is gauche to write that the likes of IBM, RCA, and Philips have as a goal and guide to action profit maximization, since they make no secret about it. But it is still more gauche to imagine that the technologies these companies produce as a means of achieving this goal are somehow valueless. Serious questions must be posed as regards the technologies that were prevented from being produced—and which were never considered—because they did not accord with the market principles of capitalist enterprise. It is, for example, an index of social value that led Thorn, upon taking over EMI, to jettison the latter's production facilities for medical scanners (diagnostic machines in which a mini-computer is harnessed to X-ray technology that are especially useful in early and accurate analysis of cancers). The brute fact was that Thorn-EMI saw less money in health treatment than in entertainment, its chairman candidly opining that the "decision to withdraw from medical electronics was announced . . . as there appeared little likelihood of achieving profits in the foreseeable future" (*Report and Accounts*, 1980, p. 4). It is crucial that we recognize that I.T. has been shaped by multinational corporations to express corporate values and priorities: that the technologies—as well as the software—which we are assured promise an information age are gestated by those endeavoring, not to bring about a community-conscious post-industrial society, but to retain and advance their own interests.

Corporate Control Shapes Who Gets What I.T.

The devotion of I.T. corporations to the precepts of the market means not only that they will manufacture only that which they are reasonably confident will bring a return they judge adequate, but also that I.T. will be made available only on a basis of ability to pay. Amid all the debate about the potential of I.T., this must be placed at the center of any realistic analysis: the genesis and application of the new technologies are framed by the principles "what is the worth of this as an investment?" and "who can afford it?" The major uptakers of I.T. are those best able to pay for it, and it has been designed and developed with the most affluent in mind: the integrated computer communications facilities are being operated by and supplied to large corporate bodies (and big spending state agencies, notable police and military forces) to better enable them to centralize, rationalize, and coordinate their dispersed activities.

In turn, these purchasers are searching to maximize their own interests, the results of which are contracting for technologies and services which are justifiable chiefly in terms of company profitability. The consequences—staff saving, increased intensity of labor, more machine pacing—which we have documented are well known in factories and offices.

In addition, I.T. enables these companies to take on broad sophisticated means of both internal and external communications, the better to transmit their vision of the world either to their own employees or to the wider society. Equally important is an increasing internationalization of affairs in the hands of transnational corporations that, in the words of Citicorp, is facilitated by their adoption of "increasingly sophisticated satellite technology" that leads to "a completely integrated market place capable of moving money and ideas to any place on the planet in a matter of seconds" (quoted in *Financial Times,* 10 May, 1982).

Powerful organizations do not merely produce and uptake the new technologies; they are also providers and users of specific kinds of information. It is a truism that, the more pertinent the information, the more expensive it will be. In this light, it is worthwhile observing that information services of a financial kind (market trends, stock exchange listings, investment data, currency flows) are produced for and made available only to those groups with the means of affording them. Thus Telerate, a computerized financial information service which supplies updated data to banks and finance institutes, is currently enjoying rapid growth on the basis of revenue from subscription fees which average some $700 per terminal per month. Telerate's data may well be important, but at that price it is by no means available to everyone. Similarly, the proliferation of on-line data bases are overwhelmingly resources for business and industrial users (because these are the most lucrative markets), and they do not come cheap.

Corporate Centralization

A few moments ago, we referred to the internalization of affairs that I.T. allows, but this amounts to much more than an integration of the world's markets. With I.T. coming from advanced capitalism's largest corporations and being most avidly used by those of similar magnitude, it is important to stress the centralization of power that the new technologies facilitate. With I.T., the reach of corporate capital is at once extended and its control enhanced. Not only within the information industry itself are fewer and fewer mega-corporations dominating the field, but also within capitalism as a whole, companies are able to take up technologies that bolster their command from the center. Whether it be sophisticated computer-communications networks, computerization of manufacture, ready access to information of international monetary flows, online systems linking data bases, or satellite monitoring, I.T. is "expected to serve nicely the world business system's requirements" (Schiller, 1981, p. 16). Both within the nation state and—with the leading industrial, financial, and service corporations—across the globe, we must pay attention to "the unparalleled centralization of business control that telematics engenders" (D. Schiller, 1982a, p. 3).

Especially at a time when commentators from Daniel Bell to Alvin Toffler rave about I.T.'s potential to decentralize modern life, when any discussion of the future is accompanied by seers announcing that we might have the electronic cottage should we so choose, we must point out the verifiable trend which is a scramble by privileged corporations to produce and apply technologies which further the centralized control they already enjoy. Across societies, the evidence is overwhelming that people yearn for more control over their lives, for more access to decision-making, more access to the means of communication, more say in the organization of work. I.T. zealots and corporate ideologues tap this yearning and promise that "technologies of freedom" (Pool, 1983), provided by colossal and impersonal corporations, will somehow enable this power to be devolved. It is a deceit, a cruel mystification, where a "decentralizing ideology masks a centralizing reality" (Barnet and Müller, 1975, p. 44). To add insult to injury, as we shall see, I.T. provides increasingly centralized businesses with the means—if *they* should so choose—to restructure their enterprises in such a way as to achieve decentralization by a corporate design which retains close surveillance of the entire operation (see Chapter 11).

Corporate Control and Public Accountability

The corporate giants that dominate I.T., that are instrumental in deciding which technologies and even what sorts of information the wider society is to have, are under-examined and poorly understood, not least because information about trans-nationals is hard to come by. Even when it is available, it is usually, and revealingly, proprietary, knowledge about the architects of the "knowledge society" being of commercial value usually far beyond the purse of the individual researcher.

In spite of this, some things are known and merit emphasis. Above all, we must stress that these corporations are not democratically accountable, their business being to pursue the private interests of shareholders rather than community requirements. As their foremost academic defender puts it, the corporation's

> purpose is not to transform the economy by exploiting its potentialities (especially its human potentialities) for development, but to exploit the existing situation to its own profit by utilization of the knowledge it already possesses, at minimum cost to itself of adaptation and adjustment (Johnson, 1975, pp. 79–80).

This, coupled with their international spread, means that they do not consider a particular area or country's needs but their own livelihood, "the contribution of direct foreign investment [being] incidental to the purpose of making profit" (p. 59). Yet the decisions they make are of great import to any society; a corporate directive to invest here rather than there, to close this plant rather than that one, to develop this product rather than another, are matters of enormous substance to people's lives. The recent spate of investment by European firms in the U.S. is an instance of this. Capital is being moved out of the host nations to North America because that is where investors foresee the best return. It has nothing to do with the requirements of their own—or the recipient—country. And the same principle applies wherever investment is or is not made, whether in Eire, the Far East, or Latin America.

This does not mean that transnationals are altogether aloof from influence. Clearly, in countries such as the U.S., West Germany, or Britain, government can exert some, at times effective, pressure, and it is for this reason that IBM—described in a *Financial Times* editorial as "perhaps the supreme example of the multinational company whose ultimate decision-making authority lies in the U.S." (19 January, 1984)—regularly advertises in Europe that it is loyal to host nations (cf. Sobel, 1981, Ch. 9). But their enormous wealth and geographical spread does provide them with enormous advantages in, for example, transfer pricing (cf. Murray, 1981), strategic planning, and in that scrutiny of organizations with extraterritorial locations is untenable (see Gray et al., 1984). Moreover, I.T. itself consolidates their power, since it facilitates the communication and control processes of transnational enterprise, while supervision of cross-border data flows is neither practical nor acceptable to many nations. Instances of the capabilities of multinational corporations abound, and in illustration we might cite the emasculation of EEC attempts to compel transnationals to inform and consult their employees on matters affecting their jobs (the Vredeling directive) by what the *Economist* described as "the most expensive lobbying campaign in the parliament's history, mounted mainly by American-based companies" (October 16, 1982, p. 73), and their disdain for the abilities of trade unions to organize internationally as a counter-weight to themselves (Roberts and May, 1974). Moreover, it is important that we bear in mind that these are overt expressions of power. The major influence of transnational capital is surely the dull compulsion they exert on governments by constraining them to act in line with market principles, for fear of losing business confidence and precipitating currency crises.

The Commoditization of Information

The corporate groups which have developed and are furthering the spread of I.T. ensure that "information is a commodity, to be packaged, distributed and sold in whatever guise and context guarantee commercial value" (Golding and Murdock, 1974, p. 227). This application of market criteria means that the front end of I.T. goods and services are tailored for business, but of course it has consequences for the domestic consumer. The predominance of this value does lead to awe-inspiring computer-communications networks and an explosion of data banks for business users, but where financial resources are more scarce what is offered is something different. For the domestic market—compared to business the sphere of the information poor, though there are significant differences within this sector—the stress is on pap, on diverting and trivialized entertainment which offends few and reaches the biggest audience possible (see Chapter 9).

Wherever one looks, information "is being put into saleable packages, made into items that are being purchased, organized in enormously efficient and impressive ways for sale" (Schiller, H.I., 1983, p. 19). In Britain, for example, a government report titled, revealingly, *Making a Business of Information,* claims that the country must "pay much more attention to information as a commercial commodity" to which end new markets should be grasped, and traditional ways of information collection and dissemination (e.g., libraries, the Central Statistical Office, education) ought to reconsider their public service outlook since "the supply of information—whether in the form of education and training, share prices, news reports, journal articles or whatever—is an area of major commercial importance with high growth potential" (ITAP, 1983, p. 39).

Information Inequality

This application of commercial tenets towards I.T. relentlessly perpetuates and generates information inequalities, chiefly separated on corporate and domestic lines. It is in this way that we are to make sense of the situation in the U.S. where one of the most predicted results of AT&T's divestiture and the opening up of the "free market" is "the certainty that local telephone bills will rise by $2 a month as a result of the break-up" (*Economist,* August 13, 1983, pp. 33-34). The position in the U.K.. is much the same: privatization coupled with liberalization of telecommunications means that

> the new company will act like any other privately owned company under the discipline of market forces. Marginal services, and even those providing a lower than average rate of return, will be cut back and if possible eliminated. Any obligations remaining on B.T. to provide service will be observed in name only; business operations will be tailored to profit optimisation (POEU, 1982).

One result will surely be that rural and domestic areas will face price rises, now that B.T. no longer has unchallenged monopoly or incentive to subsidize less rewarding areas from the most profitable business routes. Similarly, cable television will go to the better off urban and suburban areas (estimates are that it will reach only half the population by 2000) where markets are propitious, while some people—the poorest—may lose communications facilities altogether as cable incorporates telephony into the new systems when, according to an internal Department of Industry paper, those left with traditional copper pair wires in a cabled area may find these "progressively abandoned if the marginal costs of operating telephony on the cable systems become lower than the cost of maintaining the copper pair network" (quoted in *Guardian,* 25 November, 1983, p. 22).

It is here that one perceives most clearly major features of the information business as it is currently developing. The poorer members of society will have least access to I.T. and, unacknowledged yet still important, I.T. will not be developed for these people. Those without resources are of no interest to the corporate guardians of the I.T. revolution, and the information age will pass them by. At best, they will be lumped together as a "mass"—and this is at best, since many will not even qualify for the entertainments of cable television—that, which by virtue of numbers, is worth catering for in terms of lowest common denominator produce, the garbage information with which mass audiences are already familiar.

The converse of this information poor, though of course there are gradations between groups, is the information rich, and this returns us to the corporate parentage of the new technology. It is an easy error to perceive the I.T. makers and users as merely corporations, but IBM, GEC, and their ilk are private companies controlled by and for particular sorts of people—the rich—which no amount of concentration on technology or propaganda about the managerial revolution ought to disguise. The chief beneficiaries of I.T. are the leaders of the groups which have pioneered it and those best able to afford it in other corporations. Propelled by as-strong-as-ever commitment to profit maximization (Herman, 1981, pp. 112-113) and enjoying a close connection with one another through a network of interlocking directorates (cf. Zeitlin, 1974; Scott, 1979, Ch. 6; Kerbo and Della Fave, 1983), these groups have in recent years, if anything, sharpened their access to political decision-making to consolidate their economic hold (Useem, 1984; Marsh and Locksley, 1983). I.T. will do nothing if it does not secure this class dominance.

Conclusion

Faced with all of this, a few mega-corporations able to make decisions which will impinge upon our everyday lives (should we manufacture this good rather than that one? produce this program rather than another?), relentlessly operating on principles which discriminate in favor of the already rich and powerful, their reach extending even into provision of information upon which we make decisions about our personal and societal development (in television, video, educational publishing, etc.), it is easy to be overwhelmed. This is still more the case when one investigates the primary beneficiaries of the I.T. industry—large business users. Looking around, it is hard "not to be overcome and consequently paralysed by what may appear to be the emergence of a powerful and unassailable information apparatus, at the disposition of a system of concentrated, corporate capital" (Schiller, H.I., 1981, p. xvii). How else is one to respond to the news that the Citicorp corporation, a major user and producer of I.T., is able "to read world events better than the State Department" (*Financial Times*, 17 July, 1981). What else can one conclude when we witness the emergence of an information industry at once integrated and operating on a global scale, yet also capable of penetrating the individual's home? Who would not be awed by this corporate dominance at a time of acute economic and political crisis?

In advanced capitalist societies, the only force capable of counteracting this concentration—and offering some degree of accountability to the democratic process—is the state. Because it has important powers—as information provider, employer, legislative center, market and telecommunications authority, as well as political representative—it is intricately involved with the I.T. industry. We ought not to confuse this intervention with the public interest, as in some way curtailing and making answerable the I.T. corporations, but the state role is a vitally important factor to which we now turn our attention.

Chapter 8
I.T. and the State

To a much larger extent than appearance and rhetoric have been made to suggest, the politics of advanced capitalism have been about different conceptions of how to run the *same* economic and social system, and not about radically different social systems. *This* debate has not so far come high on the political agenda.

—Ralph Miliband. *The State in Capitalist Society.*
1969. Quartet, 1974, pp. 66–67.

The state is a massive presence in all advanced capitalist societies. Despite some enthusiasm for a return to laissez-faire in which its frontiers are rolled back, the fact is that, nowadays, no state can withdraw from at least major involvement in economic activity, still less from social arrangements. Its control of education budgets, its role as an employer, its duty to uphold law and order and prepare appropriate defenses, its responsibilities for key industries such as coal, gas, electricity, and water supply, its fiscal, administrative, and legislative functions, its leverage as a buyer of goods and services, and so forth, rule out disengagement. It may try to marshal its powers to create conditions in which free enterprise thrives and, in so doing, announce a crusade to loose market forces from the restrictions of excessive taxation, limitations on dividend payments, and the like, but even this involves nothing less than large-scale participation in industry, finance, and business, and it can never hope to effect withdrawal. To imagine the state being replaced by the hidden hand of the market is as risible as the Marxist faith that, come socialism, it will wither away.

In every advanced capitalist society, government has taken a special interest in technological innovation and has devised policies to stimulate and facilitate its introduction. In Britain, for example, the state is intervening to:

- create a sense of awareness and acceptance of I.T.
- provide appropriately qualified school-leavers and graduates to service I.T.
- speed the development of I.T. by funding and channelling research projects.
- integrate and consolidate disparate corporate interests to meet expected competition from foreign corporations and state institutions.
- subsidize I.T. ventures from public funds and, if necessary, instigate I.T. industries under state auspices.
- act as an especially important market for I.T. products and services, and use this power to the advantage of domestic industry.
- provide a favorable regulatory and legal environment for an information society (for example, in data collection and movement, copyright, and narrowcasting).
- help with the building of a telecommunications infrastructure.

So complex and fast-changing is this involvement with I.T.—for example, legislation to liberalize telecommunications is extensive, intricate, and subject to a host of amendments; the specifics of various types of subsidy vary between industries, departments, and from year to year; educational policies range across the school system through to universities—that description of its features can quickly get lost in minutae. Moreover, when one enters comparative analysis of Japanese, French or American policies, this is compounded by the danger that national differences, palpable though they are, take on an importance they do not merit. It is to minimize these risks that we review with a broad brush what we consider the most consequential aspects of the state's role in I.T. and, as a preliminary to sketching varieties of state response, delineate what they have in common.

Common Features of State Involvement

• State actions are guided by the requisites of market economy generally domestically, and always internationally. The market principle of production of what can be sold at a profit is the overriding determinant of state participation in I.T., and its complement is use of I.T. in circumstances that can be justified on commerical criteria. Whatever variance might be apparant between national policies and practices, all are perceived and operationalized as strategies to meet this requirement. A concommitant is that state actions towards I.T. are informed by the notion that social needs are synonymous with market diktats.

• All state share a desire to escape a world-wide recession by each nation endeavouring to strengthen its competition vis-a-vis foreign interests by adopting I.T. as quickly as possible, so that industrial restructuring will be effected before competitors. Thereby their prices may be undercut, their goods and services superceded, and their market share seized so that the successful nation might enjoy economic growth, increased employment, and prosperity by operating better on the global market.

• The search for reduced costs and/or improved products, that competitors may be bested, is connected of course to the axial role of market criteria. However, the I.T. market and the vigorous competition that is taking place therein cannot be regarded as one of open competition, both because the enormous oligopolistic groups which dominate the scene and state involvement itself often preclude the operation of competitive forces (for example, government contracts are frequently offered on a noncompetitive basis). Thus, the new technology is being developed on market criteria, but free market practices in the sense of unrestricted participation by more or less equal partners are nonexistent.

• State policies are primarily reactions to the presence and power, in the I.T. industry, of transnational corporations, notably those originating in the United States, that decisively influence the market. In France, for example, Minc and Nora have recognized this difficulty of competing with American capital, since "the omnipotence of IBM throws the game off balance." In response to the might of corporations like AT&T, IBM, and ITT, nation states outside the US (where government has felt, in spite of qualms about the Japanese threat, able to withdraw from the industry to play chiefly a supportive role—though this is no less crucial for being supportive—by serving as an outlet for I.T. products and a supplier of research and development funds, contending that competition between strong and well-placed corporations will best assure US dominance) have pursued policies aimed at counter-balancing this disproportionate power. In implementing these, the state's criteria are those of the multinationals, as Nora and Minc make clear. While warning that IBM "will participate . . . in the government of the planet," their proposals are for the state to assist in the rationalization of the French I.T. industry that will consolidate domestic producers into large units capable of effective competition with US and Japanese transnationals, to encourage tactical alliances of French companies with AT&T against IBM because the "interests of these behemoths are divergent," and generally to seek the "new growth" that will come from more "foreign trade" (Nora and Minc, 1980, p. 78, 80). Everywhere, the recommendations of the state are the same: to match the dominant transnationals by mustering internal resources that will "improve our export performance and reduce our dependence on imports" (Labour Party, 1980). The rationale is presented as self-evident, agreement to abide by the rules of multinational capital unproblematical.

Assumptions behind these strategies include:

• that the international market is an appropriate arbiter of technological innovation, and of the socio-economical organization which is its necessary complement.

• that transnational corporations either express a foreign menace to a particular nation or its own interests. That is, state policies intended to strengthen domestic capital against transnationals from abroad, by building usually bigger and more integrated units at home which are then better placed to extend further into overseas markets, rest on the assumption that transnational corporations do serve an identifiable national interest.

• that the well-known and self-proclaimed cosmopolitanism of multinational corporations is amenable to harness for national purposes.

• that the internationalization of capital and the integration of the world economy brought about by the spread of transnationals will not undermine the viability of strategies formed around the notion of a nation state.

Such assumptions and the actions they imply produce a "dog's dinner of policies" at the national level, one which at once lauds the free market in international terms and simultaneously does much to subsidize, protect, and support its own boundaries and those identified as belonging within them.

• I.T., since it will influence all spheres of society, is unlikely to be most successfully introduced by an individual or even a select few corporations operating on their own. The objectives of companies in competition with one another for particular markets cannot be assumed to serve the interests of the sum of corporations even in a particular nation. The profitability and efficiency of business in toto, which could be best served by energetic take-up of I.T., might conflict with a specific corporation's desire to retain contracts with a government department hitherto not competed for, though open tender might be to the advantage of the I.T. industry overall. Another company might wish to slow the pace of a technological innovation in order to recoup its investment by extending the product cycle, though, all in all, speed of adoption is of the essence. Yet another may attempt to forestall the entry of competitors into its domain by, for example, using its accumulated wealth to subsidize its own products at sub-market prices, undercut the insurgent and force it from the scene to the long-term detriment of the national economy. More obviously, the smooth and rapid development of common standards for communication and computer systems, while this might serve the interests of capital in general, especially in tackling overseas markets, could well be opposed by an individual corporation which wants to enter these sectors to sell its own products and services. The struggle this precipitates between corporations extending their own interests may be to the detriment of industry as a whole, since it can hinder the process of technological change and even dissipate vital resources in internecine competiton.

Because individually competing corporations do not necessarily harmonize, it is necessary for the state to try to orchestrate and rationalize the I.T. revolution in the best interests of capital as a whole. At the least, this involves an attempt to take an overall view and act accordingly by dispensing state aid where appropriate, pump-priming a company here, originating another there; offering one ministerial contract to the cheapest bid, but allocating another noncompetitively; encouraging mergers in some sectors of the industry while stimulating new entrants in another. All states to a greater or lesser degree are in this way participants in the I.T. industry, since all have a duty to serve the national interest, which requires speedy adoption of the new technology that the economy as a whole is able to withstand and ideally overcome foreign competition.

• In many cases, such is the scale of competing entities in the I.T. business that the state feels it necessary to intervene to help form mega-corporations in their homelands to support the overall interests of the economy. Since, as Olivetti observes, I.T. is a "world industry" with "competition . . . increasingly more a question of nation-systems than of individuals companies" (*Annual and Extraordinary General Meeting*, 7 April, 1982, p. 10), it is not surprising that some governments feel it serves the national interest to encourage, even to guide, consolidation of domestic capital that will gain strategic advantage both for those in the I.T. business and for other companies reliant on the prosperity of these leaders. This thinking is most evident in the practices of Japan and France, but it is present, in spite of appearances to the contrary, in the UK. Thus in the midst of liberalization (allowing competitors to enter markets once an exclusive province) and privatization (selling to private capital public holdings) of British Telecom (BT), and all the talk of state withdrawal that accompanies such measures, strategic considerations prevent the government breaking-up the network, though doubtless this would increase competition by dealing a body-blow to the monopoly. As BT chairman Sir George Jefferson successfully argued, the UK will not gain a significant share of world markets though small companies alone . . . large sectors of the world markets will only be entered by those with considerable financial and technological resources . . . [BT] is clearly one of the very few UK companies with the necessary expertise and resources to compete in these new markets . . . British Telecom, if allowed to develop dynamically, will not only be able to compete in world markets: just as importantly, it will help to create a more robust environment in which the ability of our equipment suppliers to compete internationally will be greatly enhanced (Jefferson, 25 January, 1984).

In short, government considerations of capital as a whole do not allow it to throw communications to the market. It must orchestrate the information revolution in favor of the national interest; it cannot abrogate its role of coordinator of manifold and separate interests; and therefore it cannot pursue free market policies, however much it might wish to do so.

• This orchestration involves attempts to dovetail state agencies with the needs of the I.T. industry. In Britain, for example, the public sector accounted for over half the entire market for electronics in 1982, while over 70% of the defense ministry's research and development budget went to companies which are major exporters of weaponry and heavily involved in I.T. (Britain is the third largest arms manufacturer, after the U.S. and France). These are connections between state institutions and private corporations that demand regular scrutiny for improved and sustained compatibility.

• Because an important factor in the implementation of policies to strengthen a country's competitive position is the willingness of the populace itself to change, the state takes on the role of smoothing social acceptance of the new technology. Education here plays a primary part, and the rush to install computers in primary and secondary schools, to provide courses in computer literacy, and to alert teachers to the urgency of adjusting to the information society and then transmit this message to their charges, is evidence of the state's obligations in this respect. The transition to a novel post-industrial era while a crucial continuity remains—the need to be competitive—is considerably eased by instructing the future generation that acceptance of computerization is essential to its well-being. On a wider scale, but following the same imperative of bolstering the market position of indigenous capital, the state endeavors to persuade the people as a whole that rapid adoption of I.T. is both a necessity and beneficial. In the UK, there have been extensive and well-funded awareness campaigns, funded from public monies and directed by leading politicians that have enjoyed lavish advertising resources and travelling exhibitions to meet this target. A similar story is to be told of France, where efforts to sensitize the public to computers have been a theme of government programs, while in Japan the state has for years enthused about high technology and the need to keep abreast of change of its people.

• Though the language of efficiency, rationalization, and competition appears paramount in considerations of I.T., and efforts to persuade the public to willingly accept it appear subordinate to these goals, social discipline is both a prerequisite of effective introduction of I.T. and a requirement of handling any dislocation consequent upon its adoption. To the extent that successful implementation of technological innovation requires social control, and to the extent that changes bring about social upheaval (job transfer, retraining, redundancies, etc.) that may need attention, then the state frequently plays an important role. Currently, it is the first of these functions which commands the attention of governments in advanced capitalist societies—those unfortunate enough to find themselves in the "sunset" industries in France, Germany, America, and Britain have found little solace from the state—and measures to make sure that I.T. gets adopted are considerably more material than media extravaganzas extolling the "mighty micro." These get relatively sparse treatment in discussions of the state's role in the I.T. industry, but they can be among the most pressing forms of state intervention.

For example, legislation and practice in the sphere of industrial relations is at the moment playing a critical role in facilitating technological change in Britain, since it has weakened the capacity of trade unions to negotiate by removing traditional legal immunities. The 1982 *Employment Act* forbids unions from taking industrial action unless it "wholly or mainly" relates to specific employment issues (i.e., wages and work conditions). This new law was used to effect in October and November of 1983 by Mercury Communications, which found itself blacked by telecommunications engineers who refused to interconnect the company to the British Telecom network as part of their campaign against liberalization which they feared would ultimately reduce their job security. Mercury's injunction, backed by the threat of large fines, sequestration of union funds, and imprisonment of members, led to the acquiescence of the engineers. (*Times*, Law Report, 10 November, 1983, p. 9).

Following the Mercury affair, the much more bitterly fought case between the print workers' union (the National Graphical Association) and a local newspaper publisher (Mr. Selim Shah) in Warrington also involved legislation, this time the 1980 *Employment Act*, which forbids secondary action by unionists in pursuit of an industrial dispute. Heavy picketing by the national union led to fines of £675,000 being imposed, its £13 million assets seized, and, upon the threat of national action from the union to squeeze Mr. Shah, numerous injunctions from newspaper publishers calling upon the union to revoke its call for a 24-hour strike in the printing industry or face the penalties of the law placed on secondary activities. Moreover, the union's defiance of legal rules at the outset gave legitimacy to effective and large-scale police action which constrained the mass picketing of the Shah works and rendered union attempts to halt production there ineffective, while the same illegality of the picketing made other unions hesitant to give support to the printers. The union called off its costly action early in 1984, after being defeated in its bid to uphold the closed shop in Warrington.

The use of legislation and the legal process, from policing through to the courts, is of importance as regards the introduction of new technology, and it is worth noting that both these disputes were concerned with I.T. Though the issues became camouflaged by debates about the "rule of law," technological innovation and employees' adaptation to these changes were central. The Mercury Communications issue struck at the core of communications policies in the UK, and was "based fundamentally on justified fears of worsening conditions" of engineers at a time "when technology is rapidly changing old working practices" *(Financial Times,* October 12, 1983). The Shah affair focused on the same key issue, the *Observer* noting that "at the heart of the NGA's militancy is the knowledge that with modern, computerised type-setting, the traditional craft skills of its members are no longer needed by newspaper proprietors" (4 December, 1983, p. 9).

We have reviewed the law's role in facilitating technological change for two reasons. First, because this sort of intervention, that which goes far beyond the issue of achieving attitudinal change to creation of concrete conditions favorable to technological change, gets insufficiently considered in discussions of the state's participation. Second, because it highlights the fact that the state's involvement is extensive, that to appreciate fully its intervention we should look to a wide range of policies and practices, gauging the weight of (un)employment policies, equality opportunity enforcement, or whatever to understand its role in technological change. We ought not to be surprised that the state is intimately involved. Since this technology will have a pervasive influence, the state is inevitably embroiled in manifold social and economic issues. In addition, since the strategy of all advanced capitalist governments is to place I.T. at the center of industrial restructuring in hope of economic rejuvenation, they then feel committed to do all in their power to assist in that recovery, and anything which interrupts that process, from employee recalcitrance to shortages of capital, will be perceived as an obstacle to be removed by whatever means the state can bring to bear. Though, at this stage in the book, we restrict ourselves to discussion of the more conventional aspects of state involvement in I.T. in order to show something of its scope and significance, we return to the wider issues in Part Three.

Varieties of State Involvement

There has been a range of national responses to I.T. that has two extremes. At one pole is a philosophy which is committed to Liberal political economy. This is assured that market disciplines are the best means of developing I.T. both domestically and internationally, and that private capital should take the lead. Here, the state sees itself as essentially supportive, attempting to produce regulatory policies and the like which can secure the maximum freedom of maneuver for private investments, and it tries to keep a distance from commercial affairs. Circumstances are such that this philosophy cannot consistently be upheld, but, where governments do commit themselves to Liberal doctrines, the state tries as much as possible to be guided by market forces so long as these are demonstrably beneficial to national interests. The United States is the premier instance of this outlook, and the British emulate it in important respects, though conditions inside the UK mean that there is a considerable gap between laissez-faire expostulation and practice. At the other pole is a philosophy which, while acceding to the imperatives of international markets, is convinced that the state itself must adopt a leadership role if the nation is to successfully compete. In countries such as Japan and France, the state has taken upon itself the role of entrepreneur, guiding, protecting, plotting, and prodding the indigenous IT industry in a corporatist manner (Winkler, 1976), and, on occasion, even nationalizing key corporations in search of advantage in the world economy.

France

The French state has for some time been vexed by the intrusion of American capital ever deeper into Europe, impressed by the rapid emergence of Japan as an industrial power capable of challenging even the U.S., characterized by a predilection for government planning of economic life, and aware of the special contribution information technology can make towards stimulating French competitiveness domestically and internationally. A result of these factors has been a more or less consistent policy over the past generation of trying to meet the "défi americain" by emulating Japanese policies of providing state aid and direction, especially for computing and telecommunications, in order to capture and consolidate domestic markets as a prelude to expansion abroad. There have been differences of emphasis dependent on circumstances and the political complection of governments, but there remains a remarkable constancy of strategy through the regimes of de Gaulle, Giscard d'Estaing, and Mitterand. The French ambition to become, in the words of Laurent Fabius, "the third electronic nation in the world" after Japan and America, has long been premised on what President Mitterand has described as "reconquering the internal market" in high technology by means of extensive protectionism, subsidy and support, and thereafter aggressively invading other nations (cf. Servan-Schreiber, 1968).

Its governments have insisted for a generation that France holds a majority stake in a computer manufacturing enterprise, because of its strategic significance for the remainder of industry and as a means of resisting the dominance of IBM. To this end in the 1960s it formed Compagnie Internationale de l'Informatique (CII) with an immediate subsidy of $80 million and a further $45 million before its integration into a European consortium, UNIDATA, which in turn received in excess of $130 million (Vos, 1983, pp. 37–60). When this venture was abandoned, an alliance was formed with the U.S. company Honeywell (with a 53% French stake) to make CII–Honeywell Bull, which between 1975 and 1980 was in receipt of $522 million of state subsidy plus guaranteed state purchases of almost $1 billion over those years. By 1982, Honeywell's interest had reduced to 8% and the company renamed Bull, though state aid (a further $70 million capital was injected in 1983) and preferential purchases (the state accounts for over half of France's total installed computers) continued. The upshot of such policies is that, while IBM in France has about twice the sales revenue of Bull, it holds less than 20% of central government's computer business compared to Bull's 40% (*Financial*

Times, 28 November 1983, p. 21). This preferential treatment enables Bull to rank in the top four European data processing companies, though only a minority (43%) of revenue comes from outside the domestic market.

Support for an indigenous computer manufacturer has been only one part of French strategy towards I.T. More emphasis has been placed on telecommunications as a means of regenerating the nation, because here there is not the threat from IBM. Under Giscard d'Estaing, while computing received substantial support, the ambition was to create a mass domestic market for télématique and at the same time to familiarize the populace with I.T. by replacement of printed telephone directories with cheap electronic terminals linked to computerized data banks. Though the costing of this enterprise was underestimated, and though, at first, the terminals will simply provide information regarding addresses and telephone numbers, their importance lies in the widespread introduction into society of computer terminals which can in future be enhanced by extending the data held at central computers and transmitting it on the digital network.

The Mitterand government placed still more stress on the potential for I.T. for France to regain its international stature by not only continuing with the restructuring commenced by the outgoing ministry, but also by announcing in July 1982 an £11.5 billion investment to develop electronics as a cornerstone of industrial policy. This commitment combined with the nationalization of the leading I.T. companies that led to some 50% of all electronics manufacture coming to the state (and all the dominant areas), bringing with it some 90% of research and development funds (*Financial Times*, 7 July, 1982). A few months later, the French telecommunications authority was given overall responsibility for the important office automation and computing (including Bull) side of this plan—"la Filière Electronique"—a move which stressed its key role and which was confirmed early in 1984 by the decision to proceed with the cabling of the nation, using an optical fibre network to provide TV and communications services of the most modern kind under PTT auspices.

In the late 1970s, the Christian Democrats had encouraged and advised on major restructuring of French I.T. companies that culminated in three large groups: CGE (Compagnie Générale d'Electrique): CII-Honeywell Bull being brought under the wing of the transnational conglomerate Saint-Gobain-Pont-à-Mousson, where together they secured a one-third stake in Olivetti, intent on capitalizing on the Italian company's strengths in data processing; and the Thomson electric and electronic group. Inside this trio was feverish reorganization to meet the requirements of changed technology and international competition. The state was active in much of this, not only through its stock holdings in CII-Honeywell Bull and St.-Gobain, but also by persuading ITT and Ericsson to relinquish to Thomson their controlling shares in French subsidiaries.

Mitterand's election led to the nationalization of whatever of these companies remained in private hands, and a result was that St.-Gobain withdrew from Olivetti (with CGE taking on a 10% French share) that meant French plans for data processing were undermined. However, though the redesigned strategy placed still more emphasis on telecommunications, the overall goals did not change. Even the nationalizations were guided by the aim of meeting international competition rather than political ideals, were matters of producing more effectively market-oriented companies than socialist institutions, so much so that CGE felt able to say that, while

> Ownership of the parent company was formally transferred to the French State in February 1982 [it] should be clearly stated that management continues to exercise free rein in the conduct of the Group's affairs. The course of strategic international expansion embarked upon by the prior management of the Group with such significant success is being pursued with increased vigour. Future development will continue to be on the basis of conventional business criteria (CGE. *Summary of annual reports and accounts for 1981.* May 1982, p. 4).

Faced with growing financial problems, the Mitterand government, accepting that still greater economies of scale were necessary to compete internationally and that Franco-French competition was wasteful, agreed to a reorganization of CGE and Thomson by an exchange of assets that put French telecommunications into CGE's Cit-Alcatel subsidiary, with consumer electronics, components, and military electronics under Thomson. At the same time, it has encouraged Bull to enter collaborative arrangements with overseas companies such as ICL and Siemens to improve its capabilities, a policy replicated in French searches for European alliances in telecommunications that may match U.S. and Japanese threats.

What is particularly striking about the French example is the self-conscious and articulate character of the state's role in I.T. There is a clear policy of protecting and stimulating the domestic arena, consolidating into coherent and powerful groups, and henceforth moving decisively into foreign markets. This policy might appear to some to be socialist, because of its emphasis on planning, its phobias about American transnationals, and the spate of recent nationalizations. The fact that the main elements of the policy were constructed well before Mitterand counters this argument. Rather than being socialist, the French strategy should be seen as corporatist, an example of state involvement of a directive kind determined to achieve success within the framework of an international market economy (cf. Nora and Minc, 1980).

Today, the French I.T. industry is predominantly in the hands of the state (and this public holding does set France somewhat apart from other advanced capitalist societies, though overall France has no more nationalized industry than the UK) which has concentrated telecommunications in CGE (1982 sales $9.9 billion), computers in Bull ($1.2 billion), consumer electronics and much defense electronics in Thomson ($7 billion), with Matra ($1.2 billion) playing a supporting role in weapons exports and microelectronics. Backing these state-owned enterprises are programs to familiarize the population with I.T., to support and direct research and development in key areas, notably telecommunications, to lay the domestic infrastructure for a successful move into the information age.

But however different France's domestic arrangements are for handling I.T., one thing is unmistakeable; the overriding concern of all the measures is to equip French industry with the means to withstand foreign competition. Whatever alternative ideals the current government might aspire to, it is drawn into the vortex of a swirling and threatening world market.

Japan

The French strategy is modeled on the Japanese plan for an information society. As with the French, so do the Japanese look to a post-industrial future, regarding IT as the "nervous system of the future economy" (Masuda, 1975) for which they have advanced blueprints. Behind this plan, which has been nurtured for well over a decade, lies an aggressive commercial strategy which is its raison d'etre. The aim has been to develop an indigenous computer industry and a strong domestic I.T. sector on the basis of which it would be possible to expand into foreign markets. This would replicate the successful strategy previously used by consumer electronics and automobiles.

The Japanese state has played an active and markedly directional role in laying the foundations for the country's current ascendancy in I.T., having since the early 1970s been committed to expanding knowledge-intensive industries via a strategy that is attributable in large part to what Chalmers Johnson describes as the "developmental state" which, capitalizing on historical circumstances and legacies, placed a high degree of control of the economy in the hands of government officials (Johnson, 1982). MITI (Ministry of International Trade and Industry), which emerged from the war mobilization of the nation in the early 1940s, has been intimately involved with mapping out routes for corporations in products, industrial sectors, and appropriate markets. The upshot of this close state involvement is that, in Japan, "the government and private sector do have some kind of long-range plan, some vision of the future," which means that the nation has "an industrial road map" (*Far Eastern Economic Review,* December 3, 1982, p. 47) that coordinates individual contributions, concentrates resources, and smooths potential conflicts of interest to the advantage of Japan as a whole. This has been supported by a combination of protectionism by legal methods such as licensing and foreign exchange controls, as well as straight-forward taxation disincentives; preferential purchase; cheap borrowing arrangements from state-influenced banks; selective joint deals with high technology foreign corporations; considerable state guidance and support for research and development, unencumbered by Western societies' one-sided commitment to armaments and carefully aimed at commercial prospects; and extensive state-guided and subsidized corporate cooperation in the genesis of I.T. systems.

Such has been the success of "Japan Incorporated" that other governments and corporations have become apprehensive and envious, threatening to reciprocate with the sort of tariffs and import restrictions that have helped Japanese ascendancy. The retort of Japan has been a rash of alliances with (noncompeting) corporations in Europe (Ball, 1983) and America, and a surge of overseas investment intended to forestall possible counter-measures.

However, if some nations have felt threatened by Japanese prosperity and its remarkable rise in electronics, it is this same surge that has led to the French attempts at emulation of energetic state direction of key industries and technologies. Japanese governments have not felt a need to nationalize I.T. corporations to implement national plans, chiefly because the intimacy of corporations and government is such that radical measures appear unnecessary to achieve the desired result of international competitiveness. However, they have to date effectively used NTT (Nippon Telegraph and Telephone), the state-owned telecommunications monopoly with an estimated value of £30 billion (thus seocond only to AT&T), to nurture the industry. Indeed, NTT is the lynchpin of Japanese I.T. strategy, and is at the center of plans to develop fifth generation computers and optical fibre communications technologies (notably through its four research laboratories which ally with private corporations on specified projects). NTT's lengthy association with the so-called Denden Family of thirty-odd telecommunications equipment suppliers (which includes Hitachi, Mitsubishi, Fujitsu, NEC, Sumitomo, Showa and Oki Electric) has given these substantial relief from the risks inherent in technological innovation in accounting for between 20 and 30% of their sales, as well as assuring economies of scale in production to these companies with its multibillion annual dollar annual procurement (in 1983, NTT's expenditure was $16 billion), which in turn has situated them well to benefit on foreign markets. NTT's plans to totally overhaul its network between 1981 and 2000—at an estimated cost of £60 billion—to provide an integrated information system which involves replacing all cables with fibre optics, digitalization of all operations, and expansion of data and facsimile services throughout the society, will provide a continued outlet to "family" members at the same time as it enhances the efficiency of Japanese business as a whole.

In Japan, it has been decided that NTT should begin to be privatized during 1985, but to ease the process this will be extended over several years and, to retain local control, no foreigners (including companies with bases inside Japan that are more than 50% foreign-owned) will be allowed to buy NTT shares. While the network will be liberalized to enable competitors to offer value-added services, it will remain intact, a gaint grouping of huge significance inside Japan which by extension heavily influences the overseas standing of its suppliers and customers. Though privatization appears to be a move towards allowing market forces to operate inside Japanese communications, the retention of NTT intact and the likelihood that the new company will "remain firmly under government control" (*Economist,* August 6, 1983, p. 58) attest to the fact that the Japanese state, while alert to market principles, is unwilling to take the risks of that market being open to all comers. A further restriction of foreign entry into Japanese I.T. business is the high performance specifications and demands of compatibility imposed by NTT. Thus whatever the rhetoric of the market in Japanese communications, foreign capital will be excluded and domestic suppliers favored.

In any discussion of Japan's interests in I.T., it is essential to consider not only the part played by the state, but also the nature of the *zaibatsu* corporations, all of which have been closely tied to MITI projects over the years, that dominate the economy. A legacy of pre-War Japan, the *zaibatsu* regrouped in the 1950s when anti-trust legislation was eased. Critical for this regrouping was that *zaibatsu* banks had been untouched in the general dissolution following the defeat, and were therefore able to take a lead in the restructuring of Japanese industry. Though there is some mystery about their operation (and in recent years insistent accusations of chicanery), there can be no doubt about the significance of this "highly important grouping of independent enterprises, clustering around one or several core city banks, with some co-ordination of policies, some joint action even, and personal regular meetings of the presidents" (Hirschmeier and Yui, 1975, p. 264). That *zaibatsu* groups such as Mitsubishi (86 firms in the group), Mitsui (71), Sumitomo (80), Furukawa, Fujo, and Matsushita play an especially important role in I.T., including as they do such interests as Toshiba, NEC, JVC, and Fujitsu, underlines this significance. Moreover, these trading houses are especially powerful and internationally competitive because their size and structure (vertically and horizontally integrated to a considerable degree) makes them capable of drawing on the necessary resources to compete on the world IT market that is limited chiefly to billion dollar interests.

Additionally, though *zaibatsu* are each independent of one another, they have been persuaded to cooperate on key issues. Guided by MITI and lured by subsidies, leading Japanese I.T. corporations—for example Fujitsu, Nippon Electric, Toshiba, Hitachi, Mitsubishi Electric, and Oki—have pooled resources to develop techniques ranging from microelectronics devices to very large scale integration for advanced computers since the mid-1970s. These endeavors, stimulated by the fact that, as a body, Japanese computer manufacturers "all feared IBM" (*Economist*, January 17, 1981, p. 71), continue in the ambitious state/corporate 10-year plan to pioneer fifth generation computers that was commenced in 1982.

Currently, it is a popular pastime to look to Japan in search of lessons in how to rediscover economic success (see Feigenbaum and McCorduck, 1984). Report after report in management journals focuses on either its labor relations (Dore, 1973), employment for life policies, national character, or its ability to successfully copy and market scientific advances made abroad. Few of these (e.g., Vogel, 1979) pay attention to the underside of Japanese society, its exploitive dual economy, the subjugation of women, its inadequate welfare services, its feudalistic hangovers, and the appalling culmination of the Second World War (Hane, 1982) which make the prospect of emulating the Japanese unappealing. Nonetheless, though the Japanese miracle should be understood within these contexts, there is no denying that the liason between state and private corporations has decisively influenced its emergence as a leading world power. Japan is a thoroughly capitalist society both internally and externally, yet it has managed to create a policy that mollifies potentially destructive competition between indigenous companies while they continue to tread individual paths inside Japan, and unites spearate corporations behind a coherent national plan which has been advanced by government legal, fiscal, and economic measures. The viability of all this has been considerably aided by the geographical location of Japan that has kept competitors at bay, but, as an alternative method of achieving success on the world market, the Japanese practice of intensive state involvement to hone domestic corporations has much to commend it to capitalist societies.

United Kingdom

Britain provides an enigmatic case of the relationship between the state and I.T. industry. Under the Labour government of the late 1970s, policy was developed in a way similar to the French and Japanese strategies. At that time there was a commitment from the state to lead the I.T. industry which entailed encouraging mergers in the private sector to produce large and powerful units and subsidy of key projects. In November 1978, the Labour administration committed a total of £400 million with the aim of forming an integrated I.T. industry made up essentially of four strands: Inmos (for the manufacture of semiconductors), Insac (for programming), Data Recording Instruments (for computer peripherals), and Nexos (for office equipment). These were all to be under the auspices of the National Enterprise Board (NEB), which undertook a 5-year plan of action (Willott, 1981). Labour also introduced a Microelectronics Industry Support Programme, with resources to boost private investment by offering it assistance and a Microprocessor Application Project to help educate opinion about I.T., all of which was combined with plans for the Post Office to pioneer advanced telecommunications services.

These plans suggested a coherent approach to I.T. which was determined that public resources would be used to attack foreign markets and repulse import-hungry competitors, a policy committed to creating more effective entrepreneurial organizations complemented by state measures to revitalize private sector concerns to meet an international challenge which the corporations on their own seemed unable to match.

However, in May 1979 the Thatcher government came to power doctinally opposed to state-supported, and still more to state-led, initiatives in the economy. Already a shadow industry minister had expressed the view that Conservatives were "deeply skeptical of the whole Inmos venture" when arguing that private enterprise should be left alone to develop the new technology. At the same time, disquiet was voiced about the Post Office concerning its unfair monopoly, its inefficiency, its inability to cope with rapid technological change. More generally, leading figures within the monetarist fold articulated opposition to the spread of corporatism in the UK, blamed state meddling for the decline of the nation, and called for a return to free enterprise, in which the market was supreme (Joseph, 1976).

In line with such attitudes, the new government commenced a campaign aimed at disposing of NEB assets. To this end, various companies were placed in the hands of the receiver, a 50% holding in Ferranti was returned to the private sector, as was much of British Aerospace, and the state's 25% interest in ICL was relinquished.

Still more dramatically, the Post Office was split to separate postal services from telecommunications, the latter liberalized to allow private corporations to invest in services that required access to the network, and the decision made to privatize the newly-created British Telecom in the mid-1980s. In addition, the Conservatives have approached cable and satellite development from a vigorously entrepreneurial angle.

It is this emphasis on the private sector that characterizes Conservative policy. The government would appear to consider that it is possible to emulate the American (rather than the French) model: that the market in the I.T. area will yield optimum results. However, it is important to see that the Conservative commitment to the market is not something which entails either the complete withdrawal of the state from the industry or the turning-over of I.T. to free market forces. The distinctive character of the Tory emphasis on the market is that it believes that, wherever possible, private capital should be able to take advantage of the potential for profit in I.T., and that this search for self-interest will hasten the general advance of new technology. To meet this goal, it is determined to sell off public holdings with bright sales prospects and reverse policies which try to speed I.T.'s development under state control where profit is likely to be found. However, the government does not by this necessarily stop providing state aid to I.T.—subsidies run into several hundred million pounds and, within a few months of privatization, a floundering ICL was rescued by a £200 million government loan—since to do so might jeopardize the viability of much private investment. By the same token, its measures to boost private capital in I.T. are not synonymous with a policy of allowing market forces free rein, since the Conservatives realize that the industry is nationally, and even more internationally, dominated by huge corporate ventures which are often themselves supported by their respective governments. Given the fact that Britain's largest I.T. corporation, GEC, ranks only tenth by sales in world ratings, and that the combined turnover of the six biggest UK companies ranks only with the eighth largest in the world, no British government could feel able to break up existing oligopolies in the name of encouraging indigenous competition, since it would weaken their capabilities to operate on a world scale. In this situation to allow, for example, foreign investment without restriction in British Telecom, to fail to subsidize important domestic I.T. projects, or to stop preferential purchase arrangements could endanger British interests at home and abroad. Though the Conservatives do subscribe to an ideology of the free market which entails the private ownership of capital, its unhindered movement and toleration, even welcome, of vigorous competition, and though they have shifted towards implementation of significant aspects of this world-view, other considerations and contingencies disallow its full practice and result in an uneasy mix of state intervention and a handing over of responsibility to private capital (Taylor, R., 1983).

If there is a mismatch between ideology and action among the Conservative administration, it shares with other nations the assumption that its measures will best situate the country to meet the threat of foreigners on the international market, and, thereby, it is committed to developing I.T. which meets commercial criteria. To this degree, there as a convergence with French, British, and Japanese policies, in that all accede to the demands of the global market. The British commitment to laissez-faire moves away from the more mercantilist strategies of France and Japan in that, while they identify a national interest that can be cohered either by state coordination or even nationalization, it believes that private capital, free to respond to market opportunities and challenges (within limits), can be equated with a national interest.

While they may be unwilling to become the bureaucrats of a post-industrial society, the Conservatives are not blind to the need to play some role in the I.T. industry. Their appointment of a Minister of Information Technology attests to this insight, as does reorganization within government departments "to develop a coherent national programme" which could "co-ordinate and bring together activities" involved with I.T. (R. Atkinson, Under Secretary, Department of Industry, *in* House of Lords, 1981, p. 4). Revealingly, the NEB, though having to undergo a name change (it became the British Technology Group in 1981), was not disbanded, but rather scaled down and redefined by the minister responsible as having "a catalytic investment role, especially in connection with advanced technology and increasingly in partnership with the private sector." This insistence on alliances between state enterprise and private capital is a hallmark of Conservative policies towards I.T. which, while it may satisfy supporters' claims to favor the market, underscores the difficulty of the state altogether extracting itself. Again, Inmos remained in state hands 6 years after its establishment and following a £100 million subsidy, in spite of Conservative desires to privatize it, both because investors in Britain were not prepared to pay the going rate and because bids from AT&T and Commodore of the U.S. risked passing a strategic asset to foreign ownership. Its final disposal in 1984 to Thorn-EMI allowed Conservatives to extol the free market at the same time as Inmos was secured as a national asset. Elsewhere, despite its enthusiasm for a market approach to cable television, the government has felt obliged to establish a licensing body, the Cable Authority, which is briefed both to control by foreign consortia and to show preference towards submissions to lay and operate networks which use the most advanced technologies capable of offering two-way computer services, stipulations revealing the state's reluctance to leave everything to market forces. And, in the same legislation, cable companies were excluded from providing voice communications services in order to protect the duopoly of British Telecom and the nascent Mercury Communications in this area.

Further, the state in Britain, whatever the government's complexion, has long been playing an active role in encouraging the consolidation of indigenous private industries involved in I.T. the better to resist overseas competition. This extends back to the 1960s, when there was a striking enthusiasm for big units from government, the most significant result of which was the formation of GEC. More recently, the NEB and the Department of Industry tried, during 1979, to promote a merger of Plessey's and GEC's telecommunications equipment sides, and earlier the NEB had tried to persuade STC to be absorbed by Plessey. Later on, there were no stumbling blocks put up to GEC, Racal, and Thorn takeovers, though all could have been stalled by reference to the Monopolies Commission. It is in the light of such instances of government involvement to create large units of indigenous capital that are capable of matching other giants on the world market that one should perceive the moves to privatize British Telecom, since they are in close accord. What will result will be the transfer from state holding to private investors of a de facto monopoly which will be powerful (its 1982 revenues of $10.3 billion made BT the fourth largest network in the world) and free of restraints to meet public service clauses, thus able to play a "strategic role in the development of Britain's information technology industry by spearheading a thrust by manufacturers on world markets" (*Financial Times,* October 24, 1983).

Perhaps it is through procurement policies and research and development expenditures that the British state (and still more so that of the U.S.) is intimately involved in the I.T. industry and makes decisions of profound significance for it, irrespective of political creed. Fully 40% of the UK market for I.T. is taken up by the purchases of British Telecom and the Ministry of Defence, and government provides about half of the total R&D spending, much of which goes to electronics. Because of this, a recent National Economic Development Office report could describe British I.T. companies as being "peculiarly dependent on the State," with it accounting for over half the total electronics market, absorbing at least one-third of computer capacity, funding nearly 60% of the R&D budget of electronics, and giving to electronics companies fully 46% of all government aid to industry (NEDC, 1982, p. 2, 13). Plessey for instance, in 1981, broke down its sales as 30% to British Telecom, 1% to other nationalized industries, and 20% to local and national government departments (*Report and Accounts,* 1982). These figures make it obvious that, at the least, the British I.T. industry would be radically different without state ties, and that talk of state extrication is cavalier. Proof of this was seen in the outburst of concern during 1983-84 from GEC, Plessey, and STC when the head of BT, flushed with the thought of becoming a private company and thus free to exploit the market to its best advantage, threatened to withdraw its customary contracts from the big three suppliers and search abroad for cheaper goods instead of, as at present, lodging 80% of its equipment orders with them. The same anxiety re-emerged in 1985 when BT bought Mitel, a Canadian telecommunications exchange manufacturer with plant in Britain, and with it gained capacity to supply its own equipment. An upshot was referral of the deal to the Monopolies Commission to examine the wider significance for British I.T. companies, though as a strategic move into North America the takeover is eminently sensible.

The Military Connection

In both procurement and R&D expenditures, an important expression of state involvement is the military. Military purchases—in Britain scheduled at £8 billion for 1984-85, a figure which is dwarfed by the stupendous U.S. defense budget which stood at $199 billion in 1982 compared to Britain's $24 billion, with about 30% of this going on equipment—are a most significant element of the I.T. market, since such a large proportion of these are taken up by electronics. It is difficult to estimate precisely how much defense procurement is on I.T., but any review of the categories of expenditure shows that disproportionate amounts go on guided weapons, communications, surveillance equipment, and the like. With 75% of military procurement in the UK going to British companies and a further 15% accounted for by the British share of collaborative projects (House of Commons, 16 June, 1982, vol. 1, p. vi), it is not surprising to find that, at the upper levels, British Aerospace, with total sales of £2.3 billion, took an estimated £1 billion from the defense ministry in 1983, its president conceding that BA "look(s) to Government as our core customer for military equipment" (ibid., vol. 2, p. 101), though no I.T. company of significance, with the exception of ICL, got less than £25 million in orders from the Ministry of Defence in 1981-82, and Ferranti, GEC, and Plessey occupied the ministry's top category of "over £100 million" (*Statement of the Defence Estimates*, Cmnd. 8951-1, 1983, p. 38). Since some 70% of defense contracts are noncompetitively allocated, and 60% of these go to but 10 large companies (*Economist*, February, 1984, p. 30), the sustenance corporations get from these deals that are calculated on the basis of a 20% gross profit added to capital costs will be readily appreciated.

The scale of these state purchases is of a magnitude and strategic significance (in that these are contracts for products often at the forefront of technology) that neither government nor industrial concerns can take them for granted. There is widespread agreement with A. Pope of British Aerospace that the Ministry of Defence is a "key customer," both because "without an adequate defence industrial base it is probably fair to say that the civil side of the business could well become a shadow of its current self" and because it is "a strong influence in our ability to sell our products in the world markets" (House of Commons, 16 June, 1982, vol. 2, p. 102). The Ministry of Defence is a key outlet for I.T. corporations, but from this core of military orders stems an export business in defense worth £1.8 billion in 1982-83, which contributes to British I.T. companies rarely getting less than 20% of revenue from electronic warfare supplies (Brzoska, 1983). The interconnectedness of key I.T. corporations and defense agencies forms part of what has been described as a "military-industrial complex" (Melman, 1970), and it is perpetuated by long-term relationships, in Britain notably in the National Defence Industries Council, chaired by the Secretary of State for Defence, which brings together ministers and industry representatives who themselves combine in the Defence Industries Council, and regular recruitment of leading military, political and state officials by interested concerns.

Instances such as these lead to recognition that "the defence industrial base is a significant factor in national patterns of employment, the development and use of technology and the performance of the economy as a whole" (House of Commons, 16 June, 1982, vol. 1, p. xlv); mean that the state is unavoidably embroiled in the

I.T. industry; and tempt government to intervene to use military expenditure as an instrument of economic planning. For example, it was through the desire to advance the I.T. industry in Britain more effectively that, late in 1983, the Thatcher government invited venture capitalists to seek out inventions within defense projects, currently the intellectual property of the ministry, that could be marketed successfully in the civil sector. Despite such attempts to steer defense spending, the possibility that excessive concern for military applications has hindered the development of I.T. for alternative and nowadays more lucrative markets has recently gained credibility from a number of analysts (Maddock, 1983; Kaldor, 1981; Chalmers, 1983).

It is a sobering thought that so much I.T. is for military purposes, and it should cause doubt in the minds of all those who think it is neutral that modern arms are essentially struggles over electronics, whether for command, control, and communications systems on the battlefield, within nations, or around the globe, nuclear and conventional missiles, airplanes, or satellite surveillance (cf. Barnaby, 1982; Campbell, 1982, Chs. 5-6). This military demand provides an undiminished energy for ever-more sophisticated electronics technologies—a system is outdated before it leaves the production line—and thereby a reliable and constantly renewed outlet for I.T. manufacturers (Kaldor, 1983).

Yet the relations between user and technology producer are still more intimate. When research and development funding is considered, it is evident that the military connection—and thereby the state—plays a decisive part in the very genesis of advanced technologies. As the National Economic Development Office put it:

> The UK electronics industry's biggest single customer is the Ministry of Defence. Through R&D funding it is a major, and possibly the largest, source of technology (NEDC, 1983b, p. 7).

In Britain, the £1.9 billion that the Ministry of Defence spent on R&D in 1983 accounted for a quarter of all R&D spending in the nation and absorbed half of all government expenditure on R&D (Bowles, 1982, 1983). Similar proportions are found in other advanced capitalist societies (for example, in 1980, 48% of U.S. government R&D spending went to defense, 37% in France)—though in absolute terms the U.S. far outstrips Britain, its $14 billion on military R&D in 1980 accounting for 40% of the world total in that category (Reppy, 1983, p. 24)—with the exceptions of Japan, where less than 5% of government R&D goes to defense, and West Germany, where the figure is about 10%. On a global scale, the commitment of R&D to military goals amounts to more than the sum devoted to health, food production, energy, and environmental protection. The bald fact is that the "feeding of the world's military machine is . . . the predominant occupation of the global research and development enterprise" (Norman, 1981, p. 72), and that this in turn focuses on I.T., means, not only that state agencies play an important role in the I.T. industry, but also that their priorities influence the technologies that eventually emerge from R&D projects.

A former chief scientist at the Department of Industry recently drew attention to the fallacy that in the United States the state stands aloof from corporations which alone have pioneered I.T., by pointing to the hidden subsidies that come from that country's "gigantic defence expenditure." The U.S. state expenditure on I.T. is enormous, most prominently from the Department of Defense and the National Aeronautics and Space Agency (NASA) procurement and R&D programs which spent in excess of $50 billion in 1981. Sir Ieuan Maddock continued to observe that the

> purchasing power of the Pentagon for high technology electronic products is comparable to the entire purchasing power of the UK. By concentrating *public* funds into this one industry, conscious of the need to maintain world leadership for strategic reasons, a freak industry has been produced, which spends an exceptional porportion of its turnover on research and development, is constantly outdating its most recent products and is advancing the performance/cost ratio at a pace never experienced in any industry previously (Maddock, 1983, p. 18; cf. Gansler, 1980).

Though the figures are correspondingly larger, the expenditure proportions and characteristics of the military-industrial complex are similar in both the U.S. and U.K. They can leave no observer with the illusion that, in America, the state does not play an important, albeit disguised, role in developing I.T. How could there be anything but intimacy between the likes of IBM, ITT, Hughes, GTE, and the state, when, for instance, the Reagan administration announced in 1982 an $18 billion plan to provide a communications system able to endure a nuclear war? When, in 1982, the United States Congress gave $14.5 billion to the area of communications and defense and the Secretary of Defense followed this with a request for $31.5 billion for fiscal year 1984? (Weinberger, 1983, p. 242). When, in 1982, the United States Air Force R&D budget allocated $250 million to basic electronic research? When, following the President's "Star Wars" speech in 1983, the U.S. armed forces announced a $600 million 5-year program in artificial intelligence, microelectronics, and computer architecture which *Datamation* thought likely "to become this country's response to Japan's fifth generation computing project?" (*Datamation*, February 1984, p. 48). Faced with these sorts of figures, it is not necessary to allege that military orders constitute an enormous proportion of the I.T. business in the U.S. to demonstrate that they reveal a close involvement of the state. It is impossible to precisely gauge the proportion of sales military outlets account for, since such data is shrouded in secrecy, but it can be readily admitted that it often amounts to only 10% or so of total corporate revenues (cf. Kennedy, 1983, pp. 156-161) without denying that enormous amounts of money are being spent at the state's behest in projects and R&D which is at the cutting edge of technology.

Education for the Market

President Reagan's "Strategic Computing" program indicates another dimension of state involvement in the I.T. industry, of considerable interest. The $600 million investment will be spent largely in educational institutions where academics will labor to produce new military systems. The ways in which R&D programs—and by extention state decisions that determine their allocation—shape education is under-examined, but Barnaby's estimate (Barnaby, 1982, p. 244) that 40% of the world's research scientists and engineers are involved in military R&D, even if on the high side, suggests something of these directions.

The state's requirements of military R&D may be an important influence upon education, but it shapes it in other ways too. More generally, its control over funds results in a steady pressure to ensure that education in general, and work related to I.T. in particular, is responsive to market imperatives. It is true that military expenditures on R&D are guided by strategic considerations that may well not be entirely in keeping with market precepts. However, the concern of government that military funds are made responsive to commercial needs, at the least that they provide results which can bolster the position of indigenous corporations vis-à-vis international competitors by presenting opportunities for defense exports and hopefully civil by-products, suggests that the goals may not be too far apart.

Certainly the state's insistence that education, from curricula through to research projects, follows its instructions, provides another instance of its participation in economic affairs. Over the years, the British government has been keen to use education as a means of supporting and stimulating technological change by ensuring that it is responsive to market disciplines. In practice, these policies have entailed:

• shifting resources for teaching and research away from arts, humanities, and social sciences towards science and technology. It has long been the case that the latter have received the lion's share of government funds (in 1982-1983, the Science and Engineering Research Council disposed of £235 million, compared with the £10 million of the Social Science Research Council). In addition, the SERC's £235 million was boosted by a further £400 million from government earmarked solely for R&D and teaching in I.T. (*Computing*, 23 February, 1984, pp. 30-31).

• using the pressure of public expenditure reductions to education as a whole, to encourage them to seek collaboration with and funds from the private sector. In the past few years, there has been a marked enthusiasm from government that the gap between the academic world and industry (read the market) should be bridged (ACARD, June 1983). This has been reflected in efforts to ensure that its own expenditures on education be shaped by commercial criteria (and that it spends almost three times as much public money devoted to research in private industry than in education itself facilitiates this), but it has also been evident in a number of approved moves such as "science parks," research funds being linked with industrial projects, and direct investments from private sources in universities (see Bullock, 1983).

Science parks are modelled on the lines of Stanford and Yale, and intended both to draw outside funds into education and to harmonize with commercial operations by allowing businesses to access universities and academics to participate in entrepreneurial ventures. The Alvey scheme for fifth generation computers is typical of the new mood, in that it offers public funding of 50% of total costs so long as this is matched by private capital. Direct investment in universities is as yet small (as a proportion of research funds in Britain, it is only 3%), but in straitened times it is sure to grow. Moreover, the significance of this tiny percentage is greater than might appear, when it is realized that it is targeted at the more prestigous and productive departments (for example, in 1984 IBM announced a £2 million offer to Cambridge University's engineering department which would account for two-thirds of their planned 3-year investment in the British education system). These patterns are replicated in the U.S., where the "corporate invasion of academia" (Dickson and Noble, 1981, p. 287) is even further advanced and "science for sale" proclaimed in the pages of the *Wall Street Journal* (9 February, 1982; cf. Noble, 1982).

International Cooperation?

From this review it is evident that, though each state role differs in emphasis, everywhere there are striking similarities insofar as withdrawal from this industry is untenable, talk of it even hypocritical, since governments are embroiled willy-nilly, and each and every state uses its powers, more or less actively, to stimulate, direct, and nurture affairs to meet the overriding concern of all countries—the opportunities and threats of the global market on which they compete with one another.

Nevertheless, while this depiction of interventionist and rivalrous nations is right enough, it is not the whole story, because such is the might of the U.S. and Japan that European countries feel in danger of being swamped, fear that, left entirely to their own devices, they will individually be overwhelmed by the awesome power of the two dominant powers. Because of this, the Commission of the European Communities (EEC) has been urging its members to collaborate against the American and Japanese challenge.

Recognizing that the

> world leadership of the United States industry owes much . . . to the immense procurement power of the . . . Federal Government . . . and the massive financial support which defense and space programs have given to research and development in all branches of electronics" and that "Japan's remarkable progress in world markets for electronic equipment has also been the fruit of a systematic long term national strategy supported by large Government funds" (Commission of the European Communities, 1979, p. 4)

the EEC has proposed a similar response which requires super-state measures capable of matching the resources of Japan and America. This has involved encouragement of common technical standards in communications, the establishment of the Euronet data network, and subsidies for collaborative R&D projects to counter "the fragmented nature of the European industry as a whole" and "to bring about a better integrated structure of the industry in Europe" (House of Lords, 1981, p. xviii) that will be able to compete on the world market.

The best known of these projects is the European Strategic Programme of Research in Information Technology (ESPRIT) which arranges inter-corporate cooperation in the area of "pre-competitive research" and has involved Philips, Siemens, GEC, and Olivetti, among others. In addition, the RACE (Research and Development into Advanced Communications Technologies in Europe) project began in 1985 aimed at integrating European digital networks and rationalizing strategies and systems, and a Milan summit that year endorsed the French Eureka initiative for co-ordinating research and product application in the high technology field. Complementing these positive measures has been an EEC anti-trust case against IBM in the period 1980–1984, which sought to weaken the American transnational's dominance of the European market for computers.

However, the EEC measures are restricted by two formidable constraints. The first is that the constituent nations do not regard their individual interests as being in accord with those of the Community as a whole. As a result of each country pursuing its own goals—and in the process trying to beat other European nations—any collaborative moves are compromized and weakened from the outset. The second, which also undermines individual national strategies, is the role in Europe of private corporations, especially those—all the leading ones—with multinational links. The position of these corporations subverts attempts at creating a "United States of Europe" for numerous reasons, among the more significant of which are that Japanese and American companies, notably IBM, which claims that 90% of equipment sold by it in Europe is actually made here, insist that they are truly "European," that, having manufacturing facilities inside the Community, they cannot be regarded as foreign importers; key European corporations have established collaborative arrangements with Japanese and U.S. companies (for example, AT&T and Philips), have been recipients of substantial investments from abroad (for example, AT&T has invested heavily in Olivetti), and have considerable equity in Japan and America which might encounter retaliatory measures should EEC actions threaten these two nations. It is because private corporations cannot without extreme difficulty be brought into harmony with national interests, still more because private corporations cannot readily be made to unite with other private corporations to serve the assumed common interests of Europe, that ESPRIT's "pre-competitive research" is pitched at an inchoate level and is suspect even then, since once R&D suggests marketable results, individual interests must assert themselves.

Conclusion

Examining the widespread state involvement in I.T., one is led to a number of conclusions. The first is that, whether the state participation is active or relatively passive, enthusiastically embraced or reluctantly undertaken, it is everywhere on such a scale that appeals to "leave the industry to the market" unhindered by political intervention are either naive or disingenuous (cf. Feketekuty and Aronson, 1984). This is not to say that the different strategies adopted by individual nations are unimportant. Our point is simply that empirical review demonstrates close state involvement in I.T. which can be changed but not removed, and this undermines the credibility of those who claim the market must be left alone to decide the pace and nature of technological change.

Second, and related, it is clear that state participation in I.T. is assisting the development of oligopolistic industries, which further brings into question the feasibility of free market mechanisms operating. In Chapter 7, we showed that transnational capital's dominance of I.T. meant that competition is not open, and here we have demonstrated that the state, responding to this reality, encourages the growth of enormous private and, less often, public institutions which are equipped to meet the challenges of the leading corporations and thus further restrict the market to the large and powerful.

Third, and most important, state involvement everywhere is bound by the demands of the global market in I.T., is "constrained not so much by individual companies as by an international corporate order whose normal market responses impose themselves as a co-ordinating force on national policymakers" (Herman, 1981, p. 243). Though national responses vary, all submit to the imperatives of the market as they attempt to achieve further sales beyond their shores while consolidating at home. While this often leads to paradoxical policies, to celebration of laissez-faire co-existent with protectionism, all countries are remarkably consistent in this commitment to gaining maximum advantage on the international market. The consequences are profound in that they subvert efforts to develop cooperation between countries, and restrict options for developing I.T. to those that are profitable and/or military purposes. The types of technology thus produced, the areas in which they find application, and the ways in which they are adopted result from this submission to the market, albeit that, within the nation state, market practices are flouted time and again. The situation is ironic; while state involvement thwarts the operation of market mechanisms and thereby politicizes technological innovation by revealing that social decisions influence its development, the capitulation to market principles internationally limits the room to maneuver of any nation state, and this gives credence to those who claim that technological change has its own dynamic.

Finally, we should ask whether these attempts to forge distinct national policies for I.T. are feasible, whether the concerns of corporations are identifiable with, or perhaps even inimical to, a national interest. Harry Johnson's dismissal of state involvement in high technology, on the grounds that it is motivated by "national rivalry and emulation" (Johnson, 1975, p. 10), and his celebration of the internationalism of the multinational enterprise that heralds "the dwindling of the power of the nation state relative to the corporation" (p. 83), has a point insofar as he observes that transnational capital necessarily has an outlook and domain far larger than an individual country.

But the I.T. corporations are not antipathetic to nationalist policies merely on the grounds that they orient internationally. It is because private corporations operate to maximize the interests of their shareholders that national policies, unless they submit to this principle (and it is something to which governments cannot always subscribe, since their concern must be with the economy as a whole) are undermined. The spate of investments abroad from the UK between 1979 and 1984 is evidence that private capital's interests are not reducible to those of a national entity, and it brings into question the possibility of identifying, let alone operating on, a "national interest" in an integrated world market serviced by private corporations.

Chapter 9
I.T. and the "General Public"

Home was anywhere, so long as there was a telly.

—Anthony Burgess. *1985*. Hutchinson, 1978, p. 132.

It is evident that the major beneficiaries of I.T. are and will continue to be corporate and state organizations. For the obvious reason that they have the resources and incentives to invest, most new technologies are conceived with the intention of providing for the automated office, robotic factory, and electronic battlefield. Nevertheless, though these represent the leading edge of technological innovation and account for 80% and more of the I.T. business, there is a residue which has some appeal to the producers. This is what consultants Butler Cox and Partners refer to as the "General Public"—i.e., everything else besides the few select targets already named—which they estimate will spend $18 billion in Europe in 1988 on I.T. (*Financial Times*, April 11, 1983). While this is pretty small pickings compared to that coming from corporate information networks and military systems, it is more than loose change and readily attracts commercial interest.

In addition, though at the moment the General Public represents a fairly discrete sector of the I.T. industry, it should be remembered that markets will converge as an "electronic grid" is established. This means that companies should be able with comparative ease to extend from supplying business towards servicing the General Public, while the commercial potential of the latter will increase as prospects emerge for banking, shopping, and even working via two-way terminals. It is because this has profound implications for employment procedures, patterns of consumption, and styles of life that corporations with an eye to future outlets and governments charged with managing the information revolution express keen interest in the home of the future and its integration into an information grid along which social, economic, political, and cultural relations can be mediated. At the moment there is considerable discussion about the sort of programming cable television will make available, but these far-sighted interests realize that the creation of an information infrastructure, of which cable could be a key part (though an alternative route could be through enhancement of the telecommunications network), has far wider significance.

More of the Same

Just what this forthcoming wired society portends for the General Public has exercised much media attention which speculates on seismic changes to be instigated by the "wonder chip." We do not doubt that important changes are in store, but an effect of indulgence in visions of the electronic cottage inhabited by the computer literate has been to overlook the substance of what the General Public is actually getting in the way of I.T. which, shaped by and shaping existent relationships, will have an important influence on any possibilities being made manifest. It is our view, in line with a theme of this book, that established social relations are crucial contexts within which I.T. should be placed, that the effects of new technologies owe much to their causes.

And what is striking about the innovation for the General Public—video disc and cassette, personal computer, cable, direct broadcasting by satellite, etc.—is the familiarity of it all. Despite incessant talk of revolution, almost all the hardware is an enhancement of television, and the software is devoted overwhelmingly to what we already get in abundance from the TV—entertainment. The glittering vista of an information society is dulled by the fact that for the most part the technology provides more of the same: video recorders are means of watching more TV shows (and soft pornography); cable offers more sex, sport, and movies; home computers plug into the television and are devoted almost entirely to playing infantile games like Space Invaders and Frogger which involve next to no understanding of programming; satellite stations are planned to recycle soaps and films from Hollywood. . . .

Encountering a barrage of assertions that soon we shall study at home on our computers, have cable stations devoted to round-the-clock news and current affairs, and video networks manned by and serving local communities, it is as well to emphasize that more of the same is the order of the day and there are clear signs that it will be so in the future. The Butler Cox and Partners report quoted above contains a telling estimate that fully 70% of the "European market for the New Information Technology Services for the General Public" will be absorbed by entertainment, while education will scarcely manage 8%. It does not take a bold person to forecast more gawking at the TV monitor, more organization of daily schedules around viewing, more perception of "reality" through television's output, more moving wallpaper in the living room (cf. Goldsen, 1980; Conrad, 1982).

Commercialism and Conservatism

One response to this is that, since the consumer is king, then so be it: if people express a need for more television and entertainment, then these should be met by responsive marketers. But things are nowhere near so straightforward. It is, in fact, very difficult to gauge what need is (something we discuss later), but one thing of which we can be sure is that, at the outset and even today, there was and is little if any expressed public desire for cable television, satellite broadcasting, viewdata, breakfast TV, or even home computers. Indeed, it is the lack of public enthusiasm for most of these in the U.K. that is causing crises of confidence among their backers. What has been presented is an enormous amount of hype that has done its utmost to generate commitment (most blatantly in campaigns for personal computers that exploit parental anxieties and ambitions for their children).

Asking why there has come to be so much hawking of the new technologies moves us closer towards understanding how and why I.T. for the General Public has been and is developing on particular lines, since it is to commercial concerns and their priorities that one can trace the production of what are at once novelties

and vieux jeux, and it is a consequence of the exercise of market criteria that public
need is being assiduously manufactured for much I.T. Reasons why this should be
so include:

• The success to date of television from the point of view of both manufacturers
and programmers. In the space of little more than a decade, television ownership in
Britain grew from a tiny minority to well-nigh universal, while TV viewing came to
be the major leisure activity in all advanced societies, occupying more time than
everything else bar sleeping and working, sets switched on in the typical house for
4 and more hours per day. Far and away the most successful programming has
become entertainment—soaps, game shows, movies, situation comedy—and I.T.
innovators, careful of return on their investments, are intent on using the same
formulae in the future.

• As important, and related, is the role of the chief supporters of television, advertisers and, increasingly important, sponsors. Years ago, Martin Meyer observed that
TV is "undoubtedly the greatest selling medium ever" (Meyer, 1958, p. 198), and it
has been advertisers' recognition of this power which in large part accounts for the
content of programs (entertainment as that which combines most appeal with least
contention) and the commercial viability of television stations. That television has
been subsidized in the main by advertising has meant that a major function has
been the delivery of audiences to agencies and their corporate clients, as a general
rule the bigger the better. The promise of further advertising revenues, and the
requirement of companies nowadays to "communicate" more effectively with
potential customers, has been an important stimulus to the extension of much I.T.
for the General Public. It is not, for example, expressed demand for more television
that is hastening 24-hour programming in Britain, but the prospect that breakfast-time shows will reach children and housewives in sufficient numbers to tempt
marketers to buy time to better sell cereals, toys, washing powders, and the like.
Similarly, an important stimulus for cable services is that "a wider range of advertising will be possible . . . than on independent broadcasting" (Home Office and
Department of Industry, 1983, para. 229, p. 83) that might "attract audiences
through selective programming aimed at more clearly defined groups than the mass
audiences of the major networks" (Saatchi and Saatchi Compton Worldwide, 1983,
p. 13). It is for this reason that record and fashion houses will find a music channel
worthy of support in continuously exposing promotional videos of extravagantly
attired rock groups.

• The manufacturers of television found the market for monochrome sets reaching its peak in the late 1960s and early 1970s. The introduction of color in Britain
in 1967 created a big outlet for new sets, but by the 1980s this, combined with the
increased longevity of television sets, was in turn reaching a saturation point.
Gimmicks, such as remote control and a spurt in second (chiefly for the bedroom)
and replacement sets were inadequate to solve the problem of regularity of production for manufacturers who therefore have eagerly sought new products. Video
disc, cassette, teletext, and cable are regarded as saviors to the industry in that,

refining a successful product, they assure that sales and production lines are kept bouyant while breakfast TV opens the market for "kitchen" sets. This is not to say that the new technologies are guaranteed commercial viability (in fact, losses are being made in numerous areas), but it is to observe that manufacturers have not been content or even able to wait idly for innovations to arrive and rescue declining markets. Their long-term survival and prosperity depending upon it, the likes of Sony, Hitachi, and RCA have been actively developing new generations of technologies for the home. Given the roaring success of the originals, we ought not to be surprised that the "new" are remarkably "old."

• There are huge quantities of software available in film and television libraries that has been found useful in the past, but the reusability of which is limited on conventional television (there is *some* limit to the repeats that can be placed on three networks). Cable and satellite especially can find a home for such programming, which has the enormous advantage of being extraordinarily cheap relative to modern production. The money-making life of these programs is thus extended and this appeals to the film and TV companies, while the new channels discover instant time-fillers.

New television technologies will not only provide outlets for these old materials, the more successful formats pioneered on television will also be found a special role on the new media. Therefore, movie channels are commonplace in cable operations, recycled movies and a few recent ones accounting for most if not all the output of particular channels; sports channels, covering some live performances and drawing extensively on archive material, are also popular; re-runs of the hit TV serials of the 1950s and 1960s occupy much of the time of new channels.

Commercial Criteria and Public Need

The application of commercial criteria for home I.T., which is ensuring that it is remarkably familiar, has particularly important consequences for programming. We have already touched on this, but would extend our discussion. It is tempting to argue that the emphasis on entertainment is simply an expression of the public's will, that it freely chooses from the channels and that its preferences determine an excess of movies, pop concerts, and sport. All of us are accustomed to hearing this sort of reasoning, and it has an immediate resonance.

However, this ignores powerful pressures which shape the range of choices made available to the public from which it is able to choose. Viewers' needs can only begin to be gauged when, knowing the range of possible programs available, they can then choose what they want to see. Our belief is that this range is severely constricted by market pressures. Prominent among these is commercial television's insistence on maximizing audience, *not* to satisfy viewers, but in order to sell itself to advertisers. A result of having a television system geared towards maximization of audience is neither a diversity of programming which will lead to fragmented audiences but provide for variegated needs, nor programming that is either challenging or sustained, willing to enlarge the experiences—and thereby range of choices—of the public. Rather, it presents shows of the lowest common denominator kind, ones that are fast-moving (action is crucial to hold the viewers' attention) and gimmicky, escapist, and trivial. What it leads to, it seems to us, is the mediocre television especially characteristic of the U.S. networks, programming which is watchable by anyone—and, crucially, almost everyone—but satisfying to, or demanding of, no one; where entertainment reigns supreme, news and current affairs are minimal, and serious analyses in arts and science only occasionally get a showing. This is the sort of programming that treats the public as a mass and, catering only for that with which huge numbers can identify and be drawn towards, is unavoidably superficial. Many might watch this—after all, it is by definition attention-grabbing, exotic, quirky, full of adventure, about people and things that are idiosyncratic and intriguing—but at the expense of depth of analysis or recognition of the complexities of human needs (cf. Pilkington, 1962, Ch. 3).

The saga of breakfast television's recent introduction in Britain is illustrative. Early in 1983, *TV-am* was announced as an "electronic newspaper" by its head Peter Jay, renowned economist and ex-ambassador to Washington, who enthused about its "mission to explain" the news of the day. Within 6 weeks, Jay and key members of his team were sacked, since audiences of between 800,000 and 300,000 were inadequate to attract advertising revenue at the required premium. Immediate moves were made, as *TV-am's* chief executive explained, to replace "Peter Jay's mission to explain with a mission to entertain" to boost viewing figures (quoted *Sunday Times,* 20 March, 1983). Rating rose as the program got increasingly "young and popular," frivolous and uninformative (a manikin, Roland Rat, was produced to appeal to children during the summer vacations). The present format, offending few—lacking any gravity, its "news" can scarcely cause upset—but satisfying fewer who might anticipate reportage, is a travesty of the concept of news or current affairs (cf. Leapman, 1984). It is, however, more appealing to advertisers.

Choice, genuine choice, for viewers requires that the ratings are not seen as the arbiters of television production, because the price of programming aimed at achieving only majority audiences, those needed by marketers, is the exclusion of minority interests (or at best displacement from prime-time slots) and the removal of serious, considered, or innovative programs.

We are not condemning popular television per se, since there are certain types of programming that great numbers will find appealing and which ought to be shown. In England, for example, there is a majority audience for the annual Cup Final. Nor are we objecting to entertainment as a category of television (though entertainment defined as synonymous with escapist trivia that is counterposed to education is a product of the advertisers' ideal of high audiences that are not unsettled). What we are contending is that television geared wholly to maximization of audience, to appease advertisers, is exclusionary in that, reducing the public to an undifferentiated majority, it necessarily produces programs that only have mass appeal. Because people have manifold needs both as individuals and members of groups within society, they will be badly served by such a television which limits choice to "the average of experience" (Pilkington, 1962, p. 17, para. 48). Most of us might enjoy football, but each of us is much more than this. It is thus a paradox that, while a television company gaining mass audiences can claim to be "giving the public what it wants," it can actually be delimiting choice, and thereby fulfillment of need, for the public. Our view is that such a television system—and an alternative must admit that at any given time ratings may not be so high, though its catering to the range and variation of needs should be considerably better—is consequent upon commercial modes of organization.

Historical circumstances of course modify the ways in which pursuit of the audience commodity is undertaken. Thus, in Britain, the legacy of public service broadcasting had an effect on the then Home Secretary's insistence that Channel 4, the fourth national channel, was to have a "distinctive character of its own" (*Hansard*, 18 February, 1980, col. 55), though it was to be funded by the existing commercial TV groups on a subscription basis. This has undoubtedly shaped the content of Channel 4 which has, in important areas such as news and debate, enhanced British television. Nonetheless, Channel 4 has from its outset been hamstrung by its reliance on advertisers that stems from the stricture that it "must be financially viable and self-supporting" and in no way "constitute a direct or continuing charge on public funds" (ibid., col. 51–52). Though it introduced an extra dimension of choice into British television, Channel 4 has suffered badly from its minority audiences since these are of little use to advertisers. It attempted to make a virtue of its viewers (younger, more up-market), but, attracting only about half its target of 10% of the public, advertising revenue has been low and the commercial television companies have been quick to complain of the "intolerable" burden of the subscription. Channel 4's response has been that of any commercial TV operation: it has deliberately tried to increase its ratings by offering more entertainment, rerunning American soaps and adding game shows, aping the established commercial network, and "drifting towards becoming something parliament never intended—a pale carbon copy of ITV" (*Sunday Times*, 28 August, 1983, p. 13).

Television as Publishing

This is the antithesis of the belief of those welcoming I.T. For those committed to video, cable, and satellite television, the new technologies mark the end of broadcasting and the advent of narrowcasting. Their view is that broadcast television unavoidably fails to satisfy public needs, since the limits of the bandwidths mean there is inadequate air-time to cater for all tastes. I.T.'s multiple forms of delivery (dozens of channels, video libraries, online data bases) resolves this problem of scarcity and thereby introduces a form of publishing which "let[s] television become as accessible as print" (*Economist*, July 17, 1982, p. 25) and announces the age of "Viewer Lib." As Andrew Neil put it:

> The essential fact about cable is that it removes the scarcity constraints of broadcast television. The potential capacity available to deliver programs is now almost unlimited relative to the demand for and current supply of pro-

gramming. . . . The diversity of cable allows programmers to divide the mass audience into distinct interest groups to which programmes they want to see can be directed (Neil, 1982, p. 23).

Unfortunately, commercial tenets thwart this dream of turning television into a publishing venture from which people can freely pick and choose. It is already clear that, since they who so decide have determined that "cable investment should be privately financed and market led" (Home Office and Department of Industry, 1983, p. 8), operators will either continue to court advertisers (with the promise of lengthy "infomercials"), seek subscription and pay-per-view fees, or fill their schedules with the cheapest programming. These are by no means exclusive options, but whichever way or combination of ways are adopted, most programming will be dictated by the urge to maximize audience to satisfy advertisers and/or to keep fees at a tolerable level and be compelled to recycle the sweepings of established film and television. The evidence is that, overwhelmingly cable channels are offering old movies, more sport, and popular music. In America, Home Box Office, Showtime, and The Movie Channel set the pace and churn out an unappetizing diet of entertainment, while leading U.K. cable operators are Music Box, which shows pop music, The Entertainment Channel and Premiere movie channels that have large U.S. involvement, and Sky Channel (owned by Rupert Murdoch, so no prizes for guessing the content). The assumption that more channels means a greater range of programming is false, and indeed the reverse seems to be the case (Winston, 1982). The much-touted prospect of "dance, opera, the visual arts, in-depth news" (Neil, 1982, p. 25), and any and every other variation has failed to materialize. Moreover, the dictates of commercialism, in combination with the dominance of the market by large corporations, also means that, despite promises of 12, 30, or more channels, some 80% of cable viewing in the U.S. is confined to a mere four or five amusement channels (*Financial Times,* 18 October, 1982). Given all this sameness emanating from additional channels, it is ironic that the surge in possession of video recorders in the U.K. (by late 1983, about 30% of households had one), which of all the new technologies has extended viewer choice most, is being expressed primarily (about 70%) in recording from *current* broadcast channels for watching at a more convenient time.

Sponsorship

Sponsorship is another source of revenue for I.T. services and one that has made headway lately. Somewhat less concerned with audience size than traditional advertising, the corporate body enthusiastic to be seen as a patron of the arts, friend of the athlete, and supporter of the environment is frequently a willing sponsor so long as size is proportional to "quality" of viewer. It is by no means unlikely that companies will be persuaded to contribute to programming which might allow, in some cases, the pressure of the ratings to be eased. In the United States, the Public Broadcasting Service (PBS) receives its funds in this way, notably from oil companies, and enables Americans to tune into something somewhat different than that offered on the networks. And in Britain, the past few years have evidenced considerably more corporate interest in and political encouragement for private support for television.

However, there are problems entailed with this method of extending viewer choice. Most telling is that sponsorship is a form of advertising, less direct than the orthodox practice of buying time to parade a product, but a form of selling nevertheless (Barnouw, 1978). The J. Walter Thompson Company makes no bones about it. Commenting on "trends in the new electronic media," it expresses the belief that these will "increase both the need and the opportunities for new forms of television advertising" (Syfret, 1983, p. 39), prominent among which is sponsorship. The aims might be more or less subtle—at one extreme, trying to project an image of concern for a national culture or civilization itself, the environment, or education; at another, building a TV series around a character from an advertisement for a product—but they remain the same (Ermann, 1978). The fact is that, because corporate sponsors are not involved out of altruism, and wanting the best return from their investment, they are likely to favor channeling monies into established programs, especially sport, that will get large exposure. More serious still, should they support programs of less mass appeal, funds will not come without strings (cf. Taylor, 1984). Sponsors freely decide where to spend their cash, and it does not take much imagination to realize that funds will not be forthcoming for programs critical of either the sponsor or the business system in general. No doubt there will be some worthwhile serializations of the classics, some breathtaking explorations of the "living world," and a goodly amount of pageantry, but few can anticipate an extension of contemporary drama or more social, economic, or political analysis.

Ability to Pay

While the new technologies offer much the same—but more—as before, this of course does not mean that nothing will change, and indeed the appearance of increased amounts of television and familiar programs are themselves significant. Moreover, the terms on which information in general and cable and satellite services in particular are becoming accessible mark an important shift, insofar as they heighten the emphasis of ability-to-pay criteria being applied to the distribution of the new services. To some extent, television in Britain has always demanded ability to pay (for rental or purchase of sets, the obligatory license fee which cost £4 per month in 1984), but these sums have been comparatively small, and programs to date have been available to everyone on an equal basis. Expenditures are likely to be raised considerably with the commoditization of information/entertainment services that cable and the like represent. With services increasingly being charged for at a market rate will come restrictions not only in reception of programs but also in what is produced.

This is in line with the trend to charge for information which, as noted earlier, will benefit chiefly corporate and state agencies. However, even within the relatively poor domestic sector, significant differences will be evident consequent upon supply only to those with the requisite resources. This is obvious to the makers of personal computers and online services (with which cable will ultimately combine) who carefully target their produce. At the cheaper end of this market (itself a minority one, reaching at present less than 10% of the population), are games galore—and there is a correlation between the wider diffusion of the technologies and garbage information—while in the upper reaches, where costs are high but buyers more affluent, stock market quotations, programs to simplify tax returns, home banking services, and the like are available. We have noted that rural areas will be a poor investment prospect for cable operators in comparison to the wealthy urban and suburban locales, and already in the U.K. franchises have gone to the latter and reveal a pronounced bias towards the affluent. But even within favored areas, commercial criteria may disenfranchise poorer members of the community. For example, late in 1982 it was reported that cable television would cost between £10 and £20 per month (*Guardian,* 17 November, 1982). These are prices unlikely to be affordable to large numbers of people (the old, the sick, the unemployed, the low skilled), and larger numbers will be excluded from the shopping and banking facilities cable will eventually offer.

Since the bulk of programming for cable television will be much the same as is presently offered, one could say that this is nothing to be worried about. However, there are reasons for concern. First, because of the threat to existing broadcasting entailed in commercial services (see below); second, because the long-term move towards incorporation of cable with an "electronic grid," providing a cluster of information services to the home, may mean the exclusion of the poorer members of society from what will become a crucial means of participation; third, because cable TV will offer genuine choice and improvement of information only to those with plentiful resources.

We would dwell on the final group, the younger, high-spending, and credit-worthy groups that are the darlings of the I.T. world. These are a select target for I.T. producers, programmers, and all manner of marketers on the fringes of these developments. Because they have the money to spend, it is they who will get and be able to use to advantage the premium services: the home computers which (if expensive) are versatile and powerful; the viewdata services that bring to the home worthwhile (if expensive) data; and cable channels which (if expensive) are diverse, well-produced, and unavailable to the majority.

Too much can be made of this category and the information inequality it might highlight, in view of the failure of up-market cable TV channels to make profit (CBS Cable folded its station in 1982, after its idea to supply "culture" to the appreciative and affluent failed to win enough converts). Nonetheless, even if affluent homes are unwilling to pay high subscriptions to cable companies, they will remain an attractive target to advertisers who may sponsor channels that reach them, in which case they may still receive specific programs, as *Campaign* recently noted: "If the operators are able to deliver kids and teenagers and up-market homes regularly, in sufficient numbers, then cable will be a very successful medium indeed" (26 August, 1983, p. 31). Thus, whether it is through payment of expensive subscriptions or heavy subsidy by advertisers or sponsors desirous of reaching elite audiences, variety and quality of programming on cable television will go to the better off.

Commerce and Public Service Television

What the foregoing amounts to is that new technologies are arriving in an already unequal society; it is the old story of the better off getting the better things. However, there is something decidedly different about I.T. which will influence some societies, notably Britain, which stems from the claim that it will be provided only to those who can pay and be produced only if it is calculated that it will bring an acceptable return to investors. We refer to the demise of public service broadcasting presaged by I.T. for the home.

We take public service broadcasting to be a type institutionally set apart from outside pressures of political, business, and even audience demands in day-to-day functioning; state financed but not directed by the polity; made available to, produced for the benefit of, and distributed equally to the community at large, rather than for those who can afford to pay either for subscription or sponsorship; one committed to providing high quality—by legislation required to inform and educate as well as entertain—and comprehensive services to viewers regarded as diverse minorities which are to be catered for without jettisoning provision of programming—news, current affairs, drama, documentary, sports, etc.—aimed at the whole audience; and, above all, not constrained by the imperatives of commercial operation. This may be an ideal type, though the British Broadcasting Corporation (BBC), while it has interpreted public service with particular emphases over the years, has approximated to it.

There are specific reasons for the development of public service broadcasting, not least recognition that commercial systems lead to low quality and restrictive programming, and many criticisms can be made of its paternalist and at times even authoritarian behavior (cf. Hood, 1980). Nonetheless, though the accountability of public broadcasting has been inadequate, what must be acknowledged is that the doctrine in Britain (where it affected, to a significant degree, the commercial network which commenced in the mid-1950s, 30 years after the BBC) has created a markedly greater diversity and quality of programming than its American counterpart, where the market ethos prevailed. The removal of the advertiser and the relegation of the pressure to maximize audience gave space to public service broadcasting to experiment, to produce for minorities, and to present educational and informative programs that on a commercial system would be nonstarters. Not restricted by the need to be popular at all costs, it has been able to provide a far wider range of programming than the U.S. networks, which insistently pander to majority tastes (Hoggart, 1982, 1983; Garnham, 1983).

It is this tradition which is endangered by the development of I.T. on current lines. The militantly laissez-faire Thatcher government is ideologically opposed to public service broadcasting since it is state rather than privately managed, and imposes an involuntary tax on the individual through the license fee which is spent on programs that are aloof from market disciplines such that large audiences for cheap, often imported, serials are used to subsidize small audiences for expensive, home-produced, programs in the arts and current affairs areas. The government has made clear that "obligations which apply to public service broadcasting will not be appropriate for cable," while conceding that "the growth of cable could necessitate considerable change in existing broadcasting arrangements" (Home Office and Department of Industry, 1983, pp. 85, 83). While no one, to date, has publicly advocated scrapping the public service doctrine, ministers have made much of the virtues of emulating U.S. information policies, and some have argued that advertising should be allowed on BBC radio, and the market strictures being applied to new technologies are in effect foreshadowing the demise of public service broadcasting. *Televisual* spelled it out in November, 1983:

> The ability to pay for television services . . . is manifestly a central part of Conservative thinking on cable and satellite television. However, there is no logical reason why it should not be extended to all forms of television output. There are several indicators to suggest that this is what some long-term Tory strategy is leading towards. Along the way, existing broadcast television structures would disappear to make way for a wired society in which all television material was available from a central resource bank on a strictly pay-per-view basis (p. 27).

Public service broadcasting in Britain is being undermined in at least three related ways (cf. Tracey, 1983). First, alternative television output is likely to reduce audiences for the BBC and Independent Television (ITV) channels. It is already clear that, in the U.S., cable has caused lower ratings for the networks (between 1979 and 1981, they lost over 10% of prime-time viewers), and a similar, if less drastic, fall is likely to be experienced here. When this occurs, public service TV will unavoidably be pressed to justify its revenue from the populace, since its national service will be brought into question (how can one serve the public if audiences are, say, less than 30%?). Second, the fragmentation of audiences by services for which they must pay direct will lead to demands that people only pay for what they receive from the national service rather than, as now, paying for the system as a whole through the license. Third, when and if this should happen, a predictable response of public service broadcasting is to limit minority programs and beef up popular shows which might increase audience share and enable it to claim more resources.

The existence of ITV itself exercises this pressure on the BBC, recently evidenced in its instigation of breakfast-time shows—which are hard to distinguish from *TV-am*—for the sole reason that ITV announced that it was to establish one, though the fear that BBC programs might be considerably less popular than those of ITV, making it hard to justify the fee set by Parliament which would be drawn to "free" TV subsidized by advertising, has for years been a cause of a preponderance of telemovies and soaps on BBC in peak hours. This pressure has continued and intensified in recent months, during which the BBC has placed more emphasis on light entertainment, for example by changing early evening current affairs and providing more serials that will capture viewers for the rest of the evening.

ITV, reliant on advertisers for revenue, but with public service conditions built into its structure, also fears the advent of cable and already wants to reschedule and prune less popular programs such as current affairs, education, and the arts, a few of which are transmitted at peak hours, in order to hold on to audiences for the whole evening. That is, recognizing that viewing drops in a typical evening when a documentary follows a serial, the aim is to have popular programs throughout. The reasoning is simple: since 75% of ITV's revenue is earned in peak time, it must deliver the necessary audiences without interruption if it wants to retain the confidence of advertisers in a changing situation. The change is the threat of cable tapping into ITV's audiences; the response is to take funds from rescheduled "minority" programs and invest and promote "populist" shows. As John Birt, program director of London Weekend Television explains:

> The new era of competition is likely to mean that the scope for scheduling programs of minority appeal during peak time will be limited. Indeed, soon there may be no case for it at all (quoted in *Guardian,* 29 September, 1983).

In addition, the BBC, as the most thoroughly public service broadcaster, has been strapped for funds over the past decade. A response has been to tout its wares wherever feasible, especially in America, where it appears as just another commercial competitor on the market, and an effect has been felt on programs (the glossy historical serial or documentary has become a specialty, sometimes in collaboration with Time Inc.). Still more serious, the BBC decided to break with tenets of public service TV by accepting a role in a proposed satellite subscription business to start in 1988 which will use BBC stock and take advertising. As with the shift to more popular programs on major channels the satellite service, aborted in 1985, was to have offered "jukebox telly." Moreover, a complementary pressure comes from the fact that costs of program production are heavily skewed in favor of those which capture large audiences. Jeremy Tunstall estimates that one hour's drama costs 12 times a "bought in" series or feature film (Tunstall, 1983, p. 36). Should the BBC suffer a decline in viewers and funding remain parsimonious, the pressure to save money and increase audiences by transmitting cheap entertainment will be difficult to resist. As commercial television further intrudes into Britain, the signs are that key features of public service broadcasting are in decline, with the result that there is a narrower range of programming and moves, more or less hesitant, towards operation of market lines by established but threatened institutions.

Privatization and Consumerism

There are other conditions by which I.T. for the General Public is touched and which it influences that are still more fundamental. One is the trend towards the privatization of life, the increased emphasis on home-centeredness, which is so much a feature of advanced societies. Sociologists have frequently considered the development of the "isolated nuclear family" of "mum, dad, and the kids," which is characteristic of what Raymond Williams has called "mobile privatization" (cf. Goldthorpe et al., 1969). In a well-known book, the same author has argued that the "breakdown and dissolution of older and smaller kinds of settlement" (Williams, 1974, p. 26) shaped the "applied technology" (p. 27) of television as the "box in the corner," as a machine capable of being accommodated in the living room of the modern family, though there was no inherent reason why this should have been so. We concur and observe that cable, video, and the rest have also been influenced by this trend (and, building upon existent television, they have consolidated a technology that was originally socially shaped). There is no imminent logic that has led to the manufacture of these machines in their particular forms, and the social circumstance of privatization has played an important part in shaping what is marketed as admirably suited to the contemporary family and its surroundings. It is impossible to identify a particular moment in the origination of any one technology when this social effect is operative. Impossible to be precise, but the pervasive influence of a way of life which suffuses assumptions about design, acceptability, and desire surely cannot be denied.

These new technologies for the home should not be seen in isolation. They are at one with a cluster of goods and services which have also built on and extended a home-centered style of life: washing machines, the automobile (what Mark Abrams called the "mobile living room"), the emergence of do-it-yourself equipment, home brewing, the range of kitchen appliances (microwave ovens, hobs, waste disposal units, friers, etc.) are representative of the same movement as I.T. for the home. *Campaign* describes it thus:

> Mr. and Mrs. Britain can now sit indoors with their take-away food and alcohol and view anything from *The French Lieutenant's Woman* to the type of *oeuvre* where people find their heads being nailed to the floor. Meanwhile the kids are playing TV games on the home computer, and the washing machine and dryer are taking care of one of the main chores of the week (September 2, 1983, p. 23).

It may be baldly drawn, but *Campaign* depicts an important social phenomenon which, as we discussed in Chapter 6, Jonathan Gershuny describes as an emerging "self-service society." In our view, this is an increasingly atomized society, one characterized by retreat from participation in the outside world and concern with issues of more than immediate interest. *Campaign* depicts it as the growth of "Fortress Britain," a country where, "if an Englishman's home is his castle it looks as if he's increasingly inclined to pull up the drawbridge and settle in for an evening with the modern equivalent of ministrels, troubadours and court jesters" (ibid.). It represents a move away from going out to the cinema to see a film (the TV provides that), away from using buses to visit the shops (the car provides that), away from employing a builder to convert the loft (the power tools and manuals suffice), away from going to the pub for a drink (cheap supermarkets and beermaking kits are adequate), away from trips to the football game on Saturday (cable and video are less bother and give a better picture). . . . Obviously this sketch requires qualification as to detail, but the move towards increased privatization appears unstoppable and will only be hastened by I.T.

A response to this might be acknowledgement that I.T. and related technologies are speeding along privatization, but that this simply reflects people's wants, that it is the desire for an escape from the outside world into the bosom of one's kith and kin which has brought about the "electronic fortress," offering comforts, interests, and diversions inconceivable 30 years ago. It might even be conceded that this social formation, the modern family, has affected I.T., but then argued that both I.T. and the privatized family itself are caused by the deeper pressure of people's natural feelings. Connectedly, it might be contended that the new technologies simply are better ways of doing things than previous, and, because they are improvements, people are inevitably finding them appealing.

It is hard to resist, at least initially, such arguments; the closest affections are reserved for one's immediate family, so is it not obvious that technologies will be developed to facilitate expression of these feelings? Is it not natural to desire products that allow one to be with one's nearest and dearest in the comfort on one's home? And as society has increased in wealth and technologies have become widely available, is it not natural that easier ways of cleaning the house, getting amusement, moving about the countryside, preserving foodstuffs, etc. have been taken up? Ought we not to rejoice that household goods, having declined in price by 40% during 20 years (*Economic Progress Report*, 161, October, 1983), can now be afforded by most of the population? Who but an "inverted puritan" (Hall, 1984) would want to take away wall-to-wall carpeting, refrigerators and freezers, dishwashers, the fruits of advanced industrialism, still less the institution within which the deepest-felt emotions and affections can find expression?

We would not. But analysis and understanding cannot be satisfied to leave as explanations for the new technologies and life styles they express and perpetuate the assertion that people naturally want a more privatized family life, more home-centered things and activities, and/or that they simply represent an improvement in the standard of living. They cannot be satisfied, because it is demonstrably the case that the modern family, however intense may be the emotions within it, is a social creation (see, inter alia, Leach, 1967), and equally that identifiable social processes influence both desire for and design of goods and services intended to be used in this artificial construct. To exclude from analysis such factors is to posit that society somehow ceases to exist when it comes to explanations of family relationships—as if this bedrock of society is untouched by society; or is absent in accounts of the origination of wants—yet a moment's reflection leads one to realize that few if any of the household goods nowadays regarded as necessities (TV, fridge, indoor toilets, etc.) were imagined, let alone wanted, in pre-War Britain: ipso facto, needs must have been socially manufactured; or plays no part in understanding "improvements" and "more wealth"—as if something which is socially irresistible is unaffected by society. It is our contention that the development of goods and services for the home, and the expression of desire for them, has been influenced by social relations which have consequences that reach beyond the nuclear family. Though we theorize these processes in Part Three, we may usefully sketch features of our argument here.

Central to an explanation is the concept of consumer capitalism, by which we mean to identify a privately-owned market economy for the most part committed to producing constantly renewed goods and services aimed at the individual (or rather each family unit). Of course, consumer products have long been made available, but consumer capitalism is distinguished from previous societies in a number of ways: first, in that, during earlier periods, a great deal of economic activity was devoted to more or less subsistence agriculture; second, in that, especially in the 19th century, much went to support capital goods for the development of industry and an industrial infrastructure (machinery, railways, etc.); and third, in that, while consumer goods began to become available in 18th century England (McKendrick et al., 1982), and were extensively available by the late 19th (Fraser, 1981), it was not until the post-War boom that consumer goods and services became of primary importance to the economy, and the characteristic emphasis on novelty and individual consumption moved to the forefront of the culture.

Because an important characteristic of consumer capitalism is that very large parts of the economy (not least automobiles, consumer electronics, and entertainment) are reliant on individual citizens as the outlet for goods and services, production and profitability are put in jeopardy should consumption flag or become uncertain. There is a consequent need for the stimulation and direction of consumer needs, the converse of the popular conception that people's needs determine production. Since, within consumer capitalism, "it is the process of satisfying wants that creates the wants" (Galbraith, 1968, p. 132) steps are taken, notably in market research, advertising, and packaging, but also in model changes, product design, and constant creation of novelty, to influence people, to manufacture desire in prospective customers. Consumers must be taught how and what to want, and they must be educated to want continually in the interests of an economy which goes to great lengths to give added value to what it produces (a car is not just a car, but a status symbol; a singer not just a singer, but a superstar . . .); to stir discontent in the minds of the public that is promised assuagement by buying goods and services; to teach that the unimagined is now imaginable, the imaginable a luxury, the luxurious desirable, the desirable a necessity. . . . While advertising is most self-conscious in instruction of the public, the process permeates the society and is evident in television serials, the fashion business, the design of kitchens, and the constant parading of celebrities. Can anyone be unaware of the concerted efforts being put into the creation of needs for I.T. for the home, the sophisticated advertisements for video recorders and personal computers (for the family that's going places, the discerning viewer . . .), the door-to-door peddling of cable television? In face of an avalanche of selling from advertisers through to politicians, how can the idea that consumer demand is the sole reason for I.T.'s production be seriously credited?

Consumer capitalism also stimulates an individualistic outlook and accountancy which complements the privatization of life. We are so suffused with individualism that we find it hard to imagine people ever having thought and acted in other ways; it seems instinctive that the self is the central concern, so that any criticism of how we live now is readily dismissed as nostalgia for a mythical "organic community" (cf. Clecak, 1983). By the same token, the new technologies being manufactured for private consumption appear in some way merely responsive to a natural drive. But we can begin to understand something of the social creation of individualism and the part it might play in the development of particular technologies by reflecting first on the plethora of advertisements which daily reach the public. They are overwhelmingly expressive of individualism, cajoling us to consume personally household goods, alcohol, automobiles, and the like. Second, the cult of individualism is highlighted in consumer capitalism's systematic denigration of what Daniel Bell has called the "public household," "the agency for the satisfaction of public needs and public wants" (Bell, 1979c, p. 221). This economy assiduously inculcates an outlook which perceives collective consumption—welfare agencies, public education, library services, state-owned railways, sanitation systems—negatively, as a cost imposed upon an unwilling populace rather than an alternative mode of using resources. Galbraith captured the ethos of individualism which characterizes a society premised on private consumption when he wrote that "To suggest that we canvass our public wants to see where happiness can be improved by more and better services has a sharply radical tone. . . . By contrast the man who devises a nostrum for a nonexistent need and then successfully promotes both remains one of nature's noblemen" (Galbraith, 1968, p. 219). When one compares aspects of the post-1945 mentality in Europe, something of the scale of this individualism—seen on the one hand as a retreat into home-centeredness, on the other as profound suspicion of arrangements for social consumption—can begin to be grasped (cf. Davies, 1984), as can ways in which technologies for the home affirm changed forms of consciousness.

Paradoxically, this cult of individualism is undermined—and its social constitution better understood—by modern marketing that has "plenty of agencies which aim to take money from working people by encouraging their feelings of individuality while, in fact, encouraging them to think and choose exactly like millions of others" (Hoggart, 1970, p. 45). This simultaneous appeal to and undermining of individualism by the "forces of organized domination" (Lasch, 1977, p. 149) is much more than attitudinal, since it extends into material production itself, into the assembly line mass-manufacturing of goods that are to be used for individual ends.

Associatedly, we find the cultivation of a hedonistic attitude, suggested in the term, "me-decade," as a description of the 1970s and commented on by political commentators as diverse as Daniel Bell and Christopher Lasch, which emanates from an economy which as a "calculated strategy" seeks "to promote a mood of self-indulgence in order to promote sales" (Packard, 1963, p. 152), and is witnessed in an obsessive concern for self-analysis, indulgence in material objects, and the conviction that more goods and services will resolve personal problems. In Britain, this trend has been exacerbated by the fact that the spending of those remaining in work, most of whose incomes have risen in the midst of recession, has fuelled a retail spending boom that has run through the 1980s. As those in employ consume more, the evident lack of sympathy for the 15% workless who are bearing the brunt of economic downturn is explicable. Not surprisingly, expenditure has concentrated in the area of electronics goods for the home.

In addition, consumer capitalism qua capitalism functions on the basis of ability to pay that we discussed earlier. As it encourages self-interested actors privately to consume products manufactured for this purpose, so too does it stimulate the market principle of supply only to those with the means to pay. A result is that the rash of innovations for the home are premised on this market tenet, and different modes, notably public service broadcasting, are threatened.

Finally we would recall that, in Chapter 5, we considered the likely effect of I.T. on women's work and concluded that it was likely to be negative. The condition of women, the group with major responsibility for the home and purchase of consumer goods, is particularly influenced by the enhanced TV and other electronics technologies being produced by consumer capitalism. Though the effects will doubtless be uneven, we think that the overall consequence will be confirmation of female status as subordinate to that of the male, since I.T. does nothing if it does not confirm the primacy of the home, and it is restriction to the home which has proved the major obstacle to women achieving as much as men. There are those who believe that consumer electronics have liberated women from domestic labor—and who would want to continue with the drudgery of hand-washing, sweeping of uncarpeted floors, the chore of drying clothes?—but, while clearly they have caused significant changes, these technologies have scarcely freed the housewife. In an important book, Ruth Schwarz Cowan (1983) demonstrates that the demands of housework have not lessened, though many new technologies have come available. Instead, women hoover more, wash clothers more regularly, serve a greater variety of meals. . . . We can see no reason why this should not continue. If anything, given the dangers to female employment and its amenability to performance at home via communications networks and the continuing drift towards privatization, gains made by women in recent decades may even be put at risk by a drive to resurrect the ideal homemaker, this time equipped with a battery of electronics in the "home of the future."

Conclusion

In this chapter, we have argued that I.T. for the General Public is more of the same, more television and entertainment programming which endangers public service broadcasting. Asking why this should be so, we found that the imperatives of commercial interests and organization were paramount. Further, trying to explain why these technologies encouraged a privatized lifestyle, we found it essential to recognize that nowadays the home is "intensively organized for commercial purposes"

(Mills, 1963, p. 349) and that the priorities of consumer capitalism, rather than public need, have been the major force shaping I.T., persuading people of the desirability of its possession, and exacerbating the drift to a home-centered way of life.

We do not want to replace naive explanations of new technologies as straightforward products of innate need or as technical progress with the idea that people are passive victims of the spread of consumer capitalism which determines what will be manufactured and on whom it will be foisted. On the ground, things are more complex and shifting; the retreat to the home can coexist with a good deal of neighborliness, aspects of the self-service society may involve communal organization, people do not necessarily succumb to advertisers' propaganda and the blandishments of the arcades (they often cannot afford it!), and they can put technologies to uses never envisaged by the marketers. We recognize too that people often feel that it is in their lives outside of work where real meaning is found, where they have autonomy and some control over their destinies (cf. Moorehouse, 1983).

Yet, in trying to identify the logic, presence, and something of the power of consumer capitalism, there is no getting away from the fact that in our view the contemporary emphasis on consumption is not a phenomenon that has sprung innocently from ordinary people. Just now, when negative responses to domestic I.T. are received by conservatives and radicals alike as killjoy, we insist with Jeremy Seabrook that "the question of what we have been liberated into is always more disconcerting than that of the oppressions we have emerged from" (Seabrook, 1982b, p. 141).

PART THREE

THE 'INFORMATION REVOLUTION': FROM TAYLORISM TO NEO-FORDISM

Chapter 10
Technology, Control, Crisis

Everything begins with Taylor at the turn of the century, when the "soldier-ing" of the working class became the object of attack and was brought under control.

> —Benjamin Coriat. *L'Atelier et le Chronomètre.* Paris: Christian Bourgois, 1979, p. 23.

In the ten years between 1910 and 1920 . . . every single one of the great themes of management is struck . . . And almost everything we have done since them, in theory as well as in practice, is only a variation and extension of the themes first heard during that decade.

> —Peter F. Drucker. *People and Performance: the Best of Peter Drucker on Management.* Heinemann, 1977, p. 19.

Giddy with fantasies about the Japanese fifth generation of computers, entrepreneur Sir Clive Sinclair looks to a time when "machines of silicon will arise first to rival and then to surpass their human progenitors". As robots take over the business of economic life, we will come into our inheritance:

> Freeman of Periclean Athens led not such different lives as we might live, for where we will have the machines, they had slaves who served both to teach and as menials. Thanks, perhaps, to their fine education, the freemen of Athens seem not to have found difficulty in filling their time.
>
> Just as they did, we will need to educate our children to an appreciation of the finer things of life, to inculcate a love of art, music and science. So we may experience an age as golden as that of Greece (Sinclair, 1984).

This is the vision of a successful and acknowledged businessman in the electronics industry, and it is one that, however fantastic, enjoys a degree of credibility in media, industrial, political, and even intellectual circles.

Our assessment of the Microelectronics Revolution appears cynical and unenthusiastic when compared to Sinclair's paeon. What we have documented in Part Two is the degradation and destruction of much employment, the further concentration and consolidation of corporate capital, and the imposition of its criteria and priorities on the nation state, the aggravation of existing inequalities in our society, the perpetuation of consumerist ethics, and an increasingly atomized way of life.

This is not a popular interpretation. Hard-nosed futurists commonly sweep it aside by conceding that the Information Society will have its teething problems, but claiming that ultimately it is bound to lead us out of the desert of recession and crisis into the kingdom of wealth and freedom. We shall, say the prophets, move into a "third wave" era (Toffler, 1980, 1984); the coming "telematic society" will allow us to "supersede socialist–marxist and capitalist societies" and to progress to a new "scientific society" (Poniatowski, 1978, p. 77); we may expect a new "globalism", a "neo-renaissance" auguring "the liberation of the human spirit" (Masuda, 1981, p. 69). With the future so full of promise, there is no place for our negative and pessimistic criticism. Compared to Sinclair, we are defeatist and carping. Even Luddite.

What we want to do is elaborate and justify our position and, in so doing, confront and challenge the approach of the silicon prophets. We want here to situate the evidence we have detailed in Part Two within a theoretical and historical frame work. And in so doing we want to contest the—often implicit—theoretical perspective of the various stances that we discussed in Part One of this book. For, despite the diversity of rhetorics—whether it be the hype of the futurists, the comparatively sober post-industrial sociology of Bell and his acolytes, or the materialist aspirations of subscribers to a Scientific and Technological Revolution (STR)—there is a single theoretical position at the heart of all this work.

"Progress" and Technology

A unifying thread in popular futurology, post-industrialism, and the theory of the STR is the concept of scientific and technological progress. Wilson Dizard makes this explicit when he argues that the information age reflects "a view of society as a progression towards an earthly ideal". For Dizard, the information revolution points to "an America moving beyond the conventional modernization process into an advanced evolutionary phase". And the dynamics of this modernization or evolutionary process, he suggests, "spring from the scientific revolution" 1982, p. 22, 16, 194).

In our view, the idea of progress as that which is constantly unfolding, purposeful, and beneficial draws much appeal from conflation with the concept of change. While change is open-ended and unavoidable, progress implies a positive and evolutionary direction of change. Moreover, when, as is usual, science and technology are presented as representative of this progress—they do not merely aid progress; they *are* progress—what occurs is that particular directions of change appear to be both inevitable and desirable. And this is the case even for those who wish to change society: they embrace progressive elements which mark a level of underlying advancement.

In this way, progress serves to take responsibility for historical change out of the hands of human beings who make choices, pursue interests, and exercise power, and places it in a position of being an objective process which is unopposable and unobjectionable. Thereby science and technology, the motors and indicators of progress, are, as we detailed in Part One, considered to be neutral because they are asocial, yet inevitably to be accepted. What they represent is *more*, and more in and of itself is synonymous with progress.

However, as we argued throughout Part Two, the progress now unfolding exists as the continuation of present social conditions; far from being independent of existent social relations, it is expressive of them. But because this goes unrecognized, the future we are promised is entrapped within a narrowly technological and productivist image of progress. Human welfare and social good are seen only on the quantitative scale of economic and technological expansion. In the words of Hans Jonas, "*technology* has become the dominant symbol of progress, at the least its most external measure. In that connection, progress comes almost to be equated with material betterment" (Jonas, 1981, p. 412). Technological growth, ineluct-ably advancing, displaces all other conceptions of human destiny; we see the "adaption of *all* human needs, desires, plans, and processes of thought to the technical mode" (Winner, 1977, p. 127). The machine becomes the key to human happiness and emancipation, and its logic comes to dominate social existence.

Central to our concerns in this book is the fact that technology has become so closely and exclusively identified with ideas about the "better life". As Langdon Winner has pointed out, "many historical forms of statecraft and almost all concep-tions of utopia rest on an implicitly technological model" (Winner, 1977, p. 26). And this is the case not just in the expansionist Western economies, but also in the Soviet and East European ideal of the Scientific and Technological Revolution, where utopia is an expression of the unfettered development of the productive for-ces of society. It has become difficult, near impossible, for us to wrench away ideas about a desirable human and social future from the logic of technological progress. This is all the more so in that one strong tradition of critique, Marxism, has become no more than "an 'eschatologically' radicalized version of what the worldwide tech-nological impetus of our civilization is moving toward anyway" (Jonas, 1981, p. 454). All this poses as a key problem for the critique of I.T. and the way in which it is being exploited in the advanced capitalist societies the requirement of the evo-cation of an alternative future, a utopian vision of what society could be. And, yet utopian philosophies have become impregnated with the very technological deter-minism and ethos of progress that we are seeking to question.

Luddism and Technology

The problem that we face is that science, technology, and the idea of progress have come to assume the force of truth itself. And if, during the 1970s, under the pres-sure of the ecological and radical science movements, the mythology of progress was somewhat demystified, it now threatens to reassert itself. As David Dickson and David Noble have argued, we are now witnessing "a reinvention of the idea of progress, and its specific linkage to issues of industrial innovation and productivity" —"progress", they stress, "refers to the continued development of science and tech-nology within a structure of private direction and gain" (Dickson and Noble, 1981, pp. 270, 305). Thus we have those—technocrats, politicians, businessmen—who are now telling us that "the microprocessor could be the key to Utopia", fulfilling the vision that "was in the minds of the fathers of the first Industrial Revolution two centuries ago" (King, 1982, pp. 27, 33).

This railroading necessitates that we all the more forcefully contest the ideology of progress. We should challenge this abstract and etherial idea and demonstrate that the information revolution is less about the improvement of humankind than about the quest for profit and managerial and state control. In a fine article, David Noble has observed that

technological development has become simply the blind weight of the past on the one hand, and the perpetual promise of the future on the other. Technological determinism—the domination of the present by the past—and technological progress—the domination of the present by the future—have combined in our minds to annihilate the technological present. The loss of the concrete, the inevitable consequence of the subordination of people at the point of 'production, thus has resulted also in the loss of the present as the realm for assessments, decisions, and actions. And this intellectual blindspot, the inability even to comprehend technology in the present tense, much less act upon it, has inhibited the opposition and lent legitimacy to its inaction (Nobel, 1983a, p. 10).

Partisans of technological determinism and technological progress conspire to reduce us to the role of passivity, meekly servicing what are presented as the autonomous and irresistible trajectory of technological development. At the present moment, in the face of a new technological revolution, Noble concludes that, for the most part, "the opposition suffers from a fatalistic and futuristic confusion about the nature of technological development" (ibid., p. 9).

But this has not always been the case. History provides us with examples of those who have contested the logic of technological progress. And, among these, most important is surely the Luddite movement. "The Luddities", says David Noble, "were perhaps the last people in the West to perceive technology in the present tense, and to act upon that perception . . . They did not believe in technological progress, nor could they since the alien idea was invented after them, to try to prevent their recurrence" (ibid., p. 11). The Luddities represent an important social and cultural movement, insofar as they rejected the exaltation of technology above human values and purposes.

What the Luddites saw, and what they allow us to see, is that technology, far from being a beneficent force for progress, was a vehicle of power. They experienced and understood the new technologies, not as neutral, but as a force that was inimical to their culture and way of life. What Darvall calls "the Luddites' hopeless battle against fate" (Darvall, 1934, p.216), was a struggle against something far more tangible—the technologies that had been constituted to express the values and priorities of emergent capitalism.

If we recognize this as the weight of the Luddite rebellion, that they saw through machinery to the social relations that suffused it, we might perhaps want to confront the question once put by Lewis Mumford:

But what shall we say of the counter-Luddites, the systematic craft-wreckers, of the machine: the ruthless enterprisers who, during the last two centuries, have in effect confiscated the tools, destroyed the independent workshops, and wiped out the living traditions of handicraft culture? What they have done is to debase a versatile and still viable polytechnics to a monotechnics, and at the same time they have sacrificed human autonomy and variety to a system of centralized control that becomes increasingly more automatic and compulsive (Mumford, 1971, p. 153).

If we can see technology, not as a socially neutral force, but as an expression of social and political relations—of relations of power—then we can perhaps begin to understand why the Luddites opposed progress. And, on this basis, we can better scrutinize the meaning of technological progress in the present context of the information revolution.

From Luddism to Taylorism/Fordism

In the first act of Ernst Toller's play about the Luddites, *The Machine-Wreckers*, the character Ned Lud says:

> Every man on God's earth has a right to live by the work of his hands. Every man is born free and has a right to a trade . . . A holy right! Whoever robs him of it is a thief! The masters betrayed us when they brought the steam-engine into the town! What does our handicraft count for now?
> . . . One weaver worked three spindles; the jenny drives eighteen. It robs five weavers of their daily bread. A thousand spindles, so they say, are driven by the mule. Now comes the day when Ure would lead us to the knackers' yard. "Hey, slaughter all the pack! I have the steam-engine". We must stand together. No hands turn at machines! We would live by the work of our hands, as we have always done. We are men! Engine-wages are devil's wages (Toller, 1923, p. 18).

What Ned Lud is crying out against is not technology or progress in some abstract sense. He is angry about the new political economy of *laissez-faire* which, nurturing new technologies and relations (Berg, 1980), was ripping men, women, and children out of their familiar and traditional way of life, changing them on its terms, and drafting them into factory labor.

The significance of the Industrial Revolution lies not in technological increase or economic growth, but in a much broader and inclusive process of social and cultural change that aimed to mobilize a whole population for a new way of life. In his recent book, *La Mobilization Générale*, Jean-Paul de Gaudemar (1979) develops this concept of mobilization in a way that allows us to see the history of capitalist societies in this way. His categories enable us to mark major qualitative transformations in the mode of capitalist development since the Industrial Revolution, helping us then to situate the role of technology within this broader process.

Gaudemar refers to the early 19th century, the period of the Luddites, as that of "absolute mobilization". These are the years in which the traditional way of life of the population was most systematically undermined in order to create a factory proletariat through what Sidney Pollard calls "the adjustment of labor to the regularity and discipline of factory work" (Pollard, 1963). This disciplinary process involves efforts both inside and outside the factory to produce a pliant and cooperative workforce: the penalization of vagabondage; the undermining of traditional culture (fairs, sports, etc.); the division of labor; the discipline of factory super-vision; the campaign against St.Monday and the institution of time-thrift; the in-culcation of appropriate values and ideals (especially through religion and school-ing); the shift to reliance on wages to supply the means of living; and the assult on paternal arrangements at work, in welfare, and, in distribution of produce.

During the late 19th century, absolute mobilization is replaced by the process of "relative mobilization" which initially focused more directly on relations inside the factory. In this process of transformation, earlier forms of control are deepened by an internal factory discipline in which technology begins to play a central role. Here the machines acts "as dual instrument of discipline and of increased productivity. Hence its introduction, not as an autonomous technological manna, imposing its objective rationality on the mode of production . . . but also as a solution to the disciplinary problems of the employers" (Gaudemar, 1979, p. 198). This line of de-velopment reaches its culmination with the Scientific Management of Frederick Taylor, and, classically, with the assembly line of Henry Ford. With Taylor and Ford, there appears the figure of the "mass worker", the worker divested of par-ticularity and skill, the worker subordinated to the logic of the machine.

It is to Taylor, and his part in the strategy of relative mobilization, that we now turn. "Among the 'makers of the modern world' Taylor is rarely mentioned", says Peter Drucker, "and yet he has had as much impact as Marx or Freud" (Drucker, 1976, p. 26). Taylor has indeed profoundly shaped and influenced 20th century so-ciety. We want to isolate two key dimensions of Taylorism that relate directly to our concern with I.T. In his book, *L'Atelier et le Chronomètre*, Benjamin Coriat outlines what he sees as the achievement of Taylorism. First, he argues that Taylor-ism created "an entirely new sequence in the relations of power between classes" (Coriat, 1979, p. 13). Hitherto, a significant section of labor had managed to create its own autonomous space through possession of craft skills. This was so to such an extent that the craft system had become an obstacle to corporate expansion. "In the workers' hands, Taylor argued, this practical knowledge of production had become a 'systematic soldiering' that was paralysing the growth of capital" (Coriat, 1979, p. 46). Taylor's methods were an attack on these skills and savoir-faire, a strategy of replacing the craft worker with the deskilled "mass worker", and thus an attempt to recompose relations between labor and man-agement by expropriating workers' knowledge and skill.

The second aspect of Taylorism that we find elucidated in Coriat's writing, one less known than the innovations introduced into the workshop, is its claim to pro-vide an overall strategy for American capitalism. "Taylor had developed ideas, not only about the workshop as is commonly thought, but also about economic growth" (Coriat, 1979, pp. 58-59). These ideas, hinging on Taylor's plans for increased productivity coming from scientifically managed factories, focused on procedures to handle areas of life far beyond the plant. With mass production as the root of his strategy, a corollary of Taylorism was a panoply of state and social measures to manage a new era of capitalism. These, we argue, entailed the extension of controls beyond the sphere of work.

Two fundamental aspects of Scientific Management, then: the appropriation of knowledge/skill inside the factory; and Taylorism as a broad social philosophy and political strategy for 20th century capitalism. Let us look at each—though the two are interrelated—more closely before going on to examine developments of Taylorism after Taylor.

(1) The Gathering In of Knowledge

For Peter Drucker, Taylorism "has proved to be the most effective idea of this century" (Drucker, 1969, p. 254), "the most powerful as well as the most lasting contribution America has made to Western thought" (Drucker, 1955, p. 248). Taylor's work is so important, he suggests, because it demonstrated that "the key to productivity was knowledge not sweat"; Taylor showed that "the economic pie could be enlarged rapidly by applying knowledge to work" (Drucker, 1969, p. 255). To use a different terminology, what Scientific Management sought to do was to undertake the systematic separation of manual and mental labor, in order to monopolize the latter. It was Taylor's insistence that methodical planning by management, diligent increase of its knowledge of work processes, would result in greater output. Referring to craftworkers, Taylor observed that "the knowledge which every journeyman has of his trade is his most valuable possession . . . his life's great capital" (Taylor, 1947c, p. 36). For Taylor, the problem with this "mass of rule-of-thumb or traditional knowledge" was that it was "not in the possession of the management" (Taylor, 1947b, p. 32). Taylor argued that workers "should be entirely relieved of the work of planning . . . All possible brain work should be removed from the shop and centered in the planning or laying out department" (Taylor, 1947a, pp. 98-99). It is necessary to establish a separate "planning department" in order to "concentrate the planning and much other brainwork in a few men especially fitted for their task and trained in their especial lines" (p. 66). Of fundamental importance to Taylorism is the division of head and head which meant that knowledge was to be a prerogative of management, and this for two reasons: first in order to increase productivity without increasing costs; second, to establish the control of capital over the labor process.

The chief objective of Scientific Management was to annex and control knowledge—both the *savoir-faire* of the workers and also the more systematic knowledge being produced by increasingly organized research and development—because the possession of knowledge and skill represented the possession of control and power. However, this aspect of Taylorism, crucial though it was in the genesis of capitalism, was not limited to control, within the factory, of the labor process. We should not overlook "the moral thrust of scientific management theory, its capacity to find resonance in areas of American society far removed from the shop floor" in offering "a vision of an ideal order, a new *bourgeois imaginaire*" (Whitaker, 1979, pp. 84, 78).

The idea of a planning department and a knowledge elite came to appeal to those concerned with the management, not of an individual enterprise, but of society at large. Taylor came to believe that Scientific Management could be applied to all human activities, and his successors (particularly Henry L. Gantt) sought to extend the role of expertise, efficiency, and professionalism to the broader social and political sphere. According to Haber, "the role of the consulting management engineer, upholding 'science' in the factory against the narrow vision and vested interests of worker and employer, bore some resemblance to that of the middle class reformer in society upholding the public interest against the pressures of both capital and labor" (Haber, 1964, p. 28). During the progressivist period, he suggests, "the Taylorites stepped out of the factory and projected a role for scientific management in the nation at large" (Haber, 1964, p.xi). This role centered on the importance of science, of systematized and organized knowledge, for social administration and management. Science, expertise, administration, professionalism, planning. The "engineer-administrators", with their hold on knowledge, were key personnel of an emerging *technocratic order* dedicated to maintaining an expanding capitalism and legitimating their contribution in the name of "science".

Taylor's centralized "planning department" prefigures Daniel Bell's ideas about the "knowledge elite", and the idea of "old knowledge so collected, analysed, grouped and classified into laws and rules that it constitutes a science" (Taylor, 1947b, p. 140) anticipates Bell's "intellectual technology". As we discussed in chapter 3, for Bell—and for post-industrial theorists more generally—information/ knowledge is the key to economic regulation and planning and the basis for productivity and growth which promises a qualitatively new stage of social development. It is our contention that the information society of which they dream, when seen in historical context, is the extension and intensification of Taylor's technocratic vision which likewise camouflages the interests it serves in the language of efficiency, expertise, productivity, and science.

The link between Scientific Management and post-industrial theory may be inferred from the work of one of the leading advocates of the knowledge society. For management theorist Peter Drucker, knowledge has become "the central capital, the cost center and the crucial resource of the economy" (Drucker, 1969, p. ix). In his view, "the productivity of knowledge has already become the key to productivity, competitive strength and economic achievement . . . It is the foundation and measurement of economic potential and economic power" (pp. 248-249). Drucker's depiction of the knowledge society, echoing much of Bell, has interesting origins. For the purposes of our argument, Drucker makes a telling observation: the most important step towards the knowledge economy was Scientific Management as pioneered by F. W. Taylor, because Taylor recognized that "the key to producing more was to 'work smarter'", (Drucker, 1969, p. 254). Here we have, in nuce, the so-called "knowledge theory of value": "what counts is not raw muscle power, or energy, but information" (Bell, 1976, p. 127). From Taylor's Scientific Management to the projected post-industrial society of Bell and Drucker, the common thread is that of technocracy; the assertion of science and denial of interest. In order to understand the information society, we should situate it with that current of social thought that seeks to manage and administer life through the expertise of a planning elite.

(2)Taylorism as Social Philosophy and Political Strategy

As we have suggested, Taylorism had a claim to the status of a general social theory, and we have mentioned the manner in which its stress on science facilitated its transference beyond the factory. However, there are other dimensions to what Michael Burawoy—following Reinhard Bendix—has described as Taylorism as a social philosophy. With "its emphasis on compliance and obedience to management in the pursuit of common interest", it sought to "transcend immediate political institutions by mobilizing scientism in the projection of a utopian image of a harmonious society where politics becomes superfluous" (Burawoy, 1978, pp. 279-280). At the very heart of Taylor's social program is the emphasis upon *productivity*—productivity as the key to future prosperity, harmony, and progress. For Taylor, "the economy is not made by 'capitalism' or 'socialism'. It is made by productivity" (Drucker, 1969, p. 25). In the words of Bradley Rudin:

> Taylor and his followers sought a system that would maximise production by applying science to industry and insure social peace as well. Industrial efficiency would solve the problem of industrial discontent: first, with increased production through lowered per unit costs, employers would eliminate wages as an important grievance; and second, with the workers working harder (and more efficiently), their style of life would improve—they would become a positive asset to company and community . . . In theory, if not always in practice, scientific management answered the hopes of the earlier advocates of industrial betterment and welfare work: Taylorism created a system that promised abundance, morality, *and* social control (Rudin, 1972-73, p. 70).

Productivism as the royal road to progress is a familiar theme, and one cognate to that of technocracy. Increased production generates wealth; wealth creates the basis for social harmony. This syllogism expresses the aspirations of the ideology of progress that we discussed at the opening of this chapter. Taylorism, resulting in a "tremendous surge of affluence . . . which has lifted the working masses . . . well above any level recorded before" (Drucker, 1974, p. 181), seemed to provide "the way out of the impasse of the nineteenth century" by opening up "a 'third way' between nineteenth century capitalism and nineteenth century socialism" (Drucker, 1969, p. 255). It offered, not just a social philosophy, but also a political strategy that paradoxically removed any need for politics, one that sought to outmaneuver the demands of rising socialist and communist movements by satiating the workers with the fruits of the increased productivity that Scientific Management cultivated. What Taylorism offered, according to Charles Maier

> certainly within the plant, and ultimately, according to its author, in all spheres of government and social life—was the elimination of scarcity and constraint. It therefore implied a revolution in the nature of authority: the heralded utopian change from power over men to the administration of things. . . . Ostensibly Taylor's factory could become the nucleic building block of a post-bourgeois world, or at least a secure managerial one (Maier, 1970, p. 32).

In a moment, we shall look a little more closely at the wider social significance of Taylor's activities and ideas. But, first, we again point to the similarities between the social philosophy of Scientific Management and that of Daniel Bell and the proponents of a post-industrial information society. As with Taylor, productivity is for Bell the panacea for social ills and unrest because, thanks to technical and technological advance, "Economic life could be a non-zero-sum game; everyone could end up a winner, though with differential gains" (Bell, 1976, p. 274). Post-industrial society, heralded by I.T., promises a "steady increase of wealth and a rising standard of living by peaceful means" (p. 274). Again, productivity–progress–wealth–peace. The contemporary ideologies of the information society have their tap-roots in that philosophy of productivism and progress propounded by Frederick Winslow Taylor and the ideologues of Scientific Management. Everything begins with Taylor.

(3) Fordism

"Fordism is a stage that supersedes Taylorism," writes Michel Aglietta (1979, p. 116). And it is with the achievements of Henry Ford—"one of the most thorough practitioners of Scientific Management, though he had never heard Taylor's name" (Drucker, 1955, p. 252)—that we come to see the social, political, and economic significance of processes set afoot by Scientific Management. Fordism "further developed the mechanisation of labor, increased the intensity of work, radicalised the separation between manual and mental labor, rigorously subjected workers to the law of accumulation and turned scientific progress against them as a power serving the uniform expansion of value" (Aglietta, 1979, pp. 117-118). It intensified and deepened those new forms of control that Taylor had initiated, and it did this on the basis of technological innovation. The increased productivity of Ford's assembly line was indissociable from the increase in managerial control of the labor process and of workers' lives. And what was projected as (socially neutral) progress was in fact an expression of the prevailing relations of power.

Ford himself thought in terms of "the machine concept of industry" in which "the entirety [of the labor process] may be done by machinery and the man considered only as an attendant upon the machine" (Ford, 1926, p. 52). Mechanization here is the outcome of planning operations that have studied the labor process, appropriated and supplemented the knowledge and skills necessary to assure production, and incorporated these as far as possible into technologies. Within the Fordist factory, those processes of deskilling and "gathering in" of knowledge initiated by Taylor are subsumed within a strategy of technical control (see Edwards, 1979, pp. 111-129). Fordist principles entail "the reduction of the necessity for thought on the part of the worker":

> More brains are needed today than ever before, although they are perhaps not needed in the same place as they once were. . . . We have made it unnecessary for the highest types of mental ability to be engaged in every operation in the factory. The better brains are in the mental power-plant" (Ford, 1923, pp. 80, 280).

The new mass worker is divested of skill, the ideal Ford worker being a pair of hands severed from the brain. "Some of our tasks are exceedingly monotonous . . . but then, also, many minds are very monotonous—many men want to earn a living without thinking, and for these men a task which demands no brains is a boon" (Ford, 1926, p. 160). What we have in the new automatic machinery pioneered by Ford is "a transfer of thought, skill or intelligence from person to machine" (Reitell, 1924, p. 41), and one result is that the worker is reduced to an automaton.

In the Fordist factory, knowledge—both practical and scientific—is firmly in the hands of management, and the machinery of production stands as a testament to their success in rendering it instrumental. With this technological incorporation of knowledge/skill, Fordism fulfills the ambitions of Scientific Management and, in Benjamin Coriat's terms, establishes a new sequence in the relations of power within the factory.

If Fordism, in annexing skill and know-how, deepened the hold of management in the factory through technical control, it was important for more than that. What we suggest—again following the categories of Coriat—is that it represents the emergence of a new economic sequence (based on mass production), a social and cultural transformation (a transformation of the way of life), and important changes in the role of the state in capitalist society. It is, in other words, more than just a technical revolution in the organization of the factory. Fordism represents the extension and intensification of what, following Gaudemar, we have termed relative mobization and, as such, entails not only the technological mobilization of labor within the factory, but also a restructuring of the relation between factory and outside world and a recomposition of patterns of culture, leisure, consumption, and social space. With Fordism, capital becomes increasingly involved not just in the sphere of production, but in the sphere of consumption.

As a result of the new factory discipline, which derived from the assembly line and the assiduity of corporate planners, society as a whole underwent a profound transformation. Let us look at this process a litttle more closely by concentrating on two aspects of the Fordist "revolution".

(a) Consumer Capitalism. Perhaps the most obvious and insistent fact about the new regime of mass production is that it requires mass consumption. Unless there are markets, unless there are means to purchase the new commodities that are pouring off the assembly lines, the industrial achievements of Henry Ford amount to nothing. And Ford himself knew this. As a contemporary observer noted, "the one new and revolutionary idea of Ford seemed to be his discovery that he could not sell more cars than the public could buy, and hence he devoted himself and his business not merely to the manufacture and selling of motor cars but to the manufacture and distribution of buying power" (Filene, 1932, p. 43). Those who were most percipient in the business community were aware that "the masses cannot buy adequately unless they are provided with adequate buying power, and will not buy adequately unless they have adequate leisure in which to play the part

of consumers" (p. 88). As Ford put it in his own words: "An unemployed man is an out-of-work customer. He cannot buy. An underpaid man is a customer reduced in purchasing power. He cannot buy . . . The cure of business depression is through purchasing power, and the source of purchasing power is wages" (Ford, 1926, p. 151). As significant as the Fordist assembly line is "the new theory of wages", as embodied in the Five Dollar Day (Meyer, 1981). What Ford realized is that "higher wages and lower prices mean greater buying power—more customers": "one of the objects of industry is to create as well as to supply customers. And customers are created by finding out what people want, making it at a reasonable price, and then paying high enough wages in the making so that they can afford to pay" (Ford, 1926, p. 152). This "principle of an articulation between process of production and mode of consumption" (Aglietta, 1979, p. 117) is of the essence of Fordism.

This should not be interpreted straightforwardly as economic progress fuelled by technological innovation, for what the consumerist revolution, unleashed by Ford, did was to alter traditional social relations in such a way as to reduce the hitherto independence of people from reliance on the market. This process had been underway for some time, but it was given a particular impetus by Fordism, which "simultaneously undermin[ed] the occupational community's foundations and provid[ed] the economic and ideological infrastructure for privatisation and consumerism" (Alt, 1976, p. 56). With the advent of consumerism, where once there existed a relative independence, there came into being a dependence upon marketed commodities. Moreover, mass consumption and consumerism, as the concomitant of Fordism mass production, was offered as the justification and compensation for the degradation of labor in the factory. As the conditions of life were more effectively subsumed within market relations, so were market products revered as the object of desires, the satisfaction of needs, and the symbol of progress.

As mass production grew, it became vital to ensure that markets were waiting; it became crucial to ensure the dovetailing of patterns of consumption and of production. Needs, desires, tastes must be cultivated, and they must be shaped to suit the availability of commodities. The arbitrariness of the market—its unpredictability and inexactitude of procedure in production, distribution, and selling—could no longer be tolerated. It became necessary to ensure the rational planning, administration, and coordination of production and consumption from factory to customer.

Efficient consumption could not be assured if left to the customer's whims. For this reason, by the second decade of the 20th century procedures were developed to rationalize selling. The steady movement of clothing, cigarettes, processed foods, and suchlike required the creation of ways of reaching customers, cognizing their desires and wants, and responding to these by persuasion, and even by redesigning products to make them more, or newly, attractive. In short, modern marketing was established in the early years of the century as a complement to the new processes of production (Pope, 1983). A.P.Sloan of General Motors exemplifies aspects of this extension of control beyond the plant into the customer's home itself. It was he who, in the 1920s, introduced "new elements" into the automobile industry—installment selling, used car trade-ins, annual changes of model (Sloan, 1965, p. 150). "On the basis of GM's strategy for 'upgrading' the American automobile", writes Emma Rothschild, "US auto marketing became a worldwide model for the selling of expensive consumer goods, showing business how to create and nourish demand" (Rothschild, 1973, p. 40).

If one side of "Sloanism" was an attempt to regulate distribution and to intensify consumption, the other entailed making sure the consumer was known about and open to persuasion. Information was to be sought about income levels and spending patterns, and publicity was to be disseminated to promote the appeal and desirability of the product. At the forefront of such activities would be market research departments and advertising specialists charged with responsibility for orchestrating demand. With Sloanism, corporate capital began to extend its sphere of operation deep into the society; it sought to become knowledgeable about consumer needs and lifestyles, so that it could shape them to corporate ends.

The crucial early developments of Sloanism took place in the United States. Inevitably, the spread is uneven, so any periodization is rough-and-ready, but one can point to the years following the First and preceding the Second World War as revealing distinct signs of consumer capitalism's formation. Advertising, a major indicator and reinforcement of consumerism, had become significant to corporate operations by the second decade of the century and was firmly integrated before 1939, though it came into its own in the consumer boom of the 1950s.

It is difficult to isolate the significance of advertising, since it is part of a linked series of influences, but its stress on consumption as a way of life is well documented. Raymond Williams was surely right a generation ago to discern in the replacement of the word "customer" by "consumer" something of this change that large scale capitalist production had brought about, one which revealed that "while a large part of our economic activity is obviously devoted to supplying known needs, a considerable part of it goes to ensuring that we consume what industry finds it convenient to produce . . . it becomes increasingly obvious that society is not controlling its economic life, but it is in part controlled by it" (Williams, 1965, p. 323). In examining this radical change, Stuart and Elizabeth Ewen describe advertising's role in creating a "new way of seeing" among immigrants to America who, reared for the most part in dire poverty and originally unwilling to spend because of that experience, had to be persuaded that "continual waste and spending [was] . . . a social good, driven by a cycle of continual dissatisfaction" (Ewen and Ewen, 1982, pp. 72-73).

Whatever uncertainty we may have as to advertising's precise influence, we can be sure that a new outlook began to be developed, one with which advertising closely accorded in stressing a lifestyle of consumption in order to be personally attractive, desirable, and even a worthy citizen (Schudson, 1984). Perhaps more important, we can acknowledge that corporate capital had a distinct interest in cultivating this outlook through advertising especially, since its purpose was the stimulation of sales. No one has been able to quantitatively assess advertising's significance, but the centrality to the expansion of modern capitalism of this facet of planning, whereby "consumer wants are created by the process by which they are satisfied" (Galbraith, 1979, p. 247), is unmistakable.

(b) The Plan-State. The second aspect of Fordism to which we draw attention relates to the nature of the state. Throughout the century, the state has become increasingly involved, often reluctantly but inexorably, with economic and social affairs, such that today it is pervasive. Wherever one goes, one encounters its effects, in economic activity, in social security, fiscal measures, industrial relations, schooling, etc. Its precise role and the reasons for its development are complex and frequently ambiguous, since the state responds to numerous, often contentious, forces. As a product of capitalist society, it is to be expected that it will uphold capitalist principles, but because the state is a product of real history, often the history of liberal democracy, it is also the case that its relations with capital have often been uncomfortable (Crouch, 1979). One has but to think of the resistance of business to much collective provision (public housing, welfare services, etc.), legal measures to protect employees, and nationalization to appreciate this point. Undoubtedly the state, especially through the electoral process, representing, however imperfectly, the aspirations of diverse groups, has frequently acted contrary to the advice and interests of capital.

However, if we draw attention to its uneven record, we must emphasize that, originating and operating in a market society, the state has not been an "honest broker" between conflicting partners. A primary and persistent pressure has been the goal of achieving a healthy economy, and this has entailed managing, as effectively as possible, on terms set by a *capitalist* economy, and it is to this end that government policies on currency rates, taxation, labor relations, and research and development expenditures are overwhelmingly directed. This is neither to say that different policies may not be undertaken, nor that here and there they may not be followed through, but it is to insist that the pressures of restricting them to reasonable bounds beyond which "the confidence of the market" will be shattered have been such that only in most exceptional circumstances have they been broken.

The modern state—what Negri (1978) refers to as the "Plan-State", which is recognizably deeply involved with many major economic, political, and social issues and events—emerged in the era of Fordism, as the latter created conditions that required extensive coordination and planning. Organization is a key aspect of the Plan-State which came into being in large part as an answer to the needs of the Taylor-Ford system of production (Coriat, 1979). It was obliged to play a role in the organization and management of economic and social processes by developing industrial and fiscal policies to assist in the coordination and efficacy of production; to ensure the suitability and availability of labor; to help stimulate and direct demand; to facilitate competition between particular companies and protect strategic interests; to establish an infrastructure of transport, schooling, law, etc; and generally to orchestrate and make arrangements, nationally, and even internationally, to smooth corporate operations as they expanded their spheres of influence both within and often outside the country.

Eric Hobsbawm has noted that, impelled by depression, the inter-war years resulted in "an unprecedented era of state intervention in business, which was palatable only because it was so obviously in favour of business". Documenting this participation, he continues to observe that in this period Britain "turned from one of
the least into one of the most . . . controlled economies, and largely through direct
government action" (Hobsbawm, 1978, pp. 241–242). The experience was repeated
throughout capitalist societies and was never to be seriously reversed.

During the 1930s, J. M. Keynes' advocacy of a strong and systematically interventionist state to sustain capitalism displaced laissez-faire assumptions in becoming
a new economic orthodoxy. As it did so, it both suggests the substantive changes
that were taking place and allows Coriat with justice to describe the new condition
as the "Keynesian state". As he says, "Keynes . . . finished off the building started
by Taylor and Ford. After the theory and practice of the mass production workshop, the theory and practice of the type of state and regulation that corresponded
to it" (Coriat, 1979, p. 140). With a host of obligations falling to the state demanding coordination, action, and administration of various kinds, its planning functions, as Keynes insisted, expanded enormously. And what, in effect, this emergent
Plan–State did was to translate the factory planning of Taylor and Ford and the
market planning of Sloan to the society as a whole.

For many, this Plan-State reflects merely a rational solution to the problems and
pressures of advanced industrialism. It is this image that is present in the writing of
Daniel Bell and the theory of post-industrial society. Bell argues that "the methodological promise of the second half of the twentieth century is the management of
organized complexity: the complexity of theories with a large number of variables
and the complexity of large organizations and systems which involve the coordination of hundreds of thousands and even millions of persons" (Bell, 1979b, p. 166).
This development of what he calls "intellectual technology" is only possible on the
basis of innovations in computerized information systems since its goal is "neither
more nor less, to realize a social alchemist's dream: the dream of 'ordering' the
mass society" (Bell, 1976, p. 33). Thus, "the computer is a tool for managing the
mass society, since it is the mechanism that orders and processes the transactions
whose huge number has been mounting almost exponentially because of the increase in social interactions" (Bell, 1979b, p. 172). In short, for Bell the problems
of society result from its growing complexity, and information technology is the
panacea. I.T. is the foundation for rational management, administration, and
planning procedures which range "from direct controls and policing at one end
to 'simple' information coordination at the other' (Bell, 1979b, p. 202). What
Bell sees as novel, we see as the continuation of processes belonging to the
Taylor–Ford–Keynes attempts to consolidate and extend the hold of corporate
capital. And what he sees as neutral and rational, we see as planning guided by the
imperatives of a market economy.

If the Plan-State develops organizational forms to assist the working of corporate capitalism it also has a more explicitly disciplinary purpose. Indeed, containment is a second key and complementary characteristic which often adopts an or-

ganizational form (notably in legal institutions and statutes). A prerequisite of a prosperous economy is order and stability in social arrangements, and much of the state's energies have been channelled into achieving this. Measures have ranged from surveillance of political extremists by special branches of the police and occasional incarceration of malcontents, through "beer and sandwiches" in Downing Street to facilitate agreement between trade unionists and employers, to judicious acceptance of reform when consensus might otherwise have seemed imperiled. All have entailed an expansion of the state's size and role in everyday life.

The era of Taylor-Ford-Keynes is one in which social relations have been radically transformed. The new machinery and disciplines in the factories had as their counterpart new machinery and disciplines throughout the society. While Fordism is seen by many as a higher stage in the evolution of economic, technological, and, consequently, social forms, our assessment runs counter to this technicist and productivist way of seeing. For us, Fordism, originating in the second and third decades of the century, climaxing in the 1950s and 1960s, and vibrant until the 1970s, represents not technological progress and economic growth per se, but a further stage in the development of capitalist relations. Through the modalities of assembly-line technology and the division of labor, the meticulous plotting of sales campaigns that engender consumerism, and a plethora of state acts and agencies, society is above all else mobilized to allow the further accumulation of capital by increasingly concentrated and continuously expanding corporations. It is the questioning of this systematic and comprehensive mobilization of social relations that is outlawed as irrational, idealistic, Luddite.

The Crisis of Fordism

The Information Revolution through which we are living, it is generally agreed, marks a period of crisis and upheaval. In this epochal phase of transition from an industrial to a post-industrial civilization, there are bound to be problems, just as there were in the earlier evolution from agricultural to industrial society. Crisis, it is felt, is the necessary and inevitably *by-product* of technological progress; the symptoms of crisis are the growing pains of our historical evolution. The velocity and scale of the present technological revolution are bound to be disruptive, for "computers and other information machines are . . . pulling us towards a new information society faster than we can understand where we are going" (Dizard, 1982, p. 11). The revolution has its own logic and momentum, and it is for us to adjust ourselves to this temporary and transient period of crisis in the sure knowledge that it is part of some providential destiny. Here is a remarkable faith in the cunning of reason, in the rational course of history, in the certainty of progress. The Information Age will not be born without the pains of labor, but it *will* be born—and it will emerge as a better and higher form of civilization.

This faith in the post-industrial future of an information society is matched by the certainty that industrial society has fallen into a terminal condition. The existing system, it is argued, has reached the point of exhaustion and disintegration.

Tom Stonier, for example, notes a number of symptoms of the present sickness: "pollution, impending shortages of critical resources, over-population, nuclear annihilation and repression of personal liberties by increasingly centralized governments" (Stonier, 1980b, p. 1). He goes on to suggest, however, that the threat from these problems is now "declining under the impact of advances in science and technology" (ibid.); and, more specifically, he believes that "an expanding, advanced information network presses one country after another into increased democratisation" (p. 3). I.T. is, in fact, seen by such techno-enthusiasts as a palliative for the crisis of industrialism. And the imputed virtues of the post-industrial era—decentralization, individualism, democracy, freedom, affluence, peace, ecological awareness, affluence—are wishful antitheses to the flaws of industrialism. Thus, for Curran and Curnow, I.T. has "so much to contribute to the alleviation of problems facing the world today. Applied in these positive directions, it could help to solve the world's energy crisis; enhance its reserves of food and of raw materials; anticipate and prepare for natural disasters; deepen our sources of knowledge, and enhance our level of communication with one another" (Curnow and Curran, 1982, p. 117). The technological fix! The present society is recognized as "oppressive, dreary, ecologically precarious, war-prone, and psychologically repressive" (Toffler, 1980, p. 50), and the panacea is quite simply to be found in the new microelectronics technologies.

With the above perspective, our current crisis centers upon "the death of industrialism and the rise of a new civilization" (Toffler, 1980, p. 16). While we agree that we are living through a period of crisis, we suggest that its meaning is less grand than the apostles of post-industrialism claim. It represents, in fact, a historically more localized crisis, a slump in the capitalist economy, one that deeply implicates Fordist arrangements for production and consumption. It is news to no one that, in recent years, these have experienced considerable difficulties. There are the obvious scars of recession, mass unemployment, widespread business collapse, and heightened intercorporate rivalry. These have been compounded by problems of pollution and the depletion of natural resources. Around these have arisen challenges to the legitimacy of important facets of Fordism, vexing questions posed about corporate behavior and accountability, continued social inequalities, the quality of work patterns, and environmental spoilation.

In face of this, the search is on to find an escape. Resolutions in terms of massive unemployment, limitations on wage rates, heightened competition, restraints on labor organizations, and reductions in support for welfare services are familiar, but an even longer-term solution is sought in adoption of I.T. and celebration of the Information Revolution. Where Sir Clive Sinclair sees a new Periclean Athens in the spread of I.T., we see an attempt to restore the health of advanced capitalism and perhaps establish it in new forms. Characteristics and the potential of this new regime are the substance of Chapter 11. But the essence and closing iteration of this chapter is that we should nurture doubts and skepticism about the post-industrial mirage that we are promised. We might do well to remember the Luddites and the technological progress they resisted.

Chapter 11
Neo-Fordism and the Extension of Control

> There are some who still fondly imagine that knowledge, casting the clear
> light of awareness, inspires and contains goodness within itself
>
> Dora Russell. *The Religion of the Machine Age.*
> Routledge and Kegan Paul, 1983, p. 222.

In this final chapter, we turn our attention more directly to present circumstances, the upheavals they entail, and the involvement of I.T. within them. What
follows is an examination of some of the elements of transformation and continuity
that feature in the crisis that has engulfed the Western economics for over a decade,
and which has been the cause of concerted and vigorous attempts to restructure
economic and social relationships as a way out of the impasse. Our analysis draws
together much of the discussion in preceding sections of the book to argue that,
in the present period, changes are being instigated that consolidate, deepen, and
extend established relations and modes of control. Our earlier chapters have shown
that I.T. marks the application of Scientific Management in hitherto exempted
areas, the bolstering of corporate power nationally and internationally, a renewed
emphasis on market principles in the conduct of life, and the affirmation of consumerist ethics. These continuities in themselves bring significant changes in social
relations, but there are other dimensions of the present period that suggest more
novel shifts. We characterize the situation today neo-Fordist because, while it
announces some significant changes, it perpetuates and intensifies the social relations characteristic of Fordism set underway earlier this century. The purpose of
this chapter is to review the mix of continuity and change, to assess its meaning
and weigh its consequences.

Time and Space: The Restructuring of Social Relationships

We commence by looking at the more novel aspects of change in outlining ways
in which spatial and temporal dimensions of social life are being reorganized as
part of the restructuring process.

(1), Centralization/Decentralization

A common theme in the literature on I.T. is that "automation, and the digital computer, offer possibilities either of greater centralization, or of decentralization"
(Council for Science and Society, 1981, p. 64). And, generally, the prognostica-
tion is that the new technologies will favor decentralization. Back in the 1960s,
Marshall McLuhan was already preaching this gospel: "Obsession with the older
patterns of mechanical, one-way expansion from centers to margins is no longer
relevant to our electric world. Electricity does not centralize, but decentralizes"
(McLuhan, 1964, p. 45). Today this has become received wisdom, and there is a
widespread belief that "beyond a certain level of development and economic

power, a new kind of evolution will begin, and eventually the traditional (i.e., centralized) structures will evolve into a cellular kind of decentralized structure" (Voge, 1977, p. 18).

Daniel Bell argues that the new technologies offer "a genuine *possibility* of decentralization: decentralization of work, decentralization of industrial structures" (Bell, 1980a, p. 239). Further, "the revolution in communications allows for a large diversity of cultural expressions and the enhancement of different lifestyles", for a situation in which "individuals can create their own modes of communication and their own new communities" (Bell, 1979d, p. 40). This same point is fundamental to the Nora and Minc report. Here it is argued that telematics "allows the decentralization or even the autonomy of basic units. Better still, it facilitates this decentralization by providing peripheral or isolated units with data from which heretofore only huge centralized entities could benefit" (Nora and Minc, 1980, p. 5).

In the Nora report, the essays of Bell, and most futurism, centralization and decentralization are presented as conflicting and alternative tendencies (see pp. 77-81). However, what we want to argue is that this is not so, that in fact the decentralization presently under way is taking place within a wider centralized and integrated structure. In our view, what we are getting is decentralization designed by increasingly centralized corporate capital and state agencies, and that this is something which, without I.T. to allow coordination and observation from the center, would be unthinkable. We are not alone in this thought. Years ago, Peter Drucker put it thus:

> decentralization does not mean weakening central management. On the contrary, it is a means of strengthening the top management of the corporation by enabling it to concentrate on its own corporate tasks—to make the major entrepreneurial decisions, to set policy, to allocate capital, and to develop and place key personnel . . . decentralization will work only where the central corporate management has available adequate information and dependable knowledge regarding the company's businesses. Information and knowledge set the limits to decentralization (Drucker, 1972, p. 299).

We return to the question of centralization and power later, but for the moment we want to examine two areas of social life in which the tendencies towards decentralization will be most felt: the domestic sphere and the workplace.

(a) "Fortress Britain": The Privatization of Social Life. In *The Third Wave*, futurologist Alvin Toffler argues that we are

> undergoing a fundamental decentralization of communications, as the power of the central network waves. We are seeing a stunning proliferation of cable, cassette, computers, and private electronic mail systems, all pushing in the same decentralist direction (Toffler, 1980, p. 44).

The suggestion is that the new "demassified" media (cable, CB, video, videotex) are displacing the patterns of centralization, synchronization, and standardization that characterized *mass* media. Thus, "like short-run printing presses or Xerox copiers, cable de-massifies the audience, carving it into multiple mini-publics" (p. 173). In using these new media,

> people are learning to play with the television set, to talk back to it, and to interact with it. In the process they are changing from passive receivers to message senders as well. They are manipulating the set rather than merely letting the set manipulate them (pp. 174–175).

The emphasis is upon diversity, plurality, and creativity:

> today, instead of masses of people all receiving the same message, smaller de-massified groups receive and send large amounts of their own imagery to one another (p. 176).

As another commentator suggests, the new interactive media

> have powerful decentralizing effects, effects that may spread far beyond the entertainment "small worlds" to the various real worlds. Modern mass media are often deplored for the negative effects of massive centralization. These new media will reverse this tendency, as they encourage personalization and small scale interaction in powerful ways (Levin, 1982, p. 146).

Examples of this outlook could be multiplied *ad nauseam*. Characteristically, they celebrate a new era of pluralism and flexibility and assume that the expansion of communications and information resources will promote social harmony and understanding. As Dizard has it, "in these areas, more is better; they seem to be immune to many of our usual doubts about the benefits of technology . . . noone has argued for fewer computers, telephones, or newspapers, or more restrictions on the rest of the apparatus of the information environment"(Dizard, 1982, p. 84).

In our view, the decentralizing trend about which Toffler and others enthuse represents, not a transformation, but rather the confirmation and perpetuation of tendencies already apparent in communications systems which we described in chapter 9. Thus, cable services extend and intensify the *commercialization* of leisure activities, and even subsume new spheres of life into the marketplace. They can provide access to more information (but they chiefly present entertainment), but only under market conditions: "every person his own data collector and publisher, unmediated by any authority, public or private, as long as he pays the telephone/computer service bill at the end of the month" (Dizard, 1982, p. 8).

This commercialization also entails an increasing *privatization* of social life. The fulfilment of needs and desires through social intercourse gives way to individualized consumption of commodities. The electronic grid promises to intensify the tendencies that are already apparant not just in mass media, but also in social life more widely. The prospect is of individual consumers living in isolation, strung together only by a network which offers to personalize accounts, tied by what Gorz evocatively terms the "glue of serial impotence". This is the vision depicted by *Campaign* as "Fortress Britain", the retreat into the home and the pulling up of the drawbridge on the outside world (*Campaign*, September 2, 1983).

Thereby public life and public space are eroded; "electronic communications is one means by which the very idea of public life has been put to an end. The media have . . . rendered actual contact unnecessary" (Sennett, 1978, p. 282).

Historically, there has been a tendency for communications media (particularly radio and television) to provide an increasing number of previously discrete services to the home (music, sport, news, entertainment). Domestic cable systems extend and deepen this tendency, making the television console the channel through which ever more functions take place in the household. The culmination of these developments is the conception of the "electronic household of the future" (see Tydeman, 1982), in which the home is the locus not only of information and entertainment services, but also of educational, purchasing, banking, and work activities.

Perhaps most importantly, the possibility of decentralizing these activities and functions is dependent upon the elaboration of a national, integrated communications network under the aegis of highly centralized organizations arranging entertainment, finance, and even schooling. And as social relations and functions become more and more mediated through the electronic grid, so they will become constrained by the logic and parameters, the goals and interests, which the designers of this "giant machine" will impose on users. Paradoxically, therefore, the tendency towards decentralization expresses itself, not in the autonomy of individuals, but in the increasing arrangement of social life by centralized systems. The portents are clear in the oligopolies which dominate present media, banking and retail businesses, and will be supreme in any foreseeable wired society.

(b) Productive Decentralization. It is already apparent from the above discussion that the decentralization of communications facilitates the "de-massification" not only of leisure and entertainment, but also of work and production. The concentrated mass production characteristic of Fordism, it is suggested, is giving way to decentralized and convivial modes (Thompson, 1979). Spurred on by this insight, more far-sighted entrepreneurs are promoting the idea of decentralizing industrial and organizational structures. Sir Adrian Cadbury, for one, has suggested that large, centralized structures must give way to "federations of small enterprises". Each of these smaller units, he maintains, would "only retain under its direct control those activities which are essential for the continued survival of the enterprise", bringing in services like design, computing, or security from outside suppliers. Many of these would be self-employed: "computer programmers and systems analysts for example could work from home under contract, rather than being directly employed in large offices and so decide for themselves when and for how long they will work" (*Guardian*, 9 December, 1982).

Norman Macrae of the *Economist* has argued in similar fashion that we are approaching "the end of the era of big business corporations". And, like Cadbury, he suggests that the alternative lies in contracting work out to small, satellite organizations and entrepreneurs. "A big productive and libertarian advantage of this individualization of contracts", he stresses, "is that it will surreptitiously but dramatically erode the power of the trade unions" (Macrae, 1976, p. 42).

This school of thought believes that I.T. networks could promote the decentralization of industrial and occupational structures, and encourage the burgeoning of new cottage industries providing computing and communications services. While such tendencies do represent one facet of current retructuring, they are in reality a good deal less benign and convivial than Cadbury and Macrae infer. As we have seen in chapters 5 and 7, the purpose of this commercial interest in I.T. is not to enhance the quality of life, nor is it to foster localized autonomy. For Cadbury, there is nothing intrinsically worthwhile about small-scale structures: decentralization will occur "not because 'small is beautiful', but because big is expensive and inflexible" (*Guardian,* 9 December, 1982). The same point is made by Nora and Minc; the decentralizing trend is reactive and seeks primarily to overcome problems inherent in managing large and concentrated enterprises. The overriding objective is to elaborate organizational forms that will both cut costs and reassert control over the labor force, thereby contributing to profitability.

A version of this kind of restructuring by decentralization—and one suggestive of its real implications—has already emerged in Italy. Philip Mattera has described a tendency towards "productive decentralization" in which aspects of the labor process are transferred from huge factories to small plants and even the household (Mattera, 1980; cf., Murray, 1983; Sabel, 1982, ch. 5). This process has stimulated and fed off a growth in the hidden, black, and informal, economies:

> Decentralization, in bringing about a proliferation of *lavoro nero* ("black" or precarious labor), has thereby reintroduced labor conditions reminiscent of nineteenth century Britain: working days of 16 hours, abysmal wages often on a piecemeal basis, an extremely intense pace of production, very dangerous and unhealthy working environments, and the absence of benefits and job security—in short, "managerial prerogative" run wild (Mattera, 1980, p. 68).

Mattera argues that these small, disseminated, units of production remain subordinate to large corporation: "rather than constituting a flowering of entrepreneurship, they are external departments of the big plants, or, to use the Italian term, a diffused factory" (p. 72). For private capital, the advantage of these fragmented sites is that they provide a cheaper, disorganized, and flexible labor force.

This process of productive decentralization operates not just at a regional or national level, but entails the dispersal of production on an international scale (see pp. 109-115) from metropolitan countries to areas like South-East Asia—what Lipietz refers to as a strategy of "bloody Taylorization" in the peripheral economies (Lipietz, 1982).

The possibility of decentralized or dispersed production derives from the fact that the activities of any large enterprise are constituted from a number of small and interdependent labor processes. The realization of this possibility is dependent on the organization's ability and capacity to coordinate remote sites and labor processes. Of fundamental importance for such coordination and administration are communications and information processing technologies. And it is for this reason that transnational corporations are so intent upon establishing an integrated information/communications infrastructure (D. Schiller, 1982a). As Herbert Schiller has said, "increased linkages, broadened flows of information and data, and above all, installation of new communication technology, are expected to serve nicely the world business system's requirements" (H. I. Schiller, 1981, p. 16).

The new technolgies permit large corporations to de-massify unwieldy concentrations and to manage and administrate decentralized units. According to one approving commentator, "decentralized activities can be coordinated as if they were centralized" (Keen, 1981, p. 141):

> The multinational can use its communications network to coordinate the activities of decentralized units. It may even choose to *increase* the autonomy of the affiliates because it can monitor their activities and respond to changing situations faster than before. Daily reporting of a few key figures can replace the more detailed monthly feedback. The organization can have responsiveness *and* control. Is this an increase in centralization or decentralization? The dichotomy becomes meaningless (p. 149).

Thus, an I.T. infrastructure can help overcome spatial constraints on organizations, such that it becomes possible to orchestrate widely disseminated sites of production *as if* they were centralized—flexibility is gained without loss of control. And these sites may equally be those of cheap, shadow work in the submerged or hidden economy, or those of high technology, skilled labor in electronic cottage industries.

The point is that these contrasting scenarios—systems analysts in the electronic cottage, sweated labor in Malaysia—are far from incompatible and may indeed be perfectly harmonious. For decentralization is not the fruit of technological development, but rather a strategic decision by corporate capital to overcome the disadvantages of large industrial and organizational structures that are geographically restricted. Kenneth Baker recently spelled out one of these disadvantages: "huge places of work, where the individual is swamped, are de-humanising and it is not surprising that they become the breeding ground of militant aggravation" (Baker, 1982). *Fortune* magazine reports a solution to Baker's problem:

> The expanded use of electronic "workers" has coincided with a move to smaller plants. The typical large manufacturing company today has many plants . . . vast centralized factories like Ford's huge plant near River Rouge, which had 60,000 workers in the late 1950s, are now virtually extinct. . . . Smaller plants have helped shift the balance of power toward management. As the size of plant shrinks, it becomes easier for local managers to stay in touch with their workers and to forestall situations that might lead to union activity (*Fortune*, Nov. 2, 1981, pp. 67–68).

And other difficulties of "vast centralized factories" can also be tacked—labor costs, currency fluctuations, material supplies, political opposition—from a position of power thanks to I.T.

An integrated I.T. infrastructure bestows flexibility without the loss of control to corporations which nowadays dominate the domestic and international economy. With this prerequisite their options are increased: they can choose to employ highly skilled personnel on individual contracts for specialist functions; they may use less skilled employees, fewer in number than required by traditional factory productions thanks to advanced machinery, who are isolated from other workers about whom they know little and about the company's international operations even less; or they may decide to invest in the cooperative and cheap workforces of approved Third World countries. Or they may choose to combine these options. "Information and knowledge set the limits to decentralization" (Drucker, 1972, p. 299): I.T. radically extends those limits.

(2) Labor, Leisure, and Time

Having dealt at some length with ways in which I.T. facilitates the restructuring of spatial relations and potentially eradicates geographical constraints, we want now to argue that it is not only space, but also time, that is being more colonized and structured by corporate capital. As Foucault suggests in another context, "power is articulated directly onto time; it assures its control and guarantees its use" (Foucault, 1979, p. 160). What we are concerned with here is the way in which the new technologies have begun to change the relation between labor-time and leisure-time. Since we have already discussed aspects of this issue in chapters 6 and 9, we deal with it fairly briefly here.

The main objective of the microelectronics revolution is to save employers money by reducing the need for workers' time. I.T. increases productivity, which translates, as one of its consequences, into the need for fewer workers. Now this saving of employees' time has been interpreted by some as the liberation of time and the commencement of a leisure age. We have seen that advanced capitalist societies are not going to evolve effortlessly into leisure utopias, but, in face of the popularity of "more-time-for-leisure-thanks-to-I.T." scenarios, we might usefully recall something of what leisure-time has meant in the historical development of capitalism.

As we suggested in chapter 10, the rise of industrial capitalism resulted in the uprooting of people from the relative independence and self-sufficiency that they had once achieved. Transported, as wage laborers, to the large industrial cities, they became increasingly dependent upon the wage which would be used in the market to purchase most requirements. As Elizabeth and Stuart Ewen argue:

> the home had ceased production; the factory had taken its place. People now purchased what they had once produced for themselves. Production and consumption had become distinct activities, a fundamental rearrangement in the way people apprehended their material world (Ewen and Ewen, 1982, p. 58).

In this way, not just their conditions of labor, but also their conditions of living, came under the influence of the market.

With the advent of Fordism, the period characterized by mass production and mass consumption, this process reached, as it were, self-consciousness. It did so because it became apparent that corporations would need to concern themselves, not only with internal factory relations, but also with the satisfactory marketing of products. In other words, in the era of Fordism it became increasingly obvious that efficient production was worthless without efficient consumption, and therefore "capital not only had to take hold of labor power in order to extract surplus value from it, but it also had to take hold of the sphere of reproduction to make it function on the basis of means of subsistence produced by capitalist industry" (Granov, 1974, p. 68). At this point, time—how time was used and spent—both at work *and* in leisure, became of enormous import to the modern manager.

Paradoxically, within the period of capitalist development to which Ford lends his name, people's time became more formally divided between that devoted to work and the remaining time—free time or leisure. Much of this was due to struggles for a shorter working day, but Ford himself shared the premise of sharply dividing work and place: "When we are at work we ought to be at work. There is no use trying to mix the two. The sole object ought to be to get the work done and to get paid for it. When the work is done, then the play can come, but not before" (Ford, 1923, p. 92).

However, if it is the case that work and leisure times have become discrete and separate, it is also the case that capital has sought to develop some control over leisure, since "play" has consequences for corporate viability as an increasingly important outlet for mass produced goods. Consumption needed to be regulated so as to stabilize manufacture, and to this extent it is a requirement of modern economy to try to influence how people arrange their free time. In this way, Fordism at once sharply divides work and leisure and rigorously controls time alloted to the former, where it has most power, and simultaneously strives to influence the apportionment of free time to the advantage of company sales. This is in no way to equate work and leisure time, nor to suggest that attempts to influence leisure time are anything like as effective as those applied at work. But it is to argue that a feature of Fordism is to appeal to the consumer to use free time in ways that benefit the corporation; to make the evening time to relax with a certain drink, time to watch a movie, time to go for a drive, time to redecorate the lounge.

But what of neo-Fordism and the "leisure revolution"? What is occurring now in the sphere of leisure and in the use of time? Our belief is that we shall experience the continuation of attempts to subject leisure to time-discipline, to urge people to consume more goods and services outside of their work. The proviso will be that they should be able to afford to pay the necessary premiums, something which will disenfranchise the unemployed, who suffer "enforced leisure". But for the majority there will be intensified efforts to arrange how they spend their leisure in the electronic home.

There is, however, a significant transformation emerging that does represent a notable development from the Fordist era. Chantal de Gournay suggests that "it seems doubtful whether the functional division between the sphere of production and that of reproduction will continue in its current kind and form, in view of the advent of the information society and the new communications systems. The work/home spatial ratio is bound to change" (Gournay, 1982, p. 294). We would say the same of the temporal ratio.

A virtue of the new technologies lies in their capacity to transcent some of the limitations of Fordist time-discipline. For, under Fordism, with its rigid division of the day into work time and leisure, there developed a constraining inflexibility in the use of time both in and outside work. However, with the proposed combination of work, leisure, and consumption in the future "electronic cottage", the rigid distinction between work time and free time may begin to be eroded. Domestic cable networks can facilitate the restructuring of time use on a more flexible and individual basis; they can provide the technological means to break the times of working, consuming, and recreation into pellets of any duration, which may then be arranged and rearranged in complex, individualized configurations and shifted to any part of the day or night. We already have indications of this in the experience of the new homeworkers who are connected to the office by communications terminals. Here we have "more flexible working arrangements . . . the ability to change the structure of the working day from a basically rigid routine to an individualized partitioning of time". Such "segmentation of the working day" provides the "ability to combine work and non-work activities" (Gordon, 1976, pp. 69, 70, 74). Interestingly, this flexibility comes to the group whose work is most amenable to performance from home and who are the major determiners of leisure activities—women.

The "Information Revolution" as Social Taylorism

The new technology, it has been asserted, "is rapidly assuming huge burdens of drudgery from the human brain and thereby expanding the mind's capacities in ways that man has only begun to grasp" (*Time*, February 20, 1978). Another commentator believes that "in this brave, new world around the corner, ordinary people will have access to information and powers to organize it that are just about beyond imagination now" (Stevenson, 1981, p. 507). Examples could be multiplied endlessly. This is the new mythology of the information utopia, that I.T. can be a panacea for our social ills. In our view, the adoption of I.T. is not the novelty that it is made out to be: as we suggested in Chapter 10, Taylor himself developed an economics of information and inaugurated his own "information revolution" within the factory. What we shall be discussing in the following pages is the way in which corporate capital's need and desire to control knowledge/information is extending beyond the factory to the society as a whole, thereby developing a generalized or social Taylorism. And, in our view, the so-called information explosion will not be experienced as benign, still less as liberatory. Our analysis so far suggests that the

> enormously increased quantity of knowledge does not give us greater autonomy, independence, freedom or capacity for solving the problems we meet.

On the contrary, our expanded knowledge is of no use if we want to take our collective and individual lives into our hands. The type of knowledge we hold is of no help to us in controlling and managing for ourselves the life of our community, city, region, or even household.

The expansion of knowledge rather has gone in parallel with a diminution of the power and autonomy of communities and individuals. In this respect, we may speak of the schizophrenic character of our culture: the more we learn, the more we become helpless . . . This knowledge we are fed is so broken up as to keep us in check and under control rather than to enable us to exercise control (Gorz, 1976, pp. 63–64).

(1) The Information Commodity

Back in the 1960s, an article in *Fortune* referred to knowledge as "the biggest growth industry of them all", suggesting that "the production and distribution of knowledge is a major occupation of the technically advanced nations, and may approach half the total US output by 1985" (Burck, 1964, p. 128). Now, in 1985, information or knowledge is indeed becoming central to Western economies as a means by which they all hope to escape the present recession. The information revolution has little to do with making information into a generally available resource; it has everything to do with turning it into a profitable industry. In the words of a recent British government report, the information revolution is about "making a business of information" (ITAP, 1983). And what we are witnessing, as Chapter 7 documented, at the forefront of developments, is the emergence of a new multinational industry, the creation of a vast and overlapping information business, which insists on treating its product as a commodity.

In this discussion of the commodification of information/knowledge, we want to emphasis the deregulation and privatization of the information sector that is being promoted by both the British and American governments. What this amounts to is an undermining of the status of knowledge as a "social good", an assault on the public sphere (cf. Schiller, 1984, Ch. 3). Habermas has described the public sphere thus:

> By "the public sphere" we mean first of all a realm of our social life in which something approaching public opinion can be formed. Access is guaranteed to all citizens. A portion of the public sphere comes into being in every conversation in which private individuals assemble to form a public body. . . . Citizens behave as a public body when they confer in an unrestricted fashion —that is, with the guarantee of freedom of assembly and association and the freedom to express and publish their opinions—about matters of general interest. In a large public body this kind of communication requires specific means of transmitting information and influencing those who receive it. Today newspapers and magazines, radio and television are the media of the public sphere (Habermas, 1974, p. 49).

This represents an ideal, an aspiration, and has never actually existed in its pure and pristine form. Habermas makes clear, for example, that commerce has generally worked to undermine the public sphere since when market forces enter the arena "the difference between commodity circulation and public intercourse is removed" (Habermas, 1962, p. 217). This process has roots in the commercialization of publishing and communications within capitalist societies, but it is reaching a new stage with the information revolution. The current wave of commercialization and privatization of those information and communications media that support what remains of the public sphere threatens to subvert the possibility of informed public reasoning and exchange of ideas. It offers the prospect of communication giving way to more individualized consumption (see Métayer, 1980) on an ability to pay basis.

Let us look at what challenges there are at present to the viability of a public sphere. As we argued in Chapter 9, in Britain we are seeing what may be the end of the tradition of public service broadcasting as embodied in the BBC. The development of video, cable, and satellite services threatens to steal audiences away from the existing quasi-monopoly system. It then becomes the case that diminished audiences make it difficult to justify the licence fee which finances the BBC. Especially pertinent to the present argument is the probability that many new services will be specialized and localized; the danger then is that there will be no national forum in which significant issues can be aired to the population as a whole. We would not offer an uncritical defense of British public service broadcasting, but we feel it is important to redeem what public space we have from being overtaken by market forces. A recent report from the Adam Smith Institute (1984), which suggests the privatization of the BBC, may as yet only be testing the public mood, but it would seem that such an idea does have ministerial support (*Guardian*, June 5, 1984). There is a strong lobby that seeks to give rein to market forces and to turn the public into the consumer. "Unlimited channels and competition", it is argued, "ensure that all groups with intense preferences are catered for *provided* their willingness to pay is sufficient to make it profitable to produce and distribute a programme" (Veljanovski and Bishop, 1983, p.62). This is the logic of the market in full voice, a logic that puts special interests, ability to pay, maximum consumption, and, over-ridingly, profits above all else.

But this commercial logic applies not just to public service broadcasting (Golding and Murdock, 1983). The public service status of the telecommunications industry is also under extreme threat. The aim of the recent liberalization and privatization of British Telecom is to turn it into a more sales-oriented concern, able to compete effectively on the international market (hence its mooted alliance with IBM in 1984). As it becomes increasingly apparent that BT's activities are central to the formation of an integrated I.T. network within and beyond the nation, the Thatcher government is determined that the benefits will go to business and, though it hopes the small investor will participate, experience of earlier privatization and the news that the likes of Racal and GEC are considering buying into BT suggest that the beneficiaries will be disproportionately large-scale capital. Recent innovations (the Merlin office automation range, the Satstream network), along with the activities of BT's new private sector rival

(Mercury) set up to service business customers, indicate the demise of a service to the whole country and the growth of a new, mercenary, orientation towards the corporate sector. As the Greater London Council leader has argued, "the liberalization and privatization of BT is not a move towards people's real needs, but a radical turn towards destroying the idea of public service and entrenching the power of money over people" (Livingstone, 1983, p. 3).

These are the most prominent examples, but there are other, less immediately spectacular, examples of the privatization of social knowledge/information services. In Britain, there is the hiving off of government information services to private organizations whenever possible, and the progressive privatization of government computer operations. Already the contract to disseminate statistics in computer readable form has been awarded, and there are plans to allocate part of the work of Companies House to commercial groups. Such developments threaten to bring social data and statistics into the private sphere, where they are subject to commercial imperatives (cf. Cronin and Martyn, 1984). This policy is made quite explicit by the recent Rayner Committee, which argued that "there is no more reason for Government to act as universal provider in the statistical field than any other". It goes on to argue that "information should not be collected primarily for publication. It should be collected primarily because government needs it for its own business. Information of value to business should be made available with a timeliness which maximises its value and should be charged for commercially . . . the costs of providing such facilities should be covered by appropriate charges to the individuals or bodies concerned" (Government Statistical Services, 1981, pp. 14-15).

Pressures on public libraries, one of Britain's major institutions making freely available public information, stem from a similar logic. Expenditure cuts of 20% in real terms between 1979 and 1982 (National Book Committee, 1983) have led to reductions in availability of books, magazines, and newspapers. And the minister responsible, when approached, cavalierly asks "librarians [to] look beyond their traditional sources of funds and [to] consider whether some costs may be recovered from users" (*Guardian,* 4 February, 1984). This marks an end to the traditional concept of public libraries in the U.K. and impels the introduction of charges for loans of records and tapes, for book requests, online searches, and the like (see A. R. Schiller, 1981). Much the same story is repeated at the government Stationary Office. Instructed to operate commercially, in 1983 it posted record profits—at the cost of raising prices such that reports and tables are prohibitive.

These are signs of a severe diminishment in the social availability of information. And there is no technological imperative in these cases: it is a political decision by government to shift the basis on which information is made available, one which restricts the flow of information in society, and thereby impedes social discourse and the critique of political management. As a past president of the Royal Statistical Society, Sir Claus Moser, has said: "The different user communities not only have a right to information collected and provided from public funds; it is in any case an essential part of a democratic society and of open government that available information should be widely circulated and, one hopes, used" (Moser, 1980, p. 4). The government would seem determined to restrict the range of user communities to those who can afford to pay for their data. And, in so doing, it knocks yet another nail in the coffin of the public sphere.

(2) The Scientific Management of Society
In the previous chapter, we argued that Frederick Taylor's industrial innovations, particularly as they were taken up in the development of Fordism, required managerial control, not just within the plant, but, increasingly, beyond the factory walls. We might develop this idea by reference to the work of business historian A. D. Chandler, who shows that, between the 1840s and 1920s, important parts of the American economy changed from being controlled by market forces (Adam Smith's "invisible hand") to control by the "visible hand" of managerial capitalism". Chandler's thesis is that, during these years in America, mass production and mass distribution merged as corporations grew and proceeded to vertically integrate. As road and rail communications developed inside the United States, it became possible for producers of goods to expand production and to take over responsibility for market distribution of their goods, something which had two related consequences: first, production and distribution were "internalized" within a single enterprise, and thus the "visible hand" of managerial direction had replaced the invisible hand of market forces in coordinating the flow of goods from the suppliers of raw and semifinished materials to the retailer and ultimate consumer (Chandler, 1977, pp. 285-286); second, this process stimulated the growth of modern management, whose responsibility was to coordinate, assess, and oversee the process of manufacture and distribution. The development of the "visible hand" signifies an important stage in the spread of more systematic control in society. The modern corporation reduced the arbitrariness of the market, the unpredictability and inexactitude of procedure in production and distribution, and replaced it with managerial planning, with calculation of the best means of harmonizing factory, warehouse, and transport from a central domain.

To understand the Western societies and the role of I.T. within them, it is of paramount importance to appreciate the changed features of corporate capitalism. Processes Chandler draws attention to have been encouraged by the rapid and unrelenting increase in size of corporations, their concentration into oligopolies, and geographical extension from metropolitan centers throughout the world. Today it is the case that, in line with trends we mapped in Chapter 7, advanced capitalist economies are dominated by large, generally transnational corporations (Scott, 1979). The accompaniment of this rise to prominence has been the continuation of processes of vertical, and often horizontal, integration detailed by Chandler for an earlier period. And the requisite of this systematization, planning, rationalization, call it what you will, of corporate activities has been the further emergence of "managerial capitalism", the development of "knowledge workers" whose role is to serve the interests of the large modern corporation in supervising manufacturing, coordinating distribution of produce, organizing marketing, and planning company strategy.

As with the control of the individual plant, the *sine qua non* of the managerial attempt to coordinate the cycle of production, distribution, and consumption is the appropriation and deployment of information resources. And it is here that I.T. plays a crucial role. As we have said in our discussion of productive decentralization, an integrated information network allows large corporations to orchestrate decentralized productive and administrative units *as if* they were centralized. Corporate capital is able to combine increased flexibility with greater control over the uncertainties of the environments and markets within which they operate.

Back in the 1940s, F. A. Hayek thought that the crucial problem for business was "the utilization of knowledge not given to anyone in the totality": "Knowledge of the circumstances of which we must make use never exists in concentrated or integrated form, but solely as the dispered bits of incomplete and frequently contradictory knowledge which all the separate individuals possess" (Hayek, 1945, pp. 519-520). The economic problem was that of coordinating and utilizing this knowledge. Individuals in various locations, for example, possess "knowledge of the particular circumstances of time and place" and "the method by which such knowledge can be made as widely available as possible is precisely the problem to which we have to find an answer" (pp. 521-522). There is a need for "a process by which knowledge is constantly communicated and acquired" (p. 530). Hayek was not anticipating the role of information technologies, yet they serve precisely those information needs that he was identifying. Through the new technologies, corporations, especially those that are transnationals, can coordinate information about natural resources, financial markets, technological innovation, labor markets, political conditions, and so on. This is the reason why, in recent years, we have seen a boom in "information factories" such as Reuters, TRW, and Dun and Bradstreet, and the expansion of electronic information services by leading I.T. concerns. The products of these companies are much needed by modern corporations: Datastream's 5,000 economic indicators on the Western economies, Reuter's coverage of almost 80 countries, Telerate's up-to-the-minute records of money markets are information put at a premium by today's "managerial capitalism". And while "information factories" expand to support the international market, all significant corporations take aboard I.T. systems to enable their managers to work effectively.

It is through the new information and communication systems that dispersed production can be more effectively organized. Westinghouse Corporation is precise in reporting that, in 1981,

an integrated worldwide strategic planning process was put in place, linking product and country planning efforts. A global communications center is being established to provide timely and detailed information for every part of the world. This centralization of planning and intelligence will give Westinghouse a competitive edge in the worldwide deployment of its resources (Westinghouse. *Annual Report,* 1982).

Burt Nanus has observed more generally that "the risk, complexity, and competitiveness of multinational business require that no opportunities for improvement in control and decision making be overlooked":

> In addition to coordination, rapid and effective information flows can assist decentralized local units to compete more effectively and to take advantage of the scarce managerial talents available to them. Multinational computer systems also permit the corporation to increase its maneuverability in negotiations with government, labor, suppliers, and customers, and to react quickly to uncontrollable shifts in the environment. All these opportunities—better coordination and control, improved management decision-making, more effective use of managerial resources and increased flexibility—act in concert to increase the attractiveness to MNCs of large-scale, multinational information systems (Nanus, 1978, p. 20).

As one representative from Texas Instruments has said about their own information systems: "Global production planning, manufacturing automation and control, and tracking material in transit between sites are now realities" (Craig, 1981, p. 203). When Hayek decided that the problem of information management could not be solved "by first communicating all this knowledge to a central board, which, after integrating *all* knowledge, issues its orders", but only through "some form of decentralization" (Hayek, 1945, p. 524), he could not have known how I.T. would come to successfully combine both centralizing and decentralizing tendencies.

However, corporate capital needs not only to ensure the effective coordination of production and distribution. As we have already suggested, it tries also to ensure efficient consumption of the commodities it pours out. In Chapter 10, we discussed the link between Taylorism/Fordism and the rise of consumer capitalism, and now we want to discuss this further by considering how new technologies help to promote the "scientific management" of consumption.

Much ado is made about the free flow of information for promoting greater communication, understanding, and social harmony. But cursory examination of the new communications media will reveal that, under present conditions, their primary function is not to communicate but to sell. The information revolution is largely about promoting the image of capitalist enterprises and stimulating the consumption of its products. From their early days the media of radio and television particularly have served—with the significant exception of public service broadcasting—the needs of corporate capitalism, helping to control markets by both advertising goods and services and by extolling the virtues of the market. These media have helped to bring the messages of the market into our homes and subjectivities, selling us consumer capitalism as a way of life (Barnouw, 1968, 1970).

Now, with the greater range and versatility of the new media (video, cable, satellite television, videotex) this massage of needs and desires is being rendered more sophisticated. Far-sighted managements are turning to the new electronic media to promote their cause, to burrow themselves deeper into the texture of society. Through cable and satellite television especially, they aim to circumvent the limitations of public service broadcasting and to turn the screen into a 24 hour billboard. According to the J. Walter Thompson Company, cable television offers "new or improved advertising opportunities" (Syfret, 1983, p. 30): for example, test marketing, direct response advertising, placing of advertising within specialist channels, home shopping services, "informercials", sponsored programming. What the new media allow is more advertising, more specific and targeted advertising to particular social groups, and also the prospect of global advertising.

As an important example of this strategy to control minds, appetites, needs, and fantasies, let us refer to the activities of Britain's, and one of the world's, leading advertising agency, Saatchi and Saatchi. The business of Saatchi and Saatchi is to develop and perfect the techniques of selling required by contemporary capitalism. The company conducts thorough and systematic research before undertaking a "campaign" (military metaphors pepper its "review of operations"): it "is continually examining the results of research to bring us closer to the heart of what makes consumers tick—their wants, needs, desires, aspirations" (Saatchi and Saatchi Compton Worldwide, 1983, p. 6). But Saatchi and Saatchi has come to recognize a new "need for pan-regional and world marketing" (p. 14), and therefore has resolved not only that people should be "probed deeply", but also that "research will be conducted to look for market similarities between countries". This world marketing will require advertisers to find a formula for commercials "so deep in its appeal that it can transcend national borders previously thought inviolate" (p. 10). What will be required is "analysis of all [the] demographic, cultural and media trends" so as to allow "manufacturers to define market expansion timetables . . . [to track] trends which indicate when a region is ready for attack" (p. 13). "Armed with this information", the company continues, "the most modern marketers are achieving a new perspective on world markets. From the high ground, they can survey the world battlefields for their brands, observe the deployment of their forces, and plan their international advertising and marketing in a coherent and logical way" (p. 17).

If the new media allow such global advertising, they also facilitate more localized and specific targeting: " 'Media fragmentation' has become a byword for commentators describing the new structure of the media world. This will intensify the rifle rather than the shot-gun approach to planning advertising campaigns. Advertisers will face difficult dilemmas in determining how to effectively deliver their messages, and advertising agencies will need every ounce of their specialised knowledge and expertise to capitalize on the rapid expansion of media delivery methods" (p. 19). It might be a challenge, but Saatchi and Saatchi see a great deal of promise in cable as an advertising medium which can "attract audiences through selective programming aimed at more clearly defined groups than the mass audiences of the major networks. Multinational advertisers with a specific target audience in each country will be able to reach their target segment through a cable channel concentrating on their specific interest" (p. 13).

Saatchi and Saatchi's concern for "world marketing" as the "heart of business strategy" (p. 14) stems from its emphasis on transnational corporations as its favored clients (the "major multinationals" that spent $125 billion on advertising in 1982), and is in tune with ongoing trends. The world economy is dominated by a privileged few mega-corporations, and the advertising agencies (themselves large corporations, the top 10 of which commanded multi-million dollar revenues in 1983) will increasingly be called upon to help assure their markets by better analyzing potential outlets and designing and implementing campaigns aimed at convincing people to purchase their goods and services.

As such, the strategies of the large advertising corporations, their attempts to organize and control consumption—and, thereby, people—represent the extension and intensification of the ambitions of Scientific Management. Taylor himself would have applauded the attempt by industrial and advertising corporations to orchestrate, plan, and integrate social life. With Stella Shamoon he would have recognized that "It is a small step from the rationalisation of product lines, and the centralization of production, distribution and marketing by continent, to world brands" (Shamoon, 1984). And like Taylor himself, the new corporate capital is aware of the centrality of information to the managerial project. Information must be assembled, analyzed, and disseminated. Saatchi and Saatchi are well aware that the control of customers is indissociable from the control of information: "Knowledge has value, and there is greater "value-added" during periods of turmoil and change [as now] in the business world" (Saatchi and Saatchi Compton Worldwide, 1983, p. 19).

If the individual consumer is the target of information, it is also the case that he or she can become a piece of information. It is in the nature of cable systems that they should permit interactive communication. Insofar as the client or consumer requests programming or services from the cable operator, that person is yielding up information about his or her activities, tastes, and desires. As a recent report on cable put it, cable companies "will build up over time a substantial data base on consumer incomes, television viewing patterns, and the sensitivity of different groups of consumers to the price of different programmes" (Veljanovski and Bishop, 1983, p. 76). Domestic cable systems can provide valuable information on consumer behavior, which represents a significant new development in market research and opinion polling: information can be harvested either through push-button polling, or, more surreptitiously, through the vigilant monitoring of viewing patterns by a network's central computers (thus, Warner Amex's QUBE system scans the home of each subscriber every 6 seconds). From the point of view of the entrepreneur, the beauty of this technology is that it renders the subscriber's home transparent to the curious eyes of business. What we have here is the discrete observation of each of the households that are threaded along the cableways.

As David Burnham suggests, we have here the creation of a new kind of information, "transactional information." Information is created every time we use electronic terminals, not just in the home, but also in banks, shops, and restaurants. The consequence is that it becomes possible to "pinpoint the location of an individual at a particular moment, indicate his daily patterns of work and sleep, and even suggest his state of mind" (Burnham, 1983, p. 56). The value of this constant stream of information, when aggregated, should not be under-estimated. The individual becomes constantly—and routinely—monitored and studied. The new technologies can thereby constitute "a tool to burrow into the psyches of unsuspecting customers" (p. 242). And in that way, the Scientific Management of social life as a whole takes a giant leap forward.

The extension of Scientific Management goes beyond coordination of the dispersed corporation, more intensive marketing of products and observation of customers using I.T. to gather, assess, and disseminate information. Further changes in the organizations themselves, above and beyond growth, concentration and spatial relocation, have impelled corporations, as part of the planning procedures essential to the retention and advancement of their position, to enter into what can only be described as the Scientific Management of political life itself.

Michael Useem finds a reason for this in a shift from "managerial" to "institutional" capitalism, by which he means that the advanced economies are nowadays dominated not only by large corporations, but also that these are more interconnected than before. The upshot of this is an inner circle of interlocking directorates within modern capitalism whose interests and concerns extend beyond those of any one firm. A result is a "consciousness of a generalized corporate outlook" (Useem, 1984, p. 5), which has led to the "political mobilization of business" (p. 150) during and since the 1970s. As Useem puts it, interlocks between corporations "have created a special form of social organization within the business communities of both America and Britain, an inner circle whose unique qualities equip corporate leaders to enter politics on behalf of consensually arrived at classwide interests rather than narrow, individual corporate interests" (p. 58).

What this means is that contemporary capitalism has become more cohesive and better equipped to have its views represented in politics. It has, in short, taken steps to ensure that its political influence is systematized and regularized. It has moved, as Taylor prescribed, to identify the constituents of its activities, to examine barriers to its pursuits, to scrutinize them carefully, and to make arrangments for them to be overcome so that it might operate more productively. In the days of the modern state, with widespread political regulation and considerable significance applying to government decisions, advanced capitalism has recognized the need—and, with the growth of "institutional" capitalism, has developed the basis—for effective and consistent political representation. Information and I.T. are key requirements of the political mobilization of business.

One dimension of this is the spate of corporate and advocacy advertising we have seen emerge in recent years in the commercial media. Another is the rise of sponsorship, which will be an increasingly important means of subsidizing electronic media. These are nothing less than attempts to manage corporate image, but, important though they are for continuing the unrestricted activity of business, they pale when compared to the more directly political representation of corporations.   On the one hand, this is evident in businesses' recognition that better communications both within and outside the plant are a means of getting their own way—and the boom in public relations, cultivation of media contacts, executive grooming for television appearances, corporate video productions, etc. express this perception.

On the other hand, it is apparent in corporate involvement in politics itself. The unrelenting growth, quantitatively and qualitatively, of the business lobby— with its indices of opinion leaders, significant contacts, and constant stream of press releases and leaflets—in Britain and America is testament to this. But still more significant is the intense support for and influence upon pro-business parties themselves. The "political mobilization of business" over the last decade and more, the corporate recognition that, to serve its interests as a whole, politics must be better managed than previously, has been expressed not only in substantial support for conservative political parties, subsidy of pro-business "think tanks" and the more vigorous participation in politics of bodies such as the Confederation of British Industry. It has also been witnessed in the development within the polity itself of business procedures. In particular, we would point to the way in which Saatchi and Saatchi—in our view, something of a bell-wether corporation—by its forays into the election campaigns in Britain of 1979 and 1983, has bridged a traditional gulf between politics and business by applying its expertise as a "communicator" gained in selling products to selling politicians. American politics are the epitome of this process (see Jamieson, 1984; Perry, 1984; Spear, 1984), but Saatchi and Saatchi are an index of the way politics have been changing (under pressure from business representation, but also from within from "businesslike" politicians) to become a matter of selling ideas and delivering votes, a sign that Scientific Management has entered politics itself.

Saatchi and Saatchi's campaign management tactics are well known—the careful calculation of people's attitudes; the daily polls; the targeting of posters, TV slots, and press adverts; advice on form and content of political broadcasts; elocution lessons for the Prime Minister; meticulous selection of clothing; careful arrangement of photo-opportunities and media events . . . . A corollary of this advertising mentality in political campaigns is the excessive concern for secrecy that characterizes the Thatcher government (see Cockerell et al., 1984). Another is the diminishment of politics as a "public sphere"; the avoidance of serious political debate and exchange of ideas and principles; their replacement with image-manipulation and news management.

(3) Command and Control: Surveillance and Intelligence. Thus far we have described a process of information gathering, analysis and dissemination that serves

the purposes of corporate interests chiefly by increasing the efficiency of production and marketing. Though we have seen that this involves the extension of corporate capital into wide areas of social life, the polity included, we want now to turn to a more disturbing dimension of the amassment and use of data. We are referring to the surveillance and intelligence activities of the military and the police. If information can be garnered for the purposes of commerce, it is also the case that, increasingly, it is becoming central to military and police operations, with most serious implications for the citizenry. Moreover, while there is significant difference between issues of national security and law-and-order and the corporate concerns we have previously described, there are shadowy areas of overlap—in the politically charged area of industrial relations law, in definitions of subversion, in notions of intelligence—which, at a time of crisis that is answered by a strategy of "strong state/free market",—the state forcefully intervening in society to clear away obstacles, notably organized labor, that obstruct the changes necessary to achieve profitable businesses (Gamble, 1979)—become especially pressing.

As we demonstrated in Chapter 8, "the military market has been of critical importance in the technical revolution which created the electronics industry and the dominant position of U.S. firms" (Kaldor, 1981, p. 89). One American commentator has suggested that "the entire computer market can be traced to the military, since military requirements financed and directed most of the research and development . . . In terms of markets and producers it appears that the electronics industry, the fastest growing in the economy, is thoroughly militarized" (Nathanson, 1969, pp. 210, 212). The same applies to European-based corporations, and all have a vested interest in expanding defense budgets and providing ever-new generations of I.T. to the military.

One particularly important type of I.T. produced from the military-industrial-scientific complex is Command, Control, and Communications Systems—integrated control and surveillance systems that are the "sinews and nerves of military power" (Herzfeld, 1978, p. 90). Central to the maintenance of military superiority is the capacity to monitor, observe, and act upon enemy activities and resources (Price, 1977). For some, the surveillance technologies of the military constitute the "eyes and the ears of peace", such that one can contemplate the "stabilizing role of information resources in reducing the probability of accident or surprise" (Oettinger, 1980, p. 196), and it has to be admitted that, from a position which assumes the West is never belligerent and the East always so, this has some validity. However, for us this Manichaeism will not do; in our view, intelligence and surveillance technologies undermine the possibility of peace and contribute to the paranoia that currently characterizes international politics, where each side insistently searches to gain superiority over the other. Now, with the militarization of space that accompanies the "Star Wars" phenomenon, this surveillance compulsion reaches a new phase. By far the majority (70% plus) of satellites orbiting the earth are devoted to military functions, and surveillance and early-warning feature prominently (Gray, 1983). As Mahdi Elmandjra has argued, "the conquest of space is the development of the capacity to gather, process, use, and update information with increasing reliability, effectiveness, and speed" (Elmandjra, 1984, p. 580).

Moreover, the new and old Cold Wars that have escalated the build-up of military I.T. systems not only contribute to international instability, but also have a domestic counterpart expressed at once in heightened concern for the "enemy within" and in manipulation of information handed out to the populace. It is extraordinarily difficult to estimate the internal surveillance undertaken by and on behalf of the military, but, in Britain, the existence—officially denied—of MI5, the domestic security agency, testifies that it regularly monitors its fellow citizens. Given present defense strategies it is arguable that intensive surveillance of the people is unavoidable, since those who query or protest about nuclear weapons/energy *ipso facto* are potential or actual threats to military capability (Jungk, 1979). But aside from this, available evidence in an especially secret area suggests that large numbers of people—trade unionists, political activists, students, radicals—in Britain and America are watched by military intelligence services (Leigh, 1980, Ch. 5), their telephones tapped, electronic bugs planted, personal histories scrutinized, and dossiers prepared that are readily accessed via computers. Chapman Pincher (1978) reports that MI5 has files on several million British people, and these include scores of Labour Party Members of Parliament, something of the nature of which can be gauged from the fact that Sir Harold Wilson, *when Prime Minister*, was investigated by his own security services on suspicion that he might be a Russian agent (*Observer*, 22 July, 1984).

At MI5's Mayfair headquarters, a computer file is kept on 500,000 people (Davies and Black, 1984b), but it has access to many more and often larger police files throughout the nation (the Special Branch of the police "has become virtually an extension of the security service"—Davies and Black, 1984a). Moreover, it also has permission to draw on private data banks—health records, tax, bank accounts, education, etc.—which enable it to put together a composite picture of anyone targeted.

The suggestion of a recent MI5 employee is that there have been "widening targets of domestic surveillance" (Ingram, 1984) of late. And the *Guardian* editor reports that

> The targets of surveillance have broadened from suspected terrorists . . . or self-professed enemies of the state to embrace a wide variety of folk whose views conflict with the establishment but who could not be described as subversive—the peace movement, trade unionists, supporters of political groups on the left and right. The definition of subversion has been allowed to broaden into a grey area which brings large sections of peaceful, patriotic people into the target area of state suspicion (*Guardian*, 17 April, 1984).

The integrated computer/communications systems now becoming available do much to encourage this tendency, to surveille more and more of the populace more and more systematically.

While military observation of the domestic population increases, so does manipulation of the information that it receives from and about the military. In recent years, media coverage of the Falklands Wars (R. Harris, 1983; House of Commons, December, 1982), the Soviet destruction of Korean airliner 007 (Johnson, 1983), the Grenadian invasion by U.S. troops (O'Shaughnessy, 1984, pp. 196-216), and successful efforts to formalize and normalize censorship procedures inside NATO (Beach, 1983; Schlesinger, 1984) are all indices of a management of communications agencies and their delivery systems that new technologies have done nothing to restrain and much to assist.

Surveillance is not confined to the military. As Duncan Campbell says of the British police: "traditional military doctrines on the importance of good prior intelligence—but now turned inwards on much of the British population—have encouraged police units like the Special Branch to make advances in the same direction" (Campbell, 1980, p. 66). In the manner of the military, the police now see the need to develop Command, Control, and Intelligence capacities (see Pounder and Anderson, n.d.), and, indeed, military and police surveillance overlap in the area of "subversion" (Bamford, 1983; Aubrey, 1981). At a time when the accountability of the police to democratic processes appears to be weakening, when forces are more and more centralized while their computer-communications capabilities are being enhanced and integrated locally, regionally, and nationally, yet able to access other computer systems such as tax and social security records, police surveillance and intelligence activities assume worrisome proportions (see Manwaring-White, 1983).

Surveillance may be more or less active and deliberate. On the one hand, information can be gathered comparatively passively and routinely from people's everyday transactions: financial transactions and communications records (via telephone and, in future, cable). In this way, conversations, communications, and contracts may be recorded and monitored. Peter Large has indicated the ominous breakthrough that comes with the ability to aggregrate such information by the use of computer systems:

> For two decades computers have been progressively enhancing the value of collecting information about individuals. They have made it easier to store vast amounts of data and easier to pluck the required details from the mass. But, above all, they have made it possible to build in seconds a deep individual dossier drawn from a host of angles and sources which existed previously only in isolation in filing cabinets spread around different offices.
>
> That ability to correlate apparently unconnected scraps of information is of particular value to the police and security services, and the . . . intelligence system does this through a technique called FTR—full-text retrieval.
>
> FTR is ideally suited for surveillance. It could, for instance, compile a list of all National Front members who own white Cortinas and have red hair or all short stewards who have been to Bulgaria, work in the electronics industry, and took a holiday last July.
>
> The information can be stored on disc in almost random fashion, because

the computer roams through all the material available along its storage ten-
tacles, lifting out only the items that contain *all* the key words specified by
the investigator (*Guardian,* September 23, 1980).

On the other hand, surveillance activities may be more actively undertaken.
Control agencies now seem to be shifting the emphasis in investigation "from
evidence gathering after the commission of a crime to intelligence gathering in advance of any particular crime being committed". "In this 'pre-emptive view'", argues
Duncan Campbell, "any citizen, certainly any socially uncharacteristic citizen, is
a target for suspicion and observation. This quite explicit development in police
planning has virtually put the whole of society under surveillance" (Campbell,
1980, p. 65). This move from the automation of existant data to more active
monitoring of the populace for intelligence (political sympathies, trade union
involvement, associates, etc., aspects of which have emerged with disclosure late
in 1979 of information held on police computers of Londons jurors—Leigh, 1980,
pp. 171-175—and the British Attorney-General's admission in 1984 that telephone
metering—as opposed to listening-in to conversations—of destination, timing, and
duration of calls does not require warrants) prior to offences being committed
is sound Scientific Management. To be effective, control requires not merely
post hoc review, but anticipation of actions and motives that offences may be
preempted. A consequence is that larger and larger sections of the public are
required to be known by the police, so that their behavior can be assured to fall
into line. The FBI's National Crime Information Center (NCIC), for example,
has "been converted into a nationwide system for monitoring the whereabouts
of persons merely 'of interest' to the government". Among the files are entries on
one of every 30 Americans, and it is estimated that "in a few years, these files
could grow to include dossiers on 90% of all U.S. residents with arrest records—
as many as 35 million people, or approximately 40% of the U.S. labor force"
(Bruno, 1984, p. 116).

With the restructuring currently being undertaken in all Western societies in
response to recession, and amid the social, economic, and political turmoil that
often accompanies this, it is easy for opposition to government and business policies to become equated with opposition to the state, and this opposition to the
state to be equated with subversion—to be handled by the police assisted by
computer networks that monitor, amass, and recall details of a wide variety of
"deviants"* There is here the danger that this surveillance becomes an extension

*Thus James Anderton, Chief Constable of Greater Manchester, on BBC TV's *Question
Time* (October 16, 1979): "There are at work in the community today . . . factions, political
factions, whose designed end is to overthrow democracy as we know it. They are at work in
the field of public order, in the industrial relations field, in politics in the truest sense. And I
think from a police point of view in the future. . .basic crime as such, theft, burglary, even violent crime will not be the predominant police feature. What will be the matter of greatest
concern to me will be the covert and ultimately overt attempts to overthrow democracy, to
subvert the authority of the state, and in fact to involve themselves in acts of sedition designed
to destroy our parliamentary system and the democratic government in this country". Anderton's statement was in reply to the question: "what in the panel's opinion is now the greatest
threat to the preservation of law and order in this country?"

of that undertaken inside the workplace, that police agencies come forward to ensure the control of the populace amidst severe and contentious social changes. That could mean, in the words of Edward Thompson, moving towards "a managed society, whose managing director is money and whose production manager is the police" (Thompson, 1980, p. 211).

(4) Information and Power: The World Brain and the Panopticon

We want finally to draw attention to two figures that express the modalities through which the powerful in our society seek to make information the vehicle for retaining their command.

The first is that of the World Brain or World Encyclopedia, as elaborated by H. G. Wells some 50 years ago—the dream of an unlimited, concentrated, and accessible reservoir of knowledge. According to Wells,

> an immense and ever-increasing wealth of knowledge is scattered about the world today, a wealth of knowledge and suggestion that—systematically ordered and generally disseminated—would probably suffice to solve all the mighty difficulties of our age, but that knowledge is still dispersed, unorganized, impotent (Wells, 1938, p. 47).

The knowledge systems of the world must therefore be concentrated in the World Brain, in the creation of "a new world organ for the collection, indexing, summarising and release of knowledge" (p. 59). Wells ponders "the creation of an efficient index to *all* human knowledge, ideas and achievements . . . the creation, that is, of a complete planetary memory for all mankind" (p. 60); "the whole human memory", he believes, "can be, and probably in a short time will be, made accessible to every individual", (p. 61). For Wells, "the time is ripe for a very extensive revision and modernisation of the intellectual organisation of the world" (p. 26): "this synthesis of knowledge is the necessary beginning of the new world" (p. 64). The world "has to pull its mind together" through this new kind of "mental clearing house", the World Brain.

The World Brain is an intellectual invention with considerable social and political resonance. It is one that chimes with the aspirations of global military intelligence systems, with police and surveillance agencies, with transnational corporations, with businesses like the now defunct IRIS (International Reporting Information Systems) which sought "to gather in, sort and increase in value by sophisticated analysis the vast amount of information floating around the world" (*Observer*, April 17, 1983), and with the purveyors of videotex who believe that this "can be seen as a system in which the basic structuring imposed on the information according to amount of detail and place in the subject hierarchy. . .makes the Wellsian dream practicable" (Fedida and Malik, 1979, pp. 166-167). The World Brain anticipates what we see as an emerging regime of information production, circulation, consumption, and control—an economy and politics of knowledge. Wells, of course, saw this "new encyclopaedism" as a benevolent phenomenon. We have shown that it is by no means so.

The second figure is to be found in Jeremy Bentham's conception of the

Panopticon. At the end of the 18th century, Bentham outlined his plans for an institutional architecture of control. What he devised was a general mechanism—applicable to prisons, asylums, schools, factories—for the automatic and uninterrupted functioning of institutional power. This mechanism, the Panopticon, is a building of circular structure, with a series of individual cells built around a central "well"; at the center is an inspection tower from which each of the cells could be observed and monitored. A calculated illumination of the cells, along with the darkening and masking of the central tower, endows the "inspective force" with the "unbounded faculty of seeing without being seen" (Bentham, 1843, p. 80). The essence of the Panopticon, Bentham suggests, consists in "the centrality of the inspector's situation, combined with the well-known and most effectual contrivances for *seeing without being seen*" (p. 44). What is of importance is "that for the greatest proportion of time possible, each man should actually *be* under inspection"; but it is also desirable "that the person to be inspected should always feel themselves as if under inspection", for "the greater chance there is, of a given person's being at a given time actually under inspection, the more strong will be the persuasion—the more *intense*, if I may say so, the *feeling*, he has of his being so" (p. 44). The inspector is apparently omnipresent and omniscient, while the inmates, cut off from the view of each other, are reduced to the status of "solitary and sequestered individuals". The individual is marginalized, monitored, and, ultimately, self-monitoring: "indulged with perfect liberty within the space allotted to him, in what worse way could he vent his rage, than by beating his head against the walls?" (p. 47).

Jeremy Bentham considered the Panopticon to be an architectural paradigm capable of generalization. This insight has been most fully developed by Michel Foucault (1979) in his historical and philosophical exploration of forms and relations of power. For Foucault, the Panopticon, as a mechanism and edifice for channeling the flow of power, amounts to a major landmark in the history of the human mind. Historically, it represents a bulwark against the mobile disorder of the swarming crowd, against forbidden circulations and "dangerous mixtures". The Panopticon is a form of mobilization—and here Foucault's work intersects with that of Gaudemar—the development of an architecture of control and supervision, the elimination of confusion through the elaboration of a permanent grid of power. What Bentham did was to crystallize a sea-change in the social economy of power: his contribution was part of a wider

> effort to adjust the mechanisms of power that frame the everyday lives of individuals; an adaptation and a refinement of the machinery that assumes responsibility for and places under surveillance their everyday behavior, their identity, their activity, their apparently unimportant gestures; another policy for that multiplicity of bodies and forces that constitutes a population (Foucault, 1979, pp. 77–78).

This policy, according to Foucault, was implemented through the creation of space that was at once architectural, functional, and hierarchical. The Panopticon contains "so many cages, so many small theatres, in which each actor is alone, perfectly individualized and constantly visible" (p. 200):

> the crowd, a compact mass, a locus of multiple exchanges, individualities merging together, a collective effect, is abolished and replaced by a collection of separated individualities. From the point of view of the guardian, it is replaced by a multiplicity that can be numbered and supervised; from the point of view of the inmates, by a sequestered and observed solitude (p. 201).

Within the Panoptic machine, the individual "is seen, but he does not see; he is the object of information, never a subject in communication" (p. 200). The inmate is subjected to "a state of conscious and permanent visibility that assures the automatic functioning of power" (p. 201). So insidious are the relations of power that the individual becomes self-monitoring:

> He who is subjected to a field of visibility, and who knows it, assumes responsibility for the constraints of power; he makes them play spontaneously upon himself; he inscribes in himself the power relation in which he simultaneously plays both roles; he becomes the principle of his own subjection. By this very fact, the external power may throw off its physical weight; it tends to the non-corporal; and, the more it approaches this limit, the more constant, profound and permanent are its effects; it is a perpetual victory that avoids any physical confrontation and which is always decided in advance (p. 202).

The Panopticon, then, is a "machine" that ensures the infinitesimal distribution of power, one that turns the monitored individual into a visible, knowable, and vulnerable *object*. It is a generalizable

> type of location of bodies in space, of distribution of individuals in relation to one another, of hierarchical organization, of disposition of centres and channels of power, of definition of the instruments and modes of intervention of power (p. 205).

According to Foucault, the Panopticon is "at once surveillance and observation, security and knowledge, individualization and totalization, isolation and transparency" (p. 249); it is an integrated system of surveillance/intelligence and discipline/control. As such, let us add, it is the precursor of Taylor's Scientific Management. As Gaudemar argues, "the principles set out by Taylor scarcely go beyond those set out by Bentham" (Gaudemar, 1982, p. 55). In each, we find the same project of surveillance and control.

We have spent so long on this presentation of Bentham's Panopticon because we want to argue that Foucault is right in seeing it as a significant landmark in the history of the human mind. We want to suggest that the new communication and information technologies—particularly in the form of the electronic grid towards which they are moving—permit a massive extension of that same principle of mobilization to which Bentham aspired. What these technologies support, in fact, is the same dissemination of power and control, but freed from the architectural and geographical constraints of Bentham's stone and brick prototype. On the basis of the information revolution, not just the prison or factory, but the social totality, comes to be part of the hierarchical and disciplinary Panoptic machine.

If we consider the loops and circuits of what has been termed the "wired city" or "wired society", then we can see that a technological system is being constituted to permit the centralized, and furtive, inspection, observation, surveillance, and documentation of activities on the circumference of society as a whole. Cable television networks, as we have already suggested, can continuously monitor consumer preferences for programming material, along with details of any financial or communicative transactions. We now have very many networks of state and commercial data banks which accumulate and aggregrate information on the activities, transactions, needs, and desires of individuals or social groups. And we have innumerable spy satellites and means of intercepting electronic signals that observe, record, and categorize the movement of shipping and aircraft, interpersonal and organizational communication. The population becomes *visible* and *knowable* to the various computerized "inspective forces". Here, as Foucault suggests of the Panopticon, is "a machine for dissociating the see/being seen dyad: in the peripheric ring, one is totally seen, without ever seeing: in the central tower, one sees everything without ever being seen" (Foucault, 1979, p. 202). The individual becomes the object of surveillance, no longer the subject of communication. And, like the Panopticon, the wired society too is a "system of individualising and permanent documentation" (p. 250); the observed and scrutinized individual, subject to continuous registration, becomes the object of knowledge (of files and records). Seen and known. Overcoming spatial and temporal constraints, the electronic grid promises to fulfil the dream of an "infinitely minute web of panoptic techniques" (p. 224).

We are not suggesting that there is, or will be, a single omniscient and all-seeing inspective force in the wired society. The nodal points on the electronic grid will be multiple and differential, though concentrated in key corporate and state hands. But what we *are* suggesting is that technologies have been constituted to watch and control, to control through watching. And I.T. extends this capacity. In it is perfected the ability to mobilize and control through watching and monitoring. The electronic grid is a transparent structure in which activities taking place at the "periphery"—remote working, electronic banking, the consumption of information or entertainment, tele-shopping, communication—are always visible to the electronic "eye" of the central computer systems that manage the networks. The new technologies of knowledge are also the eyes and ears of power. The Panopticon—like the World Brain—is a figure that reminds us that information and knowledge have everything to do with *power*.

Foucault describes a "carceral archipelago" which extends throughout modern society. Nowadays the "carceral texture of society" (Foucault, 1979, p. 297) he delineates has noticeably thickened and strengthened. This is what we have been concerned with in this book and what we foresee in the future: a society in which corporate capital, using the most advanced forms of I.T. that have been designed to suit its requirements and constantly talking about the imperatives and promise of a technological revolution, extends and consolidates its hold in society, strengthening its control over employees (and shedding significant numbers) while intruding further into the everyday lives of consumers both groups of whom it observes, analyzes, and schemes about that changes might be to the company's advantage and perceived as inevitable—by those likely to suffer from restructuring—or desirable—by those able to pay the going rate. Behind, often in front, and almost always in collusion with this centralized corporate capital, is arraigned a disciplinary state, equipped with the latest surveillance technologies, able to contain dissent from those minorities unwilling to accede to the market's control or unable, through unemployment and/or poverty, to participate in its technologies of abundance.

This does not have to be so—and the thrust of this book is to show that, being socially constituted, I.T. and the information society can be socially reconstituted—but we must admit in all honesty that we can see no serious dissent to what is happening. Indeed, there are many signs of resignation to the inevitable. And this is not surprising, since the power of corporate capital and the restrains of the international economy are awesome and, anyway, the negative aspects of current changes are socially skewed. Thus the unemployed are overwhelmingly from the unskilled, vulnerable, poor, and unorganized, and it is those that are taking the brunt of the recession. And the Fordism of the office will downgrade and reduce workers, but it is targeted chiefly at women, the subordination of whom has enabled men in this sphere to be assured of promotion, a career structure, and security of employment (Stewart et al., 1980). And new modes of production will strengthen corporations, but reduce the possibility and potential of workplace organization (cf. Millward, 1983), while new technologies for the home will further fragment and isolate people from one another. Add to this the information resources we have documented, which are increasingly at the disposal of corporate capital and a state closely allied to it, and one can begin to see why consumerism has appeal and why powerful forces remain entrenched and have been strengthened in recent years. In the absence of a Luddite mentality, doubtless the information revolution will proceed apace.

> It was a lamentable time for man,
> Whether a hope had e'er been his or not;
> A woeful time for them whose hopes survived
> The shock; most woeful for those few who still
> Were flattered, and had trust in human kind:
> They had the deepest feeling of the grief.
>
> —Wordsworth

References

Place of publication is London unless otherwise stated.

Aaronovitch, S. and Sawyer, M. C. *Big Business: Theoretical and Empirical Aspects of Concentration and Mergers in the UK.* Macmillan, 1975.

Abrams, P. The Sense of the Past and the Origins of Sociology. *Past and Present* (55) May 1972: 18–32.

Abrams, P. (ed.). *Work, Urbanism and Inequality: UK Society Today.* Weidenfeld and Nicolson, 1978.

Abrams, P. *Historical Sociology.* Shepton Mallet: Open Books, 1982.

ACARD (Advisory Council for Applied Research and Development). *The Applications of Semiconductor Technology.* Cabinet Office: HMSO, September 1978.

ACARD. *Technological Change: Threats and Opportunities for the United Kingdom.* Cabinet Office: HMSO, December 1979.

ACARD. *Information Technology.* Cabinet Office: HMSO, September 1980.

ACARD. *Improving Research Links Between Higher Education and Industry.* Cabinet Office: June 1983.

Adam Smith Institute. *Communication Policy.* Omega Report. Adam Smith Institute, 1984.

Aglietta, M. *A Theory of Capitalist Regulation.* New Left Books, 1979.

Albury, D. and Schwartz, J. *Partial Progress: The Politics of Science and Technology.* Pluto Press, 1982.

Aldred, C. *Women at Work.* Pan, 1981.

Aldrich, M. *Videotex: Key to the Wired City.* Quiller Press, 1982.

Alt, J. Beyond Class: The Decline of Industrial Labor and Leisure. *Telos* (28) Summer 1976: 55–80.

Amsden, A. H. (ed.). *The Economics of Women and Work.* Harmondsworth: Penguin, 1980.

Anderson, G. *Victorian Clerks.* Manchester: Manchester University Press, 1976.

Andrew, E. *Closing the Iron Cage: The Scientific Management of Work and Leisure.* Montreal: Black Rose Books, 1981.

Anglo-German Foundation. *The Effects of Changes in Working Time on Competitiveness.* Anglo-German Foundation, 1981.

Annual Investment File. *Foreign Companies in the UK and Ireland.* Richmond, Surrey: Urban Publishing Company, May 1983.

Anthony, P. D. *The Ideology of Work.* Tavistock, 1977.

APEX (Association of Professional, Executive, Clerical and Computer Staff). *Office Technology: The Trade Union Response.* APEX, 1979a.

APEX. *Composite Motion 3.* Annual Conference, APEX, April 1979b.

APEX. *Automation and the Office Worker.* Report of the Office Technology Working Party. APEX, March 1980.

Arndt, S., Feltes, J., and Hanak, J. Secretarial Attitudes Towards Word Processors as a Function of Familiarity and Locus of Control. *Behaviour and Information Technology* 2 (1) 1983: 17–22.

Arnold, E., Huggett, C., Senker, P., Swords-Isherwood, N. and Zmroczek Shannon, C. *Microelectronics and Women's Employment in Britain.* University of Sussex, Brighton: Science Policy Research Unit, 1982.

Arnold, H. L. and Faurote, L. F. *Ford Methods and the Ford Shops.* New York: The Engineering Magazine Company, 1915.

Assen, A. van and Wester, P. Designing Meaningful Jobs: A Comparative Analysis of Organizational Design Practices. *in* K.D. Duncan et al. (eds.), 1980 (q.v., below), pp. 237–252.

ASTMS (Association of Scientific, Technical and Managerial Staffs). *Technological Change and Collective Bargaining*. Discussion Document. ASTMS, n.d., circa 1979.

ASTMS. *Proceedings of Annual Conference*. ASTMS, 1979.

Aubrey, C. *Who's Watching You? Britain's Security Services and the Official Secrets Act*. Harmondsworth: Penguin, 1981.

AUEW/TASS (Amalgamated Union of Engineering Workers/Technical and Supervisory Section). *New Technology: A Guide for Negotiators*. n.d., circa 1980.

Avineri, S. (ed.). *Karl Marx on Colonialism and Modernization*. New York: Doubleday Anchor, 1969.

Baer, W. S. Telecommunications Technology in the 1980s. *in* G. O. Robinson (ed.), *Communications for Tomorrow: Policy Perspectives for the 1980s*. New York: Praeger, 1978, pp. 61–125.

Bailes, K. E. Alexei Gastev and the Soviet Controversy over Taylorism, 1918-1924. *Soviet Studies* **29**(3) 1977: 373–394.

Bailes, K. E. *Technology and Society under Lenin and Stalin*. Princeton: Princeton University Press, 1978.

Bain, G. S., Bacon, R. and Pilmott, J. The Labour Force. *in* A. H. Halsey (ed.), *Trends in British Society since 1900*. Macmillan, 1972, pp. 97–128.

Bain, G. S., and Price, R. Union Growth and Employment Trends in the UK, 1964-1970. *British Journal of Industrial Relations* **10**(3) 1972: 366–381.

Baker, K. *Towards an Information Economy*. Department of Industry, 7 September 1982.

Baker, K. *Information Technology—the Path to Greater Freedom or to 1984*. Department of Industry, 6 January, 1983a.

Baker, K. Microchips with Everything—The Power Source for Jobs. *Guardian*, 27 May, 1983b.

Ball, R. Japanese Companies Buy into Europe. *Fortune*, May 16, 1983, pp. 146–150.

Bambrough, B. Optical Character Readers in the Automated Office. *Computers and People* **29** (1-2) 1980: 19–21, 26.

Bamford, J. *The Puzzle Palace: America's National Security Agency and its Special Relationship with Britain's GCHQ*. Sidgwick and Jackson, 1983.

Banks, O. *The Sociology of Education*. Batsford, 1971.

Baran, P. A. and Sweezy, P. M. *Monopoly Capital: An Essay on the American Economic and Social Order*. (1966). Reprinted Harmondsworth: Penguin, 1973.

Barker, J. and Downing, H. Word Processing and the Transformation of the Patriarchal Relations of Control in the Office. *Capital and Class* (10) 1980: 65–99.

Barnaby, F. Microelectronics in War. *in* G. Friedrichs and A. Schaff (eds.), *Microelectronics and Society: for better or for worse*. Oxford: Pergamon Press, 1982, pp. 243–272.

Barnet, R. J. and Müller, R. E. *Global Reach: The Power of the Multinational Corporations*. Cape, 1975.

Barnouw, E. *The Golden Web: A History of Broadcasting in the United States, vol. II–1933-1953*. New York: Oxford University, 1968.

Barnouw, E. *The Image Empire: A History of Braodcasting in the United States, vol. III—from 1953*. New York: Oxford University Press, 1970.

Barnouw, E. *The Sponsor: Notes on a Modern Potentate*. New York: Oxford University Press, 1978.

Barrett, M. *Women's Oppression Today*. New Left Books, 1980.

Barron, I. and Curnow, R. *The Future with Microelectronics: Forecasting the Effects of Information Technology*. Frances Pinter, 1979.

Barthes, R. *Mythologies*. (1957). Reprinted Paladin, 1973.

Barty-King, H. *Girdle Round the Earth: the story of Cable and Wireless and its predecessors to mark the group's jubilee 1929-1971*. Heinemann, 1979.

Bass, A. Disney and the Corporate Con. *Technology Review*, October, 1983, pp. 18–21, 76.

Beach, General Sir H. *The Protection of Military Information*. Report of the Study Group on Censorship. Ministry of Defence, Command 9112. HMSO, December 1983.

Beck, E. M., Horan, P. M. and Tolbert, C. M. Industrial Segmentation and Labour Market Discrimination. *Social Problems* 28(2) 1980: 113–130.

Beechey, V. Some Notes on Female Labour in Capitalist Production. *Capital and Class* (3) 1977: 45–66.

Beechey, V. The Sexual Division of Labour and the Labour Process: A Critical Assessment of Braverman. *in* S. Wood (ed.), 1982 (q.v., below), ch. 3.

Bell, D. *Marxian Socialism in the United States*. (1952). Reprinted Princeton: Princeton University Press, 1967.

Bell, D. *The End of Ideology: On the Exhaustion of Political Ideas in the Fifties.* (revised edition) New York: Free Press, 1962.

Bell, D. (ed.) *The Radical Right.* New York: Books for Libraries Press, 1963.

Bell, D. A Rejoiner (to Tilton). *Social Research* 40(4) 1973: 745–752.

Bell, D. Reply to P. N. Sterns. *Society* 11(May–June) 1974a: 23–25.

Bell, D. An Exchange on Post-Industrial Society. *New York Review of Books,* January 24, 1974b.

Bell, D. *The Coming of Post-Industrial Society: A Venture in Social Forecasting.* (1973). Reprinted Harmondsworth: Penguin, Peregrine Books, 1976.

Bell, D. The Once and Future Marx. *American Journal of Sociology* 83(1) 1977: 187–197.

Bell, D. *The Matching of Scales.* The Louis G. Cowan Lecture. International Institute of Communications, 1979a.

Bell, D. The Social Framework of the Information Soceity. *in* M. L. Dertouzos and J. Moses (eds.), *The Computer Age: A Twenty-Year View.* Cambridge MA: MIT Press, 1979b, pp. 163–211.

Bell, D. *The Cultural Contradictions of Capitalism.* (second edition). Heinemann, 1979c.

Bell, D. Communications Technology—For Better or for Worse. *Harvard Business Review* 57 (3) 1979d: 20–42.

Bell, D. *Sociological Journeys: Essays 1960–1980.* Heinemann, 1980a.

Bell, D. Disjuncted Realms. *New Society* 54(933) October 2, 1980b: 32.

Bell, D. Introduction. *in* S. Nora and A. Minc, 1980c (q.v., below), pp. vii–xvi.

Bell, D. First Love and Early Sorrows. *Partisan Review* 48(4) 1981: 532–551.

Bennett, T., Boyd-Bowman, S., Mercer, C. and Woollacott, J. (eds.), *Popular Television and Film.* British Film Institute Publishing *in association with* The Open University Press, 1981.

Benson, I. and Lloyd, J. *New Technology and Industrial Change: The Impact of the Scientific-Technical Revolution on Labour and Industry.* Kogan Page, 1983.

Bentall, J. *The Body Electric: Patterns of Western Industrial Culture.* Thames and Hudson, 1976.

Bentham, J. *Works.* vol. 4. (ed. J. Bowring). Edinburgh: William Tait, 1843.

Berg, I. *Education and Jobs: The Great Training Robbery.* New York: Praeger, 1970.

Berg, M. *The Machinery Question and the Making of Political Economy.* Cambridge: Cambridge University Press, 1980.

Bernal, J. D. *The Social Function of Science.* Routledge and Kegan Paul, 1939.

Bessant, J. *Microprocessors in Production Processes.* Report no. 609. Policy Studies Institute, July, 1982.

Betts, P. Now for the Hard Part ... *Financial Times,* 6 July, 1982.

Beynon, H. *Working for Ford.* Allen Lane, 1973.

Beynon, H. and Blackburn, R. M. *Perceptions of Work: Variations within a Factory.* Cambridge: Cambridge University Press, 1972.

BIFU (Banking, Insurance and Finance Union). *Report of BIFU Microelectronics Committee.* Esher, Surrey: BIFU, September 1979.

Bird, E. *Information Technology in the Office: the impact on women's jobs.* Manchester: Equal Opportunities Commission, September 1980.

Blackburn, R. M. and Mann, M. *The Working Class in the Labour Market.* Macmillan, 1979.

Blauner, R. *Alienation and Freedom: The Factory Worker and his Industry.* Chicago: University of Chicago Press, 1964.

Boer, C. de. The Polls: Attitudes towards Unemployment. *Public Opinion Quarterly* 47(4) 1983: 432–441.

Bookchin, M. *Post-Scarcity Anarchism.* Wildwood House, 1974.

Bookchin, M. *Toward an ecological society.* Montreal: Black Rose Books, 1980.

Bookchin, M. *The Ecology of Freedom: The Emergence and Dissolution of Hierarchy.* Palo Alto, CA: Cheshire Books, 1982.

Boorstin, D. J. *The Republic of Technology: Reflections on our Future Community.* New Work: Harper and Row, 1978.

Bosquet, M. *Capitalism in Crisis and Everyday Life.* Hassocks, Sussex: Harvester, 1977.

Bosworth, D. L. (ed.). *The Employment Consequences of Technological Change.* Macmillan, 1983.

Bowles, J. R. Central Government Expenditure on Research and Development. *Economic Trends* (346) August 1982: 82–94.

Bowles, J. R. Research and Development: Preliminary Estimates of Expenditure in the United Kingdom in 1981. *Economic Trends* (359) September 1983: 108–111.

Boyer, R. La Crise Actuelle: Une Mise en Perspective Historique. *Critiques d' L'Economie Politique* 7–8 (April–September) 1979: 5–113.

Brady, T. and Liff, S. *Monitoring New Technology and Employment.* Sheffield: Manpower Services Commission, June 1983.

Braun, E. and MacDonald, S. *Revolution in Miniature: the history and impact of semiconductor electronics.* Cambridge: Cambridge University Press, 1978.

Braverman, H. *Labor and Monopoly Capital: The Degradation of Work in the Twentieth Century.* New York: Monthly Review Press, 1974.

Brenner, M. H. Mortality and the National Economy. A review of the Experience of England and Wales 1936–1976. *Lancet,* 15 September, 1979, pp. 568–573.

Bright, J. R. *Automation and Management.* Boston: Harvard Business School, 1958.

Briscoe, S. Employment in the Public and Private Sectors, 1975 to 1981. *Economic Trends* (338) December 1981: 94–102.

Brittan, S. A Flawed, Dangerous Nostrum. *Financial Times,* October 6, 1983.

Brock, G. W. *The Telecommunications Industry: The Dynamics of Market Structure.* Cambridge MA: Harvard University Press, 1981.

Brown, G. *Sabotage: A Study in Industrial Conflict.* Nottingham: Spokesman Books, 1977.

Brown, R. Work. *in* P. Abrams (ed.), 1978 (q.v., above), pp. 55–122.

Brown, R., Curran, M. and Cousins, J. *Changing Attitudes to Employment?* Research Paper no. 40. Department of Employment, May 1983.

Browning, H. L. and Singelmann, J. The Transformation of the US Labor Force: The Interaction of Industry and Occupation. *Politics and Society* 8 (3–4) 1978: 481–509.

Bruno, C. The Electronic Cops. *Datamation* 30(9) June 15, 1984: 114–124.

Brzoska, M. Economic Problems of Arms Production in Western Europe—Diagnosis and Alternatives. *in* H. Tuomi and R. Väyrynen (eds.), *Militarization and Arms Production.* Croom Helm, 1983.

Bullock, M. *Academic Enterprise, Industrial Innovation, and the Development of High Technology Financing in the United States.* Brand Brothers and Co., 1983.

Bunce, R. *Television in the Corporate Interest.* New York: Praeger, 1976.

Burawoy, M. Toward a Marxist Theory of the Labor Process: Braverman and Beyond. *Politics and Society* 8(3–4) 1978: 247–312.

Burawoy, M. *Manufacturing Consent: Changes in the Labor Process under Monopoly Capitalism.* Chicago: University of Chicago Press, 1979.

Burck, G. Knowledge: The Biggest Growth Industry of them All. *Fortune,* November, 1964, pp. 128–131, 267–270.

Burke, J. G. (ed.). *The New Technology and Human Values.* Belmont, CA: Wadsworth Publishing Co., 1966.

Burkitt, A. and Williams, E. *The Silicon Civilisation.* W. H. Allen, 1980.

Burnham, D. *The Rise of the Computer State.* Weidenfeld and Nicolson, 1983.

Burns, S. *The Household Economy: Its Shape, Origins and Future.* Boston: Beacon Press, 1975.

Burris, V. The Social and Political Consequences of Overeducation. *American Sociological Review* 48(4) 1983: 454–467.

Bury, J. B. *The Idea of Progress: An Inquiry into Its Origins and Growth.* (1932) Reprinted New York: Dover Publications, 1960.

Business Week The Speedup in Automation. August 3, 1981, pp. 58–67.

Callaghan, J. *Prime Minister Announces Major Programme of Support for Microelectronics.* Press Notice, 10 Downing Street, 6 December, 1978.

Cambridge Economic Policy Review. (5)April 1979. Department of Applied Economics, University of Cambridge. Farnborough: Gower Press, 1979.

Campbell, B. T. Information and the Challenge of Information Technology. *Management in Government* 37(3) 1982: 188–195.

Campbell, C. *War Facts Now.* Fontana, 1982.

Campbell, D. Society under Surveillance. *in* P. Hain (ed.), *Policing the Police. Vol. 2.* Calder, 1980, pp. 63–150.

Carey, J. W. and Quirk, J. J. The Mythos of the Electronic Revolution. *The American Scholar* 39 (Spring and Summer) 1970: 219–241, 395–424.

Carlton, D. and Schaerf, C. (eds.). *Arms Control and Technological Innovation.* Croom Helm, 1977.

Catz, P. and Heller, R. Philips Fights Back. *Management Today,* April, 1973, pp. 71–78, 146.

Caute, D. *The Great Fear: The Anti-Communist Purge under Truman and Eisenhower.* Secker and Warburg, 1978.

Central Statistical Office. *Annual Abstract of Statistics.* 108. HMSO, 1971.

Central Statistical Office. *Annual Abstract of Statistics.* 119. HMSO, 1983.

Chalmers, M. *The Cost of Britain's Defence.* Housmans, 1983.

Chancellor of the Exchequer (Nigel Lawson). *Changing Employment Patterns: Where will the new jobs be?* National Economic Development Council (83) 58, 28 November, 1983.

Chandler, A. D., Jr. *The Visible Hand: The Managerial Revolution in American Business.* Cambridge, MA: Harvard University Press, 1977.

CIS (Counter Information Services). *The New Technology.* Anti-Report no. 23. CIS, 1978.

Clark, C. *The Conditions of Economic Progress.* Macmillan, 1940.

Clecak, P. *America's Quest for the Ideal Self: Dissent and Fulfillment in the 60s and 70s.* New York: Oxford University Press, 1983.

Clemitson, I. and Rodgers, G. *A Life to Live: Beyond Full Employment.* Junction Books, 1981.

Coates, K. Wage Slaves. *in* R. Blackburn and A. Cockburn (eds.), *The Incompatibles: Trade Union Militancy and the Consensus.* Harmondsworth: Penguin, 1967, pp. 56–92.

Cockburn, C. *Brothers: Male Dominance and Technological Change.* Pluto Press, 1983.

Cockerell, M., Hennessy, P. and Walker, D. *Sources Close to the Prime Minister: Inside the hidden world of the news manipulators.* Macmillan, 1984.

Coffield, F., Borrill, C. and Marshall, S. How Young People Try to Survive Being Unemployed. *New Society* 64(1072) 2 June 1983: 332–334.

Cohen, S. and Taylor, L. *Psychological Survival: The Experience of Long-Term Imprisonment.* Harmondsworth: Penguin, 1972.

Cohen, S. and Taylor, L. *Escape Attempts: The Theory and Practice of Resistance to Everyday Life.* Harmondsworth: Penguin, 1978.

Collins, R. *The Credential Society.* New York: Academic Press, 1979.

Command 8818. *Technology, Growth and Employment.* Report of the Working Group Set Up by the Economic Summit Meeting of 1982. HMSO, March 1983.

Commission of the European Communities *European Society Faced with the Challenge of New Information Technologies: A Community Response.* Com. (79), 650 final. Brussels, 26 November, 1979.

Compaine, B. M. *Who Owns the Media? Concentration of Ownership in the Mass Communications Industry.* New York: Knowledge Industry Publications, 1979.

Comstock, G. *Television in America.* Beverly Hills: Sage, 1980.

Connor, S. Micro Misery on Mersey. *Computing,* August 13, 1981, p. 20.

Conrad, P. *Television: The Medium and its Manners.* Routledge and Kegan Paul, 1982.

Conservative Party. *Proposals for a Conservative Information Technology Policy.* Provisional Draft Report. Conservative Central Office (mimeo), 1979.

Cooley, M. Taylor in the Office. *in* R. N. Ottoway (ed.), *Humanising the Workplace.* Croom Helm, 1977, pp. 65–77.

Cooley, M. *Architect or Bee? The Human/Technology Relationship.* Slough: Langley Technical Services, 1981a.

Cooley, M. The Taylorisation of Intellectual Work. *in* L. Levidow and B. Young (eds.), *Science, Technology and the Labour Process: Marxist Studies, vol. 1.* CSE Books, 1981b, pp. 46–65.

Coote, A. and Kellner, P. *Hear this Brother: Women Workers and Union Power.* New Statesman Report 1, 1980.

Corey, L. *The Crisis of the Middle Class.* New York: Covici, 1935.

Cornford, D. and Friedman, A. Research in the UK Reveals '80s Revamp for Jobs. *Computing,* February 2, 1984, p. 23.

Cornish, E. (ed.). *Communications Tomorrow: The Coming of the Information Society.* Bathesda: World Future Society, 1982.

Coriat, B. *Science, Technique et Capital.* Paris: Seuil, 1976.

Coriat, B. *L'Atelier et le Chronomètre: Essai sur le Taylorisme, le Fordisme et la Production de Masse.* Paris: Christian Bourgois Editeur, 1979.

Coulbeck, N. S. and Shaw, E. R. *UK Retail Banking Prospects in the Competitive 1980s.* Staniland Hall Associates, 1983.

Council for Science and Society. *New Technology: Society Employment and Skill.* Blackrose Press, 1981.

Cowan, R. Schwartz. *More Work for Mother: The Ironies of Household Technology from the Open Hearth to the Microwave.* New York: Basic Books, 1983.

CPRS (Central Policy Review Staff). *Social and Employment Implications of Microprocessors.* Cabinet Office: CPRS, 1978.

Craig, L. C. Office Automation at Texas Instruments Incorporated. *in* M. L. Moss (ed.), *Telecommunications and Productivity.* Reading MA: Addison-Wesley, 1981.

Crisp, J. Surge in Foreign Investment. *Financial Times,* March 21, 1983.

Crompton, R. and Reid, S. The Deskilling of Clerical Work. *in* S. Wood (ed.), 1982 (q.v., below) pp. 163–209.

Cronin, B. and Martyn, J. Public/private Sector Interaction: A Review of Issues with Particular Reference to Document Delivery and Electronic Publishing. *Aslib Proceedings* 36(10) 1984: 373–391.

Crouch, C. The State, Capital and Liberal Democracy. *in* C. Crouch (ed.), *State and Economy in Contemporary Capitalism.* Croom Helm, 1979, pp. 13–54.

Crozier, M. *The World of the Office Worker.* (1965). Translated by D. Landau. Chicago: University of Chicago Press, 1971.

CSE (Conference of Socialist Economists). *Microelectronics: Capitalist Technology and the Working Class.* CSE Books, 1980.

Curnow, R. and Curran, S. The Technology Applied. *in* G. Friedrichs and A. Schaff (eds.), 1982 (q.v., below), pp. 89–117.

Drafter, R. and Betts, P. The scramble to diversify. *Financial Times,* 25 March, 1981.

Daglish, R. (ed.). *The Scientific and Technological Revolution: Social Effects and Prospects.* Moscow: Progress Publishers, 1972.

Dahrendorf, R. *Class and Class Conflict in an Industrial Society.* Routledge and Kegan Paul, 1959.

Dahrendorf, R. et al. *Scientific-Technological Revolution: Social Aspects.* Sage, 1977.

Damodaran, L. The Impact of Office Automation upon Job Content and Function. *in International Word Processing Exhibition and Conference.* Northwood: Online, May 1980, pp. 1–11.

Darvall, F. O. *Popular Disturbances and Public Order in Regency England.* Oxford: Oxford University Press, 1934.

Davies, A. *Where did the Forties go? A Popular History: The Rise and Fall of the Hopes of a Decade.* Pluto Press, 1984.

Davies, N. and Black, I. Subversion and the State. *Guardian,* 17 April, 1984a, p. 19.

Davies, N. and Black, I. Techniques for Eavesdropping on the Public. *Guardian,* 18 April, 1984b, p. 6.

Davies, N. and Black, I. Targets for Covert Action. *Guardian,* 19 April, 1984c, p. 6.

Davis, L. E., Cantor, R. R. and Hoffman, J. Current Job Design Criteria. *in* L. E. Davis and J. C. Taylor (eds.), *Design of Jobs.* Harmondsworth: Penguin, 1972, pp. 65–82.

DES (Department of Education and Science). *Educational Implications of Microelectronic Technology.* DES, 24 October, 1978.

DES *Microelectronics in Education: A Development Programme for Schools and Colleges.* DES, March 1979.

Dex, S. and Perry, S. M. Women's Employment Changes in the 1970s. *Employment Gazette* 92(4) April 1984: 151–164.

Dickson, D. *Alternative Technology and the Politics of Technological Change.* Fontana, 1974.

Dickson, D. and Noble, D. By Force of Reason: The Politics of Science and Technology Policy. *in* T. Ferguson and J. Rogers (eds.), *The Hidden Election: Politics and Economics in the 1980 Presidential Campaign.* New York: Pantheon, 1981, pp. 260–312.

Dickson, P. *The Electronic Battlefield.* Bloomington: Indiana University Press, 1976.

Ditton J. Absent at Work: Or How to Manage Monotony. *New Society* 22 (533) 12 June, 1972: 679–681.

Ditton, J. Baking Time. *Sociological Review* 27 (1) 1979: 157–167.

Dizard, W. P. *The Coming Information Age: An Overview of Technology, Economics, and Politics.* Longman, 1982.

Dodsworth, T. Electronics Sector Viewed as "Weapon for the Future." *Financial Times,* 7 July, 1982.

Dodsworth, T. and Taylor, P. GM takes a $5 billion Gamble. *Financial Times,* June 6, 1985.

Dordick, H. S., Bradley, H. G. and Nanus, B. *The Emerging Network Marketplace.* Norwood, New Jersey: Ablex, 1981.

Dore, R. *British Factory-Japanese Factory.* Allen and Unwin, 1973.

Dosi, G. Institutions and Markets in High Technology: Government Support for Microelectronics in Europe. *in* C. Carter (ed.), *Industrial Policy and Innovation.* Heinemann, 1981, pp. 182–202.

Downing, H. Word Processors and the Oppression of Women. *in* T. Forester (ed.), 1980 (q.v., below), pp. 275-287.

Downing, H. On Being Automated. *Aslib Proceedings* 35 (1) 1983: 38–51.

Drucker, P. F. *The Practice of Management.* Heinemann, 1955

Drucker, P. F. *The Age of Discontinuity,* Heinemann, 1969.

Drucker, P. F. *Technology, Management, and Society.* Heinemann, 1970.

Drucker, P. F. *Concept of the Corporation.* New York: John Day Co., 1972.

Drucker, P. F. *Management: Tasks, Responsibilities, Practices.* New York: Harper and Row, 1974.

Drucker, P. F. The Coming Rediscovery of Scientific Management. *The Conference Board Recorder* 13 (6) 1976: 23–27.

Drucker, P. F. *People and Performance: The Best of Peter Drucker on Management.* Heinemann, 1977.

Duff, E. and Marsden, D. *Workless.* Harmondsworth: Penguin, 1975.

Duhm, R. and Mueckenberger, U. Computerisation and Control Strategies at Plant Level. *Policy Studies* 3 (4) 1983: 261-287.

Duncan, K. D., Gruneberg, M. M. and Wallis, D. (eds.). *Changes in Working Life.* Chichester: John Wiley, 1980.

Duncan, M. Microelectronics: Five areas of Subordination. *in* L. Levidow and B. Young (ed.), *Science, Technology and the Labor Process: Marxist Studies, vol. 1.* CSE Books, 1981, pp. 172-207.

Duncan, M. The Information Technology Industry in 1981. *Capital and Class* (17) Summer 1982: 78-113.

Dunlop, J. T. and Galenson, W. (eds.). *Labor in the Twentieth Century.* New York: Academic Press, 1978.

Economic Trends (Series). Central Statistical Office, HMSO.

Economist Intelligence Unit. *Coping with Unemployment: The Effects on the Unemployed Themselves.* Economist Intelligence Unit, December 1982.

Economist Intelligence Unit. *Cable Television in Western Europe – a licence to print money.* Economist Intelligence Unit, September 1983.

Edwards, R. *Contested Terrain: The Transformations of the Workplace in the Twentieth Century.* Heinemann, 1979.

Edwards, R. The Social Relations of Production at the Point of Production. *Insurgent Sociologist* 8 (11 & 111) 1980: 109-125.

EEC (European Economic Community). *The Perception of Poverty in Europe.* Brussels: EEC, 1977.

EETPU (Electrical, Electronic, Telecommunication and Plumbing Union). *The EETPU and Technological Change and An Ideal Technology Agreement for EETPU Stewards.* Bromley, Kent: EETPU, 1980.

Electronics Location File. *Outlook for the American Electronics Industry in 1983.* Richmond, Surrey: Urban Publishing Co., January 1983.

Ellul, J. *The Technological Society.* New York: Knopf, 1964.

Elmandjra, M. The Conquest of Space: A Few Political, Economic and Sociocultural Considerations. *Third World Quarterly* 6 (3) 1984: 576-603.

Employment Gazette. Regional Civilian Labor Force Projection. 86 (9) September 1978: 1040-1043.

Employment Gazette. Census of Employment Results for June 1978. 89 (2) February 1981: 61-68.

Employment Gazette. Labor Force Outlook to 1986. 89 (4) April 1981: 167-173.

Employment Gazette. Trends in Working Hours. 90 (11) November 1982: 477-486.

Employment Gazette. Census of Employment Results for September 1981. 90 (12) December 1982: 504-513.

Employment Gazette. Labor Force Estimates for 1981. 91 (2) February 1983: 50-54.

Employment Gazette. The Unemployed–Survey Estimates for 1981 Compared with the Monthly Count. 91 (6) June 1983: 265-267.

Employment Gazette. Statistics of Redundancies and Recent Trends. 91 (6) June 1983: 245-256, 259.

Employment Gazette. Shorter Hours through National Agreement. 91 (10) October 1983: 432-436.

Employment Gazette. Census of Employment Results for September 1981. Occasional Supplement no. 1 91 (5) May 1983.

Encel, S. The Post-Industrial Society and the Corporate State. *Australian and New Zealand Journal of Sociology* 15 (2) 1979: 37-44.

Engels, F. *Socialism: Utopian and Scientific. in* L. S. Feuer (ed.), *Marx and Engels: Basic Writings on Politics and Philosophy.* Fontana, 1971, pp. 109-152.

Ermann, M. D. The Operative Goals of Corporate Philanthrophy: Contributions to the Public Broadcasting Service, 1972-1976. *Social Problems* 25 (5) 1978: 504-514.

Ernst, D. *The Global Race in Micro-electronics: Innovation and Corporate Strategies in a Period of Crisis.* Frankfurt: Campus Verlag, 1983.

European Trade Union Institute. *The Impact of Microelectronics on Employment in Western Europe in the 1980s.* Brussels: ETUI, 1979.

Evans, C. *The Mighty Micro: the Impact of the Computer Revolution.* Gollancz, 1979.

Ewen, S. *Captains of Consciousness: Advertising and the Social Roots of the Consumer Culture.* New York: McGraw-Hill, 1976.

Ewen, S. and Ewen, E. *Channels of Desire: Mass Images and the Shaping of American Consciousness.* New York: McGraw-Hill, 1982.

Fallow, W. A. *Annual Meeting of Shareholders.* Rochester, New York: Kodak, May 5, 1982.

Fedida, S. and Malik, R. *The Viewdata Revolution.* Associated Business Press, 1979.

Feigenbaum, E. A. and McCorduck, P. *The Fifth Generation: Artificial Intelligence and Japan's Computer Challenge to the World.* Pan, 1984.

Fekete, J. McLuhanacy: Counterrevolution in Cultural Theory. *Telos* (15) 1973: 75-123.

Fekete, J. *The Critical Twilight: Explorations in the Ideology of Anglo-American Literary Theory from Eliot to McLuhan.* Routledge and Kegan Paul, 1978.

Feketekuty, G. and Aronson, J. D. Meeting the Challenges of the World Information Economy. *The World Economy* 7 (1) 1984: 63-87.

Feldberg, R. L. and Glenn, E. N. Male and Female: Job versus Gender Models in the Sociology of Work. *in* R. Kahn-Hut, A. Kaplan Daniels and R. Colvard (eds.), 1982, (q.v. below), pp. 65-80.

Ferkiss, V. Daniel Bell's concept of Post-Industrial Society: Theory, Myth, and Ideology. *Political Science Reviewer* 9 (Fall) 1979: 61-102.

Ferris, C. D. quoted in *Computer Communication Review* 10 (3) 1980: 7.

Filene, E. A. *Successful Living in this Machine Age.* Cape, 1932.

Finn, D. *The Employment Effects of the New Technologies: A Review of the Arguments.* Unemployment Unit, 1984.

Floud, J. A. Critique of Bell. *Survey* 17 (1) 1971: 25-37.

Ford, H. *My Life and Work.* (in collaboration with Samuel Crowther). Heinemann, 1923.

Ford, H. *Today and Tomorrow.* Heinemann, 1926.

Forester, T. Manpower and Chips. *New Society* 46 (838) 26 October 1978: 209.

Forester, T. The Typist and the "Smart Machine." *New Society* 53 (930) 11 September, 1980: 504-507.

Forester, T. (ed.). *The Microelectronics Revolution: The Complete Guide to the New Technology and its Impact on Society.* Oxford: Blackwell, 1980.

Form, W. and McMillen, D. B. Women, Men, and Machines. *Work and Occupations* 10 (2) 1983: 147-178.

Fossum, E. (ed.). *Computerization of Working Life.* Chichester: Ellis Horwood, 1983.

Fothergill, R. The Microelectronics Education Programme in the UK. *in* J. Megarry et al. (eds.), *World Yearbook on Education 1982/83: Computers and Education.* Kogan Page, 1983, pp. 131-137.

Foucault, M. *Discipline and Punish: The Birth of the Prison.* Harmondsworth: Penguin, 1979.

Fox, A. *Beyond Contract: Work, Power and Trust Relations.* Faber and Faber, 1974.

Fox, A. The Meaning of Work. *in* G. Esland and G. Salaman (eds.), *The Politics of Work and Occupations.* Milton Keynes: Open University Press, 1980, pp. 139-191.

Fraser, R. (ed.). *Work: Twenty Personal Accounts. vol. I.* Harmondsworth: Penguin, 1968.

Fraser, W. H. *The Coming of the Mass Market, 1850-1914.* Macmillan, 1981.

Freeman, C. *Technical Change and Unemployment.* Brighton, University of Sussex: Science Policy Research Unit (mimeo), January 1978(a).

Freeman, C. *Government Policies for Industrial Innovation.* J. D. Bernal Memorial Lecture, Birkbeck College (mimeo), May 23, 1978(b).

Freeman, C., Clark, J. and Soete, L. *Unemployment and Technical Innovation: A Study of Long Waves and Economic Development.* Frances Pinter, 1982.

Friedland, W. H. and Barton, A. *Destalking the Wily Tomato: A Case Study in Social Conse-quences in California Agricultural Research.* Davis: University of California, Depart-ment of Applied Behavioral Sciences, Research Monograph no. 15, 1976.

Friedland, W. H., Barton, A. and Thomas, R. J. *Manufacturing Green Gold: Capital, Labor, and Technology in the Lettuce Industry.* New York: Cambridge University Press, 1981.

Friedman, A. *Industry and Labor: Class Struggle at Work and Monopoly Capitalism.* Mac-millan, 1977.

Friedmann, G. *Industrial Society: the emergence of the human problems of automation.* New York: Free Press, 1955.

Friedrichs, G. and Schaff, A. (eds.). *Microelectronics and Society: For Better or for Worse.* Oxford: Pergamon Press, 1982.

Fuchs, V. R. *The Service Economy.* New York: Columbia University Press, 1968.

Furnham, A. Attitudes toward the unemployed receiving social security benefits. *Human Re-lations* 36 (2) 1983: 135-150.

Galbraith, J. K. *The Affluent Society.* (1958). Reprinted Harmondsworth: Penguin, 1968.

Galbraith, J. K. *The New Industrial State.* (1967). Reprinted Harmondsworth: Penguin, 1975.

Galbraith, J. K. *The Galbraith Reader.* Deutsch, 1979.

Galenson, W. and Smith, R. S. The United States. *in* J. T. Dunlop and W. Galenson (eds), 1978 (q. v., above), ch. 1.

Gamble, A. The Free Economy and the Strong State. *in* R. Miliband and J. Saville (eds.), *Socialist Register 1979.* Merlin, 1979, pp. 1-25.

Ganley, O. H. and Ganley, G. D. *To Inform or to Control? The New Communications Net-works.* New York: McGraw-Hill, 1982.

Gansler, J. S. *The Defense Industry.* Cambridge MA: MIT Press, 1980.

Gardner, C. and Young, R. Science on TV: A Critique. *in* T. Bennett et al. (eds.), 1981 (q.v., above), pp. 171-193.

Garnham, N. Public Service versus the Market. *Screen* 24 (1) 1983: 6-27.

Garson, B. *All the Livelong Day: The Meaning and Demeaning of Routine Work.* Harmonds-worth: Penguin, 1977.

Gaudemar, J. -P. de. *La Mobilization Générale.* Paris: Editions du Champ Urbain, 1979.

Gaudemar, J. -P. de. *L'Ordre et la Production.* Paris: Dunod, 1982.

GEC (General Electric Company). *GEC 82.* GEC, 1982.

General Household Survey 1980. Office of Population Censuses and Surveys, Social Survey Division, HMSO, 1982.

Gennard, J. and Dunn, S. The Impact of New Technology on the Structure and Organization of Craft Unions in the Printing Industry. *British Journal of Industrial Relations* 21 (1) 1983: 17-32.

George, D. *England in Transition: Life and Work in the Eighteenth Century.* (1931). Reprinted Harmondsworth: Penguin, 1962.

Gershuny, J. I. Post-Industrial Society: the Myth of the Service Economy. *Futures* 9 (2) 1977: 103-114.

Gershuny, J. I. The Self-Service Economy. *New Universities Quarterly* 32 (1) 1978a: 50-66.

Gershuny, J. I. *After Industrial Society? The Emerging Self-Service Economy*, Macmillan, 1978b.

Gershuny, J. I. The Informal Economy: Its Role in Post-Industrial Society. *Futures* 11 (1) 1979: 3-15.

Gershuny, J. I. Social Innovation: Change in the Mode of Provision of Services. *Futures* 14 (4) 1982: 496-516.

Gershuny, J. I. *Social Innovation and the Division of Labour.* Oxford: Oxford University Press, 1983.

Gershuny, J. I. and Miles, I. *The New Service Economy: The Transformation of Employment in Industrial Societies.* Frances Pinter, 1983.

Gershuny, J. I. and Pahl, R. E. Britain in the Decade of the Three Economies. *New Society* **51** (900) 3 January, 1980: 7-9.

Gershuny, J. I. and Pahl, R. E. Work outside employment: some preliminary speculations. *in* S. Henry (ed.), *Can I Have it in Cash? A Study of Informal Institutions and Unorthodox Ways of Doing Things.* Astragal Books, 1981, pp. 73-88.

Giddens, A. *Capitalism and Modern Social Theory: An Analysis of the Writings of Marx, Durkheim and Max Weber.* Cambridge: Cambridge University Press, 1971.

Giddens, A. *The Class Structure of the Advanced Societies.* Second edition. Hutchinson, 1981a.

Giddens, A. *A Contemporary Critique of Historical Materialism.* Macmillan, 1981b.

Giddens, A. and Mackenzie, G. (eds.). *Social Class and the Division of Labor.* Cambridge: Cambridge University Press, 1982.

Gidlow, B. Unemployment and Technological Change. *Australian and New Zealand Journal of Sociology* **18** (1) 1982: 45-60.

Gilchrist, B., Dagli, A. and Shenkin, A. The DP Population Boom. *Datamation* **29** (9) September 1983: 100-110.

Gilison, J. M. *The Soviet Image of Utopia.* Baltimore: Johns Hopkins University Press, 1975.

Gilpin, R. *U.S. Power and the Multinational Corporation.* Macmillan, 1975.

Ginzberg, E. The Professionalization of the U.S. Labor Force. *Scientific American* **240** (3) 1979: 48-53.

Ginzberg, E. The Mechanization of Work. *Scientific American* **247** (3) 1982: 38-47.

Ginzburg, E. S. *Into the Whirlwind.* Harmondsworth: Penguin, 1968.

Giuliano, V. E. The Mechanization of Office Work. *Scientific American* **247** (3) 1982: 125-134.

Glenn, E. N. and Feldberg, R. L. Proletarianizing Clerical Work: Technology and Organizational Control in the Office. *in* A. Zimbalist (ed.), 1979 (q.v., below), pp. 51-72.

Glenn, E. N. and Feldberg, R. L. Degraded and Deskilled: The Proletarianization of Clerical Work. *in* R. Kahn-Hut, A. Kaplan Daniels and R. Colvard (eds.), 1982 (q.v., below), pp. 202-217.

GMWU (General and Municipal Workers' Union). *New Technology: Report to Congress.* Esher, Surrey: GMWU, 1980.

Golding, P. and Middleton, S. Making Claims: News Media and the Welfare State. *Media, Culture and Society* **1** (1) 1979: 5-21.

Golding, P. and Murdock, G. For a Political Economy of Mass Communications. *in* R. Miliband and J. Saville (eds.), *Socialist Register 1973.* Merlin, 1974, pp. 205-234.

Golding, P. and Murdock, G. Capitalism, Communication and Class Relations. *in* J. Curran, M. Gurevitch and J. Woollacott (eds.), *Mass Communication and Society.* Edward Arnold, 1977, pp. 12-43.

Golding, P. and Murdock, G. Privatising Pleasure. *Marxism Today*, October, 1983, pp. 32-36.

Goldsen, R. K. The Great American Consciousness Machine: Engineering the Thought-Environment. *Journal of Social Reconstruction* **1** (2) 1980: 87-102.

Goldthorpe, J. H. Theories of Industrial Society: Reflections on the Recrudescence of Historicism and the Future of Futurology. *European Journal of Sociology* **12** (2) 1971: 263-288.

Goldthorpe, J. H., Lockwood, D., Bechofer, F. and Platt, J. *The Affluent Worker: Industrial Attitudes and Behavior.* Cambridge: Cambridge University Press, 1968.

Goldthorpe, J. H., Lockwood, D., Bechofer, F. and Platt, J. *The Affluent Worker in the Class Structure.* Cambridge: Cambridge University Press, 1969.

Goodman, R. F., Smith, A. E. and Conn, E. *New Technology in the Civil Service.* Central Computer and Telecommunications Agency, February 1980.

Gordon, F. E. Telecommunications: Implications for Women. *Telecommunications Policy* **1** (4) 1976: 68-74.

Gorz, A. On the Class Character of Science and Scientists. *in* H. Rose and S. Rose (eds.), *The*

Political Economy of Science. Macmillan, 1976, pp. 59-71.

Gorz, A. *Farewell to the Working Class: An Essay on Post-Industrial Socialism*. Pluto Press, 1982.

Gorz, A. The Reconquest of Time. *Telos* (55) 1983a: 212-225.

Gorz, A. A World with its Work Cut Out for the Future. *Guardian*, 1 August, 1983b.

Gosling, W. *Microelectronics, Society and Education*. Council for Educational Technology (Occasional Paper no. 8), 1978.

Gosling, W. *The Kingdom of Sand*. Council for Educational Technology (Occasional Paper no. 9), 1981.

Gouldner, A. W. *The Two Marxisms: Contradictions and Anomalies in the Development of Theory*. Macmillan, 1980.

Gouré, L., Kohler, F. D., Soll, R. and Stiefbold, A. *Convergence of Communism and Capitalism: The Soviet View*. Miami: Monographs in International Affairs, Center for Advanced International Studies, University of Miami, 1973.

Gournay, C. de. Leisure and Cultural Activities in the Information Society. *in* L. Bannon, U. Barry, and O. Holst (eds.), *Information Technology: Impact on the Way of Life*. Dublin: Tycooly International, 1982, pp. 293-313.

Government Statistical Services. Privy Council Office Command 8236. April 1981.

Granov, A. *Capitalisme et Mode de Vie*. Paris: Editions du Cerf, 1974.

Gray, C. S. Space is not a Sanctuary. *Survival* 25 (5) 1983: 194-204.

Gray, S., McSweeney, B. and Shaw, J. *Information Disclosure and the Multinational Corporation*. Chichester: John Wiley and Sons, 1984.

Greater London Council. *Cabling in London*. Report by Economic Policy Group. GLC, December 2, 1982.

Green, K., Coombs, R. and Holroyd, K. *The Effects of Microelectronic Technologies on Employment Prospects: a case study on Tameside*. Farnborough, Hants: Gower, 1980.

Green, K. and Coombs, R. Employment and New Technology in Tameside. *Futures* 13 (1) 1981: 43-50.

Greenbaum, J. Division of Labor in the Computer Field. *Monthly Review* 28 (3) 1976: 40-55.

Greenbaum, J. *In the Name of Efficiency: Management Theory and Shopfloor Practice in Data-Processing Work*. Philadelphia: Temple University Press, 1979.

Griffin, T. Technological Change and Craft Control in the Newspaper Industry: An International Comparison. *Cambridge Journal of Economics* 8 (1) 1984: 41-61.

Groom, B. Costs of a Cashless Future. *Financial Times*, 9 July, 1982.

Guest, D., Williams, R. and Dewe, P. Workers' Perceptions of Changes in the Quality of Working Life. *in* K. D. Duncan, M. M. Gruneberg and D. Wallis (eds.), 1980 (q.v., above), pp. 499-519.

Haber, S. *Efficiency and Uplift*. Chicago: University of Chicago Press, 1964.

Habermas, J. *Strukturwandel der Öffentlichkeit*. Darmstadt: Luchterhand, 1962.

Habermas, J. The Public Sphere: An Encyclopedia Article. *New German Critique* (3) Fall 1974: 49-55.

Hacker, A. *U/S: A Statistical Portrait of the American People*. Harmondsworth: Penguin, 1983a.

Hacker, A. Where Have All the Jobs Gone? *New York Review of Books* 30 (11) June 30, 1983b: 27-32.

Hakim, C. Sexual Divisions Within the Labor Force: Occupational Segregation. *Employment Gazette* 86 (11) November 1978: 1264-1268.

Hakim, C. *Occupational Segregation*. Research Paper no. 9. Department of Employment, 1979.

Hakim, C. Job Segregation: Trends in the 1970s. *Employment Gazette* 89 (12) December 1981: 521-529.

Hall, S. The Culture Gap. *Marxism Today*, January, 1984, pp. 18-22.

Halley, R. B. and Vatter, H. G. Technology and the Future as History: A Critical Review of Futurism. *Technology and Culture* 19 (1) 1978: 53-82.

Hamelink, C. J. *Finance and Information: a Study of Converging Interests.* Norwood, New Jersey: Ablex, 1983.

Hane, M. *Peasants, Rebels and Outcasts: The Underside of Modern Japan.* New York: Pantheon, 1982.

Hanson, D. *The New Alchemists: Silicon Valley and the Microelectronics Revolution.* Boston; Little, Brown and Company, 1982.

Hargreaves, I. Why ITT Finds that Being Big is Not Big Enough. *Financial Times,* 6 January, 1982.

Hargreaves, I. The Crisis that Growth Alone Will Not Solve. *Financial Times,* January 7, 1983.

Hargreaves, I. Why Shorter Hours Are Here to Stay. *Financial Times,* January 24, 1983.

Hargreaves, I. Jobs: The Story Behind the Figures. *Financial Times,* 20 May, 1983.

Harman, C. *Is a Machine After Your Job? New Technology and the Struggles for Socialism.* Socialist Workers' Party, 1979.

Harrington, M. Leisure as the Means of Production. *in* L. Kolakowski and S. Hampshire (eds.), *The Socialist Idea.* Weidenfeld and Nicolson, 1974, pp. 153–163.

Harris, D. and Taylor, J. *The Service Sector: its Changing Role as a Source of Employment.* Center for Environmental Studies, 1978.

Harris, D. *I.T. and the Distribution Trades.* Tesco Stores (mimeo), 25 April, 1983.

Harris, R. *Gotcha! The Media, the Government and the Falklands Crisis.* Faber, 1983.

Hayek, F. A. The Use of Knowledge in Society. *American Economic Review* 35 (4) 1945: 519–530.

Henry, S. The Working Unemployed: Perspectives on the Informal Economy and Unemployment. *Sociological Review* 30 (3) 1982: 460–477.

Herman, E. S. *Corporate Control, Corporate Power.* New York: Cambridge University Press, 1981.

Herzberg, F. *Work and the Nature of Man.* Staples Press, 1968.

Herzfeld, C. M. Command, Control and Communications. *in* C. Bertram (ed.), *New Conventional Weapons and East-West Security.* Macmillan, 1978, pp. 90–93.

Hill, S. *Competition and Control at Work: the new industrial sociology.* Heinemann, 1981.

Hills, P. (ed.). *The Future of the Printed Word: the impact and implications of the new communications technology.* Frances Pinter, 1980.

Hines, C. *The 'Chips' Are Down.* Earth Resources Research (mimeo), 1978.

Hines, C. and Searle, G. *Automatic Unemployment: A Discussion of the Impact of Microelectronic Technology on U.K. Employment and the Responses this Demands.* Earth Resources Research, 1979.

Hirschmeier, J. and Yui, T. *The Development of Japanese Business, 1600-1973.* Allen and Unwin, 1975.

Hobsbawm, E. J. *Labouring Men.* Weidenfeld and Nicholson, 1964.

Hobsbawm, E. J. *Industry and Empire.* (1968). Reprinted Harmondsworth: Penguin, 1978.

Hoffmann, E. P. Soviet Views of 'The Scientific-Technological Revolution'. *World Politics* 30 (4) 1978: 615–644.

Hoggart, R. *The Uses of Literacy: Aspects of working-class life with special reference to publications and entertainments.* (1957). Reprinted Harmondsworth: Penguin, 1968.

Hoggart, R. *Speaking to Each Other, vol. I.* Chatto and Windus, 1970.

Hoggart, R. Must We be Casualties in the TV Explosion? *Guardian,* 13 September, 1982, p. 13.

Hoggart, R. *The Hunt Report and Cable Regulation: An Alternative.* Broadcasting Reseach Unit, February 15, 1983.

Holland, S. *The Socialist Challenge.* Quartet, 1976.

Home Office and Department of Industry. *The Development of Cable Systems and Services.* Command 8866. HMSO, April 1983.

Hood, N. and Young, S. *The Economics of Multinational Enterprise.* Longman, 1979.

Hood, S. *On Television.* Pluto Press, 1980.

Hoos, I. R. *Automation in the Office.* Washington DC: Public Affairs Press, 1961.

House of Commons. Second Report from the Defence Committee, Session 1981-82: *Ministry of Defence Organization and Procurement*. 2 volumes. HMSO, 16 June, 1982.

House of Commons. First Report from the Defence Committee, Session 1982-83: *The Handling of the Press and Public Information during the Falklands Conflict*. 2 volumes, HMSO, December 1982.

House of Lords. Select Committee on the European Communities, Session 1980-81: *New Information Technologies*. 27th Report. HMSO, 19 May, 1981.

House of Lords. *Report from the Select Committee of the House of Lords on Unemployment. Vol. 1–Report*. HMSO, 10 May, 1982.

Howlett, J. *Report of the National Committee on Computer Networks*. Presented to the Secretary of State by J. Howlett. Department of Industry, October 1978.

Huws, U. *New Technology and Women's Employment: case studies from West Yorkshire*. Manchester: Equal Opportunities Commission, December 1982a.

Huws, U. *Your job in the Eighties: a woman's guide to new technology*. Pluto Press, 1982b.

Huws, U. *The New Homeworkers*. Low Pay Unit, 1984.

Hyman, A. *The Coming of the Chip*. New English Library, 1980.

Hymer, S. H. *The Multinational Corporation: a radical approach*. New York: Cambridge University Press, 1979.

ICCP (Information Computer Communications Policy) Series. No.5.–*Microelectronics, Productivity and Employment*. Paris: OECD, 1981a.

ICCP No. 6.–*Information Activities, Electronics and Telecommunications Technologies–Impact on Employment, Growth and Trade*. vol. 1. Summary and Analytical Report. Paris: OECD, 1981b.

ILO (International Labor Organization). *Women workers and society: international perspectives*. Geneva: International Labor Office, 1976.

ILO *Yearbook of Labor Statistics 1982*. Geneva: International Labor Office, 1982.

Infotech State of the Art Report. *Office Automation: Analysis*. 8 (3). Maidenhead: Infotech, 1980.

Ingram, M. Trouble with Security. *New Society* 68 (1123) May 31, 1984: 349-350.

IT '82. Open Letter from Project Director. Croyden: Committee for Information Technology Ltd., October 1982.

ITAP (Information Technology Advisory Panel). *Cable Systems*. Cabinet Office: HMSO, March 1982.

ITAP. *Making a Business of Information: a survey of new opportunities*. Cabinet Office: September 1983.

ITT (International Telegraph and Telephone Corporation). *Form 10-K*. Washington DC: Securities and Exchange Commission, December 31, 1981.

Jacoby, R. *Dialectic of Defeat: Contours of Western Marxism*. New York: Cambridge University Press, 1981.

Jahoda, M. *Employment and Unemployment: a Social-psychological Analysis*. Cambridge: Cambridge University Press, 1982.

Jamieson, K. H. *Packaging the Presidency: A History and Criticism of Presidential Campaign Advertising*. New York: Oxford University Press, 1984.

Janowitz, M. Review Symposium: The Coming of Post-Industrial Society. *American Journal of Sociology* 80 (1) 1974: 230-236.

Jefferson, Sir G. Why BT Must Have the Freedom to Compete. *Financial Times*, 25 January, 1984, p. 19.

Jefferson, Sir G. *The Industrial and Employment Implications of the Cable Revolution*. NEDC (84) 34, 26 April, 1984.

Jenkin, P. 'The Unemployed Cannot Blame Automation.' *New Scientist* 97 (1346) 24 February 1983: 526-527.

Jenkins, C. and Sherman, B. *The Collapse of Work*. Eyre Methuen, 1979

Jenkins, C. and Sherman, B. *The Leisure Shock*. Eyre Methuen, 1981.

Johnson, C. *MITI and the Japanese Miracle: The Growth of Industrial Policy, 1925-1975.* Stanford: Standford University Press, 1982.

Johnson, H. G. *Technology and Economic Interdependence.* Macmillan, 1975.

Johnson, R. W. 007: Licence to Kill? *Guardian*, December 17, 1983, p. 15.

Jonas, H. Reflections on Technology, Progress, Utopia. *Social Research* 48 (3) 1981: 411-455.

Jones, Barry, *Sleepers, Wake: Technology and the future of work.* Brighton: Wheatsheaf Books, 1982.

Jones, Bryn, Destruction or Redistribution of Engineering Skills: The Case of Numerical Control. *in* S. Wood (ed.), 1982 (q.v., below), pp. 179-200;

Jones, M. G. Telecommunications Technologies: New Approaches to Consumer Information Dissemination. *The Information Society* 1 (1) 1981: 31-52.

Jones, M. G. The Challenge of the New Information Technologies: The Need to Respond to Citizens' Information Needs. *The Information Society* 2 (2) 1983: 145-156.

Jones, T. (ed.), *Microelectronics and Society.* Milton Keynes: Open University Press, 1980.

Jones, T. Consumers' Expenditure. *Economic Trends* (359) September 1983: 96-107.

Jonquieres, G. de. The Next Decade will Bring Radical Changes. *Financial Times*, 3 March, 1980a.

Jonquieres, G. de. The "Wired Society" Gamble. *Financial Times*, 1 October, 1980b.

Jonquieres, G. de. Philip Goes for the World. *Financial Times*, October 26, 1982.

Jonquieres, G. de. Anxieties Rise as the Pace Quickens. *Financial Times*, March 21, 1983a.

Jonquieres, G. de. Going for Broke to Stay Number One. *Financial Times*, August 15, 1983b.

Jonquieres, G. de. IBM's Rivals Strike Back. *Financial Times*, November 21, 1983c.

Jonquieres, G. de and Stone, J. The Magnet Loses its Pull. *Financial Times*, June 27, 1985.

Jordan, B. *Automatic Unemployment.* Routledge and Kegan Paul, 1981.

Joseph, Sir K. *Reversing the Trend.* Chichester: Rose Books, 1976.

Jungk, R. *The Nuclear State.* Calder, 1979.

Kahn-Hut, R., Kaplan Daniels, A. and Colvard, R. (eds.), *Women and Work: Problems and Perspectives.* New York: Oxford University Press, 1982.

Kakar, S. *Frederick Taylor: A Study in Personality and Innovation.* Cambridge MA: MIT Press, 1970.

Kaldor, M. *The Baroque Arsenal.* New York: Hill and Wang, 1981.

Kaldor, M. Military R&D: Cause or Consequence of the Arms Race? *International Social Science Journal* 35 (1) 1983: 25-45.

Keel, E. E. Microelectronics: Crucial Salients in the War of Technology. *Military Review*, January, 1981, pp. 43-50.

Keen, P. W. Telecommunications and Business Policy. *in* R. W. Haigh, G. Gerber and R. B. Byrne (eds.), *Communications in the Twenty-First Century.* New York: Wiley, 1981, pp. 138-153.

Kendall, P. M. H., Crayston, J., Malecki, A. M. J., Wallace A. S., and Wheatley, T. F. *The Impact of Chip Technology on Employment and the Labor Market.* Metra Consulting Group Ltd, 1979.

Kennedy, G. *Defense Economics.* Duckworth, 1983.

Kerbo, H. R. and Della Fave, L. R. Corporate Linkage and Control of the Corporate Economy: New Evidence and a Reinterpretation. *Sociological Quarterly* 24 (2) 1983: 201-218.

Ketron, R. W. Four Roads to Office Automation. *Datamation* 26 (11) November 1980: 138-140.

Kidder, T. *The Soul of a New Machine.* Harmondsworth: Penguin, 1982.

King, A. Introduction. *in* G. Friedrichs and A. Schaff (eds.), 1982 (q.v., above), pp. 1-36.

Kleinberg, B. S. *American Society in the Postindustrial Age: Technocracy, Power, and the End of Ideology.* Columbus, Ohio: Merrill, 1973.

Kleinshrod, W. A. Did All That Happen in Only Ten Years? *Administrative Management*, January, 1981, pp. 26-27, 74-75.

Klingender, F. D. *The Condition of Clerical Labor in Great Britain.* Martin Lawrence, 1935.

Kolko, J. and Kolko, G. *The Limits of Power: The World and United States Foreign Policy, 1945-1954.* New York: Harper and Row, 1972.

Kraft, P. *Programmers and Managers: The Routinization of Computer Programming in the United States.* New York: Springer-Verlag, 1977.

Kraft, P. The Industrialization of Computer Programming: from Programming to 'Software Production'. *in* A. Zimbalist (ed.), 1979a (q.v., below), pp. 1-17.

Kraft, P. The Routinizing of Computer Programming. *Sociology of Work and Occupations* 6 (2) 1979b: 139-155.

Kraft, P. and Dubnoff, S. Software for Women Means a Lower Status. *Computing*, February 9, 1984, p. 21.

Kransdorff, A. How Texaco Oiled its Administrative Wheels. *Financial Times*, October 1, 1982.

Kuhns, W. *The Post-Industrial Prophets: Interpretations of Technology.* New York: Weybright and Talley, 1971.

Kumar, K. *Prophecy and Progress: The Sociology of Industrial and Post-Industrial Society.* Harmondsworth: Penguin, 1978.

Kumar, K. The Social Culture of Work: Work, Employment and Unemployment as Ways of Life. *New Universities Quarterly* 34 (1) 1979: 5-28.

Kumar, K. Class and Political Action in Nineteenth Century England. *European Journal of Sociology* 24 (1) 1983: 3-43.

Labour Force Survey 1981. Office of Population Censuses and Surveys. HMSO, 1982.

Labour Party. *Microelectronics: A Labor Party Discussion Document.* Labor Party, 1980.

Labour Research. Multinationals Better at Exporting Jobs than Goods. 72 (4) April 1983: 97-99.

Landes, D. *The Unbound Prometheus: Technological Change and Industrial Development in Western Europe from 1750 to the present.* Cambridge: Cambridge University Press, 1969.

Large, P. *The Micro Revolution.* Fontana, 1980.

Lasch, C. *Haven in a Heartless World: The Family Beseiged.* New York: Basic Books, 1977.

Lasch, C. *The Culture of Narcissism: American Life in an Age of Diminishing Expectations.* New York: Warner Books, 1979.

Laurie, P. *The Micro Revolution.* Futura, 1980.

Laver, M. *Computers and Social Change.* Cambridge: Cambridge University Press, 1980.

Leach, E. *A Runaway World? The Reith Lectures.* BBC Publications, 1967.

Leapman, M. *Treachery?–The Power Struggle at TV-am.* Allen and Unwin, 1984.

Leigh, D. *The Frontiers of Secrecy: Closed Government in Britain.* Junction Books, 1980.

Leiss, W. *The Limits to Satisfaction: On Needs and Commodities.* Marion Boyars, 1978.

Lenin, V. I. *Collected Works, vol. 42. Supplementary Material, October 1917-March 1923.* Lawrence and Wishart, 1969.

Levin, J. A. Interactive Entertainment: The Challenge to Broadcast Media. *Telecommunications Policy* 6 (2) 1982: 143-146.

Levine, N. *The Tragic Deception: Marx contra Engels.* Oxford: Clio Books, 1975.

Levitt, T. The Industrialization of Service. *Harvard Business Review* 54 (5) 1976: 63-74.

Linhart, R. *Lénine, les Paysans, Taylor.* Paris: Seuil, 1976.

Lipietz, A. Towards Global Fordism? *New Left Review* (132) March–April 1982: 33-47.

Lipset, S. M. (ed.). *The Third Century: America as a Post-Industrial Society.* Stanford: Hoover Institution Press, 1979.

Lipset, S. M. Whatever Happened to the Proletariat? An Historic Mission Unfulfilled. *Encounter* 56 (June) 1981: 18-34.

Little Consultants, A.D. *The Emergent Real World of Office Automation.* Cambridge MA: A. D. Little, 1979.

Littlechild, S. *Regulation of British Telecommunications' Profitability.* Department of Industry, HMSO, February 1983.

Littler, C. R. *The Development of the Labor Process in Capitalist Societies.* Heinemann, 1982.

Littler, C. R. and Salaman, G. Bravermania and Beyond: Recent theories of the labor process. *Sociology* 16 (2) 1982: 251–269.

Livingstone, K. *Report by the Leader of the Council: British Telecom and the Two Nations.* Greater London Council, Council Agenda, May 3, 1983, pp. 2-7.

Lloyd, J. Automation Still in its Infancy. *Financial Times*, October 23, 1979.

Locksley, G. Europe and the Electronics Industry: Conflicting Strategies in Positive Restructuring. *West European Politics* 6 (2) 1983: 128-138.

Long, F. A. and Reppy, J. (eds.). *The Genesis of New Weapons: Decision Making for Military R&D.* New York: Pergamon Press, 1980.

Lukacs, G. *History and Class Consciousness: Studies in Marxist Dialectics.* Merlin, 1971.

Lukacs, G. Max Weber and German Sociology. *Economy and Society* 1 (4) 1972: 386–398.

Lupton, T. and Tanner, I. Work Design in Europe. *in* K. D. Duncan, M. M. Gruneberg and D. Wallis (eds.), 1980 (q.v., above), pp. 217-236.

Machlup, F. *The Production and Distribution of Knowledge in the United States.* Princeton: Princeton University Press, 1962.

Mackie, L. and Pattullo, P. *Women at Work.* Tavistock, 1977.

Mackintosh Consultants. *Mackintosh European Electronics Companies File.* Luton: Mackintosh, 1980.

Macrae, N. The Coming Entrepreneurial Revolution: A Survey. *Economist* 261 (6956) December 25, 1976: 41-65.

Macrae, N. The Third Industrial Revolution. *in* A. Neil (ed.), 1982 (q. v., below), pp. 14–17.

Maddock, Sir Ieuan. *Civil Exploitation of Defence Technology.* Report to the Electronics Economic Development Committee. National Economic Development Office, February 1983.

Maddox, B. Cable Television: The Wiring of America. *Economist* 279 (7190) June 20, 1981: 26-30.

Magrill, D. Information at the Touch of a Button. *New Scientist* 77 (1084) 12 January, 1978: 76-79.

Maier, C. S. Between Taylorism and Technocracy: European Ideologies and the Vision of Industrial Productivity in the 1920s. *Journal of Contemporary History* 5 (2) 1970: 27–61.

Malik, R. *And Tomorrow... The World? Inside IBM.* Millington, 1975.

Management and Personnel Office. *Equal Opportunities for Women in the Civil Service: a report by the Joint Review Group on Employment Opportunties for Women in the Civil Service.* HMSO, 1983.

Manley, P. and Sawbridge, D. Women at work. *Lloyds Bank Review* (135) January 1980:29-40.

Manwaring–White, S. *The Policing Revolution: Policy Technology, Democracy and Liberty in Britain.* Brighton: Harvester Press, 1983.

Marcuse, H. *Soviet Marxism: A Critical Analysis.* Routledge and Kegan Paul, 1958.

Marcuse, H. *One-Dimensional Man.* Routledge and Kegan Paul, 1964.

Marsden, D. *Workless: An Exploration of the Social Contract Between Society and the Worker.* Croom Helm, 1982.

Marsh, D. IBM and Mitterand—An Entende Cordiale. *Financial Times,* November 28, 1983, p. 21.

Marsh, D. and Locksley, G. Capital in Britain: Its Structural Power and Influence over Policy. *West European Politics* 6 (2) 1983: 36–60.

Marsh, P. *The Silicon Chip Book.* Abacus, 1981.

Marsh, P. Britain Faces up to Information Technology. *New Scientist* 96 (1335) 9 December, 1982: 634-638.

Marti, J. and Zeilinger, A. *Micros and Money: New Technology in Banking and Shopping.* Policy Studies Institute (no. 608), July 1982.

Martin, J. *Future Developments in Telecommunications.* Second edition. Englewood Cliffs: Prentice-Hall, 1977.

Martin, J. *The Wired Society*. Englewood Cliffs: Prentice-Hall, 1978a.

Martin, J. *Communications Satellite Systems.* Englewood Cliffs: Prentice-Hall, 1978b.

Martin, R. *New Technology and Industrial Relations in Fleet Street*. Oxford: Clarendon Press, 1981.

Martin, W. H. and Mason, S. *Leisure and Work: The Choices for 1991 and 2001*. Sudbury, Suffolk: Leisure Consultants, 1982.

Marx, K. *On Colonialism*. Lawrence and Wishart, 1950.

Marx, K. *Wage Labor and Capital*. Moscow: Progress Publishers, 1967.

Marx, K. *Capital: A Critique of Political Economy. vol. 1*. Lawrence and Wishart, 1970.

Marx, K. *Grundrisse*. Harmondsworth: Penguin, 1973.

Marx, K. *Early Writings*. Harmondsworth: Penguin, 1975.

Marx, K. and Engels, F. *Selected Works. vol. 1*. Moscow: Foreign Languages Publishing House, 1958.

Marx, K. and Engels, F. *Collected Works. vol. 5*. Lawrence and Wishart, 1976.

Marx, K. and Engels, F. *Collected Works. vol. 38*. Lawrence and Wishart, 1982.

Marx, L. *The Machine in the Garden*. New York: Oxford University Press, 1964.

Masuda, Y. A New Development Stage of the Information Revolution. in *Applications of Computer and Telecommunications Systems*. Paris: OECD, 1975.

Masuda, Y. *The Information Society as Post-Industrial Society*. Washington DC: World Future Society, 1981.

Mattera, P. Small is not Beautiful: Decentralized Production and the Underground Economy in Italy. *Radical America* 14 (5) 1980: 67-76.

McCartney, L. Our Newest High-Tech Export: Jobs. *Datamation* 29 (5) May 1983: 114-118.

McCuster, T. Examining the Office of the Future. *Datamation* 26 (2) February 1980: 120-121.

McDonald, S. and Mandeville, T. Word Processors and Employment. *Journal of Industrial Relations* 21 (4) 1980: 137-148.

McHale, J. *The Changing Information Environment*. Elek, 1976.

McKendrick, N., Brewer, J., and Plumb, J. H. *The Birth of a Consumer Society: The Commercialization of 18th Century England*. Europa Publications Ltd, 1982.

McLean, J. M. and Rush, H. J. *The Impact of Microelectronics on the UK: A Suggested Classification and Illustrative Case Studies*. Occasional Paper Series no. 7. University of Sussex, Brighton: Science Policy Research Unit, June 1978.

McLellan, D. *Karl Marx: His Life and Thought*. Paladin, 1976.

McLellan, D. (ed.). *Karl Marx: Selected Writings*. Oxford: Oxford University Press, 1977.

McLellan, V. Spiffy Office at Amoco. *Datamation* 26 (2) February 1980: 68, 70.

McLuhan, M. *The Gutenberg Galaxy: The Making of Typographic Man*. Routledge and Kegan Paul, 1962.

McLuhan, M. *Understanding Media: The Extensions of Man*. Abacus, 1964.

McLuhan, M. (with Q. Fiore). *The Medium is the Message: An Inventory of Effects*. Allen Lane, 1967.

McMahon, F. Word Processing—Its Effects on Female Employment. in *International Word Processing Exhibition and Conference*. Northwood: Online, May 1980, pp. 35-45.

Medvedev, Z. A. *The Medvedev Papers: The Plight of Soviet Science Today*. Macmillan, 1971.

Melman, S. *Pentagon Capitalism*. New York: McGraw Hill, 1970.

Mertes, L. H. Doing your Office Over—Electronically. *Harvard Business Review* 59 (2) 1981: 127-135.

Mészáros, I. *Marx's Theory of Alienation*. Merlin, 1970.

Métayer, G. *La Société Malade de Ses Communications?* Paris: Dunod, 1980.

Meyer, M. *Madison Avenue USA: the Inside Story of American Advertising*. Bodley Head, 1958.

Meyer, S. *The Five Dollar Day: Labor Management and Social Control in the Ford Motor Company, 1908-1921*. Albany: State University of New York Press, 1981.

Meyersohn, R. Work and the New Leisure. *Economic Impact* no. 9 (1) 1975: 44-46.

Miles, I. The Ideologies of Futurists. *in* J. Fowles (ed.), *Handbook of Futures Research.* Dorsey, Illinois: Green Wood Press, 1978, pp. 67-97.

Miles, I. *Adaptation to Unemployment.* University of Sussex, Brighton: Science Policy Research Unit, 1983.

Miliband, R. *The State in Capitalist Society: The Analysis of the Western System of Power.* (1969). Reprinted Quartet, 1974.

Mills, C. W. *White-Collar: The American Middle Classes.* New York: Oxford University Press, 1953.

Mills, C. W. *Power, Politics and People.* New York: Oxford University Press, 1963.

Millward, N. Workplace Industrial Relations. *Employment Gazette* **91** (7) July 1983: 280-289.

Molitor, G.T.T. The Information Society: The path to Post-Industrial growth. *Futurist* April, 1981, pp. 23-30.

Montgomery, D. *Workers' Control in America.* Cambridge: Cambridge University Press, 1979a.

Montgomery, D. The Past and Future of Workers' Control. *Radical America* **13** (6) 1979b: 7-22.

Moore, B. *Injustice: the social bases of obedience and revolt.* Macmillan, 1978.

Moore, T. Embattled Kodak Enters the Electronic Age. *Fortune,* August 22, 1983, pp. 120-128.

Moorhouse, H. F. American Automobiles and Workers' Dreams. *Sociological Review* **31** (3) 1983: 403-426.

Morgall, J. Typing Our Way to Freedom: Is It True that New Office Technology Can Liberate Women? *Behavior and Information Technology* **2** (3) 1983: 215-226.

Morgenbrod, H. and Schwartzel, H. *Informations–und Kommunikationstechnik verandern den Buroarbeitsplatz.* Zurich: Siemens Data Report, Heft 6, December 1978.

Morrison, H. Employment in the Public and Private Sector 1976 to 1982. *Economic Trends* (352) February 1983: 82-89.

Mosco, V. *Pushbutton Fantasies: Critical Perspectives on Videotex and Information Technology.* Norwood, New Jersey: Ablex, 1982.

Moser, Sir C. Statistics and Public Policy. *Journal of the Royal Statistical Society* A **143** (1) 1980: 1-31.

Mumford, L. *The Myth of the Machine: The Pentagon of Power.* Secker and Warburg, 1971.

Murray, F. The Decentralization of Production–The Decline of the Mass-Collective Worker? *Capital and Class* (19) Spring 1983: 74-99.

Murray, R. (ed.). *Multinationals Beyond the Market: Intra-Firm Trade and the Control of Transfer Pricing.* Brighton: Harvester Press, 1981.

Musannif, N.Y. *Chips in Retailing.* Special Report no. 138. Economist Intelligence Unit, 1983.

Myrdal, A. and Klein, V. *Women's Two Roles: Home and Work.* Routledge and Kegan Paul, 1956.

Nadworny, M. J. *Scientific Management and the Unions, 1900-1932.* Cambridge MA: Harvard University Press, 1955.

Naffah, N. (ed.). *Integrated Office Systems.* Amsterdam: North-Holland Publishing Co., 1979.

NALGO (National and Local Government Officers' Association). *New Technology: A guide for NALGO Negotiators.* NALGO, 1980.

Nanus, B. Business, Government and the Multinational Computer. *Columbia Journal of World Business* **33** (1) 1978: 19-26.

Nanus, B. Developing Strategies for the Information Society. *The Information Society* **1** (4) 1982: 339-356.

Nathanson, C. The Militarization of the American Economy. *in* D. Horowitz (ed.), *Corporations and the Cold War.* New York: Monthly Review Press, 1969, pp. 205-235.

National Book Committee. *Public Library Spending in England and Wales.* National Book League, September 1983.

NEC's Universe. Tokyo: NEC (Nippon Electric Co., Ltd), 1982.

NEDC (National Economic Development Council). *Microelectronics: Challenge and Response.*

(78) 73, NEDO, 1978a.

NEDC *Industrial Strategy*. Electronic Components Sector Working Party. Memorandum by the chairman of the Electronic Components SWP. (78) 72, NEDO, 27 November 1978b.

NEDC. *Progress Report*. Telecommunications Sector Working Party. NEDO, 1978c.

NEDC. *Progress Report*. Electronic Computers Sector Working Party. NEDO, January 1979.

NEDC. *Computer Manpower in the '80s: The Supply and Demand for Computer Related Manpower to 1985*. Electronic Computers Sector Working Party. NEDO, 1980.

NEDC. *Policy for the UK Electronics Industry*. Electronics Economic Development Committee, NEDO, October 1982.

NEDC, *Report to NEDC on the Sector Assessments*. Memorandum to the Director General. (83) 18, NEDO, 30 March 1983a.

NEDC. *Policy for the UK Electronics Industry: Review 1982/83*. Electronics Economic Development Committee, NEDO, April 1983b.

NEDC. *Crisis Facing UK Information Technology*. Information Technology Economic Development Committee, NEDO, September 1984.

Negri, A. *La Classe Ouvrière Contre L'Etat*. Paris: Galilée, 1978.

Neil, A. (ed.). *The Cable Revolution: Britain on the brink of the information society*. Visionhire, September 1982.

Nelson, D. *Managers and Workers: Origins of the New Factory System in the United States, 1880-1920*. Madison: University of Wisconsin Press, 1975.

Nelson, D. *Frederick W. Taylor and the Rise of Scientific Management*. Madison: University of Wisconsin Press, 1980.

Nevins, A. *Ford: The Times, the Man, the Company*. New York: Scribner's Sons, 1954.

Newby, H. *The Deferential Worker: A Study of Farm Workers in East Anglia*. (1977). Reprinted Harmondsworth: Penguin, 1979.

Newby, H. *Green and Pleasant Land? Social Change in Rural England*. (1979). Reprinted Harmondsworth: Penguin, 1980.

New Earnings Survey 1982. Department of Employment, HMSO, 1983.

Nichols, T. and Beynon, H. *Living with Capitalism: Class Relations and the Modern Factory*. Routledge and Kegan Paul, 1977.

Nielson, B. Online Bibliographic Searching and the Deprofessionalization of Librarianship. *Online Review* 4 (3) 1980: 215-224.

Noble, D. F. *America by Design: Science, Technology, and the Rise of Corporate Capitalism*. New York: Oxford University Press, 1977.

Noble, D. F. Social Choice in Machine Design: the Case of Automatically Controlled Machine Tools. *in* A. Zimbalist (ed.), 1979 (q.v., below), pp. 18-50.

Noble, D. F. The Selling of the University. *The Nation*, February 6, 1982, cover, pp. 143-148.

Noble, D. F. Present Tense Technology. Part 1. *Democracy* 4 (1) 1983a: 8-24.

Noble, D. F. Present Tense Technology. Part 2. *Democracy* 4 (2) 1983b: 70-82.

Noble, D. F. Present Tense Technology. Part 3. *Democracy* 4 (3) 1983c: 71-93.

Nora, S. and Minc, A. *The Computerization of Society* Cambridge MA: MIT Press, 1980.

Norman, C. *The God that Limps: Science and Technology in the Eighties*. New York: W. W. Norton and Company, 1981.

Northcott, J. and Rogers, P. *Microelectronics in Industry: Final Report: What's Happening in Britain*. Policy Studies Institute, March 1982.

Northcott, J. and Rogers, P. *Microelectronics in British Industry: the Pattern of Change*. Policy Studies Institute, February 1984.

Oakley, A. *Housewife*. Allen Lane, 1974.

Oakley, A. *Subject Women*. Oxford: Robertson, 1981.

OECD (Organization for Economic Co-operation and Development). *Equal Opportunities for Women*. Paris: OECD Publications, 1979.

OECD Observer. Women at Work: More Jobs–More Jobless. 121 (March) 1983: 27-29.

Oettinger, A. G. Information Resources: Knowledge and Power in the 21st Century. *Science* 209 (4) 1980: 191-198.

Orwell, G. *The Road to Wigan Pier.* (1937). Reprinted Harmondsworth: Penguin, 1967.

O'Shaughnessy, H. *Grenada: Revolution, Invasion and Aftermath.* Sphere, 1984.

Otway, H. and Peltu, M. (eds.). *New Office Technology: Human and Organizational Aspects.* Frances Pinter, 1983.

Packard, V. *The Hidden Persuaders.* Longman, Green and Co., 1957.

Packard, V. *The Waste Makers.* (1960). Reprinted Harmondsworth: Penguin, 1963.

Pahl, R. E. *Divisions of Labour.* Oxford: Blackwell, 1984.

Palm, G. *The Flight from Work.* Cambridge: Cambridge University Press, 1977.

Parker, E. B. Social Implications of Computer/Communications Systems. *Telecommunications Policy* 1 (4) 1976: 3-20.

Parkin, F. *Class Inequality and Political Order.* Paladin, 1972.

Parkin, F. *Marxism and Class Theory: A Bourgeois Critique.* Tavistock, 1979.

Peel, J. *Herbert Spencer–the Evolution of a Sociologist.* Heinemann, 1971.

Pelton, J. N. The Future of Telecommunications: A Delphi Survey. *Journal of Communication* 31 (1) 1981a: 177-189.

Pelton, J. N. *Global Talk.* Alphen aanden Rijn, The Netherlands: Sijthoff and Noordhoff, 1981b.

Perry, R. *The Programming of the President.* Aurum Press, 1984,

Philips *Innovation in a multinational industrial company.* Eindhoven, Holland: Philips Corp., February 1979.

Pike, A. An Industry Under Seige. *Financial Times,* 27 August, 1980.

Pilkington, Sir H. (Chairman). *Report of the Committee on Broadcasting, 1960.* Command 1753. HMSO, June 1962.

Pincher, C. *Inside Story: a Documentary of the Pursuit of Power.* Sidgwick and Jackson, 1978.

POEU (Post Office Engineering Union) *British Telecom Privatization: Evidence Presented to the Department of Industry.* POEU, August 27, 1982.

POEU *The American Experience. . . A Report on the Dilemma of Telecommunications in the USA.* POEU, October 1983.

Pollard, S. Factory Discipline in the Industrial Revolution. *Economic History Review* 16 (2) 1963: 254-271.

Pollard, S. *The Idea of Progress: History and Society.* (1968). Reprinted Harmondsworth: Penguin, 1971.

Poniatowski, M. *L'Avenir N'est Ecrit Nulle Part.* Paris: Albin Michel, 1978.

Pool, I. de Sola The New Technologies: Promise of Abundant Channels at Lower Cost. *in* E. Abel (ed.), *What's News: The Media in American Society.* San Fransisco: Institute for Contemporary Studies, 1981, pp. 81-96.

Pool, I. de Sola *Technologies of Freedom.* Cambridge MA: Harvard University Press, 1983.

Pope, D. *The Making of Modern Advertising.* New York: Basic Books, 1983.

Porat, M. *The Information Economy.* Washington DC: Government Printing Office, 1976.

Porat, M. Communication Policy in an Information Society. *in* G. O. Robinson (ed.), *Communications for Tomorrow.* New York: Praeger, 1978, pp. 3-60.

Pounder, C. and Anderson, S. *The Police Use of Computers.* Edinburgh: Technical Authors Group (Scotland), n.d., circa 1982.

Powell, D. (ed.). *Counter Revolution: The Tesco Papers, 1975-1982.* Twickenham: Hallam and Mallen, 1983.

Prais, S. J. *The Evolution of Giant Firms in Britain: A study of the growth of concentration in manufacturing industry in Britain 1909-1970.* Cambridge: Cambridge University Press, 1976.

Prandy, K., Stewart, A. and Blackburn, R. M. *White-Collar Work.* Macmillan, 1982.

Price, A. *Instruments of Darkness: The History of Electronic Warfare.* Macdonald and Jane's Publishers, 1977.

Price, R. and Bain, G. S. Union Growth Revisited: 1948-1974 in Perspective. *British Journal of Industrial Relations* 14 (3) 1976: 339-355.

Price, R. and Bain, G. S. Union Growth in Britain: Retrospect and Prospect. *British Journal of Industrial Relations* 21 (1) 1983: 44-68.

Price. S. G. *Introducing the Electronic Office.* Manchester: National Computer Center, 1980.

Pym, Sir F. The Revolution Laissez-faire and Socialism Cannot Handle. *Guardian*, 10 October, 1983.

Radice, H. (ed.). *International Firms and Modern Imperialism.* Harmondsworth: Penguin, 1975.

Rattansi, A. Marx and the Abolition of the Division of Labor. *in* A. Giddens and G. Mackenzie (eds.), 1982a (q.v., above), pp. 12-28.

Rattansi, A. *Marx and the Division of Labor.* Cambridge: Cambridge University Press, 1982b.

Reid, I. and Wormald, E. (eds.). *Sex Differences in Britain.* Grant McIntyre, 1982.

Reinecke, I. *Electronic Illusions: A Skeptic's View of our High-Tech Future.* Harmondsworth: Penguin, 1984.

Reitell, C. Machinery and its Effects upon the Workers in the Automobile Industry. *Annals of the American Academy of Political and Social Science* November 1924, pp. 37-43.

Renmore, C. *Silicon Chips and You.* Sheldon Press, 1979.

Reppy, J. The United States. *in* N. Ball and M. Leitenberg (eds.), *The Structure of the Defense Industry: an International Survey.* Croom Helm, 1983, ch. 1.

Ricardo, D. *The Principles of Political Economy and Taxation.* (1821). J. M. Dent and Sons, n.d.

Richta, R. et al. *Civilization at the Crossroads: Social and Human Implications of the Scientific and Technological Revolution.* White Plains: International Arts and Humanities Press, 1969.

Ring, T. Long Battle Looms on DHSS dp Plans. *Computing*, May 26, 1983.

Roberts, B. C. and May, J. The Response of Multinational Enterprises to International Trade Union Pressures. *British Journal of Industrial Relations* 12 (3) 1974: 403-416.

Robertson, J. Socialising with the Family Unit. *Guardian*, 30 March, 1983.

Robertson, J. A. S. and Briggs, J. M. Part-time Working in Great Britain. *Employment Gazette* 87 (7) July 1979: 671-677.

Robertson, J. A. S., Briggs, J. M. and Goodchild, A. *Structure and employment prospects of the service industries.* Research Paper no. 30. Department of Employment, July 1982.

Robins, K. and Webster, F. New Technology: A Survey of Trade Union Response in Britain. *Industrial Relations Journal* 13 (1) 1982: 7-26.

Robinson, J. Housework Technology and Household Work. *in* S. Fenstermaker Berk (ed.), *Women and Household Labor.* Beverly Hills: Sage, 1980, pp. 53-67.

Rogin, M. P. *The Intellectuals and McCarthy: The Radical Specter.* Cambridge MA: MIT Press 1967.

Rose, R. *Getting by in the Three Economies: The Resources of the Official, Unofficial and Domestic Economies.* Strathclyde: Center for the Study of Public Policy, University of Strathclyde, 1983.

Ross, G. The Second Coming of Daniel Bell. *in* R. Miliband and J. Saville (eds.), *Socialist Register 1974.* Merlin, 1974, pp. 331-348.

Rothschild, E. *Paradise Lost: The Decline of the Auto-Industrial Age.* New York: Random House, 1973.

Rothwell, R. and Zegveld, W. *Technical Change and Employment.* Frances Pinter, 1979.

Routh, G. *Occupation and Pay in Britain, 1906-1979.* Macmillan, 1980.

Roy, W. G. The Unfolding of the Interlocking Directorate Structure of the United States. *American Sociological Review* 48 (2) 1983: 248-257.

Rudin, B. Industrial Betterment and Scientific Management as Social Control, 1890-1920. *Berkeley Journal of Sociology* 17 1972-73: 59-77.

Rumberger, R. W. *Overeducation in the US Labor Market.* New York: Praeger, 1981.

Runciman, W. G. *Relative Deprivation and Social Justice: a study of social inequality in twentieth century England.* Routledge and Kegan Paul, 1966.

Russell, D. *The Religion of the Machine Age.* Routledge and Kegan Paul, 1983.

Saatchi and Saatchi Compton Worldwide. *Review of Operations.* Saatchi and Saatchi, 8 December, 1983.

Sabel, C. F. *Work and Politics: The Division of Labor in Industry.* Cambridge: Cambridge University Press, 1982.

Sachs, R. T. Matching the Technology to the Organization. *Administrative Management,* June 1981, pp. 36-39, 68.

Sahlins, M. *Stone Age Economics.* (1972). Reprinted Tavistock, 1974.

Salaman, G. *Class and the Corporation.* Fontana, 1981.

Salaman, G. Managing the Frontier of Control. *in* A. Giddens and G. Mackenzie (eds.), 1982 (q.v., above), pp. 46-62.

Samuel, R. Workshop of the World: Steam Power and Hand Technology in mid-Victorian Britain. *History Workshop Journal* 3 1977: 6-72.

Sarnoff, R. W. The Electronic Revolution. *Economic Impact* no. 7 (3) 1974.

Schaff, A. Occupation Versus Work. *in* G. Friedrichs and A. Schaff (eds.), 1982 (q.v., above), pp. 337-349.

Schiller, A. R. Shifting Boundaries of Information. *Library Journal* 106 April 1, 1981, pp. 705-709.

Schiller, D. *Telematics and Government.* Norwood, New Jersey: Ablex, 1982a.

Schiller, D. Business Users and the Telecommications Network. *Journal of Communications* 32 (4) 1982b: 84-96.

Schiller, D. The Storming of the PTTs. *Datamation* 29 (5) May 1983: 155-158.

Schiller, H. I. *Mass Communications and American Empire.* New York: A. M. Kelley, 1970.

Schiller, H. I. *Who Knows: Information in the Age of the Fortune 500.* Norwood, New Jersey: Ablex, 1981.

Schiller, H. I. The Communications Revolution: who benefits? *Media Development* 30 (4) 1983: 18-21.

Schiller, H. I. *Information and the Crisis Economy.* Norwood, New Jersey: Ablex, 1984.

Schlesinger, P. Preparing for the Next Media War. *Cencrastus* (17) 1984: 23-24.

Schonfield, A. Thinking about the Future. *Encounter* 32 (2) 1969: 15-26.

Schudson, M. *Advertising, the Uneasy Persuasion: Its Dubious Impact on American Society.* New York: Basic Books, 1984.

Sciberras, E. *Multinational Electronics Companies and National Economic Policies.* Greenwich, Connecticut: Jai Press, 1977.

Scott, J. *Corporations, Classes and Capitalism.* Hutchinson, 1979.

Scott, J. W. The Mechanization of Women's Work. *Scientific American* 247 (3) 1982: 137-151.

Seabrook, J. *What Went Wrong? Working People and the Ideals of the Labor Movement.* Gollancz, 1978.

Seabrook, J. Poverty as Metaphor—Or Why both Peter and Paul Feel Robbed. *New Society* 51 (908) 28 February, 1980: 439-441.

Seabrook, J. *Unemployment.* Quartet, 1982a.

Seabrook, J. *Working-Class Childhood.* Gollancz, 1982b.

Seabrook, J. Eldorado in our backyard. *Guardian,* 17 January, 1983.

Seguret, M. -C. Women and Working Conditions: Prospects for Improvement? *International Labour Review* 122 (3) 1983: 295-331.

Sennett, R. *The Fall of Public Man: On the Social Psychology of Capitalism.* New York: Random House, Vintage Books, 1978.

Sennett, R. and Cobb, J. *The Hidden Injuries of Class.* New York: Random House, Vintage Books, 1973.

Servan-Schreiber, J. -J. *The American Challenge.* New York: Atheneum, 1968.

Shamoon, S. Why Global Advertising "Is It". *Observer,* 23 September, 1984.

Sharpe, R. ITT's "jigsaw" takes on the Xerox "string." *Computing.* June 4, 1981, pp. 18-19.

Shepard, J. M. *Automation and Alienation: A Study of Office and Factory Workers.* Cambridge MA: MIT Press, 1971.

Siemens. *This is Siemens.* Zurich: Siemens, n.d., circa 1980.

Simons, G. L. *Women in Computing.* Manchester: National Computing Center, 1981.

Sinclair, Sir C. Coming Soon—A Robot Slave for Everyone. *Guardian,* 24 April, 1984.

Sinfield, A. *What Unemployment Means.* Oxford: Robertson, 1981.

Singelmann, J. The Sector Transformation of the Labor Force in Seven Industrialized Countries, 1920-1970. *American Journal of Sociology* 83 (5) 1978a: 1224-1234.

Singlemann, J. *From Agriculture to Services: The Transformation of Industrial Employment.* Beverly Hills: Sage, 1978b.

Sklair, L. *The Sociology of Progress.* Routledge and Kegan Paul, 1970.

Sleigh, J., Boatwright, B., Irwin, P., and Stanyon, R. *The Manpower Implications of Microelectronic Technology.* Report of the Department of Employment Manpower Study Group on Microelectronics. HMSO. 1979.

Sloan, A. P. *My Years with General Motors.* Sidgwick and Jackson, 1965.

Smiles, S. *Thrift.* (1875). Reprinted Murray, 1891.

Smith, A. *Goodbye Gutenberg: The Newspaper Revolution of the 1980s.* New York: Oxford University Press, 1980.

Smith, A. E. A Word Processing Pilot Project. *Management Services in Government* 34 (2) 1979: 86-89.

Smith, L. Matsushita Looks Beyond Consumer Electronics. *Fortune,* October 31, 1983, pp. 96-104.

Sobel, R. *IBM: Colossus in Transition.* New York: Times Books, 1981.

Sochor, Z. A. Soviet Taylorism Revisited. *Soviet Studies* 33 (2) 1981: 246-264.

Spear, J. C. *Presidents and the Press: The Nixon Legacy.* Cambridge MA: The MIT Press, 1984.

Stansell, J. Fleet Street—The Key Battle Between the Old and the New. *New Scientist* 89 (1244) 12 March, 1981: 666-668.

Stedman Jones, G. The Marxism of the Early Lukacs: An Evaluation. *New Left Review* (70) November-December 1971: 27-64.

Steinfels, P. *The Neoconservatives: The Men who are Changing America's Politics.* New York: Simon and Shuster, 1979

Stevenson, R. L. The Politics of Information. *Communications Research* 8 (4) 1981: 499-509.

Stewart, A., Prandy, K., and Blackburn, R. M. *Social Stratification and Occupations.* New York Holmes and Meier, 1980.

Stoneman, P. *Technological Diffusion and the Computer Revolution: The UK Experience.* Cambridge: Cambridge University Press, 1976.

Stonier, T. The Impact of Microprocessors on Employment. *in* T. Forester (ed.), 1980a. (q.v., above), pp. 303-307.

Stonier, T. Technological Change and the Future. *in* G. Cherry and T. Travis (eds.), *Leisure in the 1980s: Alternative Futures.* Leisure Studies Associates, 1980b.

Stonier, T. *The Wealth of Information: A Profile of the Post-Industrial Economy.* Thames Methuen, 1983.

Sullivan, T. A. and Cornfield, D. B. Downgrading Computer Workers: Evidence from Occupational and Industrial Redistribution. *Sociology of Work and Occupations* 6 (2) 1979: 184-203.

Syfret, T. *Cable and Advertising in the Eighties.* J. Walter Thompson Company, December 1983.

Taylor, B. *Eve and the New Jerusalem: Socialism and Feminism in the 19th Century.* Virago, 1983.

Taylor, F. W. *a Shop Management.*
  b The Principles of Scientific Management.
  c Testimony before the Special House Committee.
  Collected in *Scientific Management.* New York: Harper and Brothers Publishing, 1947.

Taylor, P. *Smoke Rings: the politics of tobacco.* Bodley Head, 1984.

Taylor, R. The Technical Tory U-Turn. *Management Today,* June 1983, pp. 90-96.

Terkel, S. *Working: People Talk About What They Do All Day and How They Feel About What They Do.* Harmondsworth: Penguin, Peregrine Books, 1977.

TGWU (Transport and General Workers' Union). *Microelectronics: New Technology Old Problems New Opportunities.* TGWU, 1979.

Thackray, J. How RCA lost its bets. *Management Today,* April 1976, pp. 60-63, 114.

Thatcher, M. *Speech at the Opening Ceremony of IT '82 Conference.* Press Office, 10 Downing Street, 8 December, 1982.

Thatcher, M. *Speech to the Glasgow Chamber of Commerce Bicentenary Dinner.* Press Office, 10 Downing Street, 28 January, 1983.

Thatcher, M. Interviewed by G. Bull. *The Director* 37 (2) September 1983: 22-27.

Thatcher, M. Speech at Conservative Party Conference, Blackpool, October 14, 1983 reported in the *Times,* October 15, 1983, p. 2.

Thomis, M. I. *The Luddites: Machine-Breaking in Regency England.* New York: Schocken Books, 1972.

Thompson, A. W. J. and Hunter, L. C. Great Britain. *in* J. T. Dunlop and W. Galenson (eds.), 1978 (q.v., above), ch. 2.

Thompson, E. P. Time, Work-Discipline and Industrial Capitalism. *Past and Present* (38) December 1967: 56-97.

Thompson, E. P. *The Making of the English Working Class.* (1963). Reprinted Harmondsworth: Penguin, 1968.

Thompson, E. P. *The Poverty of Theory and other essays.* Merlin, 1978.

Thompson, E. P. *Writing by Candlelight.* Merlin, 1980.

Thompson, G. B. *Memo from Mercury: Information Technology is Different.* Montreal: Institute for Research on Public Policy (Occasional paper no. 10), 1979.

Thorn-EMI 1980. Thorn-EMI, n.d.

Tilton, T. A. The Next Stage of History? *Social Research* 40 (4) 1973: 728-745, 753-760.

Tobin Foundation. *Structural Issues in Global Communications.* Washington DC: Tobin Foundation, 1982.

Toffler, A. *Future Shock.* Bodley Head, 1970.

Toffler, A. *The Third Wave.* Collins, 1980.

Toffler, A. *Previews and Premises.* Pan, 1984.

Toller, E. *The Machine-Wreckers.* Benn Brothers, 1923.

Townsend, P. *Poverty in the United Kingdom: A Survey of Household Resources and Standards of Living.* Harmondsworth: Penguin, 1979.

Tracey, M. Telecommunications' Effects on Existing Media. *Political Quarterly* 54 (2) 1983: 177-186.

TUC (Trades Union Congress). *Congress.* TUC, 1979.

TUC. *Employment and Technology.* September 1979.

Tunstall, J. *The Media in Britain.* Constable, 1983.

Turner, P. Humpty Dumpty Challenge for Women over Jobs, Pay and Training Opportunities. *Electronics Times,* 14 February, 1980, pp. 28-29.

Tydeman, J. Videotex: Ushering in the Electronic Household. *Futurist,* February 1982.

Uhlig, R. P., Farber, D. J., and Blair, J. H. *The Office of the Future.* Amsterdam: North-Holland, 1979.

Unit of Manpower Studies. *Word Processing and Employment*. Department of Employment (mimeo), 1978.

Useem, M. *The Inner Circle: Large Corporations and the Rise of Business Political Activity in the US and UK*. New York: Oxford University Press, 1984.

Veljanovski, C. G. and Bishop, W. D. *Choice by Cable*. Institute of Economic Affairs (Hobart Papers, 96), 1983.

Vines, S. and Taylor, R. The Economy under Mrs. T. *Observer*, 15 May 1983.

Voge, M. Information, Growth and Economic Crisis. *Intermedia* 5 (6) 1977: 15-19.

Vogel, E. F. *Japan as Number One: Lessons for America*. Cambridge MA: Harvard University Press, 1979.

Vos, D. de *Government and Microelectronics: The European Experience*. Ontario: Science Council of Canada, 1983.

Wainwright, H. Women and the Division of Labor. *in* P. Abrams (ed.), 1978 (q.v., above), ch. 3.

Wainwright, J. Secretaries: Light in a Dark Tunnel? *Computing*, October 7, 1982, p. 22.

Wakeham, J. Information Technology: The Department of Industry's role. *Aslib Proceedings* 34 (8) 1982: 350-357.

Wallace, M. and Kalleberg, A. L. Industrial Transformation and the Decline of Craft: the decomposition of skill in the printing industry, 1931-1978. *American Sociological Review* 47 (3) 1982: 307-324.

Warr, A. Programmed for Misery (letter). *Guardian*, 4 September, 1980.

Webb, M. The Labor Market. *in* I. Reid and E. Wormald (eds.), 1982 (q.v., above), ch. 6.

Weber, M. Politics as a Vocation. *in* H. H. Gerth and C. W. Mills (eds.), *From Max Weber*. Routledge and Kegan Paul, 1967, pp. 77-128.

Weber, M. Socialism: Speech for the General Information of Austrian Officers in Vienna, 1918. *in* J. E. T. Eldridge (ed.), *Max Weber: The Interpretation of Social Reality*. Michael Joseph, 1971, pp. 191-219.

Wedell, E. G. Deploying the Army of the Unemployed. . . . *Guardian*, 26 January, 1983.

Weinberger, C. W. *Annual Report to the Congress: Fiscal Year 1984*. Washington DC: US Government Printing Office, February 1, 1983.

Weir, M. (ed.). *Job Satisfaction: Challenge and Response in Modern Britain*. Fontana, 1976.

Wells, H. G. *World Brain*. Methuen, 1938.

Werneke, D. *Microelectronics and Office Jobs: The Impact of the Chip on Women's Employment*. Geneva: International Labour Office, 1983.

Werskey, G. *The Visible College*. Allen Lane, 1978.

West, J. (ed.). *Work, Women and the Labor Market*. Routledge and Kegan Paul, 1982.

Westergaard, J. and Resler, H. *Class in a Capitalist Society: a study of contemporary Britain*. Heinemann, 1975.

Whitaker, R. Scientific Management Theory as Political Ideology. *Studies in Political Economy* 9 (Fall) 1979: 75-108.

White, G. C. Technological Changes and the Content of Jobs. *Employment Gazette* 91 (8) August 1983: 329-334.

White, M. *Shorter Working Time*. Policy Studies Institute, 1980.

Wilkinson, B. *The Shopfloor Politics of New Technology*. Heinemann, 1983a.

Wilkinson, B. Technical Change and Work Organization. *Industrial Relations Journal* 14 (2) 1983b: 18-27.

Wilkinson, M. Why GEC Went After an Old American Family Company. *Financial Times*, 22 November, 1978.

Wilkinson, M. Larger Companies Benefit from Centralized Systems. *Financial Times*, 13 April, 1982.

Williams, C. The "Work Ethic," Non-Work and Leisure in an Age of Automation. *Australian and New Zealand Journal of Sociology* 19 (2) 1983: 216-237.

Williams, F. *The Communications Revolution*. Beverly Hills: Sage, 1982.

Williams, M. *On-line Retrieval–Today and Tomorrow:* lst International On-line Information Meeting, 13–15 December 1977. Oxford and New York: Learned Information, 1978.

Williams, R. *The Long Revolution* (1961). Reprinted Harmondsworth: Penguin, 1965.

Williams, R. *Television: Technology and Cultural Form.* Fontana, 1974.

Williams, R. *The Country and the City.* (1973). Reprinted Paladin, 1975.

Williams, R. Advertising: The Magic System. *in* R. Williams, *Problems in Materialism and Culture.* Verso, 1980, pp. 170–195.

Williams, Roger. British Technology Policy. *Government and Opposition* 19 (1) 1984: 30–51.

Williamson, B. *Class, Culture and Community: A Biographical Study of Social Change in Mining.* Routledge and Kegan Paul, 1982.

Willott, W. B. The NEB involvement in Electronics and Information Technology. *in* C. Carter (ed.), *Industrial Policy and Innovation.* Heinemann, 1981, pp. 203–212.

Wilson, H. *Labour and the Scientific Revolution.* Labour Party–Report of the 62nd Annual Conference, Scarborough, September 30–October 4, 1963. Labour Party, 1963, pp. 133–140.

Winkler, J. T. Corporatism. *European Journal of Sociology* 17 (1) 1976: 100–136.

Winner, L. *Autonomous Technology: Technics-out-of-Control as a Theme in Political Thought.* Cambridge MA: MIT Press, 1977.

Winner, L. Do Artifacts Have Politics? *Daedalus* 109 (1) 1980: 121–136.

Winston, B. Unusual Rubbish. *Sight and Sound,* Summer 1982, pp. 154–158.

Winsbury, R. *New Technology and the Press.* Royal Commission on the Press Working Paper no. 1. HMSO, 1975.

Wohl, A. D. Office Automation–The Next Battlefield. *in* Special Report: IBM–AT&T: The Coming Collision. *Datamation* 28 (8) July 20, 1982: 34–39.

Wood, S. (ed.). *The Degradation of Work? Skill, deskilling and the labour process.* Hutchinson, 1982.

Word Processing by Computer. Report of a Pilot Project at the Department of Education and Science, Darlington. Central Computer Agency, November 1978.

Work in America. Report of a Special Task Force to the Secretary of Health, Education and Welfare. Cambridge MA: MIT Press, 1973.

Young, R. Science *is* Social Relations. *Radical Science Journal* (5) 1977: 65–129.

Young, R. Science as Culture. *Quarto,* December 1979.

Zeitlin, M. Corporate Ownership and Control: The Large Corporation and the Capitalist Class. *American Journal of Sociology* 79 (5) 1974: 1073–1119.

Zimbalist, A. Technology and the Labor Process in the Printing Industry. *in* A. Zimbalist (ed.), 1979 (q.v., below), pp. 103–126.

Zimbalist, A. (ed.). *Case Studies in the Labor Process.* New York: Monthly Review Press, 1979.

Author Index

Subject Index